Women and Gender

A Feminist Psychology

Women and Gender

A Feminist Psychology

FOURTH EDITION

Mary Crawford
University of Connecticut

Rhoda Unger
Brandeis University

McGraw Hill

Boston Burr Ridge, IL Dubuque, IA Madison, WI New York San Francisco St. Louis
Bangkok Bogotá Caracas Kuala Lumpur Lisbon London Madrid Mexico City
Milan Montreal New Delhi Santiago Seoul Singapore Sydney Taipei Toronto

The McGraw-Hill Companies

Higher Education

WOMEN AND GENDER: A FEMINIST PSYCHOLOGY
Published by McGraw-Hill, a business unit of The McGraw-Hill Companies, Inc., 1221 Avenue of the Americas, New York, NY, 10020.

This book is printed on acid-free paper.

2 3 4 5 6 7 8 9 0 FGR/FGR 0 9 8 7 6 5 4

ISBN 0-07-282107-8

Publisher: *Stephen Rutter*
Sponsoring editor: *Stephen Rutter*
Developmental editor: *Kirsten Stoller*
Marketing manager: *Melissa S. Caughlin*
Lead project manager: *Susan Trentacosti*
Lead production supervisor: *Randy L. Hurst*
Designer: *Cassandra J. Chu*
Lead supplement producer: *Marc Mattson*
Photo research coordinator: *Alexandra Ambrose*
Associate art editor: *Cristin Yancey*
Photo researcher: *Christine Pullo*
Permissions: *Marty Granahan*
Cover design: *Yvo Riezobos*
Cover photo: *Dancers of the Third Age. Photographer: Dennis DeLoria.*
All rights reserved 1981 Liz Lerman Dance Exchange, Inc.
Typeface: *10/12 Palatino*
Compositor: *ElectraGraphics, Inc.*
Printer: *Quebecor World Fairfield Inc.*

Library of Congress Cataloging-in-Publication Data

Crawford, Mary (Mary E.)
Women and gender : a feminist psychology / Mary Crawford, Rhonda Unger.—4th ed.
p. cm.
Authors' names in reverse order on the first two editions.
Includes bibliographical references and index.
ISBN 0-07-282107-8 (soft cover : alk. paper)
1. Women—Psychology. 2. Feminist psychology. I. Unger, Rhoda Kesler. II. Title.
HQ1206.U49 2004
305.42—dc22 2003059540

www.mhhe.com

To our husbands
Roger Chaffin and Burt Unger
for always being there;
to our children:
Mary, Mark, and Ben
Laurel and Rachel, and our grandchildren,
Alex, Isaac, and Hannah
who represent our hopes
for the future.

About the Authors

MARY CRAWFORD is Professor of Psychology and former director of the Women's Studies Program at the University of Connecticut. She has taught the psychology of women and gender for twenty-eight years. As a faculty member at West Chester University of Pennsylvania, she earned the Trustees' Award for Lifetime Achievement. She has also held the Jane W. Irwin Chair in women's Studies at Hamilton College, served as distinguished Visiting Teacher/Scholar at the College of New Jersey, and directed the graduate program in women's studies at the University of South Carolina. Professor Crawford received her Ph.D. in experimental psychology from the University of Delaware. She is a consulting editor for *Psychology of Women Quarterly* and *Sex Roles,* the U.S. editor of *Feminism and Psychology,* and a Fellow of both the American Psychological Association and the American Psychological Society. Mary Crawford has spoken and written about women's issues for audiences as diverse as the British Psychological Society, *Ms.* magazine and the "Oprah Winfrey Show." She is the author of numerous research articles on gender and is actively involved in mentoring future psychologists. Books she has authored or edited include *Gender and Thought: Psychological Perspectives* (1989); *Talking Difference: On Gender and Language* (1995); *Gender Differences in Human Cognition* (1997); *In Our Own Words* (1997/2000); *Coming Into Her Own: Educational Success in Girls and Women* (1999); and *Innovative Methods for Feminist Psychological Research* (1999).

RHODA UNGER is Professor Emirita of Psychology at Montclair State University and Resident Scholar at the Women's Studies Research Center at Brandeis University. She received her Ph.D. in experimental psychology from Harvard University. Professor Unger was the first recipient of the Carolyn Wood Sherif Award from the Division of the Psychology of Women of the American Psychological Association. She is also the recipient of two distinguished publication awards and a distinguished career award from the Association for Women in Psychology. She has been the president of the Division of the Psychology of Women and, more recently, president of the Society for the Psychological Study of Social Issues. She has lectured extensively in the United States and abroad as a Fulbright scholar in Israel, a distinguished lecturer at the University of British Columbia, and as a visiting fellow of the British Psychological Society. She is currently the founding editor of *ASAP (Analyses of Social Issues and Public Policy)* an electronic and print journal of the Society for the Psychological Study of Social Issues, which can be found at www.asap-spssi.org. Professor Unger is the author or editor of eight previous books—the most recent of which is the *Handbook of the Psychology of Women and Gender* published in 2001. Her other books include: *Resisting Gender: Twenty Five Years of Feminist Psychology; Representations: Social Constructions of Gender; Women, Gender, and Social Psychology;* and *Female and Male.*

Contents

Preface

We wrote this book to share our excitement about the psychology of women and gender. Psychology is in the midst of a transformation into a more balanced and inclusive body of theory, research, and practice. Contemporary feminism has provided psychology with a wealth of new theoretical frameworks and scholarship. In turn, psychological research is being used to further social change to benefit girls and women. This is an exciting time for students to begin their study of women and gender, and an exciting time to be teaching in this dynamic field.

As we wrote the fourth edition of *Women and Gender,* we increasingly recognized the need to look even more at the social and cultural context of girls' and women's lives. The world has become a smaller and more dangerous place, and current political and social events will continue to have a major impact on relationships between women and men. This edition considers ethnic, racial, and cultural diversity to a greater extent than previous editions.

As *Women and Gender* enters its fourth edition, we feel more confident than ever that it is a thought-provoking and informative text that is also a great read. Through an ongoing process of dialogue with students and teachers who used the earlier editions, we have created a new shorter edition that speaks to today's students without sacrificing the depth and nuance that instructors expect from us. Because of feedback from previous editions of the book, we have added many new areas of research and eliminated much older, out-of-date material. We believe students will find that this book discusses many issues that are crucial to their lives today.

We believe in introducing students to a variety of perspectives. We try not to oversimplify research findings and social issues. Rather, we respect the intelligence of our student readers. Although many will be new to feminist concepts and psychological methods, all are capable of reasoned analysis. And we have found, along with other instructors who have used the earlier editions, that students appreciate a text that does not talk down to them. The issues are too important, and too complex, to be presented superficially.

We take up the issues students want to know about: media images, women and leadership, transgender activism, male-female differences, relationships, career success, sexuality, date rape, and eating disorders. Students are eager to discuss and debate these topics. We relate the most current and comprehensive research on each. Sometimes, we leave an issue open and unresolved, so the reader may use informed judgment to make up her or his own mind. Feminism has nothing to fear from critical thinking!

THE SOCIAL CONSTRUCTIONIST PERSPECTIVE

Even more than in the earlier editions, *Women and Gender* is grounded in a social constructionist perspective. In other words, we view gender not as an attribute of individuals but as a system of meanings in which we are all immersed. Furthermore, we regard psychology not as an abstract, decontextualized search for truth but a human enterprise shaped by culture. The social constructionist stance opens the way to critical analysis of popular culture, mass media, and everyday understandings of women and men. It also encourages critical analysis of why psychology chooses favored research topics, how it views women as objects of analysis, and how it has treated women who have made psychology their career, both historically and in the present.

The consistent social constructionist approach in this text makes it far more than just a compendium of research on sex differences or women's experiences. We draw on a huge variety of research using methods that range from case studies to surveys and experiments, and on theoretical perspectives from anthropology, sociology, and cultural studies, as well as psychology. Our social constructionist perspective organizes this wide-ranging knowledge base and fosters the analysis of women and gender in their social, cultural, and historical context.

THEMES OF THE BOOK

Four themes organize this book:

- **Gender is more than just sex.** Gender is a system of meanings related to power and status. It operates at individual, interactional, and cultural levels to structure people's lives. We examine phenomena from each of these levels—individual, internalized aspects such as gender identity and gender typing; interactional aspects such as stereotypes, attributions, and self-fulfilling prophecies; and cultural aspects such as media representations, laws, and religious teachings.
- **Language and naming are sources of power.** Aspects of reality that are named become more visible. Regaining for women the power to name is the first step in personal and social change. We analyze gender bias in naming and language use, both in ordinary language (e.g., the "generic he") and in the specialized language of psychological constructs (e.g., "premenstrual syndrome"). We also show how ongoing language change is making

women's experiences more visible. Thinking critically about language can increase understanding of how the gender system works and how it can be changed.

- **Women are not all alike.** Feminist scholars have become increasingly sensitive to the differences among women—in social class, ethnicity, age, sexual orientation, (dis)ability, and culture. Integrating diversity throughout each chapter of the book, we explore how these differences affect women's experiences, including gender socialization, adult relationships, and psychological distress and disorder. We also make use of a great deal of cross-cultural data, reflecting the transformation of psychological knowledge from its formerly white, North American, middle-class perspective. In discussing cultural differences, we avoid the ethnocentric view that presents other societies as exotic or less developed. Instead we contextualize practices that may seem strange to North American students. This depth of interpretation is especially important when discussing controversial issues such as female genital surgery. Moreover, cross-cultural data provide powerful examples of our first theme, that gender is more than just biological sex. Even phenomena thought to have a strong biological base, such as menarche and menopause, are shaped by culture.
- **Psychological research can foster social change.** Students want more than just information about the problems confronting girls and women. They want to know what is being done to resolve them, and what might be done in the future. Without an emphasis on change, studying the psychology of women and gender could promote a sense of helplessness and pessimism. In every chapter of this text, there are powerful examples of people who have been agents of change.

  Many of the problems that confront girls and women today are the result of social structures that disadvantage them. While changes in individual attitudes and behaviors, traditionally a focus of psychological research and practice, are necessary, they must be linked with changes in societies as a whole. Psychological research and theory can point the way to progressive social change.

NEW IN THIS EDITION

This edition retains and expands successful features from earlier versions. Each of the four themes is woven throughout the book; each chapter ends with a summary of how the four themes are played out in that particular chapter (in Chapter 15, the themes are summarized and contextualized). This allows students to trace the themes throughout the book and see their relevance across a wide range of topics.

- **Student friendliness.** Written by two active researchers, *Women and Gender* has always been notable for its scholarship. In this edition we have made it shorter and more student-friendly while sacrificing none of the authoritative research base that made the earlier editions so popular with instructors.

- **More effective text and chapter organization.** One result of our dual focus on student interest and scholarly depth is that we have reorganized many chapters extensively by adding new themes and topics and eliminating some areas which are no longer relevant to women today.
- **Emphasis on social change.** A third major revision in this edition is the increased emphasis on personal and social change. Although the use of psychological research to foster change has always been a theme of the book, we now make the connections between research and social policy more visible, and we highlight women and men who are agents of change. Continuing an innovation begun with the third edition, each chapter contains a boxed feature, "Making a Difference," which describes one person's efforts to bring about social justice. These features, researched and written by Mykol Hamilton, Professor of Psychology and Psychobiology at Centre College, are an exciting and unique part of *Women and Gender,* providing models of feminist activism.
- **Expanded multicultural coverage.** The new edition expands the multicultural perspective of the previous editions by adding new findings about the interactions of ethnicity, sexual orientation, gender, and social class in women's lives.
- **More coverage of women's health.** Throughout the book there is greater attention to women's health issues, reflecting the recent increase in research in this area. Rather than isolating health issues in a single chapter, we chose to stress the interaction of physical and psychological well-being, and their sociocultural specificity, by discussing health issues in context. For example, typical and atypical development of the female body is discussed in Chapters 5, 7, and 12; reproductive health issues in Chapters 5, 7, 8, and 12; the physical and psychological effects of culturally sanctioned violence against girls and women in Chapters 8 and 13; eating disorders in Chapters 2 and 14; and the social construction of mental health and illness in Chapters 8, 10, 12, and 14.

NEW COVERAGE IN EACH CHAPTER

Instructors are invited to take a look at the complete table of contents to see how comprehensive our coverage is. Here, we would just like to point out a few new areas of emphasis in each chapter.

Chapter 1: With its focus on issues relevant to diverse students, Chapter 1 is an engaging introduction to the field. It presents a variety of feminist perspectives, which are contrasted to conservative perspectives on women and gender. New to this edition is expanded coverage of third wave and global feminism, and updated references on attitudes toward feminists and feminism.

Chapter 2, "Images of Women and Men," has always been a student favorite. In this new edition we have revised the sequence so that students are presented first with material on media images and their impact before discussing stereotypes and their impact on perception and thought. The problematic aspects of women's quest for beauty and their conformity to impossible standards of weight are now presented in a multicultural and global perspective. New research on the institutional and cultural bases of various forms of sexism is highlighted. Many new illustrations and thought-provoking cartoons are included.

Chapter 3, "Doing Gender," unique to our text, shows how the belief that women and men are (and should be) fundamentally different is created and sustained in ordinary interaction through cognitive processes. In this edition, we discuss new work on stereotype threat and its impact on women's math performance. We also continue to move beyond the "double bind" by focusing on new research on perceptions of entitlement and legitimacy and how these influence the way women understand their place in the world.

Chapter 4, "The Meanings of Difference," tackles that perennial student question, "Just how different are women and men?" helping students think critically about how difference is defined, measured, and evaluated. Debates over gender differences in cognition and personality are connected to current societal issues such as women's underrepresentation in math and science careers and the undervaluing of care work done primarily by women. Along with updated material, this chapter has new research on culture and personality and on stereotype threat as it affects math performance in diverse cultural groups.

Chapter 5, "Biology, Sex, and Gender," is the most sophisticated and nuanced discussion of this topic available to students. In this new edition, we critically review recent studies suggesting a genetic basis for sexual orientation as well as new research on the many biological factors that influence human sex. Intersex and transgendered individuals are discussed from ethical as well as scientific perspectives. Finally, there is an increased emphasis on the contribution of culture in determining how sex leads to gender.

Chapter 6, "Becoming Gendered: Childhood," now includes a synthesis of theoretical and empirical work on the social construction of gender before birth and throughout childhood. New material examines the increasing polarization of girls' and boys' toys and clothing and its potential impact on gender equality. New topics include the gendering of emotion and the development of helplessness, the antecedents of gender flexibility, and how gender segregation in children contributes to the development of male dominance. This chapter integrates cutting edge information on cognitive processes and social interaction.

Chapter 7, "Becoming a Woman: Puberty and Adolescence," includes new material on the experience of adolescent girls as they encounter their changing bodies and boys' and mens' response to their sexual maturation. New to this edition is a discussion of the way the marketplace tries to speed up the sexual maturation of girls. In response to increasing biological determinist theories about puberty, we stress how ethnicity and social class interact with situational context. New topics include peers, schools, and social power and the impact of social demands on the mental health of young women. We also examine critically the questions of when and how participation in sports in good for young girls.

Chapter 8, "Sex, Love, and Romance," covers the cultural construction of sexual desire, romance, and norms for sexual behavior. We offer comprehensive coverage of adolescent sexuality, lesbian and bisexual women, the silencing of female desire, and a discussion of female genital surgery in cross-cultural perspective. Our integration of new research on sexual scripts as a function of ethnic group and social class and on HIV/AIDS and women make this chapter topical as well as comprehensive.

Chapter 9, "Commitments: Women and Close Relationships," updates its survey of heterosexual marriage, cohabitation, divorce, and lesbian relationships. Current statistics on these life paths in our own and other societies, as well as emerging relationship types such as egalitarian marriage, are presented. New to this edition is the integration of qualitative research on how couples justify and perpetuate inequality in marriage.

Chapter 10, "Mothering," analyzes the diverse experiences of women who mother, including teen mothers, lesbian mothers, and single mothers. Medical and family-centered models of pregnancy and childbirth are contrasted, and the physical and psychological consequences of pregnancy and birth are comprehensively covered. The topic of reproductive rights includes new information on the erosion of women's choices in the current political climate.

Chapter 11, "Work and Achievement," reflects the rapid change in women's work roles. The unpaid work of women in their homes is acknowledged, and the domain of employment is analyzed for gender inequality as well as opportunity. A provocative section, "Leadership: Do Women Do It Differently?" discusses up-to-the-minute research on leadership style and effectiveness. The most recent research on tokenism and its differential effects for women, men, and ethnic minorities is integrated into this edition. The chapter also features an expanded synthesis of the costs and benefits of juggling work, relationships, and family.

Chapter 12, "Midlife and Beyond," continues to emphasize the social construction of age and aging. It contains a new unit on the way menopause is used as a way to construct a medical/biological image of the weakness of midlife women, and includes the newest research findings on the negative aspects of hormone replacement therapy and the pressures to remain young and beautiful that have led women to engage in unsafe health practices. The chapter discusses the many complex role transitions of midlife and the important role of past and present poverty on women's lives. In this edition, new details on the positive aspects of growing older are provided.

Chapter 13, "Violence Against Women," written especially for this book by Jacquelyn White, Barrie Bondurant, and Patricia Donat, is organized around a model that identifies the commonalities among the various forms of violence against women: child sexual abuse, dating violence, sexual assault, and wife abuse. Its developmental contextual perspective views violence against women as occurring in a sociocultural context that supports male control of women. New to this edition is a discussion of sexual harassment in varied settings. The controversial topics of miscommunication and date rape and false memory syndrome are addressed. Most important, there is a wealth of information on what is being done to stop violence against girls and women.

Chapter 14, "Mental and Physical Health," continues its emphasis on the relationship between physical and psychological health. We have expanded our coverage of the way race, ethnicity, and social class influence the development of various psychological disorders such as depression as well as eating disorders. We have expanded our discussion of relational-cultural therapy as an important form of feminist therapy while, at the same time, explaining the similarities and differences between various forms of therapy that focus on women's lives.

Chapter 15, "Making a Difference: Toward a Better Future for Women," allows the instructor to end the course with a positive synthesis of the gains that feminist psychology has brought. This empowering chapter speaks to students about both personal and social change as a result of their involvement in feminist psychology.

At the personal level, Chapter 15 discusses research on the changes that occur in students' attitudes toward women, self-esteem, and feminist identity as a result of studying the psychology of women. It acknowledges and encourages increased personal empowerment for students.

At the societal level, Chapter 15 shows students how psychology can be used outside the classroom. It ties together the "Making a Difference" features from earlier chapters and discusses third wave feminism—the work of today's young activists. With examples of successful activism, it demonstrates how much society has changed in response to the first two waves of the women's movement.

USING THIS BOOK

Women and Gender contains a great deal of information and a sophisticated analysis of the field. However, as the wide adoption of the earlier editions at very diverse institutions shows, it is an approachable book. The fourth edition is considerably shorter and even more user-friendly. It can be read by people who have the equivalent of one course in psychology and no previous exposure to women's studies. Students find the wealth of women's own accounts of their experiences compelling. And they like the touches of humor that lighten serious issues.

The book can be used in either a chronological developmental sequence, in social/clinical clusters, or in groupings of topical issues. Each chapter can stand as a unit by itself, allowing maximum flexibility in combining them. Chapters 5–7, 9–10, and 12 have a developmental approach that covers the life span. Chapters 2, 3, and 11 are social psychologically oriented, and Chapters 4, 8, and 14 form a clinical/personality cluster.

SUPPLEMENTS

In our own teaching, we also use *In Our Own Words: Writings from Women's Lives,* (McGraw-Hill, 2001), a reader we developed specifically to connect the psychological research and theory in textbooks like our own with the voices and experiences of diverse girls and women. *In Our Own Words* is a collection of short (2–20 pages) essays, each with a distinctive personal voice. Some are humorous (Gloria Steinem's "If Men Could Menstruate"), some are poignant (Judith Ortiz Cofer's "The Story of My Body"), and all are memorable.

In Our Own Words is organized into five sections: Making Our Voices Heard; The Making of a Woman: Bodies, Power, and Society; Making Meaning; Making a Living: Women, Work, and Achievement; and Making a Difference. A section of 5–7 readings and their associated two-page introduction can be read along with a textbook chapter. For example, the section on bodies, power, and society nicely complements the *Women and Gender* chapters on "Images of Women" or "Sex, Love, and Romance." Or, students can write brief reaction papers on selections of their choice, using the questions provided at the beginning of each essay. *In Our Own Words* provides a stimulus for student interest and class discussion and an experiential counterpoint to research.

The Instructor's Manual for the new edition, prepared by Mykol Hamilton with Jennifer Lambdin and Michelle Broaddus, continues our tradition of providing the best teaching resources in the field. It features test items (multiple-choice, short-answer, and essay), current video listings, classroom demonstrations and other techniques for stimulating active involvement, sample syllabi, suggestions for using World Wide Web resources, course evaluation forms, ideas for integrating additional readings, and much more. Contact your McGraw-Hill representative for further information about supplements that accompany this text.

ACKNOWLEDGMENTS

Like the previous editions, this book came about with the help of colleagues and friends. Jackie White, Barrie Bondurant, and Patricia Donat contributed a compelling chapter on violence against girls and women to each edition. We are grateful to have their expertise on this vitally important topic. Mykol Hamilton contributed not only the Instructor's Manual but the "Making a Difference" feature. We are grateful to Mykol for taking on these sizable tasks. Her superb work will make teaching easier and more rewarding for instructors who choose our book.

Mary Crawford thanks Danielle Popp, a graduate student in social psychology at the University of Connecticut, for her dedicated help with library research. Special thanks go to our editors at McGraw-Hill: Steve Rutter, Cheri Dellelo, and Kirsten Stoller, along with project manager Susan Trentacosti, photo researcher Alexandra Ambrose, and art editor Cristin Yancey.

We wish to thank all the instructors and students around the United States, the United Kingdom, and Canada who so generously gave us feedback on the first three editions. We thank, too, the reviewers for the third edition: Helena M. Carlson, University of California, Santa Cruz; Britain A. Scott, University of St. Thomas; Samanatha Swindell, Washington State University; and Ellen Tetlow, University of Missouri, St. Louis.

We consider this book to be truly a collaborative effort. Our respective partners, Roger Chaffin and Burt Unger, have by now put in decades of effort in support of our research and writing. Their belief in the value of our work and their tangible support has sustained us through the tough spots. Our colleagues, students, and friends, too, should know that this book would not exist without your cooperation. We are grateful for the network of support that makes our work possible.

Mary Crawford
Rhoda Unger

CHAPTER 1

Introduction to a Feminist Psychology of Women

Consider the following facts and events:

- After more than 200 years of U.S. democracy, only 13 percent of U.S. Senators and 14 percent of members of the House of Representatives are women.
- In the United States, women earn about seventy-four cents for every dollar earned by men.
- The United Nations estimates that 100 million women worldwide are missing from the population—dead because, as females, they were unwanted.
- One in four U.S. college students believe that the activities of married women should be limited to home and family (down from one in two in 1970).
- Women have been heads of state in twenty-three countries around the world, yet in others they lack basic human rights such as voting and going to school.
- Women in the U.S. are far more likely than men to suffer from serious depression and eating disorders.
- Less than 5 percent of the artists in New York's Metropolitan Museum collections are women, but 85 percent of the nude paintings are of females.

What do these facts and events have in common? They demonstrate that equality has not yet been achieved. Although some things have changed for the better, a worldwide wage gap, underrepresentation of women in positions of status and power, and significant problems of violence against girls and women persist. Gender, sexuality, and power are at the core of social controversies around the world.

BEGINNINGS

We are living in an era in which nothing about women, sexuality, and gender seems certain. Entering this arena of change is a new branch of psychology that has developed research and theory about women and gender. The new branch is a form of *critical psychology*—it questions and challenges the moral, political, and scientific claims of psychology and tries to influence the direction of the field as a whole (Fox & Prilleltensky, 1997). It is usually called *feminist psychology,* the *psychology of women,* or *the psychology of gender* (Russo & Dumont, 1997; Unger, 1998; 2001). Those who use the term "feminist psychology" tend to emphasize theoretical connections to women's studies. Those who use "psychology of women" tend to focus on women's lives and experiences as the subject matter. Those who use "psychology of gender" tend to focus on the social and biological processes that create gender differences. In this book, we include all these perspectives, inviting you to explore the processes that create and maintain gender and to learn about the experiences of girls and women.

How Did Feminist Psychology Get Started?

As the women's movement of the late 1960s made women and gender a central social concern, the field of psychology began to examine the bias that had characterized its knowledge about women. The more closely psychologists began to look at the ways psychology had thought about women, the more problems they saw. They began to realize that women had been left out of many studies. Even worse, theories were constructed from a male-as-norm viewpoint, and women's behavior was explained as a deviation from the male standard. Often, stereotypes of women were unquestioned or considered to be an accurate portrayal of women's behavior. Good psychological adjustment for women was defined in terms of fitting in to gender norms. When women behaved differently from men, the differences were likely to be attributed to biology, instead of social influences (Crawford & Marecek, 1989; Kahn & Jean, 1983; Unger, 1979b).

These problems, though not universal, were very widespread. Psychologists began to realize that most psychological knowledge about women and gender was *androcentric,* or male-centered. They began to rethink psychological concepts and methods and to produce new research with women as the focus of study. Moreover, they began to study topics of importance and concern to women and to develop ways of analyzing social relations between women and men. As a result, psychology developed new ways of thinking about women, expanded its research methods, and developed new approaches to therapy and counseling.

Women within psychology were a very important force for change. They published many books and articles showing how psychology was misrepresenting women and how it needed to change. One of the first was Naomi Weisstein (1968), who declared that psychology had nothing to say about what women are really like, what they need, and what they want, because psychology did not know. Another was Phyllis Chesler, whose book *Women and Madness* (1972) claimed that psychology and psychiatry were used to control women.

Here are a few more examples of the strong critical voices of women who helped develop the new feminist psychology:

> Carolyn Sherif, 1964: "Ignorance about women pervades academic disciplines in higher education, where the requirements for the degree seldom include thoughtful inquiry into the status of women, as part of the total human condition." (cited in Sherif, 1979, p. 93)
>
> Mary Parlee, 1975: "The academic discipline (of psychology) . . . has distorted facts, omitted problems, and perpetuated pseudoscientific data relevant to women." (p. 124)
>
> Kathleen Grady, 1981: "The promise of science cannot be realized if . . . certain questions are never asked, or they are asked of the wrong people and in the wrong way, or they are not published because they do not fit accepted theories." (p. 629)
>
> Michelle Fine, 1985: "Women who represent racial and ethnic minorities, working-class and poor women, and disabled women and lesbians, need to be involved in [psychological] research. The lives of these women need to be integrated into this literature. . . ." (p. 178)

The growth of feminist psychology can be charted through many statistics. Before 1968, almost no psychology departments offered courses in the psychology of women or gender; today, more than half of psychology departments offer these courses. Psychology of women courses are often connected to women's studies programs, which began about 1970. In 2002, the National Women's Studies Association reported 736 women's studies programs in the United States. In 1974, there was not a single journal article on achievement that focused on women; in 1993, there were 161. Similar growth has occurred in the number of articles on many other topics, including rape and sexual assault, sexual harassment, and feminist therapy (Worell, 1996). In fact, the new field soon developed its own journals focusing on the psychology of women or gender: for example, *Sex Roles,* which began publishing in 1975; *Psychology of Women Quarterly,* published since 1977; and *Feminism & Psychology,* published since 1991.

The psychology of women and gender is rich and varied. Virtually every intellectual framework from Freudian theory to cognitive psychology has been used in developing new theories and approaches, and virtually every area of psychology, from developmental to social, has been affected by its critical analysis (Crawford & Marecek, 1989; Wilkinson, 1997a, 1997b). This book is an invitation to explore the knowledge and participate in the ongoing debates of feminist psychology.

Has the Women's Movement Affected Psychology?

The emergence of interest in women and gender took place in a social context marked by changing roles for women and the growth of a feminist social movement in the late 1960s. Questioning psychology's representation of women was part of the general questioning of "women's place" that was led by women's liberation activists.

The First Wave

The women's movement of the late 1960s was not the first. A previous women's-rights movement had reached its peak more than a hundred years earlier with the Seneca Falls Declaration of 1848, which rejected the doctrine of female inferiority then taught by academics and clergy (Harris, 1984). However, this *first wave* of the women's movement lost momentum in the 1920s, after women had won the vote, because women believed that voting would lead to political, social, and economic equality. Psychology's interest in sex differences and gender waned.

The Second Wave

With the rebirth of the women's movement in the 1960s, researchers again became interested in the study of women and gender. Women psychologists and men who supported their goals also began to work toward improved status for women within the field of psychology. Feminist activism made a big difference for women of this era, who had been openly discriminated against (Unger, 1998). Psychologist Carolyn Sherif remembered it this way:

> To me, the atmosphere created by the women's movement was like breathing fresh air after years of gasping for breath. . . . I did not become a significantly better social psychologist between 1969 and 1972, but I surely was treated as a better social psychologist. (Sherif, 1983, p. 280)

Activists—mostly graduate students and newcomers to psychology—formed the Association for Women in Psychology (AWP) in 1969. At about the same time, others—mostly older, more established psychologists—lobbied the American Psychological Association (APA) to form a Division of the Psychology of Women (Unger, 1998; 2001). This Division 35 was officially approved in 1973. Divisions on ethnic-minority psychology and gay/lesbian issues were established later, with the support of Division 35. Progress in incorporating women has also occurred among Canadian psychologists (Parlee, 1985) and the British Psychological Society, which now has a Psychology of Women Section (Wilkinson, 1997a).

These organizational changes have acknowledged the presence of diverse women in psychology and helped enhance their professional identity (Scarborough & Furumoto, 1987). And none too soon—women now earn 70 percent of

Ph.D.s awarded in psychology, and ethnic minorities earn 15 percent (Ballie, 2001).

The Third Wave

AWP continues to thrive as an activist organization with no formal ties to the psychological establishment. Division 35, now named the Society for the Psychology of Women, has become one of the larger divisions of APA, with about 3,000 members. Feminist theory and activism continue to develop as younger women follow up on the gains made by the second wave.

Today, the *third wave* of the women's movement tackles some of the unfinished business of the first two waves, such as ensuring reproductive freedom, ending violence against girls and women, and integrating women into politics, through groups such as the Third Wave Foundation. But third-wave groups such as the Riot Grrrls have their own agenda, too, speaking out to reclaim "girl culture," assert women's place in rock and pop music, and proclaim the joys of women's sexuality. Though the issues and the voices have changed, third-wave feminism is clearly connected to its foremothers' visions (Baumgardner & Richards, 2000).

Voices from the Margins: A History

Throughout the history of psychology, there had been criticism of psychology's treatment of women and people of color, most often voiced by members of those groups. As early as 1876, Mary Putman Jacobi completed a Harvard dissertation challenging the idea that women required special mental and bodily rest during menstruation. Jacobi noted that those who studied the supposed limitations of women were, like those who studied the supposed inferiority of people of color, hardly ever women or people of color themselves, and were very often quick to ascribe differences to nature or biology (cited in Sherif, 1979).

In the early 1900s, some of the first scientifically trained women devoted much research effort to challenging accepted wisdom about the extent and nature of sex differences. Helen Thompson Wooley conducted the first experimental laboratory study of sex differences in mental traits. In interpreting her results, she stressed the overall similarity of the sexes and the environmental determinants of observed differences, remarking daringly in a 1910 *Psychological Bulletin* article: "There is perhaps no field aspiring to be scientific where flagrant personal bias, logic martyred in the cause of supporting a prejudice, unfounded assertions, and even sentimental rot and drivel, have run riot to such an extent as here" (Wooley, 1910, p. 340). Among the women inspired by her work was Leta Stetter Hollingworth, who challenged the Darwinian view that women are innately less variable (and therefore less likely to be highly creative or intelligent) (Shields, 1982).

The work of a few early women psychologists opened the way for critical research to replace unexamined assumptions about women's "natural" limitations (Rosenberg, 1982). Determined to demonstrate women's capacity to contribute to modern science on an equal basis with men, they chose to measure sex differences in order to challenge beliefs about women's limitations. In a sense, their research interests were dictated by questions chosen by others. Faced with the necessity of proving their very right to do research, these women labored to refute hypotheses that they did not find credible (Unger, 1979a). Moreover, they worked in a social context that denied them opportunities because of their sex and forced them to make cruel choices between work and family relationships (Scarborough & Furumoto, 1987). Their story is one,

> in many ways, of failure—of women restricted by simple prejudice to the periphery of academe, who never had access to the professional chairs of the major universities, who never commanded the funds to direct large-scale research, who never trained the graduate students who might have spread their influence, and who, by the 1920s, no longer had the galvanizing support of a woman's movement to give political effect to their ideas. (Rosenberg, 1982, p. xxi)

The challenges to psychology to develop knowledge about all humanity have been present throughout psychology's history. Robert Guthrie's book *Even the Rat Was White* (Guthrie, 1976) examined the history of racism in psychology and anthropology and documented the contributions of early African-American and Mexican-American psychologists in providing less-biased views of human nature. However, the efforts of women and minorities remained voices from the margins until recently. The existence of AWP, Division 35, women's studies programs, and dozens of feminist journals make it unlikely that interest in the psychology of women and gender will fade away as it did in the 1920s. Because this new psychology clearly has developed in a social context of feminism, it is important to look closely at the relationship between the two.

WHAT IS FEMINISM?

The writer Rebecca West noted in 1913: "I myself have never been able to find out precisely what feminism is: I only know that people call me a feminist whenever I express sentiments that differentiate me from a doormat" (quoted in Kramarae & Treichler, 1985, p. 160). Exactly what is feminism and what does it mean to call oneself a feminist?

Feminism Has Many Meanings

Contemporary feminist theory has many variants (Tong, 1998). Each can be thought of as a different lens through which to view the experiences of women, and like different lenses, each is useful for focusing on particular phenomena.

What are the most influential feminist theoretical perspectives? In the United States, they include liberal, radical, socialist, womanist (woman of color), and cultural feminism. Belief in these different branches of feminism has been defined, reliably measured, and shown to predict people's behavior (Henley et al., 1998). Let's look briefly at each perspective.

Socialist feminism emphasizes that there are many kinds of divisions between groups of people that can lead to oppression. Socialist feminists believe that acts of discrimination based on social class, race, and gender are equally wrong. Moreover, it views these forms of discrimination as inseparable: sexism, racism, and classism reinforce each other, so that, for example, a poor woman of color is triply disadvantaged. This book presents many examples of relationships among different kinds of disadvantage, from teen mothers (Chapter 10) to social-class differences in gender-role learning during childhood and adolescence (Chapters 6 and 7).

Woman-of-color feminism, or *womanism,* began with criticism of the white women's movement for excluding women of color and issues important to them: poverty, racism, and needs such as jobs, health care, good schools, and safe neighborhoods for all people. Asian-American, Hispanic, and African-American women and men who are activists often choose to join forces with each other to fight racism and classism, even though the women are aware of their oppression as women (Chow, 1996). In general, womanists do not see men of color as sexist oppressors but as brothers who suffer the effects of racism just as women of color do. People who adopt this feminist perspective often point out the strengths and positive values of minority communities, such as the multigenerational support and closeness emphasized by African-American families (Chapters 10 and 12).

Radical feminism emphasizes male control and domination of women throughout history. This perspective views the control of women by men as the first and most fundamental form of oppression: women as a group are oppressed, not by their biology or their social class, but by men as a group. According to radical feminists, sexist oppression is one thing all women have in common. Radical feminist theory has fostered much research on violence against women and on sexuality, seeking to understand the sources and consequences of males' greater power (Chapters 8 and 13).

Liberal feminism is familiar to most people because it relies on deeply held American beliefs about equality—an orientation that connects it to political liberalism. From this perspective, a feminist is a person who believes that women are entitled to full legal and social equality with men and who favors changes in laws, customs, and values to achieve the goal of equality. The liberal feminist perspective has fostered research on such topics as how people react to others when they violate gender norms (Chapter 3), gender socialization (Chapter 6), and sex discrimination in employment (Chapter 11). It emphasizes the similarities between males and females, maintaining that given equal environments and opportunities, males and females will behave similarly.

Cultural feminism emphasizes differences between women and men. This perspective stresses that qualities characteristic of women have been devalued and should be honored and respected in society. Cultural feminism has been useful in understanding the importance of unpaid work contributed by women, such as child care (Chapter 11). It is often used in discussing gender differences in values and social behaviors—for example, the apparent tendency for women to be more nurturing and caring than men.

Feminism is increasingly becoming a global movement. *Global feminism* focuses on how sexist practices are related across cultures and how they are connected to neocolonialism and global capitalism. Issues of special concern to global feminists include sweatshop labor conditions, unequal access to health care and education, and forced prostitution. An important part of global feminism is the recognition that Western feminists do not have all the answers for women from other cultures. For example, in some societies, women are strongly pressured to undergo genital cutting (Chapter 8) or are required to veil their faces and bodies in public (Chapter 2). Though Western women may criticize these practices, it is important to remember that Western society also restricts women's bodily freedom and integrity through practices such as sexual harassment in public places and pressure to seek the perfect body through dieting and cosmetic surgery (hooks, 2000). Strategies for change work best if they come from within each culture, rather than being imposed from outside.

The diversity of frameworks and values in feminist thought may seem to be a source of confusion, but it is also healthy and productive. The lenses of different feminist perspectives can be used to develop and compare diverse viewpoints on women's experiences. In writing this book, we have drawn on a variety of feminist perspectives, using the lens of each as we thought it would help clarify a particular topic, sometimes comparing several feminist perspectives on an issue. However, within psychology, liberal feminism and cultural feminism have generated more debate and research than any other views. Therefore, Chapter 4 is devoted to contrasting liberal and cultural feminist perspectives on the question, "Just how different are women and men?"

Is There a Simple Definition?

Because of the plurality of definitions and viewpoints, it is perhaps more appropriate to speak of "feminisms" than "feminism." However, feminist perspectives share two important themes. First, feminism values women as important and worthwhile human beings. Second, feminism recognizes the need for social change if women are to lead secure and satisfying lives. Perhaps the simplest definition of a *feminist* is an individual who holds these basic beliefs: that women are valuable and that social change to benefit women is needed. The core social change that feminists advocate is an end to all forms of domination: those of men over women and those among women (Kimball, 1995). Therefore, perhaps the simplest definition of *feminism* is one proposed by bell hooks (1984): it is a movement to end sexism and sexist oppression. These broad definitions allow feminists to work together for political change while recognizing that ideas about how to reach their goals may differ.

Can men be feminists? Certainly! Men can hold the values we have described as feminist; they can value women as worthwhile human beings and work for social change to reduce sexism and sex discrimination. Some men who share these values call themselves feminists. Others prefer the label *profeminist,* believing that this term acknowledges women's leadership of the feminist movement and expresses their understanding that women and men have different experiences of gender.

Feminist perspectives in general can be contrasted to *conservatism* (Henley et al., 1998). Conservatives seek to keep gender arrangements as they have been in much of the recent past, with males holding more public power and status and women being more or less restricted to home and family. The conservative view has usually been justified on the grounds of biology or religion. The biological justification states that gender-related behaviors are determined by innate and unchangeable biological differences far more than by social conditions.

FIGURE 1.1. The Southern Baptist sect made the news by urging a return to female submission.
Source: Dan Wasserman. Copyright © 1998 *The Boston Globe*. Distributed by the Los Angeles Times Syndicate. Copyright 2003 Tribune Media Services, Inc. All rights reserved. Reprinted by permission.

Therefore, women should not be encouraged to try to do things that go against their "nature." For example, if women are biologically destined to be more nurturing because they are the sex that gives birth, it is unnatural and wrong for women to limit their childbearing or take on jobs that do not involve nurturing others. The religious justification (often combined with the biological justification) is that female submission and subordination are ordained by a supreme being. For example, some religions teach that women must be obedient to their husbands; others forbid contraception or grant the right to divorce only to men (see Figure 1.1).

Negative attitudes and values about women as a group constitute the form of prejudice known as *sexism.* Over the past thirty years, attitudes toward women have grown less conservative and more liberal. Women have been more liberal than men all along, but this gender difference has decreased as men's attitudes have moved in the direction of women's (Twenge, 1997). However, more subtle forms of sexism have emerged (see Chapter 2).

Sexist attitudes may lead to differential treatment of women, or *sex discrimination.* Discrimination occurs at the societal level, such as when women are paid less than men for equivalent work (see chapter 11), as well as in the form of everyday hassles, such as sexist remarks about women's bodies. Discrimination occurs surprisingly often and negatively affects women's emotional well-being (Swim, Hyers, Cohen, & Ferguson, 2001).

The Backlash against Feminism

Feminism, like other movements for social justice, has often met with resistance. Each time that feminist perspectives have gained power, there has been a backlash—attempts to put women and feminists "back in their place" (Faludi, 1991). The backlash has taken different forms at different times in history, but some characteristic patterns emerge repeatedly. These include stereotyping feminists and their ideas as crazy, outrageous, or trivial; insisting on immutable differences created by God or Nature that make social change impossible; and characterizing feminism as a mere quarrel among women. Let's look more closely at each of these forms of backlash.

Negative Stereotypes of Feminists

When first-wave feminists began organizing to win the right to vote, political cartoonists depicted them in ways that will seem very familiar today. Figure 1.2 shows suffragists as ugly, cigar-smoking, angry women who foist their babies off on men. Their uncontrolled sexuality is represented by the women

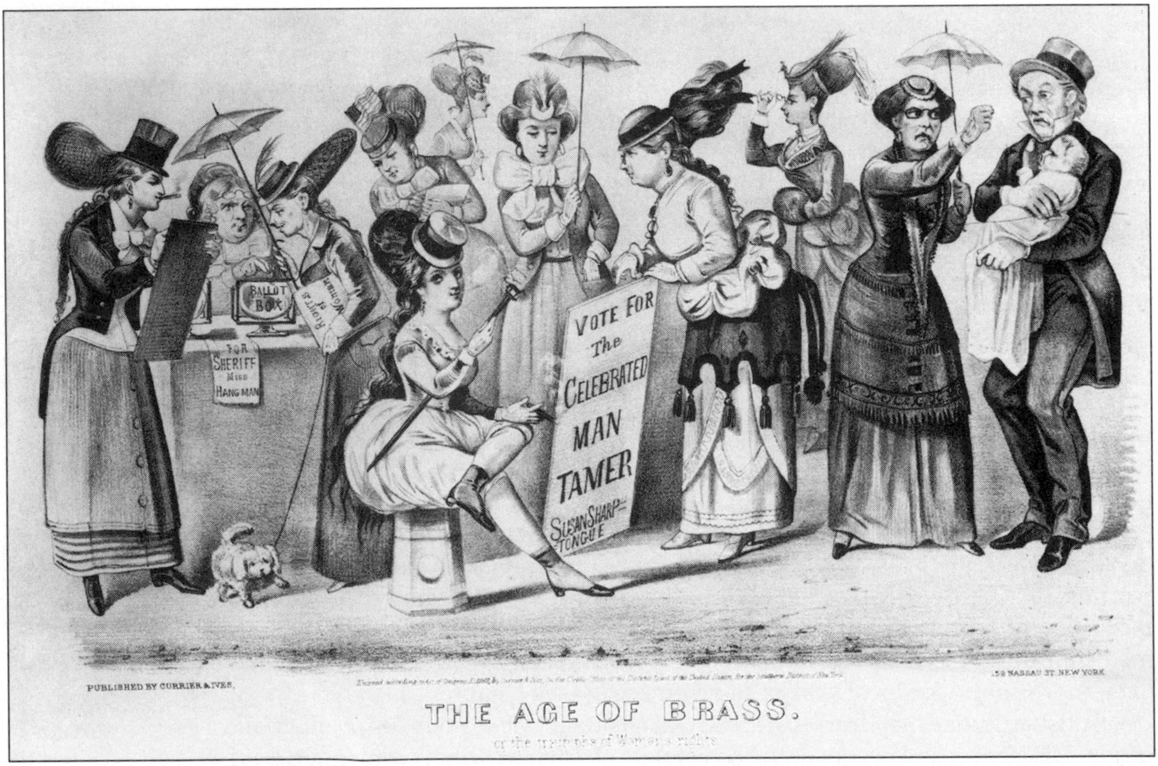

FIGURE 1.2. Backlash against first wave feminists.

whose legs are exposed. The text tells us that they are brassy, sharp-tongued man-tamers.

In the 1970s, these stereotypes resurfaced. The media image of second-wave feminists was quite negative:

> News reports and opinion columnists created a new stereotype, of fanatics, "bra-less bubbleheads," Amazons, "the angries," and "a band of wild lesbians." The result is that we all know what feminists are. They are shrill, overly aggressive, man-hating, ball-busting, selfish, hairy, extremist, deliberately unattractive women with absolutely no sense of humor who see sexism at every turn. They make men's testicles shrivel up to the size of peas, they detest the family and think all children should be deported or drowned. Feminists are relentless, unforgiving, and unwilling to bend or compromise; they are singlehandedly responsible for the high divorce rate, the shortage of decent men and the unfortunate proliferation of Birkenstocks in America (Douglas, 1994: 7).

By the 1980s, at least some women had made some gains toward equality. The media then turned to declaring feminism outdated, claiming that equal rights had been fully achieved, society was now in a "postfeminist" era, and women were abandoning feminism because it had terrible costs. In the 1980s version of backlash, everything from infertility to the breakdown of society was blamed on feminism (Faludi, 1991).

Today, the public image of feminists has both positive and negative aspects. For example, a study of British male high-school students and adult men revealed that they had "Jekyll and Hyde" views: feminists are reasonable women who just want equality, and they are ugly, man-hating lesbians who go around "banging and shouting" and just want men to "jump in the river." Surprisingly, many men held *both* these contradictory views (Edley & Wetherell, 2001). U.S. studies also show that feminists are viewed positively as women working together to achieve goals and negatively as man-hating, masculine-appearing extremists (Alexander & Ryan, 1997). Conservative commentators play to the negative view, trying to scare men and turn women away from working together for equality by referring to "feminazis" and characterizing any criticism of the status quo as "male-bashing" (see Figure 1.3).

The mixed image of feminism clearly influences women. On the one hand, college women describe feminists as strong, caring, capable, open-minded, knowledgeable, and intelligent (Berryman-Fink & Verderber, 1985; Buhl, 1989). On the other hand, being labeled "feminist" brings a certain stigma (see Figure

FIGURE 1.3. Responding to the backlash.
Source: Sylvia © 1992 by Nicole Hollander. Used by permission of Nicole Hollander.

FIGURE 1.4.
Source: Stone Soup. © 1999 Jan Eliot/Distributed by Universal Press Syndicate. Reprinted with permission of Universal Press Syndicate. All rights reserved.

1.4). In one study, women made less positive statements about the "feminist" movement than about the "women's" movement, demonstrating that simply adding the "f-word" (feminist) caused them to think more negatively about women's activists (Buschman & Lenart, 1996). When college women were asked to report their own beliefs and those of a "typical feminist," even those who identified themselves as feminists felt that the typical feminist was more extreme in beliefs that they themselves were (Liss, Hoffner, & Crawford, 2000). And many women are reluctant to label themselves feminists. In one recent study, 78 percent of college women said they were not feminists, although the majority agreed with some or most of the goals of the women's movement (Liss, et al, 2001). And even the feminists reported that they didn't always admit to being feminists in public!

Negative stereotypes have done their work: women who support gender justice seem to be quite aware that "feminist" may connote an angry woman who hates men, and "feminism" may connote an outdated ideology. What factors predict whether a woman will choose to identify as a feminist? Exposure to feminist ideas, having a generally positive view of feminists, and recognizing that discrimination exists are important. In addition, those who call themselves feminists support the goals of the women's movement, believe in collective action, and tend not to hold conservative beliefs (Liss et al, 2001; Myasovsky & Wittig, 1997).

Insisting on Differences

> If combat means living in a ditch, females have biological problems staying in a ditch for 30 days because they get infections and they don't have upper body strength. . . . On the other hand, men are basically little piglets. You drop them in the ditch, they roll around in it, it doesn't matter.

These words were spoken by the former Republican Speaker of the House of Representatives, Newt Gingrich, in 1995. Although it is disturbing that a person in high public office could profess such a simplistic stereotype (one that is demeaning to both sexes), it is not surprising. The more women accomplish in realms formerly closed to them, the more loudly it is proclaimed that they cannot and should not be doing what they are doing.

Today, women are astronauts, combat soldiers, coal miners, Supreme Court justices, great artists, and Nobel Prize-winning scientists, all the while continuing the traditional work of women: bearing and rearing children and caring for the needs of others. Yet theories and studies that purport to show that women are biologically inferior continue to receive press coverage and are used to justify women's disadvantaged status in society. Throughout this book we will critically examine theories and research claiming that women's minds (Chapter 4), brains (Chapters 4 and 5), and bodies (Chapters 7, 12, and 14) are so different from men's that women are incapable of equal achievements.

Women against Women: Feminism as a Cat Fight

One of the ways that feminists and their ideas are trivialized is to portray women as fighting with each other (Douglas, 1994). Any woman who attacks the ideals and practices of feminism is almost guaranteed a hearing in the news media. It is even better if she claims to be a feminist, and it seems to matter little if her expertise on the issues is minimal. This prevents male social theorists and political analysts from having to study and consider feminist ideas themselves and allows them to claim that sensible women see through feminism and reject it.

In the 1970s, the media ignored the many groups of women working collectively for women's rights. Instead, they focused on Gloria Steinem, a feminist journalist and activist, versus Phyllis Schlafly, a conservative activist who called feminists a "bunch of bitter women seeking a constitutional cure for their personal problems." The national debate over the Equal Rights Amendment to the U.S. Constitution was described as "women versus women" and "the war between the women." In the 1992 presidential campaign, Barbara Bush and Hillary Rodham Clinton were portrayed as polar opposites—the good wife and mother versus the selfish career woman. Today, conservative media celebrities such as "Dr. Laura" pit stay-at-home and working mothers against each other. In short, "the catfight remains an extremely popular way for the news media to represent women's struggles for equality and power" (Douglas, 1994, p. 243).

We invite our readers to think critically about the ways that feminists and feminism are portrayed in our society. It is disturbing that the media focus on the ideas of feminism only through the distortions and attacks of antifeminists (see Figure 1.5). We ask our readers to consider this question: Whose interests does it serve if a movement to end sexism is made to seem irrational, wrong, and futile?

Despite the attacks, feminism is a vital arena of theory and research. Far from holding to an inflexible "party line," feminists have always encouraged debate and a plurality of viewpoints. In writing this book, we have tried to present a variety of feminist perspectives with the goal of encouraging critical thinking about them.

METHODS AND VALUES IN SCIENTIFIC INQUIRY

Scientific research is often represented as a purely objective process in which a neutral, disinterested scientist investigates and reveals the secrets of nature. However, psychology has sometimes been anything but neutral in explaining

FIGURE 1.5. Sisterhood is complicated!
Source: © 1994 Lynda Barry. First printed in *Newsweek,* 1994. Courtesy Darhansoff, Verrill, Feldman Literary Agents.

the behavior of women. Interest in the psychology of women has led psychologists to identify specific methodological flaws in traditional research on women.

Toward Nonsexist Research

Let's look briefly at the research process. The researcher starts by generating a question to be answered by gathering information systematically. The question may originate in a theory, a personal experience, or an observation, or it may be raised by previous research. The next step is to develop a systematic strategy for answering the question—often called *designing the research.* In the design stage, a method is selected, such as experiment, survey, or case study. Research participants are chosen, materials such as questionnaires or laboratory setups are devised, and ways to measure the behaviors in question are decided on.

Next, the data are collected and analyzed so that patterns of results become clear. Statistical techniques are usually used for this task. The researcher then interprets the meaning of his or her results and draws conclusions from them. If reviewers and journal editors judge the research to be well conducted and important, the results are published in a scientific journal where they can influence future research and theory. Some research makes its way from journals into textbooks, influencing teachers and students as well as other researchers. Some even gets reported in the mass media, influencing perhaps millions of readers' and viewers' beliefs about such issues as racial differences in intelligence, sex differences in the brain, and the causes of social problems.

Biases can enter into the research process at any stage. In describing a few common types of bias at each stage, we will focus on gender-related examples. However, the principles of nonsexist research also apply to eliminating biases related to such characteristics as race/ethnicity, social class, or sexual orientation (Denmark, Russo, Frieze, & Sechzer, 1988).

Question Formulation

The process of creating research questions is perhaps the most neglected and undervalued part of the scientific enterprise. Textbooks and research courses say very little about where hypotheses come from or how to decide if a question is worth studying (Wallston & Grady, 1985). It is not surprising, then, that unexamined personal biases and androcentric theories often lead to biased research questions. Gender stereotypes related to the topic can bias the question and therefore the outcome of the study.

For example, many studies of leadership have defined it in terms of dominance, aggression, and other stereotypically male attributes. A nonstereotypical definition of leadership might include the ability to negotiate, to be considerate of others, and to help others resolve conflicts without confrontation (Denmark et al., 1988). Another example of bias in question formulation is found in the large amount of research on mothers who work outside the home. Much of it focuses on the question of whether the mothers' work endangers their children's psychological welfare. There is much less research on whether fathers' commitment to their work endangers their children's welfare or on whether mothers' employment might benefit mothers or children (Hare-Mustin & Marecek, 1990).

Designing Research

In the design phase of research, one important aspect is deciding how to measure the behaviors under study. If the measures are biased, the results will be, too. An extreme example of a biased measure comes from a study of women's sexuality. Participants were asked to describe their roles in sexual intercourse by choosing one of the following responses: "passive," "responsive," "resistant," "aggressive," "deviant," or "other." The outcome of this research might have been very different if women had also been allowed to choose from alternatives such as "active," "initiating," "playful," and "joyous" (Bart, 1971; Wallston & Grady, 1985).

Another aspect of the design phase is the choice of a comparison group. The results and conclusions of a study can be very different depending on which groups are chosen for comparison with each other. For example, one group of researchers was involved in an ongoing study of aging among a selected group of college-educated professional men. When they decided to add a sample of women, the biomedical scientists on the research team suggested that they should add the sisters of the men already in the study. Because they had the same parents, these two groups would be similar in physiological characteristics. The social scientists on the research team, however, suggested that the appropriate sample would be college-educated professional women who would be similar in social status. Although one choice is not necessarily right and the other wrong, the choice is conceptually important. The conclusions reached about gender differences in aging might be very different depending on which group of women was chosen, and the group chosen depends on assumptions about what kind of explanations (physiological or social) are most important (Parlee, 1981).

Choice of research participants is subject to many possible biases. Since the 1940s, psychology has come to rely more and more on college student samples, creating biases of age, social class, and developmental stage (Sears, 1986). Moreover, males have been more likely to be studied than females, perhaps because topics were gender-linked in the minds of researchers and "male" topics were considered more important (Wallston & Grady, 1985).

The proportion of male-only studies has decreased since the 1970s (Gannon, Luchetta, Rhodes, Pardie, & Segrist, 1992). However, subtler kinds of sex bias persist. Nearly 30 percent of psychological journal articles still do not report the gender of the participants. When researchers use an all-female sample, they are more likely to state it in the article's title, to discuss their reasons for studying women, and to point out that their results cannot be generalized to men (Ader & Johnson, 1994). It seems that psychologists believe it is important to indicate the limitations of an all-female sample, but they see nothing remarkable about an all-male sample—males are still the norm.

Other types of bias also persist. Research on ethnic-minority people of both sexes is scarce except when they are seen as creating social problems (Reid & Kelly, 1994). There is abundant research on teen pregnancy among African-American women, for example, but little research on their leadership, creativity, or coping skills for dealing with racism. Poor and working-class women, too, have been virtually ignored (Bing & Reid, 1996; Reid, 1993).

Many well-known psychologists, both female and male, have pointed out that psychology, supposedly the science of human behavior, is in danger of becoming a science of the behavior of college sophomores, and white male college sophomores at that. Feminist psychology, with its valuing of women as worthy subjects of research and its recognition of the diversity of social groupings, is providing an important corrective to this type of bias.

Analyzing Data: A Focus on Differences

Psychologists have come to rely on statistical tests in data analysis. Over the past thirty years, both the number of articles using statistics and the number of statistical tests per article have increased. Statistics can be a useful tool, but they also can lead to many conceptual difficulties in research on sex and gender (Wallston & Grady, 1985).

Statistical models lead to a focus on differences rather than similarities. The logic of statistical analysis involves comparing two groups to see if the average difference between them is "statistically significant." Unfortunately, it is not easy to make meaningful statements about similarities using statistical reasoning (Unger, 1981).

It is also unfortunate that statisticians chose the term *significant* to describe the outcome of a set of mathematical operations. As used by most people, the word means *important*, but as used by statisticians, it means only that the obtained difference between two groups is unlikely to be due to mere chance. A statistically significant difference does not necessarily have any practical or social significance (Favreau, 1997). The meaning and interpretation of difference will be discussed in more detail in Chapter 4.

Interpreting and Publishing Research Results

Psychology's focus on group differences affects the ways that results are interpreted and conveyed to others. One type of interpretation bias occurs when gender differences in performing a specific task are interpreted as evidence of a more general difference. For example, because special samples of highly gifted junior-high boys score higher on SAT math tests than similar samples of girls, some psychologists have argued that males in general have a biological superiority in math ability.

Another kind of interpretation bias occurs when the performance style more typical of girls or women is given a negative label. For example, girls get better grades in school in virtually every subject, but no one interprets this to mean that females are biologically superior in intelligence. Instead, girls' academic achievement is discounted; they are said to get good grades by being "nice" or "compliant."

Biased interpretations of gender differences lead to thinking of men and women as two totally separate categories. But it is simply not true that "men are from Mars, women from Venus." On many traits and behaviors, men and women are more alike than different. Even when a statistically significant difference is found, there is always considerable overlap between the two groups (see Chapter 4).

Problems of interpretation are compounded by publication biases. Because of reliance on the logic of statistical analysis, studies that report differences between women and men are more likely to be published than those that report similarities. Moreover, the editorial boards of journals are predominately made up of white men, who may perhaps see topics relevant to women and ethnic minorities as less important than topics relevant to people more like themselves (Denmark et al., 1988). Until feminist psychology was formed, there was very little psychological research on pregnancy and mothering, women's leadership, violence against women, or gender issues in therapy.

Bias continues after publication. Some findings are noticed by the media and others are not. Television and the popular press often actively publicize the latest discoveries about gender differences. Of course, some of these differences may not be very important, and others may not hold up in future research, but the public is less likely to hear about that, because gender similarities are not "news" (Crawford, 1989).

In summary, research is a human activity, and the biases held by those who do research can affect any stage of the process. As more diverse people become psychologists, they will bring new values, beliefs, and research questions. They can also question and challenge the biases in others' research. Feminist psychologists have led the way by demonstrating gender bias in psychological research and showing how it can be reduced.

Nonsexist research is not value free; that is, nonsexist research practices do not eliminate value judgments from the research process. Androcentric research is based on the value judgment that men and their concerns are more important and worthy of study than women and their concerns. In contrast, nonsexist research is based on the value judgment that women and men and their concerns are of equal worth and importance (Eichler, 1988).

Feminist Values in Research

Although feminist psychologists have been critical of psychology, they remain committed to it, expressing feminist values in their work (Grossman et al., 1997). What are some of these values?

Empirical Research Is a Worthwhile Activity

Although feminist psychologists recognize that science is far from perfect, they value its methods. Scientific methods are the most systematic way yet devised to answer questions about the natural and social world. Rather than abandon those methods or endlessly debate whether there is one perfect, feminist way to do research, they go about their work using a rich variety of methods, theories, and approaches. Good research on women and gender is necessary and important (Peplau & Conrad, 1989; Unger, 2001; Worell, 1996).

Research Methods Must Be Critically Examined

Feminist theorists have pointed out that methods are not neutral tools; the choice of method always shapes and constrains what can be found (Crawford & Kimmel, 1999; Marecek, 1989; Unger, 1983). For example, what is the best way to study female sexuality—by measuring physiological changes during arousal and orgasm or by interviewing women about their subjective experiences of arousal and orgasm? The two methods might produce very different discoveries about female sexuality (Tiefer, 1989).

Traditionally, experimentation has been the most respected psychological method. Psychologists like to do experiments because they can control for many outside factors that could affect results and because they can show causation (changing X causes a change in Y). However, experimental methods have been criticized for at least two reasons. First, in an experiment, the researcher creates an artificial environment and manipulates the experience of the participants. Experiments thus strip behavior from its social context (Parlee, 1979). Although laboratory studies isolate variables from the contaminating influence of real-life social processes, gender is played out in exactly those real-life processes (Crawford & Marecek, 1989). Therefore, behavior in the laboratory may not be representative of behavior in other situations (Sherif, 1979). Second, experiments are inherently hierarchical, with "the powerful, all-knowing researchers instructing, observing, recording, and sometimes deceiving the subjects" (Peplau & Conrad, 1989). The inequality of the experimental situation may be particularly acute when the researcher is male and the subject is female (McHugh, Koeske, & Frieze, 1986).

On the other hand, many important advances in understanding women and gender have come about because of experimental results. For example, experimental research has clarified the nature and functioning of stereotypes about women (see Chapter 2). Experimental research on perceptions of leadership, how power influences behavior (Chapter 3), and the evaluation of men's and women's performance (Chapter 11) has demonstrated in detail how sex discrimination occurs.

Although psychology has perhaps used the experimental method too much and too unreflectively, it should not be rejected. Just as any research method can be used in sexist ways, all methods can be used toward the goal of understanding women and gender. When the variety of methods is large, results based on different approaches can be compared with each other, and a richer and more complete picture of women's lives will emerge.

Both Women and Men Can Conduct Feminist Research

Most feminist researchers in psychology are women. The membership of APA's Division 35 is more than 90 percent female, and "women have taken the lead in investigating topics relevant to women's lives and in developing new concepts and theories to explain women's experiences" (Peplau & Conrad, 1989, p. 391). However, it is important not to equate female with feminist and male with nonfeminist. Women who are psychologists work in every area from physiological and learning to industrial and clinical psychology. Women psychologists may or may not personally identify as feminists, and even when they do, they may not bring a feminist perspective to their research. Also, male psychologists can identify as feminist. Men can and do conduct research on women and gender, and many conduct research on male gender roles. Of course, all psychologists—male and female, feminist and nonfeminist—should, at a minimum, conduct their research in nonsexist ways and work to eliminate sexism from their professional practices and behaviors.

Science Can Never Be Fully Objective or Value-Neutral

Science is done by human beings, all of whom bring their own perspectives to their work, based on their personal backgrounds. Personal experience sensitizes people to different aspects of problems (Unger, 1983). Because the values of dominant groups in a society are normative, they are not always recognized as values. When others—women and minorities, for example—question the assumptions of the dominant group, the underlying values are made more visible.

One of the most important insights of feminism is that research and the creation of knowledge do not occur in a social vacuum. Rather, each research project or theory is situated in a particular period in history and in a particular social context. The psychology of women and gender is not unique in being affected by social currents such as feminism, conservatism, and liberalism. All of psychology is so affected. Moreover, psychology in turn affects social issues and social policy through providing ways to interpret human behavior. Because psychology is a cultural institution, doing psychological research is inevitably a political act (Crawford & Marecek, 1989).

Although the effects of values on the scientific process are inevitable, they need not be negative for women. We believe that psychology should admit values, not only as sources of bias, but as a means of evaluating all parts of the research process (Crawford & Marecek, 1989; Unger, 1983). An awareness of the politics of science can help feminist psychologists use science to foster social change and improve women's lives (Peplau & Conrad, 1989).

Human Behavior Is Shaped by Social, Historical, and Political Forces

Because feminists believe that gender equality is possible, although it has not yet been achieved, they are sensitive to the ways that social contexts and forces shape people's behavior and limit human potential. Feminist psychologists try to understand not only the effects of gender, but also the effects of other systems of social classification such as race, social class, and sexual orientation. They tend to be skeptical that psychology will ever discover universal laws of behavior. Rather, they prefer to try to clarify the ways that sociocultural forces, as well as biological and intrapsychic ones, affect behavior.

Feminist psychologists respect the diversity of women and recognize that it is important to study varied groups. For example, U.S. women generally have lower self-esteem than men, but this is not true of African-American women. Such differences can show how women's psychology is affected by their social and cultural backgrounds, not just their biology.

THEMES OF THIS BOOK

Because much of psychology's knowledge about women has historically been androcentric, one task of feminist psychology is to analyze assumptions about women embedded in psychology's theories and research. Throughout this book, you will find many examples of such critical analyses, in which feminist psychologists have exposed areas of neglect, androcentric concepts and research questions, and faulty reasoning in theory and research about women.

However, feminist psychology does more than just criticize androcentric psychology. It helps create a more comprehensive and adequate psychology of women (Worell, 1996). This book draws on the work of hundreds of psychologists, both women and men, who have contributed to the ongoing process of revising—and transforming—psychology. It also draws on the work of feminist theorists and researchers in other disciplines, including philosophy, history, anthropology, sociology, political science, and literary and cultural studies.

This book, then, provides both a critique of androcentric knowledge about women and a survey of emerging scholarship. Four broad themes are woven through the book. First, we distinguish between sex and gender, conceiving gender as a cultural construction. Second, we emphasize the importance of thinking critically about language and naming. Third, we recognize the diversity of women. Fourth, we emphasize that psychological knowledge about women can and should be used to foster social change that will benefit women. Let's look at these themes in more detail.

Theme 1: Gender Is More Than Just Sex

Researchers who study the psychology of women find it useful to distinguish between the concepts of sex and gender (Unger, 1979b). Sex is defined as biological differences in genetic composition and reproductive anatomy and function. Human infants are labeled as one sex or the other, female or male, at birth, based on the appearance of their genitals. It sounds like a simple and straightforward matter, though in fact it can be surprisingly complex (see Chapter 5).

Gender is what culture makes out of the "raw material" of biological sex. All known societies recognize biological differentiation and use it as the basis for social distinctions. In our own society, the process of creating gendered human beings starts at birth. When a baby is born, the presence of a vagina or penis represents sex—but the pink or blue blanket that soon enfolds the baby represents gender. The blanket serves as a cue that this infant is to be treated as a boy or girl, not as a "generic human being," from the start.

Because gender is based on sex, the two terms have sometimes been used interchangeably. However, it is important to distinguish sex from gender for two reasons. First, equating them can lead to the belief that differences in the traits or behaviors of men and women are due directly to their biological differences, when the traits or behaviors actually may be shaped by culture. Second, keeping the concepts of sex and gender distinct can help us to analyze the complex ways they interact in our lives (Unger & Crawford, 1993).

Gender distinctions occur at many levels in society. Their influence is so pervasive that, like fish in water, we may be unaware that they surround us. Gender-related processes influence behavior, thoughts, and feelings in individuals; they affect interactions among individuals; and they help determine the structure of social institutions. The processes by which differences are created and power is allocated can be understood by considering how gender is played out at three levels: societal, interpersonal, and individual.

The Social Structural Level: Gender as a System of Power Relations

All known human societies make social distinctions based on gender. In the broadest sense, gender is a classification system that shapes the relations among women and men. The gender system influences access to power and resources (see Chapter 3). In many societies, for example, many kinds of violence against women are taken for granted (see Chapters 8 and 13). Genital mutilation, sexual harassment, rape, incest, and battering can be seen as culturally "useful" ways of controlling girls and women. The power conferred by gender is pervasive and multidimensional. Men have more public power in most societies, controlling government, law, and public discourse. By and large, men make and enforce the laws that women and men must obey.

Other ranking systems, such as race, class, and sexual orientation, also influence social power. All women and men can be classified in terms of their race, class, and sexual orientation, in addition to their gender. Feminist research and theory emphasize that these systems are connected—they operate simultaneously in social institutions and everyday interactions, often outside awareness (Weber, 1998). Being white, male, middle or upper class, and heterosexual confers advantages that often are not even noticed by those who have them (Rosenblum & Travis, 1996).

The Interpersonal Level: Gender as a Cue

People use gender cues in deciding how to behave toward others in social interactions. What happens when a person (A) meets someone (B) for the first time? Based on how B appears and acts, A decides that B is either male or female, and behaves accordingly. Why is it important to make that classification? Without it, A would not know whether to behave as though he or she were with a woman or with a man.

When people interact, the influences of sex and gender are intertwined. Not only do people use gender cues to make inferences about sex, they use perceived sex to make inferences about gender. When a man and a woman walk together into a car dealership, the salesperson is likely to direct the sales pitch to the man. Based on their appearance (gender), the salesperson decides that these two are a woman and a man (sex), assumes that they are a heterosexual couple, and acts according to his or her beliefs about which partner is more likely to make decisions about buying a car (gender). These kinds of interactions are so "normal" that they usually pass unnoticed. It is only when people "step out of line" that the gender forces shaping interaction become visible. A couple in which the woman is choosing the new car may feel quite uncomfortable as they violate the unwritten codes of gender.

Although much differential treatment of women and men (and boys and girls) happens outside awareness, research confirms that it is a reality. For example, observations in elementary school classrooms show that although teachers believe that they are treating boys and girls the same, boys receive more attention, both positive and negative, than girls do. Boys are yelled at and criticized more in front of their classmates. Moreover, in some classes, a few boys are allowed to dominate class time by interacting constantly with the teacher while most students remain silent (Eccles, 1989; Sadker & Sadker, 1994).

Research shows that the behavior of men and boys is often evaluated more positively than the behavior of women and girls. Even when a woman and a man behave in identical ways, their behavior may be interpreted very differently. Moreover, gender categorization is not simply a way of seeing differences, but a way of creating differences. When men and women are treated differently in ordinary daily interactions, they may come to behave differently in return. When they do, this re-creates the expectation that men and women ought to behave differently, reinforcing continued gender inequality (Risman, 1998). We will look more closely at these processes in Chapter 3.

The Individual Level: Gender as Masculinity and Femininity

To a greater or lesser extent, women and men come to accept gender distinctions visible at the social structural level and enacted at the interpersonal level as part of the self-concept. They become *gender-typed,* ascribing to themselves the traits, behaviors, and roles normative for people of their sex in their culture. Women, moreover, internalize their devaluation and subordination. Feminist theories of personality development (see Chapter 4) stress that characteristics such as passivity, excessive concern with pleasing others, lack of initiative, and dependency are psychological consequences of subordination. Members of subordinate social groups who adopt such characteristics are considered well adjusted; those who do not are controlled by psychiatric diagnosis (Chapter 14), violence or the threat of violence (Chapter 13), and social rejection (Chapter 3).

Much of the psychology of women and gender has consisted of documenting the effects of internalized subordination, and we will see many examples throughout this book. Laboratory and field research, as well as clinical experience, attest that, compared with boys and men, girls and women lack a sense of personal entitlement; expect less pay for comparable work; are equally satisfied with their employment even though they are paid significantly less than men; lose self-esteem and confidence in their academic ability, especially in mathematics and science, as they progress through the educational system; and are more likely to suffer from disturbances of body image, eating disorders, and depression. These differences are not "natural." They are shaped by differential opportunities and maintained in social interaction. They are the product of the gender system.

Although the distinction between sex and gender is an important one, it is relatively new in psychology, and it is not always used consistently from one book or article to another (Deaux, 1993; Gentile, 1993; Unger & Crawford, 1993). Because we (the authors) assume that virtually all human behavior is shaped by culture, we will use *gender* except when referring directly to sexual anatomy or reproduction. Differing social behaviors in women and men, for example, will be referred to as "gender differences," because they are probably not directly caused by biological sex. However, we will retain terms such as "sex discrimination" that are widely used by researchers.

Theme 2: Language and Naming Are Sources of Power

Controversies over terminology can sometimes seem like semantic hairsplitting. But language and naming are sources of power. Thinking critically about language can increase understanding of how the system of social classification called gender confers more power on males.

Aspects of reality that are named become "real" and can be talked about and thought about. Names allow people to share experiences and teach others to name their own experiences in the same way. Moreover, when certain aspects of reality are granted names, unnamed aspects become overshadowed and thus more difficult to think about and articulate. Unnamed experiences are less visible, and therefore, in a sense, less real to the social world (Berger & Luckmann, 1966).

The English language is, unfortunately, rich in linguistic sexism (Adams & Ware, 1989). One example is the traditional practice of using *he, his,* and *him* to represent both women and men—as in "Each student should bring his notebook." A great deal of psychological research has shown that the use of "generic" masculine language leads people of both sexes to think more about males (Henley, 1989).

Androcentric language omits important aspects of female experience. The negative physical changes and feelings some women experience in conjunction with the menstrual cycle have the official and scientific-sounding label *premenstrual syndrome*—but the feelings of well-being and heightened competence that some women experience around the ovulation phase of the cycle have no label. Thus, PMS has become widely accepted as "real," is readily discussed everywhere from Oprah to the college classroom, and is a legitimate topic of research. Midcycle well-being is rarely a focus of research or discussion.

Issues of language and naming can divide people. For example, one student described an ongoing feud with her roommate. The student used the term *woman* rather than *girl* for herself and others, believing that to call anyone past the teen years a girl is insulting. The roommate believed just as firmly that it is fine to be called a girl. The issue was important to both because in their choice of words they were claiming different identities. The term *woman,* like *man,* conveys adulthood, power, and sexuality; the term *girl,* like *boy,* conveys youth, powerlessness, and frivolity. "Mere words" permanently divided the two roommates (Rosenblum & Travis, 1996).

Choices about language are controversial because of their symbolic meanings. Consider these contrasting opinions of women on whether a woman should take her husband's name upon marriage:

> When I got married, it seemed a bit late in life to get used to a new last name, as I'd had mine for 35 years. I also frankly couldn't see what choosing to share your life with someone had to do with changing your name.

> I feel desperately sorry for all those young women who will never know the joy and/or soaring pride of taking their new husband's name.

> When my husband and I decided to give our daughter my last name, it seemed like a sensible plan. Having grown up in a blended family, in which different last names were the norm, keeping my own name at marriage was an easy choice. . . . Little did we know how controversial our decision would be. Routinely, people assume that my daughter is not my husband's—and when it is explained, they look at us in utter shock. They ask my husband, "Didn't you want your kid to have your name?" and say to me, "Your husband must be a really nice guy.". . . The idea that a man would give up the privilege of "passing down his name" is virtually unthinkable; the assumption that women will give up this privilege unquestioned . . . (Henry, 1998, p. E6)

Linguistic sexism and symbolism are discussed in Chapter 2. Throughout the book, there are many examples of the importance of language and naming.

Feminist scholars are not only analyzing language practices but also challenging gender bias in language use. They have caused some important changes (Crawford, 2001). For example, the American Psychological Association adopted guidelines for nonsexist language in 1977. Language change as a result of feminist activism is evident outside psychology as well. One example is the widespread use of Ms. as a parallel title to Mr. When Ms. was first proposed, it was considered dangerously radical and subjected to ridicule; now it is the norm (Crawford, Stark, & Renner, 1998). The writer Gloria Steinem perhaps best expressed the importance of the power of naming—and the influence of feminist activism on language change:

> We have terms like "sexual harassment" and "battered women." A few years ago, they were just called "life." (Steinem, 1983, p. 149)

Until recently, the public power to name has been largely in the hands of men. Men controlled the institutions of knowledge, and even if women acquired expertise, they did not acquire legitimacy. History is full of stories about learned women whose work was attributed to their fathers, their brothers, their teachers, or "anonymous."

One illustration of how a woman could have outstanding expertise and yet be denied legitimacy is the story of Mary Whiton Calkins. Despite completing an impressive Ph.D. dissertation, she was denied a Ph.D. from Harvard because she was a woman. Nevertheless, Calkins taught for many years at Wellesley College, established an experimental laboratory there, and made important contributions to psychology. Although Mary Calkins triumphed personally, her life illustrates the way even outstanding women may be marginalized. For example, she taught during her entire life at a women's college where she did not have doctoral students of her own. Under these conditions, her theories and research projects did not receive the continuity of investigation they deserved. Similar stories have been uncovered about other early feminist psychologists (Scarborough & Furumoto, 1987). The ability to have one's research and theories taken seriously and passed on to the next generation of researchers is part of the power to name.

Making a Difference

Mary Whiton Calkins (1863–1930) was the first woman president of both the American Psychological Association in 1905 and the American Philosophical Association in 1918, a founder of Wellesley College's psychology department, and a pioneer in several topics in psychology, including the self, dreams, and memory. In 1906 she was ranked as the twelfth most important psychologist in the U.S. But because she was a woman, Harvard University did not award her the Ph.D. degree she earned there more than 100 years ago. The university refuses to do so to this day. Harvard had given Calkins grudging permission to study in Hugo Münsterberg's laboratory and to attend seminars with William James and Josiah Royce, but despite passing an unauthorized Ph.D. exam given by James, Münsterberg, Royce, and other Harvard professors, Calkins did not receive a Harvard Ph.D. Petitions from famous Harvard alumni such as Edward Thorndike and Robert Yerkes led Harvard officials to respond that they saw "no adequate reason" to confer the degree. Recently, Professor Karyn Boatwright of Kalamazoo College and students Meghan Keeler, Tracy Van Tuyl, Tim Pruzinsky, and Kelly Koss brought the issue to national attention by starting a media campaign to convince Harvard to grant Calkins a posthumous Ph.D. degree. Harvard responded that although "Mary Calkins was clearly a dedicated scholar," there was "no evidence to indicate that she completed the requirements necessary to receive a Ph.D." Dr. Boatwright and the students are now gathering evidence to prove that Calkins completed her coursework. You may read about the project and send Harvard an email at http://kzoo.edu/~k00kk03/pfolio/marywhiton calkins.html.

Sources:

Justice for Mary Whiton Calkins. (Summer 2002). *The Feminist Psychologist,* p. 11.

Mary White Calkins. (2001). www.astr.ua.edu/4000WS/CALKINS.html

The "mother of psychology" deserves her doctorate from Harvard University! (2002, August). Article available at http://kzoo.edu/~k00kk03/pfolio/marywhitoncalkins.html

Theme 3: Women Are Not All Alike

Although gender is an important and universal dimension for classifying human beings and allocating power, it is not the only dimension. As discussed earlier, social class, sexuality, and race/ethnicity also serve as principles of social organization. Therefore, important though gender is, it would be a mistake to assume that all women necessarily have much in common with each other simply because they are women. A woman who is wealthy and privileged may, for example, have as much in common with wealthy and privileged men as she has with poor women. African-American and Latina women share with the men of their ethnic groups—and not with white women—the experiences of racism and racial stereotyping. Lesbians share the experience of being in a sexual minority with bisexuals and gay men, not with heterosexual women. Dimensions such as age and (dis)ability are relevant, too. The viewpoints and concerns of older women and disabled women are not necessarily the same as those of young, able-bodied women. Studies of different groups of women can help us to understand how biological, social, and cultural factors interact to influence behavior.

Yet creating a psychology of all women is not an easy task. If women of color are studied only in comparison to a mythical "generic" (white, privileged-status) woman, researchers are implicitly making white women the norm, just as previous generations of psychologists made men the norm (Greene & Sanchez-Hucles, 1997; Yoder & Kahn, 1992). It is important to study each group of women within its own cultural context.

In writing this book, we have tried to respect and express the diversity of women's experiences. As we worked on the book together, we noticed that feminists have often used metaphors of gender as a lens or prism through which to view the social structure (Bem, 1993; Crawford & Marecek, 1989; Unger, 1990). Viewing psychological and social phenomena through the lens of gender allows us to see aspects of social reality that are otherwise obscured. However, like any lens, gender can reveal only some features of the social landscape. Lenses such as race, class, and age reveal other, equally important features. Feminist psychologists do not want to copy the limitations of androcentric psychology by replacing "male as norm" with "white-middle-class-heterosexual female as norm."

Theme 4: Psychological Research Can Foster Social Change

Traditionally, psychologists have focused on changing individuals. They have developed techniques to change attitudes, increase insight and self-understanding, teach new behavioral skills, and reduce or eliminate self-defeating thinking and behaviors. They have applied these techniques in a variety of educational and therapeutic settings. This book shows many examples of how feminist psychology has adapted and used these techniques.

However, research on women and gender indicates that there are limits to the power of individual change. Many problems that confront women are the result of social structures and practices that put women at a disadvantage and interfere with their living happy, productive lives. Social-structural problems cannot be solved solely through individual changes in attitudes and behavior; rather, the social institutions that permit the devaluation and victimization of women must also be changed. Therefore, throughout this book we discuss the implications of psychological research for changing institutions such as traditional marriage, language use, child rearing, the workplace, and the institution of psychology itself. Chapter 15 focuses on individual and structural change.

Social changes are not always for the better. Sometimes policies that solve problems for one group create problems for others (McGrath, 1986). For example, the Communist regimes in Eastern Europe reduced the individual freedoms of everyone. These governments were toppled. New, more democratic regimes, such as those in Poland, however, have voted to eliminate legal abortion and equal rights for women. Thus, women's freedoms are curtailed in these new democracies. What is defined as progress depends on who is writing the definition.

Psychological research draws on the real world of people living in complex social contexts. It isolates aspects of that world for systematic study. When researchers and textbook writers examine the implications of psychological research for changing women's social environments and opportunities, they return the isolated aspects to their context. Thus, a circle is closed, and psychological research is potentially more useful for women.

OUR GOALS FOR OUR STUDENTS

We, the authors of this book, have changed, both personally and professionally, as a result of our involvement in the psychological study of women. Rhoda Unger wrote:

> Once upon a time I was a confirmed behaviorist. In principle, this meant that I believed effects derived from orderly determinist causes, that the subjective aspects of behavior were irrelevant, and that the best studies required maximal distance between experimenter and subject. In practice, this meant that my first major research, my doctoral dissertation, involved making lesions in the caudate nucleus of rats and examining their effects upon temporal and spatial alternation by means of operant conditioning procedures. If I thought of sex professionally at all, I saw it as a variable which could neither be manipulated nor controlled and therefore of very little scientific interest. Even the rats were male. (1989, p. 15)

Like Rhoda Unger, Mary Crawford started out as a psychologist believing that good science demanded a separation of personal or social concerns from scientific problem solving. Her dissertation was an analysis of species-specific reactions in rats and their effects on classical and operant conditioning. She writes:

> More and more, my research seemed like a series of intellectual puzzles that had no connection to the rest of my life. In the lab, I studied abstract theories of conditioning, accepting the assumption that the principles were similar for rats and humans. In the "real world," I became involved in feminist activism and began to see things I had never noticed before. I saw sex discrimination in my university and knew women who struggled to hold their families together in poverty. Trying to build an egalitarian marriage and bring up my children in nonsexist

ways made me much more aware of social pressures to conform to traditional gender roles. I began to ask myself why I was doing a kind of psychology that had so little to say about the world as I knew it. I turned to the study of women and gender in order to make my personal and intellectual life congruent and to begin using my skills as a psychologist on behalf of social change.

Both of us have worked for social change on behalf of women—for reproductive rights, gender equity in education, peace and nonviolent conflict resolution, nonsexist marriage and child raising, and gender-fair language. We have helped communicate psychology to the general public through speaking and writing on feminist issues. These commitments have raised fresh questions and provided us with new insights on women and gender.

Today, we value our early research for teaching us how to go about scientific inquiry systematically and responsibly, but we have changed our views about what the important questions in psychology are and which theoretical frameworks have the most potential. We have chosen to specialize in the study of women and gender, and to write this book, in the hope that we may contribute to the creation of a new, transformed psychology.

A study of fifty-one distinguished feminist psychologists suggests that our experience of professional and personal change through feminism is not unusual. Asked to describe their experience of feminism, these psychologists indicated that, to them, feminism meant valuing women and their experiences, a concern with equality of power, the need for change and activism, and the idea of gender as a social construct. Their focus on women and gender in their research and teaching was part of a feminism whose meaning was "much more than the dictionary would suggest . . . a lived, conscious, changing experience." Researcher Ellen Kimmel noted the transformative power of feminist thought among her research participants and in her own life. Her summation can apply to the women who wrote this book as well: "Feminism (whatever it is and all that it is) transformed my life by connecting it to my work and gathering the disparate parts of myself into a whole" (Kimmel, 1989, p. 145).

Rhoda Unger has taught the psychology of women for thirty years and Mary Crawford has taught it for twenty-nine years. Together, we have introduced thousands of students, both women and men, to feminist psychology. Our students have differed in their racial and ethnic backgrounds, age, life experience, and sexual orientation. Their personal beliefs and values about feminism, women, and gender varied a great deal. In short, our students have been a diverse group of people. We have welcomed that diversity, and in this book we try to reflect what we have learned from it. Whatever your own background, we welcome you, our newest students, to the study of women and gender.

Perhaps because of our own experience of change through learning about women and gender, our goals for our students involve changes in knowledge, thinking skills, and attitudes. We hope that you, like many of our students before you, will experience growth in at least some of the following areas as a result of your studies:

- *Critical thinking skills.* By studying the psychology of women, you can learn to evaluate psychological research critically and become a more astute, perceptive observer of human behavior.

- *Knowledge and understanding about social inequities.* The focus is on the gender system, sexism, and sex discrimination. However, gender always interacts with other systems of domination, such as racism and heterosexism.
- *Empathy for women.* You may come to appreciate the experiences and viewpoints of your mother, your sisters, and your women friends better. In addition, women students may experience a heightened sense of sisterhood with all women.
- *Desire to work toward social change that benefits women—and a commitment to do so.*
- *The ability to see the larger context of women's lives.* The psychology of women is linked to their place in society and culture.
- *The understanding that "women" is a complex category.* Women are a diverse group and must be studied in the context of their lives.

There is one thing, however, that we cannot offer you as a consequence of studying women and gender: closure. A first course in women and gender, our students tell us, raises as many questions as it answers. Acquiring knowledge is an ongoing process, for professional researchers as well as for college students.

> Feminist psychology and feminism in general seem to be at the point of trying to piece together the individual parts of a quilt. The overall pattern of the quilt that we want to create is still emerging. No one knows what a feminist psychology will look like. . . . We are beginning to piece the separate parts together—to explore the kinds of stitching to use in connecting the pieces and how to place the separate pieces into the pattern. But we have not stopped questioning the process of quilting itself (Gentry, 1989, pp. 5–6).

Perhaps most important, the quilt is already useful, and the conversations around the margins are vibrant.

SUGGESTED READINGS

BAUMGARDNER, JENNIFER, & RICHARDS, AMY. (2000). *Manifesta: Young women, feminism, and the future.* New York: Farrar, Straus, and Giroux. Third-wave feminists talk about how the women's movement has evolved, describe the social and political changes that the third wave is working for, and share their vision of a world of true equality. This book has humor, passion, and a great list of resources for activism.

CRAWFORD, MARY & UNGER, RHODA. (2001). *In our own words: Writings from women's lives* (2nd edition). New York: McGraw-Hill. A rich collection of diverse voices on women's lives: a mother whose daughter was stalked and murdered, a "brave new family" with one child and four gay parents, an Asian-American woman on the politics of cosmetic surgery, a transgendered person on being a "gender outlaw," feminist Gloria Steinem on "If Men Could Menstruate"—and many more.

HOOKS, B. (2000). *Feminism is for everybody: Passionate politics.* Cambridge, MA: South End Press. An African-American feminist writes about the development of feminist thought and its impact on diverse women.

CHAPTER 2

Images of Women and Men

What picture do you see when someone asks you to think of a "woman"? Do you think of the images shown on TV or in the movies? Or do you think of individual women you have known—your mother or a favorite teacher? As you can see from the picture in Figure 2.1, womanhood is not a simple category.

Women vary in age, ethnicity, and social class as well as in many other dimensions. Images of women also differ across cultures, and they vary within our own culture over time. These images are neither fleeting nor trivial. They are used as models by which women (and men) are judged as worthy members of their sex. These idealized images often become anchors for psychological identity and serve as a basis for self-perception and self-esteem (Gilmore, 1990).

Media images of women differ greatly from the picture of real women in Figure 2.1. In the media, portrayals of women emphasize their bodies and set exacting physical and sexual standards. Women who are found deficient or deviant according to media standards may be stigmatized and shamed. Women who fail to meet minimal standards of femininity (such as older or disabled women) may be denied a gender identity at all. They are invisible in our culture's images of women.

Although images of women are not constructed in the same way by all societies, gender is a category that exists in all cultures. Most societies tend to exaggerate biological differences by clearly differentiating gender roles and defining the proper behavior of women and men as opposite or complementary. Images of women convey these cultural demands. The way a society pictures its women can never be considered trivial or meaningless.

FIGURE 2.1. Who is the real woman? Women come in all sizes, colors, and varieties.

MEDIA IMAGES OF WOMEN AND MEN

Biased images of women are found in every form of the mass media—in children's picture books, storybooks, and textbooks, in the movies, on television, and in magazine fiction. And some of the most pernicious images of women are found in advertising. Biases are measured by the disproportionate number of males to females portrayed, the gender-specificity of the traits that males and females display, the limited behavioral roles of women compared with the roles of men, the smaller number of occupations in which women can be found, and the different physical characteristics associated with each group (Unger, 1979a).

Things have not changed as much as one might expect. For example, an article a few years ago in *The New York Times* (1997) noted that there are still more male than female characters in the movies and on TV; that 49 percent of the men were shown working outside the home versus 28 percent of the women; and that women were much more likely than men to talk about romantic relationships. Seventy-eight percent of the performers in music videos are male.

What Do the Media Show?

Comic Strips

Biased images of men and women in the comics pages of newspapers may be particularly insidious. The comics are easily accessible to young children, and because readers do not take the material seriously, they may be unaware of the sexist messages they are receiving (Figure 2.2).

Images of men and women on the comics pages are seriously distorted. Males appear more frequently as both central and minor characters. The least visible women are ethnic minority women: Although comic strips have im-

FIGURE 2.2. Turning the tables.
Source: Rhymes with Orange. © Hilary B. Price. Reprinted with Special Permission of King Features Syndicate.

proved their gender representations in recent years and have become more ethnically diverse, daughters continue to be found less frequently than sons in comic strips involving black families (LaRossa, Jaret, Gadgil, & Wynn, 2001).

One pair of researchers examined three Sunday comics ("Blondie," "The Born Loser," and "Dennis the Menace") over three decades (Brabant & Mooney, 1986, 1997). They found that images of women in passive roles declined significantly in these comics between 1974 and 1994, but women were still shown as significantly more passive than men. The major change over a twenty-year period was that women were shown wearing aprons less often. Men were never portrayed as wearing aprons, not even when Dagwood helps Blondie in her catering business!

The same researchers also investigated more contemporary comic strips in which the wife works outside the home (Mooney & Brabant, 1987). Even in these less traditional comics, husbands were more likely to be portrayed outside the home than wives were. Career women in these comics were portrayed as critical, worried, and having stressful, sleepless nights.

Women in the News

Women are much less often featured in the news media than men are. Men were solicited for comment on newspaper front pages 75 percent of the time, whereas women were quoted only 25 percent of the time (Hernandez, 1994). Another survey of both major and minor newspapers found that stories about women accounted for only 15 percent of the front-page stories ("A Survey Finds Bias," 1996). Men dominated the local news and business pages as well. Most of the front-page stories were written by men (67%), as were the op-ed or equivalent pieces (72%). Women were portrayed negatively much more often than men in both small and large newspapers (30% versus 12%). Even the positive images of women and men were not equivalent. Nearly half of the positive portrayals of women in the major papers (such as *The New York Times* or *The Washington Post*) featured women as entertainers, whereas 82 percent of the positive portrayals of men were as authorities, experts, or opinion makers.

The news media appear to treat women in politics particularly harshly. When Geraldine Ferraro was the Democratic candidate for the U.S. vice presidency in 1984, political cartoons often showed her as a threatening or dominating figure who reduced Walter Mondale, the presidential candidate, to helpless submission (Miller, 1993). Most women in politics are ignored. For example, female senators receive little news space, even in their home states.

When women are mentioned, their physical appearance and clothing are commented on more frequently than those of comparable men, no matter what the news story is about (Foreit et al., 1980). (See Chapter 3 for more examples of this practice.) For example, a quip about Shannon O'Brien (who recently lost her bid to become governor of Massachusetts to a man) was circulated widely. It suggested that "she looked like every man's first wife." The news media also focused on the appearance of Linda Tripp (a major figure in the Clinton sex scandals) with endless comments about her weight, hair, and dress. In contrast, the media made almost no comments about the personal appearance of Special Prosecutor Ken Starr, who was, like Tripp, middle-aged and very average in looks and attire (Rivers, 2000).

Women on the Sports Pages

Women are more likely to be featured in sports rather than in political news, but women athletes still receive less coverage than male athletes. For example, women were featured on the cover of *Sports Illustrated* four times in 53 issues in 1996. There was also much less coverage of women's than men's sports events during the 1996 Olympics (Eastman & Billings, 1999). Ironically, 1996 had been named the year of women in sports. Data from the 2000 Olympics have not yet reached the pages of professional journals, but there is no reason to believe much will change. The neglect of female athletes starts early. Boys and young men receive more and longer articles than girls and young women in the sports pages of high school and college newspapers (Sagas, Cunningham, Wiglety, & Ashley, 2000).

When women are featured in the sports news, their images are likely to be distorted. Stories focus on their physical attractiveness rather than on their ability and accomplishments. One study demonstrated that this emphasis detracts from how the athletes are perceived. Undergraduates who read fictitious newspaper profiles about male and female Olympic athletes neither liked nor had favorable impressions of them when the articles focused on their attractiveness rather than their achievements (Knight & Guiliano, 2001). Media images of male athletes tend to glorify their strength and power, even their violence. In contrast, media images of women athletes focus on feminine beauty and grace (so they are not really athletes) or on their thin, small, wiry, androgynous bodies (so they are not really women) (Lorber, 1993a), as Figure 2.3 illustrates.

Male and female athletes are even named differently in stories about them. First names are most likely to be used for women athletes and for male black ath-

FIGURE 2.3. The bias against mature femininity in figure skating is illustrated by Michelle Kwan (on the right) who has lost successive Olympic gold medals to younger, less mature girls (most recently to Sarah Hughes on the left).

letes nearly as often. Only white male athletes are routinely referred to by their last names (Messner, Duncan, & Jensen, 1993). This pattern of under-representation and trivialization of women in sports has even been found in Sweden—a nation committed to gender equality. Swedish women athletes are occasionally referred to as girls, but more frequently as ladies or young ladies. In contrast, male athletes are always referred to as men or guys. Male athletes were also referred to by their last times almost twice as often as female athletes were (Koivula, 1999).

Sexism on the TV Screen

Every time you turn on your TV you get a dose of sexism. Sexist biases in both children's and adults' television programs have been demonstrated repeatedly (Ward & Carruthers, 2001). One study found, for example, that 57 percent of all the characters on comedy shows were men, and this figure rose to 71 percent in action/adventure shows (Davis, 1990). Female characters are usually younger than male characters by an average of ten years, and men are four times more likely than women to have gray hair. The age difference is particularly noticeable among television news anchors (Figure 2.4).

Television commercials are much more sexist than the programming. Women in TV ads are about four times more likely to be provocatively dressed than men are (Davis, 1990). Women are particularly likely to be presented as sex objects in advertisements delivered during weekend afternoon sportscasts whose audience is primarily men (Craig, 1992). Women in these weekend ads are almost never shown without an accompanying man. When they are not models or sex objects, they are generally shown taking care of men—as hotel receptionists, secretaries, or flight attendants.

FIGURE 2.4. A cartoonist's view of differing standards of age and appearance for women and men.
Source: Six Chix. Reprinted with Special Permission of King Features Syndicate.

TABLE 2.1 Authority and fulfillment of characters in 1992–1994 television commercials by race/ethnicity and gender. This table shows who appears in TV advertising and what roles they play. Both race and gender are important, but the analysis compares only black and white actors since other groups appear in too small numbers to be analyzed. There were only 29 Latino/as and 50 Asian Americans in this sample of nearly 2,500 characters in the ads.

	White (*N* = 2058)		*African American* (*N* = 257)	
	Men	Women	Men	Women
Authority				
Aggressive (%)	13.91[a,b]	9.51[a]	37.78[a,b]	11.11[a]
Active/instrumental (%)	41.72[a,b]	29.61[a]	59.26[a,b]	31.31[a]
Passive/emotional (%)	20.71	24.54[b]	19.26	11.11[b]
Employed (%)	27.61[a]	13.91[a]	22.96	16.16
Order-giver (%)	32.14[a,c]	17.09[a]	16.13[c]	6.25
Fulfillment				
Cross-sex interaction (%)	56.82[a,b]	72.87[a,b]	39.36[b]	50.00[b]
Sex object (%)	7.59[a]	25.80[a,b]	6.67	10.10[b]
Spouse (%)	6.31[c]	7.97[c]	2.22[c]	3.03[c]
Home setting (%)	26.23[a,b]	39.12[a,c]	13.33[a,b]	30.30[a,c]
Parent (%)	9.17[a]	14.27[a]	8.15	10.10
Child (%)	9.89[c]	9.08	5.34[c]	11.34

[a] $p < .05$ for difference between men and women within race (Fisher's exact test, two-tailed).
[b] $p < .05$ for difference between White and African American within gender (Fisher's exact test, two-tailed).
[c] $p < .10$ for difference between White and African American within gender (Fisher's exact test, one-tailed).

Source: Adapted from S. Coltrane & M. Messineo (2000). "The perpetuation of subtle prejudice: Race and gender imagery in 1990s television advertising," *Sex Roles. 42.* Reprinted by permission of Kluwer Academic/Plenum Publishers.

Images in TV commercials are racist as well as sexist. In a content analysis of more than 1,600 commercials associated with highly rated shows, researchers found that characters in these commercials enjoyed more prominence and had more authority if they were white or male (Coltrane & Messineo, 2000). In general, TV programs of the 1990s tended to show white men as powerful, white women as sex objects, black men as aggressive, and black women as inconsequential. There were not enough representations of Latinos/Latinas or Asian Americans to perform an analysis (see Table 2.1).

The characters in TV commercials do not have to be human to demonstrate sexist biases. Most of the animated characters who act as spokespersons for products are male (Peirce & McBride, 1999). Commercials featuring animated characters may be more effective promoters of sexism because they are watched more than other advertising and are more easily remembered. The characters are "cute and likable like the Keebler Elves or strong and powerful like Mr. Clean. What they are not is female. As does the Energizer Bunny, 'he' keeps going and going and going" (p. 967).

Similar sexism in TV commercials has been documented in other cultures as well. In the United Kingdom (Furnham & Bitar, 1993), Portugal (Neto & Pinto,

1998), and Kenya (Mwangi, 1996) as well as in the United States, males predominate in TV commercials, women are portrayed as younger than men, and women are more likely to be shown in traditional, domestic roles. Gender inequities in TV portrayals were particularly strong in Hong Kong and Indonesia. Authoritative male voice-overs in commercials also remained a bastion for men in studies done on five continents over twenty-five years (Furnham & Mak, 1999).

Sexism in Magazines

Despite thirty years of modern feminism, magazine images of women have changed little. Only one stereotype of women has declined over the past forty years: many more ads show them in work settings outside the home (Busby & Leichty, 1993). But this trend is offset by the trend toward displaying women as decorative and sexualized (73% of all ads). They are routinely shown as being "checked out" by men, inspecting or touching themselves, flirting, or wearing

FIGURE 2.5 This ad represents a sexy woman as a bottle of beer. It is representative of many ads that link women's bodies with addictive drugs such as alcohol and cigarettes. Absolut Vodka ads have been particularly likely to dehumanize women and, disturbingly, elementary school children are reported to collect and swap these ads.

FIGURE 2.6. Fetish or fashion? Pamela Anderson achieved fame and fortune on the TV series "Baywatch," in great measure, because of her implant-augmented breasts. Interestingly, she has since announced that the

OUR OWN POLYMORPHOUS APPETITES THAT IF HE WERE AROUND TODAY, WINCHELL
ESQUIRE 83

implants would be removed. At about the same time, teenaged singing star Britney Spears stated that she would have her breasts surgically enlarged.

something revealing (Coltrane & Messineo, 2000). Many ads feature just a part of a woman's body or show a woman's body morphing into a product (Kilbourne, 2000) (Figure 2.5).

Standards of taste seem to be rapidly falling in today's magazine advertisements. For example, the number of women who are shown partially clad or nude has increased (Kong, 1997; Plous & Neptune, 1997). *Newsweek* magazine (1999) discussed the trend toward maximizing breast cleavage with a headline titled "Finding the Inner Swine." Pornography-like images, such as those in Figure 2.6, have little to do with pictures of real women!

In magazine ads, as in other media, gender and race are intertwined. For example, black female models are shown wearing the majority of animal prints—particularly those patterned after a predatory animal (Plous & Neptune, 1997). There was no difference in the amount of body exposure for black and white models. But both black women and white women were nearly four times as likely to be exposed as either African-American or Euro-American men were.

Music Videos

Some of the most overtly sexist and racist images of women and men can be found in music videos. One study, for example, found that when the portrayals of men and women are compared, men engaged in significantly more aggressive and dominant behavior; women engaged in significantly more implicitly sexual and subservient behavior; and women were more frequently the object of explicit, implicit, and aggressive sexual advances (Sommers-Flanagan, Sommers-Flanagan, & Davis, 1993). Viewers were given the message that romance, sexual attraction, and sexually suggestive activity are the only important human activities.

Music videos aimed at predominately African-American rather than white audiences also feature men more than women. The level of sexual aggression and derogation aimed at women in gangsta rap is enormous. Women are frequently called bitches or ho's, and images of rape and assault are common. Such lyrics have psychological consequences. For example, when male students who were unfamiliar with this type of music read the lyrics, they expressed more adversarial sexual beliefs than participants who had not read sexually violent material (Wester, Crown, Quatman, & Heesacker, 1997).

Pornography

The worst images of women of color are found in pornography. Although pornography treats women in general as mere objects for male sexuality, women of color are treated even more negatively than white women. For example, white women are seen as objects, whereas black women are portrayed as animals. Animals may be treated even more harshly than objects. They can be "economically exploited, worked, sold, killed, and consumed" (Collins, 1993b). In an analysis of X-rated videos, black women were the recipients of a significantly greater number of verbally and physically aggressive acts than white women (Cowan, 1995).

Asian-American women are also stereotyped in pornography, but their image is one of a "special sexuality" that is both more exotic and more subservient

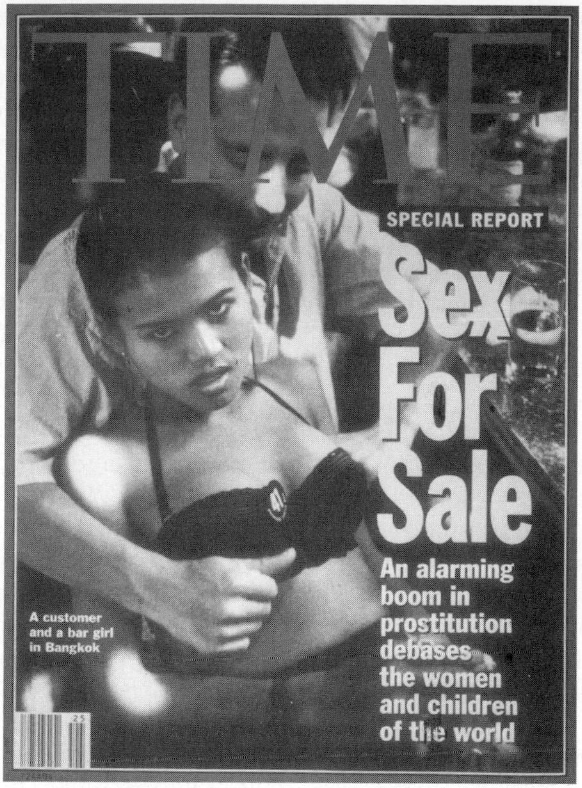

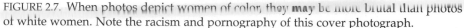

FIGURE 2.7. When photos depict women of color, they may be more brutal than photos of white women. Note the racism and pornography of this cover photograph.

than that of women from other ethnic groups (Root, 1995). The media exploit images of Asian women as prostitutes even when they purport to criticize them (see Figure 2.7).

Selling Beauty, Selling Whiteness, Selling Sex

We live in a world where *looks-ism*—the favoring of people who are perceived as physically attractive—is one of the most pervasive but denied forms of prejudice and where the standards for an American beauty remain white and blond. In U.S. television commercials, one in four white women is shown in a provocative pose or in provocative attire compared with one in ten African American women and one in fourteen men (Coltrane & Messineo, 2000). One might be cheered by the lower exploitation of black women, except that it is part of a larger pattern of excluding them from images of fantasy consumption and personal fulfillment.

Although "whiteness" is unattainable to women of color, its possibility is being sold all over the world through the global marketing of glamour. The version of *Elle* (a French fashion magazine) distributed in China and Tibet pictured

Asian models inside but white models on the cover (Etcoff, 1999). In a story about Brazil, a *New York Times* article commented that a stranger familiarizing himself with the country through its magazines would "mistake this racial rainbow of a country for a Nordic outpost . . . slender blonds smile from the covers and white faces dominate all but sports glossies (Schemo, 1996, p. A13)." Similarly, *telenovelas* (Spanish language soap operas) depict the main characters, especially the most desirable ones, as racially white. Working-class characters as well as less-desirable individuals are shown as darker, with more indigenous features (Pacheco & Hurtado, 2001).

As North American movies, television programs, magazines, and commercial beauty products are increasingly marketed throughout the world, the North American beauty ideal is becoming an international one, part of a "global culture machine," where each woman is encouraged to aim to be "whiter, more Western, more upper-class." Women factory workers in Malaysia are provided with makeup classes by their employers, and many Asian women undergo eyelid surgery to Westernize their eyes (Kaw, 1994).

Women in India and the People's Republic of China have been the target of aggressive marketing of cosmetics that glorify American standards of beauty. In response, women are beginning to disrobe in ads in Chinese magazines (Johansson, 2001), and beauty contest winners have become important role models in India (Munshi, 2001). In spite of the health risks, women in Kenya buy skin-lightening creams (Lacey, 2002). Presumably, these women are taking their cues from advertisements such as one from a working-class, predominantly black neighborhood in Philadelphia. A large billboard pictured three glamorous African-American women. All are very light-skinned, thin, and young, with dainty noses and soft-looking hair. The words underneath the picture were "Philadelphia's Faded Beauties"; the billboard advertised skin bleach.

Women of color bear a greater burden than their white counterparts as looks-ism combines with sexism and racism to stigmatize them as unattractive. Black women, even more than white women, describe feeling ugly. In one study, 70 percent of black women believed that black men prefer very light-skinned women (Bond & Cash, 1992). Darker skin color predicts lower self-esteem among African-American women (Thompson & Keith, 2001). Lower self-esteem scores were more likely to be found in dark-skinned women from working-class backgrounds and dark-skinned women who were judged unattractive.

In fact, the standard of attractiveness glorified in the U.S. media and exported elsewhere is impossible for all but a few to attain. The chances are high that the women one sees portrayed in *People Magazine's* "50 most beautiful people" will have "a body resculpted through gym workouts, advice from personal trainers, liposuction, and possibly implants (Etcoff, 1999, p, 223)." Only 3 to 5 percent of all U. S. women can achieve the physical appearance of a "real" fashion model (Thompson, Heinberg, Altabe, & Tantleff-Dunn, 1999). But even real fashion models do not measure up:

> When model Veronica Webb was asked how long it took her to make her natural beauty, she replied "Two hours and two hundred dollars . . . I could never make myself look the way I do in a magazine." (Etcoff, 1999, p. 13)

THE IMPACT OF MEDIA SEXISM

Images, Beliefs, and Behavior

Do sexist images in the mass media matter? Biases in advertising cannot be dismissed as trivial. Advertisements occupy almost 60 percent of all newspaper space, 52 percent of magazine pages, and 17 percent of prime-time television (Collins & Skover, 1993). The visual media may be particularly effective for both creating and evoking biased beliefs about women because people are less likely to monitor their responses to pictures than to words. After all, it's just entertainment!

One important tool used by researchers who have demonstrated the effects of media content is *meta-analysis*—a statistical technique that allows researchers to combine and evaluate the results of many studies on the same topic (see Chapter 4). Meta-analyses demonstrate that experimental studies that expose people to media content consisting of traditional images and roles increase people's acceptance of gender stereotypes (Herrett-Skjellum & Allen, 1996). These analyses have also found that people who watch television heavily give more sexist responses to questions about the roles of men and women than people who watched less TV (Signorielli, 1989).

The consistency and stability of images of women and men may lead people to believe that there is a social consensus about gender. It is difficult to remember who is left out—older women, "imperfect" women with disabilities, and all those women who cannot or will not participate in making themselves attractive to men.

Body Image and Self-Esteem

Exposure to unrealistic images of women has negative consequences for women and men. In general, women score lower than men on measures of bodily self-esteem. Their scores become even lower after exposure to photos of female models (Grogan, Knott, & Gaze, 1996). In this study, men's self-esteem also fell after exposure to pictures of male models. This may be equality, but is it progress?

In one survey of more than 800 U.S. college women, 72 percent reported that they were repeatedly teased or criticized about their looks, their weight, or both (Rieves & Cash, 1996). Teasing or criticism usually began in late childhood or early adolescence and lasted for an average of 6.6 years. The most commonly ridiculed attributes were features of the face or head (45%) and weight (36%). Almost all the women who reported being teased also reported being distressed by it, and 41 percent felt it had been detrimental to their body image. These self-reports were consistent with research that shows a correlation between the frequency of teasing and negative body image (Cash, 1995).

Some feminist researchers have argued that the pervasive objectification of women's bodies is a major source of low body esteem. *Objectification theory* refers to the idea that girls and women internalize others' (usually male) perception of their physical appearance, causing them to relate to themselves as "observers" who see their bodies in need of habitual self-monitoring and manipulation (Travis & Meginnis-Payne, 2001). Research findings support the important role of self-objectification in women's lives. For example, the relationship among body surveillance, body shame, and body esteem is stronger for women than for men. Those women who are more conscious of body surveillance are also more likely to be ashamed of their bodies, to perceive a greater discrepancy between their actual and ideal body weight, and to have lower body esteem. When their objectified body consciousness scores were controlled, however, differences between women and men on these measures disappeared (McKinley, 1998; McKinley & Hyde, 1996).

The media contributes to the objectification of women. But it is difficult to determine how much the popular media contributes to girls' and women's negative body image because it is almost impossible to find anyone who has escaped media influence. However, one intriguing study of the Old Order Amish—who own no televisions, do not go to the movies or read modern magazines—found no differences between young women and men in either body dissatisfaction or the accuracy of perceptions of body size (Platte, Zelten, & Strunkard, 2000).

The Social Importance of Looks

Good looks are an asset for both males and females. So many positive social judgments are made about physically attractive people that researchers coined the phrase "What is beautiful is good!" (Dion, Berscheid, & Walster, 1972). But physical attractiveness is more salient in judgments about females than in judgments about males. Most images of women in the media are beautiful images. Female bodies are displayed more than male bodies and judged more harshly.

In a study of college women (Cash, Ancis, & Strachan, 1997), women who accepted traditional views of female sexuality showed the greatest investment in their appearance, internalized societal standards of beauty more fully, and endorsed more problematic assumptions about the pivotal importance of their appearance in their lives. The connection between traditional views about gender relations and a concern with appearance should not be surprising given how many cultural messages about female beauty people encounter every day.

Good looks are more important to men than to women in evaluating a potential date, and especially important in a prospective sexual partner (Nevid, 1984). One analysis of 800 personal ads for same- and other-sex romantic partners found that men were more concerned with physical characteristics, whereas women were more interested in psychological factors (Deaux & Hanna, 1984). Neither race, sexual orientation, nor social class affected women's tendency to mention thinness in personal advertisements (Epel, Spanakos, Kasl-Godley, & Brownell, 1996).

Beauty may represent a kind of power for women (Unger, 1979a). They may be able to barter their looks for financial security or other material resources. Attractive women raise the prestige of men. Men are evaluated more highly when they are presented as the boyfriends of attractive, rather than unattractive, women (Bar-Tal & Saxe, 1976). Curiously, men paired with attractive women are not necessarily seen as more physically attractive—instead, they are seen as better people. People seem to infer that these men must have something going for them to win such an attractive "prize."

The media not only reflect ideal images of appearance, but also teach them. For example, popular comedies convey the message that heavier women are unattractive, undesirable, and laughable. Researchers found that in 18 prime-time situation comedies, males made significantly more negative comments about or to heavier-than-average female characters. Eighty percent of these comments were followed by audience reactions such as laughter, "oohs," or giggles (Fouts & Burggraf, 2000). Thus, insulting heavier women is reinforced by the approval of the audience. Women who are exposed to ideal media images of women are more negative about their own weight when men are present than when they are not (Henderson-King, Henderson-King, & Hoffmann, 2001).

Girls and women learn that no matter how hard they try, they can never measure up. Over the past few decades the ideal body shape has (literally) shrunk. Measurements of Miss America contestants and *Playboy* centerfold models became steadily thinner from the 1950s through the 1990s (Spitzer, Henderson, & Zivian, 1999). There was no such trend for male models in men's magazines (Petrie et al., 1996).

The curvaceousness of movie actresses and models in women's magazines has also been declining since about 1950 (Silverstein, Perdue, Peterson, & Kelly, 1986), until many models look as though they are starving. Advertisers call this

Making a Difference

Jamie Lee Curtis (1958–), movie star and author of five children's books, is known for her sexy, beautiful body. So where's the risk in posing in her underwear for *More* magazine? The 2002 photo shoot was daring because Curtis insisted the magazine give her real body equal time. For the glamour photo, as is customary, a large team (13 people) united to make Curtis look impossibly good—a creative director, a photographer and three assistants, a hair stylist, a makeup artist, two fashion stylists and an assistant, a prop stylist and an assistant, and a manicurist. In the "natural" shot, Curtis posed with no makeup or fancy hairdo, no airbrushing or retouching, no seductive posturing. Why did she allow her "True Thighs" to be revealed? Because she believed the movie and beauty industries' use of artifice to portray women in a state of unreachable perfection makes it difficult for women to celebrate their bodies no matter their size and shape. Curtis stated, "There's a reality to the way I look without my clothes on. I don't have great thighs. I have very big breasts and a soft, fatty little tummy . . . It's insidious—Glam Jamie, the Perfect Jamie, the great figure, blah, blah, blah. And I don't want the unsuspecting 40-year-old women of the world to think that I've got it going on. It's such a fraud." She confessed to other imperfections in the article, such as feelings of inferiority, a past addiction to painkillers, and a history of plastic surgeries, liposuction, and botox injections. *More* readers were thankful for Curtis's revelations—the issue sold record numbers, and hundreds of women wrote in expressing gratitude that Curtis had shared her flaws and shown that cover girl looks are a façade.

Sources:

Dateline NBC Website. (2002). Jamie Lee Curtis keeps it real. http://ww4.lhj.com/lhj/story.jhtml?storyid=/templatedata/lhj/story/data/jamieleecurtistruethighs_08212002.xml&categoryid=/templatedata/lhj/category/data/Celebrity/Archive_General.xml

Oldenberg, A. (2002, August 2). Jamie Lee Curtis bares the truth. *USA Today*, p. B1.

Wallace, A. (2002, September). True thighs. *More*, 90–95.

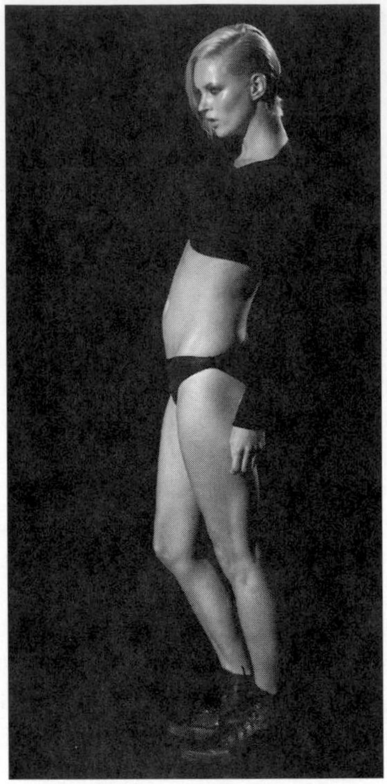

FIGURE 2.8. This photo accompanied an article titled "The Tyranny of Skinny, Fashion's Insider Secret," which notes that "real women don't wear size 2."

the "waif look" (see Figure 2.8). The "Barbie look" is also unattainable for most women. Researchers who scaled Barbie and Ken to adult height determined that the probability that a real, human woman would have the same proportions as Barbie is about 1 in 100,000 (Norton, Olds, Olive, & Dank, 1996). It is more possible for a man to be built like Ken, with odds of only 1 in 50.

At the same time that images of ideal female bodies became thinner, the body size and shape of average young adult North American women and men became heavier. Thus, actual body size has become increasingly different from that promoted by the media. Furthermore, the media depicts the difference between young men and women as huge, whereas the differences between young women and men were actually quite small (Spitzer et al., 1999). It is not surprising that many girls and women develop distorted perceptions of their bodies. They may believe themselves to be wider or fatter than they really are, exaggerating descriptions of their "huge" thighs, breasts, or stomachs (Hoyt & Kogan, 2001).

The ideal of waiflike slimness seems to affect white women more than African American women. African-American women may be protected from excessive concern about weight by their conviction that black men prefer small-figured women less than white men do (Molloy & Herzberger, 1998). They are probably correct: African-American men have been found to be more inclined than Euro-American men to desire larger, heavier women (Cunningham, Roberts, Barbee, Druen, & Wu, 1995).

In the U.S. population overall, individuals who are conservative, individualistic, and believe in a just world are especially likely to have antifat attitudes (Crandall, 1994). Such individuals are also more likely to be white. Within the African-American community, heavier women are not necessarily considered unattractive. This ethnic-related difference may be related to social class. In one study, African-American women of higher social status valued thinness as much as white women, whereas those of lower social status perceived a heavier body size as attractive. They did not judge themselves "overweight" unless they were much heavier than the weight that would have triggered this judgment in the other groups of women (Allan, Mayo, & Michel, 1993).

Standards of thinness were as extreme as they are now at only one other time in the last hundred years: during the 1920s, when an epidemic of eating disorders appeared among women (Silverstein, Peterson, & Perdue, 1986). Is history repeating itself? Eating disorders among women are discussed further in Chapters 7 and 14.

CROSS-CULTURAL SIMILARITIES AND DIFFERENCES IN IMAGES OF WOMEN

In some ways women are seen the same way in cultures around the world. There are cross-cultural similarities in the personality traits attributed to women and the traits attributed to men. Overall, males are seen as higher in extraversion, conscientiousness, emotional stability, and openness, whereas females are stereotyped as higher in agreeableness (Best, 2001). Female attractiveness is seen as more important than male attractiveness in all the countries that have been studied (Buss, 1989). No society has been found to be gender-blind.

Religious Fundamentalism and Images of Women

But gender stereotypes around the world are not all alike. One important variable is religion. For example, in one study of twenty-five nations, some adjectives were associated with women in all the countries studied (Williams & Best, 1990). Women were seen as sentimental, submissive, and superstitious; men were seen as adventurous, forceful, and independent. But in countries with a high percentage of Catholics, women were viewed more favorably. They were seen as nurturant parents and sources of order. In Muslim countries, images of women were more different from images of men and stereotypes about women were more unfavorable than those typically found elsewhere.

Islam holds that social order depends on paying careful attention to differences based on gender (Reineke, 1989). Men live in the public sphere and worship in the mosque, whereas women remain in the private sphere—the home—where they also pray. Reports from the United Nations indicate that the position of women in Islamic countries is still poor in terms of education, health, and even life expectancy.

Of course, there are important variations within Islam and among Islamic countries. In fundamentalist Islamic countries, if a woman must leave the seclusion of the home to enter the public sphere, she must be veiled from head

FIGURE 2.9. Women in Afghanistan are no longer forced to wear the burqa, but many still choose to do so because they fear the sexual responses of men when they leave their homes without it.

to toe (see Figure 2.9). When Afghanistan was governed by the Taliban in accordance with extreme fundamentalist views of women, the consequences were tragic. Women were not permitted to work outside their home or to go to school. Women physicians were not allowed to practice and male physicians could not treat women outside of their family; women and girls received almost no health care.

Fundamentalist forms of other religions also attempt to control the bodies and behaviors of women. Ultra-orthodox Jewish women, for example, are enjoined to wear long-sleeved dresses, high necklines, and thick stockings even in the heat of a Middle Eastern summer. Although this is supposed to be good for their souls (and the souls of the men whom they might tempt if their bodies were more exposed), it has not been good for their health. Recent studies in Israel have found that forty percent of *haredi* (ultra religious) women are deficient in vitamin D because of inadequate exposure to sunlight (Siegel, 2001). High levels of social dominance orientation (Heaven, 1999) and high levels of religiosity (Harville & Rienzi, 2000) appear to be associated cross-culturally with hostility toward women and opposition to gender equality.

Cultural Contradictions

Under some circumstances the U.S. government is also willing to control women's bodies. Women serving in Saudi Arabia have been ordered to wear an *abaya* (similar to the burqa pictured above) when they leave their military bases

(Saunders, 2001). The woman who went public to protest this policy, Air Force Lieutenant Colonel Martha McSally, was also the first woman to fly a combat mission into enemy territory. However, she was not permitted to drive a car in Saudi Arabia. The U.S. government says it wants to respect the customs of an ally, but do you think it would permit such discrimination against African-American troops stationed abroad?

The preceding story indicates a contradiction in U.S. culture. Apparent contradictions in how a culture treats women can be especially puzzling. For example, women's roles are marginalized in Israel, but women are also drafted into its army and hold major public policy positions. Although women's bodies and attire are tightly controlled in many Moslem countries, both Pakistan and Bangladesh have had women prime ministers. It is important to do more cross-cultural studies, but these studies are likely to leave many questions unanswered.

STEREOTYPES: AN OVERVIEW

Images of women and men are conveyed by myths and fairy tales as well as by pictures and religious texts. These images may be the source of attitudes and beliefs; they may reflect and maintain stereotypes, the conventional wisdom about the characteristics of a group of people.

When was the last time you heard remarks such as "Beautiful, but dumb!" or "You can never be too rich or too thin"? Statements of this sort reflect stereotypes. Stereotypes are acquired without consent or conscious awareness. In all countries studied, a general developmental pattern has been found. The acquisition of gender stereotypes typically began before the age of 5, accelerated during the early school years, and was completed during adolescence (Williams & Best, 1990). Many people are unaware of stereotypes because they are so pervasive. There are few gender-fair or gender-free images with which to contrast them.

This section focuses on the cognitive aspects of stereotypes, exploring how stereotypes are measured and how they are put together as cognitive constructs. We examine the differences between stereotypes about women and men as general categories and stereotypes about various subcategories of men and women. Later we look at some of the ways stereotypes are conveyed by language, the impact of stereotypes on people's behavior, and the question of whether gender stereotypes have changed.

What Are Stereotypes?

Surprisingly, the term *stereotype* was not invented by a psychologist. It was first used by Walter Lippmann (1922), a noted journalist of his day, to describe a kind of behavior. He defined stereotypes as culturally determined pictures that intrude between an individual's cognitive faculties and his or her perceptions of the world. (Lippmann appears to have borrowed the term from a kind of curved printing press in which the type had to be deformed to fit its structure.) Stereotyping is still viewed as a process that distorts reality, but most psychologists see these distortions as part of the normal process of concept formation. They are necessary because we need to construct general categories from all the information we receive. Stereotypes save the perceiver time and energy at a cost of oversimplifying their targets.

Although the word *stereotype* has become part of our everyday language, it has some specific meanings when used by a psychologist. Stereotypes occur whenever individuals are classified by others as having something in common because they are members of a particular group or category of people. Early studies (Fernberger, 1948; Kirkpatrick, 1936; Sheriffs & McKee, 1957) demonstrated that *gender stereotypes,* defined as consensual beliefs about the different characteristics of men and women, were widely held, persistent, and highly traditional. Gender stereotypes, like other stereotypes, have the following characteristics:

- Groups that are the targets of stereotypes are easily identified and relatively powerless.
- People largely agree about the characteristics of a stereotyped group.
- Stereotypes imply a covert comparison between groups, to the disadvantage of the stereotyped group.
- Stereotypes do not represent individuals accurately, although cognitions about groups are sometimes related to their actual characteristics.
- Misperceptions appear to be the product of information processing; however, motives to preserve one's self, one's group, and the social system in which one lives are also important.
- Misperceptions are difficult to modify, even when the person who holds the stereotype encounters many disconfirming examples.
- People are largely unaware that they stereotype, and they deny that stereotypes characteristic of their group apply to themselves.

These points will be discussed more fully in this chapter. It is particularly important to keep in mind, however, that it is the consistency and apparent universality of gender stereotypes that makes them so dangerous. They are destructive because they influence perceptions independent of the individual characteristics of members of the stereotyped group. They weigh down these individuals, anchor interactions with them, and hold them back (Fiske, 1993).

Stereotypes about Women and Men

Individual beliefs are not the same thing as stereotypes. A belief becomes a stereotype when the majority of people in a population choose a particular quality as characteristic of a particular group. For example, most people believe that women are less competent in math and science than men. The extent to which this belief influences the way people perceive and evaluate men and women differently may come to influence their relative abilities in these areas (see Chapters 3 and 4). Stereotypes appear to be more like forms of social consensus than individual judgments.

The way psychologists measure gender stereotypes illustrates their social nature. In a classic study (Broverman, Vogel, Broverman, Clarkson, & Rosenkrantz, 1972) researchers developed a questionnaire made up of 122 pairs of adjectives that were antonyms; that is, each member of the pair was opposite in meaning to the other. The pairs consisted of words that are commonly used to describe people's personality traits, such as sneaky/direct, passive/active, submissive/dominant, and so forth. Respondents were asked to indicate the extent to which each pair described a normal male, a normal female, and themselves, forcing them to choose between adjectives in describing the target individuals.

If no stereotypes exist, people should assign traits at random and no pattern will emerge. The researchers defined a trait as gender stereotypic only if at least 75 percent of individuals of each sex agreed that the adjective described the average man *or* the average woman. Even with this conservative definition, they found high agreement for more than eighty traits. These beliefs were not affected by the age, religion, education level, or marital status of the participants. People from a large variety of groups, when forced to make a choice, select different traits for men and women.

The researchers found two groups of traits: an instrumental dimension that was considered to be characteristic of typical males, and an affective dimension considered to be characteristic of typical females. *Instrumentality* includes traits such as active, objective, independent, aggressive, direct, unemotional, dominant, and competent. These traits appear to describe a person who can manipulate the world effectively. *Affective traits* include warm, expressive, and sensitive. These traits appear to describe a person who is nurturant, is concerned about others, and cares more for people than for things. These patterns in gender stereotypes are still relevant today.

When people think about females and males, they think about more than just their personality traits (Kite, 2001). They also consider role behaviors (financial provider, meal preparer), physical characteristics (sturdy, graceful), and occupations (construction worker, telephone operator) (Deaux & Lewis, 1984). But perceptions in these areas are closely associated with each other. For example, characteristics associated with women might include taking care of children and having small bones, as well as being warm and emotional. Stereotypes about females and males appear to consist of a tight network of associations that extends to virtually all aspects of human beings.

Physical appearance seems to be much more important than traits, roles, or behaviors in triggering stereotypes. This should not be surprising: physical appearance is the first information people have when they meet a new person. Information about appearance is acquired within the first one-tenth of a second of seeing someone (Locher, Unger, Sociedade, & Wahl, 1993). The perception occurs so rapidly that people seem to be unaware of how much information they have acquired. Therefore, they tend to deny the extent to which physical appearance influences their perceptions of others.

Stereotypes and Subtypes: The Many Meanings of Being a Woman

Suppose you were asked to list the attributes of mother. What would you say? Are women seen as warmer than men because they are perceived as mothers (a social role they occupy) rather than because they are women (the more global category)?

One group of researchers addressed this question by asking people to list attributes for various subtypes of women and men (Deaux, Winton, Crowley & Lewis, 1985). They examined perceptions of the sexes in terms of their different roles, such as mother and father; their occupations, such as housewife or blue-collar worker; and their physical characteristics, such as strong or graceful. The researchers found that the same number of associations was generated for various social roles, occupations, and physical characteristics. The researchers were also able to calculate the degree of overlap between various images of women and men by measuring the extent to which the same descriptor (sensitive, strong, etc.) appeared on lists for different roles or occupations. For example, they found that there was more overlap between people's perceptions of mother and parent than father and parent. Similarly, the terms assigned to woman were closer to labels attached to mother and grandmother than the words used to describe man were to father or grandfather. In fact, there was no relationship between the description of man and grandfather. Using an entirely different methodology, these studies also suggested that relational roles are very meaningful in conceptions of women but much less so for conceptions about men.

The same technique was also used to measure the beliefs about four subtypes of women and men. The four subtypes of women were housewife, athletic woman, businesswoman, and sexy woman. The four subtypes of men were athletic man, blue-collar working man, businessman, and macho man. The most frequent concepts generated for each type are found in Table 2.2.

Male targets were all viewed as equally unlikely to engage in female occupations or to have female physical characteristics. They were all seen as equally likely to perform masculine role behaviors and not to perform feminine role behaviors. In contrast, each of the four female subtypes showed substantial variation from the generic "woman" and from each other. Businesswomen, for example, were viewed as more likely to engage in masculine roles and to have masculine traits. At the same time, they were seen as less likely to engage in feminine roles, to have female physical characteristics, or to have feminine traits. In contrast, housewives were seen as high in terms of their possession of feminine role behaviors and low for both male and female occupations and masculine traits. The housewife stereotype appears to bear the closest resemblance to people's global stereotypes about women in general (Eckes, 1994).

Three important conclusions can be drawn from these data. First, stereotypes about particular types of women and men appear to be just as strong as stereotypes about men and women as global categories. Second, stereotypes about women appear to be more strongly differentiated than stereotypes about men. Men are like each other and not like women. Third, perceptions about women and men appear to be conceived in terms of opposites.

Gendering Race and Class

Most of the individuals used in early studies of stereotypes were white and middle class. Researchers now understand that images of women (and men) are differentiated by race and class. One study, for example, provided undergraduates with the labels "white woman," "middle-class woman," "black woman," and "lower-class woman" and asked the students to assign adjectives

TABLE 2.2. Most Frequent Attributes Associated with Different Kinds of Women and Men

Woman	*Man*
Attractive	Strong
Feminine	Hides feelings
Smart	Acts macho
Sensitive	Sexy
Emotional	Muscular
Housewife	*Blue-collar working man*
Cleans things	Factories
Cooks	Hard worker
Takes care of kids	Middle-lower class
Motherly	Uneducated
Busy	Union member
Athletic woman	*Athletic man*
Muscular	Muscular
Good body	Healthy
Strong	Strong
Aggressive	In shape
Masculine	Good body
Sexy woman	*Macho man*
Good figure	Muscular
Long hair	Hairy chest
Good dresser	Moustache
Nail polish	Attractive
Pretty face	Self-centered
Businesswoman	*Businessman*
Smart	Wears suits
Nice clothes	Office with view
Unmarried	College education
Hard-working	Smart
Organized	Good appearance

Source: From K. Deaux, W. Winston, M. Crowley, & L. L. Lewis. "Level of categorization and content of gender stereotypes," *Social Cognition*, 3, pp. 145–167. Copyright © 1985. Reprinted by permission of The Guilford Press.

to each group in a "manner that best describes society's stereotypes of the group" (Landrine, 1985). Participants offered different stereotypes for each group although all the adjectives used were stereotypically feminine. White women were rated significantly higher than black women on dependent, emotional, and passive (traits that resemble those identified in earlier studies). Lower-class women were rated significantly higher than middle-class women on confused, dirty, hostile, inconsiderate, and irresponsible. The stereotypes of white women and middle-class women were most similar to the traditional stereotypes of women in general.

Black women are evaluated considerably less positively than white women by white respondents. They are seen as louder, more talkative, and more aggressive than Euro-American women in general, although they were also seen as more straightforward than their white counterparts (Weitz & Gordon, 1993). Black women were rated as more masculine in traits and roles than white women and much more masculine in physical characteristics. There appears to be no difference between black and white women in ratings involving occupations. However, women of both races were seen as closer to each other than either was to men of their own racial category (Deaux & Kite, 1985).

Recent studies indicate that the effects of race and class on gender stereotypes have not disappeared. White respondents continue to view both male and female African-Americans in terms of masculine and negative stereotypes (Niemann, O'Connor, & McClure, 1998). Perhaps most disheartening is the popularity in the media of stereotypes about "welfare mothers." (Bullock, Wyche, & Williams, 2001). Although the largest group of welfare recipients in the United States is poor children, media depictions usually focus on their mothers, who typically are single and unlikely to be white. "The poster mother for welfare reform spends her days painting her nails, smoking cigarettes, and feeding Pepsi to her baby" (Douglas & Michael, 2000, p. 67).

LANGUAGE AND STEREOTYPES

Verbal Images of Women and Men

Just as pictorial images put women in their place, the English language contains a large variety of sexist as well as racist words. Linguistic analyses reveal persistent negative biases against women. For example, these analyses trace various forms of debasement in female-gender words (Schultz, 1975). The mildest form of linguistic debasement occurs when the female member of a word pair that was previously reserved for people in high places comes to refer to people at any level of society. Thus, the word *lord* still refers to the deity and a few Englishmen, but anyone may call herself a "lady." Other examples of this process are *sir/madam* and *master/mistress:* the female terms have been debased into words with sexual connotations. Whether a woman is a "madam" or a "mistress," her identity is still based on her relationship with men as a sex object.

Terms of endearment addressed to females have also undergone debasement. A *tart* was originally a small pie or pastry, then a term of endearment; next it became a term applied to young women who were sexually desirable, then to those who were deemed careless of their morals, and finally, it became a word meaning prostitute. Words denoting boys and young men have not been debased in this way.

To a surprising extent, terms referring to women resemble those referring to children. Excluding any negative connotations, words like *doll, honey, pussycat,* and *baby* can apply equally well to women or children (particularly girl children). Our language, like our culture, equates adulthood with manhood (Graham, 1975). There is a clear distinction between the words *boy* and *man* that does not exist between *girl* and *woman.* A boy greatly increases his status when he becomes a man, whereas a girl is seen as losing status and bargaining power when her youth is lost. Language echoes gender stereotypes when it encourages females to cling to girlhood as long as possible.

Power relationships between men and women are reflected in gender-specific slang vocabulary, too. One study found that college students of both sexes use more sexual slang to describe women than men (Grossman & Tucker, 1997). The most commonly chosen terms to describe women were *chick, bitch, babe,* and *slut.* The most commonly chosen words to describe men were *guy, dude, boy,* and *stud/homey.* Men (especially those in fraternities) are especially likely to use sexually degrading terms for female genitals and to describe sexual activity in aggressive terms (Murnen, 2000). The effects of this kind of language on women's sexuality is discussed in Chapter 8.

Derogatory names are even more likely to be aimed at women from ethnic outgroups. A historical inventory of terms for women of various ethnic groups found many negative terms that alluded to women of color. These terms often referred to stereotyped physical differences from white women (in terms of skin color, hair texture, or shape of eyes), made derogatory sexual allusions, or used food and animal metaphors (Allen, 1984).

Some of the mechanisms that operate in the linguistic distortion of gender-specific words have been categorized (Graham, 1975):

- Labeling what is considered to be an exception to the rule—woman doctor, male nurse, career girl. This process is known to linguists as *gender marking.* The term *feminine logic* is a particularly sexist example of this kind of label.
- Trivializing female gender forms—poetess, suffragette (instead of suffragist). Many university women's sports teams have names similar to those of the men's teams with the addition of "ette" or "Lady."
- "His virtue is her vice"—mannish attire or aggressive female, butch.
- Exclusion, which may be the most pervasive mechanism. The use of *man* in its extended sense, as in *mankind* or "the child is father to the man," may be one of the major sources of the perceived lack of relationship between "woman" and "adult."

Does Sexist Language Matter?

The battle against the generic use of masculine words such as *mankind* and *he* was probably the most visible aspect of the fight that second-wave feminists waged against sexist language. Newspaper columnists ridiculed their criticism of sex-biased language as trivial for years. (One favorite butt of humor is the "personhole cover.") But researchers have demonstrated that sex-biased language has wide-ranging effects.

For one thing, even supposedly neutral linguistic usages such as the generic "he" distort how people think. For example, when undergraduates read sentences aloud that used *he, he/she,* or *they* and then described the images that came to mind, both sexes produced a disproportionate number of male images to the supposedly generic *he* (Gastil, 1990). Male students also gave male images when *he/she* was used. Only *they* appeared to function as a true generic pronoun.

Use of the generic pronoun *he* seems to make men and women think of males first, even when the context implies both sexes (Gastil, 1990). One researcher (Henley, 1989) examined twenty studies in which people of various ages—from 6 years to adult—were presented with the masculine form used for both sexes. The pictures selected or drawn, the names used for the persons referred to, the subjects of stories, the answers to questions about the sex of the people referred to in stories, and the imagery seen was predominantly, and often overwhelmingly, male.

It appears that we think of people as males. But do we also think of males as people? One creative study asked students to write a short paragraph about the most typical person they could imagine and then give that person the "perfect typical name" (Hamilton, 1991). The instructions were gender neutral. Nevertheless, only 25 percent of the students in the study described and named a female.

More generally, gender bias in language influences comprehension and memory. The number of correct answers given by women to questions about a science-fiction story (read out loud) was higher when it contained unbiased forms than when it contained masculine forms (Hamilton & Henley, 1982). Both male and female students who read an exclusively male version of the "Ethical Standards of Psychologists" (in contrast to one that used "he or she" or no gender-specific words at all) rated a career in psychology as less attractive for women than for men (Briere & Lanktree, 1983). Some of these effects occur even when participants are unaware that any linguistic manipulation has occurred. Thus, women's memory of essays 48 hours later was worse when the essays were written with masculine generics than when they were written with unbiased grammatical forms, in spite of the fact that participants had not noticed which pronouns had been used (Crawford & English, 1984).

Making Meaning

Does sexist language also influence behavior? The answer appears to be "yes!" One early study found, for example, that women's interest in job positions was influenced by the wording of advertisements (Bem & Bem, 1973). This research led to a change in job titles in a major telephone company. Similar changes in language include the shift from "mailman" to "mail carrier" and from "stewardess" to "flight attendant." The gender ratio of these occupations has changed as well.

Language reflects and constructs social reality. Groups may differ in how they see and how they describe that reality. For example, groups of undergraduate women who differed in ethnicity showed few differences in self-evaluations (Landrine, Klonoff, & Brown-Collins, 1992). But they differed in the meaning they attached to the adjectives they used. In other words, they appeared to be more similar than they actually were because they were using the same words with differing meanings. For example, women of color were most likely to define *assertive* as "Say whatever's on my mind," whereas white women were most likely to define it as "Stand up for myself."

The same word may have different meanings when applied to members of groups with differing levels of status and power. For example, the word *aggressive* has been found to indicate "physical violence" when applied to a construction worker and "verbal abuse" when applied to a lawyer (Kunda, Sinclair, & Griffin, 1997). When women and men engage in the same activities, they may also be evaluated by shifting standards (Biernat & Kobrynowicz, 1999). Thus, when participants viewed the same five aggressive acts by a man or a woman and were asked to describe them, the most frequent description of the woman was bitch or bitchy, whereas the most frequent response used to describe the man was aggressive (although asshole and jerk were close behind). These studies demonstrate how important language is in how we think about the world. Terms introduced or made popular by the women's movement that have changed many people's views are "sexual harassment" and "domestic violence" (see Chapter 13). To paraphrase a comment by Gloria Steinem—women used to think these were just part of life.

STEREOTYPES AS SOCIAL DEMANDS

Gender Stereotypes and Social Attributions

Stereotypes serve as messengers about the appropriate social roles and behaviors of women and men. As discussed earlier, gender stereotypes consist of a network of associations involving personality traits, social roles, behaviors, and physical characteristics. They have a prescriptive as well as a descriptive function. Stereotypes inform people about what behavior ought to be.

Because of their complex interlocking nature, stereotypes can influence assumptions about the behaviors of males and females in a variety of contexts. It is, in fact, difficult to find conditions in which the identical behavior of women and men is viewed similarly by observers. Gender-blind social judgments appear to be rare.

The prescriptive aspect of stereotypes is conveyed primarily by the different attributions people make about others on the basis of their gender. *Attributions* are assumptions about why people behave the way they do. If one believes that women and men have different causes for the same behaviors, these beliefs can lead to different expectations about future behaviors. It is through such expectations that stereotypes operate as a means of social control (for more about how this can produce discrimination against women, see Chapters 3 and 11). Here we focus on factors that influence assumptions about the social acceptability and social deviance of women and men.

The Many Effects of Physical Appearance

Physical appearance is one of the major sources of information that people use when they are making stereotypic judgments about others. No physical characteristic is too trivial! One study found, for example, that people rated photos of brunette job applicants as more capable than the same applicants wearing a blond wig (Kyle & Mahler, 1996). The suggested average starting salary for blond women was $23,792 versus $27,478 for brunettes. Blondes may be seen as having "more fun," but they are certainly not offered more money with which to do so.

People appear to be more sensitive to facial differences among women than among men. They make more refined distinctions, offer more extreme positive and negative ratings, and show more consensus about female faces than about male faces (Schulman & Hoskins, 1986). Facial expression also affects the ratings of women more than men. Women who smiled were seen as more attractive than those who did not. The absence of a smile had a greater effect on perceptions of women than of men. Nonsmiling women were rated as less happy, less warm, less relaxed, and less carefree than the average woman (Deutsch, LeBaron, & Fryer, 1987). These findings illustrate how even minor deviations from social expectations can result in negative social judgments.

There is overwhelming evidence that women are much more severely stigmatized for obesity than are men (Crandall, 1995; Crocker, Cornwell, & Major, 1993). This stigma produces economic costs. Overweight women earn less money than their non-overweight counterparts (Sargent & Blanchflower, 1994). They are even less likely to receive support for college from their parents who, nevertheless, support their overweight sons as well as their sons and daughters who are not overweight (Crandall, 1995). Heavyweight women and men are both underrepresented in colleges, but in the case of heavy men, it is not because of their parents' prejudices.

A stigma is much more likely to be attached to weight in white populations than in black populations. When African-American women were asked to evaluate the qualities of professional models dressed in fashionable clothing, they did not stigmatize large women. This was especially true when they rated large black women. In contrast, white women rated heavier models, especially large white women, as lower than average in attractiveness, intelligence, job success, relationship success, happiness, and popularity (Hebl & Heatherton, 1998).

Stereotypes and Social Deviance

Variations in physical attractiveness also influence perceptions of social deviance (Unger, Hilderbrand, & Madar, 1982). For example, less-attractive women were seen as more likely to be involved in a radical student organization than in student government and as more likely to be lesbian. Less-attractive men were also seen as more likely to be involved in radical politics and to be studying for a feminine-typed occupation, such as librarian, rather than a traditionally masculine field. There were no important differences between the judgments made by men and women. Respondents appeared to be unaware that their judgments were based on the attractiveness of the people in the photographs.

Inferences of homosexuality are made more frequently about women who are perceived to be physically unattractive (Dew, 1985). Women who held conservative attitudes about gender roles were particularly likely to associate homosexuality with those women to whom they had given the worst evaluations on physical appearance. Less-attractive women are perceived as more masculine, and women who are described as masculine are perceived as more likely to be homosexual than women who are described as feminine (Storms, Stivers, Lambers, & Hill, 1981).

Homosexual individuals of both sexes are most frequently described in terms of the stereotypic characteristics of the other sex (Kite & Deaux, 1987). Gay men are sometimes seen as similar to heterosexual women. To a lesser extent, lesbians are seen as similar to heterosexual men. This belief in the inversion of gender-related characteristics in gays and lesbians is inaccurate but very strong (see Chapter 5). Although stereotypically masculine and feminine traits may exist independently within the same individual (defined as androgyny), perceptually these characteristics are organized as polar opposites. It is difficult for people to recognize, for example, that a woman can feel sexual desire for another woman and still like makeup, work as a flight attendant, and be timid rather than prefer to wear overalls, work as a mechanic, and be assertive.

The more people deviate from gender-typed qualities, the more they are punished. People who violate all categories of gender stereotypes (appearance, traits, and roles) are disliked most, followed by those who are incongruent in two categories. Which categories' expectations they violate does not matter (Cano & Kite, 1998). Single violations are not seen as serious, but at some point, multiple violations become unacceptable.

Males face more social penalties for gender deviance than females do (Kite, 2001). Being gay is associated with being feminine even more than being lesbian is associated with being masculine. Because masculinity has higher status, gay men may be doubly penalized for accepting socially devalued roles. Many more negative attitudes are held about gay men than about lesbians, especially by men (Kite & Whitley, 1996).

Men perceive themselves as conforming to masculine norms more than women perceive themselves as conforming to normative demands for femininity (Twenge, 1999). Being feminine appears to be relatively simple. It involves a combination of having a socially approved attractive appearance and a high number of expressive traits. Masculinity is a more complex mix of gender-related attributes. It involves a combination of low expressiveness, sports interest, more male friendships, sitting with knees far apart, and conservative attitudes toward feminism. These characteristics are associated with social dominance as well as masculinity.

STEREOTYPES AND SEXISM

Ambivalent Sexism

Stereotypes about women contain both positive and negative judgments. In general, women appear to be liked better than men but are not seen to be as competent (Eagly & Mladinic, 1993). Some men, known as *ambivalent sexists,* appear to compartmentalize these views of women (Glick & Fiske, 1996). Their views include a *hostile sexism* that acknowledges the competence of women who challenge their power in society but that also sees them as manipulative, cold, and aggressive. At the same time, ambivalent sexists maintain idealized images of women in their traditional roles as wives and mothers. This idealization (called *benevolent sexism*) is also sexist because it sees women as lovable but unable to take care of themselves.

These two components of ambivalent sexism can be illustrated by a few items from the scale devised to measure them. Items that are part of the hostile sexism scale include

> "Women seek to gain power by getting control over men."
> "Most women fail to appreciate fully all that men do for them."

Items that are part of the benevolent sexism scale include

> "Women should be cherished and protected by men."
> "Many women have a quality of purity that few men possess."
> (Glick & Fiske, 1996)

Ambivalent sexists generate polarized images of women. Like nonsexist men, they view career women as intelligent, hardworking, and professional, but they also perceive them to have negative interpersonal qualities such as aggression, selfishness, greed, and coldness (Glick, Diebold, Bailey-Werner, & Zhu, 1997). Ambivalent sexist men reported that they feared, envied, were intimidated by, or felt competitive toward career women. In contrast, nonsexist men viewed career women as confident and honest and expressed admiration for them. Both sexists and nonsexists agreed that homemakers are caring, loving, and nurturant; however, sexist men frequently reported "a wealth of positive emotions toward homemakers—warmth, trust, respect, and happiness" (Glick et al., 1997). Ambivalent sexists may be particularly resistant to attitude change because their favorable feelings toward traditional women enable them to deny their prejudice against women and the role of power in their relationships with women.

Sexism and Discrimination

Ambivalent attitudes about women who deviate from traditional roles may explain why some women are penalized even when their "deviant" behaviors are appropriate for their occupational role. *Hopkins v. Price Waterhouse* (a case that came before the U.S. Supreme Court) illustrates the biasing effect of stereotypes. When Ann Hopkins came up for review for promotion to partner in a major accounting firm, her aggressive (and very successful) strategies were interpreted as "overbearing, arrogant, self-centered, and abrasive." She was denied the promotion, despite the fact that she had brought more money to the company than any other person proposed for partner that year—$25 million (Fiske, Bersoff, Borgida, Deaux, & Heilman, 1991). She was denied the position because of "interpersonal skills problems" that could be corrected, a supporter told her, by walking, talking, and dressing more femininely. In contrast, an opponent suggested she needed to go to "charm school."

A group of researchers in cognitive social psychology served as expert witnesses in this trial. They testified that stereotyping is most likely to occur in situations in which the target person is isolated or one of a few of a kind in an otherwise homogeneous environment. (See the discussions of tokenism in Chapters 3 and 11.) Stereotyping also increases when members of a previously omitted group move into jobs that are nontraditional and when there is a perceived lack of fit between the person's social category and his or her occupation. And, finally, stereotypes are most likely to occur when evaluative criteria are ambiguous (Fiske et al., 1991).

The situation at Price Waterhouse met all these conditions. At the time, the company had 27 women partners out of a total of 900, or 3 percent. Moreover, the traits considered desirable in a manager—aggressive, competitive, driven, and masterful—are still not considered desirable in women (Heilman, Block,

Martell, & Simon, 1989). Finally, in the Price Waterhouse partnership process, hearsay information was given equal weight with the opinions of people who had more intensive contact with the candidate. There were no corporate policies prohibiting sex discrimination and no corporate awareness that sex discrimination was inappropriate (Fiske et al., 1991).

The Supreme Court decided in favor of Ann Hopkins. Its ruling stated:

> "Nor . . . does it require expertise in psychology to know that if an employee's flawed interpersonal skills can be corrected by a soft-hued suit or a new shade of lipstick, perhaps it is the employee's sex and not her interpersonal skills that has drawn the criticism." (*Hopkins* v. *Price Waterhouse* 1989, p. 1793, cited in Fiske et al., 1991)

The ruling also stated: "We sit not to determine whether Ms. Hopkins is nice, but to decide whether the partners reacted negatively to her because she is a woman" (p. 1795). Finally, the ruling pointed out the impossible dilemma for women that such stereotypes produce. "An employee who objects to aggressiveness in women but whose positions require this trait places women in an intolerable Catch-22: out of a job if they behave aggressively and out of a job if they don't" (p. 1791). The social processes that create such dilemmas (also known as *double binds*) are described in Chapter 3.

The Persistence of Stereotyping: Cognitive Factors

Stereotypes of socially stigmatized groups, including women, appear to cluster into judgments of (1) sociability/warmth and (2) competency (Goodwin & Fiske, 2001). Housewives, for example, are seen as nice but incompetent. Some social psychologists argue that perceptions of women's competence are primarily influenced by their status in society, whereas perceptions of their sociability/warmth are influenced by whether they are seen to compete or cooperate with men (Glick & Fiske, 1999).

Women are divided into subtypes on the basis of their social roles. A subtype that is high in niceness but low in competency includes not only housewives but also the elderly, those who are mentally retarded, and people with physical handicaps (Goodwin & Fiske, 2001). Another subtype includes career women and feminists, who are seen as competent but not nice. Women in this subtype violate conventional gender expectations, do not meet heterosexual needs, and challenge societal power relations.

Career woman and *feminist* appear to have become words that target women who are not nice and not feminine enough (Fiske, Xu, & Cuddy, 1999). As in the Anne Hopkins case, behaviors, such as self-promotion, that raise women's competency ratings reduce ratings of their attractiveness and hireability (Rudman, 1998; Rudman & Glick, 1999). Recent newspaper articles report that an increasing number of women college professors are being denied tenure because they "don't fit" into their departments (Lewin, 2002). They are charged with being "noncollegial" because they are aggressive and self-promoting—characteristics that might be applauded in their male colleagues.

The existence of subtypes helps explain why stereotypes persist despite the many disconfirming examples that people encounter every day. For example, what happens when a person meets a feminine woman who is an excellent athlete or a student leader who is also warm and sensitive? When people encounter individuals who disconfirm their beliefs about members of a group, they often find it easier to reclassify these persons than to change their beliefs about a whole category. The women might be seen as sexy or as future careerists. The response to each subtype depends on the beliefs of the observer.

In an experiment that illustrates the way subtyping works, researchers examined the attitudes toward women that were held by different groups of men (Haddock & Zanna, 1994). The different groups constructed different images in response to the label "woman." Right-wing authoritarian men (these individuals have submissive attitudes toward established authorities, show a general aggressiveness toward persons "targeted" by those authorities, and adhere tightly to social conventions) did not share the positive evaluations of women held by other groups of men because unlike other men, they did not respond to the label *woman* with the image of a housewife. Instead, for authoritarian men, *woman* elicited an image of a feminist and triggered negative evaluations. The authoritarian men had more negative beliefs about feminists and saw them as possessing many values that they disliked. Ambivalent sexist men are also more likely than nonsexist men to generate a large number of subtypes of women and to make more extreme judgments about different subgroups (Glick et al., 1997).

Some disconfirming cases are better than others at challenging stereotypes. Change in stereotypes is promoted by many examples of otherwise typical group members who engage in one atypical behavior. Change is also facilitated when the disconfirming behavior occurs repeatedly in many different settings. For example, women who are fighter pilots, rock climbers, and construction workers have undermined the stereotype that women cannot do tough, demanding work (Fiske & Stevens, 1993).

Measuring Modern Sexism

Until recently, few differences had been found between those who hold negative biases against women and those who do not. In part, this was because psychologists had looked at attitudes about women as a group rather than at more particular images or attitudes toward subtypes of women. Recent studies have revealed correlates of sexism in both women and men. For example, high scorers on right-wing authoritarianism have traditional gender-role identity and attitudes. They also rate political events associated with women as less important, and they see women as having high power and influence in society (Duncan, Peterson, & Winter, 1997). They express more antiabortion views in essays and are punitive toward women seeking abortion. Men with high levels of male self-esteem (those who place a high value on their own masculinity) appear to find feminism particularly threatening (Burn, Aboud, & Moyles, 2000).

Openly admitting that one believes women are inferior to men is not easily done in the early part of the twenty-first century. However, prejudice persists in disguised forms. To study modern forms of sexism, researchers have devised new measurement tools such as the neosexism scale and the modern sexism scale, which probably measure related biases (Campbell, Schellenberg, & Senn, 1997).

The *neosexism scale* focuses on the conflict between egalitarian values and residual negative feelings toward women (Tougas, Brown, Beaton, & Joly, 1995). Neosexism is related to old-fashioned sexism, but scores on the neosexism scale predict attitudes toward symbolically important issues such as affirmative action better than old-fashioned sexism scales do. Neosexist beliefs appear to be triggered by self-interest. For example, they were stronger among employees of a firm committed to affirmative action than among university students.

Some individuals who oppose affirmative action do so because they believe that sexual equality already exists. People who score high on a *modern sexism scale*—a scale designed to measure covert sexism—tend to show such perceptual biases (Swim, Aikin, Hall, & Hunter, 1995). They overestimated the percentage of women in several male-dominated occupations. They also believed that gender segregation in the workforce (see Chapter 11) is due to biological or natural differences between the sexes (Swim & Cohen, 1997).

IS THE GLASS HALF EMPTY OR HALF FULL?

Are negative attitudes toward women increasing or declining? The answer depends on how change is measured. On the one hand, scores on the Attitudes toward Women Scale (Spence & Helmreich, 1978)—the first scale to measure attitudes about the political, economic, and social equality of women and men—have become more feminist over the past twenty years (Twenge, 1997). Men are less liberal in their attitudes than are women, but gender differences have been decreasing since the early 1980s.

On the other hand, the evidence suggests that gender stereotypes have changed little over the past thirty-five years. One study replicated in 1978 a study of gender-role concepts that had first been published in 1957 (Werner & LaRussa, 1985). The researchers used the same 200-item checklist with the same number of respondents at the same university (Berkeley) at which the earlier study had been conducted. They found that 62 percent of the adjectives that had been significantly assigned to men in 1957 were still part of the male stereotype in 1978. Of the adjectives that had been used to describe women in 1957, 77 percent were still part of the current stereotype. In no case did an adjective shift between men and women over the two decades between the studies, although some adjectives dropped out and some new ones appeared. The major change was that there were fewer negative stereotypes about women. Roughly equal numbers of favorable and unfavorable adjectives were assigned to women and men. A more recent study that examined the gender stereotypes of college students from 1974 to 1991 also found no substantive change (Lueptow, Garovich, & Lueptow, 1995).

The reduction in negative stereotypes about women should perhaps be a cause for joy. However, this change seems to be due to the assignment of positive communal qualities such as helpfulness, warmth, and understanding to women. Unfortunately, perceptions that women possess these qualities did not influence respondents' attitudes toward the equality of women and men. In other words, women are thought of as very nice people but not as worthy as men of equal rights, roles, and privileges (Eagly & Mladinic, 1989). Overall, neither sex is seen as "better" than the other, but men are viewed more favorably than women in dynamic terms such as activity and strength (Williams & Best, 1990).

Furthermore, undergraduate women still encounter one to two sexist incidents per week—incidents that had an emotional impact on them according to their daily diaries (Swim, Hyers, Cohen, & Ferguson, 2001). The incidents included reflections of or demands for traditional gender roles such as "You're a woman, so fold my laundry" or "Don't worry your pretty little head about those complex insurance forms" (p. 36); demeaning comments such as the label "bitch" or "chick"; sexist jokes; exclusion from conversations; or sexual objectification.

Changes in behavior lag behind the endorsement of gender-egalitarian beliefs. Women and men show the greatest resistance to change in the area of male–female relationships (Spence & Hahn, 1997). In their relations with men, women admitted to deliberately acting "feminine" as much or more than men admitted to acting "masculine" (Sherman & Spence, 1997). Traditional ideology about gender roles may be linked to social desirability for women. Such "new old-fashioned girls" do not see it as necessarily a bad thing for men to initiate dates, offer women seats on the bus, or offer admiring looks or glances to strange women (Theriault & Holmberg, 1998). (See Figure 2.10.)

Beliefs about the differences between men and women function at many psychological levels. They help preserve a sense of self, structure interpersonal relationships, and maintain the legitimacy of social systems (Jost & Banaji, 1994). They are maintained by a variety of cognitive and behavioral processes (see Chapter 3).

The connections between perceptions and reality are complex. Biases in information gathering, encoding, and memory processes are important for understanding stereotypes, but so are contemporary societal practices that discriminate against women. For example, although the work world has changed dramatically, sex segregation of occupations remains strong. If current societal arrangements underlie stereotypes, changes in cognitive biases will not occur (because the current biases are valid in terms of how the real world works).

FIGURE 2.10. The media's focus on looks limits beliefs about other domains of achievement for women.
Source: Stone Soup. © 2001 Jan Eliot/Distributed by Universal Press Syndicate. Reprinted with permission of Universal Press Syndicate. All rights reserved.

Thus, those interested in social change will have to look beyond cognitive biases. In his landmark book on prejudice, Gordon Allport (1954) attributed being a target of stereotypes to historical as well as psychological circumstances. Whether you are a target depends to a great extent on the relative power of your group. Groups do not exist in a social vacuum. The issue of power will be discussed more fully in Chapter 3, but it can never be ignored.

Finally, we all have some responsibility for change. Negative attitudes toward feminists have implications for all women—whether or not they label themselves as feminists. Many women understand that if they express complaints about women's status, note some form of inequality, or report sexual harassment, they can expect to be perceived negatively. Negative judgments are likely to focus on aspects of likability—on traits that are important for interpersonal relationships. These perceptions have a silencing effect on women and help maintain the status quo. Will the information in this chapter help you find a voice?

CONNECTING THEMES

- *Gender is more than just sex.* Gender stereotypes exist inside people's heads as forms of cognitive bias. They are maintained through interactive processes involving both the person and society. The consistent and universal representation of women and men as different helps generate these biases. In turn, cultural images of the sexes are used to justify sexist perceptions.
- *Language and naming are sources of power.* Nothing in a culture can be regarded as trivial. Differences in the pictorial and linguistic representations of men and women influence how people perceive and think about the world. Declines in stereotyping are facilitated by naming. Naming brings into focus that which has been invisible.
- *Women are not all alike.* The global stereotypes of "women" and "men" are too broad. Subtypes exist based on physical characteristics, roles, race/ethnicity, and class. It is important to investigate both the similarities and the differences between perceptions about different groups of women and men.
- *Psychological research can foster social change.* Stereotypes are almost "pure" forms of social construction. Cognitive social psychology can help us understand the psychological mechanisms underlying these constructions and how constructs are related to current social realities.

SUGGESTED READINGS

ETCOFF, NANCY (1999). *Survival of the prettiest: The science of beauty.* NY: Anchor Press. Although we do not always agree with the individualist and evolutionary perspectives in this book, it is an excellent review of what we know about the biological, social, and cultural bases of physical attractiveness. It includes much information about the nonreality of ideal beauty and the impossibility for ordinary women to meet its impossible standards.

MUNSHI, SHOMA (Ed.). (2001). *Images of the "modern woman" in Asia: Global media, local meanings.* Richmond, Surrey, UK: Curzon Press. The articles in this book have a more cultural studies perspective than most students of psychology are used to. However, many of articles complement theory and research from psychology and also add a multicultural perspective to the selling and consumption of beauty.

WEITZ, ROSE (Ed.). (2003). *The politics of women's bodies: Sexuality, appearance, and behavior* (2nd edition). New York: Oxford University Press. A well-chosen set of articles from a social constructionist perspective. It focuses on the way appearance affects all aspects of women's lives.

CHAPTER 3

Doing Gender

"Who am I?" This is a question that is much simpler to ask than to answer. Psychologists interested in identity have been analyzing this question for more than thirty years (Gordon, 1968). People answer it in both predictable and idiosyncratic ways because everyone has many forms of identity. For example, if we, the authors, answered this question, we would probably list woman, feminist, mother, wife, professor, middle-aged, European-American, middle-class, and so on. The order might vary from time to time, and there would be some differences between us, but gender would always be high on the list.

Why is gender such a central part of identity? It is important because it is a major way by which society classifies people. Furthermore, gender is internalized so that people use its "rules" as a way of defining themselves and evaluating their own behavior. Although these rules differ across cultures, psychologists are uncovering some underlying similarities.

This chapter focuses on the ways gender is created and maintained by social processes. This is why we call the chapter "Doing Gender." It may be a little difficult to get used to the idea of gender being something that you "do." Most people think about masculinity and femininity as something that comes naturally. But most gender differences have a "now you see them, now you don't" property. It is almost impossible to determine how an individual will behave based solely on her or his gender. Instead, people change their behaviors based on who they perceive themselves to be (identity or self-image), how they want others to see them (self-presentation), who else is present and what they are perceived to want (social demands), and the general societal context and ideology about gender (norms). Gender is a kind of performance, and the actors must learn their lines and cues. Like good acting, gender is best performed when it appears most natural.

Gender and power are intimately connected in the social world. As two early feminist researchers stated:

> . . . it is in social interaction that women are constantly reminded of what their "place" is and here that they are put back in their place, should they venture out. Thus, social interaction serves as the locus of the most common means of social control employed against women. By being continually reminded of their inferior status in their interactions with others, and continually compelled to acknowledge that status in their own patterns of behavior, women may internalize society's definition of them as inferior so thoroughly that they are often unaware of what their status is. Inferiority becomes habitual, and the inferior place assumes the familiarity—and even desirability—of home. (Henley & Freeman, 1989, p. 457)

It is not always pleasant to find out how gender works, but an awareness of gender can protect women and girls from the negative consequences of living with sexism. In this chapter, we discuss the social processes that maintain women's place. The last part of this chapter examines some of the ways in which strong women have redefined themselves and changed some of the ways of doing gender.

GENDER AS A SOCIAL CATEGORY

The social processes by which gender is constructed are complex, but a growing body of experimental research allows one to disentangle the factors involved. Although these studies examine behavior in artificial situations, they support the arguments of feminists. They show that interpersonal processes involving gender help to maintain a pattern of male dominance. Moreover, the large number of social mechanisms involved and people's relative unawareness of them help to convince both women and men that androcentric reality has a basis in the natural world.

The Categorization Process: Gender and Social Roles

An ingenious experiment illustrates how people construct social categories with properties analogous to those of women and men (Hoffman & Hurst, 1990). Participants were asked to imagine a planet that had two kinds of people—Orinthians and Ackmians—who performed different jobs on the planet. Most of the members of one group worked in the industrial centers of the city. Most of the other group stayed home and raised children. Participants were then asked about the personality characteristics of the people in the two jobs. They were also asked why they thought there was an unequal distribution of the two groups in these jobs. Participants reported that they believed each group had personality characteristics that suited them for a particular kind of work.

Pretend that the Orinthians and Ackmians are men and women. Because people have limited experience with men and women in the same roles, they tend to explain gender roles as though they are due to personality differences. They assume that people are in various roles because they want to be. Roles, however, force people to behave in particular ways regardless of their individual qualities. Nevertheless, people tend to confuse the actor and his or her role (TV actors who play villains often complain about being yelled at in public). Confusion between actor and role explains why people are surprised when a female executive or pro athlete acts "like a man."

Further evidence that social roles influence perceptions of gender comes from a study that asked participants to imagine the average man or woman of the recent past (1950), present (2000), or future (2050). As gender roles were seen to converge, traditional stereotypes decreased (Diekman & Eagly, 2000). However, the convergence imagined for the future resulted primarily from giving women masculine traits. Men were seen as only moderately likely to increase in feminine characteristics.

The Importance of Gender as a Category

People construct social divisions even when the rationale for doing so is either trivial or arbitrary. For example, in one study students put people into different groups on the basis of whether or not they liked abstract art or whether they consistently overestimated or underestimated the number of dots on a slide (Wilder, 1986). Gender, race/ethnicity, and age appear to be particularly important cues for categorizing others, perhaps because of the visibility and relative permanence of these categories.

Early studies revealed that people almost always notice whether another person is female or male. People also have difficulty ignoring sex in favor of other aspects of another person that might be more useful to them. Consider a classic study in which people who were waiting at a subway station were asked if they had just purchased a token. If they had, they were told that a study on eyewitness reports was being conducted, and they were asked to describe the token seller by listing characteristics for the purpose of identification. Of the characteristics mentioned, the sex of the token seller—in this case, female—was always included. It was given as a first or second characteristic 100 percent of the time. In fact, it was given first 75 percent of the time and was displaced to second position only by race (in this case, African-American). "As if to underscore the prominence of sex as a characteristic, the one respondent who couldn't offer any description said, 'I can't even remember whether it was a man or a woman' " (Grady, 1977, p. 4).

The participants in this study apparently thought that sex was a very important characteristic to mention for purposes of identification. Of course, it isn't important in any statistical sense. By naming sex, one only distinguishes a person from about 50 percent of the population. Most people have many more individuating characteristics—glasses, hair color, freckles, and so forth.

The major importance of sex as a social category has been documented by more recent studies, too. In one study, when men and women were asked to identify different males and females in a group on the basis of what they had said (other cues were also varied—such as hair length and color of clothing), sex was the primary category used (Lorenzi-Cioldi, 1993). People are more likely to categorize others by their sex than by their race (Stangor, Lynch, Duan, & Glass, 1992). They are also more likely to confuse individuals of the same sex than individuals of the same age, race, role, or name (Fiske, Haslam, & Fiske, 1991). And they are more likely to notice when people break a gender prescription than when they "fail to act their age" (Fiske & Stevens, 1993).

Box 3.1 Brown Buttons and Gray Buttons at a Singles Bar

The scene is a "singles" bar located in a middle-sized town. Some people are dancing in one section of the room. Others are sitting or standing around the bar drinking and socializing. An individual with brown shirt buttons (Brown Buttons) walks purposefully toward a person with gray shirt buttons (Gray Buttons) and begins a conversation. After a few minutes, Brown Buttons asks Gray Buttons to dance. Gray Buttons agrees, and they begin to move to the dancing area.

?

As they start to dance, Gray Buttons says to Brown Buttons, "You are a good dancer. I don't come across many people who dance this well."

"Thank you" says Brown Buttons with a slightly embarrassed smile. "I think you dance well too."

"What do you do for a living?" asks Gray Buttons.

"I'm a high school teacher," answers Brown Buttons. "And you?"

"I'm a research technician," says Gray Buttons, "but I'm thinking of getting into computers."

As the music comes to an end, Gray Buttons says, "You are a very interesting person. I'd like us to talk some more . . . why don't we sit over here?" motioning to a small table in the corner.

?

They've been sitting for quite a while. Brown Buttons orders drinks again, and they continue to talk. . . . "I'm really fascinated by your life; I'd like to get to know you better."

"That's interesting," says Gray Buttons. "I find you exciting too, but I'm not sure that I'm able to handle too much familiarity now. I'm really interested in pursuing my career. . . ."

?

"I understand your position," says Brown Buttons, "but I'd really like to see more of you."

"I'm going to think about it," says Gray Buttons. "Why don't we stop off at my place? Perhaps we'd both get some perspective over coffee and. . . ."

Source: From John and Sussman, "Initiative taking as a determinant of role reciprocal organization," in *Representations; Social Constructions of Gender,* edited by Rhoda Unger. Copyright © 1989 Baywood Publishing Company, Inc. Reprinted with permission.

When gender is not available as a social category, people invent it. An ingenious study illustrates the process by which people construct gender. College students were given a story in which two individuals, "Brown Buttons" and "Gray Buttons," took turns furthering the progress of a relationship (John & Sussman, 1984–1985). At various points in the narrative, conversational dominance shifted from one protagonist to the other and back again. At each of these transitions, respondents were asked to guess the sex of Gray and Brown Buttons. You can see some of this dialogue in Box 3.1. At each question mark, you may select the sex of the participants.

Did you think Gray Buttons was a man or a woman? How about Brown Buttons? At various points during this dialogue, people in the study changed back and forth between male and female labels as social dominance shifted from one character to the other. They changed labels even when doing so meant that they had to give up their previous labels and "resex" characters.

Many people seem to have difficulty accepting the idea that people can take turns engaging in gender-inconsistent behaviors during a social encounter. They see masculinity and femininity as complementary aspects of gender that reproduce sex. When one person was perceived as a man, the other was perceived as a woman. No one conceived of both of the actors as the same sex.

Customary representations of reality do not leave any room for ambiguity of sex or gender. Physically androgynous targets are viewed as more likely to be sexually deviant and as less attractive than individuals whose identity is clearer (Madson, 2000). Sexual ambiguity makes most people uncomfortable. For example, in Ursula LeGuin's *The Left Hand of Darkness*—a story that takes place in a world in which people can alternate between sexes—one of her most startling lines is "The king was pregnant."

Cognitive Tricks with Social Categories

People try to make the world an orderly, predictable place and use a variety of strategies to achieve that end. In particular, they use stereotypes (see Chapter 2) and social categories to explain the way people behave. These constitute a form of cognitive bias. Such cognitive biases operate inside the head of the observer, and they would be less of a problem if they would stay there. But biased beliefs based on social categories are communicated to others and influence their behavior.

Stereotypes and explanations based on social categories are often functional; they save users time and energy in making decisions about the people they meet. But they are usually based on limited information and can lead to broad generalizations that are incorrect. Nevertheless, they are very persistent, in part because they are deeply embedded in how people think, biasing such cognitive processes as attention, encoding, and recall.

Selective Attention and Encoding

People routinely encode information about others based on their perceived race and sex. When asked to recall the speakers from a conversation they had heard, students were less accurate in distinguishing between members of the same social category (either race or sex) than between members of different categories (Taylor, Fiske, Etcoff, & Ruderman, 1978). All the women (or all the men) seemed to "look alike." The students did not intend to use race or sex as a strategy to remember particular people. In fact, the one student who admitted using race was very apologetic about having done so.

People tend to minimize differences within groups and exaggerate differences between them. Within-group characteristics are also exaggerated in inverse proportion to the size of the minority subgroup present. When few members of the minority subgroup are present, their characteristics are seen as more stereotypic of their social category. Thus, people saw women as more feminine and men as more masculine when few other members of their sex were present in a group (Taylor et al., 1978). Women and blacks were just as likely as men and whites to make social judgments about the minority group.

Status and power help shape the perception of social categories. High-status groups are much more likely than low-status groups to receive favorable trait evaluations (Jost & Banaji, 1994). Furthermore, subordinate groups are perceived as more homogenous than dominant groups (Cabecinhas & Amancio, 1999). For example, when men and women were asked to identify different males and females in a group on the basis of what they had said, both men and women had more difficulty distinguishing between female target persons than between male target persons (Lorenzi-Cioldi, 1993). Thus, both women and men acknowledged the greater personal distinctiveness and individuality of males.

Selective Recall

People's attitudes toward women and men can influence what they remember about them. People systematically distort their recollections about individuals from a particular category to make them resemble their stereotypes. For example, when students who read a long story about the life of a woman named Betty K. were subsequently informed that she was living either as a lesbian or with a male partner, they "remembered" more events that supported their interpretation of her sexual identity (Snyder & Uranowitz, 1978). Respondents who learned that Betty K. had a lesbian lifestyle remembered more events in her life that reflected stereotypic beliefs about lesbians; for example, that she had not dated in college. Similarly, people were more likely to recall having seen "librarian-like" qualities in the behavior of a person when she was portrayed as a librarian rather than as a waitress (Cohen, 1981).

Individual differences in beliefs about women and men can influence what people remember. For example, those who believed in women's rights made fewer errors when remembering which traits differentiated between two women than did those with more traditional attitudes. More traditional individuals made fewer errors for male than for female targets (Stewart, Vassar, Sanchez, & David, 2000). These kinds of memory distortions are what makes political disagreements so difficult to resolve.

Behavioral Confirmation and the Self-Fulfilling Prophecy

Cognitive biases are not just passive perceptions. When people interact with someone, they look for information that will confirm their beliefs about that person's social category. For example, when students were informed that they would be interviewing a person who was either an introvert or an extrovert, they chose questions that would confirm the social label they had been given (Snyder & Swann, 1978b). It is only a small step from generating questions that confirm expectations to acting in a way that produces the behavior that one expects. This process is known as a *self-fulfilling prophecy.*

Creating Self-fulfilling Prophecies

How does a self-fulfilling prophecy occur? One component involves *self-presentation,* the attempt to behave in a way that evokes a particular image in others. People are often motivated to confirm the beliefs that others have about them. Based on what they think others want, they change their self-presentation. One early study that applied this concept to gender asked women students to describe themselves to a male partner whose stereotype of an ideal woman was said to conform closely to either a traditional or nontraditional type (Zanna & Pack, 1975). The attitudes of these women had been measured earlier. When the partner was desirable (good-looking and attending an elite university), the women presented themselves more in terms of his ideal type, regardless of their actual attitudes. The women performed better on tests of intellectual competence when the desirable partner was portrayed as having non-stereotypic views about women. Women also altered their self-presentation when they believed they were to be interviewed by a sexist rather than a nonsexist potential employer (von Baeyer, Sherk, & Zanna, 1981). When women believed that they were to be interviewed by a sexist man, they wore more frilly clothing, more jewelry, and perfume to the interview.

It seems reasonable that people should change their appearance to maximize the potential rewards in a social interaction. However, the participants in these studies did not yet know anything about the man's behavior, which existed only in their imaginations. Nevertheless, the women changed their self-presentation to conform to what they believed to be the expectations of powerful or desirable men. Of course, men may also change their self-presentations when they react to implicit demands. For example, in one recent study, college men expressed more profeminist attitudes in public discussion groups than did men in groups where their privacy was assured (Rosell & Hartman, 2001).

A second component of self-fulfilling prophecies is *behavioral confirmation* (how people's actions produce the behaviors they expect from others). For example, in the earliest study on gender and self-fulfilling prophecies, being labeled physically attractive improved women's social competence (Snyder, Tanke, & Berscheid, 1977). Male college students had a short conversation by telephone with women whom they had been led to believe were either physically attractive or unattractive. Photographs had, however, been assigned to the female partners at random. And the women were unaware that their male partners had received false information about their physical appearance. Nevertheless, judges (who heard only the women's part of the conversation) rated those women who had been labeled as physically attractive as more friendly, sociable, and likable than those who had been labeled as less physically attractive. Presumably, the women were responding to subtle cues in the men's conversations. A more recent study replicated these results, although it found that the effects of the attractiveness manipulation waned as the men gained more information about their partners (Valentine, Blankenship, Cooper, & Sullins, 2001).

Many traits traditionally associated with men and women may be influenced by self-fulfilling prophecies. For example, men who expected to interact in a competitive game with a man who had been labeled as hostile initiated more aggressive interactions with him (Snyder & Swann, 1978a). In turn, their behavior induced more aggression from him than from a supposedly nonhostile partner. When the target individuals in this study were led to believe that their aggressive behavior reflected their own personality characteristics, they maintained their increased aggressiveness in subsequent competition with new partners. If, however, the targets were informed that their behavior reflected their partner's behavior, they did not continue this higher level of aggression with new partners.

This finding illustrates one of the most potent elements of the behavioral confirmation process. If a person *internalizes* the new behavior generated by behavioral confirmation, both that person and the perceiver may come to share perceptions about what he or she is like. "What began in the mind of the perceiver will have become reality not only in the behavior of the target but also in the mind of the target" (Snyder & Swann, 1978a, p. 151).

Perpetuating Stereotypes

Self-fulfilling prophecies help perpetuate stereotypic beliefs about women (Skrypnek & Snyder, 1982). Consider an experiment in which unacquainted pairs of men and women were asked to negotiate a division of labor on a series of work-related tasks. Students were located in different rooms and communicated by means of a signaling system. Some of the men were told that they were interacting with a male partner, some with a female partner, and some were not informed about the sex of their partner. During the first part of the study, the men were given the opportunity to choose how the tasks were to be divided between themselves and their partner.

Men were more likely to choose the more masculine tasks when they believed their partner was a woman than when they either believed he was a man or had no information about gender. When both partners initially chose the same task, the men were much less willing to let their partner have the preferred task and switch to the alternative when they believed she was a woman.

As long as the men were the initiators in the situation, all their partners provided behavioral confirmation for their beliefs. The "sex" to which the partners were assigned rather than their actual sex influenced their behavior! "Male" partners chose more masculine tasks and "female" partners chose more feminine tasks. Even when the male initiators no longer had the opportunity to guide the negotiations, many of their partners continued the behaviors of the sex to which they had originally been assigned.

This study clearly shows how one person's belief about the sex of another and the traits associated with this belief channel their interaction to confirm stereotypes. At the same time, this experience probably confirms and strengthens the perceiver's stereotypes about women and men in general—stereotypes that he or she will carry into new situations and act to confirm.

This study also reaffirms the idea that people seem unable to tolerate ambiguity in their sexual categories. People whose sex was unlabeled behaved in a manner that was indistinguishable from those who were labeled as male. This is because the male participants adopted similar behavioral strategies when they thought their partner was a man and when the partner's sex was unknown. As discussed in Chapter 2, when gender is unspecified, people are assumed to be male. In other words, maleness is the normative condition.

Although few studies on the self-fulfilling prophecy have been conducted recently, social psychologists have developed techniques that uncover the kind of nonconscious processes that may underlie it. Most of these studies have been conducted using the *implicit attitudes task,* which measures the speed with which participants make judgments about combinations of two concepts (Greenwald & Banaji, 1995). For example, in a series of word combinations presented by a computer, participants who respond faster to the combination of "male-good" than to the combination of "female-good" are evaluated as having an automatic gender bias in favor of men. Researchers using this technique have found that men who anticipated an interaction with a female superior revealed negative biases against women; that is, they tended to respond more slowly to the word combination "female-good" than to the combination "male-good" (Richeson & Ambady, 2001). In contrast, men who expected to interact with a female subordinate or a woman of equal status to themselves showed a pro-female bias.

Stereotype Threat

The research discussed so far examines the ways in which social interactions construct individual behaviors. Recently, social psychologists have studied how systemic beliefs about marginalized groups can also lead to behavioral confirmation. These studies have focused on how cultural beliefs about women and African-Americans negatively influence behavior in important cognitive domains. The work is based on a theory of *stereotype threat* developed by Claude Steele and his colleagues at Stanford University (Steele, 1997; Steele & Aronson, 1995). Some of the important features of stereotype threat are the following:

1. Stereotype threat affects the members of any group about whom there exists some generally known negative stereotype.
2. Stereotype threat is triggered when a negative stereotype about one's group becomes relevant to oneself or one's behavior.
3. Stereotype threat is not always present. It varies from group to group and for the same group in different settings. People may move to groups in which the relevant stereotype does not exist or settings that do not activate the stereotype. Paradoxically, stereotype threat most affects those individuals who care about their performance in the threatened domain.
4. The stereotype may influence one's behavior even if one does not believe in the stereotype.
5. Efforts to disprove the stereotype may be daunting because these stereotypes are so widely disseminated that they must be constantly disproved in one setting after another.
(Adapted from Steele, 1997, pp. 617–618).

What makes this theory so interesting is the evidence that supports it. Although some of the research involves African-Americans and other ethnic minorities, our discussion will focus on research on women. It has been found, for example, that gender stereotypes involving advanced quantitative skills can handicap women who take tests in this area. These studies manipulated the degree of stereotype threat by varying the information available to test takers. They found that women underperformed in comparison to men on difficult (but not on easy) math tests. However, when the test was described as not showing gender differences, sex-related differences in performance disappeared (Spencer, Steele, & Quinn, 1999). When stereotype threat was increased by informing participants that the test produced gender differences, women performed substantially worse than equally qualified men did (see Figure 3.1). This study suggests that stereotype threat may be high for women when they take difficult math exams under standard conditions.

Stereotype threat is most potent when tests are at the very edge of students' abilities. For example, female and male college students performed equally well when difficult math problems were presented numerically. When the same problems were presented as word problems (an area that women find more difficult), informing test takers about gender differences induced significantly poorer performance only for the women. Further studies indicated that under threat, women had difficulty in formulating problem-solving strategies (Quinn & Spencer, 2001).

Stereotype threat may be activated without explicit information about tests and performance. When participants were shown commercials that depicted females in traditionally stereotypic roles, women performed less well on the word-problem test. They performed as well as men when they saw counter-stereotypic commercials prior to the testing situation (Quinn & Spencer, 2001). Women also performed less well than men when they were the only female to take a difficult math test in three-person groups. Women who took the test in all-female groups performed significantly better (Inzlicht & Ben-Zeev, 2000). Even women who took the test in a female-majority condition (two women and one man) showed moderate but significant deficits. Men performed equally well on the math test under all conditions.

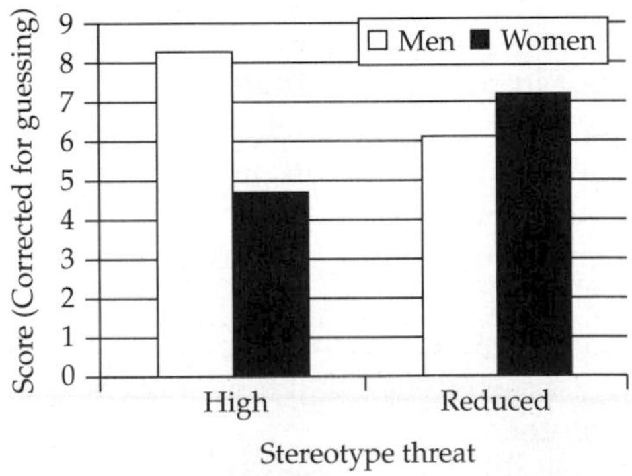

FIGURE 3.1. Performance on math test as function of stereotype threat and gender. Notice that women actually outperform men when they are not reminded of stereotypes that women cannot do math.

Stereotype threat appears to be heightened by identification with a group to whom the negative stereotype applies. When test performance was linked to gender, women with high levels of gender identification performed worse than men on a math test, whereas women with lower levels of gender identification performed as well as men (Schmader, 2002). When gender was not linked to test performance, women's performance was equal to men's, regardless of the importance they placed on gender identity.

White males, too, can be placed under stereotype threat. When white male college students were told that Asians generally did better than whites on the difficult math test they would be taking, they performed significantly less well than comparable males who were not under threat (Aronson, Lustina, Good, Keough, Steele, & Brown, 1999). These studies show that the situational threat of negative stereotypes is sufficient to impair performance even among groups that are not chronically stereotyped.

Under usual circumstances, however, negative stereotypes are more likely to exist about individuals from subordinate groups. Even at elite institutions such as Harvard, female undergraduates in male-dominated academic areas (engineering, math, and science) reported higher levels of discrimination and stereotype threat than did women in fields dominated by females (Steele, James, & Barnett, 2002). They were also more likely to report that they were considering a change in their major. The behavioral consequences of stereotype threat help to confirm and maintain traditional beliefs about the unsuitability of women for technical and scientific careers (see Chapters 4 and 11).

GENDER DIFFERENCES AS STATUS DIFFERENCES

Status and Power

To understand fully how gender functions to distinguish and stratify people, we must consider concepts such as social power (sometimes abbreviated as "power"), ascribed status, and achieved status. *Social power* is control over events or resources that other people value (Molm & Hedley, 1992). It is an attribute of relationships, not individuals. Because of authority, legitimacy, or expertise, bosses have more power than their employees, teachers have more power than their students, and doctors have more power than their patients. Social power differs from *social influence* because social power implies the use of some kind of coercion, such as the loss of a salary or a poor grade.

Status refers to a person's potential ability to influence or control others. Sociologists distinguish between two kinds of status: ascribed and achieved. *Achieved status* is based partly on the role one performs in an organization or a family—for example, boss versus secretary, father versus mother, or professor versus student. How well one performs one's role is also a component of achieved status.

Ascribed status describes and predicts relations between categories of people in terms of the rewards, benefits, or compliance they give each other. In other words, ascribed status defines who is supposed to have more social power in society. Unlike achieved status, ascribed status is not based on how well people function in their roles. Ascribed status is usually based on inherent characteristics and cultural norms. Status is conferred because of a person's group membership, not his or her personal characteristics. In the United States, race/ethnicity, age, social class, and sex are all determinants of ascribed status. The relative value of these characteristics is determined by others' definitions, not one's own.

Ascribed status is usually described in hierarchical terms—some people possess more or less status than others. Think of a posh restaurant in New York City. A tourist from the Midwest has difficulty getting a waiter's attention no matter how elaborately he gestures. A suave customer from Wall Street obtains obsequious service with a flick of a wrist. Obviously, the latter gentleman has ascribed status. Similarly, women's suggestions and comments tend to be ignored. To get the same amount of recognition as men, women often have to be more persistent, sometimes leading to the perception that successful women are "pushy," "mouthy," and "difficult."

In any group or social system, individuals are typically differentiated from one another according to one or more dimensions involving ascribed or achieved characteristics. Sex, as an ascribed characteristic, conveys status and power. It has been argued that "maleness" is a diffuse status characteristic—associated with greater power, prestige, and social value than "femaleness" (Cohen, Berger, & Zelditch, 1972; Unger, 1976, 1978).

Status differences contribute to perceptions about the traits that individuals possess. In a study that illustrates this process, participants read descriptions of a fictional Amazonian society consisting of the Ngwani and the Gunada (Conway, Pizzamiglio, & Mount, 1996). The society was described as stable, peaceful, and cooperative; both groups worked in the same fields. The Ngwani were described as having higher social status (bigger huts), which was justified by their religious belief that they were descendants of the first man and woman. The Gunada had lower religious status and raised the Ngwani's children. When participants were asked to evaluate the traits of each group, the Ngwani were seen as more competent and the Gunada were seen as more pleasant. A subsequent study compared the gender-related traits attributed to men and women as well as to the Ngwani and Gunada. Researchers found that the same traits were attributed to men and the high-status Ngwani (Conway & Vartanian, (2000). And except for some forms of passive aggression (for example, nagging and whining), the same traits were attributed to women and the low-status Gunada. It is surely no coincidence that the more powerful group was seen as having traditionally masculine traits, whereas the less powerful group was seen to have traditional feminine qualities.

Ascribed status characteristics cannot easily be changed by the behavior of individuals. For example, if women lack power because of their roles as child bearers or child rearers, they should gain power as a result of changes in these roles (for example, if men had an equal share in child care). If, however, their relative lack of power is a result of who they are, women will continue to lack power even in "male" roles. These competing hypotheses can be tested. Researchers have looked at gender differences in many kinds of behavior. Far more often than not, men engage in behaviors that convey high social power, whereas women's customary behaviors convey lower social status and power.

When women violate status norms, they are regarded as socially deviant and are penalized for their behavior. In this section, we will examine a number of behavioral areas and point to parallels between gender and status.

Gender and Nonverbal Behavior

Many nonverbal behaviors vary by gender and sometimes vary by status as well. One study, for example, examined how pairs of men, pairs of women, and mixed-sex pairs interacted during a 10-minute task in which each pair constructed a domino structure for a contest (Lott, 1987). Under these conditions, women behaved the same way regardless of whether their partner was a man or another woman. In contrast, men distanced themselves more from female than from male partners by turning their faces or bodies away and by placing the dominoes closer to themselves than to their partners. In fourteen of the seventeen mixed-sex pairs in which the structure was closer to one partner than to the other, it was closer to the man than to the woman. Paper-and-pencil measures had not revealed any evidence of prejudice or gender stereotypes among these college students. However, the men's nonconscious behaviors seemed to reflect their sense of greater status relative to women.

The people with more social power are usually men. Do the ways men customarily behave toward women reflect gender-typed behaviors or their usually superior status in social settings? In most studies, status appears to be more important than sex. One important area of investigation is conversational dynamics. For example, women lean away from the group and smile when speaking significantly more than men do (Kennedy & Camden, 1983). People in low-status positions are also more likely to smile in group settings (Hecht & LaFrance, 1998). Gender differences in smiling are greatest in face-to-face interactions and in situations that encourage self-conscious social displays, such as in a posed photograph (Hall, LeBeau, Reinoso, & Thayer, 2001). Women appear to feel a greater obligation to smile than men do (LaFrance, 2001).

Smiling, in turn, has interesting consequences. People are more likely to be interrupted when they lean away, smile, or do not look at the other people in the group. By interrupting, higher-status individuals can gain the floor and restrict the contributions of lower-status group members. In most groups, men are more likely than women to interrupt others. Even in groups where men and women attempt to interrupt at roughly the same rate, these behaviors are associated with status differences as well. In one study, for example, researchers found that the men interrupted women more than men. Men were also more successful when interrupting women than men (Smith-Lovin & Brody, 1989). These findings illustrate how displays of power by men are socially reinforced.

Women who interrupt others cannot be so sure of social support. When students rated videotapes of interactions between two men, two women, or a man and a woman, although the videotapes were identical in script features, students rated a woman who interrupted a man as ruder, more irritable, and more self-concerned than in other scenarios (LaFrance, 1992). Interactions in which a woman interrupted a man received more negative ratings than any other pairing. Male and female raters agreed that there was something wrong with this situation. The woman appeared to have broken more than a conversational rule. She had violated an accepted social policy concerning appropriate behavior by those who have less power. This kind of social regulation makes it less likely that women will emerge as leaders of mixed-sex groups. Thus gender differences in group settings not only reflect status and power differences but also help to perpetuate them.

There has been no decline in gender differences in conversational interruptions despite the increased presence of women in public life. Men make considerably more intrusive interruptions than women do (Anderson & Leaper, 1998). *Intrusive interruptions* are active attempts by the previous listener to usurp the current speaker's conversational turn.

Women are generally better at decoding nonverbal cues than men are (Hall, 1985). This difference is consistent with subordinate status, in which it is important for lower-power individuals to adapt their behaviors to the demands of more dominant individuals. This gender difference may, however, be more a function of motivation than ability. When students were paid for their empathetic accuracy, the performance of both men and women improved and gender differences disappeared (Klein & Hodges, 2001).

Helping and Gender Norms

Gender differences also parallel status/power differences in helping and being helped. Helping is a particularly useful form of social behavior for demonstrating mechanisms of gender construction because it can be studied unobtrusively.

Who Helps Whom?

Like many other social behaviors, helping reflects and maintains gender distinctions (Eagly, 1987). Men are only somewhat more helpful than women, although women are, indeed, more likely to be the recipients of help.

When are women helped more than men? Men received priority for service in department stores even when they arrived at the same time as a woman customer (Stead & Zinkhan, 1986; Zinkhan & Stoiadin, 1984). The men were assisted first twice as often as the women were. When the salesclerks (mostly women) were asked about this difference, they gave answers that reflected gender stereotypes, such as "Women shop around more," "Men are more serious buyers," "Men need more help than women," or "Men are easier to deal with."

When norms about female dependency are evoked, however, women are helped more than men (Piliavin & Unger, 1985). For example, women were helped more than men when they needed to change a flat tire, when they had a car break down on the highway and needed someone to relay a call for them, or when they asked for travel directions. Men also helped women more than men when there was some potential danger for the helper, such as assistance with a staged theft. Such conditions are consistent with definitions of help in terms of heroism and chivalry—both aspects of the normative masculine role. Men did not help more than women when the situation called for empathy or social support.

Maintaining and Upsetting Hierarchical Relationships

Helping is related to status as well as to gender. For example, in a study of more than 2,500 physicians in Norway, both male and female respondents reported that female physicians were given less help by nurses than their male counterparts (Gjerberg & Kjobsrod, 2001). A large-scale survey of financial service employees found that even when black women and white women had jobs in which they controlled organizational resources, they received less work-related help from their co-workers than did white men (McGuire, 2002).

What happens when a woman needing assistance has higher status than the man? In one experiment, men and women college students interacted with a man or woman who was introduced as either their supervisor or their subordinate (Dovidio & Gaertner, 1983). They were told that this individual (actually a confederate) had either more or less ability than they did. Before the students worked with this person on the task that was supposed to be the object of the research, he or she "accidently" knocked a container of pencils to the ground. The researchers unobtrusively measured helping by the number of pencils the students helped the confederate pick up.

Status but not ability influenced the frequency with which women were helped. Both women and men helped women supervisors less than women subordinates but did not discriminate between male supervisors and subordinates. Ability, not status, influenced the degree to which men were helped. Men and women helped high-ability men more than those with low ability, but helped low- and high-ability women equally as often.

White men have also been found to be more reluctant to help black male supervisors than black male subordinates (Dovidio & Gaertner, 1981). Relative ability had no effect on helpfulness toward black men, although the high-ability white confederate was helped significantly more than his low-ability counterpart.

These studies illustrate some important points about how sex and race interact with status in our society. First, people in a higher-status group appear to be unwilling to recognize ability differences in individuals with a lower status than their own. White men helped other white men whose abilities were supposedly greater than their own, but did not appear to notice superior abilities in either white women or black men. Second, when traditional role relationships were threatened (by the experimenters' conferring supervisory rank on a woman or an African-American man), helping declined. Third, discrimination is frequently masked by people's desire to behave in a socially desirable manner. Studies such as these, which use indirect and unobtrusive measures, indicate high levels of covert sexism and racism among college students. The potential for discrimination is greater than many people believe.

The Effects of Being Helped

Help-seeking, like helping, is related to roles and status. Women and men with high self-confidence are particularly reluctant to seek help from others (Fisher, Nadler, & Whitcher-Alagna, 1982). They resist being helped by people who have greater resources or power than they do and prefer to be helped by someone who expects to be repaid.

Seeking help from others involves social costs that can be very threatening to individuals' perceptions of their own status and competence. One recent field study, for example, examined help-seeking by physicians and nurses regarding a new computer system within a large hospital (Lee, 2002). Individuals reported less help-seeking when they were men in male-oriented occupations and when the task was seen as central to the organization's core competence.

Being helped reduces self-esteem, whereas being helpful raises it (Nadler & Fisher, 1986). Men who received unsolicited help from another student actually performed less well on a subsequent task than men who received no such help (Daubman & Lehman, 1993). People who habitually seek help from others appear to trade a short-term gain for a long-term loss. Being helped not only lowers their self-esteem but also increases their sense of dependency, making them more likely to seek help yet again. Women are socialized into perceiving themselves as helpless and dependent. They are more likely to be helped than men under some circumstances, and this reinforces their belief that they need help. The long-term consequences may include the creation of gender-biased vulnerability to some forms of emotional distress (see Chapter 14).

Doing Gender, Doing Emotion

Gender differences in emotion are also a product of social construction. In a number of studies, Stephanie Shields (2002) has demonstrated that women are perceived to be the more emotional sex, that women who are described as "emotional" are viewed more negatively than comparable men, and that men are expected to have more emotional control than women. Such beliefs are maintained largely by excluding anger—an emotion much more frequently expressed by men—from definitions of emotion.

People have a great deal of difficulty overcoming their gender stereotypes about emotion. When asked to evaluate the emotions portrayed in photographs of women and men, respondents consistently rated women as sadder and less angry than men. Even women whose photographs portrayed unambiguous anger were rated as presenting a mixture of anger and sadness (Plant, Hyde, Keltner, & Devine (2000). These perceptions appear to function without conscious awareness (Goos & Silverman, 2002).

One major way that women and men present themselves as feminine or masculine is through the use of gender-appropriate emotional displays (Shields, 2002). In keeping with gender stereotypes, women encode happiness better than men, whereas men are able to encode anger better than women (Coates & Feldman, 1996). The ability to portray happiness so that people could distinguish it from other emotions was associated with higher popularity for women, but not for men. In contrast, the ability to demonstrate anger was associated with higher popularity for men, but not for women. In a large-scale survey of people's responses to feeling angry, men were more likely than women to report that aggressive responses would elevate their mood (Harris, 1992).

This gendered use of emotional cues is learned early in childhood (see Chapter 6). Boys tend to interact in large, status-oriented groups characterized by conflict, competition, and self-promotion. Girls tend to interact in smaller, intimate groups in which conflict is more covert; open expression of anger is less useful to them. Preschool girls' anger, but not distress, has been associated with rejection by their peers (Walter & LaFreniere, 2000). In contrast, boys' anger was positively related to popularity with their peers.

The expression of specific emotions is associated with status and entitlement as well as gender. When college students read vignettes about high- and low-status employees who received performance evaluations, they believed that high-status individuals should feel more anger over negative outcomes, whereas low-status people should feel more sadness or guilt (Tiedens, Ellsworth, & Mesquita, 2000). In response to positive outcomes, high-status people were expected to feel more pride and low-status people more appreciation. The students also inferred status from the emotions expressed. Independent of sex, angry and proud people were seen as high status, whereas sad, guilty, and appreciative people were viewed as lower in status.

The ability to show anger is a form of social power. Anger can be helpful to men in both politics and business (Tiedens, 2002). For example, respondents supported President Clinton more when they saw him expressing anger about the Monica Lewinsky scandal than when they saw him expressing sadness about the episode.

GENDER AND THE USE OF SOCIAL POWER

Masculine and Feminine Power

Attempts to influence or use power in groups carry strong gender-role prescriptions. One study examined 100 behaviors associated with dominance and 100 behaviors associated with submissiveness to see if these behaviors were gender stereotyped. Examples of dominant behaviors included: "I set goals for a group" and "I resist conceding an argument." Examples of submissive behaviors included: "I do not complain when I was overcharged at the store" and "I accepted verbal abuse without defending myself." Although dominant and submissive acts were perceived as equally desirable (or undesirable) for men and women to perform, respondents expected that dominant acts would be more frequently performed by typical men and submissive acts by typical women (McCreary & Rhodes, 2001).

Traditionally masculine forms of power, such as being decisive or speaking assertively, appear to be less effective when used by women than when used by men. For example, women speak more tentatively when interacting with men with whom they disagree than when interacting with other women under the same circumstances (Carli, 1990). This use of tentative speech appeared to be functional for women even though both men and women judged a woman who spoke tentatively to be less competent and knowledgeable than a woman who spoke assertively. Men were influenced to a greater degree by women who spoke tentatively than by those who spoke assertively. Women who spoke tentatively were less effective with other women.

Similar results have been found when women confederates present a persuasive message after endorsing either a traditional and subordinate role for women or a less-traditional role. "Traditional" confederates were judged as less competent by both women and men. Nevertheless, they exerted more influence over men than the more competent, "nontraditional" advocates did, and they had more influence over men than women (Matschiner & Munen, 1999).

In another study, women who exhibited a competent style were seen by male raters as less likable, more threatening, and less influential than men exhibiting the same style (Carli, 1999). Resistance to a woman's competence was reduced if she "tempered" it with displays of friendliness and warmth (Carli, 2001).

Double Binds and Their Implications

These findings illustrate a classic *double bind.* When women use tentative language as a subtle influence strategy, it compromises their perceived competence and makes it difficult for them to persuade other women. If they use more assertive language, however, they find it difficult to influence men. Because most influence attempts in the real world take place in mixed-sex situations, there is no behavior by which a woman can "win."

Many double binds are constructed around gender categories (see Figure 3.2). They occur when traits or roles are polarized as irreconcilable opposites and it is assumed that a person cannot have both (Jamieson, 1995). Thus, a woman who demonstrates a traditionally male quality such as strength or competence is seen as unfeminine.

One reason women use indirect power strategies is their anticipation of unfavorable reactions from men. These assumptions are not unfounded. In a study of emergent leaders in mixed-sex groups, female leaders received more negative emotional responses—such as furrowed brows, tightened mouths, and nods of disagreement—when they made the same contributions as male leaders. Women's contributions to the group also received fewer positive responses such as smiles and nods of agreement (Butler & Geis, 1990).

Reports from real life reinforce the message of laboratory studies. For example, both male and female university students viewed women instructors as more incompetent than men when they received negative evaluations from them. Ratings were not affected by the instructor's sex if the students received praise, and negative evaluations did not affect students' ratings of male instructors (Sinclair & Kunda, 2000). Similarly, the researchers found that African-American instructors were disparaged only when they delivered a negative evaluation. The students seemed to be trying to salvage their self-esteem by using stereotypes that they would not use if their self-image had not been threatened.

FIGURE 3.2. Double binds and their consequences.
Source: Signe Wilkinson. © 2002 The Washington Post Writers Group. Reprinted with permission.

Female professors are caught in another double bind: They can be perceived as having status or as being accessible, but not both. One study found that women professors are accorded less status than their male counterparts. The probability of being addressed by the title "doctor" was significantly higher for male than for female professors (Takin, Sanchez, & Stewart, 2001). But female professors who were addressed by their title rather than their first name were also seen as less accessible by their students. There was no effect of term of address on perceptions of male faculty. Male competence and power is taken for granted by both sexes. Both women and men give themselves lower performance ratings when interacting with a man rather than a woman, even when there are no differences in actual performance (Carli, 1999). For women to be considered as competent in group interactions, participants must be given explicit evidence of their clear and substantial superiority (Shackelford, Wood, & Worchel, 1996).

Penalizing Nonconforming Women

Both women's and men's behaviors in groups are consistent with gender role prescriptions that men should have power and expertise. People who violate gender roles are seen as less socially acceptable (Kite, 2001). They are often stigmatized or seen as socially deviant. *Stigmatization* refers to the process of responding to a person in terms of some physically negative or socially undesirable characteristic. People react to the characteristic rather than to the person.

Who Is Penalized?

Men are often influential even when they violate traditional norms, but women are penalized even when they perform very well. In one set of studies (Wahrman & Pugh, 1972, 1974), for example, a man or a woman (who were confederates of the experimenter) violated rules about turn-taking and reward allocation at various times during trials involving problem solving. Early nonconformity by a man led co-workers to consider him more influential and desirable, although the nonconformist was disliked more than a man who went along with the group. In contrast, the earlier a woman violated the rules, the less she influenced the group and the more disliked and less desirable as a co-worker she became. The best liked of all the confederates was the conforming woman. Competent nonconforming women were preferred less than incompetent nonconforming men—even though the group as a whole benefited from competent performance.

Similarly, more recent studies show that both women and men dislike a woman who disagrees with them more than they dislike a man who does so, and they are less likely to be persuaded by her. Direct disagreement by a woman evokes more overt expressions of hostility or tension than the same behavior by a man (Carli, 2001). Aggressive women are also evaluated more negatively than aggressive men are (Barber, Foley, & Jones, 1999).

Women are vulnerable to stigmatization because of their social subordination. They are not in a good position to define the rules that evaluate their own behavior. They can violate norms about women's inferior status in many ways, such as having a position that confers power over men, behaving aggressively, or telling men what to do. It is the woman's claim to authority rather than her competence that evokes some men's hostility.

Stigmatizing Feminists

The terms "feminist" and "career woman" have become synonymous with stereotypes of women who are not nice and not feminine enough (Fiske, Xu, Cuddy, & Glick, 1999). Feminists and businesswomen are two of the groups seen as competent (with the related traits of being intelligent, confident, competitive, and independent) but not warm (with traits such as sincere, good-natured, and tolerant). Other groups perceived to have this combination of traits are rich people, Asians, Jews, and Northerners. These groups are disliked because of the probability that they will compete with dominant groups. In contrast, out-groups seen as warm but not competent include retarded people, housewives, disabled people, blind people, house cleaners, migrant workers, and welfare recipients. These groups evoke paternalism rather than hostile prejudice.

Negative constructions of "feminists" and "feminism" may be a way for privileged men to maintain their power. One interesting qualitative study analyzed the responses of forty-six professional men in Scotland to four vignettes depicting current gender issues (Riley, 2001). The men simultaneously attempted to incorporate feminist values and to reject people associated with the feminist movement. (For example, they used the word *stuff* to refer to feminist arguments and complaints; they proclaimed the need for feminist groups and then criticized them for being coercive and for excluding men; they portrayed feminists as extremists and avoided any discussion of men's social power.) These privileged men engaged in a kind of liberal rhetoric that minimized historical oppression of women, made it difficult to see the impact of feminism on contemporary society, and ignored their own privilege.

What Are the Penalties?

Being termed a "feminist" can trigger a variety of negative social behaviors. Men are more likely to dislike a woman who confronts a sexist remark than one who does not (Dodd, Giuliano, Boutell, & Moran, 2001). In a study in northern Italy, men were more likely to send sexually harassing pornographic images via computer to female partners who espoused egalitarian gender beliefs (Dall'Ara & Maass, 1999). This behavior occurred when the experimental situation was designed to be a competitive one that threatened male superiority. The men also made fewer attempts to persuade their female partner when they believed she held egalitarian rather than traditional beliefs. These kinds of punitive responses may explain why, although most women said they would confront a sexist remark, when given the opportunity to do so, the majority do not (Swim & Hyers, 1999).

A major way of dealing with stigmatized individuals is to exclude them from important social interactions. Even women who have attained high professional status may be excluded. For example, a woman physician at a major medical school reported the following:

> Several times, my male colleagues used my records of my patients to do research. It's never occurred to them to ask me to participate on these projects or to ask my opinion about diagnoses. I know I'm doing a good job, but I feel very isolated professionally. (From Benokraitis & Feagin, 1986, pp. 92–94)

FIGURE 3.3. Linda Mabry resigned from Stanford Law School because "I came to the conclusion that it's just a hostile climate for women and people of color."

A more recent example comes from an article in the *Chronicle of Higher Education* that discussed the resignation of Linda Mabry (Figure 3.3) from her position as a professor at Stanford Law School:

> What finally triggered her resignation, she said, was learning that the law school was planning to open a new program in her area of expertise—international business law—and hadn't consulted her. . . . She first learned of the new program "when I read a flyer inviting students to a meeting. . . . It was as if I were invisible."(Mangan, 1999, p. A12)

Verbal aggression is also used as a form of social control to maintain gender norms. Targets are not chosen at random. Women who are "out of place" are more likely to be the targets of male aggression. For example, highly placed women such as Hillary Rodham Clinton and Martha Stewart have been the recipients of vicious verbal attacks disguised as "humor."

Humor is not just funny. Sexist humor leads to greater tolerance of a sexist event among men who are already hostile to women (Ford, 2000). Within groups, joking is a status-related activity. Men, high participators in group discussions, and those who are more likely to interrupt others are likely to use humor that differentiates between groups and individuals (Robinson & Smith-Lovin, 2001).

Aggressive humor is sometimes described as "teasing." However, when college students of both sexes were asked to describe their responses to being teased, both women and men remembered the teasing as unpleasant and threatening (Kowalski, 2000). Women more than men reported that their self-esteem was lowered by the teasing. In contrast, perpetrators remembered incidents involving teasing as harmless and funny.

It is difficult for women to present themselves as both nice and capable in order not to be punished for being overbearing and dominant. The need to pay attention to this delicate form of impression management may produce anxieties that, in turn, diminish task performance. The desire to appear nice may also help maintain female subordination such as the tendency to defer to men in social interactions (Ridgeway & Erickson, 2000). It should not be surprising, therefore, that women in college have difficulty viewing themselves as people who will possess power in the future. They are less likely than comparable men to see themselves as political leaders, chief executive officers, or directors of scientific research centers (Lips, 2000). Realistically, perhaps, they see such roles as producing problems with their gender roles and their relationships.

WOMEN AND MEN DOING GENDER

Sex, Gender, and Behavior in Groups

One cannot simply blame men's prejudice for women's lower power within many groups. The perceptions and behaviors of both women and men interact to maintain male dominance. For example, researchers observed students interacting in four-person mixed-sex groups (Wood & Karten, 1986). When they were given information only about each other's name and sex, men were perceived by themselves and by other group members to be more competent than women. Men also engaged in a greater amount of active task behavior (giving information and opinions), whereas women showed more positive social behaviors (agreeing and acting friendly).

Women and men in these groups also responded differently to the positive and negative behaviors of others. When a positive act occurred, women were more likely to respond with another positive act (especially if the initiator of the action was another woman), whereas men used the positive action as a cue to begin task-related behavior (Wood & Rhodes, 1992). If, on the other hand, someone behaved negatively within the group, men were much more likely to respond negatively, especially when the initiator was another man. Women rarely responded at all to negative actions. The consequence of these gender-related differences was that the men tended to elevate the level of conflict within a group, whereas the women sought to avoid conflict. These studies indicate that the addition of women to decision-making institutions might reduce global conflict.

Barriers to Change

Beliefs about greater male competence and social power are difficult to change. Men in one study, for example, did not change their beliefs about their own ability even when they were told that they had less ability than their partner. Women, in contrast, formed either weak or strong expectations about their own ability depending on the experimenters' manipulations (Foschi & Freeman, 1991). The men appeared to be unwilling to accept the authority of others when it conflicted with their standards for themselves.

Men's perceptions of women are also difficult to change. When no experimental intervention took place in problem-solving groups involving spatial judgments, women deferred to men significantly more often than men deferred to women (Pugh & Wahrman, 1983). Researchers used many interventions designed to reduce men's influence, but very few worked. Both women and men agreed that men were more competent than women. The only way that the experimenters were able to change this traditional pattern was to rig the task so that women performed better than men. Under these circumstances, women became more influential and men became less. However, these supposedly superior women still did not gain a significant advantage over their male partners. Instead, a woman had to perform much better than a man to be seen as just as good!

The perceptions and behaviors of both men and women must be altered for changes in group processes to occur. In one attempted intervention, token women leaders were pretrained for a stereotypically masculine problem-solving task (Yoder, Schleicher, & McDonald, 1998). But the women were able to influence their groups only when their expertise was also legitimated by a male experimenter.

Under some circumstances, women's contributions to their groups can be evaluated fairly. One such condition appears to be participation in a task for which there are explicit criteria for success—for example, figuring out what items are needed for survival during a NASA moon mission. In this task, solo women (women in otherwise all-male groups) were evaluated positively by the men in their group and suffered no performance decrement (Fuegen & Biernat, 2002). Interestingly, compared with other participants, the solo women reported feeling more entrapped by stereotypes and more visible within their groups, and they asked more questions about the task. Their greater number of questions apparently led others to perceive them as highly involved in the group task and to give them positive evaluations.

Why Don't Women Change?

We have seen that gender and role are intertwined. Roles conferring authority and power are played by men while women occupy subordinate positions. Women, on the other hand, are seen as more likable than men and are assigned roles that emphasize their interpersonal skills (Glick & Fiske, 1999). At present, men and women compete in some roles and cooperate in others. Some men polarize them as likable but incompetent or as competent but cold and aggressive. Women's awareness of this double bind may explain why some are reluctant to change their behavior..

It is difficult to induce women to behave in a dominant manner in group situations. In one study, for example, groups of two men and two women (with a group leader who received three times as much credit for class participation than the other members of the group) were formed (Ellyson, Dovidio, & Brown, 1992). Groups were either (1) told that the leader had received the unanimous vote of everyone in the group; (2) told that the leader had received more votes than others, but the vote was split; or (3) given no information about leadership selection. Women leaders displayed lower levels of visual dominance except when they were told that their leadership was the result of a unanimous vote. Men, in contrast, displayed high visual dominance even when their position was not secure. The women leaders appeared to question their own legitimacy.

By behaving in a nondominant manner, the women created a self-fulfilling prophecy. Observers who were not aware of the leadership conditions in the study rated the women in insecure leadership positions as significantly less powerful than comparable men. Only the women who were unanimously authorized in their leadership displayed high visual dominance and were perceived to be as powerful and competent as the men. Similar effects occur even when members of the group have expressed beliefs in egalitarian gender roles. In the majority of the mixed-sex groups observed, men participated more in group discussion and were more likely to be selected as the leader (Sapp, Harrod, & Zhao, 1996).

There are clearly some rewards for being likable. For example, both men and women rated women as being most attractive and powerful when they are trying to be liked (DeBlasio, Angiro, Orbin, & Ellyson, 1993). In contrast, they were rated as less attractive by men when they displayed power. The wish to be liked by the positive regard of men may account for the finding that 44 percent of the women surveyed approved of benevolent but not hostile sexism (Kilianski & Rudman, 1998). Benevolent sexism has three major components: protective paternalism (women ought to be rescued first in an emergency); complementary gender differences (women are purer than men); and heterosexual intimacy (every man should have a woman he adores) (Glick & Fiske, 2001). *Equivocal egalitarians* (women who accepted inequality as long as they saw themselves as benefiting from it) supported the status quo more than those women who condemned all forms of sexism (see Figure 3.4).

Women who score high in belief in benevolent sexism tend to prefer strategies that maximize their indirect power over men rather than to exert power themselves. For example, they used more cosmetics when preparing for a romantic date than women who did not endorse such beliefs (Franzoi, 2001). But indirect power strategies that attract men may backfire and undermine women's sense of competence. For example, one study found that women's self-ratings of the creativity of their art projects were significantly lower if a

FIGURE 3.4. Having it all: only in the comics.
Source: Stone Soup. © 2001 Jan Eliot/Distributed by Universal Press Syndicate. Reprinted with permission of Universal Press Syndicate. All rights reserved.

male authority figure was flirtatious rather than neutral (Satterfield & Muehlenhard, 1997). The women's self-confidence may have been reduced because they had another rationale (attraction) for his praise of their work.

The Token Woman

Stereotypes and social demands based on gender can be particularly potent when there is only one woman in an otherwise homogenous group of men. This situation is sometimes known as *tokenism,* but social psychologists frequently use the term *solo status.* Individuals experience solo status when they are the only member of their social category in a group. Field studies and surveys show that members of socially disadvantaged groups, such as women and racial/ethnic minorities, have more negative experiences as solos than do members of privileged groups such as whites and men (Thompson & Sekaquaptewa, 2002).

Tokens are likely to be seen by themselves and others as representatives of their social category rather than just group members. More attention is paid to them than others, and they are more aware of their own behaviors in the group. These processes make potential stereotype threats more potent and are particularly detrimental to public performance. For example, both women and African-Americans performed more poorly than white men when they took an oral exam before an audience made up only of members of the other sex or race (Sekaquaptewa & Thompson, 2002).

Even highly selected women may show negative effects from solo status. Solo women in U.S. army leadership training groups rated themselves more negatively than did male members of their groups, and the effect persisted throughout the leadership course. In groups with more than one woman, male-female differences disappeared after the first day of class or were not reliable at any point during the course (Biernat, Crandall, Young, Kolbrynowicz, & Halpin, 1998).

Solo status has markedly different consequences for women and men. For example, men who were minorities in their group rated themselves as more masculine than men in groups in which they were the majority (Swan & Wyer, 1997). Minority status also increased the masculinity of women's self-ratings. Others in the group also saw men as more masculine when they had solo status, whereas women were perceived to be least feminine when they had solo status (Crocker & McGraw, 1984). These findings can be explained by men's motivation to identify themselves with a higher-status group when they perceive themselves as vulnerable. Women, in contrast, may avoid thinking of themselves in terms of attributes associated with their lower-status social category.

Women do not like being tokens. College women who anticipated being the only female member of their group preferred a different group, wished for a change in the sex composition of their group, and expected more gender stereotyping than nontoken women (Cohen & Swim, 1995). There were no differences in preferences between token and nontoken men. However, token men anticipated more positive stereotypes than token women. Their expectation of stereotyping was positively correlated with their expectation of becoming leader of their group. Women's anticipation of stereotyping, on the other hand, was negatively associated with their belief that they might become the group's leader. These women did not actually have to be tokens for tokenism to affect them. The mere anticipation of being a token (even in a cooperative problem-solving group) induced negative expectations about the experience.

These expectations appear to be accurate. Various studies have found that solo women were unlikely to be selected as group leaders; overall group satisfaction was lowest when a lone woman was present; and gender-related issues were most likely to be raised in groups that included only one woman (Crocker & McGraw, 1984). Solo men, on the other hand, tended to be integrated into their groups as leader, resulting in smoother group functioning. Gender stereotypes about men's domination and women's subordination help explain why lone men are likely to be chosen as group leaders.

Gender, Leadership, and Legitimacy

Men are more stressed by threats to their status than women are (Brinkerhoff & Booth, 1984). They appear to be even more threatened by a woman's authority than by her competence. When a woman is portrayed as having authority over men of the same age and social class, she is seen as reducing their status rather than enhancing her own (Denmark, 1980) (see Figure 3.5).

One recent study indicates that the higher respect accorded men accounts for much of the gender discrimination that women encounter (Jackson, Esses, & Burris, 2001). Respect was only moderately correlated with either positive or masculine qualities. Instead, people apparently give greater respect to men as a result of living in a social world where men habitually occupy most positions of status and power.

In the past, women who attained high positions of leadership in government and industry sometimes questioned their own legitimacy. For example, fifty French and Norwegian women leaders interviewed about their accomplishments rarely described them as due to their own efforts, even though they knew how competent they were (Apfelbaum, 1993). Instead, they explained

THE LOCKHORNS
"I FEEL SO INFERIOR SINCE WOMEN BECAME EQUAL."

FIGURE 3.5. Equality depends on one's point of view.
Source: The Lockhorns. © 1992. Reprinted with Special Permission of King Features Syndicate.

their positions in terms of circumstances. Many of the older French women leaders felt that they were a "token woman" who had achieved power as a result of some male authority. Their loneliness was highlighted by the absence of any mention of family in their lives. Their narratives stressed their marginality and their sense that they lacked control over their destiny.

The second generation of French women leaders (who had had the first group as role models) and the Norwegian women leaders (who made up a much larger percentage of the leadership in their country) had a much greater sense of their own legitimacy. Their growing numbers contributed to changes in cultural norms about women in leadership. The positive implications of these findings are clear. Changes in circumstances can produce rapid changes in women's lives.

Because women are perceived to be less competent than men, it is not surprising that they emerge as leaders of groups far less often than men (Eagly & Karau, 1991). The reluctance to select women as leaders is particularly strong in

Making a Difference

Mary Edwards Walker (1832–1919) was the only woman ever to win the Congressional Medal of Honor, the nation's highest military award. As a young woman, Walker was a feminist and a proponent of dress reform for women, wearing ankle-length pantaloons called "bloomers" under her dresses. While serving in the Union Army during the Civil War, she carried two pistols, wore men's pants under her skirt, and sported a men's uniform jacket. In later life she lectured on women's rights while wearing men's formal wear, including a top hat. Professionally, Walker was a physician, the second American woman to graduate medical school, in 1855. In her 1856 marriage ceremony to fellow doctor Albert Miller, Walker wore men's clothing, did not promise to obey her husband, and kept her own name. The couple's joint medical practice failed, largely because of the public's lack of acceptance of a woman doctor, and thirteen years later they divorced. When the Civil War broke out, Walker volunteered as an army physician, but was not commissioned. Throughout the war, she worked as a nurse, a surgeon, and possibly a spy, and was taken prisoner in 1864. She was exchanged months later "man for man" for a Confederate officer, a fact of which she was very proud. President Andrew Johnson signed an order to award Walker the Medal of Honor in 1865. The medal was revoked in 1917, as were the medals of 900 others, two years before Walker's death. Walker refused to return the medal, wearing it until she died. Due to the efforts of Walker's granddaughter, President Jimmy Carter reinstated the medal in 1977. In 1982 a postage stamp was issued to honor Mary Walker.

Sources:

Golden Ink. (2002). Mary Edwards Walker: A North Georgia notable. http://ngeorgia.com/people/walker.html

The History Net. Mary Edwards Walker. (2003). http://womenshistory.about.com/library/bio/blbio_mary_edwards_walker.htm

St. Lawrence County, NY Branch of the American Association of University Women. (2000). Mary Edwards Walker: Civil War Doctor. www.northnet.org/stlawrenceaauw/walker.htm

Snyder, Charles McCool. (1977). *Dr. Mary Walker: The little lady in pants.* Stratford, NH: Ayer Co.

Women's Internet Information Network. (2000). Dr. Mary Edwards Walker—Surgeon, Spy, Suffragette, Prisoner of War, Proponent of Style and Congressional Medal of Honor Winner. www.undelete.org/military/mil3walker.html

U.S. politics. Thirty-seven women have been elected presidents or prime ministers of a nation since 1960 (see Table 3.1), but there has never been a viable woman candidate for the presidency of the United States. In recent years the

TABLE 3.1. Women Who Have Been Elected Heads of State Since 1960

Leader	Country	Office	Elected
1. Siramavo Bandarannike	Sri Lanka	Prime Minister	1960
2. Indira Gandhi	India	Prime Minister	1966
3. Golda Meir	Israel	Prime Minister	1969
4. Isabel Peron	Argentina	President	1974
5. Margaret Thatcher	United Kingdom	Prime Minister	1979
6. Maria de Lourdes Pintasilgo	Portugal	Prime Minister	1979
7. Lidia Geiler	Bolivia	President	1979
8. Vigdis Finnbogadottir	Iceland	President	1980
9. Eugenia Charles	Dominica	Prime Minister	1980
10. Milka Planinc	Yugoslavia	President	1982
11. Corazon Aquino	Philippines	President	1986
12. Gro Harlem Brundtland	Norway	Prime Minister	1986
13. Benazir Bhutto	Pakistan	Prime Minister	1988
14. Ertha Pascal-Trouillot	Haiti	President	1990
15. Violeta Chamorro	Nicaragua	President	1990
16. Mary Robinson	Ireland	President	1990
17. Khaleda Ziaur Rahman	Bangladesh	Prime Minister	1991
18. Edith Cresson	France	Prime Minister	1993
19. Tamsu Ciller	Turkey	Prime Minister	1993
20. Kim Campbell	Canada	Prime Minister	1993
21. Hanna Suchocka	Poland	Prime Minister	1993
22. Agathe Uwilingiymana	Rwanda	Prime Minister	1994
23. Chandrika Bandaranaike Kumaratunga	Sri Lanka	President	1994
24. Claudette Werleigh	Haiti	Prime Minister	1995
25. Ruth Perry	Liberia	President	1996
26. Shiekh Hasina Wajed	Bangladesh	Prime Minister	1996
27. Janet Jagan	Guyana	Prime Minister	1997
28. Jenny Shipley	New Zealand	Prime Minister	1997
29. Mary McAleese	Ireland	President	1997
30. Ruth Dreifuss	Switzerland	President	1998
31. Jennifer Smith	Bermuda	Prime Minister	1998
32. Vaira Vike-Freiberga	Latvia	President	1999
33. Mireya Elisa Moscoso de Arias	Panama	President	1999
34. Helen Clark	New Zealand	Prime Minister	1999
35. Tarja Halonen	Finland	President	2000
36. Gloria Macapagal-Arroyo	Philippines	President	2001
37. Megawati Sukarnoputri	Indonesia	President	2001

Sources: P. Norris (1997). Women leaders worldwide: A splash of color in the photo op. In P. Norris (Ed.). *Women, media, and politics.* NY: Oxford University Press (pp. 149–165) table on p. 150. www.capwip.org/participation/womenheadsofstate; www.wedo.org.5050/heads.

number of women in U.S. public life increased rapidly. As we write this, women in the United States have served as both secretary of state (Madeline Albright) and attorney general (Janet Reno), and an African-American woman (Condaleezza Rice) is currently serving as national security advisor. For the first time, a woman (Nancy Pelosi) has been elected a leader of her party in Congress. Still, only about 25 percent of all the legislators in Congress are women.

It has sometimes been argued that women are not elected to leadership positions because they lack necessary experience and skills. Of course, it will be difficult for them to acquire skills if they are not given the opportunity to learn them. The news media still do not take women candidates seriously. Following are some descriptions of female and male candidates for the U.S. Senate taken from the pages of *The New York Times:*

> 59-year-old Ms. [Diane] Feinstein faces another race in 1994 . . . no doubt she will rely, as she has done in the past, on the assets of her husband, Richard C. Blum, an investment banker.
>
> The 42-year-old Ms. [Patty] Murray lives in the Seattle suburb of Shoreline, where in addition to her two children, age 12 and 15, she cares for her aging parents.
>
> Ben Nighthorse Campbell . . . at age 59, he is striking for his appearance, with steel-gray ponytail and string ties.
>
> Dick Kemphorne, the 41-year-old mayor of Boise. . .
>
> Lauch Fairchild, 64, a businessman and farmer . . .
>
> Russell Feingold, 39, has served in the Wisconsin state senate for 10 years, where he specialized in judicial affairs.

"Where occupation was the defining feature of the male candidates, it was a secondary characteristic of the females. Not a single male candidate was identified as married, divorced, or single. . . . Like the women, the male Native American was characterized differently, here by appearance." (Jamieson, 1995, p. 170).

Leadership styles continue to be seen as masculine. Therefore, female leaders face a dilemma. If they emulate a masculine leadership style, their male subordinates will dislike them. If they adopt a stereotypically warm and nurturing feminine style, they will be liked, but may not be respected.

The dilemma for women is heightened by the media's greater emphasis on women's looks than men's. One researcher found that mature-faced men were seen as more influential and attractive, no matter how they behaved. However, women leaders were perceived as attractive either when they were baby-faced and submissive or when they had a mature face combined with dominant behavior (Keating, 2002). She proposed two faces for the first female president of the United States (Figure 3.6). One face is a composite of the faces of two current female leaders with a relatively indirect nonverbal self-presentation style (Elizabeth Dole and, to a lesser extent, Hillary Rodham Clinton). The other face is a composite of two leaders with a relatively direct, status-enhancing self-presentation style (Margaret Thatcher and Madeline Albright). Which one will it be and how long will it be before a female leader can transcend yet another double bind?

FIGURE 3.6. The face on the left is a composite of two current women leaders—Hilary Rodham Clinton and Elizabeth Dole—with relatively indirect leadership styles. The face on the right is a composite of two women leaders—Madeline Albright and Margaret Thatcher—with more direct leadership styles. The researcher suggests that facial cues provide information about status and influence voters. However, indirect and direct style appears to be less of a consideration when people make decisions about male leaders.

Moving Beyond the Double Bind

Experimental research is better at locating problems than in providing solutions for them. Most of this research has been conducted with women college students who may be more concerned about being liked than being powerful at this point in their lives. However, double binds often lead to no-win solutions. What strategies may be helpful to deal with them?

One important way for women to avoid being defined by others is to recognize the way double binds are constructed and become active agents in defining themselves. Techniques used by successful women politicians include reframing (critiquing the conventional rhetoric used to describe women's options). In discussing double binds involving marriage, for example, one female candidate pointed out:

> If we are single, they say we couldn't catch a man. If we are married, they say that we are neglecting them. If we are divorced, they say we couldn't keep him. If we are widowed, they say we killed him. (Jamieson, 1995, p. 190)

Other useful strategies include recovering the stories of strong women (as we have done in the boxes throughout this book) and reclaiming language; for example, words such as *sexism, ageism,* and *homophobia* condemn behaviors that might be tolerated if unlabeled. Sometimes language can be recast. For example, a feminist man devised the word *himbo* to indicate both male images designed for women, such as the model Fabio, and those constructed for men, such as Sylvester Stallone (Kimmel, 1996). Recasting language is particularly effective if one can do it with humor.

INTERNALIZING NORMS AND INTERPRETING DISCRIMINATION

To use strategies similar to those just discussed, women must recognize the extent to which their status is still unequal to that of men. This is a very painful process, and many women prefer to ignore or deny evidence of discrimination. The extent to which women accept beliefs and behaviors that are detrimental to themselves is one of the most problematic aspects in the study of the psychology of women.

The Denial of Personal Discrimination

Sometimes men describe themselves as victims of sex discrimination, although fewer men (8.5%) than women (20%) do so. Men who report personal discrimination tend to have For men, reports of personal discrimination were associated with low self-esteem and high personal assertiveness. For members of privileged groups, perceptions of discrimination may be an attempt to explain declines in historical privilege. These men are making a comparison to a better past. In contrast, women are making a comparison to a past that is worse than the present (Kobrynowicz & Branscombe, 1997).

Many women deny personal discrimination. One large survey of adults in a Boston suburb found no significant differences between employed women and men in measures of job-related grievances, satisfaction, or deservedness (Crosby, 1982). Subjective equality persisted even though employed women made significantly less money than employed men with equivalent jobs. These women reported no sense of personal discrimination, although they were keenly aware of gender discrimination in general. In other words, they knew that discrimination against women existed, but only against "other" women.

There are a number of explanations for women's denial of discrimination against themselves. Sometimes women lack the information needed to make comparisons (Crosby, 1984). It is often more difficult to get information about the salaries of one's co-workers than about their sexual habits! Also, people make more favorable judgments about themselves than about others, even when they are using the same information (Unger & Sussman, 1986).

Women with a high need for approval are especially hesitant to acknowledge that they have been discriminated against. Drawing attention to discrimination may be difficult for these women because they are aware of potential stigma. Dominant group members dislike members of devalued groups who report being the victims of discrimination (Dijker, Koomen, van der Heuvel, & Frijda, 1996).

Furthermore, shifting standards of evaluation sometimes make it difficult for individuals to determine whether discrimination has occurred (Biernat & Kobrynowicz, 1999). Many evaluations use subjective language that permits people to judge others with reference to their gender. In one study women who were objectively judged to earn, on average, about $9,000 less per year than men were seen as more financially successful. They were doing nicely for "someone of their gender." (Biernat, Manis, & Nelson, 1991).

Studies have consistently found that women pay themselves less than men do when allocating rewards between themselves and others (Major, 1994). In the absence of comparative information, women perceived less money as fair pay for their work and paid themselves less money than men did. Even women at elite universities buy into these beliefs. In a recent study at Yale University, students generated five thoughts to the question: "Do you think it would be better or worse if most shopping were done from home computers rather than in stores?" (Jost, 1997). After writing these essays, the women rated themselves as less sophisticated, less original, and less insightful than the men did. They also gave themselves $1.51 (18%) less pay for work viewed by independent judges as similar in quality and quantity to that of the male students. Women's willingness to give themselves lower pay for work that is identical to that of men reflects cultural norms about the relative lower worth of women.

Procedural Stigma

Women's awareness of their membership in a subordinate category may explain their feeling of undeservedness. In an ingenious experiment, men and women received rewards that they were told were based either on their performance or on their sex (Heilman, Simon, & Repper, 1987). Women's, but not men's, self-perceptions were negatively affected by selection based on sex. When given rewards based on sex, women devalued their leadership performance, took less credit for successful outcomes, and reported less interest in remaining as leader of their group. They also characterized themselves as more deficient in general leadership skills.

These effects have not declined over the past fifteen years. A recent study led women to believe that they had been selected as leaders in a team problem-solving task either because of their sex, because of their sex and their ability, or at random. The women who believed they had been selected because of their sex performed significantly worse on a subsequent problem-solving test than women from either of the other two groups (Brown, Charnsangavej, Keough, Newman, & Renfrew, 2000). Reward based on a gender category had no effect on men's view of themselves or their worth (perhaps because it is a meaningless distinction for them because they are the normative category). These studies have obvious implications for affirmative action programs in which members of subordinate groups are told that they have received their positions because of their social category. In a second another study by these researchers, students' suspicion that they had benefited from race-based preferences in college admissions was negatively related to their grade-point average (Brown, et al., 2000).

Women's devaluation of their own worth appears to be a common response to sex-based categorization. The term *procedural stigma* has been used to describe how being selected by way of procedures perceived as unfair leaves the person selected feeling stigmatized. The target individuals' perceptions reflect similar perceptions in others. For example, when women undergraduates read a story in which a woman protagonist received a research award, they expected poorer subsequent evaluations when they believed that the selection criteria had included preferential treatment based on sex (Nacoste & Lehman, 1987).

Women students have sometimes told us that they would rather not know so much about how things are stacked against their sex. However, awareness of the sexist bias of others sometimes reduces its negative impact. For example, explicit standards for ability wiped out college students' expectations that men would do better than women on a "male" task (Foddy & Smithson, 1999). In a study in which college-age males as well as businessmen were shown video clips of women leading groups, women were perceived as better leaders if they had been reminded to adopt a "male" style of leadership (Kawakami, White, & Langer, 2000).

Differential Responses to Discrimination

Women are more aware than men of every aspect of gender discrimination (Schmitt, Branscombe, Kobrynowicz, & Owen, 2002). Perceptions of discrimination harm the psychological well-being of women but not of men (See Chapter 14). Women sometimes attempt to cope with these negative consequences by increasing their identification with women as a group.

Under other circumstances, women may respond to perceived discrimination by distancing themselves from feminine stereotypes. Women who were forewarned that there was a high probability that a prejudiced man would evaluate them wrote different essays about what their lives would be like ten years in the future than women who had not been so warned. These essays, however, provoked more negative evaluations than the essays of women who were not told of probable prejudice. The essays were judged as less family focused, less feminine, and less nice by evaluators who were unaware of the experimental conditions (Kaiser & Miller, 2001).

Both privileged and disadvantaged groups are aware that some groups are treated less well than others and that society gives men and whites higher status than women and ethnic minorities (Sidanius & Pratto, 1999). Members of disadvantaged groups, however, report more serious forms of discrimination, and they report encounters with prejudice and discrimination over a wider variety of contexts (Branscombe, 1998). Differences in perceptions about the pervasiveness of discrimination can lead members of privileged groups to see prejudice as relatively controllable and discrimination as infrequent and easily avoidable.

One's place in the social hierarchy shapes how one views discrimination. Members of low-status groups face an unhappy choice between favoring members of their own group or endorsing the superiority of high-status groups. This superiority is justified by the prevailing social ideology. In one study, women who believed in the legitimacy of the status differences in our society (as measured by their belief in a just world and their scores on tests of social dominance) had a more ambivalent response to a female victim of gender discrimination than women who held less system-justifying beliefs. Men who held such beliefs showed more consistently negative views toward a victim after reading a newspaper account of a woman who was suing her university for sex discrimination (Jost & Burgess, 2000).

Another recent study found that the more women and African-Americans endorsed the ideology of individual mobility (the idea that any individual can get ahead if they work hard), the less likely they were to believe they had been discriminated against when they were penalized by members of higher status groups (Major, Gramzow, McCoy, Levin, Schmader, & Sidanius, 2002). In contrast, the more European Americans and men endorsed individual mobility, the more likely they were to characterize penalties from members of lower-status groups as discrimination. This study indicates that those members of marginalized groups who endorse an individualist ideology may underestimate discrimination.

In short, perceptions about discrimination and explanations for it are influenced by both the place of the beholder and the beholder's ideas about what determines that place. Compared with members of privileged groups, members of disadvantaged groups (especially those with a sense of collective identity) are more likely to see discrimination as a reflection of systemic rejection and devaluation by the dominant culture (Branscombe, Schmitt, & Harvey, 1999). This is, of course, the perspective of most feminist theory.

Doing Gender Across Cultures

These and similar studies challenge the belief that prejudice and discrimination reflect merely personal perceptions and behaviors. Sexism, whether hostile or benevolent, is an ideology that justifies inequality between groups.

Cross-cultural studies have found that belief in benevolent or hostile sexism predicts which traits are associated with women and whether these traits are seen as positive or negative (Glick et al., 2000). Benevolent sexism allows men to maintain a positive self-image as protectors and providers who care for the women in their lives. In nations that had high benevolent sexism scores, women were seen as warm, sweet, and sensitive, and these traits were evaluated positively. In nations that had high hostile sexism scores, women were seen to be high in such negative traits as sly, touchy, and selfish. Overall, hostile sexism also predicted negative attitudes toward career women, whereas benevolent sexism predicted positive attitudes toward homemakers.

Both hostile and benevolent sexism scores were highly associated with measures of gender inequality developed by the United Nations (see Figure 3.7). These measures assess women's participation in a nation's economy and political life. They also compare males and females in terms of health and longevity, adult literacy and years of schooling, and standard of living. Across cultures, men's sexism scores were strongly related to gender inequality (Glick & Fiske, 2001).

Women usually score lower than men on measures of benevolent and hostile sexism, but in the four countries with the highest sexism scores (Cuba, Nigeria, South Africa, and Botswana), women endorsed benevolent sexist beliefs more than men did. Acceptance of paternalism may be the only "helpful" ideology available to women in such a hostile cultural climate. They may fear the open antagonism that is reserved for those members of subordinated groups who fail to defer or who question existing ideologies (Glick & Fiske, 2001).

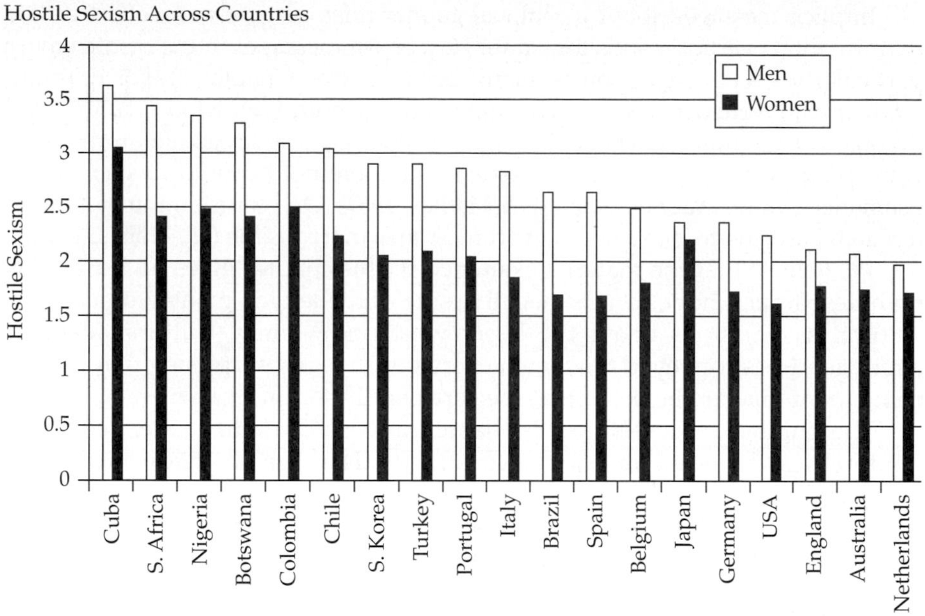

FIGURE 3.7. Hostility toward women is not just a problem for individuals. This graph shows how levels of hostile sexism varies across cultures and, therefore, shows the normative level of misogynism that may be tolerated.

Combating Social Myths

Although many gender-related differences in social behaviors are constructed through social interactions, people continue to believe in innate gender differences. One could call these beliefs *social myths.* Members of both the dominant and the subordinate group share these myths. The myths determine views of the world that are believed to be objectively "true." They are maintained because each person does not create his or her social reality anew but must use cultural beliefs to understand and justify all the forms of inequality in which he or she is involved (Tajfel, 1984). Deeply entrenched social myths protect the individual from cognitive conflict.

Figuring out how to effect change is not easy. Traditional perceptions about men and women sometimes disappear when people are reminded about their egalitarian gender-related beliefs (Porter, Geis, Cooper, & Newman, 1985). Explicit messages about gender ideology can also be effective. U.S. women who were explicitly informed that traditional gender roles require women to be modest about achievement became significantly less modest in their subsequent responses (Cialdini, Wosinska, Dabul, Wheatstone-Dion, & Heszen, 1998). Those women who reacted most strongly to the manipulation also anticipated that they would not be particularly modest about their future achievements.

Implicit messages about traditional gender roles may be more effective and harmful than overt demands for conformity. Sexist messages in the media have a particularly strong impact on women's behavior (see Chapter 2). For example, women who were exposed to advertisements that portrayed women in their traditional role as homemakers subsequently reported less favorable attitudes toward political participation than women who were not exposed to such advertisements (Swarz, Wagner, Bannert, & Mathes, 1987). One contribution of feminist research has been to make such covert messages more visible (cf., Norris, 1997).

We believe that the material examined in this chapter gives us reasons for both despair and hope. On the negative side of the ledger, many women share cultural assumptions about the lesser worth of women. Cultural ideology about gender is conveyed to women every day. It is not surprising that women come to internalize the belief that they are less important than men.

The findings discussed in this chapter are also cause for hope. People are not totally at the mercy of external constraints. They are not passive recipients of social forces. They are also active agents of social change. Women working together have made great changes in social institutions.

Only a few years ago, the media were full of a story about a major breakthrough at the Massachusetts Institute of Technology, or MIT (Goldberg, 1999; Zernike, 1999). The women scientists there had banded together and used their scientific skills to demonstrate pervasive discrimination against women (see Box 3.2). They found differences between men and women in the amount of laboratory space allotted to them as well as in faculty salaries and pensions. The women worked five years on their report (which was on MIT's website). Their evidence clearly convinced the president, Charles Vest, who said: "I have always believed that contemporary gender discrimination within universities is part reality and part perception. True, but . . . reality is by far the greater part of the balance" (Zernike, 1999, p. F4).

Ironically, some of the fifteen tenured women who worked on the report secretly worried that they might not be as good as the men. The opposite was true. Forty percent of these women had been named members of the National Academy of Sciences or the Academy of Arts and Sciences (organizations that elect as members the very best scholars in their fields). It was only by talking to one another that they learned that their shared sense of marginality was not due to personal inadequacy. They also found that the men did not dislike women. In making decisions about awards and promotions, they just liked their male buddies more.

This victory should be celebrated, but, as the report notes, things are just as bad at comparable institutions such as Harvard or the California Institute of Technology. It will take communal efforts to make changes there, too. University campuses are certainly not gender-blind. In a random sample of 340 university students, 31 percent of the females versus 10 percent of the males reported being intimidated on the basis of their sex, religion, or academic ability (Sands, 1998). Most of this intimidation came from fellow students.

The process of change requires changes in consciousness to make changes in social structures, which, in turn, change attitudes and perceptions. Real social change will take place only when there are changes in both inner and outer reality.

Box 3.2 The Story Behind a Successful Fight on Gender Bias

The story began in 1994 when MIT told Nancy Hopkins, a prominent DNA researcher, that it would discontinue a course that she had designed that was now required for 1,000 students a year. She had worked for five years to develop that course. In the previous two years, a male professor had joined her in teaching it. The man, MIT informed her, was going to turn the course into a book and a CD-ROM without her.

Hopkins drafted a letter to the president of MIT about how she felt women researchers were treated. When she discussed it with a woman colleague, she asked to sign it, too. They decided to poll every tenured woman in the School of Science to see if what they had experienced were individual problems or part of a pattern.

They were surprised to find out how fast they got their answers. Within a day they had talked to all 15 tenured women (there were 197 tenured men) and agreed that there was a problem and that something had to be done. True to their fields, they looked first at the data (see graphs).

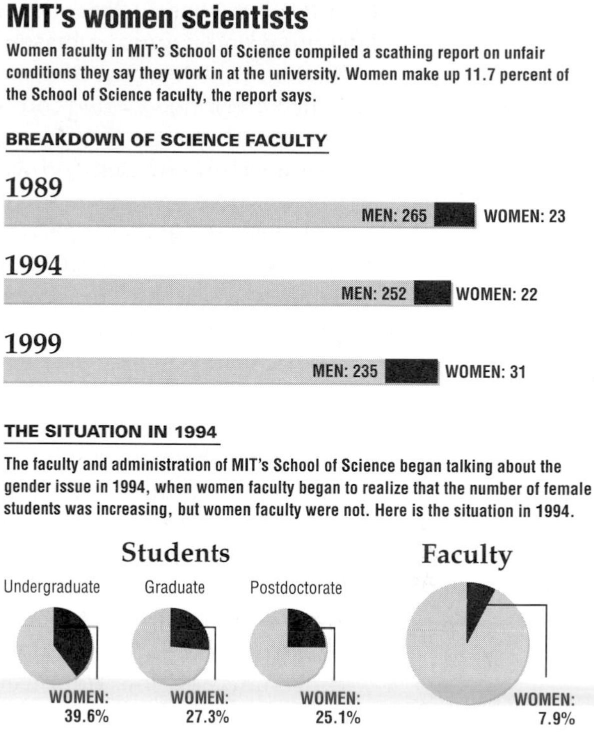
MIT's women scientists
Women faculty in MIT's School of Science compiled a scathing report on unfair conditions they say they work in at the university. Women make up 11.7 percent of the School of Science faculty, the report says.
BREAKDOWN OF SCIENCE FACULTY
1989
MEN: 265
WOMEN: 23
1994
MEN: 252
WOMEN: 22
1999
MEN: 235
WOMEN: 31
THE SITUATION IN 1994
The faculty and administration of MIT's School of Science began talking about the gender issue in 1994, when women faculty began to realize that the number of female students was increasing, but women faculty were not. Here is the situation in 1994.
Students
Faculty
Undergraduate
Graduate
Postdoctorate
WOMEN: 39.6%
WOMEN: 27.3%
WOMEN: 25.1%
WOMEN: 7.9%

Source: Study on the Status of Women Faculty in Science at MIT.

Individually, some women said they had sensed discrimination but feared that they would be dismissed as troublemakers or that their work would suffer from the distraction of trying to prove their point. "These women had devoted their lives to science," Hopkins said. "There was the feeling that if you got into it, you weren't going to last; you'd get too angry."

But the hurdles were already costing them time and making them miserable. All fifteen women crowded into the dean's office to ask for an investigation. The dean checked their numbers and became an immediate convert. He boosted the women's salaries an average of 20 percent and eliminated the requirement that they raise part of their salaries from grants. He also appointed a committee that spent five years gathering data. Their report was released in March 1999 and posted on MIT's Web site. It acknowledges that there is evidence of "subtle differences in the treatment of men and women," "exclusion," and, in some cases, "discrimination against women faculty." The inequities included salaries, space, research, and inclusion of women in positions of power. An underrepresentation of women making key decisions had bred male "cronyism" that for women meant "unequal access to the substantive resources of MIT."

In addition to salary, space, and resource increases, MIT plans to have a 40 percent increase in the number of women with tenure next year, bringing the percentage to above 10 for the first time. The institute also corrected some pensions, one by $130,000 and another by $80,000.

"I was unhappy at MIT for more than a decade," one woman told the committee. "I thought it was the price you paid if you wanted to be a scientist at an elite university. . . . After . . . the dean's response, my life began to change. . . . My research blossomed, my funding tripled. Now I love every aspect of my job. It is hard to understand how I survived—or why."

Source: From "MIT Women Win a Fight Against Bias" by Kate Zernike, *The Boston Globe,* March 21, 1999. Reprinted courtesy of The Boston Globe.

CONNECTING THEMES

- *Gender is more than just sex.* This chapter emphasizes how sex as a category is used to construct gendered distinctions. This process begins with perceptual and cognitive biases that lead individuals to expect different behaviors from women and men. People act to confirm these expectations, which are, indeed, often confirmed by others' self-presentational strategies. These behaviors in turn, reinforce gender-biased views about the differing characteristics of men and women.
- *Language and naming are sources of power.* Naming (in the sense of deviance and stigma) can be used to delegitimize women who exercise social power or possess public authority. However, naming (in the sense of conscious awareness) can also reduce the extent to which gender-biased views of the self are internalized.
- *Women are not all alike.* Sex is not the only social category that is used to produce and maintain distinctions between groups of people. Other categories with similar effects are race/ethnicity, age, and disability. It is important to remember that most of the effect of these categories on behavior is a result of normal cognitive and social psychological processes rather than deliberate discrimination.
- *Psychological research can foster social change.* A model of gender as a social construction is a positive step in the movement for social change. This model argues that gender-related traits and behaviors are situationally constructed and help maintain the societal status quo. As more women move into positions of power in the public arena they will change perceptions about the relationship between gender and status and, therefore, help create more egalitarian social systems.

SUGGESTED READINGS

JAMESON, KATHERINE HALL (1995). *Beyond the double bind: Women and leadership.* Although the media references are slightly dated, this is a very important book by an expert on the media and politics. It reviews the many double binds that women encounter and suggests strategies for moving beyond them.

JOST, JOHN T. & MAJOR, BRENDA (Eds.). (2001). *The psychology of legitimacy: Perspectives on ideology, justice, and intergroup relations.* New York: Cambridge University Press. This book is a collection of papers from a conference at Stanford. Although not all the chapters are not on gender, many summarize recent work by researchers cited in this chapter. These chapters expand psychology's perspective away from individuals to a more systemic perspective.

SHIELDS, STEPHANIE A. (2002). *Speaking from the heart: Gender and the social meaning of emotion.* New York: Cambridge University Press. A book that examines the social construction of emotion and gender by a well-known social psychologist who has done much empirical work in the area. The book draws from many popular as well as scholarly sources and is engaging, thoughtful, and provocative.

CHAPTER 4

The Meanings of Difference

Our language and our stereotypes portray men and women as "opposite sexes." Most people believe that women and men differ in many important ways. But what are the "real" differences between boys and girls or women and men in traits, abilities, and behaviors?

Often, students of psychology want "the facts and just the facts," and they expect the science of psychology to be able to provide those facts. However, the study of group differences is not just a matter of establishing facts; understanding these differences may depend more on interpretation of evidence than on the evidence itself.

Some differences between groups, like those between brown-eyed and blue-eyed people, do not matter in Western society. Other differences, like the ones in Figure 4.1, matter very much. These differences have social and political consequences; they represent dimensions of privilege versus disadvantage (Morgan, 1996). For each dimension, there is clearly a "good" and a "bad" end. In the case of gender, what is male and masculine is valued more highly than what is female and feminine.

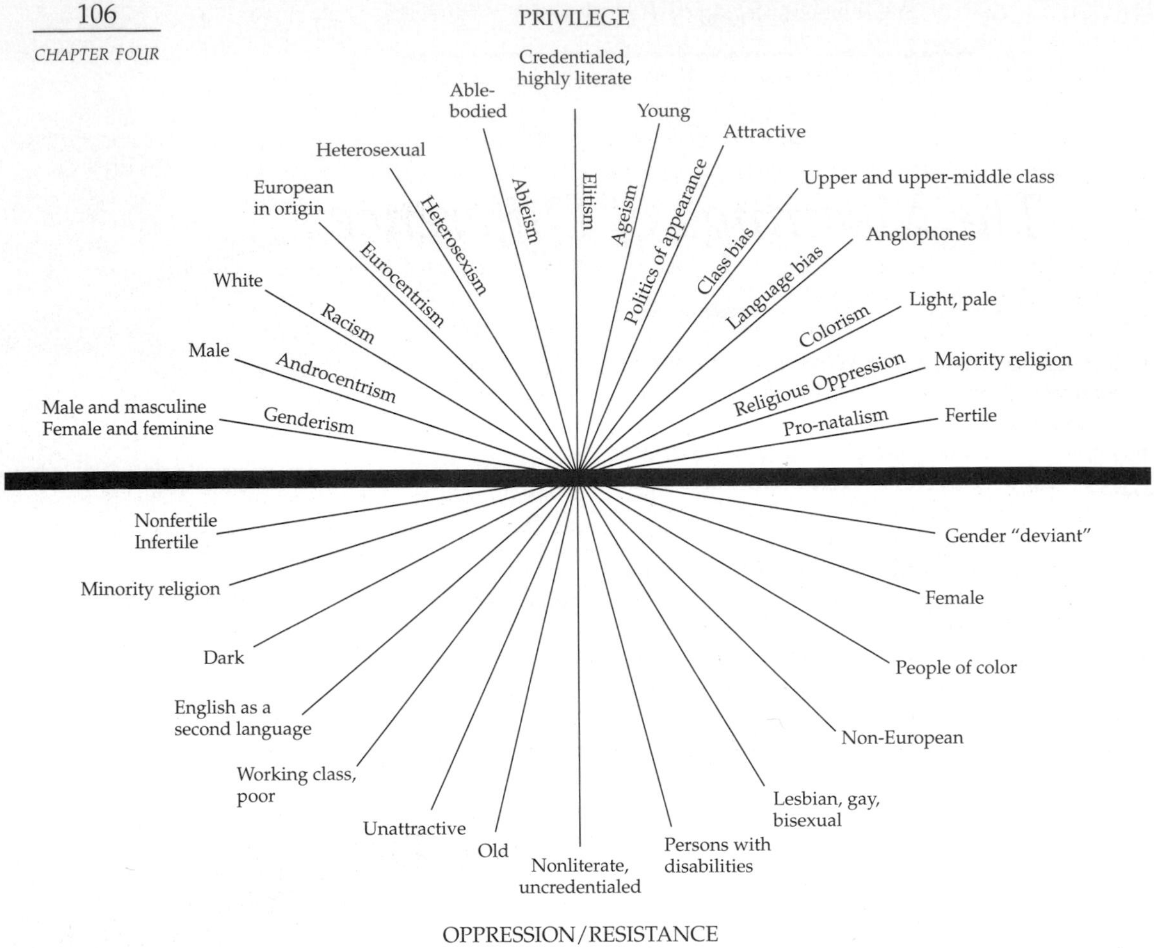

FIGURE 4.1. Intersecting dimensions of privilege and oppression.
Source: From *The Gender Questions in Education: Theory, Pedagogy, and Politics* by Ann Diller. Copyright © 1996 by Westview Press, a member of Perseus Books, L.L.C. Reprinted by permission of Westview Press, a member of Perseus Books, L.L.C.

In feminist theory and political movements, there have long been two ways of thinking about gender-related differences (Kimball, 1995), grounded in liberal and cultural feminism respectively (see Chapter 1). *The similarities tradition* claims that women and men are very much alike in intelligence, personality, abilities, and goals. This tradition stems from liberal feminism and is used to argue for equality of the sexes. After all, if men and women are far more alike than different, shouldn't they be treated equally?

The *differences tradition* claims that there are fundamental differences between women and men that should be recognized and honored. This tradition, stemming from cultural feminism, is used to argue that society should give more recognition to the activities, traits, and values of women. After all, if taking care of other people and relationships (traditionally feminine characteristics) were rewarded as much as dominance and personal ambition (traditionally masculine characteristics), wouldn't the world be a better place?

Both these ways of thinking have been used to generate research and to form political strategies. Debates about which approach is better have gone on for a long time. In this chapter we explore both traditions, looking at important research from each. The goal is not to decide which tradition is better. Rather, we hope you will decide that there is value in both—that "double visions are theoretically and politically richer and more flexible than visions based on a single tradition" (Kimball, 1995, p. 2).

A FOCUS ON SIMILARITY: WORKING FOR EQUALITY

Psychologists who work within the similarities tradition have tried to show that gender differences in ability or skills are either nonexistent or much too small to explain gender differences in power, prestige, and income (Kimball, 1995). They point out there has been a lack of agreement in *defining* difference, problems in *measuring* difference, and issues of *values and interpretation* in understanding results. This tradition has generated a great deal of research on gender and cognitive abilities, using standard psychological research methods and statistical analysis.

Making a Difference

Amy Cohen describes her former self as "this nonconfrontational person, just very agreeable." But when Brown University violated Title IX of the Education Amendments of 1972, a federal gender equity law, she came out fighting. In 1991, Cohen, now a second-grade teacher, had just been elected gymnastics team captain at Brown. Suddenly the university declared it was cutting the team due to budget problems. Appeals to the athletic director and team efforts to raise money led to limited reinstatement of the women's team, but also to a series of broken promises ("The athletic trainers can't treat you for injuries [after all] because you're not a varsity team," "you can't use this locker room"). Finally, Cohen and thirteen others brought a lawsuit. As Cohen discovered, only a small percentage of universities are in compliance with Title IX in regard to athletic allocations. Six years and about $3 million later, the Supreme Court agreed that Brown University was in violation of the amendment. Cohen argues that people, whatever their sex, gain incalculably from sports, and that to say that girls' enjoyment of athletics isn't as great as boys' is ridiculous. "If you spend $80,000 recruiting football players and $25 recruiting gymnasts, then should you be surprised if you get 100 football players and 2 gymnasts? Should you then say that people just love football so much more? No. You say you get what you looked for." Fortunately for all of us, due to Cohen's strength and perseverance, women and girls are now a little closer to getting what we're looking for.

Source: Woman of the Year: For Rescuing Title IX for College Women. (1998, January/February) *Ms.*, pp. 52–54.

Defining Difference and Similarity

Determining the facts about gender differences sounds relatively easy: a psychologist measures a group of women and a group of men for a trait or an ability and computes the average difference between the groups. There is a long tradition of this kind of research. Between 1967 and 2002, *Psychological Abstracts,* which lists published journal articles in psychology, indexed 50,393 articles on human sex or gender differences!

You might think that with all these studies, some definitive answers would emerge. However, the meaning of "difference" can be very ambiguous. Suppose you were at a party where you overheard someone explain why there are more men than women judges in the United States by saying, "Let's face it, women just don't reason like men. When it comes to reasoning ability, they just don't have what it takes." Your first reaction might be that this is just an outdated stereotype. Your second reaction might be to ask yourself what evidence could be brought to bear on this claim.

The speaker (let's call him Mr. Pompous) has asserted that there is a gender-related difference in reasoning, a cognitive ability. Before we examine the evidence, let's consider what he might have meant. One interpretation is that all men and no women have the ability to reason—in other words, that reasoning ability is dichotomous by sex. If the entire population of men and women could be measured on a perfectly valid and reliable test of reasoning ability, the two sexes would form two nonoverlapping distributions, with the distribution for women being lower. This hypothetical situation is shown in Figure 4.2a. *But despite a hundred years of research on gender-related differences, no one has ever discovered a psychological trait or cognitive ability on which men and women are completely different.*

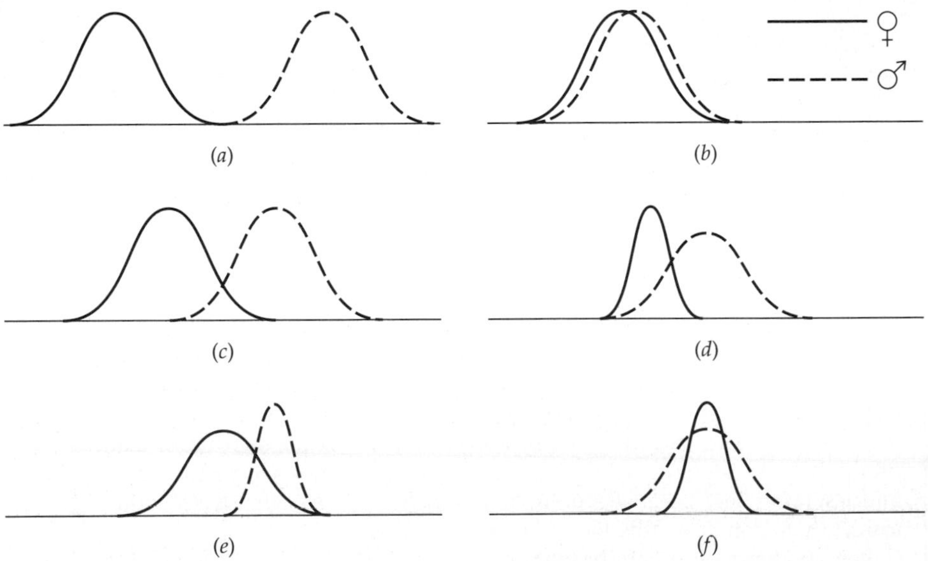

FIGURE 4.2. Some possible distributions of reasoning ability in females and males.
Source: Unger, R. & Crawford, M. (1996).

Because it would be ridiculous to argue that women are categorically inferior in this way, Mr. Pompous probably means something else when he talks about "difference." Perhaps he means that there is a mean, or *average* difference, such that the mean for women is slightly lower (Figure 4.2b) or very much lower (Figure 4.2c) than the mean for men. However, an average difference doesn't tell us very much by itself. Sets of distributions can have the same differences in means but large differences in *variability*, defined as the range or "spread" of scores. Figure 4.2d shows males more variable than females and 4.2e shows females more variable than males. Looking at the areas in which males' and females' distributions do not overlap in each set shows that the meaning of difference is different for each. That is, the proportion of women who score below the lowest-scoring men and the proportion of men who score above the highest-scoring women differ greatly from one set of hypothetical distributions to the next.

Moreover, these are not the only possible population distributions. Women and men could be equal on average, but one sex could be more variable, as shown in Figure 4.2f; here, the area where females and males overlap is larger than those where they do not.

Most research on gender-related differences reports a mean (average) difference between a sample of women and a sample of men, with statistical tests to determine whether the difference is *statistically significant* (unlikely to have occurred by chance). The concept of statistical significance is not the same as the ordinary meaning of "significant." A difference may be statistically significant, yet be trivially small and useless in predicting differential behavior in other situations. In other words, statistical significance is not the same as importance.

How large does a statistically significant difference have to be before we are justified in labeling men and women more different than similar? Should the importance of a difference be judged in terms of average scores, in terms of how much variability exists between scores for each gender, or in how much the distributions for women and men overlap? And how do we compare the results of several studies of the same trait or ability when the results vary? How many studies are sufficient to settle a question? How consistent must the results be? Is it important to measure the trait or ability in people of different age groups, social classes, ethnic groups, and cultures—or is it safe to assume that what is true for North American college students is true for all people? The answers to these questions involve value judgments about the meaning of difference.

Measuring Differences

Suppose a psychologist wanted to test Mr. Pompous's claim that there is a gender difference in reasoning ability. She might compare a sample of women and a sample of men on a standard test of reasoning, matching the two groups on any other factors that might affect reasoning ability, such as years of education. She would compare the average scores of her two groups with an appropriate statistical test to determine whether the difference she obtained was likely to have occurred by chance.

The logic of experimental design and hypothesis testing leads psychologists to put more weight on findings of difference than on findings of similarity. Statistical tests allow psychologists to be fairly confident that when a difference is judged to exist, the conclusion is an accurate one. But when a difference is not found, psychologists cannot know for certain that there is no difference in the population; the result could be just a failure of this experiment to detect the difference. They may conclude that they should try again, not that the hypothesis about a difference was wrong. Relying on similar logic, as discussed in Chapter 1, professional journals are less likely to publish articles that report similarities between women and men than they are to publish reports of differences. The possibility of overemphasizing differences is a built-in limitation of hypothesis testing. Furthermore, problems in research design are common (Deaux, 1984; Grady, 1981; Jacklin, 1981; Maccoby & Jacklin, 1974; Parlee, 1981; Unger, 1979b), and some researchers charge that many reported gender differences are distorted or exaggerated (Grady, 1981).

What are some of the flaws in difference research? Some studies have measured behaviors of only one sex and have erroneously drawn conclusions about differences between the sexes—for example, measuring the relationship between hormonal levels and mood only in women and concluding that only women show such relationships. Of course, it is impossible to demonstrate a gender difference (or similarity) if only one group is studied (Jacklin, 1981). Other flaws include researchers' tendency to overgeneralize from limited samples to all women and men and to conclude that a gender-related difference is due to innate or biological factors when such factors have not been measured.

Examples of these mistakes are easy to find. The eminent psychologist Harry Harlow, who studied behavior in primates, found evidence that male rhesus monkeys are more aggressive than females. The problem with his research arose when he used this evidence to explain the behavior of boys and girls in biological terms:

> There is reason to believe that genetic variables condition similar differences in human primates. The gentle and relatively passive behavior of most little girls is a useful maternal attribute, and the more aggressive behavior of most little boys is useful preparation for the paternal function of protection. (1971, p. 6)

When Harlow's own research showed that female monkeys reared in abnormal environments were much more aggressive than those reared normally, he was not convinced of the importance of environmental influences. Instead, he ignored the implications of his own data and resorted to stereotypes:

> Negative feedback, however, quickly suppresses this aggression. Females win their way into male hearts and minds through passive resistance and social sophistication. In our society females usually attempt to combine love and marriage with social security. . . . Young males prefer action and young females prefer active attention. (1971, pp. 90–91)

Not only had Harlow failed to study biological factors in aggression, but he hadn't even studied girls and boys. Instead, he generalized from his research on rhesus monkeys!

One of the most persistent sources of bias in gender-difference research is the difficulty of separating gender from all the other factors it is related to in our society (Jacklin, 1981). The interaction of gender with other factors leads to *confounding,* in which the effects of two or more variables are mixed, and it becomes impossible to decide which variable is causing experimental effects.

For example, suppose we were matching participants for our imaginary experiment on reasoning ability. We would certainly not choose a male sample with college degrees and compare it with a female sample of high-school graduates. Obviously, the different backgrounds and experience of the two groups could account for differences in reasoning ability. But even when a researcher attempts to measure comparable men and women, it is often hard to decide what characteristics should be matched. Suppose researchers compared female and male college students. Although a sample of male and female college students can be matched on level of formal education, the women and men may have very different backgrounds in mathematics, science, and the liberal arts (Eccles, 1989) and may be concentrated in different majors. These differences may be irrelevant to some research questions but crucial to others.

Many psychologists believe that a technique called *meta-analysis* can resolve some of the issues of definition and measurement in research on gender differences. Basically, meta-analysis uses quantitative methods to summarize the results of research done by different people at different times (Hedges & Becker, 1986). It allows researchers to integrate the results of many studies on a single topic and to assess the magnitude and consistency of difference effects statistically (Hyde & Linn, 1986).

In doing a meta-analysis, the investigator first identifies all relevant studies on a topic. The next step is to summarize the results of each study in a common unit of measurement. There are different degrees of statistical significance, and the results of some studies may be stronger than others. In meta-analysis, studies can be distinguished from one another in terms of the magnitude of the gender-related difference. Finally, meta-analysis allows researchers to group studies by subcategory and thereby assess the influence of variables other than gender. For example, if a researcher did a meta-analysis of studies on gender and reasoning ability, she might categorize the studies according to the type of task used or whether there was time pressure in the situation. Perhaps the gender difference occurs only when the task is male-oriented or when there is time pressure. A variable that interacts with another variable to change its effect is called a *moderator variable*.

Many psychologists, especially those who work within the similarities tradition, see meta-analysis as a useful technique for studying gender differences (Eagly, 1987; Hyde & Linn, 1986). It helps researchers interpret data from large numbers of studies and allows them to estimate the size of a gender-related difference. It simplifies the study of other variables that interact with gender—which is important because there almost always are other factors involved (Hyde & Linn, 1986).

But meta-analysis cannot wholly compensate for the biases in the original studies or ensure "objective" interpretation (Unger & Crawford, 1989). Reviewers must still decide which studies are relevant and whether several measures of the same construct (such as different tests of reasoning ability) are measuring the same thing. Moreover, there could be an overlooked source of bias common to all the studies in a meta-analysis, which could lead to an overall conclusion that is biased (Hedges & Becker, 1986). If all the tests of reasoning ability used in research happened to be biased toward men, for example, a false "gender difference" might show up in a meta-analysis.

No statistical technique can resolve all problems of interpreting differences. Meta-analysis can show which variables moderate the occurrence of gender differences, but it does not allow conclusions about the *causes* of the differences. Moreover, there is still room for disagreement about how big a difference must be to count as an important one. The meaning of observed differences is still at issue. We now turn to areas of research where debates about similarity, difference, and their interpretation are ongoing.

DIFFERENT OR SIMILAR? GENDER AND MATH ABILITIES

The general pattern in cognitive skills is one of gender similarity (Maccoby & Jacklin, 1974). However, math ability and achievement is one of a very few areas where standard psychological research shows consistent gender differences. In this section we look at ongoing controversies about these differences in mathematics performance.

There are two widely used ways to measure math ability and achievement: school achievement and performance on standardized tests such as the SAT-M. On standardized tests, boys come out ahead. In school achievement, girls come out ahead. From elementary school through college, girls and young women of all ethnic groups get better grades than boys and young men, even in areas in which the boys score higher in ability tests. Girls are less likely to repeat a grade, get assigned to special education classes, or get in trouble over their behavior or schoolwork, and they are more likely to take honors and AP classes, make the honor roll, and be elected to a class office (Coley, 2001; Hyde & Kling, 2001). Their higher academic achievement is rarely interpreted to mean that girls are more intelligent. Rather, it is argued that girls may get their higher grades by being quiet and neat, following directions, and trying hard to please their teachers. This may be an example of devaluing feminine characteristics.

Are Mathematics Ability and Performance Gender-Linked?

Girls' performance on standardized math tests is better than boys' in the elementary school years; in high school they perform equally or slightly less well than boys (Hyde & Kling, 2001). Just a short time ago, in the 1940s to 1960s, the differences in favor of boys were much larger. Today, the similarities outweigh the differences, and there is a lot of overlap between the distributions of males' and females' scores.

There is, however, a well-documented difference favoring males in *advanced* mathematics performance. Every year, more than 1 million high school students take the Scholastic Assessment Test, or SAT. For the past thirty years, boys have scored consistently higher on the math portion of the SAT than girls. In national math talent searches using the SAT and similar tests, far more boys than girls are identified as gifted, and the gifted boys score higher than the gifted girls (Benbow & Stanley, 1980; Hyde & McKinley, 1997). The gender gap in SAT-M scores occurs within every ethnic group tested (White, Black, Hispanic, and Asian-American), and extends to the GRE test, which is used for admissions to graduate school (Coley, 2001).

What a puzzle for psychological research to unravel! Girls start out liking math and believing that girls are better at it than boys (Boswell, 1985). They do better than boys on standardized tests in math and get better grades. Yet, by the time they are in high school, they score lower on advanced math. As you might expect, the development of this difference cannot be attributed to just one or two causes. Rather, many interacting factors may be responsible. We will examine girls' confidence in their math abilities and their opportunities to learn math. We also look at stereotypes about math as a male domain and hypotheses about biologically based differences in ability.

What Factors Influence Mathematics Performance?

Gender in the Classroom

In the past, the single biggest influence on math performance was that girls took fewer math courses (Chipman & Thomas, 1985). Fortunately, college-bound girls now are just as likely as their male counterparts to take four years of math. The exception is Hispanic girls, who still take somewhat less high school math than Hispanic boys (Coley, 2001).

Even when they take the same courses, boys and girls experience different worlds in the classroom. At all grade levels, a few males often dominate classroom interaction while other students are silent and ignored (Eccles, 1989) (see Figure 4.3). Gender interacts with race: white males get the most attention from teachers, followed by minority males and white females; minority females get the least attention of any group. This discrimination takes a toll: African-American girls become less active, assertive, and visible in class as they move through the elementary grades (Sadker & Sadker, 1994).

Sexism in the classroom may be benevolent (Hyde & Kling, 2001). Teachers may "protect" the feelings of girls by not calling on them for difficult questions or by praising their appearance, not their performance. Sexism can also be hostile.

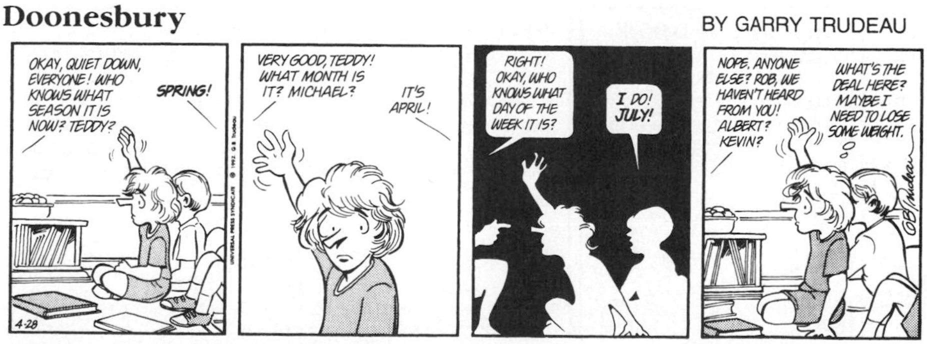

FIGURE 4.3. Sexism in the classroom.
Source: Doonesbury. Copyright © 1992 G. B. Trudeau. Reprinted with permission of Universal Press Syndicate. All rights reserved.

For example, girls experience sexual harassment from their peers and teachers more often than boys and they fear it more (AAUW Educational Foundation, 2001). Sexism and its effects are evident in the voices of young women interviewed by Myra Sadker and David Sadker:

> "In my science class the teacher never calls on me, and I feel like I don't exist. The other night I had a dream that I vanished."
>
> "I have a teacher who calls me 'airhead' and 'ditz.' I used to think I was smart, but now I don't know. Maybe I'm not. What if he's right? The more he treats me like an airhead, the more I think maybe I am." (Sadker & Sadker, 1994, p. 135)

Gender inequity that can affect math and science performance extends to out-of-school experiences as well. Boys are more likely to participate in activities such as chess clubs, math clubs, summer computer courses, and science camps. In short, boys are more likely than girls to have a math-enriched environment that encourages math achievement and self-confidence.

Low Confidence, Low Self-Expectations

Girls' lower confidence about their math abilities is a consistent finding in many studies, although meta-analysis shows that the difference is not large (Hyde, Fennema, Ryan, Frost, & Hopp, 1990). By the time they are in junior high, girls are losing their early confidence that they can do math as well as or better than boys, and their change in attitude is independent of their actual performance (see Figure 4.4). Although their grades remain better than boys' grades, girls rate themselves lower in math ability, consider their math courses harder, and are less sure that they will succeed in future math courses (Eccles et al., 1985). For adolescent girls, self-esteem is less tied to confidence in their academic ability than it is to confidence in their physical attractiveness to boys (Eccles et al, 2000). (For more on gender and ethnic differences in overall self-esteem, see Chapter 7).

FIGURE 4.4. Math performance depends on the situation!
Source: Foxtrot. Copyright © 1995 Bill Amend. Reprinted with permission of Universal Press Syndicate. All rights reserved.

Parents of girls probably play a part in these attitude changes. Parents attribute a daughter's success in math to hard work and effort, and a son's success to talent. They view math as more difficult for daughters and more important for sons. Research in both Germany (Tiedemann, 2000) and the United States (Eccles, 1989) shows that parents' stereotypes predict children's later beliefs about their math abilities. Boys learn that they have natural talent in an important area, and girls learn that hard work cannot entirely make up for their lack of ability!

Math as a Male Domain

Close your eyes and visualize a mathematician. Chances are your image is of a cerebral-looking man with glasses and an intense but absentminded air—an Einstein, perhaps. Early research showed strong stereotypes that math was for men, and "dorky" men at that. When elementary and senior high school students were asked about their perceptions of people in math-related careers such as science, engineering, and physics, they described white-coated loners, isolated in laboratories, with no time for family or friends (Boswell, 1979). Not surprisingly, female mathematicians were stereotyped as unattractive, masculine, cold, socially awkward, and "overly intellectual" (Boswell, 1985).

The gender deviance of math for girls is heightened by a lack of role models. Beyond junior high, math and science teachers are predominantly men. Very few girls learn about great women mathematicians like Emmy Noether, who provided the mathematical basis for important aspects of relativity theory (Crawford, 1981). Few young girls or boys have opportunities to offset negative influences through personal contact with women mathematicians and scientists.

In the past, it was thought that the belief that "math is for men" was held largely by girls and women, and that it deterred them from choosing math courses and math-related activities. However, a meta-analysis of math attitudes has shown that *males* hold this belief much more strongly than females do (Hyde et al., 1990). This finding suggests that gender-related influences on math choices work at the interactional and social structural levels at least as much as at the individual level. In other words, we can no longer conclude that women exclude themselves from math and science because they believe that math is not for them. Rather, their underrepresentation in these fields may be at least partly due to males' beliefs that math is not for women. Such beliefs can create self-fulfilling prophecies (Chapter 3), as males may behave in ways that put subtle pressure on the girls and women they interact with.

Stereotype Threat

One way that beliefs about gender and math ability may have an effect is through stereotype threat. As described in Chapter 3, when people know that there is a negative stereotype about their group's abilities, the pressure caused by their fear of confirming the stereotype can interfere with their performance. Stereotype threat clearly works its damage on the performance of women in math. When college students were given a tough math test after being told that men and women typically do equally well on it, the women and men achieved similar scores. Another group of students took the same test after being told that significant gender differences were expected. In this group, the men outperformed the women. A third group was given the test with no mention of gender similarities or differences (similar to an SAT testing situation). In this group, the men also outperformed the women (Spencer, Steele, & Quinn, 1999).

These results suggest that the gender gap in math performance is at least partly due to stereotype-influenced beliefs and expectations. When people believe that men will do better than women on a math test (either because they're led to by the experimenter or because they have learned this belief elsewhere), they tend to produce the expected results. However, when the stereotype of female inferiority is explicitly challenged, women perform as well as men.

Taking a test in the presence of men may activate stereotype threat for women. In one study, students were tested on difficult math problems in small groups composed of all men, all women, or different male/female combinations. When tested with other women, women got 70 percent of the items correct. When the group was one-third male, their scores dropped to 64 percent. And when they were outnumbered by men, they got only 58 percent correct. Group composition had no effect on the men's performance (Inzlicht & Ben-Zeev, 2000). It seems that being in the minority hinders women's performance by increasing anxiety and stereotype threat.

When stereotype threat is activated, it interferes with women's ability to generate good problem-solving strategies (Quinn & Spencer, 2001). College women in male-dominated areas (math, science, and engineering) report higher levels of discrimination and stereotype threat than women in female-dominated areas (arts, education, and social science) and are more likely to consider changing their major (Steele, James, & Barnett, 2002). Of course, women who pursue math and science careers are in the minority for most of their working lives.

What happens when gender and ethnicity both foster negative stereotypes? In a study of 120 Latino and white college students, math performance was affected by ethnicity-based stereotype threat for Latinos of both sexes and by gender-based stereotype threat for Latina and white women. Latinas were affected by both (Gonzales, Blanton, & Williams, 2002). Women can be disadvantaged by multiple or salient identities when they are connected to stereotype threat.

Ethnic and gender stereotypes sometimes contradict each other. Asian women, for example, may be stereotyped at different times as not good at math (because they are female) and good at math (because math ability is stereotypically attributed to Asians). To see how these contradictory stereotypes affected math performance, researchers manipulated the salience of Asian-American women's gender or ethnic identity by having one group fill out a questionnaire about gender and another a questionnaire about ethnicity before taking a math test. A control group filled out a general questionnaire that did not reference ethnicity or gender. As predicted, women in the ethnicity-primed group did best on the math test; those in the control group did next best; and those in the gender-primed group did worst (Shi, Pittinsky, & Ambady, 1999).

Biological Perspectives

Some psychologists believe that differences in math achievement reflect biological influences. Gender differences, especially in advanced mathematical reasoning, may be in part determined by genetic contributions, hormonal influences, or differences in brain structure (Benbow, 1988; Geary, 1996). So far, however, no one has been able to specify exactly what the biological differences are or how they might work to produce performance differences. The existence of a sex-linked gene for math ability has been ruled out (Sherman & Fennema, 1978). But possible connections between these biological influences and intellectual performance continue to be explored (see Chapter 5).

Overgeneralization and a rush to "biologize" results are unfortunately frequent in research on gender-related differences. For example, recall that boys are much more likely than girls to be identified as gifted in national math talent searches. Based on this evidence, two prominent researchers concluded: "Sex differences in achievement and in attitude toward mathematics result from superior male mathematical ability which may, in turn, be related to greater male ability in spatial tasks" (Benbow & Stanley, 1980, p. 1264). Although they had not investigated biological causes in any way, the researchers suggested that biology was at the root of the difference because environmental factors were equated: their (junior high) boys and girls had taken the same number of math courses. But as two mathematics professors swiftly pointed out, environmental factors were not ruled out by Benbow and Stanley's study:

> Anyone who thinks that seventh-graders are free from environmental influences can hardly be living in the real world. While the formal training of all students may be essentially the same, the issues of who helps with mathematics, of what sort of toys and games children are exposed to, of what the expectations of parents and teachers are, and of a multitude of other factors cannot lightly be set aside (Schafer & Gray, 1981, p. 231).

Indeed, biological and cultural influences can rarely be separated. Even among boys and girls identified as gifted in math and science, the majority do not pursue math and science careers. Among those who do, the influences that shape their choices seem to be similar. In one study, male and female graduate students in math and science who possessed "world class" talent had similar test scores and grades as young people selected in giftedness tests. The world-class graduate students were distinguished from the other young people by strong scientific interests and values and exceptional persistence in pursuing their goals. Gender differences were minimal on these attributes (Lubinksi, Benbow, Shea, & Eftekhari, 2001). Clearly, ability alone does not determine intellectual growth and career choice.

Ironically, media emphasis on biological explanations may contribute to the sociocultural causes of math deficits in girls and women. When Benbow and Stanley's (1980) article speculating about biological factors in math achievement was published in the prestigious journal *Science,* it was seized on by the popular press and reported in highly misleading stories (see Figure 4.5). An interesting field study compared the attitudes of parents who had heard about the article with those who had not (Eccles & Jacobs, 1986). (Because Eccles's research on math attitudes and performance was under way at the time, she had a sample of parents whose attitudes toward their daughters' abilities she had already measured.) Reading about "scientific evidence" for a "math gene" favoring boys led mothers of daughters to lower their estimates of their daughter's abilities. We have already noted the important effects of parents' beliefs on their children's self-assessments.

Do Males Have a Math Gene?

Can girls do math as well as boys? All sorts of recent tests have shown that they cannot. Most educators and feminists tude Test normally given to high-school seniors. In the results on the math portion of the SAT—there was no appreciable dif-

Newsweek, Dec. 15, 1980

The Gender Factor in Math

A new study says males may be naturally abler than females

Until about the seventh grade, boys and girls do equally well at math. In early high school, when the emphasis Julian C. Stanley of Johns Hopkins University, males inherently have more mathematical ability than females.

Time, Dec. 15, 1980

Male superiority

Are boys born superior to girls in mathematical ability? The answer is probably Yes, say Camilla Persson Benbow and Julian C. Stanley, researchers in the department of psychology at the Johns

The Chronicle of Higher Education, December, 1980

Are Boys Better At Math?

New York Times, Dec. 7, 1980

BOYS HAVE SUPERIOR MATH ABILITY, STUDY SAYS

Boys are inherently better at math than girls, according to an eight-year study of 10,000 gifted students. Coun-

Education U.S.A., Dec. 15, 1980

SEX + MATH = ?

Why do boys traditionally do better than girls in math? Many say it's because boys are encouraged to pursue

Family Weekly, Jan. 25, 1981

Study suggests boys may be better at math

WASHINGTON (UPI) – Two psychologists said Friday boys are better than girls in math reasoning, and they urged educators to accept the fact that something more than social factors is re-

Ann Arbor News, Dec. 6, 1980

FIGURE 4.5. Media messages: Biased reporting of a gender-based difference.
Source: From Eccles and Jacobs's, "Social Forces Shape Math Attitudes and Performance," *Signs,* 11, pp. 367–389, 1986. University of Chicago Press. Reprinted by permission of the authors.

What Are the Implications for Society?

The evidence shows that males are more likely to achieve in advanced (but not elementary or intermediate) mathematics. Researchers in the similarities tradition have minimized the size and importance of this difference, pointing out that it is an *average* difference, and the overlap between females and males is much greater than the difference between them. Moreover, they argue that when differences occur, they are probably the result of differential experiences and socialization. We are all so used to living in a gendered world that it is hard for us to appreciate the pervasiveness of gender differentiation (see Chapter 6). We grow up being given gender-typed toys: dolls and play jewelry for girls; microscopes, building sets, and computers for boys. We are told that boys are better at math, science, and reasoning. Because U.S. society tries so hard to make girls and boys different, it is surprising that cognitive differences are not larger and more general than they are. Research from other societies shows that gender differences are not universal—for example, there is no difference in math skills between high school girls and boys in China (Huang, 1993).

Research on social influence on math performances suggests that researchers who want to test for gender differences should first match their male and female research participants on relevant background experiences rather than just matching for age or grade in school. Otherwise, a "gender" difference simply reflects the fact that being a boy or a girl is correlated with particular experiences (Crawford & Chaffin, 1997; Hyde, 1981). One way to help young girls develop their cognitive abilities is to provide them with computers and "boys' toys." "We may be shortchanging the intellectual development of girls by providing them with only traditional sex stereotyped toys" (Halpern, 1992, p. 215).

The purpose of standardized tests like the SAT is to predict performance in college. But although women score lower on these tests, they get better grades than men in college. The tests thus underpredict women's performance (Rosser, 1987; Stricker, Rock, & Burton, 1992). Testing activists have charged that a test that underpredicts the performance of more than half the people who take it should be considered consumer fraud (Rosser, 1987, 1992). This *female underprediction effect* compromises women's right to equal education under the law (Hyde & Kling, 2001).

The consequences of the underprediction effect are serious (Hyde & Kling, 2001). Nearly all four-year colleges and universities use test scores in admissions decisions. Because women's college grades are higher than their test scores predict, some women are rejected in favor of male applicants who will do less well in college. Moreover, women lose out on millions of dollars in financial aid because more than 750 organizations use test scores in awarding scholarships (Sadker & Sadker, 1994). Girls also lose out on opportunities to participate in special programs for the gifted. Finally, an individual's test scores affect her self-confidence and her future academic goals (Rosser, 1992; Sadker & Sadker, 1994).

Most of the research on cognitive abilities has been based on standard research methods. But feminist theorists have questioned some assumptions of such methods. One criticism is that psychological research lacks *ecological* ("real-world") *validity* because it examines behavior outside its normal social context. For example, performance on a standardized test may have little relevance to most jobs or everyday thinking skills. If the importance of a task itself is unproven, the importance of a gender difference in the task becomes even more questionable.

At least one testing specialist maintains that standardized tests are deeply androcentric:

> Excluded are whole areas of human achievement that contribute to success in school and work. . . . Such characteristics and skills as intuition, motivation, self-understanding, conscientiousness, creativity, cooperativeness, supportiveness of others, sensitivity, nurturance, ability to create a pleasant environment, and ability to communicate verbally and nonverbally are excluded from standardized tests. . . . Content that is not tested is judged less valuable than that included on tests. (Teitelbaum, 1989, p. 330)

Although standardized tests are supposed to be objective, they are written by subjective human beings who reflect the values of their society. Furthermore, test takers bring to the test different feelings about themselves and the test, and thus interpret items differently. There is no such thing as a value-free test (Teitelbaum, 1989). Because many important decisions are made on the basis of testing in our society, more research is needed on the tests themselves and how they produce similarities and differences among groups.

THE SIMILARITIES TRADITION: WHY IT MATTERS

It is not always easy to see the values and assumptions underlying our cultural practices. Much of what people believe about gender is learned and expressed at a nonconscious level (Bem & Bem, 1971). Students also learn that science is value-free and scientists are objective, impartial seekers of truth. But values and beliefs related to gender have always affected scientific research (Harding, 1986). A brief review of the history of gender and racial issues in science will help clarify the interconnections between values and practice.

Values and Ideology in Research: What Are the Lessons of History?

Throughout most of Western history, the intellectual and moral inferiority of women was seen as self-evident. The first systematic empirical research on women conducted by scientists of the late nineteenth century took women's inferiority as a given and was aimed at uncovering its biological determinants (Gould, 1980; Hyde & Linn, 1986; Russett, 1989; Shields, 1975). In an era of agitation over women's rights, members of the dominant social group needed to document the inferiority of other groups in order to defend the status quo. "You are women and hence different," was the message conveyed. "Your differences disqualify you for the worldly roles you seem, most unwisely, to wish to assume" (Russett, 1989, p. 23). Sometimes the scientists' antifeminist bias was expressed directly; one British anthropologist presented a "scientific" paper denouncing the "superficial, flat-chested, thin-voiced Amazons, who are pouring forth sickening prate about the tyranny of men and the slavery of women" (cited in Russett, 1989, p. 27).

Then (as well as now), sexism, racism, and class bias were often intertwined and the brain often was the battle site (Bleier, 1986). First, researchers asserted that the inferiority of women and people of color was due to their smaller brains. One prominent scientist asserted that many women's brains were closer in size to those of gorillas than to the brains of men (cited in Gould,

1981). Similarly, scientists measured cranial size in skulls representing various "races" and concluded that the races could be ranked on a scale of cranial capacity (and hence intelligence) with darker people such as Africans at the bottom, Asians intermediate, and white European men at the top. The brain-size hypothesis foundered when it occurred to scientists that, by this criterion, elephants and hippos should be much more intelligent than people. They then turned to the ratio of brain size to body weight as a measure of intellectual capacity. Little more was heard of this measure when it was discovered that women fared better than men by it.

Giving up on gross differences such as brain size, scientists turned to examining supposed differences in specific regions of the brain. When it was believed that the frontal lobe was the repository of the highest mental powers, the male frontal lobe was seen as larger and better developed. However, when the parietal lobe came to be seen as more important, a bit of historical revisionism occurred. Women were now seen as having similar frontal lobes but smaller parietal lobes than men (Shields, 1975).

When size differences in brain regions proved impossible to document, the debate shifted to the variability hypothesis. It was asserted that men, as a group, are more variable—in other words, that although men and women may be similar on average, there are more men at the extremes of human behavior. Variability was viewed as an advantageous characteristic that enabled species to evolve adaptively. The variability hypothesis was used to explain why there were so many more highly intelligent men than women. Only men could achieve the heights of genius. (The prediction of greater incidence of mental deficiency among males was virtually ignored.)

The history is similar for another type of research, the measurement of human abilities, which began in the nineteenth century with Sir Francis Galton's studies of physical variation and motor skills (cited in Hyde & Linn, 1986). Galton measured height, grip strength, and reaction time because he thought they reflected mental ability. When physical abilities failed to correlate with intellectual functioning, the mental testing movement was born. When tests of mental ability failed to demonstrate male intellectual superiority, scientists returned to the variability hypothesis to explain how apparent similarity reflected underlying difference, claiming that men and women might be equal on average, but only men appeared at the upper end of the distribution of mental ability (Hyde & Linn, 1986; Shields, 1982).

Some of the first generation of women who became psychologists worked to dispute these claims. For example, Leta Hollingworth and Helen Montague examined the hospital records of 2,000 newborn infants to test the variability hypothesis. Others examined gender-related differences in emotionality and intelligence (Wooley, 1910). Few differences were found. However, widespread beliefs about innate gender differences in mental abilities persisted. Today, the search for biological differences underlying intellectual functioning continues (see Chapter 5).

The history of attempts to find biologically based sex differences illustrates some important points about the study of group differences. Much of this history shows haphazard testing for a wide variety of differences. Of course, the number of possible group differences is infinite, and demonstrating the existence of one or many gives no information about their causes. Moreover, the "truth" discovered by science is historically and contextually limited. It is easy to see how the racist and sexist prejudices of past eras led researchers to search for justifications of the inferiority of women and people of color. It is less easy to see how personal values affect the work of contemporary scientists, but such influences surely exist. Although people could be grouped in any number of ways, in practice only a few—such as race and gender—are usually chosen. There seem to be no "separate but equal" classification schemes available. The traits attributed to women and minorities are less positive and socially desirable than the traits attributed to men. Because white men remain the norm by which others are judged, research is easily enlisted in support of the social status quo.

Women, Minorities, and Math/Science Careers

Despite gains for women in other areas, math, computer science, and engineering are still among the most male-dominated careers. In most of the world, women—both white women and women of color—are still far more likely to be found doing the support work of science as technicians and assistants than being in charge of a research program (Kimball, 1995).

Women who persevere in scientific careers face discrimination. Although they may start out with similar jobs as their male peers, a gap appears and widens as time goes on. Research (reviewed by Kimball, 1995) shows that women scientists typically earn about 25 percent less than men and are twice as likely to be out of a job. These differences are not due to the women publishing less, taking time out to have children, or other individual factors. Rather, they seem to reflect built-in structural biases in the scientific professions. The higher the level, the fewer women. Only about 2.5 percent of Nobel Science Prize winners and 3 percent of members of the prestigious U.S. National Academy of Sciences are women.

Researchers in the similarities tradition have tried to demonstrate that, given the same opportunities, women can do math and science as well as men. By questioning the size of cognitive differences and examining how they are socially produced, researchers in the similarities tradition have made a contribution toward equality. Yet, equality has not been achieved, although women, particularly white women, have made some very real gains. The belief persists that math and science are male domains; women of color continue to be extremely underrepresented in science; and discrimination against women persists (Look back at the MIT example in Box 3.2.)

Hypotheses about female inferiority seem to keep turning up, despite lack of evidence (Shields, 1982). Rather than focus further research effort on debating how big or how real gender differences are, some psychologists have proposed alternative approaches. For example, psychologists could study exceptions to the average, such as girls with very high math abilities, and determine what experiences have influenced them and what cognitive strategies they use (Halpern, 1986). Or they could explore how differences are produced by social causes or focus on how to equalize opportunity for girls (Hyde & Lynn, 1986). Figure 4.6 shows one attempt to increase girls' interest in science careers.

HIGH SCHOOL CHEMISTRY LED HER TO A LIFE OF CRIME.
As Director of the Delaware State Police Crime Lab, forensic microscopist Julie Willey catches murderers, rapists and thieves by analyzing hair and fiber specimens. It's a job she has today because, in high school, she didn't think it was uncool to take chemistry.
There's a whole world of interesting jobs in science out there. Find out how you can turn your daughter on to them.
Call 1-800-WCC-4-GIRLS. Or visit us on the Internet at http://www.academic.org.
EXPECT THE BEST FROM A GIRL.
THAT'S WHAT YOU'LL GET.
Ad Council
Women's College Coalition

FIGURE 4.6.

THE DIFFERENCES TRADITION: CELEBRATING WOMEN

Compared with the similarities tradition, the differences tradition reflects a very different view of what it is to be a woman. Based on theories of personality, this approach claims that there are fundamental differences between the sexes and that the characteristics of women should be honored and respected.

Psychologists working within the differences tradition have focused on positive human characteristics such as being interdependent and caring for others' needs. They claim that these characteristics have been underappreciated because they are associated with women and femininity. They stress that if we take seriously women's ways of being in the world, we can imagine—and begin to construct—better worlds for all. Equality within the present system is not the primary political goal of the differences tradition. That is, women should not settle for being equal in a man's world. Rather, the goal is to create "a different, more humane world that incorporates traditional feminine values as a central human focus" (Kimball, 1995, p. 7).

Within the differences tradition, researchers study gender differences and how they are created in particular social contexts. They look closely at women's lives to see how women's experiences create a uniquely feminine psychology. One of the central experiences of many women's lives is motherhood, and this has been closely studied to see how it produces gender differences. For our first example of research in the differences tradition, we look at a feminist psychoanalytic theory of mothering and the development of gender differences. We then turn to a theory of gender and moral reasoning, and finally to a theory of gender and power.

Nancy Chodorow: A Feminist Perspective on Mothering

One of the most influential theorists concerned with women's place in society is Nancy Chodorow (1978, 1979). Her theory attempts to explain why women do most of the child care and nurturing in many societies. How do women develop the skills and the desire to become mothers? Chodorow proposes that the crucial events underlying the development of gender identity and subsequent gender differences in nurturing occur in the first two years of life.

According to Chodorow (and other psychoanalytic theorists) the infant has no "self"—it cannot distinguish between itself and its caretaker (usually the mother). Because the infant is helpless, it is psychologically merged with the mother as she meets its every need. Infants must go through a gradual process of differentiation in which they come to perceive boundaries between themselves and their primary love object (see Figure 4.7).

Developing a self is not automatic or invariable. It requires psychological and cognitive maturation (such as the ability to understand that objects exist independently of the child's presence). Most important, the self develops *in relation to the primary caretaker.* As the mother leaves and returns, meets (or fails to meet) the infant's needs, asserts her own needs, and interacts with other people, the infant comes to perceive her as separate, to make a "me/not me" distinction: "Differentiation occurs in relationship, separateness is defined relationally: 'I' am 'not you'" (Chodorow, 1979, p. 67).

FIGURE 4.7. An infant's sense of self develops in relationship with a caring adult.

Developing a separate sense of self is an essential task for every human infant. What does this process have to do with the development of gender differences? Because most child care is done by women, female infants experience a caretaker who is like them in a very fundamental way. They can define themselves in terms of that similarity; they move from "I and you are one" to "I am like you." Their distinction between self and other ("me" and "not-me") is overlapping and fluid, built on their primary sense of oneness with the mother.

Girls grow up with a sense of similarity to and continuity with their mother, and a sense of connection to others in general. Boys, however, must learn the more difficult lesson that their gender identity is not-female, or not-mother. Because mother has been the first object of love, and because fathers are likely to be less involved with their infants, boys develop an identity based on defining themselves in opposition to all that is feminine: femininity becomes negative and masculinity positive.

These gender differences in identity have important consequences. Boys who define masculinity as the opposite of femininity grow into men who devalue women and believe in the superiority of whatever qualities they define as masculine. They deny and repress their needs for closeness and connection with others, which reduces their ability to be warm, loving fathers and leads them to be satisfied with less intimacy.

Women, on the other hand, tend to define themselves in terms of their relationships with others and to feel a need for human connectedness. Their greater relational needs cannot be entirely satisfied by a man (especially one preoccupied with separateness and independence!). So women have babies, satisfying their needs for connectedness in the mother–infant bond.

The cycle is repeated as another generation of boys and girls defines gender in relation to female caretakers. Differences in social roles follow, for as long as women are responsible for children, their opportunities in the wider world will be curtailed. Chodorow titled her book *The Reproduction of Mothering* to indicate her thesis that masculine-feminine identities and roles are not biologically determined but are reproduced in every generation by social arrangements.

Women's experiences as mothers are central to Chodorow's theory; indeed, she views the female practice of mothering as the source of not only gendered personalities but also the division of labor in society. The theory does not devalue mothering or suggest that women should try to be more like men. Mothering is viewed as a positive goal for women, one that satisfies important needs. Yet the theory does not claim that mothering is instinctive or inherent in women's nature. If men nurtured and cared for young children, they too would develop relationship skills and a sense of connection, and these qualities would be socially reproduced in their sons.

There are some limitations to this approach. First, it assumes that children are all brought up in nuclear families and does not ask how development might differ in other kinds of families. Cross-culturally and historically, a nuclear family pattern is the exception, not the rule. Chodorow acknowledges that there are cross-cultural differences in child care, but she believes that these differences affect only the details and not the basic process of forming a self.

Another kind of diversity not addressed by Chodorow's theory is sexual orientation. Obviously, not all women are heterosexual. Because the theory claims that women have greater relational needs than men, it implies that women might tend to turn toward each other for friendship, connectedness, and sexual/affectional bonds, rather than to less-satisfying relationships with men. Chodorow, however, glosses over this implication of her theory and views heterosexuality as the only normal outcome of feminine development (Rich, 1980).

Chodorow's theory is a serious attempt to explain why so many women want to be mothers and are willing to sacrifice other aspects of their lives to do so, and why so many men resist involvement in relationships and fathering. She explained these stereotypical differences in terms of psychosocial processes that create gender-specific unconscious needs. Despite criticisms, this intriguing theory has stimulated research and scholarship (Heenan, 2002).

Carol Gilligan: A Theory of Moral Reasoning

One of the most important kinds of reasoning and thinking people do in everyday life concerns issues of right and wrong. Psychologists have studied moral reasoning to find out how it develops and how people reach conclusions about moral issues.

Lawrence Kohlberg (1981) suggested that a child's conception of right and wrong should depend on the child's stage of cognitive development, just as other kinds of reasoning and thinking do. He studied moral development in children and adults by posing hypothetical dilemmas like the one in Box 4.1 and carefully analyzing the answers people gave. For Kohlberg, the reasoning behind the solution was more important than the solution itself, because it revealed different levels of moral development.

Kohlberg's research led him to propose a theory of moral development that consists of three levels of moral reasoning, from least to most mature: *preconventional, conventional,* and *postconventional* morality. Within each level, there are two stages. As you can see from Box 4.2, children start out with a moral orientation based on avoiding punishment (e.g., Heinz should not steal because he might get caught by the police). By the time they reach middle childhood, most people have moved to a conventional orientation based on gaining approval from others (Heinz should not steal because it's not nice and people won't like him) and, later, on rules and laws (Heinz should not steal because there are laws against stealing). Only a few people move beyond conventional morality to the postconventional level, where moral reasoning is based on internalized ethical principles. For example, they might argue that stealing the drug is a morally valid choice because human life should be worth more than financial profit. People who deliberately chose to violate segregation laws during the civil rights movement provide real-life examples of postconventional morality.

In Kohlberg's early research, boys and men tended to achieve at least stage 4 moral thinking, whereas girls and women were more likely to stop at stage 3. In other words, women seemed to have a less mature and less developed sense of morality. Carol Gilligan (1982) criticized this conclusion. First, she pointed out, Kohlberg's early research was conducted entirely with male participants and their responses became the norm by which girls and women were later evaluated. Second, the dilemmas posed by Kohlberg may have been easier for boys and men to relate to because they frequently involved men as the principal actor

Box 4.1 How Would You Resolve This Dilemma?

In Europe, a woman was near death from a very bad disease, a special kind of cancer. There was one drug that the doctors thought might save her. It was a form of radium that a druggist in the same town had recently discovered. The drug was expensive to make, but the druggist was charging ten times what the drug cost him to make. He paid $200 for the radium and charged $2,000 for a small dose of the drug. The sick woman's husband, Heinz, went to everyone he knew to borrow the money, but he could get together only about $1,000, which was half of what it cost. He told the druggist that his wife was dying and asked him to sell it cheaper or let him pay later. But the druggist said, "No, I discovered the drug and I'm going to make money from it." Heinz got desperate and broke into the man's store to steal the drug for his wife.

Do you think that Heinz should have stolen the drug? Was his action right or wrong? Why?

Source: Submitted text excerpt from *Essays on Moral Development: The Philosophy of Moral Development* (Volume 1) by Lawrence Kohlberg.

in the moral drama. The hypothetical dilemmas also might not reveal much about moral behavior in real-life situations. For all these reasons, Gilligan proposed, Kohlberg's theory may be an inadequate map of female development.

Gilligan went on to develop her own theory of women's moral development. In one study of real-life moral reasoning, Gilligan interviewed women who were pregnant and considering abortion. She chose the abortion situation because it provides examples of ethical decision making by women and also because it brings up a central conflict for women:

> While society may affirm publicly the woman's right to choose for herself, the exercise of such choice brings her privately into conflict with the conventions of femininity, particularly the moral equation of goodness with self-sacrifice. Although independent assertion in judgment and action is considered to be the hallmark of adulthood, it is rather in their care and concern for others that women have both judged themselves and been judged. . . . When a woman considers whether to continue or abort a pregnancy, she contemplates a decision that affects both self and others and engages directly the critical moral issue of hurting. (1982, pp. 70–71)

Like Kohlberg, Gilligan found preconventional, conventional, and postconventional levels of moral reasoning in the people she interviewed. However, the basis for each level is different (see Box 4.2).

At level I, women are concerned with survival, and their immature responses, derived from their feelings of being alone and powerless, may seem selfish. One 18-year-old, for example, saw the decision only in terms of her own freedom. On the one hand, having a baby would provide "the perfect chance to get married and move away from home." On the other hand, it would restrict her freedom "to do a lot of things" (p. 75).

Box 4.2 Levels and Stages of Moral Development According to Lawrence Kohlberg and Carol Gilligan

I. Preconventional morality
Kohlberg:
- Stage 1: Obeying rules in order to avoid punishment
- Stage 2: Obeying rules to get rewards

Gilligan: Concern for oneself and survival

II. Conventional morality
Kohlberg:
- Stage 3: "Good girl" orientation: obeying rules to gain approval
- Stage 4: "Law and order" orientation: rigid conformity to society's laws and rules

Gilligan: Concern for one's responsibilities; self-sacrifice and caring for others

III. Postconventional morality
Kohlberg:
- Stage 5: Obeying rules because they are necessary for social order, but with understanding that rules can be changed
- Stage 6: May violate society's rules or laws if necessary to meet one's own internalized standards of justice

Gilligan: Concern for responsibilities to others and to oneself; self and others as interdependent

Source: Kohlberg, 1981; Gilligan 1982.

At level II, women think primarily in terms of others' needs. The conventional morality of womanhood tells them that they should be prepared to sacrifice all for a lover or a potential baby. When their own and others' needs conflict, they may face seemingly impossible dilemmas. One 19-year-old, who did not want an abortion but whose partner and family wanted her to have one, posed the conflict:

> "I think what confuses me is it is a choice of either hurting myself or hurting other people around me. What is more important? If there could be a happy medium it would be fine, but there isn't. It is either hurting someone on this side or hurting myself." (p. 80)

When women reach the final level of moral development, they resolve the conflicts between their own and other's needs not by conventional feminine self-sacrifice but by balancing care for others with healthy self-care. Because the woman is acting on internalized ethical principles that value relationships, caring is extended both to self and others. A 29-year-old married woman, already a mother, struggled to take into account the strain on herself and her family posed by her pregnancy and concluded:

> "The decision has got to be, first of all, something that the woman can live with, . . . and it must be based on where she is at and other significant people in her life are at." (p. 96)

Gilligan's experiences in listening to what women said about moral issues convinced her that the type of morality studied by Kohlberg (and more common in men) is an *ethic of justice,* whereas the type she discovered (more common in women) is an *ethic of care.* Rather than judge women as morally deficient by a male norm, Gilligan believes researchers should recognize that women and men have different but equally valid approaches to moral issues. (For this reason, her book on moral development is titled *In a Different Voice.*) For both men and women, the highest levels of development should integrate the moralities of rights and responsibilities, incorporating both justice and caring.

Gilligan's ideas about moral development have generated a great deal of research and criticism. Some have questioned her use of the abortion dilemma. Comparing women's resolution of real-life abortion dilemmas to men's resolution of hypothetical Heinz-and-the-drug dilemmas may be an invalid "apples-and-oranges" method. Reasoning in the highly stressful abortion situation may not generalize even to women who haven't faced it, let alone to men (Code, 1983). Moreover, many of the women in Gilligan's interviews were in exploitative relationships (O'Laughlin, 1983). What appears to be a gender difference in moral reasoning could reflect women's subordinate social position and lack of power; in other words, perhaps the ethic of care and responsibility is expressed by less-powerful people generally rather than just by women (Hare-Mustin & Mareck, 1988; Tronto, 1987).

At a minimum, critics argue, the moral reasoning of women and men should be assessed in situations that are as comparable as possible. For example, the male partners of the pregnant women in Gilligan's study could have been interviewed on their moral conflicts about abortion (Colby & Damon, 1983). Other researchers have pointed out that Gilligan did not use well-defined measures or a standard scoring procedure and that she selected parts of the interviews to illustrate her ideas rather than presenting her data systematically (Broughton, 1983; Nails, 1983). Reviews of other research suggest that when women and men are compared directly and factors such as level of education are controlled, the stages of moral reasoning do not differ by gender (Ford & Lowery, 1986; Walker, 1984, 1986). Moreover, a recent meta-analysis has shown women and men are more similar than different in their use of justice and caring viewpoints when solving moral dilemmas (Jaffee & Hyde , 2000).

The debate over theories of difference such as those of Chodorow and Gilligan's is, in part, a debate over whether the similarities or the differences tradition is the best approach. But psychologists from both traditions would probably agree that Carol Gilligan's theory has eloquently described a "different voice"—a moral orientation that Kohlberg's research did not discover. Whether the different voice is a *woman's* voice is still being debated.

Jean Baker Miller: A Theory of Power and Gender Differences

Jean Baker Miller (1986) has looked closely at the relationship between power and feminine personality. She proposed that because women are a subordinate group in society, they develop personality characteristics that reflect their subordination and enable them to cope with it.

Miller analyzes the effects of power differences on personality formation. Women have been socially defined as unequals, similar to other "second-class" groups, which are labeled as such because of their race, religion, or social class. Once a group is defined as inferior, the dominant group justifies its inferiority by labeling it as deficient. Just as people of color are stereotyped as less intelligent and poor people are stereotyped as lazy, women are stereotyped as emotional, illogical, and so on.

Dominant groups define acceptable roles for subordinates, which usually involve services that the dominant group members do not want to perform for themselves. Thus, women, minorities, and poor people are relegated to low-status, low-paying jobs that often involve cleaning up the waste products of the dominant group or providing them with personal services. Roles and activities that are preferred are closed to subordinates. Subordinates are said to be unable to fill those roles, and the reasons given by the dominants usually involve subordinates' "deficiencies" of mind or body. In our society, the status and pay accorded nurses, teachers, homemakers, and child-care workers versus physicians, attorneys, carpenters, and auto mechanics reflect devaluation of "women's work," and it is easy to find people who believe that women are unsuited for certain prestigious or demanding jobs.

Because dominants control a culture's arts, philosophy, and science, they have the power to define "normal" personality and relationships. Dominants define inequality as normal and justify it in terms of the inferiority of subordinates.

> It then becomes "normal" to treat others destructively and to derogate them, to obscure the truth of what you are doing by creating false explanations, and to oppose actions toward equality. . . . if pressed a bit, the familiar rationalizations are offered: the home is "women's natural place," and "we know what's best for them anyhow." (Miller, 1986, pp. 8–9)

When subordinates behave with intelligence, independence, or assertiveness, they are defined as exceptions to the rule or abnormal. If women take direct action on their own behalf, they risk economic hardship, social ostracism, and psychological isolation—"even the diagnosis of a personality disorder" (Miller, 1986, p. 10). Moreover, women are controlled by violence and the threat of violence (see Chapter 13).

Being a subordinate has psychological consequences, too, according to Miller. Subordinates are encouraged to develop psychological characteristics that are useful and pleasing to the dominant group, and the ideal subordinate is described in terms of these characteristics, which

> form a certain familiar cluster: submissiveness, passivity, docility, dependency, lack of initiative, inability to act, to decide, to think, and the like . . . qualities more characteristic of children than adults—immaturity, weakness, and helplessness. If subordinates adopt these characteristics they are considered well-adjusted (1986, p. 7).

To survive, women become highly attuned to the dominants, able to "read" and respond to their smallest behaviors—perhaps the origins of "feminine intuition" and women's reputation for using manipulative "feminine wiles."

Another consequence of subordination is that women learn to monitor and worry about their relationships, to transmute anger into hurt feelings, chronic fatigue, or depression, and to try to influence others' behavior by indirect or extreme methods. Even if they recognize their anger, they may not act on it. Because direct assertive behavior toward a dominant may be dangerous, devious methods or emotional outbursts may seem preferable (Travis, 1988a). Moreover, women may come to accept the dominant group's untruths about women. According to Miller, there are a great many women who believe, consciously or not, that they are less important than men. Finally, subordination sets up internal conflicts as women struggle to reconcile their own perceptions of reality with the interpretations imposed on them by men.

Miller's approach has been criticized for ignoring ethnic, social, and cultural diversity among women. All women are not equally oppressed and powerless, and some men are low in status and power. Furthermore, "If the only reason women value care is because they are oppressed, then feminists are in the very awkward political position of glorifying women's oppression if women's caring is valued" (Kimball, 1995, p. 111).

THE DIFFERENCES TRADITION: WHY IT MATTERS

Research and theory on women's unique experiences and psychological issues have been very influential in creating the interdisciplinary field of women's studies. The differences tradition has raised interesting and important questions for future feminist scholars.

Should Humans Be More Like Women?

Researchers in the differences tradition argue that women and their characteristic activities must be reappraised (Chodorow, 1979; Gilligan, 1982; Jordan, Kaplan, Miller, Stiver, & Surrey, 1991). Women have been assigned the task of fostering others' development in relationships—of empowering others. In our society, women are expected to be nurturing, to take care of children, old people, ill people, and, of course, men. Women are expected to use their intellectual and emotional abilities to help others. Yet they have not been encouraged to value these interactions and activities, which may be underpaid on the job (see Chapter 11) and taken for granted at home (see Chapter 10).

Psychology and its theories have failed women by devaluing their strengths, according to researchers in the differences tradition. Many psychological theories of human development focus on *autonomy* as the end point. That is, the ideal adult is seen as one whose sense of self is entirely separate from others and who is independent and self-reliant. Close relationships (e.g., the infant–mother relationship) are characterized negatively in terms of dependency and lack of a differentiated self.

But very few people are truly autonomous, and when individuals appear to be so, it is usually because many other people are quietly helping them. The idea that psychological development is a process of separating from others may be an illusion fostered by dominant men. Perhaps instead of the John Wayne/Clint Eastwood ideal of the autonomous man, theories of human development should stress human connection and caring. Feminist theorists have articulated alternatives to the notion of the autonomous self, such as the notion of personality development within relationships (Jordan et al., 1991; Miller, 1984b), the self defined in terms of caring and responsibility (Gilligan, 1982), and fluidity in self-development (Kaplan & Surrey, 1984).

From this perspective, the criteria for human development should include the ability to engage in relationships that empower others and oneself. Empathy, not autonomy, is the ideal (Jordan et al., 1991). By this measure, women would be revalued, and problems and deficiencies in men's development would become visible. Researchers in the differences tradition believe that the close study of women's experience may lead to a new synthesis that will better encompass all human experience.

The Politics of Difference

Celebrating women's connection to others, mothering, and the ethic of care seem like positive ways to think about gender. But what are the political consequences of linking caring to women in this way? If we accept the view that women are more connected and caring, it is easy to expect that *all* women *should* show these traits, and that there is something wrong with women who put limits on caring. Yet women have moral responsibility to themselves, as well as to others (Gilligan, 1982). The ethic of care may encourage women to sacrifice themselves to others. Should a woman's decisions about an unwanted pregnancy be based only on avoiding distress to her boyfriend or parents? Should a woman stay in an abusive relationship because she feels responsible for her partner's well-being? Glorifying women's connectedness and caring is problematic if it diminishes women's ability to meet their own needs.

Assigning caregiving to women also may prevent men from developing their capacity to nurture, inhibiting them from becoming fully human. Some feminist theorists have suggested that women will never achieve legal and social equality until men become full partners in the nurturing roles so necessary in relationships, families, and society (see Chapter 10). Yet, as long as women take on most of society's caring tasks, there is little incentive for men to change.

Another problem with the difference tradition is that it puts gender in the spotlight but does not incorporate other differences. For example, Gilligan's research looked for the "different voice" only as a gender difference, ignoring the question of how a person's social class, ethnic community, or religion might affect her moral orientation (Auerbach, Blum, Smith, & Williams, 1985). But women are not alone in articulating the ethic of care; for example, it is often expressed by African-American men as well (Stack, 1986).

A person's identity is shaped by many cultural forces, not just by gender. One broad distinction between cultures is that some societies encourage the development of an *independent* sense of self, whereas others foster an *interdependent* self (Markus & Kitiayama, 1991). The United States and Western Europe hold up the independent ideal: each individual is seen as unique, and the task of each individual is to fulfill his or her potential and become an autonomous person. Much of the rest of the world has a very different ideal: individuals are seen as connected in a web of relationships, and their task is to maintain those connections by fitting in, staying in their proper place, and building reciprocal relationships with others. As one South African woman of color put it:

> There is no word for "identity" in any of the African languages . . . perhaps there is good reason for this. In English the word "identity" implies a singular, individual subject with clear ego boundaries. In Africa . . . ask a person who he or she is, a name will quickly be followed by a qualifier, a communal term that will indicate ethnic or clan origins. To this day, African bureaucracies use forms that require the applicant (for a passport, a driving license (etc.) . . .) to specify "tribe" (Mama, 2002, p. 7).

Cultural differences in the self are aptly expressed in contrasting proverbs from the United States and Japan:

The squeaky wheel gets the grease. (U.S.)

The nail that sticks up gets hammered down. (Japan)

These cultural differences affect many aspects of daily life. For example, college students in Japan reported feeling generally happier when they were experiencing emotions tied to interconnections, such as friendly feelings toward another. American college students, on the other hand, were happier when experiencing emotions tied to separateness, such as pride in an achievement (Kitiayama, Markus, & Kurokawa, 2000). In another study, the self-concepts of Japanese students, because they were more dependent on their connections to others, changed more across situations than did the self-concepts of American students. Japanese students also said more negative things about themselves because interconnected cultures rely partly on individuals' self-judgments to keep them in line with the group, whereas American culture encourages impressing others with one's accomplishments (Kanagawa, Cross, & Markus, 2001).

Does the interdependent self sound a lot like the description of women in the differences tradition? Both the cross-cultural research and the feminist differences tradition spotlight aspects of identity that were long ignored by

Western psychology. These alternative conceptions of the self raise questions of how culture, ethnicity, and gender interact to produce identities. And they challenge all of us to explore differences without labeling one orientation superior to another.

CAN SIMILARITIES AND DIFFERENCES BE RECONCILED?

Gender differences and similarities are not just attributes of individuals. They are the socially constructed product of a system that creates categories of difference and dominance. One theme of this book is that gender is more than just sex. It is a system of social classification that operates at the sociocultural, interactional, and individual levels. Researchers in both the similarities and the differences traditions have recognized that sociocultural aspects of gender govern access to resources; for example, social forces work to keep women out of careers in math and science and to overvalue the attributes of dominant groups in society. Both traditions also recognize that gender can become internalized—as when women come to think of themselves as bad at math and good at nurturing.

Individual feminists may feel an affinity for either the differences or the similarities tradition (Hare-Mustin & Marecek, 1990). And a particular kind of research may be useful for a specific political goal. But both traditions have an important place in feminist theory. Whether we are making comparisons by gender, culture, or some other category, similarities *and* differences can be shown, and they both have strengths and limitations (Kimball, 2001). Becoming familiar with both traditions can help address a very important question: How is the gender system made invisible so that socially produced gender seems inevitable, natural, and freely chosen?

CONNECTING THEMES

- *Gender is more than just sex.* When gender differences in cognitive abilities and performance emerge, they are always preceded by differences in social environments and experiences. The similarities tradition argues that these differences would diminish or disappear with equal opportunity and gender-fair environments.
- *Language and naming are sources of power.* The similarities tradition has demonstrated that what counts as an important difference depends on the values of the observer. The difference tradition, by celebrating feminine qualities, has made previously devalued traits and behaviors the subject of new attention and respect.
- *Women are not all alike.* On every cognitive skill or ability tested, there is much more variability *within* each sex than *between* the sexes. Comparisons of different ethnic and social groups within and across cultures suggest that diversity in cognitive skills and personality is strongly related to sociocultural factors.

- *Psychological research can foster social change.* History tells us that "sex differences" have often been created and used to keep women "in their place." The similarities tradition encourages a focus on equity for girls and women in family, work, and educational settings. The differences tradition turns the table by suggesting that women's characteristics are strengths, not weaknesses.

SUGGESTED READINGS

HARE-MUSTIN, RACHEL T., & MARECEK, JEANNE (Eds.). (1990). *Making a difference.* New Haven: Yale University Press. A sophisticated analysis of how psychology has represented male and female as oppositions and an argument that it is time to move beyond conceptualizing gender as difference.

KIMBALL, MEREDITH. (1995). *Feminist visions of gender similarities and differences.* New York: Harrington Park. By delving into the complexities of research on gender similarities and differences, this book shows how the tension between them can be fruitful. A thoughtful example of good feminist theory, with connections to justice and social change.

RUSSETT, CYNTHIA E. (1989). *Sexual science: The Victorian construct of womanhood.* Cambridge, MA: Harvard University Press. Gender and racial differences were twin obsessions of Victorian science. In a time when women and people of color were demanding civil rights, science was used to "prove" their biological inferiority. The history of this era is fascinating in itself—and also encourages analysis of the political aspects of contemporary sex difference research.

CHAPTER 5

Biology, Sex, and Gender

> Alex A. was labeled a girl when he was born in 1971, although his genitals were ambiguous. When Alex was a year or two old, his mother noticed that his phallus was enlarged, and by the time he could speak he called it "my penis." At puberty his voice deepened, and he began to be called "he-man" by other kids. He did not develop breasts, but by age thirteen, he was menstruating irregularly from his phallus. A rural doctor put him on estrogen, and he developed small breasts and considerable body hair. In his late teens Alex was sent to an endocrinologist who asked him whether he had ever taken hormones. At this point, Alex did not even know what hormones were. The doctor said: "I think you should change to a male" and gave him a prescription for testosterone. But Alex never filled it. . . . "We [mother and I] didn't know what was going on." Alex's mother was encouraging him to "try and grow breasts."
>
> When Alex was twenty-four, his breasts were starting to enlarge. Another physician said: "We can make you a girl" and bolstered this suggestion with the argument, "You know, women can even be managers now." Alex was told that his clitoris could be reduced and that ultrasound revealed a uterus. In spite of the doctor's recommendation, Alex does not want to go this route. . . . He feels like a male and has no idea what his problem is. (Adapted from Kessler, 1998, p. 1)

What sex is Alex really? The answer depends on how sex is defined. Some of the common-sense notions about sex that are challenged by Alex's story are the following:

- If an organism has a sex (and some lower organisms do not), it must be either male or female.
- There are only two sexes.
- Within any individual, there are strong and consistent relationships between sexual anatomy, physiology, sex-related behaviors, and gender identity.
- Within a given individual, sex is always permanent.

However, sex, like gender, is much less simple than common sense might suggest.

WHAT IS SEX AND WHAT ARE THE SEXES?

Despite the fact that everyone talks about sex, very few people try to define it. About all they agree on is that *sex* represents a division of reproductive labor into specialized cells, organs, and organisms. Evolutionary psychologists also focus on the reproductive aspects of sex. They see organisms as the way for the egg and sperm to create other eggs and sperm. Some evolutionary psychologists reduce almost all social behaviors to reproductive strategies (cf. Buss, 1995). They generalize freely between insects, lower mammals, primates, and human beings. However, different species differ in their reproductive arrangements. There are no clear theories to help us to determine when a particular animal is a useful model for human reproductive strategies (see Gowaty, 2001 and Travis, 2001 for critical discussions of the value and limitations of evolutionary psychology).

Animal studies demonstrate that even the most basic aspects of sex are neither fixed nor universal. Two separate sexes, for example, do not always exist. Many invertebrates (e.g., earthworms and oysters) have both kinds of *gonads* (the organs that make either eggs or sperm). Even among species that have two sexes, sex is not always fixed at birth. Some fish and birds can be made to change sex, producing eggs or sperm after a period during which they produced the other kind of germ cells (Diamond, 1993). Some fish change spontaneously from fertile female to fertile male if no males are around. A few vertebrates even manage to reproduce with only one sex. An all-female species of whiptail lizards is of particular interest to researchers (Crews, 1987a). In this species, there are no males, and the females reproduce from unfertilized eggs that contain the same genes as those of their single parent (a process sometimes called *cloning*). This species separates reproductive biology from reproductive behavior. Although there are no males and no sperm, courting behaviors supposedly characteristic of males have been retained. The pseudo-male behaviors encourage reproduction much as male courtship behavior does in species with two sexes. These species are not simply scientific curiosities. Studying them allows scientists to ask, How fundamental is the relationship between various biological components of sex and sex-related behaviors? How different are the sexes?

Although females in at least one all-female species show the complete range of behaviors associated with males in related species, most biologists and evolutionary psychologists classify many behaviors of males and females as *dimorphic* (having two forms or bodies). This categorization is misleading because no single behavior can be found exclusively in either males or females.

Supposedly dimorphic behaviors such as nurturance or aggression are best viewed in probabilistic terms. In other words, these behaviors are more easily elicited or expressed in one sex or the other but may be found in either sex under some conditions. Separating behaviors into "male" and "female" is a false dichotomy, created by ignoring all the exceptions to the rules.

Even the so-called male and female hormones are not found only in one sex; androgens and estrogens influence both males and females. Furthermore, it is now well known that the androgen testosterone is converted into *estradiol* (a form of estrogen) by neurons in some structures of the brain. Interestingly, it is estradiol that induces masculine behavior in some mammals (Fitch & Denenberg, 1998). Nevertheless, stories about the division between the sexes persist. For example, in the 1990s researchers found that "male" hormones influence normal women's bodies (Angier, 1994). In reporting this research, the popular press stressed the negative effects on women of excess "male" hormones. This kind of media bias reinforces cultural beliefs about absolute distinctions between the sexes (see Figure 5.1).

Alex's story shows that sex is not always an all-or-none phenomenon. Instead, biological sex is determined through an orderly sequence of steps. Each step depends on the one that preceded it. For most people, all the succeeding steps are determined by the first event in the sequence: whether the egg was fertilized by an X- or Y-bearing sperm (see Figure 5.2). Under normal conditions,

FIGURE 5.1. Biologically determinist explanations of different interests in women and men. Cartoons may be funny, but they also reflect cultural beliefs.
Source: Baby Blues. © Baby Blues Partnership. Reprinted with Special Permission of King Features Syndicate.

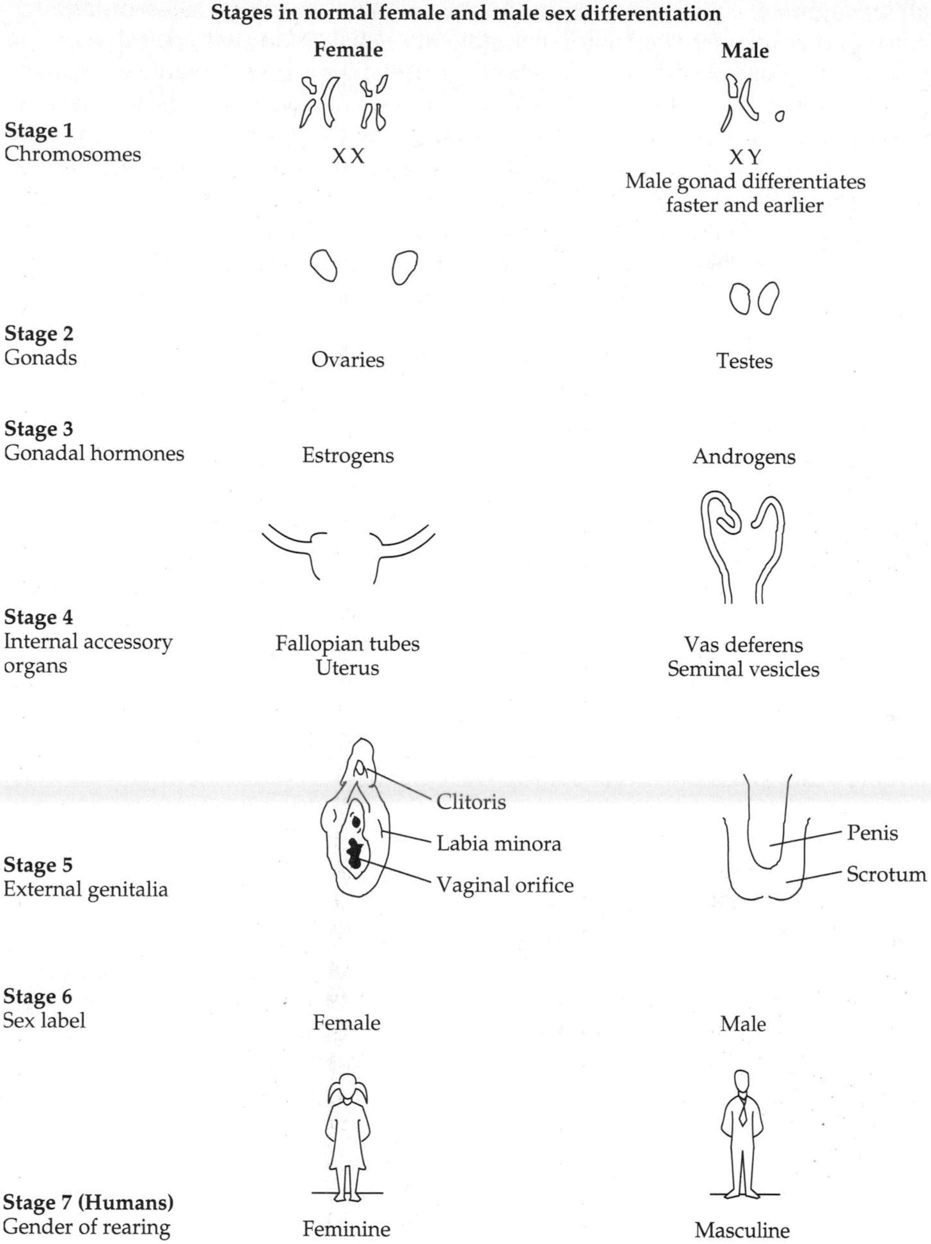

FIGURE 5.2. The many stages of sex determination: (1) chromosomal sex; (2) gonadal sex; (3) hormonal sex; (4) sex of the internal accessory organs; (5) sex of the external genitalia. In human beings, the sex label assigned at birth and the socialization associated with that label are also very important for gender identity.
Source: Reprinted with permission from Alina Wilczynski.

all the steps are consistent with one another. For this reason, it has been difficult to recognize that sex has many components—such as sexual anatomy, sexual physiology, sex-related behaviors, and gender identity. The study of animals and of humans (like Alex) in whom sex-related characteristics are inconsistent with each other has made it clear, however, that although most people are wholly male or female, there is no one biological characteristic that always determines sex.

The study of people who are sexually inconsistent may reveal a great deal about how various components of sex relate to one another and to gender identity and behaviors. According to one estimate, as many as 2 percent of newborn infants have some inconsistency in the various components of sex (Blackless, Charuvastra, Derryck, Fausto-Sterling, Lauzanne, & Lee, 2000). *Intersex* individuals (those whose sexual characteristics are incomplete or inconsistent with each other) generate medical, ethical, and social dilemmas. Before we explore such sexual inconsistencies, let's review what is known about typical prenatal development.

PRENATAL DEVELOPMENT

Chromosomal, Gonadal, and Hormonal Sex

The first stage in the determination of sex in mammals is the presence of either two Xs or an X and a Y chromosome in the fertilized egg. Human beings have twenty-three pairs of chromosomes, with one of each pair inherited from each parent. Twenty-two pairs of these chromosomes (the *autosomes*) are roughly identical in size and shape. The *sex chromosomes* differ, however, in that females have two X chromosomes that are similar in size and shape to the autosomal chromosomes, whereas males have one X chromosome and a Y chromosome that is only a fraction of the size of the other chromosomes. Genes on both the X and the Y chromosomes are involved in sexual differentiation as are genes on some autosomes (Aaronson, undated). But the Y chromosome carries little information with one important exception: a gene (SRY) that causes the formation of the *testes*—the male gland that produces sex hormones and sperm (Sinclair et al., 1990).

Male and female human embryos develop identically during the first few weeks of gestation. Because the reproductive systems of females and males develop from the same embryonic origins, each part has its developmental counterpart, or *homologue,* in the other sex. (You can easily identify some of these homologous structures by comparing the male and female internal and external reproductive systems in Figures 5.2 and 5.3.) If a Y chromosome is present, the gonads begin to grow faster and to develop into testes.

Shortly after the testes are formed, they begin to secrete a number of hormones (androgens) that act on the internal and external structures to produce what are considered to be male characteristics, such as a penis and scrotum. One hormone (*MIH, or Mullerian duct inhibiting hormone*) prevents the development of an oviduct, uterus, cervix, and the deepest part of the vagina. A second hormone, *testosterone,* is responsible for the masculinization of the male internal genital tract,

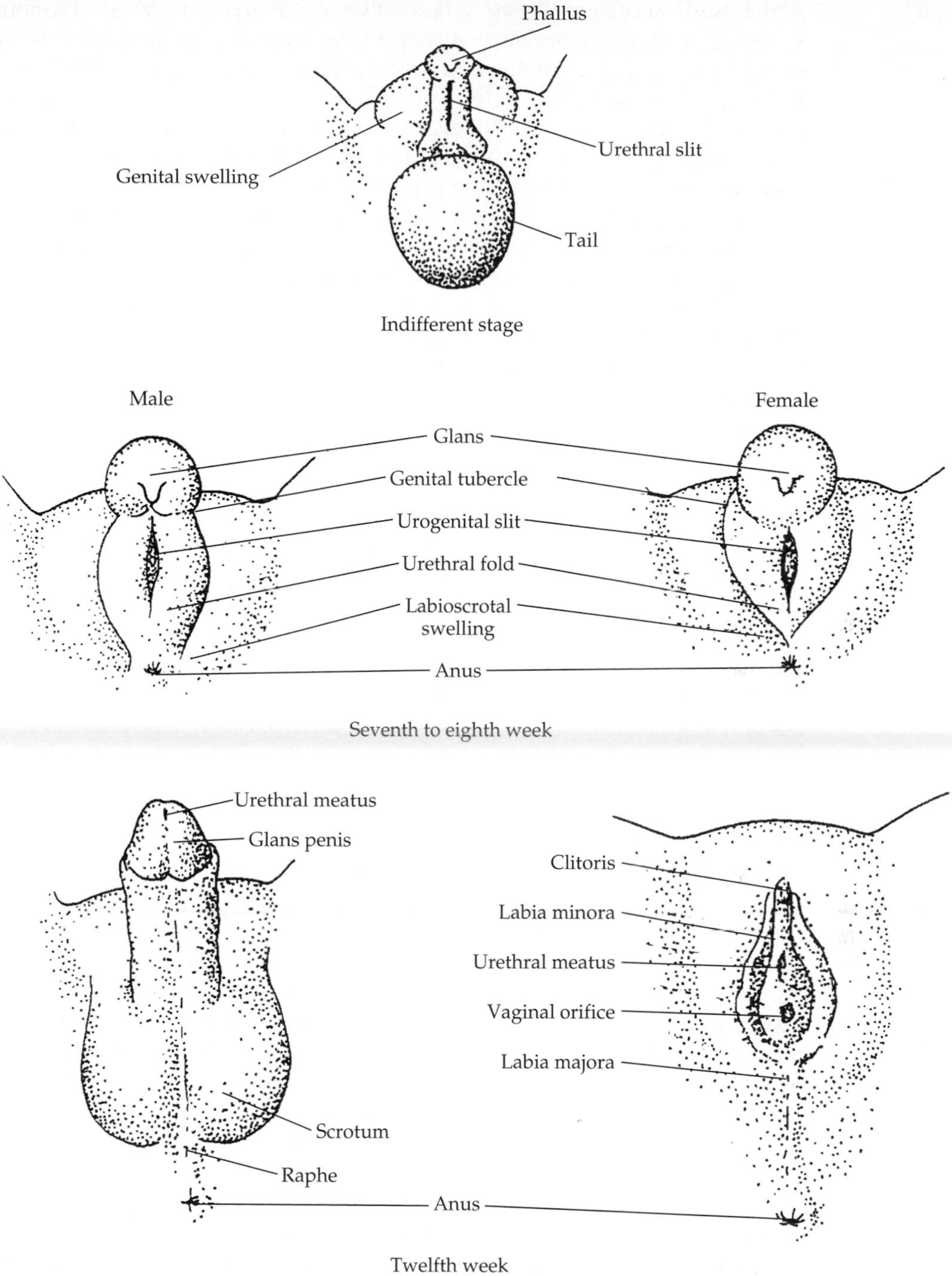

FIGURE 5.3. The development of the female and male genitalia from the undifferentiated or bipotential gonad during early fetal development.
Source: Reprinted with permission from Alina Wilczynski.

and a third, *dihydrotestosterone* (a derivative of testosterone), causes development of the male external genitalia—fusion of the scrotum and growth of the penis (Gorski, 1999). All three of these substances must be present prenatally to produce an anatomically complete male.

Many developmental biologists state that the embryo develops in a female direction if the Y chromosome is absent. An alternative to this so-called default model argues that parallel genetic pathways exist for testis formation and for ovarian formation. However, formation of the *ovaries* (the female gland that contains the eggs and produces estrogens) occurs after the female external structures are far advanced in development, and estrogens play a role at a later stage in the development of females than androgens do in the development of males (Fitch & Denenberg, 1998). A second X chromosome is necessary, however, for female fertility. Those who lack one X chromosome have nonfunctional gonads and no uterus despite their superficially female external appearance.

A number of different hormones must be present to produce an anatomically typical female or male. In later fetal life, androgens are produced primarily by the testes (with a smaller contribution from the adrenal glands), and estrogens and *progestins* (hormones that support pregnancy) are produced mainly by the ovaries. Both sexes are exposed to hormones produced by the mother during pregnancy. Although males and females are exposed to different amounts of each hormone, all three types are found to some degree in both sexes (Collaer & Hines, 1995).

Because the various sex hormones influence parts of the reproductive system independently of one another, human beings with mixed or ambiguous genitalia are not particularly rare (see Table 5.1). In fact, so-called normal female and male genitalia are not that different either, as Figure 5.3 shows. Even after the fetal gonads begin to be distinguishable (by the second month of pregnancy), several more weeks are necessary before it is possible to see the differences.

Sexual Differentiation of the Central Nervous System

Are there sex differences in the human brain? Researchers cite the same studies to argue that there are no consistent or conclusive differences (Devor, 1996) or that there are many sex differences in human brains similar to those found in lower mammals (Collaer & Hines, 1995). We must be very careful neither to deny the possible importance of biology nor to assume that biology is unaffected by the physical and social environment. Most responsible researchers take an interactional approach, arguing that the environmental-biology distinction is a false dichotomy. One noted neuroscientist neatly summarized the impossibility of separating social and biological factors; he argued that "while it is possible to have either biological or psychological measures of a particular behavior, biology operates through psychological mechanisms and any change of behavior must also have an effect on the brain (Breedlove, 1994, p. 391)."

A series of studies on rats has provided a good example of how biology and the social environment can interact to produce sex-related differences (Fausto-Sterling, 1997). Rat mothers lick the anogenital area of their male offspring more than that of their female offspring. Their licking is stimulated by an odor

TABLE 5.1. Approximate Frequencies at Birth of Various Intersex Conditions

The following statistics are drawn from the work of Dr. Fausto-Sterling and her colleagues. Note that the frequency of some of these conditions such as congenital adrenal hyperplasia, differs for different populations. These statistics are approximations.

Not XX and not XY	One in 1,666 births
Klinefelter (XXY)	One in 1,000 births
Androgen insensitivity syndrome	One in 13,000 births
Partial androgen insensitivity syndrome	One in 130,000 births
Classical congenital adrenal hyperplasia	One in 13,000 births
Late onset adrenal hyperplasia	One in 66 individuals
Vaginal agenesis	One in 6,000 births
Ovotestes	One in 83,000 births
Idiopathic (no discernable medical cause)	One in 110,000 births
Iatrogenic (caused by medical treatment, for instance progestin administered to pregnant mother)	No estimate
5 alpha reductase deficiency	No estimate
Mixed gonadal dysgenesis	No estimate
Complete gonadal dysgenesis	One in 150,000 births
Hypospadias (urethral opening in perineum or along penile shaft)	One in 2,000 births)
Hypospadias (urethral opening between corona and tip of glans penis)	One in 770 births
Total number of people whose bodies differ from standard male or female	One in 100 births
Total number of people receiving surgery to "normalize" genital appearance	One or two in 1,000 births

Source: From Blackless, M., Charuvastra, A., Derryck, A., Fausto-Sterling, A., Lauzanne, K., & Lee, E., 2000. "How sexually dimorphic are we? Review and synthesis." *American Journal of Human Biology, 12,* 151–166.

related to the level of testosterone in the pups' bloodstream. As adults, these rats took less time to ejaculate than pups raised by mothers who had their ability to smell removed and, therefore, did not stimulate their male pups' genital region. Their pups also had fewer motor neurons in a part of their hypothalamus associated with sexuality than did males raised by intact mothers (Moore, Dou, & Juraska, 1992). Is sexual behavior in male rats biologically or socially controlled? The answer is not one or the other, but *both* in a complex pattern of interaction.

The jury is still out on the source of many so-called sex dimorphisms in the human brain. Researchers do not yet understand the relationship between structure and function in most of the neural areas in which sex differences have been found. Nor do they understand the role that environmental factors play in their development. Remember that the social environment is not sex-neutral even for newborn rats! And with the exception of an absolute size difference between the brains of newborn girls and boys (with considerable overlap of the distributions for the two sexes), no sex differences in neural structure have been found at birth (Breedlove, 1994).

Sexual Orientation and Genetics

The question of whether the sexual orientation of humans is genetically determined has also been explored a great deal in recent years. Animal models are of little use here because no experimental treatment has produced animals who show a marked preference for partners of their own sex (Breedlove, 1994). Sexual behavior in lower mammals is largely controlled by hormonal conditions before birth. There is little, if any, relationship between their rigid sexual behaviors and human sexual activity.

Science still does not have a good definition of sexual orientation. Nevertheless, researchers are looking for evidence of a "gay gene." Evidence for a genetic contribution to same-sex desire comes from studies showing that gay and lesbian individuals recur among family members at a rate much higher than chance (Diamond, 1995). If such genes exist, however, the genetic determinants of same-sex preference are not the same for women and men. Families with a large number of lesbians do not have a larger than average number of gay men. And families with a large number of gay men do not have a greater-than-average number of lesbians in them.

If one of a pair of identical twins of either sex is lesbian or gay, at least 50 percent of the time the other is also likely to be lesbian or gay (Bailey, Pillard, Neale, & Agyei, 1993; Hamer, Hu, Magnuson, Hu, & Pattatucci, 1993). One study even located a set of female triplets in which the two sisters from a single egg were both lesbians, and the third sister, who was a fraternal twin, was heterosexual (Whitam, Diamond, & Martin, 1993). However, current reviews of the area suggest that there is little convincing evidence that biological factors determine sexual orientation in women (Baumeister, 2000; Veniegas & Conley, 2000).

The evidence of a genetic component to sexual orientation is stronger for males. Same-sex orientation in males has sometimes been associated with the presence of a gene found on a particular part of the X chromosome. Gay men have been found to be more likely to have gay uncles on their mother's, but not on their father's, side of the family (LeVay & Hamer, 1994). And in one study of forty pairs of gay identical twins, thirty-three shared a genetic marker on their X chromosome (Hamer et al., 1993). But these studies must be looked at cautiously. Many of them have not been replicated by independent researchers (Zucker, 2001).

Even if the research was replicated, these studies do not indicate complete genetic determinism For example, seven pairs of gay twins in Hamer's study did not share the predicted genetic marker. And in studies where both twins did not have the same sexual preference, the heterosexual twin appeared to have no same-sex desires at all—he was neither bisexual nor sexually ambiguous (Diamond, 1995). If one brother was gay, adoptive siblings were also gay at a rate higher than chance (Brelis, 1999). Such findings indicate that other factors must be important, too. But it is unlikely that headlines will proclaim: "Environment Modifies Sexual Orientation!"

DOES THE HUMAN BRAIN HAVE A SEX?

Sex and Neural Laterality

Scientists in the past used supposed differences between the brains of women and men to construct a case for female inferiority in cognitive skills (see Chapter 4). Today, the search for biological sex differences underlying intellectual functioning continues. For example, a number of researchers have proposed that female brains are less lateralized than those of males. *Lateralization* refers to the degree to which brain functions are specialized in the right or left hemisphere. In right-handed people, the left hemisphere is usually dominant for language skills as well as motor control; the right hemisphere, on the other hand, is more dominant in spatial activities. The brains of left-handed people appear to be less specialized than those of right-handed people (or better balanced, depending on your point of view).

Lateralization differences between males and females are much smaller and more elusive than lateralization differences between left- and right-handed people; nevertheless, lateralization differences between males and females are often used to "explain" sex-related differences in cognitive abilities such as mathematics and spatial ability (Kimura, 1999). For example, in normal populations, there is no evidence that left-handers have any more difficulty in acquiring mathematical skills than right-handers. The idea that a left brain/right brain distinction is importantly related to intellectual abilities is selectively used to explain the behavior of normal women—but not normal left-handed people. Of course, handedness, unlike sex, is not a distinction of great social and political importance in contemporary American culture (Unger, 1979b).

Attempts to demonstrate sex-related differences in laterality are complicated by complex interactions among age, the consistency with which one hand is preferred for various activities, sex, and sexual orientation (Fitch & Denenberg, 1998). One recent study, for example, found a consistent relationship between spatial ability and handedness—but only in bisexual men (Cohen, 2002). Studies of the relationship between hand preference and sexual orientation are also inconsistent. Some studies have found a greater probability of left-handedness among gay than heterosexual men; others found no such relationship, although they did find more left-handedness among lesbians than among same-sex heterosexual controls (Mustansky, Bailey, & Kaspar, 2002).

Despite weak research support, respected scientists and important institutions of scholarship continue to look for sex differences in the size of various parts of the brain. One recently popular area is the *corpus callosum*—a structure that links the two sides of the brain. Despite much attention, however, a recent meta-analysis found no significant differences between the sexes in total callosal size or shape (Bishop & Wahlsten, 1996).

Sexual Orientation and the Brain

Some researchers believe that the brains and behaviors of gay men resemble those of heterosexual women (this is an example of a *sexual inversion hypothesis,* which is also found in stereotypes about lesbians and gay men as discussed in Chapter 2). Researchers interested in the biological bases of sexual orientation often compare differences between gay and straight men to differences between straight women and men (see, for example, Lippa, 2002). This research is based on the idea that gay men have feminized brains (more like heterosexual women) and lesbians have masculinized brains (more like heterosexual men).

Several investigators have claimed to have found differences in various parts of the brains of gay and straight men (Allen & Gorski, 1992; LeVay, 1991, Swaab & Hofman, 1990). Some studies have found differences in the hypothalamus and the corpus callosum. These studies have been criticized for their small sample size, lack of replicability, and the fact that many of the gays who were studied had died of AIDS (Fausto-Sterling, 1992).

Dramatic headlines followed the publication of the first claims to have found differences between the brains of straight and gay men; for example, "The Biology of What It Means to Be Gay" (*The New York Times*), "Zone of Brain Linked to Men's Sexual Orientation" (*The New York Times*), "What Causes People to Be Homosexual? Study Pinpoints a Difference in the Brain" (*Newsweek*), "Are Gay Men Born That Way?" (*Time*), "Homosexuality and Biology" (*Atlantic Monthly*). The media's enthusiastic response illustrates the popularity of biologically determinist explanations for any kind of sex-related difference. It also shows the continued assumption that being male equals being human. Although none of the researchers found a difference in the brains of lesbian and heterosexual women (indeed, few have looked for one), several of the headlines generalized the results from gay men to lesbians.

Why do misleading findings persist in both the popular and scientific media? First, people tend to believe evidence in the "hard" sciences, such as physiology and biology, more than evidence from the "soft" sciences, such as psychology or sociology. Structures are seen as more real than processes are. Second, biological effects are believed to be less reversible than social effects. This belief has major consequences for the way people think about others and the kinds of social policies they espouse. Beliefs in biological determinism, political conservatism, and the inequality of the sexes are associated (Unger, 1996). Although researchers interested in neurology and physiology are aware of the major effects of the environment on biological processes, reports in the popular and professional media de-emphasize the importance of learning. Biological sex differences are often seen as fixed and used to argue against a need for social change (Unger, 1984–1985) (see Chapter 4). Such biases perpetuate sexist beliefs that, in turn, lead to practices that produce the "evidence" that supports them.

The Relationship between Biology and Behavior

Recently, some biologically oriented researchers have begun to stress that "nature needs nurture" (Wallen, 1996). Some of the most interesting work in this area examines the role of environment on sex-related differences in primates.

This research shows that the early "childhood" experiences of monkeys have an impact on behaviors that are also influenced by hormones and that are usually regarded as sexually dimorphic.

For example, findings on primates illustrate the importance of early environmental factors on reproductive behavior. Rhesus monkey males raised only with other males showed a lower frequency of *mounting* (climbing on the back of another animal and thrusting with the pelvis) compared with heterosexually reared males. In contrast, females raised in an all-female environment mounted more than heterosexually reared females (Wallen, 1996). Paradoxically, single-sex environments increased the similarity between males and females in this behavior.

Male and female monkeys raised under abnormal conditions (alone, with only brief access to other monkeys) rarely achieve normal sexual postures even as adults. When monkeys were studied under more normal group conditions, sex differences in these behaviors were no longer found. Similarly, high levels of threat behavior by male monkeys were found only in those who had been deprived of their mothers and had limited access to their peers. Aggression was inhibited by either peer socialization or by the moderating influence of parents. The only sex-related behavior that was largely uninfluenced by rearing conditions was rough-and-tumble play. In every environment where play has been examined, male primates engage in more rough-and-tumble play than females do (Wallen, 1996). Levels of such play are also influenced by the presence or absence of prenatal androgens (female monkeys who are exposed to androgens before birth are more active than untreated females, whereas males who were deprived of androgens prenatally were less active than normal males). The role of play in monkey (or human) social development is not known. Recent research suggests, however, that boys' tendency to engage in more rough and active play than girls may help shape gender roles in humans (Maccoby, 1998) (See Chapter 6).

Other supposedly dimorphic behaviors are also influenced by the social environment. One researcher, for example, looked at sex-related differences in the parenting of rhesus monkeys (Gibber, 1981). She found that male and female monkeys looked at, approached, and picked up "stranded" newborn monkeys to an equal extent when they were alone. However, when both a male and a female were present, females did virtually all the parenting behavior. Many of the males who had shown nurturant responses when alone did not do so in the presence of a female.

These studies indicate that monkeys of both sexes are capable of a wide variety of behaviors that have been linked with only one sex. In social situations, however, they appear to "take the easy way out" and let the more experienced sex get involved. Similarly, most men will wait for a woman to change a baby's diaper—but no one believes that a man would be unable to change a diaper if no women were around.

ATYPICAL HUMAN SEXUAL DEVELOPMENT

We have argued against overgeneralizing from animal to human studies. It is unethical, however, to do experimental studies of human sexual differentiation. Therefore, clinical cases in which the various components of sex are not consistent with each other are the only way to explore the relationship between biological sex and psychological aspects of gender in human beings.

Learning about people with sexual anomalies helps show how individuals who do not conform perfectly to dualistic sexual categories deal with a gender-divided world. The major reason for scientists' interest in these individuals is, however, the clues they provide to the origin of sexual identity and other gender-related behaviors in typical human beings. By looking at people for whom the various components of sex are inconsistent, researchers try to figure out what factors must be present for a particular behavior to occur. They ask questions such as: What is the effect of absent or additional sex chromosomes on sex-related behaviors? Are sex hormones necessary for an individual to identify strongly as a male or female? And what happens to an individual whose external sex is different from that of his or her internal structures?

It is important to be cautious in generalizing from people who vary from the norm to sexually consistent human beings. People for whom the multiple determinants of sex do not coincide may be more sexually flexible than other people. It may be easier for them to shift their sexual identities than it is for people whose sexual characteristics are consistent. Furthermore, individuals who

FIGURE 5.4. Moving beyond nude photographs with dots over the faces. Do the intersex people in this photograph look different from anyone else?
Source: Chrysalis: The Journal of Transgressive Gender Identities, Vol. 2, #5 Fall 1997/Winter 1998, p. 57.

come for treatment may not even be a representative sample of people with the same sexual variation. People who seek or are sent for treatment are often more adversely affected than others with the same characteristics.

It is also difficult to determine what is "normal" in this area. People do not carry around signs saying, "I am a man" or "I am a woman." As discussed earlier, 1 to 2 percent of all live births may involve some sort of sexual inconsistency. Many of these cannot be found by simple observation of the genitals. Figure 5.4 is a photograph of a group of intersex people. What cues could be used to separate them from other people? As Alex's story showed, medical authorities do not always agree about an individual's sex. And a person may not always agree with the experts' opinion.

All sex-related characteristics do not necessarily have the same origin. Some characteristics have everything to do with the society in which one lives and little to do with biology. The sexual profile of any individual includes at least five components, which Diamond (1995) abbreviates as *PRIMO* (see Table 5.2). People for whom a sexual profile is being assembled are asked questions about the kinds of clothing they wear, what sex their friends are, and so on. These questions are about gender patterns and roles, which have everything to do with the society in which one lives and little to do with biology. They are also asked about their sexual identity (either directly or by means of drawings) as well as about the sex (or sexes) of the persons to whom they are attracted erotically. Their reproductive structure is examined, and they are asked about their sexual functioning, such as their sexual drive. These aspects of sexuality can be relatively independent of each other even in people who do not question their own sex or gender. The study of intersex individuals can reveal a great deal about how various components of sex and sexuality are related. As we explore several types of sexual inconsistency, think about what a sexual profile might look like for individuals with each condition. But remember that such a profile may vary between cultures even for individuals with the same condition.

Extra or Missing Sex Chromosomes

Recall that under normal circumstances, human beings possess twenty-two pairs of autosomes and one set of sex chromosomes. During the development of the egg or sperm, however, it is possible for one of these chromosomes to be

TABLE 5.2. The Parts of a Sexual Profile (PRIMO)

Name	Examples
Gender **P**atterns and Roles	Favorite toys; occupational preferences
Reproductive Structure	Kind of phallic structure present; form of accessory structures such as scrotum or labia
Sexual **I**dentity	Perceptions of oneself as male or female
Reproductive **M**echanisms	Subjective perceptions about sexuality such as level of sexual desire or presence or absence of orgasms
Orientation	Sex to which one is erotically attracted

Source: Diamond, "Biological aspects of sexual orientation and identity," *The Psychology of Sexual Orientation, Behavior, and Identity.* Copyright © 1995.

dropped or for an extra one to be added. What happens to the individuals who, as a result, have XO, XXY, or XYY chromosomes?

Turner's Syndrome: Can One Be a Female without Estrogen?

One abnormality that affects sexual development is known as *Turner's syndrome.* Individuals with this disorder usually have only one unmatched X chromosome. The incidence of Turner's syndrome is approximately 1:2,000 to 1:5,000 births (Collaer & Hines, 1995).

Because the missing chromosome could have been either an X or a Y, people with Turner's syndrome are classified as XO. They are usually identified as female on the basis of their external genitalia. During a critical period of prenatal development, they lack ovarian hormones. At birth, individuals with Turner's syndrome usually appear to have normal female genitalia, but they have no ovaries and no uterus. During adolescence, breasts fail to develop, and pubic hair does not grow. Their internal reproductive structures are undeveloped, with ovaries represented only by fibrous streaks of tissue. Individuals with Turner's syndrome do not menstruate and, of course, they are sterile. They are also unusually short (rarely reaching more than four and a half feet in height as adults).

People with Turner's syndrome are particularly interesting because they show how development occurs in the absence of any sex hormones except those produced by the mother before birth. Some findings parallel those of animal experiments: in the absence of any gonadal influences, differentiation takes a female direction. However, people with Turner's syndrome are not simply unusual females. They are essentially neither male nor female individuals whose external genitalia are similar to those of females. They are defined as females because of the inadequacy of a binary classification system for sex.

Individuals with Turner's syndrome provide researchers with an opportunity to examine the psychological effects of the sex of assignment and rearing independent of the biological influences usually associated with that sex. A number of studies have looked at their psychological and behavioral responses (Collaer & Hines, 1995). People with Turner's syndrome have often been described as being slightly retarded. Their verbal abilities are relatively unimpaired, but their performance on visual and spatial tasks is significantly below normal. They may have difficulty orienting spatially and performing numerical calculations.

The bases for these deficiencies are unknown, although they have sometimes been ascribed to the lack of a Y chromosome. The Y chromosome, however, is not known to carry any genes besides those for male sex determination. Recent research suggests that the cognitive difficulties of those with Turner's syndrome may be due to attentional and memory deficits rather than the absence of sex hormones (Collaer & Hines, 1995).

Although their central nervous systems have not been exposed to any gonadal hormones during gestation, individuals with Turner's syndrome identify themselves as female. As children they appear even more feminine than other girls. They show less interest and skill in athletics, fight less, and have a greater interest in personal adornment. In one study, despite the handicap of their stature and infertility, which all of the older Turner's syndrome girls knew about, all but one explicitly hoped to get married one day. They all reported daydreams and fantasies of being pregnant and wanted to have a baby to care for. All but one had played with dolls exclusively, and the exception preferred dolls even though she played with boys' toys occasionally (Money & Ehrhardt, 1972). These findings suggest that a feminine gender identity can develop without any help from prenatal gonadal hormones that might influence the brain.

How do we explain these results? The only obvious physical difference, and sometimes the only external sign, of XO individuals is their small size. Other aspects of their physical immaturity may not become obvious until adolescence. It is likely that these children will not be reinforced for their skill in athletics or fighting. Size is also a cue for status and power among children. Because children with Turner's syndrome tend to be consistently much smaller than their peers, they probably have low status and power as well.

There is no clear evidence that the personality and behavioral differences between XX and XO individuals are socially determined. But the lack of a second X chromosome may not be directly responsible for these effects, either. Factors such as activity level and body image and its social consequences should be considered in addition to biological variables.

XYY and XXY Males: What Is the Power of the Y Chromosome?

Both scientists and ordinary people tend to overestimate the extent to which biology determines behavior. An excellent example is the case of the so-called criminality syndrome. Individuals with an extra Y chromosome (XYY) were first reported in 1965 among the inmates of institutions for violent, dangerous, and aggressive patients. No physical abnormality was reported except for excessive height. XYY males tend to be tall, averaging over six feet.

Many similar studies have now been carried out in prisons in Europe and the United States, and it has held true that the frequency of XYY males confined for crimes of violence is about ten times greater than the percentage of XYY males found among a sample of newborn infants. This result led a number of investigators to conclude that the extra Y chromosome predisposed these men toward excessive aggression and violence. Such conclusions are an example of an extreme form of biological determinism.

These studies were biased by the fact that they took place in an institutional setting. They had, therefore, no information about the XYY men who are not societal problems (the greater number). Chromosomal factors, moreover, do not rule out social influences as well. Since XYY men tend to be taller than the average, it is possible that their extra height imposes psychosocial stresses that make violent, aggressive behavior more likely. Their height may also make any aggression more effective and reinforcing.

A Danish study of criminality among XYY males is particularly important because it is free of many of the biases found in other studies. The study was possible because of the excellent records kept in the small country of Denmark. The researchers (Witkin et al., 1976) examined *all* available records on almost all men 28 to 32 years of age born in Copenhagen whose height was within the top 15 percent of the height distribution of Danish males. They found twelve XYY and thirteen XXY men in this group. The researchers also obtained information on any crimes committed by these men, the educational level they had attained, and the results of an intelligence test used to screen army recruits.

Individuals with an XXY chromosomal composition (also known as *Klinefelter's syndrome*) served as a comparison group for the XYY males. XXY individuals are also taller than average, but the presence of an extra X chromosome produces a smaller penis and testes and feminization of the hips, with some breast development. The testes fail to enlarge at puberty, the voice remains rather high-pitched, and pubic and facial hair remain sparse.

Because of the feminizing effects of an extra X chromosome, the researchers expected XXY men to engage in fewer violent aggressive acts than either XY or XYY males. They found that chromosomal composition, by itself, was not highly related to the probability that a man would be convicted of a crime. Height was also not related to the probability of being convicted of a crime (criminals were actually shorter than their noncriminal counterparts). Those of low socioeconomic status—irrespective of their chromosomal composition—were more likely to have been convicted.

The most important findings of this study were that both XXY and XYY males had significantly lower scores on army intelligence tests and lower educational levels than XY males did. For each group, men with criminal records rated substantially lower in both measures of intellectual function than men without criminal records. These findings seem to imply that the somewhat higher rate of criminality among XYY males may be due to their moderately impaired mental function. The hypothesis that an extra Y chromosome is related to aggression was definitely not supported. In fact, the only violent crime committed by any man with extra chromosomes was the physical attack on a woman committed by an XXY male.

The case of the so-called criminality syndrome illustrates the danger of overestimating biological causality. At about the time of the first discovery of XYY males among exceptionally violent criminals, a pathological killer, Richard Speck, sneaked into a nurses' dormitory in Chicago and brutally murdered eight student nurses. A newspaper claimed that he had been "born to kill" because he was XYY. This turned out to be untrue—he was XY—but the false report was widely circulated and believed. Several proposals were made for the mass screening of newborn boys to detect those with XYY and to provide them with special education and psychological counseling to counteract their supposed "killer instinct." This could have produced a self-fulfilling prophecy, creating problems for XYY people because others believed them to have severe problems with aggression. The results of the Danish study indicate, however, that the rate of criminality is related more to income and intellectual functioning than to sex-chromosomal composition.

What Do the Sex Chromosomes Tell Us about Sex?

Perhaps because the X and Y chromosomes carry relatively little information, missing and extra sex chromosomes appear to be the most common form of chromosomal abnormality in human beings. Many people may be completely unaware of their unusual chromosomal nature. Chromosomal composition appears to have little direct effect on sexual identity or orientation, although it may influence characteristics such as intelligence, height, and physique, which, in turn, influence the way people are treated by others.

Society's ignorance about the role of the sex chromosomes has had tragic results for women who compete in world-class athletic events such as the Olympics. Women who were found to have a Y chromosome in some of their cells (this is common enough that several such women are usually identified at most major international sports events) were routinely denied the opportunity to participate (Lorber, 1993a). Only women are tested to see if they are "female enough" to compete. Men are not tested. The purpose is to prevent women from having to compete unfairly with individuals who have male advantages in size and strength. However, there is no evidence that sex chromosomes affect sports prowess (Birrell & Cole, 1990). The International Amateur Athletic Federation has urged that sex be determined by simple genital inspection (Kolata, 1992).

Prenatal Hormones and Sex Differentiation

When people are born with a mixture of male/female organs, it is usually due to an excess or absence of androgens during critical periods of prenatal development. The presence or absence of these hormones influences the development of internal reproductive structures and the appearance of the external genitalia. But do these conditions also influence the brain and behavior?

Congenital Adrenal Hyperplasia: What Is a Normal Female?

Individuals with *congenital adrenal hyperplasia (CAH)* lack an enzyme needed to build certain adrenal steroids. As a result of this missing enzyme, steroids such as testosterone and *progesterone* (a hormone, produced in large amounts by the ovaries during pregnancy, that has masculinizing properties) build up during prenatal life. The incidence of this genetic disorder is estimated

Making a Difference

Cheryl Chase (b. 1956) grew up withdrawn and lonely, stigmatized and harassed by other children. She had been born with a large clitoris, was labeled a boy at birth, and was treated as a boy until age 1½. Then a new set of "expert" physicians relabeled her as a girl and removed her clitoris. Chase, on doctors' advice, was kept in the dark about her intersexuality and history of sex change. In middle age she finally understood that her difficult childhood was likely due to her parents' ambivalent attitude toward her, which had been encouraged by the medical perspective of intersexuality as a shameful secret. Chase then began to speak about her history and soon met others with similar experiences. She founded the Intersex Society of North America (ISNA) in 1993. ISNA holds that cosmetic genital surgery on infants is harmful because: (1) it is sexually mutilating, (2) it conveys that the child is a misfit who would not be acceptable without plastic surgery, and (3) many intersexed people reject the gender assigned by doctors and feel doubly robbed by early surgery. ISNA emphasizes the importance of open and honest disclosure concerning intersexuality as well as peer and professional mental health support for intersexual children and their families. They also believe an intersex person might quite rationally choose not to undergo any medical interventions, considering the body they are born with to be normal for them, a variant rather than an abnormality. Chase and her colleagues at ISNA are working toward the end of the notion that it is monstrous to be different.

Sources: Intersex Society of North America, www.isna.org.
Colapinto, J. (1997, December 11). The true story of John/Joan. *Rolling Stone*, 54–97.
Renshaw, D. C. (1999, March 31). Lessons from the intersexed. *Journal of the American Medical Association*, 1137–1138.
Cowley, G. (1997, May 19). Gender Limbo. *Newsweek*, 64–66.

to be about 1 in 13,000 births ((Blackless et al., 2000). A related disorder occurs in females whose mothers received doses of progesterone during pregnancy to prevent a threatened miscarriage. The two groups seem to be similar, suggesting that any behavioral effects are due to prenatal masculinizing hormones.

Females with CAH have two normal X chromosomes and normal ovaries, uterus, and fallopian tubes. However, their external genitalia look more or less like those of male infants (see Figure 5.5). Changes in the genitalia range from

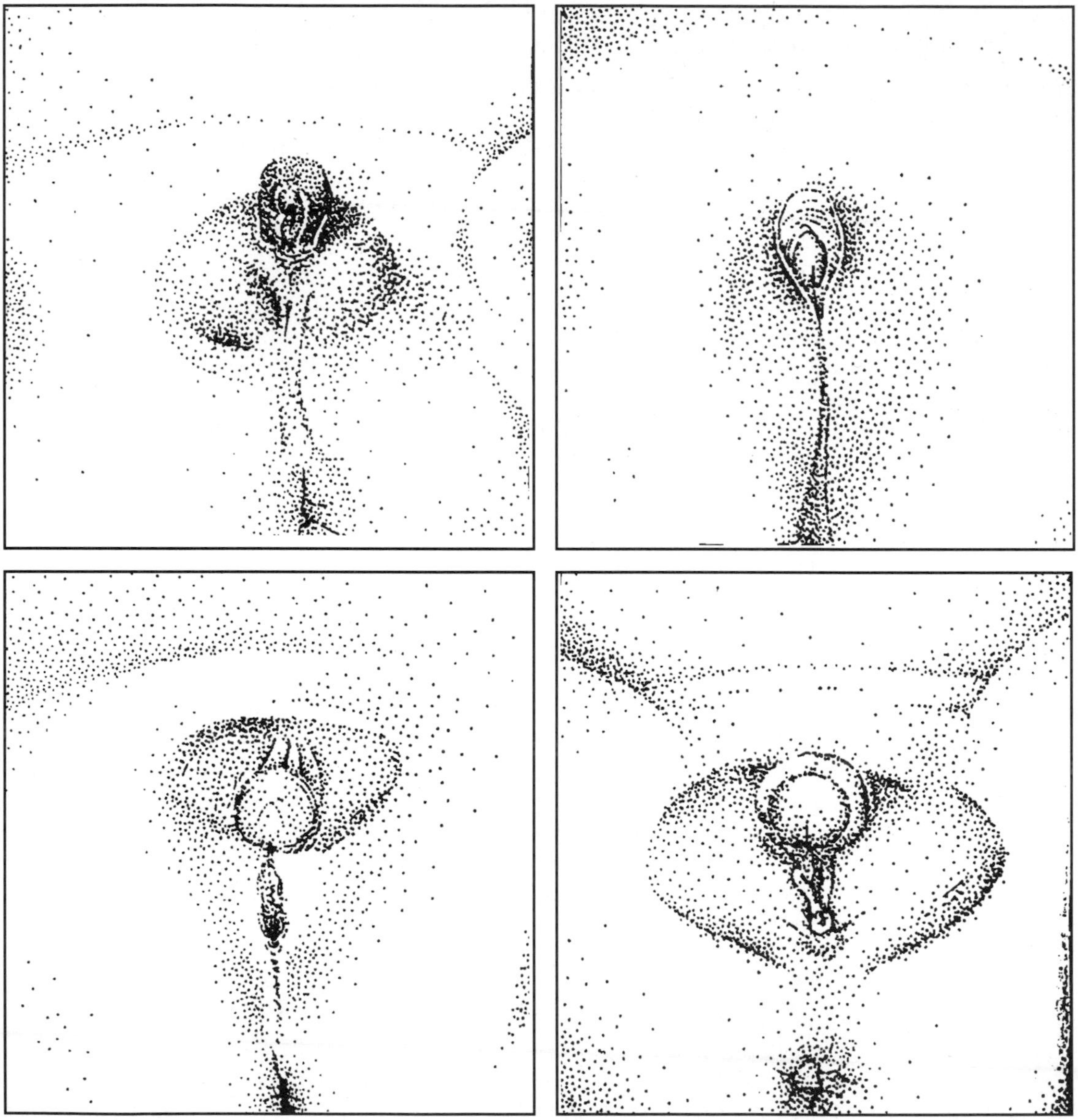

FIGURE 5.5. Genitals are not always clearly "male" or "female." Here are examples of the external genitals of several intersex infants.
Source: Reprinted with permission from Alina Wilczynski.

an enlarged clitoris to fusion of the lips of the labia, producing what appears to be an (empty) scrotum. Some individuals have complete closure of the urethral groove and a penis that is capable of becoming erect.

Until rather recently, sex was assigned to newborn infants on the basis of inspection of their genitalia. Thus, two individuals with equivalent ambiguities might have been classified differently. In the United States, at least, this kind of misassignment no longer occurs for individuals with CAH. Because of knowledge about gonadal structure and chromosomal composition, most affected individuals are raised as females. In spite of a somewhat enlarged clitoris, their internal structures tend to be normally female, and many of them are fertile. If those girls who need it receive proper therapy (with cortisol), they experience pubertal development at the normal age, and their sexual functioning and fertility are not impaired in adulthood.

Because all CAH females receive a heavy dose of masculinizing hormones during fetal life, their sexual identity, gender-related behaviors, and sexual orientation are of great interest. Girls with CAH have been found to identify firmly as girls and women. However, compared with other girls (either matched unaffected females, unaffected siblings, or individuals with other clinical disorders), they typically engage in more intense active outdoor play, associate more with male peers, and tend to be identified as "tomboys" by themselves and others. They prefer "masculine" to "feminine" toys beginning in their nursery school years (Berenbaum & Hines, 1992). These behavioral differences are probably related to the higher activity levels that they also show from an early age.

When ten-year-old girls with CAH were compared with tomboys and with their unaffected sisters, their gender identity was more like that of their sisters than that of the tomboys (who had been recruited as controls with no known intersexuality). The researchers concluded that these girls with CAH had female-typical gender identity (Berenbaum & Bailey, 1998). None of their behaviors would be considered abnormal for a girl in our culture. Girls with CAH have not been found to be any more aggressive than comparison girls, nor do they show what some researchers consider a "malelike" cognitive profile—better spatial-perceptual than verbal abilities (Collaer & Hines, 1995).

Findings regarding the sexual preferences of women with CAH are more complicated. Although most women with CAH are heterosexual, several studies have reported increased same-sex or bisexual fantasies and behaviors in comparison to their unaffected sisters or female relatives. In one study, 44 percent of CAH women 21 years or older had desired or experienced sex with a female partner, but none of their sisters had done so (Dittmann, Kappes & Kappes, 1992). Another study found that CAH women had fewer sexual experiences with men than did their female relatives (Collaer & Hines, 1995). However, many of these women had undergone clitoral reduction, and their sexual behavior may have been a result of surgical damage rather than a direct effect of prenatal androgens on sexual orientation. In general, most of these individuals live as women, although their sexual preferences appear to be more varied than those of the women who served as controls (Zucker, 2001).

These studies suggest that the effects of prenatal masculinizing hormones on human females are complex. Most of these women do not question their identity as females. Their sexual orientation appears to be more idiosyncratic.

Some of these women were heterosexual, some had same-sex preferences, and some were bisexual in orientation, just like women who have not been subjected to masculinizing hormones. Some gender-related behaviors, especially those associated with a high energy level, appear to be influenced by the level of male steroids present prenatally. It is important to stress, however, that most of the women interviewed expressed satisfaction with themselves as females. In sum, prenatal androgens do not appear to influence gender identity in females, although the question of whether they influence sexual preference is still unanswered.

Androgen Insensitivity: What Does the Y Chromosome Do?

The *androgen insensitivity syndrome (AIS)* is an inherited condition of individuals with an XY chromosomal composition. It is caused by a gene on the X chromosome that prevents embryonic tissues from responding to testosterone either partially or completely. Individuals with *complete AIS* have female external genitalia and an incompletely developed vagina, but no uterus or fallopian tubes. Those with *incomplete AIS* have ambiguous genitalia similar to those shown in Figure 5.5, with a structure that could be called either a large clitoris or a small penis. Internally, they are similar to normal males in appearance, although the testes contain unusual cells and are present in the abdominal cavity rather than the scrotum.

Individuals with complete AIS are totally unresponsive to testosterone. However, their bodies (like those of other males) produce estrogens. Without testosterone to counteract them, estrogens induce breast development and feminine contours at puberty. Individuals with AIS often appear to be very attractive women. The Y chromosome carries information that is not completely mediated by testosterone. Thus, persons with AIS tend to have male height. Their breast development is normal and appears to result from the action of estrogens produced by their testes (if they are still present) and their adrenal glands. Pubic and axillary hair tends to be sparse or absent. Of course, having no uterus, these individuals do not menstruate and are sterile.

In the past, individuals with AIS were classified as female and raised as girls. Even when the male chromosomal pattern of infants with partial AIS was recognized, many physicians continued to argue for "clitoral" reduction and surgical construction of a vagina on the grounds that boys with an inadequate penis would be ridiculed and be unable to function in manly roles (Kessler, 1998).

Because it is a rare disorder, relatively few studies of the behavior of people with AIS have been conducted. An early survey of the clinical data on ten such individuals reported that they show a high preference for a traditionally feminine role. Eighty percent preferred the role of homemaker over an outside job; 100 percent reported having dreams and fantasies of raising a family; 80 percent reported playing primarily with dolls and other girls' toys. They rated themselves high in affectionateness and fully content with the feminine role (Money & Ehrhardt, 1972). Adults with this syndrome tend to take up occupations that put a high premium on an attractive feminine appearance and behavior, such as modeling and acting. Apparently, the most attractive female body may be that of a genetic male.

Although there are no data suggesting that people with AIS have any difficulty identifying as females, their lack of ability to reproduce may influence others' view of them. For this reason, people with AIS may be especially anxious to keep their biological status a secret. Consider the case of a strikingly attractive Latina teenager who sought medical information as to why she (like many members of her maternal family for at least four generations) was unable to menstruate and conceive. This family "curse" had led her parents to give up everything and emigrate to the United States. Imelda said:

> In Mexico, the girls are treated like royalty when they get their period. But those of us who are unable to have children are treated like slaves. We are forced to serve the others, to care for them, to cook and clean for them. We can't marry. And then, when we become too old to work, we are banished from the houses of our relatives (Marion, 2000).

In the United States, Imelda and her sisters have many more options. But this case and others discussed next demonstrate how impossible it is to deal with biological issues in isolation from social and cultural norms.

5-Alpha-Reductase and 17-Beta-Hydroxysteroid Dehydrogenase Deficiency: Biology versus Culture?

There have been several studies of individuals who have one of two rare genetic defects with the tongue-twisting names given in the preceding heading. Briefly, affected individuals lack one of several enzymes that aid in the conversion of testosterone to *dihydrotestosterone*—the androgen that masculinizes the external genitalia, including fusion of the scrotum and growth of the penis. Individuals who lack these enzymes are born with normal testes and male internal structures combined with female-appearing or ambiguous external genitalia that are quite similar to the ambiguous structures of girls who have been exposed to prenatal androgens (see Figure 5.5). When methods for determining chromosomal sex are unavailable, they may be identified and raised as girls.

Males with these enzyme deficiencies are, however, masculinized during childhood or at puberty when their normal testes pour increasing amounts of testosterone into their systems. The testosterone produces deepening of the voice, enlargement of the penis and testicles, erections, and ejaculation from a urethral orifice at the base of the penis (Imperato-McGinley & Peterson, 1976; Peterson, Imperato-McGinley, Gautier, & Sturla, 1977). Such males would appear to provide a perfect test for examining the effect of socialization versus biological factors in the development of sexual identity and gender roles because they are biological males who have been raised as females throughout childhood. The interesting question is: What happens to their identity when their sex of rearing and their physical properties diverge at a relatively late point in their lives? Or, how reversible is sexual identity?

One study examined a group of thirty-eight related individuals with the disorder in a rural region of the Dominican Republic (Imperato-McGinley, Peterson, Gautier, & Sturla, 1979). In this isolated group, 5-alpha-reductase deficiency is so common that it has a name: *guevedoce,* or "testes at twelve." In the first nineteen cases, individuals with this disorder were reared unambiguously as girls, but in later cases, persons with the deficiency were recognized early and treated as special. What is surprising is the striking ease with which these people shifted gender at puberty. Seventeen successfully assumed a masculine identity and fifteen were married, suggesting a much later capacity for sexual identity reversal than studies on other sexually ambiguous people would indicate is possible. The researchers believe that the shift was made possible by the prenatal masculinization of the brain in these individuals; that is, their "male" brains were able to overcome easily many years of feminine socialization (Imperato-McGinley et al., 1979; Imperato-McGinley, Pichardo, Gautier, Voyer, & Bryden, 1991).

As you can see, nature-versus-nurture arguments are still alive and well in the area of sexual development and behavior. Some researchers have challenged that a more intensive analysis of these data suggests that the shift from feminine to masculine identity was not as simple as it first appeared. For example, the individuals are described as realizing that they were different from other girls sometime between the ages of seven and twelve (Rubin, Reinisch, & Haskett, 1981). This realization took place shortly after the age at which children in this culture are encouraged to segregate by sex for play and domestic tasks. They shifted their gender identity over several years and initiated sexual intercourse with young women at the same age as those affected males who had been raised as boys.

Other isolated populations of individuals with this disorder have been studied in New Guinea (Herdt & Davidson, 1988) and Gaza (Diamond, 1999). (Groups of individuals with the same recessive genetic disorder tend to accumulate in isolated areas with much intermarriage between relatives.) Unfortunately, it is difficult to test questions of nature versus nurture in these cultures because of linguistic difficulties and differences in sexual norms. In Gaza, for example, close examination of the genitals of newborn infants is not usual even in communities where this intersex condition is fairly common. Researchers do not know whether anyone recognized differences in these children's genitals at an early age. They also do not know whether assumptions about the stability of sex are similar to those found in other cultures where such conditions are rare.

Culture plays a role in sexual identity even when development differs drastically from the norm. There are advantages to living as a male in all the cultures studied. Anthropological investigations of the Dominican population have indicated, for example, that social class affects how intersexed people take on adult male roles. Individuals from poor families are likely to drift into marginal occupations, including prostitution, whereas similarly affected individuals from well-to-do families marry and purportedly "father" children with their wives (Tobach, 2001).

As in the Dominican Republic, the genetic abnormality is common enough in parts of New Guinea to have received a colloquial name—*Turnim man.* This society actually has three linguistic terms for sex: male, female, and an ambiguous compound word that emphasizes a complex relationship between genital anatomy and gender identity (Herdt & Davidson, 1988). People in the third category are not treated like other males. Unlike other boys their age, they are excluded from initiation into male societies, although they are sometimes granted a religious identity as a shaman (Herdt, 1996).

A strong case may be made for a biological priming of sexual identity in these individuals. Consider the following report on people from Israel and Gaza whose genitals begin to masculinize between ages three and seven:

> Intersex persons interviewed claimed to be aware of not being girls/female from an early age on. This was often verbally expressed even before genital masculinization was recognized. Demonstrated male behaviors by an intersexed child were often cause for parents to first become aware of the condition. The older individuals that remained living as women did so due to cultural conditions which prevented their switching. They were fully aware they were male but considered themselves socially restrained from switching to live as men and believed that they were thus also fulfilling the will of Allah. Their sexual orientation, as that of all those that switched to living as males, remained gynecophilic [i.e., attracted to women]. (Diamond, 1999, p. 12 of manuscript)

Studies of XY children with other syndromes that produced ambiguous genitalia and who were assigned as females in infancy also indicate prenatal influences on male gender identity (Phornphutkul, Fausto-Sterling, & Gruppuso, 2000; Reiner, 1999). Despite having their testes removed early in life, many such children reassign themselves as males during late childhood or early adolescence. Prenatal androgens may act on the brains of genetic males to induce a sense of bodily maleness. This combined with the average higher activity level encouraged by prenatal hormones may lead affected boys to see themselves as male in spite of some degree of feminine socialization. Their sexual orientation follows the pattern found in most males with a normal prenatal chemistry.

Cross-Sex Rearing in Prenatally Normal Males

The studies discussed so far suggest that sexual identity in males, at least, is not easily changed by socialization. These studies were not available when John Money (1974) began working with a case whose bizarre aspects seem more suited to a science fiction story than to scientific annals. Identical male twins experienced normal development before birth. In infancy, however, an accident during circumcision resulted in near-total destruction of one twin's penis. The parents were advised to reclassify the child as female, and this was formally done at the age of 17 months.

The sex reassignment was based on the opinion that a child without a penis would be able to function more adequately as a female than as a maimed male. One psychiatrist predicted the twin's emotional future in the following words:

> He will be unable to consummate marriage or have normal heterosexual relations; he will have to recognize that he is incomplete, physically defective, and that he must live apart. (Colapinto, 1997, p. 58)

The decision to change this child's sex of assignment was also supported by studies suggesting that children identify with the gender in which they are reared if the label is assigned within the first two or three years of life and the child is treated consistently as either a male or a female from then on (Money & Ehrhardt, 1972).

Think about both the conceptual bases and the ethical implications of this sexual reassignment. First, it reflects our cultural bias about the primacy of the penis. Anyone without a functional penis is not considered to be truly male. Experts were willing to subject this child to additional surgery (including castration or removal of his healthy and functional testes as well as construction of a vagina) and lifelong hormonal replacement therapy because they believed he could not function as a male without a penis. The experts also did not question whether the reassigned "woman" would have sexual pleasure with men or women or whether she would consider herself a "normal" female without menstruation or the ability to bear children.

When a sex change is done for male-to-female transsexuals, it is done with their informed consent. This child was not old enough to give consent and, in fact, as of age 13, had not yet been told about the sex reassignment. Given the higher status of males, it is possible the child might have preferred to remain a male even without a penis. On the other hand, perhaps he would have chosen to be a functional female rather than a maimed male. What would you have done?

After the sex change, the parents changed the "girl" twin's clothing and hairdo. "She" was also encouraged to help her mother with housework, in contrast to her brother. Although the "girl" had many tomboyish traits, she was encouraged to engage in less rough-and-tumble play than her brother and to be quieter and more "ladylike." The boy responded by being physically protective of his "sister" (Money & Ehrhardt, 1972).

This case appeared to provide strong evidence that most traditional gender differences are socially learned. However, when the twin was seen at age 13 by a new set of psychiatrists, she was said to be beset by problems (Diamond, 1982). The reports stated:

> At the present time the child refuses to draw a female figure and when asked to draw a female, refuses, saying it's easier to draw a man.
>
> The child . . . has a very masculine gait, er, looks quite masculine, and is being teased by each group that she attempts to make overtures toward . . . they will call her cavewoman and they make reference to the fact that she is not particularly feminine.
>
> At the present time, she feels that boys have a better life. That it's easier to be a boy than it is to be a girl. She aspires to masculine occupations, wants to be a mechanic. (Diamond, 1982, p. 183)

This latter statement might be made by many adolescent girls (see Chapter 7).

This case disappeared from public scrutiny for many years. It resurfaced in both the medical archives (Diamond & Sigmundson, 1997) and as a somewhat sensational article in *Rolling Stone* titled "The True Story of John/Joan" (Colapinto, 1997), and as a popular book, *As nature made him: the boy who was raised as a girl* (Colapinto, 2000). Contrary to earlier reports of Joan's femininity, her twin reported:

> "I recognized Joan as my sister," Kevin says, "but she never, ever acted the part. She'd get a skipping rope for a gift, and the only thing we'd use that for was to tie people up, whip people with it. Never used it for what it was bought for. She played with my toys: Tinkertoys, dump trucks. Toys like this sewing machine she got just sat."
>
> "When I say there was nothing feminine about Joan," Kevin laughs, "I mean there was nothing feminine. She walked like a guy. She talked about guy things, didn't give a crap about cleaning house, getting married, wearing makeup. . . ." (Colapinto, 1997, p. 64)

At 18 years of age, Joan sought and received surgery to reconstruct a penis and scrotum. She also had a mastectomy to remove the breasts created by her treatment with estrogens. At age 23 he married a woman three years his senior who had three children. He works in a well-paid factory job and enjoys taking his adoptive sons on fishing trips. He has an acceptable sexual life, but unnecessary medical treatment has taken its toll. The original accident prevented John from fathering children without artificial intervention. Subsequent castration made it impossible for him to father children in addition to reducing his sexual pleasure. He resents it now and regrets these losses.

Other XY males assigned and raised as girls have also run into problems (Diamond, 1999). In a long-term follow-up, one researcher stated that two years into his study, all six children were closer to boys than girls in their attitudes and behaviors. Two of them spontaneously (without being told about their chromosomal status) switched back to being boys. He commented that it would be wrong to say that these children wished to be boys or felt that they were boys in girl's bodies; they believed they were boys (Reiner, quoted by Colapinto, 1997). In contrast, boys with a very small penis who are reared as boys appear to live sexually satisfactory lives as heterosexual males without surgery (Diamond, 1999). Studies like these have led the American Academy of Pediatrics to announce that medical staff and parents should refrain from immediately assigning a gender to newborns with genital abnormalities until the child's condition can be thoroughly reviewed (American Academy of Pediatrics, 2000).

Dealing with Genital Anomalies

Intersex individuals have begun to question the rigid two-sex system. Some have joined with the Intersex Society of North America (ISNA), which publishes a newsletter and maintains an excellent website. This group's goal is to "end the idea that it is monstrous to be different" (Colapinto, 1997). Some of its members have publicly acknowledged their genital ambiguities to help others to see them as people rather than as medical curiosities. Members of the group include Cheryl Chase, a leading activist, who was born with a somewhat vaginalike opening behind a male-like urinary tract and a phallic structure that could be described as either an enlarged clitoris (if she was assigned as a girl) or a small penis (if assigned as a boy). See "Making a Difference" on p. 153 for more about Chase.

A major aim of ISNA is to abolish all cosmetic genital surgery on infants. Physicians have assigned sexually ambiguous infants to a sexual category based largely on how well they could construct an adequate genital appearance and function for a member of that category. Their assumptions are sexist—with an emphasis on sexual function for those who are ascribed as males and on reproductive function for those who are labeled females (Dreger, 1998; Fausto-Sterling, 2000; Kessler, 1998). Their decisions to assign an infant as a male or a female have been largely based on the size of the infant's phallic structure. Figure 5.6 shows the size difference between a medically acceptable penis and a clitoris—one and a half centimeters (Kessler, 1998). Most people are not aware of how large a "normal" phallic structure should be. When, for example, college students were interviewed about the normal phallic size of newborn girls and boys, they imagined a much smaller size gap between the largest clitoris and the smallest penis than physicians did. The researcher asked: "Would people like these notice that an infant's genitals were the 'wrong' size unless told so by a physician?" (Kessler, 1998, p. 100).

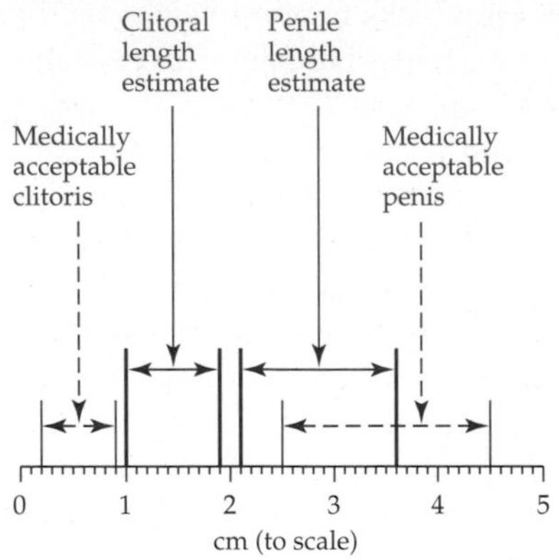

FIGURE 5.6. The size of a normal penis and clitoris at birth and students' estimates of the size of newborn's penis or clitoris.

The language used by physicians to describe the genital anomalies of newborn infants illustrates commitment to a two-sex schema. They described an overly large clitoris as "disfiguring and embarrassing" and stated that, "Female babies born with an ungainly masculine enlargement of the clitoris evoke grave concern in their parents." And they indicated that they would attempt to preserve the capacity for erotic stimulation and sexual gratification if it "does not interfere with cosmetic, psychological, social, and sexual adjustment" (Kessler, 1998, pp. 35–37).

Genital anomalies are rarely life threatening. Newborns are unlikely to be embarrassed by them. And newborn infants cannot consent to surgery that may have irreversible effects on their ability to enjoy sex or have children. The surgery appears to be designed to help parents deal with cultural norms that dictate they must have a boy or a girl. A growing number of experts argue that surgery should be withheld until the child has formed a sexual identity and can give his or her informed consent (Diamond, 1999; Gruppuso, 1999; Kessler, 1998).

Changing Identity

Transsexualism

Tens of thousands of people firmly believe that they were born with the bodies of the wrong sex. This phenomenon is known as *transsexualism.* Many *transsexuals* maintain that they have been discontented with their identity from earliest childhood. Their belief is not easily influenced by any form of psychological therapy.

These people are not psychotic. They are not confused about the actual biological condition of their bodies, but believe that their psyches are consistent with the body of the other sex. A number of transsexuals have had successful careers before seeking gender reassignment. For example, Jan Morris, a well-known writer, was James Morris and wrote the story of her transition from male to female in the best-selling book *Conundrum* (1974). Rene Richards (pre-

FIGURE 5.7. Deirdre McCloskey—a noted economist—who shifted from male to female. Some feminist economists worry whether her egalitarian views on economics will be taken seriously now that she is a woman.

viously Richard Raskin), an eye surgeon, made headlines when she attempted (unsuccessfully) to play on the women's professional tennis circuit after having played on the men's circuit. More recently, well-known economist Donald McCloskey and important pianist David Buechner became Deirdre McCloskey and Sara Buechner (Jacobs, 1998; Wilson, 1996). (See Figure 5.7).

It has been estimated that there are 30,000 transsexuals worldwide, 10,000 of whom are believed to live in the United States (Grimm, 1987). Male-to-female transsexuals appear to outnumber female-to-male transsexuals, but this estimate may be inaccurate because many female-to-male transsexuals do not opt for genital surgery (since it is expensive and an acceptable-looking penis is almost impossible to construct). They often self-masculinize by using testosterone (Devor, 1996). Other researchers believe that the reason for the sex disparity is that primarily androcentric cultures are less accepting of variant masculine role behaviors. Thus, men who deviate in some ways may come to feel that they are not men at all. In contrast, it is socially acceptable in many countries for women to wear pants, carry briefcases, and enjoy sports. What would people think about a man who wears dresses, carries a purse, and enjoys needlepoint?

People who are *sexually dysmorphic* (whose self-concept does not fit their sexual biology) may range from those who simply dress in the other sex's attire in the privacy of their homes (known as *cross-dressers*) to those who undergo extensive surgery to make their bodies consistent with their psychological sex.

Clinics that perform sex-change surgery usually require the individual to live successfully as a member of the other sex for at least a year. "Passing" seems to be more a matter of attire, hairstyle, voice, mannerisms, and gestures than any extensive physiological change. In fact, it has been estimated that two-thirds of the cross-dressing population have not gone as far as surgery but are nonetheless living as members of the other sex on a full-time basis (Grimm, 1987). They typically take years to change sex and go through a gradual readjustment to their changing body image and societal reactions to it (Bolin, 1996).

Transsexuals do not necessarily transcend traditional masculine-feminine dichotomies. Until recently, many male-to-female transsexuals adopted an exaggerated stereotypical version of feminine dress and behavior. They wore more elaborate clothing and makeup than most women. In *Conundrum,* Jan Morris (an ex-war correspondent who went on expeditions to Mount Everest) tells how she liked to be helped on and off trains with her luggage following sex-change surgery.

The medical establishment appears to encourage such stereotyping. The more feminine the appearance and behavior of the applicant, the more likely his request for surgery will be granted. Male-to-female transsexuals are required to divorce their spouse before sex-change surgery to prevent a legal lesbian marriage (Bolin, 1996). Surgical treatment of transsexuals actually confirms traditional social constructions of masculinity and femininity. It opts for massive, permanent changes in the body rather than acceptance of the idea that roles and bodies may be independent and that the connection is imposed by the cultural standards for each sex.

Follow-up reports on sex-change surgery indicate relative satisfaction with the new body. Change in sexual orientation is less consistent. In one intensive study of seven male-to-female transsexuals, only one was exclusively heterosexual (defined by attraction to biological males). Three were exclusively lesbian and lived with women who did not define themselves as lesbian, one was bisexual living with a self-defined lesbian, and two were living with each other (Bolin, 1996).

Some reports from those who have undergone sex-change surgery highlight the importance of gender roles in ways that may be invisible to those who have not changed sex. In one study, female-to-male transsexuals complained of their difficulty in finding intimacy in their friendships with men, although they had no difficulty establishing or maintaining sexual or romantic relationships with women (Devor, 1996). Another study found that women who took a male body gained in economic status, whereas men who took a female body lost status (Blanchard, 1985). Even for the same person, being a man (no matter how it is achieved) is associated with a higher income.

The Transgender Movement

Some transsexual and intersex individuals have moved from personal to societal change. The *transgender movement* challenges an obligatory two-sex system and argues that transgender people must be viewed as people rather than as sexual curiosities. They question the idea that there is any necessary relationship between gender, the genitals, and other markers of sexuality. They want to create a worldview that allows for the possibility of numerous genders and multiple social identities (Bolin, 1996; Califia, 1997).

Some of these people do not want to call themselves "women," but do not want to become "men." One of the most visible and articulate proponents of this viewpoint is Kate Bornstein, a male-to-female transsexual who wrote *Gender Outlaw: On Men, Women and the Rest of Us* (1994). Here is the way she describes herself:

> I know that I'm not a man, about that much I am very clear, and I've come to the conclusion that I'm probably not a woman either, at least not according to a lot of people's rules on this sort of thing. The trouble is, we're living in a world that insists we be one or the other—a world that doesn't bother to tell us exactly what one or the other is. (Bornstein, 1994, p. 8)

Bornstein calls the idea that "we are trapped in the wrong body" a myth:

> I'll bet that's more likely an unfortunate metaphor that conveniently conforms to cultural expectations, rather than an honest reflection of our transgendered feelings. (Bornstein, 1994, p. 66)

Those in the transgender movement question the need for people to be equipped with penises and vaginas appropriate to their gender and suitable for heterosexual intercourse. They often violate the rules by which sex and gender are constructed in our society. Many people find their questioning of the "natural" order disturbing. But rules about what a particular sex can wear and with whom they may have sexual relationships have changed greatly over time and often appear quite arbitrary (Fausto-Sterling, 2000). (See Figure 5.8).

Gender Blending and Body Image

The transgendered movement aims to change society. But many individuals who question sex or gender are more concerned about their own personal choices and lives. Women appear to be much more flexible in many aspects of sex than men are. They appear to be more able than men to maintain same-sex or bisexual orientations without questioning their fundamental identity as women (Devor, 1996). Of course, they are also permitted much more latitude in gender roles. For these reasons, women appear to be much less active than gay men and male-to-female transsexuals in the transgender movement.

Some women represent themselves as men without engaging in any kind of medical or surgical treatment. One example was Billy Tipton—a jazz musician who lived as a man until he died (Middlebrook, 1998). Tipton married several times and engaged in sexual activity with his wives, who claimed to have been unaware of his femaleness. There are also women who are often mistaken for men but see their sex as female and their gender role as compatible with being a woman. They may or may not be lesbians. These women do not pass as men in a consistent or purposeful fashion. But because of their height, body build, and nonverbal behaviors, they are often mistaken for men or boys during brief impersonal encounters (Devor, 1987).

Gender-blending women (such as those described in the preceding paragraph) often explain their gender nonconformity by saying that they oppose traditional standards of femininity and like the advantages they gain through maleness. For example, as men they gain freedom of movement, a feeling of safety on the streets at night, and safety from the threat of rape.

FIGURE 5.8. This cartoon is not funny! Cartoon history of changes in views about intersexuality.
Source: "Managing Intersexuality—an Historical Perspective" from *Sexing the Body: Gender Politics and the Construction of Sexuality* by Anne Fausto-Sterling. Copyright © 2000 by Basic Books, a member of the Perseus Books Group. Reprinted by permission of Diane DiMassa and Basic Books, a member of Perseus Books, L.L.C.

How can women be mistaken for men? Men are the unmarked or normative gender in our culture. Thus, individuals who do not clearly designate themselves as women by their clothing, cosmetics, and adornment will be perceived as men unless the physical markers of femaleness are overwhelmingly

FIGURE 5.9. In order to portray the sexes as biological opposites, we ignore fairly common exceptions to the rules. Frida Kahlo was willing to portray herself with a faint mustache—a female characteristic that is omitted from portraits of less beautiful (or honest) women.

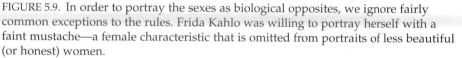

obvious (Devor, 1996). Gender-blending women demonstrate how, in everyday life, sex may be irrelevant to the ascription of gender. Assumptions about the separateness of the sexes permit people to explain away any lingering misaligned bodily cues. For example, a prominent chest on a woman who has been identified as a man may be seen as large pectoral muscles or simply fat on the upper body. Similarly, facial hair is ignored in a woman (see Figure 5.9). Women who suffer from polycystic ovarian syndrome—a disorder which produces menstrual irregularities, infertility, and heavy hair growth on the face and body—regard the hair growth as the worst part of the disorder (Wilmott, 2000).

Gender-blending women are neither transsexuals nor do they suffer from any kind of biological disorder. However, their lives illustrate the social pressures that produce ambivalence about gender. As girls they enjoyed physical activity, and they were tomboys throughout their early years. The majority played mostly with boys or were loners (these stories are similar to those told by female-to-male transsexuals and some lesbians as well). About half of the gender blenders came from homes where their fathers acted as though they would have preferred them to be sons. Many were tall. This combination of behavioral preferences and physical characteristics appears to have led them to become "gender blenders."

Body image may play an important role in the development of sexual identity. Physical attractiveness in childhood has been associated with the development of a feminine gender identity in boys (Zucker, Wild, Bradley, & Lowry, 1993). Girls with a masculine gender identity are perceived as less attractive than feminine girls by raters who are unaware of their gender identification (Fridell, Zucker, Bradley, & Maing, 1996; McDermid, Zucker, Bradley, & Maing, 1998). One of the more obvious (but frequently neglected) truisms in the study of the biological bases of behavior is that one cannot remove the organism from his or her environment. The organism's body structure (and in the case of human beings, social reactions to that structure) forms part of that environment.

If individuals' gender identity conflicts with desirable bodily norms for a member of their sex within a society, they may have gender identity problems. Lack of attractiveness is a major stigma for females in our society. Girls with CAH who were *virilized* (made more biologically male) showed higher masculinity scores than their less-affected counterparts (Zucker, 2001). It should not be surprising, therefore, that unattractive Joan would reject her feminine role. It is a simple fact of binary logic that if you feel everything is wrong the way you are, maybe the correct way is the other way.

CULTURAL CONSTRUCTIONS OF GENDER

Not all cultures agree with the idea that all people are either men or women. Earlier in this chapter we discussed the alternative sexual category of "Turnim man." Other traditional societies, such as the Zunis, also see sex as naturally malleable. They believe that a series of interventions, begun before and continuing after birth, are necessary to ensure that the child will have a sex (Roscoe, 1996). Many Native American societies constructed alternative genders, independent of a person's physical body.

One such category is called the *berdache*—biological males who adopted the clothes and some of the roles of women and who had sexual relations with other men. They could, however, revert back to the masculine role without penalty or switch back and forth between roles. Male berdaches have been documented in nearly 150 North American Indian societies (Roscoe, 1996). Their behavior does not fit our society's norms for homosexuals, transvestites, or transsexuals (Williams, 1987). For example, berdaches do not appear to question their biological maleness, and they do not invariably cross-dress. In their societies, not all homosexuals are berdaches. Moreover, berdaches were not expected to have sex with each other, but only with "normal" males.

One extensive participant-observer study of berdaches concluded that some traditional Native American societies are neither as biologically reductionist nor as bipolar in their gender system as current Western cultures are (Williams, 1986). The berdache can be seen as a third, alternative gender. This gender was defined by occupational role, not biology. (Berdaches were often involved in creative arts and crafts and were seen to be especially talented and original.) This gender was often conferred by religious authorities before the child was physically mature. Spiritual authorization was more important than cross-dressing, and many berdaches dressed in combinations of male and female attire (Roscoe, 1996). In contrast, some transsexuals in our society are very uncomfortable about combining male and female attire (Hill, 2000).

The berdache role is part of a broader gender system of male and female inequality. In Native American societies that valued the berdache, women also had high status. Men who became berdache had an enhanced status. Because women were valued, androgyny was allowed to men. In contrast, if women were devalued by the society, feminine characteristics in men were denied and the berdache role was not an institutionalized part of these American Indian cultures (Williams, 1986). Fewer than half the societies that had male berdaches had female berdaches—women who acted out some aspects of the masculine role (Roscoe, 1996). This omission may also be related to status. It is difficult for women to acquire the privileges of maleness.

Interestingly, a category for "social males" exists in isolated rural villages of Albania and Montenegro (part of what used to be Yugoslavia). Under certain special circumstances—for example, when there are no surviving male children—a young woman may be permitted to wear men's clothing and do the work of a man, including military service (Gremaux, 1996). Such women are known as "pledged virgins" rather than "women" (see Figure 5.10). They gain the legal and social status of men by giving up sexual experience.

FIGURE 5.10. Albanian pledged virgin who had served in the military. In a number of cultures, sex is determined by the ability to reproduce, and sex assignment may be more flexible for those who do not engage in sexual activity.

Alternative cultural arrangements involving differing assumptions about what constitutes sex and the potential of additional sex/gender categories are quite common in non-Western societies. Many Polynesian societies have a category of "gender liminal" persons who are thought to excel in artistic skills such as weaving mats. Although they cross-dress occasionally and have sex with men, their membership in the category is determined by their behavior in domestic and social areas. Like the berdache, they can opt out of the category through marriage (Besnier, 1996).

There have also been studies of *hijiras*—a sect found in northern India. Men became hijiras through their impotence with women. Hijiras include individuals who would be defined as intersex, transsexual, or homosexual in our own society. What is important about hijiras is their legitimized role in a society that defines personhood in terms of the ability to reproduce. They are seen as "not men" because their male organ does not work and as "not women" because they cannot bear children. In earlier periods, the group had religious functions and were supposed to castrate themselves and dedicate their "useless male organs" to a mother Goddess. Currently, many hijiras hide the fact that they have kept their genitals (which would make them unfit for religious rituals) and function mostly as prostitutes who take the receptive role with other men. They wear women's clothing, prefer women's occupations, and take female names. Unlike traditional Indian women, however, they also engage in dancing, cursing, and smoking in public (Nanda, 1996).

Varying cultural constructions of sex and gender are intriguing. They provide alternatives to current beliefs about a stable biological core to which one simply adds deviations to broaden the picture. Instead, they show that sex can be unstable and culturally specific.

The simple word *sex* hides great complexity. Sex is used to refer to reproductive category, physiological properties, reproductive and nonreproductive behaviors, and, in human beings, our sense of who we are. It also refers to a system of categorization that differs from one culture to another.

But even if discussion is limited to the biological aspects of sex, it is probably impossible to determine what causes a person to be male or female. Instead, think about sex as neither entirely nor permanently male or female. The view that the sexes are opposite to each other is just one of many possible viewpoints. Sexual dichotomies are a result of both androcentric and ethnocentric bias. It may sound strange, but try thinking about "all" the sexes rather than the two sexes for a while!

CONNECTING THEMES

- *Gender is more than sex.* Just as gender is more than just sex, "sex" is more than just sex, too. Studies of various animal species and sexually anomalous human beings indicate that an individual's sex is a composite of biological and social factors. Probably no one single factor determines maleness or femaleness.
- *Language and naming are sources of power.* The assumption that males and females are "opposite" sexes is a good example of the power to name. Beliefs about biologically determined differences between the sexes are

maintained by the media's attention to findings about the anatomical bases for such differences and its lack of attention to social and environmental factors.

- *Women are not all alike.* All cultures do not think about sex and gender the same way we do. Human beings with the same biologically induced anomalies may have different experiences based on their culture's beliefs about sex and gender. The connections between biology, physical appearance, social roles, and sexual preference may be neither stable nor universal.
- *Psychological research can foster social change.* Biology is a double-edged sword in the cause of social change. For example, biological arguments can be used to define homosexuality as morally acceptable (because it is not a matter of choice) or as a reason to commit mass murder (homosexuals were routinely killed by the Nazis because of their alleged biological inferiority). Equality is a political and social issue, not a biological one. Whatever their biology, everyone deserves equal rights under the law.

SUGGESTED READINGS

FAUSTO-STERLING, ANNE. (2000). *Sexing the body: Gender politics and the construction of sexuality.* New York: Basic Books. This book is by a molecular biochemist who is one of the leading critics of reductionist views of sex. It is current, knowledgeable, and clearly written.

KESSLER, SUZANNE J. (1998). *Lessons from the intersexed.* New Brunswick, NJ: Rutgers University Press. A brief and clearly written book that takes a critical look at the medical response to intersex infants and the social assumptions that underlie medical and surgical practices.

LEGUIN, URSULA. (1969). *The left hand of darkness.* New York: Ace Books. This award-winning science fiction novel takes place in a world in which the same person can be either male or female. It challenges our assumptions about the relationship between sex and gender.

CHAPTER 6

Becoming Gendered: Childhood

- **Acquiring Gender: A Developmental Perspective**
  Social Learning
  Gender Schema
  Interactive Models of Gender Development
- **How Do Parents View Sons and Daughters? Gender Bias**
  The Preference for Sons
  Attributions about Infants
  The Eye of the Beholder: Fathers' versus Mothers' Perceptions
  The Gendering of Emotion
  The Socialization of Helplessness
- **How Does Society Foster Gender Typing?**
  Gender and Children's Clothing
  Gender and Toys
  Sexism in Books for Children
  Gender and Animated Cartoons
  The Impact of Gender Labels
  Learning Adult Roles
- **Sex Segregation**
  The Development of Single-Sex Groups
  The Impact of Peers: Group Dynamics and Gender Differences
  Social Mechanisms for Maintaining Boundaries
  Social Dominance and Social Influence
- **The Socialization of Social Behaviors**
  Aggression, Assertiveness, and Dominance
  Facilitating Male Aggression
- **Gender Role Scripts for Boys and Girls**
  Learning to be Male
  The Values of Being a Tomboy
  Negative Aspects of Hyperfemininity
- **Resisting Gender Rules**
  Flexibility Begins at Home
  The Effect of Ethnicity and Class
  The Case for Positive Social Deviance
- **Connecting Themes**
- **Suggested Readings**

Early one midsummer's night, Daddy Sam settled on the plush gold carpet in the nursery to play with Baby while the evening bath was being prepared. Reaching for Baby's teddy bear, he slowly and rhythmically bounced it toward

Baby, softly saying, "Here comes Teddy! Teddy's coming to see you! Look, look at Teddy. He's coming to play with Baby." Giggling in delight, Baby opens her arms to hug the oncoming teddy bear. Next door, a different Daddy and a different Baby played on the nursery floor. Holding Baby's teddy bear, Daddy John marched the bear resolutely toward Baby in a series of quick, controlled movements, mock growling, "Here comes Teddy! Teddy's coming to *get* you! Better get Teddy, before *he* gets *you!*" Screeching at the challenge, Baby reaches out and tumbles on his now captive Teddy. (Brooks-Gunn & Mathews, 1979, pp. 5–6)

What does this scenario show? Even when fathers are apparently playing the same game, they can treat infant boys and girls differently. And it shows how babies respond to the behaviors of their parents. Even in infancy, gender does not exist in a social vacuum.

How do babies become gendered? At first glance the answer to this question seems obvious—infants are born either male or female. As Chapter 5 discussed, however, that answer is misleadingly simple. Most children can be assigned an unambiguous sex based on their anatomy at birth. But are they also born with the behavioral tendencies considered characteristic of that sex? There is only weak documentation for behavioral differences during the first weeks of life, and few consistent sex-related differences appear during the first year. Nevertheless, by the time they are 2 years old, most children can label their own gender correctly, recognize many gender stereotypes, and show traits and behaviors considered appropriate for their own gender. By the end of childhood, girls and boys differ in their personality traits, preferred roles, and beliefs about their future lives. This chapter examines both theories and research that explain in detail how children acquire gender.

ACQUIRING GENDER: A DEVELOPMENTAL PERSPECTIVE

A number of theories try to explain what happens during the early years that leads to the establishment of gender. Most researchers no longer try to explain the development of gender differences in terms of psychodynamic processes (cf. Freud, 1933/1965). One exception is Nancy Chodorow, whose ideas were discussed in Chapter 4. The focus in this chapter is on two theories that have generated a great deal of empirical research on how children learn to be boys and girls. Although neither social learning nor gender schema theory explains all the processes by which children acquire gender, together they explain a great deal.

Social Learning

Social learning theories explain children's development of gender identity and gender-typed behaviors as the result of moment-to-moment, day-to-day interactions between the developing child and his or her immediate social environment—mother, father, and other caretakers; the media; school; and playmates. This theory proposes that gender typing, just like other social and cognitive behaviors, is learned through reinforcement, punishment, observation, and imitation.

There is considerable evidence that parents do reward and punish some behaviors differently for girls and boys. You can probably think of examples from your own experience. Our students tell us that, in their families, boys were less likely to be punished for being messy or careless and more likely to be rewarded for achievement in sports and school. Girls were rewarded for being thoughtful of others' feelings, looking pretty, and taking good care of their possessions and appearance. These students' memories are consistent with systematic research.

Considerable evidence also supports the view that children learn by imitation. A classic study illustrates how children might learn to be aggressive through both reinforcement and imitation (Bandura, 1965). In this study, children were shown one of three films. In all the films, an adult behaved aggressively by hitting and kicking a large toy clown. In one film, the adult was rewarded; in another, the adult was punished; and in the third, no specific consequences followed the aggression. The children were then given the opportunity to play with the toy clown. Just as social learning theory predicts, children imitated the aggressive behavior most when it had been reinforced; that is, children who had seen the first film were more aggressive than those who had seen either of the other films. Overall, boys were more aggressive than girls. In the next part of the experiment, children were offered small treats for performing as many of the adult model's aggressive behaviors as they could remember. Here, all children were more aggressive, and girls were, overall, nearly as aggressive as boys.

The experiment shows that children do imitate adult models even when the children are not directly reinforced for doing so. In particular, they imitate models who are themselves reinforced. Furthermore, children may learn a behavior through observation but show no evidence of that learning until the behavior is reinforced—like the girls in the second part of the experiment.

The second major claim of social learning theory is that children identify with—and therefore imitate—their same-sex parent in preference to the other parent. Although it sounds reasonable, little evidence supports this idea (Bussey & Bandura, 1999). Children do not selectively imitate their same-sex parent.

Gender Schema

A second major theory about how children become gendered is based on *gender schema,* which are knowledge structures about aspects of sex and gender that guide thinking and behavior. Gender schemas encourage children to behave consistently with the gender to which they are assigned (Martin & Dinella, 2001). The processes through which children conceptualize sex and gender during development and how these knowledge structures guide their thinking and behavior are the focus of schema theory.

Children develop gender schema because society places such a heavy emphasis on gender distinctions. These distinctions encourage children to pay attention to, remember, and use information about gender. Almost from birth, sex is a salient perceptual distinction. For example, infants as young as 3 months of age look at photos of male infants longer than at those of female infants (Shirley

& Campbell, 2000). Between 8 and 12 months of age, infants look at a slide of an adult female face associated with a high-pitched voice longer than at slides that mismatch images and voices (Poulin-Dubois, Serbin, Kenyon, & Derbyshire, 1994; Patterson & Werker, 2002).

It is not clear how infants develop the ability to make gender distinctions or even what cues they use to make them. But it is clear that young children acquire an astonishing amount of information about gender categories by the time they are two years of age. They look at stereotype-inconsistent photos more than at consistent ones; they select gender-appropriate dolls when imitating male or female adult activities; and they can sort photos by gender (Powlishta et al., 2001). Recent studies suggest that children show an awareness of gender categories as early as 18 months of age (Powlishta, Sen, Serbin, Poulin-Dubois, & Eichstedt, 2001).

Children understand some things about the concepts of sex and gender long before others. By the time children learn to speak, they have already acquired *gender labels.* This term refers to the child's ability to categorize correctly his or her own sex or that of another person. In one study, by 24–28 months, 61 percent of the children tested could correctly label their own gender and 54 percent could correctly label other children's gender (Campbell, Shirley, Heywood, & Crook, 2000).This stage is called *gender identity.*

Next, children learn how to categorize by means of gender. In its simplest form, this means linking gender labels to objects, traits, and behaviors. When a child learns to "know" that dolls are "girls' toys" or that "boys like to play rough," he or she is using a simple gender schema. Such schemas can be used to organize the child's own preferences for play, toys, and even playmates. By the time children are between [illegible] and [illegible] months of age, they show a great deal of knowledge about gender-appropriate toys and clothes; they also prefer gender-appropriate toys as well as same-sex playmates (Martin & Little, 1990).

Many children have developed rudimentary stereotypes about the sexes by the age of 30 months. The stereotypes involve appearance (girls have long hair); emotions (girls cry a lot), and behaviors (boys play with trucks). Children also remember information better when it is consistent with their own sex schema, such as the actions of a child who is the same sex as themselves (Martin & Dinella, 2001).

Later, children acquire the concept of *gender stability*—the idea that one's sex remains stable over time. Before this stage the child may believe that boys can grow up to be mommies and that people can change sex by changing their hair styles or clothing. At age 2, one of our own children maintained stubbornly that the "real" difference between boys and girls was that only girls wear barrettes!

Usually around 7 years of age, children develop an understanding of *gender constancy*—they know that gender is permanent (P. Smith, 1987). Gender constancy is not a simple result of social learning. It requires a certain level of cognitive maturity before a child knows that she or he is, and always will be, one sex or the other. Recent studies suggest that the age at which children achieve gender constancy is not related to their awareness of gender stereotypes or other concepts involving gender (Powlishta, Sen, Serbin, Poulin-Dubois, & Eichstedt, 2001).

Gender schema are complicated, and knowledge in one area may not reflect knowledge in another. Researchers have not found a relationship between preferences for gender-appropriate toys and activities (*gender typing*) and accurate labeling of one's own sex (Campbell, Shirley, & Cargill, 2002). Children's level of gender understanding also does not appear to be well related to their degree of gender typing (Hort, Leinbach, & Fagot, 1991; Golombok & Fivush, 1994; Martin, 1999).

Gender schemas do not develop in the same way for every child, and some gender differences are puzzling. In general, girls seem to develop schemas about gender-appropriate labels and roles earlier than boys do, whereas boys acquire gender stereotypes (especially those prescribing male activities) at an earlier age than girls. Many kinds of information about gender are missing from the schemas of both boys and girls during the earlier stages of cognitive development.

Children's gender schemas are not the same as those of adults. Preschool children exaggerate differences between males and females and see them as opposites. Some researchers have characterized this kind of thinking as *essentialist* (see Table 6.1). Hair length, clothing design, color, and choice of accessories are cultural mechanisms designed to polarize the sexes. It takes a long time before children recognize that these differences are the result of social decisions rather than physical laws. When preschoolers accept the idea that children who violate gender rules exist, they view them negatively, even as morally wrong (Gelman & Taylor, 2000). Until the age of 9 or 10, children see gender as similar to physical characteristics—as an intrinsic property of human beings (Taylor, 1996). Only later do they perceive that social factors may influence gender.

Young children develop gender schema that are much broader than simple toy selection and play preferences. For example, when preschoolers were asked whether objects were more likely to be associated with one sex than the other, they believed that bears were for boys and butterflies were for girls (Leinbach,

TABLE 6.1. Essentialist versus nonessentialist views about the nature of gender differences.

Essentialist	Nonessentialist
Discovered	Invented
Biological	Social
Inherent in individual	Product of social interaction
Unalterable	Easily changed
Enduring	Transient
High inductive potential	Low inductive potential
Nonobvious/underlying differences	Superficial differences
Universal	Individual
Mutually exclusive traits	Overlapping traits
Alpha bias (exaggerating male-female differences)	Beta bias (minimizing differences)

Source: From S. A. Gelman & M. G. Taylor (2000, p. 172). Gender essentialism in cognitive development (pp. 169–190). In P. H. Miller & E. J. Scholnick (Eds.), *Toward a feminist developmental psychology.* NY: Routledge.

Hort, & Fagot, 1997). They also believed that tall fir trees were for boys and rounded maple trees were for girls. In another study, researchers painted a tea set brown and put spikes on the teapot. They cut off the mane of a long-haired pastel pony, painted it black, and gave it spiked teeth. All of the children said these were boys' toys, and several of the boys said they wanted them for Christmas presents (Hort & Leinbach, 1993).

Interactive Models of Gender Development

The processes that mold gender are truly developmental in nature. Both the age of the child and the social environment to which the child is exposed must be taken into account. Seemingly identical social messages do not have the same meaning at different ages. The child changes in reaction to these messages and, consequently, interprets them differently. In this sense, the meaning of gender is a function of both gender schemas and social learning. Information about gender distinctions is everywhere and children use this information to develop gender schemas. Because learning gender schemas is equivalent to learning social norms, there are few individual differences, and children acquire a sense of their own gender in quite orderly stages (see Table 6.2).

Societal definitions of what is gender-appropriate behavior change as the child matures. For example, most people do not expect little girls to wear makeup and high heels, although some think it is "cute" when they do so. But adolescent girls who refuse to wear makeup may be labeled as unfeminine. The process by which gender is constructed is *interactive,* which means that development reflects a continuing interplay between the child and the environment.

Boys and girls are treated differently even before birth. Differential treatment produces behavioral and cognitive differences that, in turn, lead to different social consequences for each sex, making them still more different. Think of the process of gender construction in terms of the saying, "As the twig is bent, so the tree will grow." Little differences become larger as the child grows, until one forgets that the sexes were originally not very different at all.

Children are acutely aware of both their similarities to and differences from others (Powlishta, 1995a). They use this information to help construct a sense of self. The media provides many opportunities for children to learn messages about gender-appropriate appearance, roles, and behaviors. Partly because of the repetition of these messages, gender becomes a central dimension in the way children classify themselves and others. Thus, although gender typing may appear to be due to children's cognitive stage, it is also a reaction to the gender distinctions made by everyone around them.

Most cultures are not neutral about sex and gender. Female traits, roles, and behaviors are less highly valued in most, if not all, societies. As girls become aware of the relative status of masculinity and femininity, they may also recognize the economic and occupational advantages of being male. How then do girls come to value their devalued role enough to want to follow it? Many girls are "tomboys" throughout middle childhood. This identity is a major site of resistance to the devalued aspects of being female.

In the rest of this chapter, we take a closer look at the processes through which children become gendered. Depending on the age of the child, sometimes social learning and sometimes cognitive mechanisms are more important. There

TABLE 6.2. Percentages of Children Showing Gender-Related Behaviors

Task	Age of child (in months)			
	18 mos.	24 mos.	30 mos.	36 mos.
Cognitive skills				
Gender self-labeling (percentage correct)		68%	88%	93%
Labeling of friend		43%	37%	39%
Nonverbal sorting (placing pictures in boxes)	48%	56%	69%	84%
Sorting to verbal cues	22%	67%	90%	96%
Correct use of gender words				
Mom/Dad		98%	97%	100%
boy/girl		75%	88%	98%
man/woman		53%	79%	94%
he/she		42%	79%	91%
her/him		27%	63%	83%
Stereotype learning				
Clothes (percentage identifying correctly)		37%	59%	74%
Toys		24%	38%	53%
Tasks		—	32%	39%
Occupations		—	27%	35%
Preference behavior				
Percentage of time spent with same-sex toys	32%	42%	45%	62%
Percentage of time spent with other-sex toys	25%	25%	25%	21%
Percentage of same-sex photo choice as playmate			33%	52%
Sex of actual playmates (percentage same sex)		57%	67%	73%

Source: From P. A. Katz, "Raising Feminists," *Psychology of Women Quarterly, 20,* pp. 323–340.

is no period in a child's life when he or she is free from messages about gender. Although the specific mechanisms involved may vary, some themes recur throughout childhood:

- Males are the more valued sex.
- Pressure for conformity to gender roles occurs earlier and is stronger for boys than for girls throughout the childhood years.
- Parents appear to be largely unaware of the extent to which they treat their young sons and daughters differently.
- Differential treatment of boys and girls appears to be consistent with producing a pattern of independence and efficacy in boys and a pattern of emotional sensitivity, nurturance, and helplessness in girls.

- The child is not a passive recipient of gender socialization but actively participates in this socialization through his or her views of self, expectations, and behavioral choices.
- People are largely unaware of how the culture as a whole mandates dichotomies based on gender and punishes those who do not conform to social expectations.
- All social subsystems—parents, teachers, peers, and especially the media—provide consistent models of gender difference.

Look for these patterns from birth through the middle years of childhood.

Although the meaning of gender changes as the child grows, not all changes represent progress. Children acquire more and more gender biases as they mature. This means that the majority of children become increasingly sexist and, thus, fit "better" into a sexist world.

HOW DO PARENTS VIEW SONS AND DAUGHTERS? GENDER BIAS

The Preference for Sons

Gender before Birth

Even before a child is born, gender stereotypes are at work. There are many folk recipes for determining whether a pregnant woman is carrying a boy or girl. These predictions are, of course, correct 50 percent of the time. They include ideas about the pregnant woman's placidity, complexion, and health as well as the level of activity of the fetus. The birth of a girl is predicted by more negative or less desirable characteristics.

These folk beliefs about pregnancy mirror a widespread preference for males. There is still some preference for male children in the United States and Canada, although this changed greatly during the latter part of the twentieth century. The stated preference for sons appears to be due primarily to men's responses. In one study, 86 percent of male college students surveyed said they would prefer a son if they could have only one child, whereas only 42 percent of the female students had such a preference (Pooler, 1991). Men preferred sons over daughters for their firstborn child, as the majority in a three-child family, and as their only child (Hamilton & Mayfield, 1999). Like men, women preferred a firstborn son and sons as the majority in three-child families but did not prefer a son as their only child. Only pregnant couples did not indicate this preference for males.

A recent survey of Canadian women found that most had no preferences about the sex of first or subsequent children. However, among those women with a sex preference, more preferred a firstborn son than a daughter (McDougall, DeWit, & Ebanks, 1999).

Stated responses may, however, underestimate the actual preference for firstborn sons. Behavioral studies indicate more male favoritism. For example, a study in Germany videotaped the equivalent of a day's interactions between mothers and fathers and their 3-month-old infants. As expected, parents spent more time with firstborn than later-born children, but they spent more time with firstborn sons than daughters (Keller & Zach, 2002).

Although the preference for sons may be declining in North America, it is still strong in the developing world. Surveys in Botswana, Tunisia, and Morocco indicated that women, as well as men, prefer sons (Campbell & Campbell, 1997; Obermeyer, 1996). This desire for sons is strongly associated with the desire to ensure the survival of at least one male child. In Israel, when infant survival was ensured, the preference for males and for a larger number of children declined (Okun, 1996).

Preference for boys is most extreme in Asian countries such as Korea and Taiwan and in the Middle East. Daughters are described as "water spilled on the ground" in Taiwan and as "maggots in the rice" in China. In some Arab cultures, an unexpected pause in the conversation might be followed by the comment, "Why the silence? Has a girl been born?" (Sohoni, 1994). The reasons given for the preference for sons were similar in all the countries investigated: continuation of the family name, economic reasons (including support of parents in old age), and as companions for fathers. In all the countries surveyed, men showed a greater preference for boys than women did (Arnold & Kuo, 1984).

Selective Mortality: The Missing Girls

Probably the most compelling evidence demonstrating the preference for sons are data on voluntary abortion. Advances in prenatal sex determination allow parents to learn the sex of their prospective offspring during the first few months of pregnancy. In Asian societies, where the preference for sons is most extreme, selective abortion of female fetuses is also extreme. Estimates indicate that several million female fetuses were aborted in Asia during the last two decades of the twentieth century (Miller, 2001).

Sex-selective abortion is not officially sanctioned. In India, for example, ultra-sound tests for the purpose of abortion have been banned. However, the practice has barely gone underground, and signs advertising ultrasound tests are quite visible (Dugger, 2001). Early figures from the 2001 census indicate that the number of female fetuses being aborted continues to increase, especially in the richest states, where more people can afford tests and abortions (Dugger, 2001). In one cluster of villages, the number of female births has dropped to 770 per 1000 male births.

Sex-selective abortion is consistent with ancient cultural norms permitting female infanticide (Watts & Zimmerman, 2002). Evidence of female infanticide has been found as early as the first century B.C. in ancient Greece (Rouselle, 2001). Sex-biased infanticide has been practiced by about 9 percent of the world's cultures, and more often than not, the unwanted sex has been female (Hrdy, 1988).

The preference for males is also expressed less directly through discrimination. In a number of cultures, boys are breast-fed twice as long as girls (see Figure 6.1). In many societies, men and boys eat first, and whatever is left is then distributed to the women and girls. Invariably, women and girls eat less food, which is of inferior quality and nutritive value (United Nations, 1991b). Based on demographic information, the United Nations has estimated that more than 100 million females are missing from the world's population (Sen, 1990).

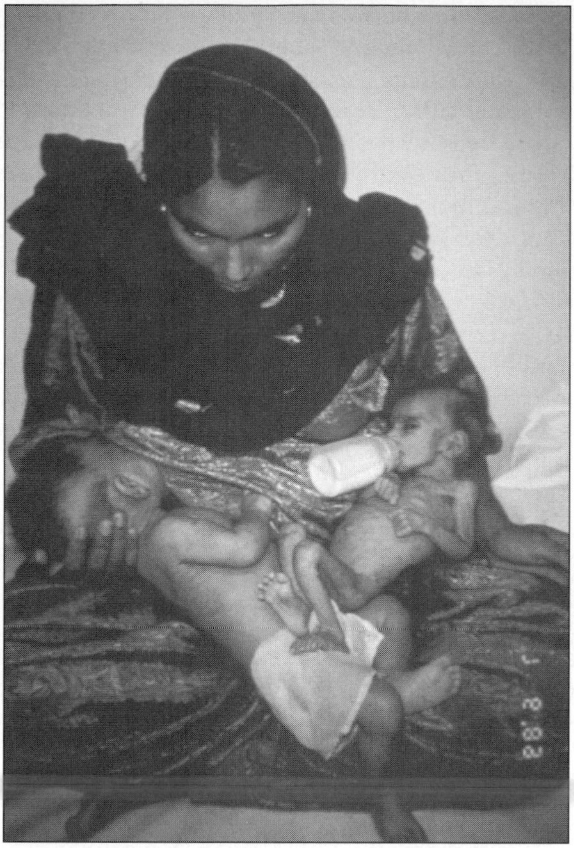

FIGURE 6.1. A mother's grief. This photo from Islamabad, Pakistan, tells a poignant story about the age-old bias in favor of the male child. The child being bottle-fed is a girl. Her twin brother was breast-fed. The woman was told by her mother-in-law that she did not have enough milk for both the children, so she should breast-feed the boy. The infant girl died the next day.

The selective preservation of male infants is beginning to have major social consequences in those countries where it has been practiced most intensively (China, South Korea, and India). According to estimates from the Chinese Academy of Social Sciences (Agence-France Press, 1999), with the current gender ratio of males to females, 111 million Chinese men—a number greater than the entire population of Mexico—cannot hope to find a wife. We presume that this will make daughters more valuable, but it is impossible to predict what other impact such an excess of males will have on this society.

Attributions about Infants

Many characteristics besides sex could be used to describe an infant, such as its size, its coloring, the presence or absence of hair, and so forth. But popular culture mandates attention to the sex of the newborn. When one of the authors had her first child, she found it impossible to locate a gender-neutral birth announcement.

One innovative birth announcement compared the baby to a new model car. Nevertheless, even this relatively gender-neutral announcement was pink and proclaimed "It's a girl!" rather than "It's a beautiful baby!"

The sex of a child is his or her most conspicuous feature at birth. A study conducted in English delivery rooms found that 82 percent of the parents' comments within twenty minutes of the baby's birth were made about the infant's sex (Woollett, White, & Lyon, 1982). Fathers more than mothers differentiate between their newborn sons and daughters (Power, 1981).

Parental stereotyping of their children begins at birth. Parents rate newborn daughters as finer-featured, less strong, more delicate, and more feminine than newborn sons (Karraker, Vogel, & Lake, 1995). Mothers use more neutral terms to describe their infant one week later, but fathers continue to use gendered descriptors. Fathers' stereotyping of infants has declined recently but has not disappeared.

Even birth congratulation cards reflect gender stereotypes. One study looked at girl and boy cards from eighteen stores in four municipalities (Bridges, 1993). Visual images of activity were more commonly shown on boy cards; verbal messages of sweetness and sharing were more likely on girl cards.

Despite these different responses to females and males, young infants show few, if any, consistent sex-related differences. One exception is activity level. Meta-analysis indicates that male infants are more active than female infants. The researchers argue that this difference appears to be biologically based (see Chapter 5). However, expectations and experiences probably act on this small biological difference to produce the much larger gender differences in activity found during childhood (Campbell & Eaton, 1999).

A recent experimental study demonstrates how expectations may influence children's motor performance. The researchers found that the mothers of 11-month-old boys overestimated their performance in a novel situation (crawling down steep and shallow slopes), whereas the mothers of girls underestimated their performance. In fact, the girls and boys had identical levels of motor performance (Mondschein, Adolph, & Tamis-LeMonda, 2000). In later childhood, gender differences in motor performance emerge, but this study shows that they do not do so in a social vacuum.

The Eye of the Beholder: Fathers' versus Mothers' Perceptions of Young Children

Although behavioral differences between baby boys and girls are minimal, parents treat their sons and daughters differently from the earliest days of life. Parents consistently promote differences in activities and interests in their sons and daughters. They also respond differently to girls' and boys' emotional and social behaviors.

The evidence for gender-differentiated socialization is stronger today than it was fifteen years ago, in part because researchers have paid greater attention to the role of fathers. Meta-analysis of a large number of studies indicated that fathers differentiate between their sons and daughters much more than mothers do (Lytton & Romney, 1991). These studies may even be underestimating the extent of fathers' gender traditional beliefs. More traditional fathers have been found to be under-represented in research on families (Costigan & Cox, 2001).

Gender stereotypes are maintained even as children grow older and display individual differences in their behavior. In a sample of parents of 2-year-olds in Great Britain, for example, fathers more than mothers saw their children as conforming to gender stereotypes (McGuire, 1988). Boys, in particular, were stereotyped by their fathers. More than two-thirds of the boys' fathers saw them as very masculine, whereas only 40 percent of the girls' fathers saw them as very feminine. Even for these very young children, the commonest masculine attribution was physical ability or athletic skill. Feminine attributes for girls usually involved comments about physical attractiveness, appearance, caring doll play, gentleness, and doing housework.

There is evidence that parents' gender ideology has an impact on their sons' and daughters' behavior. A recent meta-analysis found a relationship between parents' gender beliefs and their children's behavior (Tenenbaum & Leaper, 2002). Specifically, parents with more traditional gender beliefs were more likely than parents with more nontraditional beliefs to have children with gender-typed cognitions about themselves or others. This relationship was present in children at almost every age—from one year through college.

The Gendering of Emotion

How do parents communicate their expectations and beliefs about gender? A great deal of recent research has focused on parent-child conversations in the early years. Again, parents differ in their interactions with their daughters and sons.

When parents were asked to tell their 4-year-old child stories about growing up, fathers told more stories with autonomy themes to sons than to daughters, and gender-traditional parents told more stories with achievement themes to their sons than to their daughters (Fiese & Skillman, 2000). The researchers were particularly struck by the prevalence of "getting into trouble" stories told by fathers to their sons. These stories may be meant as warnings about the dangers associated with independence, but they also provide models of male autonomy.

Parents also treat emotions differently in conversations with daughters and sons. Parents used a greater number and variety of emotion words when talking to their 40-month-old daughters than when they spoke to sons of the same age (Kuebli & Fivush, 1992). Although 4-year-old girls and boys did not differ in their emotional vocabulary, by 70 months of age the girls used a larger emotional vocabulary than the boys did (Adams, Kuebli, Boyle, & Fivush, 1995).

Parents also tend to emphasize different emotions when they talk to their daughters and sons. They mentioned the sad aspects of events more with girls than boys (Kuebli & Fivush, 1992). In home visits, researchers asked each parent separately to talk about four specific past events during which their 40- to 45-month-old child experienced happiness, anger, sadness, and fear (Fivush, Brotman, Buckner, & Goodman, 2000). Both parents discussed the emotional aspects of sadness more with girls than boys, although the girls were not talking about sadness more than the boys. By middle childhood, however, when girls narrate their experiences, they report feeling sad more than boys do (Buckner & Fivush, 1998). It is possible girls are learning to ruminate about sadness—a process that has been associated with depression (see Chapter 14).

Conversational style influences children's understanding of the relative importance of particular experiences. For example, children whose parents elaborated about the past in conversations (which occurred more often in conversations with daughters than sons) remembered more about their experiences (Reese, Haden, & Fivush, 1993). When children are in preschool, mother-daughter dyads were found to be much more likely to discuss other children and their behaviors than were mother-son pairs. Mothers were especially likely to make emotional references when discussing interpersonal relationships with their daughters (Flannagan & Perese, 1998). In contrast, the mothers of sons had more emotionally elaborate discussions on topics related to learning (Flannagan, Baker-Ward, & Graham, 1995). Thus, girls may be learning that other people's feelings are an important part of their school day, whereas boys may be learning to focus on achievement.

In short, gender-differentiating communications are part of the way parents do gender with their children. The emotions expressed are consistent with gender stereotypes discussed in Chapters 2 and 3. Boys are encouraged to model achievement, independence, and autonomy, whereas girls are encouraged to model emotionality in general, interpersonal closeness, dependency, and sadness.

Children also acquire beliefs about emotions that are consistent with this pattern of parental socialization. Preschoolers of both sexes were found to believe that females were much more likely to feel sad than were males and that men were incapable of expressing sadness (Karbon, Fabes, Carlo, & Martin, 1992). They also believed that men became angry more frequently and intensely than women did.

Are boys more likely than girls to get angry? Social location appears to be a better predictor of anger than gender. Compared with rural youngsters, urban children reported more anger in their responses to hypothetical situations such as being hit with a stick by accident or not being invited to a party (Buntaine & Costenbader, 1997). However, boys from both locations reported more aggressive responses (such as hitting, kicking, and punching) than girls, whereas girls suggested sulking and pouting as responses to the same experiences. Boys were also less likely to consider intent. They expressed the same level of anger regardless of whether the event was due to an accident or happened on purpose.

Females of all ages (6–12, 14–16, and adults) also reported more fear than males in response to stories portraying frightening or anger-provoking situations (Brody, Lovas, & Hay, 1995). Both sexes reported more fear of males than females. However, girls' fear of both sexes was more intense than boys' fear of males. Females of all ages felt more vulnerable than males did. Their sense of vulnerability may be due to their lower status and power, their smaller physical size, or their socialization as the "weaker sex."

The Socialization of Helplessness

Both parents and other adults appear to believe that girls require more help than boys. Studies in the home have found that fathers are more likely to hold their year-old daughters in contrast to their sons and to give them toys (Snow, Jacklin, & Maccoby, 1983). An observational study of families visiting a zoo, an amusement park, or a nursery rhyme theme park reported that male toddlers were more likely to be allowed to walk alone than female toddlers were (Mitchell, Obradovich, Herring, Tromborg, & Burns, 1992).

The belief that little girls need help more than little boys do was dramatically illustrated by a clever experiment titled "Sex Differences: A Study of the Ear of the Beholder" (Condry, Condry, & Pogatshnik, 1983). While performing an unrelated task, young men and women heard a tape recording of an infant waking up next door. They had previously been told that the infant was a boy or a girl. Although they denied any belief about differences in fragility between girls and boys, the young women responded more quickly to a "girl" than to a "boy." Young men responded equally slowly to infants regardless of their gender.

Children also act on gender stereotypic emotional cues associated with helplessness. When 10- to 11-year-old girls and boys were given a scenario involving helping a friend who was angry, sad, or fearful, sadness was given almost exclusively as a reason for helping. Both boys and girls were less willing to help an angry friend. This study informs us as much about acceptable emotions as about perceived need. Sadness (associated with females) was seen as a reason for help, whereas anger (associated with males) was seen as a reason to deny help. A sex difference in helping was found for only one emotion: fear. When the protagonist was described as fearful, boys were especially likely to give this as a reason for *withholding* help (Terwogt, 2002). Because at this age, friends are almost always of the same sex as the child, boys may be stigmatizing other boys for admitting to fear.

If girls are seen as sadder and more fearful than boys, they will be helped more quickly and more often. By being taken care of more often, girls learn that they are needier than boys. Greater adult assistance confirms their belief in their own helplessness.

By the time they are 4 years of age, girls have been found to be more willing than boys to ask for help from a teacher in solving a difficult puzzle (Thompson, 1999). There were no gender differences in puzzle-solving ability. Moreover, girls' help-seeking did not predict their ability to solve the puzzle, although boys' help-seeking did. Early experiences with the results of help-seeking may have already reinforced girls' and boys' beliefs about their self-efficacy. These experiences lead to self-fulfilling prophecies in which girls are more willing to present themselves as helpless and then have their beliefs confirmed by help from others. These girls receive less valid feedback about their abilities than the boys whose help-seeking behavior appears to be determined by their current needs.

HOW DOES SOCIETY FOSTER GENDER TYPING?

Gender and Children's Clothing

Gender-typed messages are everywhere. Without making the request explicit, researchers on child development find it is virtually impossible to get parents to provide a neutral environment when dressing their young child. For example, even in the first few days of life some infant girls are brought to the laboratory with pink bows tied to their wisps of hair or taped to their little bald heads.

One set of researchers categorized the clothing found on infants in shopping malls. Baby girls were dressed in pink, puffed sleeves, ruffles, and lace, whereas boys were dressed in blue or sometimes red, but nothing ruffled or pink (Shakin, Shakin, & Sternglanz, 1985). Similar gender-related differences in clothing colors have been found among young children in French-speaking Canada (Pomerleau, Bloduc, Malcuit, & Cossette, 1990).

Gender-typed clothing ensures gender-appropriate treatment from strangers. (If you want to see for yourself just how important this aspect of appropriate identification is, deliberately "mis-sex" an infant the next time you are in a public place.) Few if any behaviors distinguish infant girls and boys. In neutral clothing it would be difficult to tell them apart. Knowledge of their sex may not be sufficient to guarantee that strangers react differentially to them. A review of studies involving neutrally clothed infants who were labeled either "male" or "female" indicated that adults did not consistently react differently to them based on their label (Stern & Karraker, 1989).

Appropriate distinctions are very important if two genders are to be constructed (see Figure 6.2). Gender-appropriate behaviors must be elicited from the infant and reinforced when they occur. Girls' more delicate and restrictive attire can inhibit play and promote gender-stereotypic behavior.

Costumes for apparently gender-neutral celebrations such as Halloween also show how images for little girls and boys are managed and mandated. In a fascinating study titled "The pink dragon is female," one researcher analyzed 469 ready-made costumes for children, as well as those offered as sewing patterns (Nelson, 2000). Less than 10 percent of the costumes were gender-neutral. Girls' costumes clustered in a narrow range depicting beauty queens, princesses, and other exemplars of traditional femininity, from "Colonial Belle" to "Blushing Bride" or "Pretty Mermaid" (see Figure 6.3).

In contrast, boys' costumes depicted characters battling historical, contemporary, or supernatural opponents, such as "Bronco Rider," "Dick Tracy," "Sir Lancelot," "Hercules," or "Servo Samurai." Boys were also more likely to portray villains such as "Captain Hook" or "Rasputin," and monsters, such as "Frankenstein" or the "Wolfman."

There was an especially large gender difference in costumes depicting agents of death, such as "Dracula," "Devil," or "Grim Reaper." These boys' costumes were often embellished with weapons, blood, or body parts. The names

FIGURE 6.2. No comment.
Source: Jump Start by Robb Armstrong. Reprinted by permission of United Feature Syndicate, Inc.

FIGURE 6.3. There may not be quite as much unanimity among real-life girls as is shown in this comic strip, but girls' Halloween costumes clearly differ in meaning from those of boys. Try making your own observations next Halloween.
Source: Cathy. Copyright © 1996 Cathy Guisewite. Reprinted with permission of Universal Press Syndicate. All rights reserved.

of the few costumes for female villains emphasized their erotic nature—"Sexy Devil" or "Bewitched"—or their harmless charm—"Little Skull Girl" or "Pretty Little Witch."

These differences applied to children's costumes for every age. Although Halloween costumes may seem like harmless fun, they are again providing models of appropriate gender roles that are difficult for children to evade. It is also interesting that although everyday children's clothing appears to be relatively neutral (jeans are only subtly gendered), expensive clothing for children, such as those advertised in the Sunday *New York Times Magazine,* show great gender differentiation in the same direction as Halloween costumes (see Figure 6.4).

Gender and Toys

Who Gets What?

Most parents deny any intention to distinguish between their sons and daughters, but gender stereotyping in toy selection can take place without parental awareness. Researchers examined the furnishings and toys found in the rooms of forty-eight boys and forty-eight girls under the age of 6 on the assumption that whatever differences were found would indicate parental ideology regarding gender (Rheingold & Cook, 1975). Gender differences in several categories of toys were impressive. The number of vehicles for the boys was 375 versus 17 for the girls. No girl's room contained a wagon, boat, kiddie car, motorcycle, snowmobile, or trailer. Only eight of the boys' rooms contained a female doll, compared with forty-one of the girls' rooms.

FIGURE 6.4. Girls are fragile princesses and boys are superheroes—complete with fake muscles. Even everyday clothing for children are gendered. This boy can easily get ice cream on his jacket, whereas the girl's lollipop looks more like a fashion accessory.

A study conducted fifteen years later (Pomerleau et al., 1990) found similar, although somewhat less dramatic, gender differences in these two categories of toys for younger children ranging from 5 through 25 months of age. Girls had 3.9 dolls compared with an average of 1.2 for boys. Boys, in contrast, had an average of 10.3 small vehicles each, whereas girls had 3.5. There were no differences between girls and boys in the number and variety of toys.

After many years of relative neutrality, toy marketing has become aggressively gender-biased in recent years. A story in *The Wall Street Journal* recounted the experiences of one mother who went to Toys "R" Us to buy a train for her 3-year-old daughter (Bannon, 2000). She found two new toy sections in her suburban megastore—one labeled "Girl's World" with magenta shelves stocked with dolls, kitchen toys, and makeup kits and another labeled "Boy's World" with red shelves filled with action figures, Tonka trucks, and walkie-talkies. The trains were, of course, in the boys' section. The mother said she felt as if she had been transported back to the 1960s.

Toys and Tots: Teaching Preferences

Marketers believe that it is again safe to emphasize gender differences in products and pitches aimed at children (see Figure 6.5). Marketers claim that they want to "celebrate" the differences between girls and boys, but their products create gender-typed play patterns that have long-term implications. Mattel made headlines when it marketed a pair of gender-specific computers for children ages 4 to 12:

> The pink-flowered Barbie computer and the royal blue Hot Wheels computer each came packaged with 20 software titles. But many more of the titles in the Hot Wheels package were educational—leading to public criticism of the toy company. Mattel said it wasn't trying to slight girls, but that there are simply more Barbie software titles than Hot Wheels software available, and so there wasn't as much room in the Barbie package for educational titles. (Bannon, 2000, p. B1)

In view of massive gender distinctions, it should not be surprising that many children display gender-stereotyped toy preferences by 18 to 24 months of age. Parents encourage gender-typed play both directly and indirectly. At age 2 most boys and girls will play with trucks, blocks, and kitchen utensils, but parental responses to this play may vary with gender. Both mothers and fathers are more likely to pay attention to the block play of their sons than of their daughters.

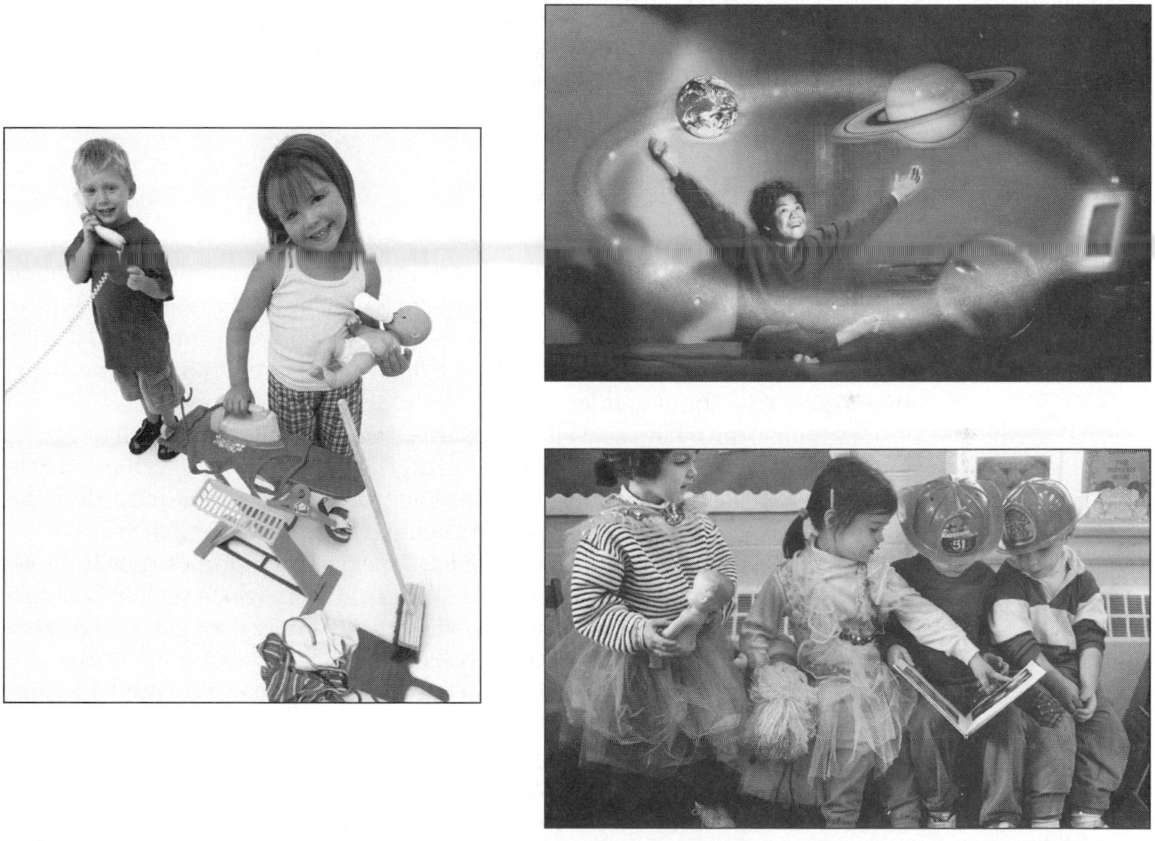

FIGURE 6.5. Toys communicate preferred activities and future roles. These ads are examples of "his," "her," and "their" toys. The latter category is very interesting because boys and girls are equal only in imaginary scenarios. Even when they are together in the kitchen, he is talking on the phone. It is unfortunate that these ads cannot be reproduced in color since the amount of pink in ads for girls' toys is quite sickening.

One study videotaped parent-toddler pairs playing with six different sets of toys for 4 minutes each (Caldera, Huston, & O'Brien, 1989). The parents' initial nonverbal responses to the toys were more positive when the toys were stereotyped for the child's and parent's sex than when they were not. Children showed greater involvement when playing with stereotypically gender-appropriate toys, even when parental behavior was taken into account. They were less interested in gender-inappropriate toys even when no alternative toys were available. Some parents had difficulty complying with the instructions to play with all the toys: "One father with his daughter opened a box of trucks, said 'Oh, they must have boys in this study,' closed the box, and returned to playing with dolls" (Caldera et al., 1989, p. 75).

Different types of toys elicit different kinds of play. As we have shown, different toys are made available to girls and boys from an early age. But even very similar toys can provide cues for gender-different behaviors. In one study, parents were provided with two baby dolls and a stuffed clown and were asked to play with their 20-month-old toddler for 4 minutes (Caldera & Sciaraffa, 1998). Parents of girls called more attention to the dolls, whereas parents of boys called more attention to the clown. They also played with these toys differently. Regardless of the sex of the child, baby dolls elicited more nurturance and caretaking from the parents than the clown did. In other words, parents who give their children baby dolls are also providing them with lessons in stereotypic feminine behavior.

Sexism in Books for Children

Where do children acquire gender stereotypes? They are learned from parents and peers, but like adult stereotypes (Chapter 2), they can also be found in every form of media designed for children. The most obvious source of information about the gender appropriateness of toys comes from toy advertisements. But toy commercials are only the tip of the iceberg in terms of powerful covert messages about gender-appropriate roles and behaviors.

Traditional fairy tales as well as modern stories for children are full of gender stereotypes. In many fairy tales, women are especially desirable when they are passive. In some, like "Snow White" or "Sleeping Beauty," they are most desirable when they are unconscious. Disney's feature cartoons for children, such as *The Little Mermaid, Beauty and the Beast,* and *Aladdin,* appear to provide more positive roles for females, but closer scrutiny reveals the old narrative in which selfless, beautiful girls are rewarded by the love of a prince they barely know (Douglas, 1994).

Analyze some of your favorite fairy tales from a feminist perspective. You may find yourself asking whether anyone in her right mind could possibly want to be a fairy-tale princess. They are either passive victims or decorative figures or must die in order to be loved. If they resist these roles, they are punished or portrayed as evil or mad (Sapiro, 1994).

Despite improvements, readers for the early school years still portray many gender-stereotyped roles. As in traditional fairy tales, a common theme is the female character's need to be rescued. (When not rescued by boys or men, she is rescued by an animal.) "Girls are shown as being very brave while waiting for rescue, but they still cannot help themselves out of trouble" (Purcell & Stewart, 1990, p. 184). Boys, in contrast, almost never have to depend on anyone.

Early reading texts also stereotype personality traits. A recent study of readers for first, third, and fifth graders found that male main characters are much more likely to be portrayed as aggressive, argumentative, and competitive than female characters. Males are also less likely to be shown expressing affection or tender emotions. Nearly 30 percent of female main characters, but only 8 percent of male characters, were shown as passive (Evans & Davies, 2000). It is also troubling that a number of stories involved out-of-control boys and angry men. The researchers concluded that male and female characters are being portrayed the same way they were twenty years ago.

The story is much the same in picture books. A recent analysis of award-winning picture books for children found, for example, that males continue to be portrayed as more powerful and active than females (Turner-Bowker, 1996). When females or female animals appear in book illustrations, they are less likely to be alone than are male characters (Gooden & Gooden, 2001). Most of the female roles remain traditional ones, such as mother, grandmother, or washerwoman, although some women were shown as doctors, chefs, and milk vendors. Males were rarely shown as caring for children or shopping for groceries and never as doing housework (Gooden & Gooden, 2001). However, even when there were no differences in roles, females were portrayed as passive-dependent as often as they were fifty years ago (Kortenhaus & Demarest, 1993). Young girls were still valued for their beauty, whereas older women were characterized as hags or witches or given barely visible domestic roles.

Gender and Animated Cartoons

The characters in animated cartoons also model gender stereotypes. In one study, male characters were found to appear more frequently, to be given more prominence, and to talk significantly more than female characters (Thompson & Zerbinos, 1995). They also displayed more ingenuity, were more often both the perpetrators and the victims of physical and verbal aggression, showed more leadership skills, interrupted more, and so on. Female characters were more often shown as attractive, affectionate, and concerned about interpersonal relationships. Males were more likely than females to be shown in some sort of recognizable job (31% of the time as compared with 13% of females). Female characters were shown as caregivers 46 percent of the time, whereas males were never shown in this role.

The researchers noted some improvements in the treatment of female cartoon characters. Since 1980, the number of main female characters has risen, and females are portrayed in somewhat less stereotypic ways. But male characters continue to do everything much more than female characters do because they appear so much more often.

The Impact of Gender Labels

Do the Media Matter?

It is difficult for children to avoid or evade stereotypic images. Are children influenced by these representations?

When children aged 4 through 9 were interviewed, they recognized that there were more males than females in cartoons and that the males talked more as well as engaged in more violent and silly/amusing behavior than females (Thompson & Zerbinos, 1997). Girls were more sensitive to the subtle interpersonal messages being communicated. Boys did not see the violent activities in cartoons as having anything to do with their relationships with girls, whereas girls saw the male characters as teasing and making fun of girls. Girls made comments such as "boys think they are the smartest" and "try to catch girls." Boys described the girl characters as "going out on dates," "follow what boys say," and as saying "I'm pretty."

Other research suggests that what children see and hear through the media does make a difference. Children who watch commercial rather than educational TV have been found to have a greater knowledge about gender stereotypes (Bigler, 1997). Watching commercial TV is also associated with gender-role rigidity in the way children distort or forget stereotype-inconsistent information (Signorella, Bigler, & Liben, 1993). Children who watched the most TV (four or more hours per day) had the most stereotyped views about appropriate work for females and males (Signorielli & Lears, 1992). Those children who noticed the largest number of stereotypes on TV also selected more gender-stereotypic jobs for themselves (Thompson & Zerbinos, 1997). For boys, the most frequently selected jobs were firefighter, police officer, and athlete; for girls, nurse and teacher. Boys whose favorite cartoons were continuing adventures selected more masculine-stereotyped occupations than other boys.

Are the gender differences in children's clothes, toys, and media portrayals mirrored in children's own behavior? Years of detailed studies by scores of researchers offer us portraits of just what that behavior is. How do boys and girls differ in the toys they prefer and in the games they play? When and how do these differences develop, and how do children respond to the implicit demands that they follow gender labels in their choices?

Gender-Typed Preferences

Psychologists can measure children's preferences at an early age with nonverbal methods. For example, 18-month-old children look longer at photos of gender-typed toys—dolls for girls and vehicles for boys (Serbin, Poulin-Dubois, Colburne, Sen, & Eichstedt, 2001). By 24 months of age, toddlers look longer at stereotype-inconsistent photos (girls with vehicles or boys with dolls) than at consistent photos (Powlishta et al., 2001). In a further study, toddlers were asked to choose a male or female doll to imitate masculine, feminine, or gender-neutral activities such as shaving, vacuuming, or sleeping (Poulin-Dubois, Serbin, Eichstedt, Sen, & Beissel, 2002). Twenty-four-month-old girls, but not boys, picked male dolls for masculine activities and female dolls for feminine activities. Boys showed their awareness of appropriate gender roles somewhat later—at 31 months.

Although these studies were conducted in Canada, there is reason to believe that they reflect global patterns of gender distinctions. A recent study in France found that 2-year-old girls chose more objects to handle and play with when the objects were related to females (doll, iron, basket, stroller, baby bottle, dressing table, jewels, a tea set, and a store) than when they were related to males (robot, pistol, garage, helicopter, jeep, small airplanes, workbench, construction set, and train). The boys chose equal numbers of objects associated with males and females (Le Maner-Idrissi, 2001).

Preschool-age children have not yet become completely gender-typed, but most children have developed preferences for gender-typed toys and play by age 3. Girls spend significantly more time playing with so-called feminine toys and less with masculine toys, whereas the reverse pattern is found in boys (Powlishta, Serbin, & Moller, 1993). There is, however, considerable within-sex variability and between-sex overlap in play patterns. For example, girls spent 5 to 22 percent of the observed time intervals playing with masculine toys, compared with 5 to 71 percent for boys. In contrast, boys spent 0 to 47 percent of their time playing with feminine toys, compared with 18 to 54 percent for girls.

Girls' toy choices became gender-typed more gradually than those of boys. Only 29 percent of the girls requested stereotypical feminine toys at age 3 versus 73 percent at age 5 (Powlishta et al., 1993). It is difficult to determine whether gender typing in toy preference among young children is a cause of or a response to parental gift-giving behavior. However, children were less likely to receive toys they requested for Christmas when the toys were atypical for their sex (Etaugh & Liss, 1992).

Gender differences in preferences have also been found for all forms of the communications media. Boys as young as 3 to 5 years of age show a greater preference than girls for TV programs with violent content (Cantor & Nathanson, 1997). Girls show more fear than boys in response to frightening scenes on television (Valkenburg. Cantor, & Peeters, 2000). Gender differences are also found in preschool children's preferences for fairy tales. By age 4, girls preferred romantic themes, whereas boys were significantly more likely to prefer stories with violent themes (Collins-Standley, Gan, Yu, & Zillmann, 1996).

When young children gather in play groups, boys are more likely to enact fictional superhero roles shown on TV, such as Power Rangers. Girls are more likely to portray familial characters such as Rug Rats. The overall effect of commercial TV is to promote children's preferences for gender-stereotyped toys and activities (Edwards, Knoche, & Kumru, 2001).

Early gender differences extend to the use of leisure time. By age 3 or 4, girls spend more time than boys on personal care, social interactions, and chores. On weekends, when one might expect that activities depend on individual preferences, girls spent more time on art and music, whereas boys spent more time watching cartoons and playing video games. Gender differences in video game play increased sharply between the ages of 2 to 7 (Huston, Wright, Marquis, & Green, 1999). Diverging interests are most noticeable among older children. Older boys spend more time watching sports programs on TV and playing electronic sports games. Older girls spend more time watching relationship dramas on TV and little time playing video games (Wright et al., 2001). As we discuss later, video games tend to be violent and may contribute to gender differences in aggression.

Gender Labels As Social Demands

By the time they are 3 years of age, children are aware of the socially prescribed nature of the kind of toys with which they play. In keeping with the more rigid demands for gender-role conformity from boys than from girls, three-fourths of all the 3- to 5-year-old boys in one study requested gender-stereotypic toys for Christmas (Robinson & Morris, 1986). A high proportion of slightly older boys (4 to 5 years of age) told interviewers that their fathers would think that playing with feminine toys was "bad" (Raag & Rackliff, 1998). Boys who believed this chose more gender-typed playthings than other boys. The researchers did not have any information about the fathers' actual attitudes, but these boys did not report that anyone other than their fathers would respond to the gender typing of their toys.

Children avoid toys that are considered appropriate for the other sex. When preschoolers were exposed to three boxes of gadgets that were labeled for the same sex, for the other sex, or for both sexes, they explored the gadgets less, asked fewer questions about them, and recalled their names less frequently when they were labeled for the other sex rather than for their own (Bradbard & Endsley, 1983). Children avoid toys considered appropriate for the other sex even when they are very attractive (Martin, Eisenbud, & Rose, 1995). One expert on child development calls this "the hot potato effect." It is probably best illustrated by the following story:

> A boy in their laboratory school had been playing with a race-car and its driver when the driver's helmet fell off revealing long blond hair. The driver was a woman. The boy dropped the race-car like it was a hot potato. (Martin, 1999, p. 49)

In another story about children's responses to gender-inappropriate toys, the researchers who conducted the study reported: "Two boys and six girls overtly reacted to the treatments by (1) seeking reassurance that they could play with the other-sex labeled objects; (2) making negative statements about the other-sex labeled objects ('Yuck, girls!'); and/or (3) refusing to look at, repeat the names of, or move near the table containing the other-sex labeled objects" (Bradbard & Endsley, 1983, p. 257). Such behaviors obviously limit children's opportunities to learn about all aspects of their world (see Figure 6.6).

Boys who engage in cross-gender play are particularly likely to receive less positive attention and more criticism from their peers. They are often ignored and left to play alone. An example of this isolation is provided by an anecdote from another group of researchers regarding a boy

FIGURE 6.6 Gender dichotomies limit the opportunities for girls and boys to play together.
Source: Baby Blues. © Baby Blues Partnership. Reprinted with Special Permission of King Features Syndicate.

> who spent many hours in his preschool class playing with the doll house and furniture. He played alone. Because of parental concern, the teacher inquired what he was doing, only to learn that he was playing "moving man." No one—children, teachers, or parents—could see the sex-appropriate truck for the sex-inappropriate doll house and furniture. (Wynn & Fletcher, 1987, p. 84)

It has been suggested that play is the work of children. Different kinds of toys provide children with different opportunities for the rehearsal of adult roles. Play preferences that become rigidly stereotyped at an early age limit the kinds of experience that children have. It is more difficult to engage in active, adventurous play if one's only toys are dolls. But some girls subvert gender-appropriate toys. The following is a true story that happened to one of the authors of this text. Her 4-year-old daughter demanded a Barbie doll. Her feminist mother reluctantly acceded to the request. You can imagine her delighted surprise when she found her daughter and two friends in the backyard playing with their dolls—they had taken off all the dolls' clothing and were tossing them like darts at a target they had made from a cardboard box.

Learning Adult Roles

Gender stereotypes of toys and play are well known. Toys rated by college students as well as parents as most appropriate for girls were those associated with domestic tasks (a toy vacuum cleaner and kitchen center); beauty enhancers (such as a makeup kit and jewelry); and items useful for child care (a cradle, stroller, and dollhouse). Barbie was number 2 on the list—just below the makeup kit. The toys rated as most appropriate for boys were, in order: football gear, GI Joe, boxing gloves, a Ninja warrior set, toy soldiers, a gun, and a construction set (Campenni, 1999). What messages about future roles and occupations are being conveyed to boys and girls?

Behaviors associated with the nurture of infants and young children appear to be particularly problematic for boys. One early researcher suggested that boys appear to *unlearn* affectionate responses to babies. She found equal amounts of interest and affection for baby humans and baby animals in 3-year-old girls and boys. By age 5, however, boys began to withhold their warm response to young infants, although they continued to show interest and concern for kittens and puppies. The girls' behavior did not change (Berman, 1980). In a later study, children were shown action sequences of children either diapering or shaving a teddy bear. Afterward, some toddler boys refused to play with the diapering props (Bauer, 1993). They appeared to have a clear idea about who was supposed to be doing the diapering—and it was not them!

Some time between 4 and 6 years of age, both black children and white children learn what the "correct" gender-appropriate responses toward infants are. When 5-year-olds were asked to pose for photographs with a same-sex peer and with an infant, girls stood significantly closer, smiled more, and touched the baby more often than boys did (Reid, Tate, & Berman, 1989). The gender differences that appeared when children were asked to enact the same-sex parental role are particularly informative. Girls asked to act as "mommy" moved closer to the infant, while boys asked to act as "daddy" actually stood farther from the infant than when they had posed with the infant without any instructions. This study illustrates why the study of children's play is so interesting. Stereotyped play influences the way children visualize future adult roles. And, as we noted earlier, children's stories seldom show boys engaged in any form of domestic activity.

Views about work outside the home also remain gender stereotyped. When preschoolers were asked what jobs they would like to have when they grew up, girls chose traditionally female occupations such as teacher and nurse, whereas boys chose traditionally male occupations such as truck driver or police officer (Trice & Rush, 1995). The occupations rated as most masculine were car mechanic and airline pilot; most feminine were clothes designer and secretary. In a subsequent study, researchers used these occupations to find out how preschoolers would feel if they had a gender-consistent or inconsistent occupation when they grew up (Levy, Sadovsky, & Troseth, 2000). Both boys and girls reported that they would be happier if they grew up to have a gender-consistent occupation. However, girls also reported more negative emotions associated with the feminine occupations. No boys expressed anger, disgust, or sadness about the masculine occupations.

In another study, 6- to 11-year-old children gave higher status to masculine jobs and expressed greater interest in jobs culturally associated with their own sex. This finding was not due simply to an awareness of gender stereotypes. Older children rated novel jobs shown with male workers as having higher status than the identical jobs portrayed with female workers (Liben, Bigler, & Krogh, 2001).

Similar occupational stereotyping has also been found in Australian children (Durkin & Nugent, 1998). Although most children saw most activities as doable by anyone, 5-year-old boys were least likely to indicate that they could be a nurse, wash clothing, or sew (the most stereotypic feminine activities), whereas 5-year-old girls were least likely to indicate that they could fix cars or put out fires (the most stereotypic masculine activities).

Occupational aspirations became more stereotypic for the same boys as they progressed from the second through the sixth grade (Helwig, 1998). By sixth grade, 93 percent of the boys reported that they aspired to a traditionally masculine occupation. In contrast, stereotypic aspirations declined for girls as they grew older. Although 58 percent of the girls reported interest in a traditionally feminine occupation in second grade, by sixth grade, the figure had dropped to 30 percent. In sixth grade, 49 percent of these girls reported interest in a traditionally male, high-prestige occupation such as vet, doctor, and lawyer.

Parents' behavior that has no obvious relationship to adult careers may influence their children's gender typing of various occupations. For example, girls who were given traditionally feminine chores and toys were found to have more feminine occupational preferences than both girls and boys who were assigned so-called masculine chores (Etaugh & Liss, 1992). Traditional boys' chores (e.g., errand running or lawn mowing) permit more independence and autonomy than traditional girls' chores (e.g., dish washing or taking care of younger siblings). Socialization of gender differences in autonomy begin early. Mothers employ control without autonomy with girls in the early school years (6 to 11), but grant autonomy along with control with boys of the same age (Pomeratnz & Ruble, 1998).

SEX SEGREGATION

The most important consequence of the gender typing of toy and play preferences may be to set limits on the sex of the children with whom a child customarily plays. Throughout their childhood years, children usually play with same-sex peers, a pattern called *sex segregation.* Extensive research shows when and how this pattern develops.

The Development of Single-Sex Groups

Beginning at a very young age, children begin to play more with same-sex peers. Recent observations indicate that same-sex preferences may be appearing at an earlier age than before, possibly because of children's greater exposure to sexist media and their earlier experiences with day-care and other preschool programs. Same-sex preferences now begin as early as 2 years of age (Powlishta et al., 2001). Observations in day-care centers indicate that at this age, girls begin to make friendly overtures to other girls at a level above that of chance. Boys show a preference for same-sex peers about a year later.

These same-sex preferences increase steadily during the preschool years (Martin & Fabes, 2001). By the age of 35 months, 62 percent of the girls and 21 percent of the boys played with same-sex children at above-chance levels (Moller & Serbin, 1996). By the age of 53 months, over 80 percent of the children observed showed clear same-sex preferences. Only 10 to 15 percent of the children's social interaction time was spent with children of the other sex (Martin & Fabes, 2001).

There appears to be little initial relationship between children's preference for same-sex playmates and other measures of gender typing, such as preference for masculine or feminine toys or proximity to a teacher (Powlishta et al., 1993). Same-sex preferences in early childhood appear to be mediated more by *behavioral compatibility* than by cues about gender. Sex-segregating girls were seen by their teacher as more socially sensitive, and segregating boys were seen as more active and disruptive than other children (Moller & Serbin, 1996). Young boys become more aroused than girls in highly physical, competitive contexts and have greater difficulty regulating their arousal (Fabes, 1994; Fabes, Shepard, Guthrie, & Martin, 1997).

Among older preschoolers, same-sex preferences produce as well as reflect sex-related differences in play. Thus, play with same-sex peers was greater during the second semester of an observational study of 4- to 5-year-old children than during the first. The researchers suggested that a *social dosage effect* was operating. For both boys and girls, playing with same-sex peers contributed to more gender-typed behavior (Martin & Fabes, 2001).

By the age of 4 or 5, gender differences in play styles are obvious. When pairs of children were given the opportunity to play with similar toys that were either stereotypically feminine (a doll house and doll figures) or masculine (a pirate ship with figures), pairs of girls tended to engage in *constructive play* (using a plan to reach some goal); pairs of boys were more likely to engage in *repetitive play,* involving simple muscular movements (Neppi & Murray, 1997). Boys' play involved adventurous themes with both kinds of toys, whereas girls had adventures only with the masculine toy. When a girl and boy were paired, there was a tendency for the boys to refuse to follow the leads of girls during play with the pirate ship. These pairs tended to engage in parallel rather than cooperative play, so few attempts at leadership or dominance occurred. Boys' preference for other boys is accentuated when children play physically active and competitive games (Boyatzis, Mallis, & Leon, 1999).

Although these researchers did not report any gender differences in beliefs or behaviors, older boys have been found to maintain sex segregation more than girls do. In one study of 8- to 10-year olds engaged in a puzzle completion task, girls contacted other girls more than twice as often as boys, but boys interacted with other boys by a whopping ratio of forty to one (Powlishta, 1995b). These play patterns are not entirely maintained by different interests; even in sex-segregated groups, children often play with neutral toys and in neutral settings (Martin & Fabes, 1997).

Sex segregation has been found cross-culturally, too (Edwards & Whiting, 1988). As in the United States, it increases from early to middle childhood. Sex segregation is greater when many children are available as potential playmates and when children are in same-age rather than mixed-age groups. Sex segregation is enhanced by games involving territoriality and high physical activity (Kelle, 2000). It is also higher in situations that have not been structured by adults. The separation of girls and boys in friendships and in casual encounters is central to daily life in elementary schools. When they choose seats, select companions for work or play, or arrange themselves in line, elementary schoolchildren frequently cluster into same-sex groups. At lunchtime, boys and girls often sit separately and talk matter of factly about "girls' tables" and "boys' tables." Playgrounds have gendered spaces: boys control some areas and activities, such as large playing fields and basketball courts, and girls control smaller enclaves, such as jungle-gym areas and concrete spaces for hopscotch and jump rope (Thorne & Luria, 1986). In the United States, sex segregation in elementary and middle schools accounts for more separation than race does (Graham & Cohen, 1997).

The Impact of Peers: Group Dynamics and Gender Differences

By the time children reach the first grade, boys and girls are socialized into two virtually nonoverlapping groups of peers. Preference for same-sex companions does not have to be supported by adults. It is maintained by the children themselves.

Sex segregation is partly maintained by children's beliefs about what their peers will think about them. Both preschoolers and children in the early grades of elementary school (between 41 and 82 months of age) believed that others would be more likely to approve of their behavior when they played with same-sex rather than other-sex children (Martin, Fabes, Evans, & Wyman, 1999). This belief became stronger with age. The stronger their belief, the more children played with same-sex partners.

Children not only favor their own sex, but also devalue children of the other sex and avoid activities associated with them. Same-sex peers appear to be the most potent agents in separating the sexes. Both girls and boys patrol sexual boundaries. In one study, whatever their activity, girls responded positively to other girls about twice as often as to boys. Boys responded positively to other boys more than twice as often as to girls, except when the boys were engaged in a traditionally feminine activity (Fagot, 1985a).

When the continuation of an activity was used as the criterion for the effectiveness of the reinforcement, girls were found to be influenced by other girls and by teachers, but less by boys. Boys were influenced by other boys, but less by girls or by teachers. Boys were not influenced at all by girls or teachers if they were engaged in male-preferred activities (defined as rough-and-tumble play or play with transportation toys, large blocks, or carpentry tools). In other words, boys engaged in male-preferred activities appear to have developed a group structure that resists the social demands of anyone except other boys.

The behaviors of children within same-sex groups also support separation of boys and girls. By the time they are in third or fourth grade, children have developed gender-differentiated speech styles. Boys brag and insult their opponents more during both mixed- and same-sex competition (checkers). They are also more verbally aggressive during collaborative play with puppets (Leaper, 1991). Girls talk off-topic, interrupt, and laugh more in same-sex dyads than they do in mixed-sex dyads or more than boys do under any condition. Boys make more demands and use more self-promoting speech in their interactions with girls than girls do. Although boys do not appear to dominate their conversations, girls seem to be less happy and less engaged when they are interacting with boys than with other girls (McCloskey & Coleman, 1992).

Social Mechanisms for Maintaining Boundaries

The avoidance of other-sex playmates is closely controlled by group processes, especially among boys. Boys tease other boys for being a "sissy" more than girls tease other girls for being a "tomboy" (Edwards, Knoche, & Kumru, 2001). Marginal or isolated boys are verbally taunted with the term "fag." Elementary schoolchildren may not understand the adult meaning of the latter term (which they use essentially as a synonym for "nerd"), but sexual idioms are a major resource that children draw on to maintain sex segregation (Thorne & Luria, 1986).

In a context of teasing, the charge that a particular boy "likes" a particular girl (or vice versa) may be hurled as an insult. Children have great difficulty countering such accusations. Here is an example from a conversation with an adult observer in a Michigan school:

> Susan asked me what I was doing, and I said that I was observing the things children do and play. Nicole volunteered, "I like running, boys chase all the girls. See Tim over there? Judy chases him all around the school. She likes him." Judy, sitting across the table, quickly responded, "I hate him. I like him for a friend." "Tim loves Judy," Nicole said in a loud sing-song voice. (Thorne & Luria, 1986, p. 186)

Sexual and romantic teasing reflects social hierarchies. The most popular children and the pariahs—the lowest status, most excluded children—are most frequently mentioned as targets of "linking." Linking someone with a pariah suggests shared contamination and is an especially vicious tease.

Boundaries between boys and girls are also emphasized and maintained by rituals such as cross-sex chasing. When boys and girls chase each other, they become, by definition, separate teams. Group labels override individual identities: "Help, a girl's chasing me!" "C'mon, Sarah, let's get that boy." "Tony, help save me from the girls" (Thorne & Luria, 1986, p. 187).

Sometimes, cross-sex chasing is structured around rituals of pollution, such as "cooties," when individuals or groups are treated as contaminating or carrying germs (see Figure 6.7). Female pariahs—the ultimate school untouchables because of their sex and some added stigma such as being overweight or very poor—are sometimes called "cootie queens" or "cootie girls." On the other hand, "cootie kings" or "cootie boys" do not seem to exist.

In short:

> Gender-marked rituals of teasing, chasing, and pollution heighten the boundaries between boys and girls. They also convey assumptions which get worked into later sexual scripts: (1) that boys and girls are members of distinctive, opposing, and sometimes antagonistic groups; (2) that cross-gender contact is potentially sexual and contaminating, fraught with both pleasure and danger; and (3) that girls are more sexually-defined (and polluting) than boys. (Thorne & Luria, 1986, pp. 187–188).

Heterosexual teasing and oppositional games reinforce patterns of outgroup hostility and ingroup favoritism that remain important in relationships between adult males and females (see Chapter 3). By middle childhood (among children 8 to 12 years old), children respond much more negatively to a provo-

FIGURE 6.7. Fear of female pollution can be found in comic strips as well as schoolyards.
Source: Marvin by Tom Armstrong. © NAS. Reprinted with Special Permission of North American Syndicate.

cation by a peer of the other sex than to a similar provocation by a same-sex peer. Children reported that they liked other-sex provocateurs less and tried less to get along with them (Underwood, Schockner, & Hurley, 2001).

With such social processes operating, it is hardly surprising that friendships between girls and boys among 7-year-olds are very rare (Gottman & Parker, 1987). These rare friendships had been maintained over several years—most commonly since about the age of 3. By age 7 most such friendships had gone underground. The boys and girls seldom acknowledged one another at school but continued to play together mainly in the privacy of their own homes. At what age did you stop associating with the other sex on a regular and public basis?

Social Dominance and Social Influence

Gender differences are also status and power differences. Children learn about gender-related differences in power early. By the age of 3, boys in several Australian day-care centers were found to use high-power strategies, such as the domination of toys or territory, in their conflicts with both boys and girls (Sims, Hutchins, & Taylor, 1998). Girls used such strategies with other girls, but they used lower-power strategies, such as persuasion, in conflicts with boys. These differences are maintained as children get older. At age 7, both black boys and white boys in the United States use controlling acts and domineering exchanges in their interactions with other boys. Girls are more likely to use a mixture of collaborative and informative behaviors with other girls as well as with boys (Leaper, Tennenbaum, & Shaffer, 1999).

The characteristics of boys' play promote their dominance in group situations. For example, researchers examined dominance behavior in groups of four children (two boys and two girls) playing with a movie viewer that was designed to allow only one child at a time to see the movie (Charlesworth & La Freniere, 1983). In these groups, boys generally achieved the dominant position. On the average, boys spent three times as much time in the viewing position as the girls. Another study on all-boy and all-girl groups found that the tactics used to attain dominance differed. Boys usually obtained dominance by shouldering other children out of the way, whereas dominant girls usually managed by greater use of verbal persuasion (Charlesworth & Dzur, 1987). The implication of these studies is that the techniques adopted by dominant girls for gaining control in all-girl groups do not work very well with boys. It should not be surprising, therefore, that researchers consistently find that boys are more influential over group decisions than are girls (Lockheed, 1985).

What does all this mean? Some researchers have suggested that sex segregation is due to incompatibility between girls' and boys' interactional styles (Maccoby, 1998). But these interactional styles may reflect status and power rather than gender differences. Boys' and girls' groups are social categories with different levels of status and power (see Chapter 3). The major problem is not the children's behavior but the cultural system that supports the existence of unequal categories (Thorne, 1993).

Aggression, Assertiveness, and Dominance

Boys are clearly more physically aggressive than girls are from an early age. However, researchers who distinguish between physical aggression and *relational aggression* (disrupting a peer's ability to interact socially) argue that when acts of relational aggression are taken into account, boys and girls may be equally aggressive.

Relational aggression may be more characteristic of females than of males. Relational aggression by preschoolers can take the form of covering one's ears when a peer is talking to signal that she or he is being ignored or telling a peer that he or she will not be invited to one's birthday party unless a toy is shared. Girls are more likely to be the targets of relational aggression, whereas boys are more likely to be the targets of physical aggression (Crick, Casas, & Ku, 1999).

Because of sex segregation, children mostly interact with others who are the same sex as themselves. Sex-related differences in aggression may occur, therefore, because children learn to harm others in ways that will damage the social goals of same-sex peers (Crick & Rose, 2000). Boys' aggression potentially damages the victim's dominance status in his peer group. Girls' hostile acts potentially damage close relationships and feelings of social inclusion. Relational aggressive acts by girls that use a peer's self-disclosure increase from the third through the sixth grade. At the same time, acts of overt physical aggression decline.

Indirect forms of aggression associated with dominance (sometimes called assertiveness) are more characteristic of boys than girls. The socialization of dominance in males begins at an early age. For example, mothers accept greater assertiveness from sons than daughters. They used different ways of dealing with opposition from their 4- to 5-year-old daughters and sons. In turn, their daughters used justifications more and an explicit "no" less than sons did (Eisenberg, 1996). Preschoolers seem to be aware of their parents' gender-differentiated reactions to disobedience. Girls believed that an adult would be more annoyed by a simple "no" than by defiance, whereas boys believed defiant answers were more annoying (Leonard, 1995). Their beliefs were consistent with mothers' reports of what kind of oppositional behavior would produce a confrontation. Boys learn that they can be forceful as long as they do not overtly challenge maternal authority, whereas girls may get into trouble for simple assertiveness.

The line between assertiveness and aggression can be very fine. By the age of 10, boys expect less parental disapproval for aggression than girls of the same age do (Perry, Perry, & Weiss, 1989). Adolescent boys also believe more than girls do that aggression increases self-esteem and that victims do not suffer (Slaby & Guerra, 1988). Male models of successful aggression are readily available (see Figure 6.8). For example, when men engage in violence on television, they are equally likely to hurt others as to be hurt themselves, but for every ten women who hurt others, sixteen women are hurt (Signorielli, 1989).

Compared with girls, boys are socialized to tease more frequently and to handle teasing more effectively (Kowalski, 2000). Teasing is neither trivial nor random. Teasing is more frequent and hostile when initiated by high status and

FIGURE 6.8. Realistic violence from a popular TV show which draws more male than female viewers.

familiar others and by males (Keltner, Capps, Kring, Young, & Heerey, 2001). It is more likely to be used against children who are less popular or who regularly violate rules regarding the maintenance of gender boundaries (Leaper, 2000b).

Boys use at least some forms of covert aggression when they interact with girls. Researchers may have underestimated the extent to which covert forms of aggression regulate contact among children. When third- through fifth-graders were presented with scenarios exemplifying peer harassment, more than a third of the girls and boys reported having had an entrance blocked by someone. More boys than girls reported having someone remark about their "hot outfit" or having people whisper about them as they passed by. More than 75 percent of the boys thought these scenarios would make a boy feel "good" or "proud," whereas only 12 percent of the girls saw them as positive and 10 percent reported that the girl would be afraid. (Murnen & Smolak, 2000). Studies like this suggest that sexual harassment begins in childhood.

Facilitating Male Aggression

Toys and games marketed for boys facilitate aggression. Even elementary school children are aware of the connection. They rate commercials featuring traditional boys' toys as more aggressive than those featuring traditional girls' toys. At the same time, boy-toys were rated by both girls and boys as more desirable than girl-toys (Klinger, Hamilton, & Cantrell, 2001).

When various forms of aggressive play are made available to children—for example, violent video games—both boys and girls who played such games showed more aggression in subsequent observations (Kirsh, 1998). Boys play computer games more than girls and prefer more violent games (Buchman & Funk, 1996; Funk & Buchman, 1996). Although both boys and girls indicated a preference for games with a violent content, boys preferred those with realistic human violence, whereas girls preferred cartoon and fantasy violence. A majority of the boys and about one-third of the girls agreed that "the fighting games are mainly for boys." Playing video games was related to popularity for boys but not for girls. A boy who did not like video games was seen as "not very cool."

Like violence on TV (see Figure 6.8), video games encourage sexism as well as aggression. A recent content analysis of thirty-three of the most popular Nintendo and Sega Genesis games found that traditional gender roles and violence were central to many of the games (Dietz, 1998). In 28 percent of the games, women appeared as sex objects, with large breasts and skimpy clothing. They were also shown crying and needing help, particularly in videos directed at younger players.

Of the thirty-three games sampled, only five (15%) portrayed women as heroes or action characters. And even these women wore stereotypically female colors or clothing. For example, the hero princess in Super Mario II wore a long pink dress and a tiara on her long hair. About the "best" thing that could be said about these videos is that there were no females at all in 41 percent of them.

Games oriented around masculine interests such as wars, battles, crimes, and destruction lead girls to see computing as a male domain. There have been recent attempts to create video games for girls for whom "shoot 'em up simply won't do" (De Witt, 1997). These games reproduced gender stereotypes about girls' behavior. They included games with names such as "Let's Talk about Me" in which a girl can keep a diary, determine her personality, or alter her wardrobe. Mattel introduced the "Barbie Fashion Designer." Some of the software designed for girls is packaged in pastel colors to make it more attractive to them. This may make some girls more interested in computers, but do you consider this progress?

GENDER ROLE SCRIPTS FOR BOYS AND GIRLS

Learning to Be Male

Boys' avoidance of cross-gender toy play is stronger than that of girls and remains strong throughout childhood. There are many social demands for boys' conformity. When 3- to 5-year-old children were asked: "What would your _______ say if you played with (other gender)'s toys?" (children were asked about their mother, father, day-care worker/baby sitter, sisters/brothers, and best friends) more boys than girls reported one or more sources who would think cross-gender-typed play was bad (Raag, 1999).

Not surprisingly, boys are more influenced by gender distinctions than are girls. They form a greater number of gender stereotypes at an earlier age than girls do. White middle-class boys showed a greater level of gender stereotyping than either black middle-class or white working-class boys did (Bardwell, Cochran, & Walker, 1986). Peer acceptance appears to become more closely tied to gender-appropriate play for boys than for girls as they move into the later elementary school years (Moller, Hymel, & Rubin, 1992). Older girls become more flexible and older boys less flexible than their younger counterparts (Katz & Boswell, 1986). Part of the reason for this difference is that little girls are permitted more latitude in their attire, toy preferences, and behaviors than little boys are.

Ironically, girls and women are probably permitted more latitude because boys and men are seen as the more valuable sex (thus, requiring greater attention to their socialization) and because masculine activities are regarded as having higher status than feminine ones (Feinman, 1981). Both girls and boys assigned more positive attributes to males than to females (Urberg, 1982). People can understand why a little girl might prefer to engage in stereotypically masculine activities, but a boy who prefers stereotypically feminine activities is regarded as doubly deviant. He is engaged in activities that are not only considered gender inappropriate but are also perceived to have low status.

There is more pressure on little boys than on little girls to conform to gender-stereotypic demands. Being told they do anything "like a girl" is a powerful negative message for boys. Here is one story from a man who excelled in high school and college athletics.

> Later, at home, my father informs me that two boys on the team throw like girls, and that I, unfortunately, am one of them! By the next practice, he tells me, we will have corrected that problem. That evening, with glove and cap securely in place, I anxiously face my father on the front lawn. And we play catch, for quite a while. I am concentrating, working hard to throw correctly ("like a man"), pulling my arm back as far as I can and snapping the ball overhand, just past my ear. When I do this, it feels very strange . . . but I am rewarded with the knowledge "that this is how men throw the ball." If I learn this, I won't embarrass either myself or my father. When at times I inadvertently revert to what feels like a more natural and more easily controllable throwing style . . . I am immediately rewarded with a return throw that sails far over my head and lands two or three houses down. "Run, Run after that ball! You won't have to chase it anymore when you quit throwing like a girl!" . . . I learned very rapidly how to throw properly. But it wasn't really having to run after the ball that taught me; it was the threat to my very fragile sense of masculinity. The fear—oh, the "fear" of being thought a sissy, a "girl"! (Messner, 1994, pp. 29–30)

Children appear to acquire information about the greater importance of gender conformity for boys at an early age. In a study comparing the impact of sex, gender typing of interests, and labels such as tomboy or sissy (Martin, 1989), 7-year-olds used interests, labels, and sex to determine a playmate's desirability. Older children disliked children described as sissies more than any other group of potential playmates. Third- to sixth-grade boys were very intolerant of cross-gender behaviors in other boys (Zucker, Wilson-Smith, Kurita, & Stein, 1995).

When college students were given information about children, they also gave more negative evaluations to nonconforming boys than to girls (Martin,

1990). They expected nonconforming boys to be less well adjusted and more likely to be homosexual when they grew up, but they expected tomboys to convert to more traditional behavior. Preschool teachers are also less accepting of cross-gender role behaviors and aspirations in boys than in girls (Cahill & Adams, 1997). Like college students, their attitude was related to homophobia. Even in sex-egalitarian societies such as Finland, parents viewed cross-gender boys more negatively than cross-gender girls and saw them as less well adjusted (Sandrabba & Ahlberg, 1999).

Undergraduates did not consider sissies and girls to be very similar (Martin, 1995). They saw sissies as having fewer masculine and more feminine traits than traditional girls. Sissies were seen as being gentle, neat and clean, crying a lot, and being easily frightened.

What do you think of when you hear the word *sissy?* It probably does not have the same positive meanings associated with the word *tomboy.* Tomboys are girls who wear jeans, climb trees, and play baseball. Sissies are boys who are absent from these activities. They are defined as much by what they do not do as by what they do. It is not necessary for a boy to play with dolls to be called a sissy. It may be enough if he does not engage in rough-and-tumble games or verbally aggressive horseplay. Judgments about sissies versus tomboys reflect societal judgments about the relative value of traditionally masculine and feminine characteristics.

The Values of Being a Tomboy

Who is a tomboy? It might be easier to answer the question, Who isn't a tomboy? There are many more tomboys than sissies. In fact, being a tomboy may be a normal part of girls' development. It is a label that many women proudly claim. In one questionnaire given to women college students, junior high school students, and a sample of women in a shopping mall, more than half of the respondents reported having been tomboys in childhood (Hyde, Rosenberg, & Behrman, 1977).

A high proportion of tomboys has been found in several other studies. In a recent three-generational study that sampled undergraduates, their mothers, and their grandmothers, 67 percent said that they had been tomboys during childhood (Morgan, 1998). They reported that they became tomboys at an average age of 5.8 years and stopped at an average age of 12.6 years.

There were few differences between generations on the behaviors associated with the tomboy label. At least 75 percent of these self-identified tomboys mentioned involvement in sports, active outdoor play, and interest in so-called boys' toys, such as trucks, skateboards, and action figures. Their identification was based on doing "boy stuff" rather than a rejection of doing "girl stuff." Another recent study found that 7-year-old girls who had been identified as tomboys by their parents were more like their brothers than their sisters in their toy preferences, activities, and choice of male playmates. Contrary to some beliefs, they showed no evidence of mental health problems and were seen as just as attractive as their sisters (Bailey, Bechtold, & Berenbaum, 2002).

Considering the status conferred on masculine activities versus feminine ones, it is surprising that most girls and women do not retain such preferences.

Nevertheless, the average age of puberty and the age at which most girls report abandoning their tomboy identity (12.6 years) are almost the same. Most women did not, however, report puberty as a major factor in their behavioral change. Nor did they report a loss of interest in cross-typed activities. Social pressures were the most important reason given for stopping (Burn, O'Neill, & Nederend, 1996; Morgan, 1998).

The popular media sometimes portray tomboys as oddities. An article in *Allure* magazine on celebrity women who had been tomboys concluded:

> These days, beautiful celebrities who claim that they spent their childhood climbing trees and scraping knees are about as common as models who own restaurants. Here ten erstwhile tomboys come clean about their dirty past. (O'Connor, 1995, p. 68)

But being a tomboy brings many benefits.Young girls who identify as tomboys show a more varied set of traits and behaviors than girls who conform to gender stereotypes. They were more likely to have been selected as popular and described as having leadership skills (Hemmer & Kleiber, 1981). They were also more creative than other girls on a test of finding uses for everyday objects (Lott, 1978).

Girls who have been tomboys are more likely than other girls to continue to participate in sports during later childhood. Self-rating as a tomboy was associated with an orientation toward competition and winning in games (Guiliano, Ropp, & Knight, 2000). Girls who continued their involvement in sports reported that they received encouragement to do so from a variety of sources such as mothers, siblings, friends, and coaches (Weiss & Barber, 1995). The encouragement of fathers was more important than that of mothers (Brown et al., 1989). However, the active involvement of mothers in physical activity was also an important determinant of girls' continued involvement.

Negative Aspects of Hyperfemininity

The opposite of being a tomboy is buying into traditional femininity as it is constructed in the United States and western Europe. There is no name for girls who take this path, so they may be difficult to recognize. One example is the beautiful young woman in Figure 6.9, who is actually a child of 5—JonBenet Ramsey.

JonBenet was found strangled in her wealthy parents' home the day after Christmas in 1996. Because this was a very lurid and visible murder, all the news media published similar photographs of JonBenet. There were many photographs available because she had participated in children's beauty pageants for several years before her death.

Does JonBenet look cute in her photo? Is her premature sexualization problematic? One author estimates that the beauty pageant business involves more than 100,000 children under the age of 12 in the United States:

> little girls caked with makeup, adorned with dyed, coiffured, helmetlike hair, performing childish burlesquelike routines under the direction of overbearing parents. There appears to be little concern on the part of many of these parents about the possible negative consequences of dressing their children up in provocative clothing, capping their teeth, putting fake eyelashes on them, and having them perform before audiences in a manner that suggests a sexuality well beyond their years. (Giroux, 1998, p. 272)

FIGURE 6.9. A 5-year-old femme fatale. JonBenet Ramsey in makeup and costume for a children's beauty pageant. No age seems too young for females to be portrayed as sexually seductive.

The popular media in the United Kingdom are also full of pictures of alluring little girls who look seductively at the camera (Walkerdine, 1998). The pictures bear a startling resemblance to images found in child pornography (see Figure 6.10).

Although these little girls claim that they love the beauty pageants, it is difficult to make a case that they are truly free agents. In order to win, they require the services of professional costumers, hairdressers, makeup artists, dance teachers, and voice coaches. Although we know of no studies of these girls' self-images, it is difficult to believe that they will have high self-esteem when so many body alterations are required to make them "beautiful." Girls, in general, have higher levels of body dissatisfaction, a greater discrepancy between ideal and current self, and lower levels of self-esteem than boys (Wood, Becker, & Thompson, 1996). These findings are consistent with self-esteem differences between adult women and men (Major, Barr, Zubek, & Babey, 1999). Lower self-esteem among females than males has been reported at younger and younger ages. Premature sexualization of little girls eliminates their childhood and presents an image of beauty that is unattainable by adult women.

Games aimed at girls encourage premature sexualization. An article in the *Dallas Morning Press* described a new board game called "Sealed with a Kiss" (Rosenfeld, 1995). The girls move markers with the picture of a teenage "hunk" around the board and the first girl who receives five kisses wins the game. An-

FIGURE 6.10. Although U.S. laws do not permit the use of child pornography, open advertisements of eroticized little girls are permitted in some cultures.

other toy marketed during that Christmas season was a pink "Dream Phone" that encouraged girls to dial the phone numbers of "cute guys." The first girl to figure out which one had a crush on her wins.

Consumer organizations in some Muslim countries such as Malaysia have called for a ban on the import of Barbie dolls (Assunta & Jallah, 1995). They claim that the doll gives children a warped perception of beauty and attractiveness. They blame Barbie for girls' excessive concerns with fashion and their bodies. Some comic strips in the United States have echoed their concern (see Figure 6.11).

By the time they are 9 years old, white girls have significantly more weight concerns and body dissatisfaction than black girls or than boys (Thompson, Corwin, & Sargent, 1997). Is it surprising that eating disorders have been documented for younger and younger girls in the United States (Phillips, 1998)?

RESISTING GENDER RULES

Psychological interventions designed to counter sexism in children have often been ineffective (Bigler, 1999). They tend to produce context-specific behaviors that persist for only a short time. Like adults, children may ignore individualizing or disconfirming information and maintain their stereotypes (Jones & Bigler, 1996). Girls are usually more responsive to intervention attempts than boys are. This may be because boys have more to lose by a change in the status quo or because a majority of intervention attempts have been conducted by female researchers (Katz & Walsh, 1991).

It is also possible that what children take away from an intervention may not be what the investigator intended. Calling attention to gender in a gender-neutral context may increase children's gender stereotyping (Bigler, 1995). Like other stereotypes, cognitions about gender are difficult to change.

Similarly, short-term manipulations within schools have been ineffective in changing the cultural context that maintains sex segregation. Still, many girls (and some boys) resist conforming.

Flexibility Begins at Home

How do girls resist gender socialization? Some processes that increase gender flexibility in children begin at home.

Differences in parental ideology about gender roles seem to have some effect. For example, children from egalitarian families (self-identified as sharing parental responsibilities) adopted gender labels later during the second year of life and showed less gender-role knowledge at age 4 than other children (Fagot

Making a Difference

Anuradha Koirala (1949–) of Nepal rescues girls from brothels after their families have sold them into prostitution: she gives them a place to live, an education, and information about the trade in girls so that they can share their knowledge when they return to their villages. "My goal is to make Nepal wholly free from the slave trade in girls," Koirala says. Currently, 5,000 to 7,000 girls are sold into sex slavery each year, many of them under the age of 10. A large number leave the brothels only after becoming infected with HIV/AIDS or other STDs. Koirala, a former schoolteacher, founded the rescue organization Maiti Nepal in 1993. Maiti has opened a children's home, a school, and a hospital for women and children infected with HIV and AIDS. As of August 2002, the group had rescued more than 700 girls, intercepted hundreds more before their families could sell them, and put 15 criminals behind bars. Koirala makes a feminist analysis of the problem. She says that although many people believe the selling of girls is due to poverty, the fact that girls are treated worse than boys in Nepal shows that the problem goes beyond a lack of money. Daughters are valued less than sons are because they leave home when they marry and because the family must pay a dowry. Girl-traffickers exploit the situation by offering a "good job" to the daughter, and then selling her into the sex trade instead. For its work in rescuing girls and improving the lives of girls and women, Maiti won the 2002 World's Children's Prize and the 2002 Reebok Human Rights Award, and in October of that year, the king of Nepal appointed Koirala as the country's Assistant Minister for Women, Children, and Social Welfare.

Sources:
Anderson, J. W. The crusader behind Maiti Nepal: Mrs. Koirala. *The Washington Post.* Available at www.maitinepal.org/diretor.htm
Asiad, B. (2002, August 15). Anuradha's odyssey. *The Katmandu Post.* Available at www.kantipuronline.com/archive/kpost/2002-8-15/kp_midweekpost.htm#Anuradhais%20odyssey.
Chand appointed Prime Minister. (2002, October 12). *The Rising Sun Nepal.* Available at www.nepalnews.com.np/contents/englishdaily/trn/2002/oct/oct12/
Kleming, S. Nominated for the World's Children's Prize: Maiti Nepal. Available at the World's Children's web site www.childrensworld.org/wcpswe/2002/nominerade/nepal/engelska/maiti.asp
Nkosi and Maiti Nepal shared the jury's prize in 2002! Available at the Earlier Winners site of the World's Children's website http://childrensworld.org/wcpswe/winners/engindex.asp
Wagoner, G. (2002, November 2). Help for Maiti Nepal. http://home/swipnet.se/snf/reebok.html

FIGURE 6.11. Does Barbie make girls want to grow up faster?
Source: Baby Blues. © Baby Blues Partnership. Reprinted with Special Permission of King Features Syndicate.

& Leinbach, 1995). Girls whose parents had fewer stereotypic attitudes showed a trend toward more independent coping skills than daughters from more traditional families (Hoffman & Kloska, 1995). If they were middle class, they showed higher scores on standardized achievement tests.

What a mother does also has an impact on her child's beliefs about gender roles. Mothers in nontraditional occupations seemed to foster nontraditional aspirations in both their preschool daughters and sons (Barak, Feldman, & Noy, 1991). In contrast, mothers who have stereotypic beliefs about gender differences discourage active toy play in their daughters but not in their sons (Brooks-Gunn, 1986). Alarmingly, daughters of mothers who had strong gender-typed beliefs had lower IQ scores at 24 months than did those with less rigidly gender-typed mothers. The assignment of tasks in the home also makes a difference. In almost all cultures surveyed, girls are more likely to be assigned tasks that involve domestic and child-care responsibilities. In less-developed countries, both boys and girls are under the supervision of women who use children's labor to assist them in their often heavy work (Bradley, 1993). As they reach middle childhood, however, the boys usually leave home to perform tasks that often involve other boys (Whiting & Edwards, 1973). For example, boys in rural cultures do more of the care and feeding of animals. In urban cultures, they are more likely than girls to run errands or deliver goods and services.

In the United States, the most gender-flexible preschoolers came from homes where the division of domestic tasks was less stereotyped than in the average home (Katz, 1996). Their parents granted these children more independence and were less demanding, less authoritarian, and warmer than parents of more gender-typed preschoolers.

Gender-related differences in task assignment obviously cannot occur if there is only one child in a family or all the siblings are of one sex. Thus, girls who were only children showed a higher preference for masculine activities than other girls, although their level of performance was still well below that of the average boy (Burns and Homel, 1989). Women who have achieved a high degree of prominence in science and math are more likely to have been only children or to have had only female siblings (Anderson, 1973). Similarly, a study in England found that the choice of science O levels (roughly equivalent to the selection of majors in U.S. colleges) by young women declined as their number of brothers increased (Abrams, Sparkes, & Hogg, 1985).

The Effect of Ethnicity and Class

Some groups of children are more influenced by gender rules than others. In many studies, the strongest gender-typed patterns are exhibited by white boys (Katz, 1996). These are the individuals who are most privileged by the current status quo. Researchers studying 5- to 12-year-old children in a summer day camp found that high-status boys (those from wealthier white families) took the lead in maintaining gender boundaries (McGuffey & Rich, 1999). They used verbal and physical sanctions directed at both girls and boys to keep them from playing with each other. Girls did not appear to influence the boys' status system.

There have been relatively few studies of ethnic differences in gender cognitions. In general, these indicate that black children are less likely to stereotype (Bardwell et al., 1986). They may also have a different definition of appropriate gender roles than white children. Until recently, working outside the home was more a part of the expected feminine role for African-American than for European-American women (McGoldrick, Garcia-Preto, Hines, & Lee, 1989). African-American 8- to 10-year-old girls and boys have also been found to be equally responsive to infants, unlike European-American children of the same age (Reid & Trotter, 1993).

Social class differences in gender typing also exist. A large study of U.S. adults indicated that men, older persons, and poor persons were more gender-traditional in their assignment of household chores to children (Lackey, 1989). Studies in Australia (Burns & Homel, 1989) also indicated that children in homes with a higher socioeconomic level were less gender-typed in terms of chores.

These findings are consistent with older findings indicating that working-class children showed more gender-stereotypical behaviors than middle- or upper-class children did (Unger, 1979a). Girls, however, are less influenced by the social class of their parents than boys are. For working-class girls, resisting gender may also mean resisting other undesirable aspects of their social class. It may be of some interest to you that both authors of this textbook are from working-class families.

Gender, ethnicity, and class intertwine. People of color and people from working-class origins in general have less access to societal rewards. These limits may, however, help them to be more flexible than individuals from dominant groups. White middle- and upper-class males, in particular, have the most to gain by identifying with traditional prescriptions about gender.

The Case for Positive Social Deviance

Children who defy societal pressures for gender conformity appear to have had support from a variety of sources over a long period of time. They must also be able to ignore a considerable amount of pressure exerted against them because of their social deviance.

Girls who resist becoming gendered continue to take math and science courses and to compete in sports. Such activities help to maintain the self-esteem needed to fight pressures toward conformity. Highly creative and achieving women have a high ability to tolerate deviance (Helson, 1978). It was helpful if they did not have brothers. Because fathers seem to be important sources of gender differentiation, their encouragement was also important. But many activist women in psychology also mention the important role of their mothers in structuring their active participation in social causes (Unger, 1998a). African-American mothers have socialized strong daughters for many years (see Chapter 7).

Strong female role models are important. Until recently, few models of high-achieving women were available to most girls (see Chapter 11). Girls often find meaningful role models in the most improbable places. For example, one of the authors (Unger, 1988) examined the childhood heroes of women who were leaders in Division 35 of the American Psychological Association. These women had been recognized for both their professional achievements and their feminism. The role model that was most frequently reported (by almost 50% of those surveyed) as an important influence in their childhood was Nancy Drew. Why would a group of intelligent, independent women select the heroine of a series of books written by formula, with little intellectual merit? As a number of these women pointed out, Nancy drove her own car, had adventures, and solved mysteries. And, anyway, who else was available?

A series of statements from a group of women writers, artists, scientists, and scholars brings life to these issues:

> The journey begins, as usual, with my parents—one an attorney and one a teacher. Both were exceptionally able to hand on their experience, their enthusiasms, and their intellectual curiosity. However, they were also "bridge-builders." Firmly committed to the ideal of equality, they did not see a chasm between those who worked with their heads and those who worked with their hands (or between intellectuality and action). "Oh, for goodness sake," my mother used to say, "life is not only in books! Put that down, go outside, and look at the world!" My father said, "You will be narrow-minded if you don't work." (Kay Hamod, historian, p. 12 in Ruddick & Daniels, 1977)

> The family member who most consistently sustained me was my mother. Though she burdened me with some of her fantasies and expectations about my future, she also freed me from a debilitating pressure to accept the dictates of femininity as usual. She urged me to have a more intellectually gratifying life than she felt she had had. I need not imitate her life, she said, as long as I did something that was both respectable and excellent. If she encouraged me, my father did not discourage me. Indeed, he paid the bills for the ambiguously supportive and straightforwardedly expensive women's college I attended (Catherine Stimpson, literary scholar, p. 74)

> My mother and father never doubted my ability to take care of myself. I had been a loved and trusted child. I was a successful and much-admired student. I was not in the habit of asking for help. The realm of art and ideas, a mystery to my parents, was respected, but not basic. I would build my life on these things, but I would take care of the practical side of living, too. (May Stevens, artist, p. 104)

> As I mentioned, I was not prepared for the discovery that women were not welcome in science, primarily because nobody had told me. In fact, I was supported in thinking—even encouraged to think—that my aspirations were perfectly legitimate. I graduated from the Bronx High School of Science in New York City where gender did not enter very much into intellectual pursuits; the place was a nightmare for everybody. We were all, boys and girls alike, equal

contestants; all of us were competing for that thousandth of a percentage point in our grade average that would allow us entry into one of those high-class, out-of-town schools, where we would go, get smart, and lose our New York accents. (Naomi Weisstein, experimental psychologist, pp. 242–243)

As you can see, these women were encouraged by their parents, and their gender-inappropriate traits and behaviors were taken seriously by others and, thus, by themselves.

The penalties that girls pay for "proper" socialization may be severe. But boys also pay a price for their socialization. Internalization of rigid gender roles can lead to psychological distress for men as well as women (see Chapter 14). Psychological disorders appear to be highly gender-specific in our society. Whereas girls are socialized for dependence and passivity, boys are socialized for over-independence and a lack of close ties. Women's problems with achievement (Chapter 11) are paralleled by men's problems with relationships (Chapters 8 and 9). Women's problems may actually be easier to "cure."

There is a limit to the amount of change that any one individual can effect. If you choose to become parents, you will (we hope) make every effort to minimize gender typing of your daughters and your sons. But as long as socialization takes place in a sexist society, boys and girls will have difficulty escaping gender categories. As the number of people who are exceptions to the "rules" continues to increase, however, they may serve as reinforcers of further gender nonconformity in their peers.

CONNECTING THEMES

- *Gender is more than just sex.* Gender is a fundamental factor in the construction of girls' and boys' beliefs and behaviors. Gender determines how one labels oneself and others, what toys and games are considered appropriate, and, somewhat later, serves as a basis for the segregation of boys and girls into largely separate cultures. Gender is acquired as a result of both social learning and cognitive developmental processes that use sex as a basis of categorical distinctions.
- *Language and naming are sources of power.* What is impressive about gender socialization is the lack of awareness of both children and adults of the processes involved. The similarity in stages of gender understanding and the lack of individual variability in gender typing is consistent with the idea that gender socialization is primarily the acquisition of societal norms.
- *Women are not all alike.* Both ethnicity and social class seem to affect gender typing in boys and girls. Those who have the most to gain from the cultural status quo (white middle-class boys) seem to be most rigidly bound by social norms mandating the separation of the sexes.
- *Psychological research can foster social change.* Children take an active part in maintaining gender categories and supporting stereotypically appropriate behaviors for both sexes. Social change in this area requires both individual and structural change. The growing number of young women (and young men) who challenge traditional gender rules indicates that societal change in the direction of greater gender flexibility is possible.

SUGGESTED READINGS

JENKINS, HENRY (Ed.). (1998). *The children's culture reader.* New York: New York University Press. A cultural-studies perspective on the way popular culture portrays and constructs children's behavior. Includes material on issues that are not usually found in psychology textbooks, such as articles on producing erotic children, reaching juvenile markets, and not-so-trivial comic books.

MILLER, PATRICIA & SCHOLNICK, ELLEN (Eds.). (2000). *Toward a feminist developmental psychology.* New York: Routledge. This book includes review chapters by a number of leading, current researchers in child development. Some chapters are a little difficult, but they are thought provoking and worth the effort.

THORNE, BARRIE. (1993). *Gender play: Girls and boys in school.* New Brunswick, NJ: Rutgers University Press. This book is an engaging and thoughtful account of a series of ethnographic studies on children during their unstructured activities in school. It gathers all the author's previously published material in one place and offers us insightful ideas from outside the laboratory.

CHAPTER 7

Becoming a Woman: Puberty and Adolescence

"I was nervous about school," Christy said. "I wanted to prove I was as cool as the other kids. I wanted a boyfriend to take me to the parties that the popular girls got invited to. I knocked myself out to get into that crowd. . . . I realized right away that being smart was trouble. I felt like I was 'severely gifted.' I got teased a lot, called a brain, and a nerd. I learned to hide the books I was reading and pretended to watch television. This one guy in my math class threatened to beat me up if I kept breaking the curve." (Christy, age 14, in Pipher [1994], p. 203)

"All five hundred boys want to go out with the same ten anorexic girls." She said, "I'm a good musician, but not many guys are looking for a girl that plays great Bach preludes. . . . Boys get teased if they even talk to me," she moaned. (Monica, age 15, in Pipher [1994], p. 147)

"I blame my training for my eating disorder," Heidi continued. "Our coach has weekly weigh-ins where we count each others' ribs. If they're hard to count, we're in trouble." (Heidi, age 16, in Pipher [1994], p. 166)

"I hate my mother. She's such a witch. Sometimes I think if I have to live with her the next four years till I graduate from high school I'll go crazy. . . . She tries to control my life. She makes me clean my room and go to church on Sunday. She forces me to eat meals." (Jana, age 14, in Pipher [1994], p. 249)

Do any of these girls' words sound familiar? They are comments made to Mary Pipher, a therapist who works with adolescent girls. Although these teenagers seem to have more severe problems than most young women do, their brief remarks summarize common conflicts remarkably well. Many of these conflicts are triggered by rapid bodily change.

On average, the physical changes in girls as they mature from a juvenile to an adult body are greater than those for boys, and girls' maturation is more visible. As a result, adolescence is more problematic for girls than for boys. Identity is learned through comparisons. Girls compare themselves to other girls as well as to boys. Of course, boys also judge their bodies as they make the transition from childhood to adulthood, but because of biology, most girls must make such comparisons at a younger and more vulnerable age.

Biological events do not take place in a social vacuum. Society (often in the form of their peers) teaches girls what kinds of bodies are valued, and society is ambivalent about the value and meaning of the mature female body. Meanwhile, society also teaches girls the adult roles for which they are suitable as they confront other social milestones, such as the transition from elementary to junior and senior high school. As girls internalize society's judgments about feminine roles, stereotypes can lead to problems with self-esteem and school achievement. Relationships with their peers can also place special stress on adolescent girls. Sexual objectification influences their relationships with other girls as well as their relationships with boys. Problems such as excessive concern about appearance that might seem to be issues for individuals may in fact reflect general social issues, such as ambivalence about the role of women.

In recent years, feminist researchers have examined the context of female development during adolescence. They have focused on how home and school environments contribute to the formation of gender stereotypes and how gender-related behaviors are shaped by peers. But definitions of femininity and the experience of adolescence vary by ethnic group and social class. Examining these variations illuminates the social construction of gender during adolescence and its relationship to biology. They show, once again, that biology is not destiny. Just as males and females are different in some ways, females are also quite different from each other.

The physical, sexual, and social changes in girls that occur during early and middle adolescence are so large that they produce a discontinuity in their development. Differences emerge between the self-perceptions of girls and boys that could not have been predicted from events during childhood. These perceptions come both from the different biological events that occur during puberty and from the different social meanings attached to these events. In particular, contradictory social messages are much more likely to be applied to the mature female than to the mature male body.

WHAT HAPPENS DURING PUBERTY?

Puberty is the period of the most rapid physical growth that human beings experience. We grew faster only at one time when we were not aware of our growth—during prenatal development and the early months of postnatal life. The word *puberty* is derived from the Latin word *pubescere,* which means "to become hairy." In contrast, the word *adolescence* is derived from the Latin word meaning "to grow up" (Brooks-Gunn & Petersen, 1983a).

The origin of these two words points to their different meanings. Puberty involves physical events such as the growth spurt, changes in body composition, and the development of secondary sexual characteristics. Every normal individual in every society experiences puberty some time between late childhood and the middle teenage years. In contrast, adolescence is culturally defined.

In the United States and western Europe, adolescence is defined as the period between childhood and maturity. But in societies in which children are expected to do adult work as soon as they are physically able to do so, there is no such stage as adolescence. Adolescence is the product of an affluent mid-eighteenth-century society in which a falling infant mortality rate, a growing population, and the need for a smaller workforce produced a surplus of young people (Hollin, 1987). This period has become more important as the age at which individuals are able to take on adult roles and the age at which they are permitted or expected to do so have moved further apart.

Puberty in Girls and Boys

Puberty differs for girls and boys in a number of important ways. First, the timing of pubertal changes is different. On the average, girls begin and complete puberty two years before boys. Second, the quantity and quality of change are different for girls and boys. During puberty, differences in height, body composition, and physical configuration between males and females increase. It is sometimes difficult to distinguish the sex of children's bodies without inspecting the genital area, but the physical sex of teenagers is usually quite obvious.

The most important physiological difference between girls and boys during puberty is *menarche*—the onset of menstruation. Although this is a relatively late event in girls' physical maturation, it has a great deal of personal and social meaning. In purely physical terms, menarche conveys the information that a girl is sexually mature and able to bear children.

The ages at which puberty begins and ends depend on which physiological measure we use. By any measure, however, puberty takes a long time. Some physiological changes begin in the bodies of girls and boys long before they can be seen. For example, the level of *gonadotropins* (hormones produced by the pituitary gland that stimulate the ovaries or testes) in the bloodstream usually begins to rise when children are about 7 or 8 years old. The end of puberty is marked by a stabilization of gonadal hormone levels in the mid to late teens. Thus, in hormonal terms, puberty lasts about 10 years.

Puberty is more typically defined in terms of external changes. For girls, the growth spurt (produced by the stimulating effect of gonadal hormones on growth centers in the long bones) may begin as early as age 9. Most girls reach their adult height by 14 to 16 years of age. Boys, in contrast, usually start their growth spurt after age 11 and may continue to grow until their late teen years.

Variations in Timing

There is a great deal of variation in the timing of the bodily changes associated with puberty. Girls differ greatly in the age at which their external appearance begins to change and the time it takes for the changes to be completed. For example, in some early-maturing girls, the beginning stages of secondary sexual characteristics such as breast buds and pubic and axillary (underarm) hair may appear as early as 8 years of age. However, the average age at which breast buds appear for American girls is 11 and may be as late as 13 years (Brooks-Gunn, 1988). For unknown reasons, African-American girls begin puberty about 9 months earlier than their European-American counterparts. Their average age at menarche is also younger (12.1 versus 12.9 years). However, by the time they enter middle-school, most girls in the United States show visible signs of breast development and growth in height (O'Sullivan, Graber, & Brooks-Gunn, 2001).

It takes approximately four and a half years for an average girl to progress from breast buds to complete breast development, but some girls do so in less than a year and a half (see Figure 7.1). Moreover, some girls never reach what is considered the final stage of breast development (large, well-defined, fatty breasts).

Remember that girls' and boys' progression through puberty is different in timing as well as in specific physiological events. Girls usually experience their growth spurt and the onset of secondary sexual characteristics earlier than boys. Thus, an early-maturing girl is not only different from other girls but is also way ahead of her male classmates. By contrast, a late-maturing girl is in synchrony with her male peers (Brooks-Gunn, 1988).

Premature Puberty

In recent years there has been a great increase in the number of young girls who enter puberty prematurely (see Figure 7.2). There is no clear medical explanation for the increasing number of elementary school girls who have begun to develop breasts and pubic hair. (Pesticides, chemicals, and hormones added to food as well as substances secreted by fat cells are suspects.) There is also little information on the long-term health consequences of premature puberty. However, these little girls' social problems are obvious.

Their problems appear to be exaggerations of those encountered by girls who begin puberty at a more normal age. Their mature bodies make them uncomfortable with other girls their age, and some are not permitted by their parents to wear bathing suits or participate in sleepovers. Mature female bodies also attract the

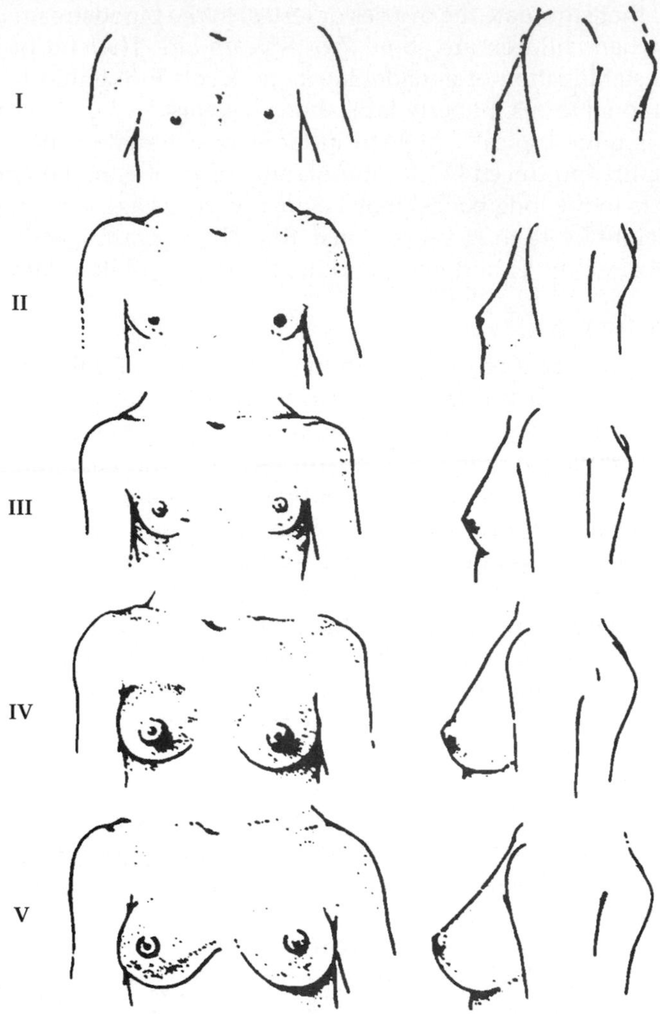

FIGURE 7.1. Breast stages during adolescence.

attention of older boys. One well-developed 13-year-old stated that "boys follow her around like dogs." We do not know the potential psychological effects of premature sexual development in little girls who "should be reading fairy tales, not fending off wolves" (Lemonick, 2000, p. 68). They are not likely to be positive.

The "Fat Spurt"

Girls experience a rapid gain in fat as well as height around puberty. Their average weight gain is twenty-four pounds, which is deposited largely in the breasts, hips, and buttocks. Prepubescent boys and girls are similar to each other with respect to lean body mass, skeletal mass, and body fat. By maturity, however, females have twice as much body fat as males (Warren, 1983).

Fatty tissue appears to be necessary for sexual maturation. Menarche usually occurs when about 24 percent of the body mass is composed of fat (Frisch, 1983a). Girls require a critical amount of body fat in order for menarche to oc-

FIGURE 7.2. This is a rather shocking image of precocious puberty, but think about what it means for a girl's childhood to look like a woman.

cur (Frisch, 1983b). During their adolescent growth spurt, girls' body fat increases 120 percent, compared with a 44 percent increase in lean body weight. (In contrast, boys' bodies grow mostly more muscle tissue.) This increase represents a relative as well as an absolute increase in fatty tissue. For girls at age 18, fat is 27 percent of total body weight.

Menarche

The age at which girls began to menstruate is often noted in diaries, letters, and medical records. These sources show that the average age of menarche has declined over the last 100 years. In mid-nineteenth-century Britain, the average age of menarche was 15½ to 16½ years. Upper-class women began to menstruate six months to a year earlier on average than working-class women. The delay among working-class women was explained as due to poor nutrition and hard living (Frisch, 1983a).

Girls in the United States in 1871 who began to menstruate at 11½ to 12½ years of age were considered to be cases of precocious puberty (Frisch, 1983a). The average age of menarche today is 12½ years. If one considers menarche the end of childhood or the beginning of sexual maturity, this change over the past century represents a significant shortening of childhood even for girls who do not experience premature puberty.

Some researchers believe that the tendency for menarche to occur earlier over the past hundred years is due to better nutrition during childhood. Girls simply reach the critical weight sooner. Weight gain is, of course, one of the few pubertal changes over which teenagers have some control. Severe dieting or intense athletic activity can delay menarche. Nevertheless, almost every young woman reaches menarche by the age of 16 (Frisch, 1983b).

Menarche is actually only a late step in a long series of changes. It typically occurs after girls have stopped growing at their peak velocity, when their breast development is nearly complete, and after they have gained a great deal of body fat. All these bodily changes are important determinants of how a girl is viewed by others and how she feels about herself. However, menarche carries particularly important messages because it is the most sudden and dramatic event during sexual maturation.

The messages that girls receive about the meaning of menarche are quite contradictory. For example, face slapping is part of some cultural traditions:

> [My mother] slapped me in the face. It's a Jewish tradition . . . for luck! I thought I had done something terrible. And then she hugged me. A lot of mixed feelings here! She told me it was for good luck, that was the Jewish tradition. (Costos et al., 2002, p. 55)

Such an ambivalent response can evoke anxiety. But more positive responses can also be problematic. For example, Andrea, a working-class 17-year-old, told one interviewer that she was "embarrassed" and "felt like an idiot" when her mother told her father and grandparents that she had started her period, and her grandmother congratulated her for being a woman (Martin, 1996).

Girls who had received no information about menstruation report much more negative experiences of menarche:

> I was babysitting and I just like got home. And I just like was screaming! 'Caus, ummm, I ran upstairs and I didn't know what it was 'cause I got home late one night, and I was just going to the bathroom, and I ran upstairs 'cause I didn't know what it was . . . and then she's [my mother's] like, "Don't worry about it, it's just your period." (Martin, 1996, p. 22)

Many girls are ambivalent about the onset of menstruation. In one study, a group of seventh-graders were shown the beginnings of stories based on passages from Judy Blume's book *Are You There, God? It's Me, Margaret,* a book that focuses on puberty. The story about menarche was:

> "Mom—hey, Mom—come quick!" When Nancy's mother got to the bathroom she said: "What is it? What's the matter?" "I got it," Nancy told her. "Got what?" said her mother.

Virtually all the girls recognized that "it" was Nancy's period. When the girls were asked, "How did Nancy feel?" half ranked "scared" first, whereas 39 percent ranked "happy" first, and no girl ranked "sad" first. Happy and scared were also the most popular second choices. Their responses suggest that girls feel both happy and frightened about menstruation (Petersen, 1983).

Despite their anxiety about menarche, girls also engage in a certain amount of menarcheal competition. The basis for this competition is the status that girls gain when they attain "womanhood." Because womanhood carries more mixed messages than manhood, girls are more ambivalent about maturation than boys are. Contrast these two statements about puberty—one from a 15-year-boy and one from a 15-year-old girl:

> I was glad when I finally got taller and older. Being older you just get to do more, go out and stuff.
>
> I didn't know what it [puberty] meant. So am I supposed to be like a woman now? Or what? It seemed so awkward to be like a little girl with breasts. I couldn't have both, but I didn't want to be a woman, but like I didn't, it didn't feel right to me. It felt really awkward, but there wasn't anything to do about it. (Martin, 1996, p. 19)

Young adolescent girls seem to believe that menarche will produce a sudden and momentous transformation into mature womanhood. But physical maturity for females in our society carries mixed messages. It is desirable to become an adult, but for women, youthful bodies are more valued than they are for men. And physical maturity can provoke parental fears about premature sexuality and consequent restrictions on girls. It should be no surprise, therefore, that girls are ambivalent about an event they see as the symbol of womanhood.

FEMALE ANATOMY AND CULTURE

The Conspiracy of Silence

Fifty percent of all cultures have some kind of ritual to publicize the fact that a girl has reached menarche. Our culture pays little public attention to the onset of menstruation, but cultural invisibility does not mean that the event is of little personal or social importance.

Although women spend as much as 25 percent of their adult years menstruating, both menarche and menstruation are still largely taboo as subjects of public discussion. For example:

> Hallmark manufactures no cards that say, "Best Wishes on Becoming a Woman." Rather than celebrate coming-of-age in America, we hide the fact of the menarche, just as we are advised to deodorize, sanitize, and remove the evidence. (Delaney, Lupton, & Toth, 1988, p. 107)

A survey conducted by Tampax in 1981 found that two-thirds of Americans believed that menstruation should not be talked about at social gatherings or in the office, and one-fourth thought it was an unacceptable topic even for the family at home (Delaney et al., 1988). Mothers are more reluctant to name the genital organs of their daughters than those of their sons and tend to do so at a much later age. There is no acceptable word for female sexual parts, which are stereotyped as unpleasant, smelly, and unattractive (Lees, 1997).

Even today, many young women know little about their bodies, and they are especially ignorant about their genitals (Martin, 1996). This is particularly true for girls from English working-class families. One such young woman reported to an interviewer:

> I never have [looked at my genitals]. Once I started using tampons I was just like "Oops I guess that's the place where everything happens." I never looked. (Martin, 1996, p. 21)

When asked whether she had ever been to a gynecologist, another 17-year-old from a working-class family replied:

No and I want to but I'm afraid to. I don't want to like (spreads her arms apart), you know (giggling) that's gross! (Martin, 1996, p. 22)

Menstruation is often characterized as an embarrassing event, one that needs to be concealed, and as a hygienic crisis. Until 1972, ads for sanitary protection products were banned from TV and radio (Delaney et al., 1988). In a recent study of objects designed to elicit disgust and revulsion, researchers found that 46 percent of their male and female participants refused to put an unused tampon (unwrapped in front of them) to their lips, 69 percent refused to put it in their mouth, and 3 percent would not even touch it (Rozin, Haidt, McCaulay, Dunlop, & Ashmore, 1999).

Menstruation continues to stigmatize women. Another recent study looked at the responses of people who interacted with a confederate who "accidently" dropped either a tampon or a hair clip from her purse (Roberts, Goldenberg, Power, & Pyszczysnski, 2002). The woman who dropped the tampon was considered less competent and was liked less. Participants also tended to sit farther from her. There were no gender differences in the responses.

Women are aware of the negative social impact of menstruation, and their awareness may lead to poor self-presentation strategies. In one study, menstruating women were interviewed by a male confederate. Those who thought that he was aware of their condition believed that he liked them less, yet they were less motivated to make an impression on him than those who believed he had not been informed. Nonmenstruating women were more positive about the interviewer and more motivated to present themselves well than either group of menstruating women (Kowalski & Chapple, 2000).

Advertising of menstrual products has become more visible in recent years, but a content analysis of these ads concluded that they heighten adolescent girls' insecurities, maintain secrecy and shame, and perpetuate negative views about menstruation (Simes & Berg, 2001). Many current ads in teen magazines are designed to dispel beliefs about menstruation as a hygienic crisis and alleviate adolescent girls' concerns about loss of virginity through the use of tampons. However, 38 percent of the ads still stress secrecy—exemplified by ads with headlines such as "No One Ever Has to Know You Have Your Period" and "It's New, It's Neat, and So Discreet" (Merskin, 1999). Seemingly open and positive ads inform young women that they "risk humiliation and disgrace if any signs of their femaleness should seep through their clothing" (Merskin, 1999, p. 954).

Femininity as a social construction requires a body that does not leak. Perhaps the ideal female body is one that does not menstruate at all. Although Depo-Provera is supposed to be used for birth control, it has also been advertised as keeping women "menstruation-free." We do not know the long-term health risks of these hormones (see Chapter 12).

With such ads, it should not be surprising that adolescent girls are concerned about how to conceal sanitary products from others. They also worry about being "discovered" and humiliated through odor or staining their clothes (Kissling, 1996). Menstrual taboos that persist in Western societies include refraining from exercise, showers, and sexual intercourse, as well as hiding the fact of menstruation entirely (Reame, 2001). But how does a young woman in junior or senior high school find time and private space to change pads or tampons so she won't "show"? As one young girl said:

> In school it's hard: teachers don't want to let you out of the classroom, and give you a hard time. In seventh grade I didn't carry a pocketbook or anything—wow!—How do you stash a maxipad in your notebook and try to get to the bathroom between classes to change? It was like a whole procedure, to make sure nobody saw, that none of the guys saw. (Martin, 1987, pp. 93–94)

These problems may be intensified by ignorance and disgust with dealing with genitals:

> My sister told me about using tampons. My sister is a lot older than I am. So at first I didn't like the idea of having to go anywhere near touching myself. I thought it was sick!" (Martin, 1996, p. 29)

When today's college students report their experience with learning about menarche and menstruation, they usually tell negative stories regardless of whether their mother or teacher was the source of information. Complaints about their teachers included unwillingness to discuss menstruation, time limits for discussion, and the presence of peers in group learning situations that led to embarrassment (Beausang & Razor, 2000).

Fifty-nine percent of one group of college students reported that the first person they told about menstruation was their mother, but 64 percent reported that they had received negative messages from her and 68 percent reported that they knew nothing about their mothers' menstrual experiences (Costos, Ackerman, & Paradis, 2002). These researchers believe that the poor quality of mother-daughter communication in this area helps to perpetuate traditional gender roles and adversely affects relationships between women.

Menarche, Menstruation, and Popular Culture

Neither menarche nor menstruation has received much attention in American literature. One of the first explicit references to menarche may be found in *A Tree Grows in Brooklyn*, a novel published in 1943 about growing up Irish, female, and poor in New York City in the early twentieth century. The following passage exemplifies many of the themes already discussed, such as instant transition to womanhood, pain, secrecy, and the consequences of female sexuality.

> She went upstairs to the flat and looked into the mirror. Her eyes had dark shadows beneath them and her head was aching. She lay on the old leather couch in the kitchen and waited for Mama to come home.
>
> She told Mama what had happened to her in the cellar. She said nothing about Joanna. Katie sighed and said, "So soon? You're just thirteen. I didn't think it would come for another year yet. I was fifteen."
>
> "Then . . . then . . . this is all right what's happening?"
>
> "It's a natural thing that comes to all women."
>
> "I'm not a woman."
>
> "It means you're changing from a girl into a woman."
>
> "Do you think it will go away?"
>
> "In a few days. But it will come back again in a month."

"For how long?"

"For a long time. Until you're forty or even fifty." She mused awhile. "My mother was fifty when I was born."

"Oh, it has something to do with having babies."

"Yes. Remember to always be a good girl because you can have a baby now." Joanna and her baby flashed through Francie's mind. "You mustn't let the boys kiss you," said Mama. (Smith, 1943, p. 212)

Menstruation is rarely mentioned in most forms of popular culture. The one allusion we could find in the comic strips conveyed a negative stereotype (see Figure 7.3). One feminist media critic was able to locate four recent movies with a menarche scene as well as a number of televised situation comedies. The movies (which included *My Girl, A Walk on the Moon, Boys Don't Cry,* and *Carrie*) emphasized the frightening aspects of menstrual blood, a sudden recognition that girls and boys are really different, and the need for concealment—especially from males. TV scenes of menarche also highlighted difference and secrecy; only an episode from *Roseanne* emphasized the role of choice in the management of both menstruation and adult female roles (Kissling, 2002).

Breast Development

Unlike menarche, which can be hidden or denied, breast development is easily observed. More than one-half of elementary or junior high school girls who were in the middle of their breast development reported having been teased about it (Brooks-Gunn, 1987b). The most frequent teasers were mothers, fathers, and girlfriends. When asked to indicate how they felt when teased, 8 percent reported being upset, 22 percent embarrassed, and 22 percent angry. None of the girls reported being pleased!

Some of the teasing about breasts has a ritual quality. One sociologist reported: "Once in a classroom and several times on the playground I saw a girl or boy reach over and pull on the elastic back of a bra, letting it go with a loud snap followed by laughter" (Thorne, 1993, p. 142). Sometimes this shaming ritual may be followed by little jokes such as "I see you're wearing a Band-Aid!" The adult staff at these schools generally ignored bra snapping.

FIGURE 7.3. A not-so-subtle reminder of the stereotype that women's moods change as a function of their menstrual cycle.
Source: Zits. © Zits Partnership. Reprinted with Special Permission of King Features Syndicate.

Some comments by working-class British teenage girls illustrate the discomfort generated by the gaze of their male peers:

> I was self-conscious [when I developed breasts], I still am. I don't know. It's just the boys. Some of them, how they react and stuff, just like if you're bigger and stuff like that, some of the boys, I know some. It's aggravating!—Wendy

> When I started to get them and now that I have them, I wish I didn't have them 'cause they're a pain. "'Cause like you have to worry about them when you get dressed in the morning. If you don't. . . . well, I'm just, I mean, I am self-conscious about my chest. I wish I was little again where you know, no one really worried about it and guys didn't really care as much and all that stuff. You know now it's the first thing they check out!"—Jill (Martin, 1996, pp. 31–32)

Pubertal girls are often embarrassed or angered by parental discussion of their breast growth or purchase of a bra (Brooks-Gunn & Zehaykevich, 1989). One director of a private elementary school for girls has speculated that fourth- and fifth-graders are much more disturbed about the loss of their childish bodies than grownups think (Delaney et al., 1988). She cited the sloppy big shirts and sweaters common to this age group—no matter what the prevailing style—as evidence of their anxieties.

As in other areas having to do with the body, girls' physical maturation puts them in a double bind. Breasts are viewed as a necessary part of an attractive woman's body, but there seems to be no such thing as "perfect breasts." One magazine advertisement illustrated this point clearly. It stated, "Your breasts may be too big, too saggy, too pert, too flat, too full, too far apart, too close together, too A cup, too lopsided, too jiggly, too pale, too padded, too pointy, too pendulous, or just two mosquito bites." With the advertiser's product, however, young women were assured "at least you can have your hair the way you want it." One advertisement for cosmetic breast surgery shows a beautiful small-breasted woman standing naked at a mirror covering her breasts with her hands and saying: "It was the one area in my life where I always felt deprived."

In one unusual case, British parents agreed to pay for their 15-year-old daughter's breast enlargement as her 16th birthday present. The young woman was reported to have wanted the surgery since she was 12. In a letter to a tabloid, she wrote:

> Every other person you see on the television has had implants. . . . If I want to be successful I need to have them too—and I do want to be successful, though I don't know at what at the moment." (Bellaby, 2001)

This young woman's viewpoint may only be at the extreme end of a continuum. One survey of more than 450 English adolescents found that attractiveness was positively associated with being "pretty" and "thin" and negatively associated with "non-voluptuousness" (Dittmar, Lloyd, Dugan, Hallwell, Jacobs, & Cramer, 2000). The contradiction between being thin and having a sexy body may be impossible to resolve without recourse to cosmetic surgery.

While puberty is forcing young girls to adapt to their new bodies, their social world is also changing. Adolescent boys and girls spend more time with their peers of both sexes than children do. During the teenage years, peer groups increase in size and complexity.

How do adolescents relate to their peers? Research has uncovered interesting differences not only between boys and girls but also among racial groups and social classes. These differences show up in the friendships adolescents form, their experience of harassment and bullying, and their reactions to the transition from elementary to middle or high school.

Friendships

As Chapter 6 discussed, girls, more than boys, are socialized to value relationships. Friendship is more important to girls than to boys. Girls spend more time with their friends, have smaller groups of friends, and expect more kindness, loyalty, commitment, and empathy from their friends than boys do (Brown, Way, & Duff, 2000). Girls in late adolescence (eleventh and twelfth grades) rated their relationships as stronger, more interpersonally rewarding, and more stressful than boys did.

Male and female friends are valued differently by the two sexes. Boys reported that their friendship with their best female friend was more interpersonally rewarding than with their best male friend and rated the quality of friendships with same- and other-sex peers equally. Boys' self-esteem did not correlate with the quality of their friendships. In contrast, girls' self-esteem was positively correlated with the quality of their relationship with their best male friend, but was not related to the quality of their friendships with other girls (Thomas & Daubman, 2001). (This study did not distinguish between romantic and platonic relationships.) Boys reported greater support from male than from female friends, whereas girls reported equal support from friends of both sexes (Kuttler, LaGreca, & Prinstein, 1999).

Girls' friendship patterns vary with ethnicity and class. White middle-class girls seem to have the most difficulty in their friendships with other girls. In one study, 95 percent of white girls reported that competition with other girls was an issue. Only 15 percent of girls of color reported problems of competition, and only 31 percent reported problems with jealousy compared with 81 percent of white girls (Brown et al., 2000). Unlike white middle-class girls, white working-class and black adolescent girls do not appear to compete with each other for status.

It is very common for white middle-class girls to define themselves against other girls.

> Most teenage girls posit an "other girl" when they talk about social and sexual relations. Good girls treat other girls bad, bad girls derogate girls who have a different vice or more stigmatized identity: drugs instead of sex, lesbianism instead of promiscuity, bisexuality instead of lesbianism. Or, other girls are traitors to their gender—two facers or backstabbers. You have to keep your eye on them all the time. (Thompson, 1994, p. 228)

White working-class girls appear to have fewer problems with friendship than their more privileged classmates. Their relationships with other girls may be solidified by the threat posed by teachers and, ironically, by their exclusion from the rewards of safety and security offered to those who come closest to the cultural ideal of femininity. Privileged girls, in contrast, have difficulty negotiating between competition for individual success and solidarity with friends (Brown, 1998).

Harassment and Hostility

Sexual objectification and sexual harassment of girls in school begins early. By middle school, heterosexuality has become a fundamental organizing principle of peer culture (Eder, Evans, & Parker, 1995) (see Chapter 8). Boys begin to perceive girls as sexual objects for conquest and compete with other boys for sexual achievements. Girls become more concerned with their appearance and more vulnerable to concerns about their status as desirable sexual objects (Tolman & Brown, 2001). Girls who do not fit peer standards may be teased and harassed. Even in elementary school, sexual harassment decreases body esteem (Smolak & Striegel-Moore, 2001).

Relationships between the sexes can be very hostile during adolescence. Extensive research in English schools shows a great deal of verbal abuse of girls by boys (Lees, 1993). A double standard of terminology referring to girls' and boys' sexuality maintains male dominance. The word that illustrates this asymmetry more clearly than any other is *slag*. Although it is supposed to refer to promiscuity, it is often used in ways not related to actual sexual behavior. A girl may be called a slag if she wears too much makeup, if her skirt is slit too high, or if her clothes are too tight. Unattractive or unfashionably dressed girls are never called slags, although other degrading terms are used for them. The term *slag* is ambiguous: it implies that the woman is both contemptible and sexually desirable. It is used by both boys and girls to exert sexual and social control.

Until recently, educators ignored the "invisible school curriculum" that is based on a white, middle-class, heterosexual, and male standpoint (Tolman & Brown, 2001). In this curriculum, girls' major route to status is through male judgments of their physical appeal. Many strong girls are socially isolated during adolescence because their difference threatens their peers' culture (Pipher, 1994).

Nearly 70 percent of the young women surveyed in one study reported being teased or criticized—mostly in terms of their appearance (Rieves & Cash, 1996). (Table 7.1 lists the humiliating themes and the most probable teasers.) Here are some graphic descriptions by Canadian high school students (Larkin and Popaleni, 1994):

> This guy and his brother went on in their sick way of having fun by rating young women as they passed by in the hallway. I told the guy he was sexist and by rating young women as they passed by . . . he was making them uncomfortable. He said "Just for saying that, I give you a zero."

> I came across a stack of boards in the corner of the art classroom with graffiti written all over them. I expected to read "So and so, 100% true love" or the names of people's favorite bands, but as I looked at the graffiti I saw a picture

TABLE 7.1. The Foci and Perpetrators of Recurrent Appearance Teasing/Criticism during Childhood and Adolescence

Foci	(%)	Teasers	Ever (%)	Worst (%)
Face and head	45	Mother	30	11
Hair	12	Father	24	6
Lower torso	11	Brother(s)	41 (79)	17 (33)
Mid torso	2	Sister(s)	22 (36)	5 (8)
Upper torso	19	Other relatives	23	4
Muscle tone	1	Friends	47	16
Weight	36	A specific peer	31	13
Height	17	Peers in general	62	28
Clothes/attire	13	Teachers	6	0
Hands/feet	3	Other adults	20	1
General appearance	10			
Miscellaneous	6			

Note: The percentages in parentheses are based on only those participants who have brothers (n = 79) or who have sisters (n = 93) rather than on the entire sample.
Source: Rieves & Cash (1996).

of a naked woman (no arms, head, calves, or knees) with her legs wide open showing her vagina, anal opening and breasts. I was shocked to see such explicit graffiti in my favorite class. I never thought anyone from our school could draw such violent pictures of women in the classroom and not have anyone say or do anything about it. Other people must have seen it because the room is used by three other classes. [To me] that picture says "Rape is OK, sexual abuse is OK," and this is what I'm scared of the most. (p. 220)

Adolescent girls are often harassed while other people watch. Teachers and school officials often downplay the significance of sexual harassment among students. They may even stand by while girls are harassed in front of them in classrooms and school corridors (Stein, 1995). The boys' behavior is frequently dismissed as an adolescent prank, a rite of passage conducted primarily by boys for other boys, or an awkward attempt at sexual teasing. One investigator who spent two years visiting an urban middle school reported that "girls and women in the school found themselves solving the problem of male violence quietly, covertly, and without making any public fuss" (Pastor, McCormick, & Fine, 1996, p. 21). Both girls and boys witness harassment going on in front of adults and peers without any obvious consequences.

Victims of harassment are selected because they violate norms about appearance, mental maturity, or gender identification. Once students are viewed negatively in one of these areas, their classmates assign them negative characteristics in the other areas as well (Brown et al., 2000). Adolescents thought to be lesbian or gay are frequent targets (Boxer, Cook, & Herdt, 1999). Lesbian and gay teens often experience intense social isolation that interferes with their academic achievement as well as their personal development (Hunter & Mallon, 2000).

Boys are more likely to bully girls than to bully other boys, and boys' bullying is more public than girls'. Social bullying by girls is more relational—victims are ignored or may have rumors spread about them. Girls are also more likely than boys to use teasing and ridicule when bullying (DeZolt & Hull, 2001).

Popular girls are more likely than other girls to form exclusive peer groups that help secure and maintain their social position. They are also more likely to tease other girls. Social bullying (also known as relational aggression) among girls increases during the middle- and high-school years.

School Transitions, Gender, and Self-Esteem

The transition from elementary to middle or high school brings boys and girls into contact with a new and larger cohort of peers, including many individuals who are older than themselves. Gender-role flexibility declines following school transitions. Boys acquire more rigid ideas about gender roles than girls do—especially in terms of masculine traits (Alfieri, Ruble, & Higgins, 1996).

The transition to a new school is difficult for many girls; it appears to affect girls more than boys. After the transition, girls' relationships with their peers were more unstable than those of boys. Both girls and boys lost old friendships and built new ones, but girls were more likely than boys to nominate previously unfamiliar peers as friends (Hardy, Bukowski, & Sippola, 2002).

Large-scale longitudinal studies conducted in several cities found that the shift from elementary to junior high school and then to high school lowered the self-esteem of girls (Simmons & Blyth, 1987). Girls reduced both school participation and leadership after the transition into a large junior high or middle school. This drop occurred again in high school. Girls who made two such changes remained impaired when compared with boys and girls who had made one transition from a K–8 elementary school to high school.

More recent studies suggest, however, that the gender differences in self-esteem following school transitions are quite small and that many girls do not experience a loss during this period. Loss in self-esteem is more of a problem for some ethnic groups than for others. For example, no gender differences in self-esteem have been found among African-Americans (Eccles, et al., 2000), a pattern that appears to be unique to this group. In contrast, Latinas, who express the highest level of self-esteem in elementary school, report less confidence than other girls in their talents, abilities, physical appearance, and relationships with others by the time they reach high school (Phillips, 1998). Thus, these effects do not appear to be due to minority status, but are related to specific aspects of black, white, and Latino culture.

Why would the transition to a large impersonal environment at an early age have a greater impact on some groups of girls than on boys or on other girls? There are several possibilities, but one focuses on the fact that self-esteem is tied to different activities for adolescent boys and girls. Although ratings of physical attractiveness, math ability, and social ability with peers were related to self-esteem for both sexes after a school transition, lack of confidence in physical attractiveness was a much stronger predictor of a decline of self-esteem for adolescent girls. Academic anxieties and worries were stronger predictors of reduced self-esteem for adolescent boys. African-American girls were more confident than European-American girls in their physical attractiveness, popularity, femininity, and ability to perform "masculine" skills. These differences in confidence explained the differences between the groups in the relationship between gender and self-esteem (Eccles et al., 2000).

Where, in turn, do these differences in confidence between white and African American girls come from? As we discuss in the next section, a large part of the answer may come from different standards for appearance among different groups. These, in turn, may be related to differences in mother-daughter communication and familial values.

WEIGHT, BODY IMAGE, AND MENTAL HEALTH

A recent development among girls is to focus on the body as a project. A feminist historian examined the diaries of adolescent women over the past hundred years (Bromberg, 1997). Girls in earlier eras described their ideas for self-improvement in terms of becoming more disciplined in their studies, learning better manners, or getting along better with their parents. Beginning in the last twenty years, however, self-improvement has been described primarily in terms of bodily change. This period coincides with the time when the mass media began their narrow focus on thinness as the major determinant of attractiveness in women. These trends appear to have major effects, especially on white middle-class girls.

Weight Concerns and Body Esteem

Girls are becoming concerned about their bodies at younger and younger ages. This trend reflects marketing practices that stress sexy teen fashions for girls as young as 8-years old (see Figure 7.4). Stores such as The Limited Inc. feature make-up, bell-bottom pants, tank tops, and other "cool stuff" for 6-to-12-year olds. This kind of advertising may explain why children constitute a growing market for fitness clubs and personal trainers in big cities like Los Angeles and New York (Bannon, 1998).

Beginning in elementary school, girls are more dissatisfied with their weight and shape than boys are. Body dissatisfaction increases as girls move into adolescence. Boys are also concerned about body weight during puberty, but they are more likely to gain muscle than fat. It also requires a greater degree of overweight for boys to become dissatisfied with their bodies (see Figure 7.5). Over the past thirty years, gender differences in body satisfaction have increased (Smolak & Striegel-Moore, 2001).

Although increases in body fat are necessary to maintain normal reproductive functioning, weight gain cannot be viewed merely as a physiological matter. An increase in weight has severe negative consequences in today's society. Weight gain causes young women to deviate from the ideal thin female body and accentuates their difference from the normative lean male body.

A national survey conducted in 1995 of ninth- through twelfth-grade students found that 34 percent of girls (compared with 22 percent of boys) per-

FIGURE 7.4. These clothes send the wrong messages about the sexuality of girls age 8 and older—the target of this company's advertising.

ceived themselves as overweight (Phillips, 1998). Sixty percent of girls—nearly two out of three—were trying to lose weight at the time of the survey. For many girls and young women, being thin is linked with being in control. Thinness is valued because it signifies triumph over the body and its desire to eat (Malson, 1997). This idea is illustrated by the comments of these young women:

> Teresa: Passivity is linked in my mind to being fat and to being indulgent, to being out of control.
>
> Zoe: I felt like such a loser because I felt like I couldn't control my weight because I was overweight. So there must be something wrong with me because you know, oh well, I didn't have enough self-control.
>
> Emma: I want to lose the fat. . . . I hate it being in me and it feels completely alien and I just want it away. You know, I want it off. It just doesn't feel like it should be part of me. . . . you know. It feels all wrong, I . . . just do feel like this big, monstrous sow.
>
> Jane: I just wanted to get rid of all this weight an' it made me feel I was better 'cos there was less fat . . . as if there was less bad. (Malson, 1997, p. 235)

It is unlikely that these girls will achieve their goals because the ideal standard for the female body is characteristic only of girls in the earliest phases of

FIGURE 7.5. It's all in the mind, not the body!
Source: Stone Soup. © 2000 Jan Eliot/Distributed by Universal Press Syndicate. Reprinted with permission of Universal Press Syndicate. All rights reserved.

puberty and of Barbie dolls. Researcher Kelly Brownell, whose 7-year-old daughter owned six Barbies, determined just how impossible this doll's dimensions are. He calculated that if a normal, healthy woman wanted to look like a life-size Barbie, she would have to grow nearly a foot in height, add four inches to her chest, and lose five inches from her waist (Discover, 1996).

Some Sources of Weight Concerns

Concern about weight begins at home. Both boys and girls whose fathers comment on their weight are more likely than other children to become constant dieters, but parental comments seem to influence girls more than boys because the comments are reinforced by peers, teachers, and coaches (Smolak & Striegel-Moore, 2001). For girls of all ages, parental comments and teasing influence body image. Both fathers' and mothers' encouragement to lose weight influences adolescent girls' dieting practices. However, mothers are more likely to help girls to diet, engage in diets with them, criticize their weight, and compliment their figures (Wertheim, Mee, & Paxton, 1999). These findings indicate that a gender-linked culture of dieting-related values and behavior is transmitted across generations.

Many factors apparently contribute to body dissatisfaction among adolescent girls. One large-scale prospective study, for example, found that being overweight, perceived pressure to be thin, internalization of a thin ideal, and lack of social support predicted body dissatisfaction in adolescent girls (Stice & Whitenton, 2002). Another large-scale study of Australian adolescents found that in the ninth grade, perceived popularity with peers influenced girls' body satisfaction and strategies for losing weight (McCabe, Ricciardelli, & Finemore, 2002). A third study, also conducted in Australia, found significantly fewer seriously committed dieters among girls who attended all-girls' schools (Huon, Gunawardene, & Hayne, 2000).

Popularity for teenage girls is a mixed bag. Girls who were nominated as popular by their peers are more likely to have lower body esteem and to engage in disordered eating than less popular girls (Lieberman, Gauvin, Bukowski, & White, 2001). Popular girls are also more likely to form exclusive peer groups that help secure and maintain their social position. Girls' preoccupation with weight and body shape is correlated with that of their friends (Paxton, et al., 1999).

Ethnicity, Class, and Weight Concerns

Weight concerns among adolescent girls in the United States are widespread. Far more females than males diet. In every socioeconomic class studied, the majority of young women, upon reaching full sexual maturity, wished that they were thinner (Dornbusch, Gross, Duncan, & Ritter, 1987). More than 70 percent of white women within normal weight ranges have been on a diet (Thornberry, Wilson, & Golden, 1986). However, more affluent young women are most likely to have bought into the belief that one "can be neither too rich nor too thin." Privileged young women are more likely to wish to be thinner—even after the actual level of fatness has been controlled for statistically (Dornbusch et al., 1987).

The cultural equation of thinness and attractiveness plays a major role in constructing differences between females and males during adolescence. As you read earlier, the decline in self-esteem among girls after puberty is partially related to perceptions about attractiveness. Academic self-concepts are not as important for these young women's self-esteem (Eccles et al., 2000).

But the relationship between perceived attractiveness and self-esteem has been found mainly in white adolescents (Tashakkori, 1993). Beliefs about parental closeness were a better predictor of self-esteem for African-American adolescents. Mother-daughter relationships remain close after puberty in African-American families (Fine & Macpherson, 1992). Black girls spoke frequently about how much they learned from their mothers. They spoke about their mothers' strength, honesty, ability to overcome difficulties, and ability to survive. African-American mothers actively teach their daughters to resist the assault of dominant standards about attractiveness and self-worth (Ward, 1996). African-American girls report their mothers as their greatest source of emotional support, and most conflicts between mothers and daughters seem to be about minor everyday issues such as cleaning up around the house (Cauce et al., 1996).

Increase in body fat appears to be more problematic for European-American than for African-American girls (Halpern et al., 1999; Ge et al., 2001). Black girls also report more positive body images than either white or Latina girls. A 1996 survey of 11- to 17-year-old girls found that 40 percent of the black girls studied considered themselves attractive or very attractive compared with only 9.1 percent of the white girls (Phillips, 1998).

Recent studies suggest, however, that concern about body weight has crossed both class and ethnic boundaries. In one large sample of low-income African-American teens, for example, about 50 percent of the girls reported that they would like to lose weight. Although working-class African-American girls had better body esteem than white or middle-class black girls, they still had lower esteem than their male peers (Grant, Lyons, Landis, Cho, Scudiero, Reynolds, Murphy, & Bryant, 1999).

Paradoxically, young black women may have been somewhat protected from the effects of unrealistic weight standards by racism and classism. The current American standard of thinness applies mainly to white women (see Chapter 2). This management of weight is designed to position women within an elite class (Bordo, 1993). The evidence of growing discontent among ethnically diverse teenage girls is disheartening.

Excessive concern with the control of weight has major implications for young women's health. According to a report by the National Council for Research on Women, girls 7–17 years old are now the heaviest users of diet pills (Phillips, 1998). Furthermore, weight concerns and dieting are strongly associated with smoking initiation among girls (Phillips, 1998). For example, a recent study in London of teenage girls with eating disorders found that beginning to smoke was linked to weight gain during puberty and to other practices designed to prevent weight gain, such as vomiting (Crisp, Sedgwick, Halik, Joughin, & Humphrey, 1999). Overall, smoking is on the rise for girls, and the rate of smoking has increased much more rapidly among young women than among young men. In 1991, 13 percent of eighth grade girls reported smoking; in 1996, the number jumped to 21 percent. However, black girls are much less likely to smoke than girls of other races; white girls are more likely to use cigarettes than girls of any other racial group.

Eating Disorders, Depression, and Puberty

Excessive concern for weight has also been tied to eating disorders such as anorexia and bulimia (discussed in chapter 14). These disorders have the highest mortality rate (10%) among all types of psychiatric disorders. According to a report commissioned by the National Council for Research on Women, girls and women account for 90 percent of all cases of eating disorders (Phillips, 1998).

Body dissatisfaction increases as girls move through adolescence. Middle-school girls with high body dissatisfaction or weight concerns are likely to develop problematic eating attitudes and behaviors in later adolescence (Smolak & Striegel-Moore, 2001). Although eating disorders occur in all ethnic groups, white girls most often develop them, followed most closely by Latinas.

A recent meta-analysis indicates that dieting is not consistently related to the development of an eating disorder, but young women who have internalized a thin-ideal appear to be at risk (Stice, 2002). Ultra-thin media images do not affect all young women the same way. One ingenious study randomly assigned either a subscription to a fashion magazine or no subscription to two groups of adolescent girls. Subsequent follow-up found that only those girls who (1) perceived pressure to be thin, (2) were dissatisfied with their bodies, and (3) lacked social support were adversely affected by exposure to ultra-thin media images in magazines. Their less vulnerable peers were not influenced by these images (Stice, Spangler, & Agras, 2001).

Depression and eating disorders have also been linked (Stice & Bearman, 2001). For example, girls who had high body dissatisfaction scores at ages 13 to 16 were much more likely to develop a major depression four years later (Stice, Haywood, Cameron, Killen, & Taylor, 2000). Girls who uncritically adopt conventional images and understandings of white femininity—often but not exclusively white middle-class girls—are at particular risk both for eating disorders and depression (Tolman & Brown, 2001).

Although there are no sex-related differences in depression before puberty, girls have higher rates of depression beginning at 13 years of age (Hankin & Abramson, 2001). The rate of depression in females increases during the teenage years and persists into young womanhood. Despite cultural differences in gender-role ideology, similar sex-related differences in depression beginning at the same age have been found in Norway (Wichstrom, 1999) and Mexico (Benjet & Hernandez-Guzman, 2001).

The reasons for the gender differences in depression that begin in early adolescence are complex. They may result from a combination of differences in biosocial events during puberty or in the processing of emotions (see Chapter 6). Different domains of vulnerability may also be important for the development of depression in adolescent females and males because they cannot change their social environments as easily as adults can.

Current theories about gender differences in depression emphasize that individuals are most stressed by those negative events that involve a domain that is important to them. Perceived physical attractiveness and body satisfaction are more important for girls during early adolescence than they are for boys. When an adolescent girl encounters a negative event in this domain (such as a classmate making belittling comments about her weight and hairstyle), she is likely to attribute the comments to stable and global causes ("I will always be fat and ugly"), infer that other negative consequences will follow from the event ("I will never go to the prom or get married"), and derive negative self-concepts from it ("I am worthless") (Hankin & Abraham, 2001). As young women enter puberty and become targets for sexual objectification, they are likely to encounter an increased number of such negative events. Girls who derive their self-worth from physical appearance report both lower self-esteem and higher levels of depression (Harter, 1999).

Early-maturing girls (those who reach menarche before the age of eleven and a half) have the highest rate of depressive symptoms (Ge, Conger, & Elder, 2001). Boys and premenarcheal girls have similar depression scores (Hayward, Gotlib, Schraedly, & Litt, 1999). The impact of pubertal timing appears to be due to the effect of menarche on weight gain (Streigel-Moore, McMahon, Biro, Schreiber, Crawford, & Voorhees, 2001). In a study of more than 3,500 students in seventh through twelfth grades, researchers found that pubertal growth was linked to perceptions of being overweight by adolescents of both sexes. However, pubertal growth had a greater effect on girls' perceptions of being overweight (Ge, Elder, Regnerus, & Cox, 2001). As discussed earlier, these perceptions are not completely unrealistic: puberty does result in more fat tissue in girls than in boys. And body fat has been associated with a lower probability of dating, even among girls who are not obese (Halpern, Udry, Campbell, & Suchindran, 1999).

Early versus Late Maturation

The relationships we have described among factors such as the timing of menarche, weight gain, body concern, gender, ethnicity, and the risk for depression illustrate the complicated interactions between biological processes and social meanings. These interactions are further demonstrated when we take a closer look at how variations in the timing of puberty influence how teenagers view themselves and how they interact with their peers.

For example, researchers have found many differences in how early- and later-maturing girls experience adolescence. Early-maturing girls date more than late-maturing girls in middle and junior high school (Brooks-Gunn, 1988). Early-maturing eighth-grade girls were more likely to report having a boyfriend, talking with boys on the phone, dating, and "making out" than their less mature peers (Crockett & Petersen, 1987). They may also engage in "adult behaviors" such as smoking, drinking, and sexual intercourse at an earlier age, probably because their friends are older (Magnusson, Strattin, & Allen, 1985). Early menarche is also associated with substance abuse (Stice, Presnell, & Bearman, 2001).

Early puberty has negative implications for girls' academic performance. In a large-scale longitudinal study of students in sixth through tenth grades, researchers found that pubertal girls performed less well in both sixth and seventh grade (Simmons & Blyth, 1987). They had significantly lower grade-point averages and poorer reading and math achievement scores than later-maturing girls. These effects are the flip side of these girls' greater popularity and social acceptance (see Figure 7.6). These effects are also gender specific. Romantic involvement has been found to be related to poorer academic performance only for girls (Brendgen, Vitaro, Doyle, Markiewicz, & Bukowski, 2002).

The effects of the timing of maturation for girls are complex. This complexity probably reflects the mixed nature of womanhood as constructed by our society. Becoming an adult in our society does not bring with it the same social advantages for a woman as it does for a man. The premature sexualization of early-maturing girls puts them at risk in terms of involvement in activ-

FIGURE 7.6. The relative importance of dating versus scholastic achievement during the high school years.
Source: Funky Winkerbean. © Batom, Inc. Reprinted with Special Permission of North American Syndicate.

ities with peers who are socially more experienced than they are themselves. The difficulties of the early-maturing girl illuminate the contradictions implicit in being a mature woman in our society.

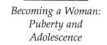

HOW DO GIRLS DEAL WITH THE STRESS OF ADOLESCENCE?

Silencing and Other Forms of Resistance

Some girls appear to lose their confidence and a clear sense of identity during adolescence. Self-silencing and taking one's knowledge underground are costly strategies that adolescent girls use to remain accepted by others (Brown & Gilligan, 1992, 1993). In repeated interviews, girls from an elite private girls' high school appeared to lose their ability to take their own experience, feelings, and thoughts seriously (Brown & Gilligan, 1993). One girl, for example, used the phrase "I don't know" 112 times in her eighth-grade transcript—more than three times more frequently than in the previous year, although the interviews were of the same length. These girls appear to be struggling with the conflict between authenticity and relatedness. To stay true to themselves, they risk being seen as neither "nice" nor "normal" by others.

Silencing may be more common among privileged European-American teenage girls who have the most to gain by "buying into" the gendered status quo. Young urban women of color, for example, create safe spaces for each

Making a Difference

Teenager ***Kelli Peterson*** cofounded the Gay Straight Alliance (GSA) at East High School in Salt Lake City, Utah, in 1996 because she was tired of hiding the fact that she was a lesbian and was concerned that other high school students were experiencing the same loneliness, shame, and fear. Peterson was not prepared for the subsequent media maelstrom. She became the center of a long-running national news story about the lengths to which conservatives would go to oppose the GSA. The local school board finally voted to ban all clubs from campus rather than allow the GSA to meet, despite unflattering national publicity and massive protest by gay and straight students from many Salt Lake City schools. Peterson appeared on the national news and made the cover of at least one magazine: she was recently featured in a documentary film titled *Out of the Past,* which aired on PBS stations around the country. In 1996, Utah's legislature passed a law allowing rental of school property for group meetings, and the GSA has been meeting on campus ever since. This is a victory of sorts, but Peterson's goal was never to prevent other student support or activity groups from meeting. Conservative parents and politicians believe clubs like the GSA are dangerous recruiting tools for homosexuals, but as Peterson stated at a meeting of the Utah Senate and Salt Lake City School Board, "I did not start this group to recruit. . . . I started this group to end the misery and isolation of being gay in high school."

Sources: Sahagun, L. (1996, February 22). Utah board bans all school clubs in anti-gay move. *Los Angeles Times,* p. 1.

Gay alert, drop everything. (1997, April 27). *The Economist,* p. 31.

Dupre, J. (Producer/Director). (1996). *Out of the Past,* [Film.]

other, secure from adult authorities, whom they believe to be intrusive and controlling. Young African-American women may also resist silencing by becoming "loud" and oppositional in order to counter their invisibility in largely white schools (Fordham, 1993). However, this form of resistance (which is more collectivist than individualistic) can also result in disengagement from education and the loss of an opportunity to acquire power in white society. Many forms of resistance have both positive and negative consequences.

Dealing with peer pressure requires collective action. One group of English working-class girls described the ways they dealt with male harassment (Lees, 1997). Their most effective forms of resistance involved verbally challenging the terms of abuse or collectively resisting the insults. Occasionally, girls did take action against the boys, as shown in the following account:

> The boys love coming into the girls' changing rooms. This boy, right, we made a decision next time he comes in, grab hold of him and start taking his clothes off and see how he feels. All the girls were watching him. He never comes back. (Lees, 1997, p. 32)

In another example of collective action, 13-year-old girls in a resident dance school in Canada became activists through a series of focus groups dealing with discomfort about their changing bodies (Piran, 2001). They noted that there were condom machines in the boys' washrooms, but no tampon dispensers in the girls' washrooms. They were able to get school authorities to make the necessary change.

Collective action can be an important strategy for girls dealing with a sexist system. Researchers have found, for example, that black girls in the United States were protected from the negative effects of school transitions if they transferred schools with a group of thirty or more peers (Simmons, Burgeson, & Reef, 1988). The size of the peer network had no impact on the negative consequences of school transition for white girls, who have a less collectivist orientation than African-American girls.

Friends can also provide a buffer from relational violence. But problems with same-sex friends may add to the difficulties that white middle-class girls encounter during adolescence. In contrast, white working-class and black adolescent girls use communal teasing about romantic and sexual relationships within their peer group as a way to distance themselves from the dominant culture in school as well as to resist dominant definitions of appropriate femininity (Brown et al., 2000).

Is Participation in Sports Protective?

What experiences make girls feel good about who they are? In a diverse population of adolescents, girls were most likely to mention athletics as the area that made them feel best (46%). Other aspects of their lives that made them feel good were involvement in arts-related activities (19%), service to others (14%), and simply playing (13%).

Preferred activities were influenced by ethnicity, wealth, and where the girls lived. Native American and Asian-American girls were most likely to mention athletics as an activity that made them feel good about themselves. Affluent girls, especially those who lived in cities, were more likely to mention an arts-related activity such as music, painting, dance, or drama. Urban areas are most likely to provide opportunities for these activities, especially for those whose families can afford to pay for them (Erkut, Fields, Sing, & Marks, 1997).

Ethnicity and class were also related to the reasons girls gave about why an activity made them feel good. More affluent European-American and Asian-American girls were more likely than other girls to cite mastery as the reason. For Native American girls and Latinas, mastery was inversely related to social class, and there was no relationship between class and mastery in the reports of African-American girls. It seems that social class produces different experiences for girls from various ethnic groups.

Girls from different locations also gave differing reasons for why they enjoyed particular activities. For example, African-American and Asian-American girls were more likely than other girls to say that an activity made them feel good because they enjoyed it. However, those girls who lived in rural areas or on reservations were more likely to say that an activity made them feel good because it gave them the opportunity to be with friends. Because particular ethnic groups are more likely to be found in some locations rather than others, researchers must take care not to confuse context or differential opportunity with ethnic differences.

When female college students reported on their sports involvement during adolescence, greater participation in sports predicted higher self-esteem—but only if the young women also saw themselves as physically competent, had a favorable body image, and were flexible in their gender roles. In the absence of positive views about themselves, early sports participation had little benefit and even undermined self-esteem (Richman & Shaffer, 2000). A recent meta-analysis of thirty-four studies comparing female athletes and non-athletes found no differences in eating problems between the groups if the athletes had participated in sports in high school. But this study also found a small but significant increase in the rate of eating disorders among female college athletes compared with their nonathletic peers (Smolak, Murnen, & Ruble, 2000).

These studies suggest that sports involvement is also a mixed bag for women. How does one account for the negative as well as the positive effects? All sports are not alike. Eating disorders were more prevalent among women who participated in dance/performance activities, such as cheerleading and aerobics, but not among swimmers or runners—sports in which performance is more important than appearance. Some comparisons also showed a protective effect for young women who participated in sports but did not compete at an elite national or international level (Smolak et al., 2000).

Some sports seem to contribute to *body shame*, the acceptance of cultural standards for female appearance, and the belief that the individual can control that appearance. Young women who participated in sports that objectify the female body (cheerleading, dance team, gymnastics, and synchronized swimming) had a higher level of body shame than those who participated in sports that do not focus on appearance and femininity, such as golf, lacrosse, crew, field hockey, or basketball (Parsons & Betz, 2001).

Physical activity, independent of sports participation, has more positive effects. Young women who participated in regular physical activity reported higher levels of personal efficacy, a greater sense of control in their interpersonal experiences, and greater instrumentality (ability to control the physical world) than their less active peers (Parsons & Betz. 2001).

Involvement in sports is less problematic for teenage boys. Skill in sports appears to enhance boys' self-esteem and may help support them in school transitions because it provides a sizeable peer group with whom to interact. In sixth and seventh grades, boys report much more confidence in their sports abilities than girls do. Gender differences in sports confidence are much larger than actual differences in sports-related skills (Eccles, Barber, Jozefowicz, Malenchuk, & Vida, 2000). These findings suggest that encouraging girls to become involved in team sports may minimize the problems associated with sexual objectification and provide psychological and social benefits during a very vulnerable period in their lives.

ARE BARRIERS TO GENDER EQUALITY FALLING?

Are Cultural Constructions Changing?

The cultural factors that make adolescent girls more vulnerable to social stress do not appear to have changed as a result of the feminist movement. Although some of the following studies are old, they are interesting because of their historic perspective. For example, gender stereotyping among boys and girls was not significantly less in 1982 than in 1956 (Lewin & Tragos, 1987). Boys emphasized gender-role differences and symbols of male dominance more than girls did. They also had more traditional attitudes toward the social, economic, and political rights of women than girls did (Galambos, Petersen, Richards, & Gitelson, 1985).

Boys were more traditional than girls in all national groups sampled in a cross-cultural study (Gibbons, Stiles, & Shkodriani, 1991). However, an unusual pattern has been found for African-American adolescent males. They appear to combine traditional attitudes about male gender roles with less conservative attitudes about female gender roles (Pleck, Sonenstein, & Ku, 1994). They are, for example, likely to disagree with the statement that it is better for everyone if the man earns money and the woman takes care of home and family.

The popular media to which young women are exposed certainly do not present them with images of equality. One study examined the number of pages of *Seventeen* magazine that were devoted to various themes for the years 1961, 1972, and 1985 (see Table 7.2). Although the number of pages on male-

TABLE 7.2. Percentages of Editorial Pages Given to Selected Topics in *Seventeen* Magazine

	1961	1972	1985
Appearance	48.0	52.0	46.0
Home	9.0	10.0	11.0
Male-female relations	7.0	2.7	6.5
Self-development	7.5	16.6	6.8

female relationships decreased and the number of pages on self-development increased in 1972 (possibly as a result of the feminist movement of the late 1960s), by 1985 the percentage had returned to the 1961 figures (Peirce, 1990).

A further analysis of *Seventeen* by the same researcher (Peirce, 1993) found that more than 60 percent of the articles in each issue were on fashion, beauty, food, and decorating. Most of the fiction showed males and females in gender-traditional occupations. In this example, the heroine, a high-school sophomore, suddenly finds herself with a boyfriend:

> "Now I was someone with a future. . . . Until now I'd been a kid, stumbling along. . . . A few weeks ago I'd been a zero and now I had a boyfriend!"

When it turns out that the boy is involved with someone else, the protagonist comments:

> "Now I didn't have a boyfriend anymore, an Ivy-League, advanced math, possible husband-in-a-big-modern-house boyfriend." (Peirce, 1993, p. 64)

"Fortunately" for this young woman, there is another boy waiting in the wings. One could hardly call these images self-actualizing!

Magazines designed for teenagers in Europe do not seem to be much better than those published in the United States. One investigator recently compared the first six issues of a magazine for teenage boys published in the Netherlands with one for teenage girls. She found that 40 percent of the girls' magazine was devoted to such female stereotypic topics as fashion, beauty, love, and romantic fiction. Another 10 percent consisted of "tips" on interior decorating, needlework, and recipes. In contrast, more than 30 percent of the boys' magazine was devoted to tips on travel; a regular feature called "Wheels" on cars, motorcycles, and so on; and a feature on films, compact discs, and computer games (Willemsen, 1998).

Even rather unlikely forms of entertainment have a sexist agenda. Two researchers analyzed so-called slasher films (which also appeal primarily to adolescents). Although female and male victims were portrayed equally frequently and were as likely to die in an attack, female nonsurvivors wore significantly more revealing and provocative clothing, were more likely to be shown undressing, nude, or engaging in sexual activity, and were shown as promiscuous more than females who survived (Cowan & O'Brien, 1990).

Other studies have found that women who wear heavy makeup are rated as more immoral and more likely to be sexually harassed than those who use less makeup (Workman & Johnson, 1991). However, these women are also seen as more attractive and feminine. These images construct a double bind similar to the one found in the use of the term slag discussed earlier in this chapter. Adolescent girls are being told simultaneously that they should appeal to the sexual fantasies of men, but also that such appeal is dangerous. Young women are expected to have a "great body" but not to draw too much attention to active sexuality, which is "normal" only for males (Tolman & Brown, 2001).

Contradictory cultural constructions of womanhood are imposed during a particularly vulnerable period. Young women must deal with biological change (with its mixed set of cultural meanings) while negotiating their path into adulthood. Very few women report that they wish to return to their teenage years. Men appear to have found them more satisfactory. Neither of us would like to be 13 again.

Working Together toward Gender Equality

Many of the young women discussed in this chapter have developed individual strategies of resistance to sexist constructions. Collective strategies are even more effective. In recent years, girls have become an outspoken voice in the women's movement, often by making use of computer technology. A growing number of girls' "zines" critique mainstream magazines for girls and offer their own, often subversive, images of current culture (see Figure 7.7).

For example, *Teen Voice Online* is a teen magazine for adolescent girls that encourages audience participation and invites submissions of creative writing and book and music reviews. It can be found at www.teenvoices.com. Another website, Club Girl Tech (girlstech.com), contains positive news articles about girls and has a search engine to help viewers find other websites for girls. *American Girl Magazine,* found at www.americangirl.com/ag/ag/cgi, includes a forum for girls to share ideas, information, and volunteer experience.

A number of women's organizations are also supporting research and action on behalf of girls. These include the American Association of University Women's Educational Foundation, The Ms. Foundation, the Women's College Coalition, and The National Council for Research on Women. The latter organization financed the publication of *The Girls Report: What We Know and Need to Know about Growing Up Female* (Phillips, 1998). This publication includes a fourteen-page re-

FIGURE 7.7. Transgressing cultural rules of gender—girls' zines as a site of resistance.

source guide to books, media, and programs for and about girls. Thirteen now is not the same as thirteen was in the past or what it will be in the future. Technology offers the promise that young women no longer need to feel isolated in a hostile environment.

CONNECTING THEMES

- *Gender is more than just sex.* Adolescence is an excellent example of the way biological sex and the many social aspects of gender interact. Perceptions about a young woman's body can influence her in ways that seem largely beyond her control.
- *Language and naming are sources of power.* Adolescence involves both naming and not naming. Recent observational studies demonstrate that the relationships between boys and girls during this period may have a larger power dimension and be much more verbally abusive than researchers had previously thought. Some young women may respond to the ambivalence of being a mature woman in a society that devalues women by silencing themselves, losing self-esteem, and/or becoming depressed.
- *Women are not all alike.* Because adolescence is a socially constructed category (in distinction to puberty, which is a biological event), it is expressed quite differently by young women from different social classes and racial/ethnic groupings in our society. White middle- and upper-class girls appear to be most vulnerable to the stresses produced by normative definitions of mature femininity. For example, they are more affected by school transitions and are more likely to suffer from eating disorders than are working-class girls or those from ethnically marginalized groups.
- *Psychological research can foster social change.* Although male dominance is a social norm, strong girls can challenge the normative social structure. Peer groups of assertive young women are very effective agents of change. They are making use of new technologies to critique current cultural systems.

SUGGESTED READINGS

JOHNSON, NORINE G., ROBERTS, MICHAEL C., & WORELL, JUDITH (Eds.), (2000). *Beyond appearance: A new look at adolescent girls.* Washington D.C.: American Psychological Association. This book contains a number of useful chapters by current leaders in research about female adolescents. It is particularly good at integrating issues of race/ethnicity and class into discussions about the personal, social, and educational problems of girls and young women.

MARTIN, KARIN A. (1996). *Puberty, sexuality, and the self: Boys and girls at adolescence.* London: Routledge. This brief book examines the impact of puberty on both sexes through interviews and analysis. It looks at how adolescents construct their sense of the self and how these constructions are influenced by the social meaning of puberty.

PHILLIPS, LYNN. (1998). *The girls report: What we know and need to know about growing up female.* New York: The National Council for Research on Women. This timely and comprehensive report covers important material on health, sexuality, violence, and schooling. It also provides an extensive resource guide for parents, social policy makers, and everyone interested in eliminating gender inequality in the United States.

CHAPTER 8

Sex, Love, and Romance

Sex, love, and romance seem like natural events—instinctive, unlearned, and universal. For example, think about a kiss. Perfectly natural, right? In Western societies, kissing is seen as an instinctive way to express love and increase arousal. Yet in many cultures, kissing is unknown. When people from these cultures hear about our kissing customs, they agree that these practices are dangerous, unhealthy, or just plain disgusting. When members of one African community first saw Europeans kissing, they laughed and said, "Look at them—they eat each other's saliva and dirt" (Tiefer, 1995, pp. 77–78).

Strange as it may seem, sex, like kissing, is not a natural act. In other words, sexuality is not something that can be understood in purely biological terms. Instead, it is a social construct.

HOW IS SEXUALITY SHAPED BY CULTURE?

Individuals develop their own sense of sexual identity and desire in the context of their particular time in history, their social class, ethnic group, religion, and prevailing set of gender roles (Foucalt, 1978; Rubin, 1984). Every culture throughout the world controls human sexuality (Hyde & DeLamater, 1997). Because men have more social and political power, this control usually works to their benefit. For women, cultural constructions of sexuality lead to an ongoing tension between pleasure and danger (Joseph & Lewis, 1981; Vance, 1984a).

What Are Sexual Scripts?

Each individual has a biological capacity for sexual arousal, but people learn rules that tell them how to have sex, with whom they may have it, what activities will be pleasurable, and when the individual is—and is not—allowed to take advantage of the biological potential for sexual enjoyment (Gagnon & Simon, 1973; Radlove, 1983). Together, the repertoire of sexual acts that is recognized by a particular social group, the rules or guidelines for expected behavior, and the expected punishments for violating the rules form the basis of *sexual scripts* (Laws & Schwartz, 1977).

The sexual scripts women and men learn can be thought of as schemas for sexual concepts and events. For example, when college students were asked to list what people would typically do on a first date, they agreed on things like worry about appearance, get dressed, go out, get to know each other by joking and talking, try to impress date, kiss goodnight, and go home. These first-date scripts featured men asking for the date and initiating physical contact (Rose & Frieze, 1989). Sexual scripts are used in guiding one's own behavior and in interpreting others' behavior.

Sexual scripts operate at societal, interactional, and individual levels. They are part of cultural institutions (e.g., sexual behaviors are regulated by law and religion), they provide norms for interpersonal behavior (e.g, the first-date script), and they are internalized by individuals (some behaviors come to be seen as exciting and others as disgusting). They are influenced by race and class as well as by gender (Mahay, Laumann, & Michaels, 2001). Table 8.1, based on a national U.S. sample, shows some normative scripts that differ among ethnic groups. Throughout this chapter, we consider women's sexuality and intimate relationships in terms of both biological potentials and the influences of society's sexual scripts.

How Do Sexual Scripts Differ across Cultures?

There is tremendous variability in cultural scripts about sex, love, and romance. For example, people in the United States believe that love is necessary for marriage. But in most of the world, marriages are arranged by family members, not

TABLE 8.1. Societal scripts about sexuality differ in American ethnic/racial groups, even when social class is accounted for.

	Ethnic/Racial Group					
	African-American		*Mexican-American*		*White*	
Sexual Script	Male	Female	Male	Female	Male	Female
There's been a lot of discussion about the way morals and attitudes about sex are changing in this country. If a man and a woman have sex relations before marriage, do you think it is always wrong, almost always wrong, wrong only sometimes, or not wrong at all? (% Wrong)	25.5	38.3	27.7	41.8	21.6	30.3
What if they are in their teens, say fourteen to sixteen years old? In that case, do you think sex relations before marriage are always wrong, almost always wrong, wrong only sometimes, or not wrong at all? (% Wrong)	67.6	83.2	75.9	92.4	73.5	84.6
My religious beliefs have shaped and guided my sexual behavior. (% Agree)	49.5	69.2	51.8	60.9	44.4	56.6
I would not have sex with someone unless I was in love with them. (% Agree)	43.3	77.0	56.6	78.3	53.1	76.4

Source: Adapted from Mahay, J. W., Laumann, E. O., & Michaels, S. (2001). Race, gender, and class in sexual scripts. In E. O. Laumann & R. T. Michael (Eds.), *Sex, love, and health: Private choices and public policies* (pp. 197–238). Chicago: University of Chicago Press.

by the bride and groom. Romantic love may be viewed as irrelevant or even destructive. In a study of college students in eleven cultures (India, Pakistan, Thailand, Mexico, Brazil, Japan, Hong Kong, the Philippines, Australia, England, and the United States), participants were asked whether they would marry someone they were not in love with, if the person had all the other qualities they desired. In India and Pakistan, about half said yes. In Thailand, the Philippines, and Mexico, about 10 to 20 percent agreed. However, in the other countries, including the United States, only a tiny minority of people said they would marry without love (Levine, Sato, Hashimoto, & Verma, 1995). Within each country, male and female respondents were quite similar in their beliefs.

Culturally influenced beliefs and expectations about sexuality lead to ethnic group differences in sexual behavior. For example, compared with American college students, Chinese students start dating at a later age, date less often, and are less likely to have sex with their dates (Tand & Zuo, 2000). A comparison of Asian and non-Asian students in a Canadian university showed that the Asian students were more conservative in their behavior (for example, they were less likely to have had sexual intercourse or to masturbate, and they had fewer partners if sexually active) (Meston, Trapnell, & Gorzalka, 1996). In another study, ethnically diverse girls in grades six to eight in the United States were asked what is the "best" age to have sex for the first time. Asian-American girls gave the highest average age (21.74 years) and the African-American girls the lowest (19.16 years). However, for all groups, the more a girl believed she could succeed in school and work, the less likely she was to predict early sexual activity for herself (East, 1998). Clearly, sexual scripts are part of larger life scripts, both of which are shaped by a person's social group and perceived opportunities.

THE SCIENTIFIC STUDY OF SEX

Starting about a hundred years ago, sex came to be seen as an acceptable topic for scientific study. For better or worse, educated people in Western societies can now compare their own sexual behavior with what the "experts" say is normal (see Figure 8.1).

Nineteenth-century research on sexuality was conducted mainly by physicians, who frequently reported case studies of people with sexual problems. Some of these pioneer researchers were social reformers who wanted to make society more tolerant of sexual variation; others condemned "deviant" sexual practices. By the early twentieth century, anthropologists such as Margaret Mead began to study sexual behavior in other cultures. Evidence of the enormous cross-cultural variability in sexual norms and practices helped create an understanding that there is no one way of being sexual that is "natural" for human beings.

Another important method of studying sexual behavior is to ask questions through surveys and interviews. When Alfred Kinsey and his colleagues conducted surveys of sexual behavior in the 1950s (Kinsey, Pomeroy, & Martin, 1948; Kinsey, Pomeroy, Martin, & Gebhard, 1953), sex became a matter for public discussion. Kinsey (a zoologist whose previous research was on insect behavior) even appeared on the cover of *Time* magazine. His books created a furor because they "pointed to a vast hidden world of sexual experience sharply at

FIGURE 8.1. What does it take to be average?
Source: Sylvia. © 1987 by Nicole Hollander. Used by permission of Nicole Hollander.

odds with publicly espoused norms" (D'Emilio & Freedman, 1988, p. 286). Religious leaders disapproved of Kinsey's research, but the majority of the public approved of scientific research on sexuality, and other surveys followed.

Kinsey's studies used samples that were not random, and his respondents were all white, disproportionately young, and well educated. Many other sex surveys have also used unrepresentative samples, but the recent National Health and Social Life Survey (NHSLS) (Gagnon, Laumann, & Kolata, 1994; Laumann & Michael, 2001) used good scientific methods and a representative sample of more than 3,400 English-speaking Americans.

By the 1960s, researchers had added another method for gaining information about sexuality: direct observation. William Masters, a physician, devised ways of measuring physiological changes during sexual activity—using instruments to measure heart rate, muscular contractions, and vaginal lubrication—and developed a laboratory procedure for observing sexual behavior. With Virginia Johnson, he studied the physiology of sexual responses using medical and graduate students, his own former patients, and women and men of all ages, both single and married, who volunteered because they needed to earn money or wanted to contribute to medical research (Masters & Johnson, 1966). A later study (Masters & Johnson, 1979) used similar procedures with gay men and lesbians as volunteers. In both studies, the participants were mostly white and well educated. And, of course, people who would feel uncomfortable having sex under observation in a laboratory were not studied. Masters and Johnson, however, did not consider the representativeness of the sample important, because they believed that the basic physiology of sexual behavior is similar in all human beings.

Sex surveys and observational research provide two kinds of information about sexuality. Surveys describe *normative,* or typical, practices; direct observation yields descriptions of individual physiological responses to sexual stimulation. Both kinds of knowledge can be useful, but both have their drawbacks.

With surveys, it is difficult to obtain representative samples, and participants may misremember or distort their accounts. There is also a danger that people who read the results of surveys will interpret their own behavior in terms of the supposedly normal behavior reported by others. It is important to remember that no survey is ideologically neutral; the questions asked and the people chosen as respondents can bias the results toward a particular social construction of sexuality.

In laboratory studies using direct observation, sex is conceptualized as a set of biological responses to stimulation. But desire and arousal are not simply reducible to blood pressure changes and muscle contractions. An emphasis on biology to the exclusion of subjective experience and social context may imply that biology is (and should be) the primary determinant of social arrangements. Ideally, sex researchers should study *both* subjective experiences and physiological measures to understand sexual activity in social and cultural contexts (see Figure 8.2). Leonore Tiefer, a feminist psychologist and sexologist, has articulated a vision for the future:

> Feminist research on sexuality would begin by adopting a collaborative stance, using participants' subjective perceptions to enrich objective measurements, and planning research to benefit the participants as well as the researchers. Re-

"NOT BAD, PHILLIP. CLOUD EIGHT."

FIGURE 8.2. A subjective measure of sex?
Source: © Martha F. Campbell. Reprinted by permission.

search would be contextualized to as great a degree as possible, since no understanding of sexuality can emerge from any study that ignores the social, demographic, and cultural features of participants' lives. . . . The assumption would be that we are studying sexualities, and looking for ways that all women are alike would play no part. (Tiefer, 1988, p. 24)

ADOLESCENT SEXUALITY

How Does Sexuality Emerge in the Teen Years?

With puberty comes a surge in sexual interest and behavior. During the last forty years, there have been large changes in patterns of sexual activity in the teen years, both in the United States and around the world:

- More teens are having sexual intercourse outside of marriage.
- The increase has been greater for girls.
- First intercourse is occurring at an earlier age, on average.

However, there are ethnic group differences in the United States in age of first intercourse, and there are large variations from one country to another (Hyde & Delamater, 2003).

In the 1940s, only about 33 percent of females and 71 percent of males had intercourse outside marriage by the age of 25 (Kinsey et al., 1948, 1953). Today, about 79 percent of males and 74 percent of females are sexually experienced by age 19 (Hyde & DeLamater, 1997). The gender gap in sexual experience has almost disappeared; however, boys still have first sex at an earlier age than girls, despite reaching puberty at a later age. African-American teens have first-time sex at around 15.5 years of age, and whites at around 17 years; Latinos vary, with Cuban-Americans and Puerto Ricans at 16.6 and Mexican-Americans at 17. More than one in five teens experiences first intercourse between the ages of 11 and 14 (Becker et al., 1998).

Comparisons of countries around the world show that the average age of first intercourse is similar (between 16–18 years in most countries). However, the percentage of unmarried women who have intercourse is lower in Latin American countries than in the United States or Africa, due to the influence of Catholicism. Increasingly, the influence of North American mass media around the world is contributing to changing sexual values and behavior, so that intercourse outside marriage is becoming more widespread globally (Hyde & DeLamater, 2003).

What Factors Influence the Decision to Have Sex?

Many factors, both biological and social, are implicated in adolescents' choice to become sexually active. Puberty is occurring earlier, and marriage is occurring later (see Chapters 7 and 9), so there is a longer time between biological readiness for sexual activity and society's approval of it.

The initiation of sexual behavior depends very much on social factors. For both boys and girls, one of the strongest predictors of sexual activity is the *perceived* level of sexual activity of their best friends (DiBlasio & Benda, 1992; Furstenberg, Moore, & Peterson, 1986; Miller et al., 1997). In a study of more than 1,300 poor, urban middle schoolers, those who became active during sixth grade were more likely to believe that their peers were sexually active and that joining in would make them more popular (Kinsman, Romer, & Schwarz, 1998). But it is not just poor urban youth who are influenced by their beliefs about others' sex lives—most teens are. In other words, teens start having sex partly because they think their friends are doing it. In fact, perceptions about what peers are doing are more important predictors than the peers' actual behavior (Brooks-Gunn & Furstenberg, 1989). This raises troubling questions of free choice versus peer pressure, with differential effects on girls (Aarons & Jenkins, 2002). In all racial and ethnic groups in the NHSLS, women were significantly less likely than men to report that their first sex was wanted (Laumann & Michael, 2001).

Parents have some influence on teens' sexual behavior (Miller et al., 1997). In a study of urban African-American teens, girls' delaying of first intercourse was related to time spent with their mother, and boys' was related to time with their father (Ramirez-Valles, Zimmerman, & Juarez, 2002). Both African-American and white girls who feel close to their parents and talk to them about sex engage in less sexual behavior than girls who do not (Murry-McBride, 1996).

Parent-child communication may have different effects on boys and girls. For example, one study found that whereas mothers' ability to communicate with sons and daughters was associated with later intercourse, sons' discussions with their fathers were related to earlier intercourse (Kahn, Smith, & Roberts, 1984). Because of the double standard for sexuality in our society, fathers may encourage their sons' sexual activity as part of sexual scripts endorsing male potency.

Although adults are quick to attribute teens' behavior to "raging hormones," the relationship between hormones and sexual activity is complex. Hormonal levels have a strong effect on the level of a girl's sexual interests, but only weak effects on her sexual behaviors (Udry, Talbert, & Morris, 1986). An earlier age of menarche has been associated with earlier sexual activity among both black adolescents and white adolescents (Smith, 1989; Zelnick, Kantner, & Ford, 1981), probably due to social pressures. In other words, girls who have more mature bodies become more sexually attractive and spend more time dating; girls with high rates of dating are equally likely to have intercourse, regardless of their age at menarche. Late-developing girls are more likely to become sexually active sooner after menarche than earlier-developing girls (Cusick, 1987). Although both groups are presumably at the same level of hormonal development at menarche, late-developing girls are in a social environment where sexual activity has already become normative for girls of their age.

Are Teens Having Safer Sex?

Traditional sexual scripts focus on men's needs and condone male power and control in relationships. As a result, women often may be unable to assert a claim to safety during sexual activity (Chrisler, 2001; Gomez & Vanoss-Marin, 1996). The consequence is an increased risk of unwanted pregnancy (see Chapter 10) and sexually transmitted diseases (STDs). These include bacterial infections such as chlamydia and gonorrhea and viral infections such as herpes, genital warts, and HIV, which causes AIDS. All these STDs are transmitted by genital, anal, or oral sexual contact, and all can have serious health consequences beyond their immediate symptoms (Amaro, Raj, & Reed, 2001; Chrisler, 2001). Although STDs are a risk for sexually active people in any age group, teens are particularly vulnerable because they tend to have more partners and because they are inconsistent in using protection. One in four sexually active teens acquires an STD (Becker, Rankin, & Rickel, 1998).

The AIDS epidemic continues. The World Health Organization estimates that more than 40 million people worldwide are infected, almost half of whom are women. In the United States, women now account for 25 percent of AIDS cases. Women of color are most at risk. Although black and Hispanic women together are less than 25 percent of U.S women, they account for 78 percent of AIDS cases among women. The most common means of transmission for women is sexual intercourse with an infected man (38%) followed by injection drug use (25%). HIV/AIDS is now the third leading cause of death for African-American women aged 25–44, and the fifth for all women in the same age group (Centers for Disease Control, 2002; Hyde & Delamater, 2003). Yet until recently, women were either ignored in HIV research and intervention or blamed for passing AIDS on to men and babies (Amaro et al, 2001).

Condoms are the most effective means of preventing HIV infection during sexual contact. But many people do not use condoms consistently, even when they know about their effectiveness in reducing STD risk. For example, interviews with

187 18- to 35-year-old Puerto Rican women in New York revealed that 64 percent engaged in unprotected sex with their primary partners (Dixon, Antoni, Peters, & Saul, 2001). In a study of ninety-eight African-American women college students, 65 percent had never or rarely used condoms, although they knew about condom effectiveness (Mays & Cochran, 1988). In a study of white college students, 38 percent never used condoms (Boyd & Wandersman, 1991). Studies in many cultures show that large proportions of young heterosexuals still engage in unprotected sex. For example, a Nigerian study of a large sample of adolescents showed that only 21 percent of the girls and 36 percent of the boys used condoms, although they knew about condom effectiveness in STD prevention (Araoye & Adegoke, 1996).

Among teens in developed countries, the main reason for not using protection seems to be that safer sex is inconsistent with the romantic, spontaneous sex of scripted fantasies. In a study of 162 Australian students, 39 percent never used condoms even for casual sex with new partners, although they rated this activity as high risk. The strongest factors determining both men's and women's condom use was their concern that it would destroy the romance and their fear of negative implications ("What will he/she think of me if I start talking about condoms?") (Galligan & Terry, 1993).

College students underestimate their AIDS risk because they use inaccurate decision rules (Malloy, Fisher, Albright, Misovich, & Fisher, 1997). For example, many believe that it is OK to have unprotected sex with someone they know well and like (Williams et al., 1992). They may judge their risk of AIDS based on their partners' appearance ("He doesn't look sick" or "She is too good-looking to have AIDS"). And although they may use condoms for first-time sex with a new partner, they believe that when they are in a relationship, they do not have to worry about protection from STDs (Hammer, Fisher, Fitzgerald, & Fisher, 1996; Misovich, Fisher, & Fisher, 1997). Of course, all these beliefs are dangerous. Young people tend to have a number of partners during the college years; even if they are monogamous while in each relationship, their partners may have engaged in risky behavior in the past. In relationships, people are in effect having sex with every other person their partner has had sex with. Even if they do not have intercourse, other activities such as oral sex can transmit STDs. Because people value relationships and want to trust their current partner, they may refuse to recognize the risks (Joffe, 1997; Misovich et al., 1997).

What can be done to reduce risky sexual behavior? Psychologists have developed strategies that work for a wide variety of groups, including urban minority teenagers and college students (Fisher & Fisher, 2000; Fisher, Fisher, Misovich, Kimble, & Malloy, 1996; Fisher, Williams, Fisher, & Malloy, 1999). Successful strategies depend on giving people *information* about how AIDS is transmitted, increasing their *motivation* to reduce their own risk, and teaching them *specific skills and behaviors.* These skills and behaviors might include practice in talking about condoms with a partner, avoiding drinking or drug use before sex, or learning how to buy and use condoms.

What works depends on the norms of the group. For example, messages that stress risk to the individual may work better in more individualistic cultures, whereas messages that stress harm to one's family may work better in more collectivist cultures (Murray-Johnson, Witte, Liu, Hubbell, Sampson, & Morrison, 2001). General appeals to "Just Say No" or to "Practice Safer Sex" simply do not change behavior. Most important, researchers need to develop feminist approaches that recognize the diverse realities of women's lives: male control of sexual decision-making, violence by male partners, dependence on men due to poverty, and drug addiction are all factors in risky behavior by women. Empowering women to control their own bodies is key to their sexual health (Amaro et al., 2001).

EXPERIENCING SEXUALITY

First Intercourse: Less Than Bliss?

North American culture is more ambivalent and restrictive about women's sexuality than some European cultures, and this may affect how American young women experience their first sexual encounter. In a study of more than 400 American and Swedish college women, the Americans expressed significantly more negative reactions to their first experience of sexual intercourse (Schwartz, 1993). In a study of 1,600 American college students, women reported more guilt and less pleasure than men. When asked to rate the pleasure of their first sexual intercourse on a 1 to 7 scale, the women gave it an average score of 2.95 (Sprecher, Barbee, & Schwartz, 1995).

The gap between the ideal and the real is highlighted in the following two accounts. The first is from a Harlequin romance novel. The second is from a sexual autobiography written by a college sophomore, reproduced here exactly as she wrote it.

> For a long timeless moment Roddy gazed down at the sleeping figure, watching the soft play of moonlight on her features . . . Gently he pulled back the blankets and lay down beside the motionless girl. She turned in her sleep, one hand flung out towards him. Tenderly he stroked a dark strand of hair from her face, then pulled her into his arms. . . . Still half drugged from brandy and sleep, she found herself stroking his hair. "Such a perfect dream," she murmured, her eyes already beginning to close again.
>
> "No dream, my lady," and Roddy's mouth found hers, silencing her words. Tenderly he slipped the ribbon straps of her nightdress over her shoulders, and her body arched up towards him as his fingers traced a burning path across her breast. A groan vibrated deep in her throat as he threw her nightdress to the floor. Then his body was pressed along hers and she gasped at the feeling of skin on naked skin, the soft hair on his chest raising her sensitivity to such a pitch she felt she couldn't bear it any longer . . .
>
> Driven now only by pure instinct, she moved against him, raining kisses down on his hair-roughened skin, tracing her fingers down the hard strength of his muscled chest. His breathing became ever more ragged, his hands slipping under her to pull her closer still, and she gave a tiny cry of surrender as he finally claimed her body, her fingers digging his shoulders as they moved together in frenzied rhythm. A vast well seemed to surge up within her, and as the room exploded into fragmented light she heard a voice crying "I love you". . . (Elliot, 1989, pp. 116–118)

> I don't think I will ever forget the night that I did lose my virginity. It was this past September (September 7th to be exact). My boyfriend and I had been going out for six months. I met him at a party late that night, but, by the time I had gotten there, he was extremely drunk. We came back to my room because

my roommate was not going to be there. We always slept together without making love so, it wasn't like we had those intentions on that night. Well, my boyfriend was very drunk and very amorous to say the least. Once we got into bed, I knew exactly what he had in mind, he was all hands and lips. I figured that we might as well have sex. . . . So, I made the decision to let him do whatever he wanted. For the actual act of sex itself, I hated it the first time. Not only was it painful but, it made a mess on my comforter. I hated my boyfriend at that time. I actually kicked him out of my room and sent him home. I was upset for a lot of reasons: My boyfriend was too drunk to remember the night so, I had made the wrong decision in letting him do whatever he wanted; there had been no feelings involved; I hadn't enjoyed it in the slightest; I had lost my virginity and betrayed my parents. I was upset for just a couple of days.

After that first night, the sex between my boyfriend and myself has been great. (Moffat, 1989, pp. 191–192)

How Do Women Experience Orgasm?

Describing sexual response in terms of frequency or physiology hardly gives a complete picture. The subjective response is equally important. Women who do not have a great deal of sexual experience are sometimes unsure about whether they have had an orgasm because they do not know how it is supposed to feel. Men, with their visible erections and obvious ejaculatory response at orgasm, need have no doubt when the event occurs.

One way to get an idea of the subjective experience of orgasm is to ask women to describe their own behaviors and sensations. Shere Hite (1976) collected lengthy surveys from more than 3,000 women, but this represented responses from only about 3 percent of the questionnaires she distributed. There is no way to know how accurately the women who chose to respond represent all women. The major strength of Hite's work is that she used open-ended questions, and many of her respondents wrote lengthy, detailed answers. A few sample descriptions of orgasm are given in Box 8.1.

Is the experience of orgasm different for women and men? Research suggests that the experiences are similar. In a study in which college students were asked to write descriptions of their orgasms, judges (psychologists and physicians) could not reliably distinguish women's and men's descriptions (Vance & Wagner, 1976). In another study, students chose adjectives from a list to describe their experiences of orgasm (Wiest, 1977). Again, there were no significant differences in responses by women and men. These similarities fit well with Masters and Johnson's (1966) emphasis on male-female similarities in the physical sexual response cycle.

Evils of Masturbation or Joys of Self-Pleasure?

Stimulating one's own genitals is a very common sexual practice. Traditionally, this practice was given the clinical term *masturbation*, which made it seem like a disorder. Indeed, masturbation was thought to cause everything from dark circles under the eyes to insanity. However, the majority of people today believe that it is neither harmful nor wrong (Oliver & Hyde, 1993). More positive terms for masturbation include *self-pleasuring* and *self-gratification*.

Women usually masturbate by stimulating the clitoris, either by hand or with a vibrator. Other methods include pressing the clitoral area against a pillow or using a stream of water while in the bath or shower. Most women who masturbate engage in sexual fantasies while doing so. Hite's survey respondents described both their techniques and their fantasies (see Box 8.2).

There is a persistent gender difference in masturbation experience. Kinsey's survey showed that virtually all males, but only about 60 percent of females, reported having masturbated to orgasm. Not only were women less likely to have masturbated, but also those who did began at a later age than the men. A meta-analysis has confirmed that this difference persists. Curiously, women do not report more negative attitudes toward masturbation, but they are definitely less likely to do it (Oliver & Hyde, 1993).

Experience in self-pleasuring has positive effects on women's sexual satisfaction. For example, in a study of married women aged 18 to 30, those who had experienced orgasm through self-gratification had more orgasms with their partners, greater sexual desire, more rapid arousal, higher self-esteem, and greater marital satisfaction than those who had not (Hurlbert & Whittaker, 1991). Self-pleasuring can be an important way for a woman to learn about her pattern of sexual arousal and satisfaction. Through practice, she can learn what fantasies are most arousing, what kinds and amounts of stimulation are most enjoyable, and what to expect from her body. For these reasons, sex therapists

Box 8.1 Women's Accounts of Orgasms

"There are a few faint sparks, coming up to orgasm, and then I suddenly realize that it is going to catch fire, and then I concentrate all my energies, both physical and mental, to quickly bring on the climax—which turns out to be a moment suspended in time, a hot rush—a sudden breathtaking dousing of all the nerves of my body in Pleasure—I try to make the moment last—disappointment when it doesn't."

"Before, I feel a tremendous surge of tension and a kind of delicious feeling I can't describe. Then orgasm is like the excitement and stimulation I have been feeling, increased, for an *instant,* a hundred-fold."

"It starts down deep, somewhere in the 'core,' gets bigger, stronger, better, and more beautiful, until I'm just four square inches of ecstatic crotch area!"

"The physical sensation is beautifully excruciating. It begins in the clitoris, and also surges into my whole vaginal area."

"It's a peak of almost, almost, ALMOST, ALMOSTTTT. The only way I can describe it is to say it is like riding a 'Tilt-a-Whirl.' "

"Just before orgasm, the area around my clitoris suddenly comes alive and, I can't think of any better description, seems to sparkle and send bright dancing sensations all around. Then it becomes focused like a point of intense light. Like a bright blip on a radar screen, and that's the orgasm."

"There is an almost frantic itch-pain-pleasure in my vagina and clitoral area that seems almost insatiable, it is also extremely hot and I lose control of everything, then there is an explosion of unbelievable warmth and relief to the itch-pain-pleasure! It is really indescribable and what I've just written doesn't explain it at all!!! WORDS!"

Source: From *The Hite Report* by Shere Hite. Copyright © 1976 by Shere Hite. Published by Simon & Schuster. Reprinted by permission of the author.

frequently use education in self-pleasuring for women who are unable to experience orgasm with a partner (LoPiccolo & Stock, 1986). Feminist writers have encouraged women to use self-gratification as a route to erotic skill and sexual independence (Dodson, 1987). The woman who can enjoy solo orgasms is not dependent on a partner for sexual pleasure and can enjoy sexual satisfaction without risk of pregnancy or STDs.

LESBIAN AND BISEXUAL WOMEN

So far, the discussion in this chapter has been about heterosexuality because it is the dominant, socially approved form of sexual expression and the one that has clear, pervasive scripts. We turn now to other sexual identities and experi-

Box 8.2 Women's Accounts of Masturbation

"To masturbate, I almost always need to be turned on by something like pornographic literature (and believe me it's hard to find anything halfway decent). I lie in bed, on my back, slide out of my panties or pajama bottoms because I like to be free to move. I rub my two middle fingers up and down and around the clitoral area. Sometimes I put two fingers of my other hand into my vagina. I rub for a few seconds and tense up my body. I can usually feel a definite fuzzy feeling when I know the orgasm is coming on and then I rub harder, mostly up and down. My legs are apart. The vaginal area is usually moistened as a result of my pornographic reading, otherwise I use spit or, very rarely, cold cream. I usually arch my back slightly when I am really turned on, at which point I take the fingers of my other hand out of my vagina and I push down on the uterine area just above the pubis."

"I lie down and begin to fantasize in my mind my favorite fantasy, which is a party where everyone is nude and engaging in group sex, lovely, lovely sex, all positions, kissing, caressing, cunnilingus, and intercourse. After about five minutes of this I am ready, very lubricated. I lift one knee slightly and move my leg to one side, put my middle finger on or around the clitoris and gently massage in a circular motion. Then I dream of being invited to this party and all those delicious things are happening to me. I try to hold out as long as possible, but in just a minute or two I have an orgasm. It is very simple, all in the mind. After the first orgasm I do not fantasize any longer, but concentrate entirely on the delicious feeling in my vagina and surrounding areas, continuing the same movement of my finger, but slightly faster and in about one minute I have another orgasm. I am very quiet, but do moan some during each orgasm. After several orgasms in this manner I start thinking of what's for dinner and the party is over."

"I don't masturbate like anybody else I ever heard of. I make a clump in the bedding about the size of a fist (I used to use the head of my poor teddy bear, but since I became too old to sleep with a teddy bear, a wad of the sheets has to suffice) and then lie on my stomach on top of it so that it exerts pressure on my clitoris. I then move my hips in a circular motion until I climax—very simple. It works with legs apart or together—either one, although when I am in a particularly frenzied state, together sometimes feels better. I usually end up sort of with my weight on my knees and elbows, so I can't do too much else with my hands."

Source: From *The Hite Report* by Shere Hite. Copyright © 1976 by Shere Hite. Published by Simon & Schuster. Reprinted by permission of the author.

ences. First, we look at sexual orientation in historical and social context; then we describe the process of developing a personal identity as a lesbian or bisexual woman.

A Social History of Lesbianism

The term *homosexual* was coined in the mid-nineteenth century. Although the term was applied to both women and men, it was defined as the inability to have a "normal" erection—a notable example of androcentrism in scientific thinking (Money, 1987b)! Throughout the nineteenth century, many women in North American society had intense friendships in which they spent weeks at each others' homes, slept in the same beds, and wrote passionate and tender letters to each other describing the joys of perfect loving harmony and the agonies of parting. These relationships sometimes were part of a lifelong commitment. No one labeled these women homosexuals or lesbians (Faderman, 1981; Smith-Rosenberg, 1975). Of course, we have no way of knowing how many of these relationships involved genital sex. They certainly involved romance, attachment, and intimacy.

By the early twentieth century, lesbianism came to be seen as a serious form of pathology. The lesbian was "sick" with a grave "disease." The change in attitude may have come about because women were beginning to demand political and social equality with men. First-wave feminists were campaigning for women's education and the vote, and more women were entering the workforce. When women's friendships and attachments to other women had the possibility of leading to real alternatives to heterosexual marriage and dependence on men, they were stigmatized and controlled. Feminists in particular were likely to be diagnosed as suffering from the newly invented disease of lesbianism (Kitzinger, 1987).

The medical and psychiatric establishment continued to evaluate lesbianism as pathological until the second wave of feminism in the late 1960s. Responding to pressure from women's liberation and gay liberation activists, the American Psychiatric Association conceded that there is no evidence that homosexuality in itself is a disorder and removed this "sexual deviation" from its official manual of psychiatric diagnoses in 1973. Overnight, millions of people who had had a psychiatric disorder became normal, a compelling example of the power of social institutions to construct—and reconstruct—reality.

Research has tended to echo society's model of lesbianism. When lesbianism was labeled a form of pathology, research by physicians, psychiatrists, sexologists, and psychologists focused on theories of causes (note that there is little research on the causes of heterosexuality), on juicy details of the deviant behaviors, and on various approaches to "curing" the disorder (Kitzinger, 1987). Bisexuals were usually lumped with gay men and lesbians or ignored altogether (Rust, 2000). The results of the first survey research on lesbians were controversial and shocking. Kinsey et al. (1953) found that 28 percent of the women he interviewed had engaged in some sort of lesbian sexual activity; 13 percent had had at least one sexual experience with another woman leading to orgasm. This is quite a lot of "pathological" women.

Kinsey had emphasized that every human being has the capacity to respond sexually in both heterosexual and homosexual ways. Indeed, later laboratory research showed that the pattern of physiological change in the sexual response cycle is the same regardless of whether one's partner is a woman or a man (Masters & Johnson, 1979). By the 1980s, lesbian sex came to be seen as more satisfying than heterosexual sex. Kinsey noted that his respondents reported greater consistency in having orgasms in lesbian sex than in heterosexual sex. Masters and Johnson (1979) suggested that women are better at making love to women than men are, and that lesbians have more satisfying relationships.

The effects on individuals of these rapid changes in the social construction of lesbianism can only be guessed at. Women born in the first decades of the twentieth century have seen lesbianism transformed from an official psychiatric disorder to a "lifestyle choice" in their own lifetime.

Still, societal attitudes about gays, bisexuals, and lesbians remain negative. About 60 percent of Americans believe that sexual relations between two same-sex adults are always or almost always wrong, down from 81 percent in 1973 (Hyde & DeLamater, 2003). Studies in several countries—including the U.S., Norway, and Turkey—show that men's attitudes are more negative than women's (Anderssen, 2002; Herek, 2002; Sakalli, 2002). In more than 70 countries around the world, same-sex sexual acts are illegal and may be punished by imprisonment, beatings, or execution (Kitzinger, 2001). In the United States, anti-gay discrimination and harassment are common.

The ideology that denies or denigrates any nonheterosexual behavior has been termed *heterosexism* (Herek, 1993). Highly heterosexist people are likely to hold authoritarian attitudes in general and to endorse social power hierarchies (Basow & Johnson, 2000; Whitley & Lee, 2000). Just as racist ideology is used to justify prejudice and discrimination against people of color, heterosexist ideology is used to justify antigay prejudice and discrimination and to discourage lesbians and gay men from becoming socially visible.

Defining Sexual Orientations

Contemporary definitions of lesbianism reflect the political and social complexities of the category. Some definitions focus on lesbianism as a refusal to accept male dominance:

> Lesbian is a label invented by the Man to throw at any woman who dares to be his equal . . . who dares to assert the primacy of her own needs. (Radicalesbians, 1969, cited in Kitzinger, 1987, p. 43)

Others focus on intimacy and attachment:

> . . . a woman who loves women, who chooses women to nurture and support and to create a living environment in which to work creatively and independently, whether or not her relations with these women are sexual. (Cook, quoted in Golden, 1987, p. 20)

Still others emphasize the individual's self-definition, as well as her behavior:

> . . . a woman who has sexual and erotic-emotional ties primarily with women or who sees herself as centrally involved with a community of self-identified

lesbians . . . and who is herself a self-identified lesbian. (Ferguson, quoted in Golden, 1987, p. 21)

Today, *sexual orientation* is considered to be a multidimensional concept involving erotic identity, affectional relationships, behavior, fantasies, and emotional attachments. Sexual relationships are only one component, and not always the most important one. Often, the various components are inconsistent within a given person (Hoburg, Konik, Crawford, & Williams, in press; Rothblum, 2000).

Definitions of bisexuality reflect this complexity. A bisexual woman is capable of emotional and sexual attachment to both women and men. However, traditionally some researchers and clinicians have maintained that there is no such thing as a "true" bisexual, implying that they are just confused or indecisive and will eventually decide to be either gay or straight (Rust, 2000). Bisexuals may feel that they fit in with neither gay nor straight culture. They may be accused by the gay community of wanting to avoid the stigma of the homosexual label and of using cross-sex relationships to hide from their own homosexuality (Ault, 1996; Rust, 1993; 2000).

Some feminists argue that bisexuality is a revolutionary concept because it challenges the "little boxes" of sexual orientation and pushes society beyond dualistic thinking about sexuality (Firestein, 1998). Indeed, some people adopt bisexual identities to reflect their gender politics—they are attracted to *people*, not gender categories of males and females—or as a challenge to the belief that everyone can be neatly labeled (Rust, 2000). Nevertheless, individuals identifying as "bi" face difficult choices about how to present themselves in everyday life (Ault, 1996).

It is clear that women do not always mean the same things when they say "I am a lesbian" (or bisexual). A study done in England compared the explanations or stories about the experience of lesbianism given by forty-one self-identified lesbians ranging in age from 17 to 58 (Kitzinger, 1987). Five viewpoints emerged from a close comparison of the accounts.

The first viewpoint was the idea of lesbianism as personal fulfillment. Women who viewed themselves primarily in this way were sure of being lesbians, were unashamed of their orientation, and thought of themselves as happy, healthy individuals:

> I have never stopped feeling relief and happiness about discovering myself and, you know, accepting about myself and finding all these other women, and it means that I'm happy almost every day of my life. . . . I've never regretted being a lesbian. . . . I mean, at least one was alive, you know, and doing things one was meant to do, doing things that were natural to one. (Kitzinger, 1987, p. 99)

A second viewpoint defined sexual preferences in terms of love: lesbianism was seen as the result of falling in love with a particular person, who just happened to be a woman. Though defining themselves as lesbian, these women felt that they could or would have a heterosexual relationship if they fell in love with a man. A third viewpoint had to do with the feeling of being "born that way," yet resisting sexual labeling:

> I'm me. I'm . . . a social worker; I'm a mother. I've been married. I like Tschaikowsky; I like Bach; I like Beethoven; I like ballet. I enjoy doing a thousand and one things, and oh yes, in amongst all that, I happen to be a lesbian;

> I love a woman very deeply. But that's just a *part* of me. So many other lesbians seem to have let it overtake them, and they are lesbians first and foremost. (Kitzinger, 1987, p. 110)

The fourth view identified women who came to lesbianism through being radical feminists:

> It was only through feminism, through learning about the oppression of women by men and the part that the enforcement of heterosexuality, the conditioning of girls into heterosexuality plays in that oppression, it was through that I decided that whatever happens I will never go back to being fucked by men. My resolution to choose sexual partners from among women only, that decision was made because I'm a feminist, not because I'm a lesbian. I take the label "lesbian" as part of the strategy of the feminist struggle. (Kitzinger, 1987, p. 113)

A final view identified women who saw their sexual orientation as a sin or weakness—a "cross to bear." These women were sometimes ashamed of being lesbians, said they would not have chosen it and would be happier if they were heterosexual.

This study explores the multiple meanings women give to their sexuality and its relationship to the rest of their lives. Each of the ways these women subjectively experience their sexuality has both costs and benefits for the individual.

Developing a Lesbian or Bisexual Identity

The process of *coming out,* or accepting lesbianism as a part of one's identity, may be slow and erratic. Gay, bisexual, and lesbian adolescents do not have an easy time. They are at higher risk for low self-esteem, emotional isolation, poor school performance, dropping out, and a variety of other problems. The suicide rate for lesbian and gay youths is two to three times higher than for other adolescents (Black & Underwood, 1998).

Coming out can take place at any time from middle childhood to late middle or old age. When it occurs later in life, it has been likened to a "second adolescence." One woman, who came out as a 56-year-old grandmother, explained: "I simply did not know there was any other way to live than heterosexual. I knew I was pretty miserable, but I just accepted that as part of the way things had to be" (Lewis, 1979, p. 19). Being out is related to greater social support, improved relationships, and lower psychological distress in lesbians of all ages (Jordan & Deluty, 2000; Morris, Waldo, & Rothblum, 2001).

Women may first come into contact with lesbians or the idea of lesbianism in many ways. Before the gay-rights movement, same-sex activity often occurred in a social vacuum. One woman recalled: " I was 16 when I first got sexually involved for about four years on and off. . . . I didn't think of it as being anything weird. I just thought of it as being neat, really something terrific. . . . I thought it was a unique thing we were doing" (Ponse, 1978, p. 187). Young women still struggle with the meaning of their desire for another woman and the dangers it represents (Ussher & Mooney-Somers, 2000). However, they now may read about the topic in the media or connect with a lesbian community and get involved in gay activism or politics.

Women's sexual identity seems to be (at least potentially) very fluid and changeable (Bohan, 1996; Golden, 1987; Rust, 1993, 2000). Some women identify first as heterosexual, then as lesbian, later as bisexual. Others go through these changes in reverse. And labels and behaviors don't necessarily match. Some women say they are lesbians although their behavior is heterosexual or bisexual; still others say they are heterosexual although their behavior is lesbian or bisexual. Some women experience their sexual orientation as freely chosen, whereas others see it as beyond their control. Women's racial or ethnic identification is also intertwined with their development of a sexual identity.

In interviews with women college students, every possible grouping of feelings and activities existed within sexual identification categories (Golden, 1987). Among women who identified themselves to the researcher as lesbians, there were some who were sexually inexperienced, some whose sexual behavior was exclusively with other women, some with heterosexual experience, and some with bisexual experience. Like those who identify as lesbian, women who identify themselves as bisexual show a diversity of actual experience (Shuster, 1987). In a study of young urban lesbians and bisexuals aged 14 to 21 years, self-identification had changed over time for many of the young women. More than half who identified as lesbian had identified as bisexual at some time in the past, and the majority had had sexual activity with both other women and with men (Rosario et al., 1996). In the first longitudinal study of lesbian and bisexual women, participants were first interviewed when they were 16–23 years old and again two years later. Half had changed their self-identity more than once, and one-third had changed between the two interviews—more evidence for the fluidity of women's sexual identities and behaviors (Diamond, 2000).

Almost all the research on lesbian and bisexual women has relied on all-white or predominantly white samples. Does identity development differ for women of different ethnic and racial backgrounds? Focusing on Latina lesbians, one researcher noted:

> Because as a Latino she is an ethnic minority person, she must be bicultural in American society. Because she is a lesbian, she has to be polycultural among her own people. The dilemma for Latina lesbians is how to integrate who they are culturally, racially, and religiously with their identity as lesbians and women. (Espin, 1987a, p. 35)

Latina lesbians are perhaps more likely to remain in the closet, keeping their orientation secret from family and friends, than white lesbians because most members of their ethnic group strongly disapprove of lesbians. However, families who become aware of a daughter's lesbianism are unlikely to openly reject or disown her. They will remain silent, tacitly but not openly accepting the situation (Castaneda, 2000).

In a questionnaire study of sixteen Latina (Cuban-born) lesbians, the respondents, like white participants in previous research, showed a wide range of subjective understandings of their lesbianism. They also wrote eloquently about the difficulty of integrating their ethnic and sexual identities. This woman had earlier said that being a Cuban and being a lesbian were equally important to her:

> I guess that if the choice were absolute, I would choose living among lesbians . . . but I want to point out that I would be extremely unhappy if all my Latin culture were taken out of my lesbian life. . . . I feel that I am both, and I don't want to have to choose. (Espin, 1987a, p. 47)

In interview studies, African-American lesbians also have described issues of integrating multiple identities and group memberships: as lesbians, as members of the black community, and as part of the larger culture with its racism, sexism, and heterosexism:

> Diane (hesitated) to discuss her lesbian feelings while in college. The college she attended was predominantly White, and Diane relied a great deal on the Black community there for support. She considered that coming out to these individuals might jeopardize her acceptance in this group. Although Diane continued to explore her lesbian feelings internally, she also continued to date men. Several years later, as she did begin to come out to others, she feared that identification as a lesbian might pull her away from what she considered her primary reference group—Black Americans. (Loiacano, 1993, pp. 369–370)

African-American families typically give strong support to their members in their struggles with racism, but may not have the same perspective about heterosexism. Also, African-American religious groups have often been silent on issues of sexual orientation (Greene, 2000). Moreover, community values emphasize childbearing as a central role for women (Hatton, 1994). The small samples used in research to date make it difficult to generalize about African-American lesbians and underscore the need for more research within the black community (Hatton, 1994). However, it is clear that, like other women of color, black lesbians "face the challenge of integrating more than one salient identity in an environment that devalues them on all levels" (Greene, 2000).

Asian-American lesbians, too, face issues of multiple identity. Within Asian cultures, being a lesbian is viewed as a rejection of women's most important role, that of wife and mother. Moreover, the implication is that the lesbians' parents have failed and that the child is rejecting not only family values but Asian culture. In a study of nineteen Asian-American lesbians, the majority felt more comfortable in the lesbian community than the Asian-American one and reported that they had experienced more frequent discrimination as Asians than as lesbians. The researcher speculated that perhaps the stereotype of the passive but exotic Asian woman is so strong that the possibility that an Asian woman could be a lesbian is rarely considered; therefore, Asian lesbians experience more discrimination as women and Asians than as lesbians (Chan, 1993).

In a cross-cultural study of identity development, women aged 18 to 35 in Brazil, Peru, the Philippines, and the United States were asked, "At what age did you realize that you would be heterosexual (or homosexual)?" In all four countries, lesbians reached this point of identity development at a later age than heterosexuals (Whitam, Daskalos, Sobolewski, & Padilla, 1998). Little is known about factors that contribute to developing a healthy lesbian identity. One study asked more than 60 lesbian national leaders about factors that contributed to their successful coming-out process. These women mentioned being part of a gay community, using self-help and counseling, and acceptance by their families as important (Bringaze & White, 2001).

More research is needed on how women integrate sexual identity with other aspects of their sense of self. One model for integrating identities comes from Native American cultures, where there is a tradition of accepting different sexualities, as Chapter 5 discussed. Anthropologists have used the term *berdache,* but some gay, lesbian, and bisexual Native American people prefer the term "two-spirit" to describe themselves. Traditionally, two-spirit people were a part of the community; by taking the traditional name, Native Americans who are gay, lesbian, or bisexual feel that they are returning to their communities (Wilson, 1996).

ROMANTIC LOVE AND SEXUAL PLEASURE

Romantic Love as a Cultural Script

Although there are few societal scripts for healthy homosexual relationships, heterosexuality is strongly scripted. One pervasive source of heterosexual scripting is the romance novels displayed in virtually every supermarket and shopping mall bookstore. Each of their covers features a woman (always young, white, beautiful) gazing rapturously up into the eyes of a tall, strong, handsome man. Their titles and their plots tell women that "Love Is Everything."

According to publishers' surveys, romance novels are read by almost 40 million American women. They account for 56 percent percent of mass-market paperback sales in the United States. More than 2,200 new titles are published every year. Romance novels aimed specifically at adolescents have been sold through school book clubs since about 1980, gaining in popularity every year. Although most romance novels are published in the United States, England, and Canada, their readership is global (Puri, 1997).

No one would claim that these novels are great literature. They follow a predictable script: "Woman meets (perfect) stranger, thinks he's a rogue but wants him anyway, runs into conflicts that keep them apart, and ends up happily in his arms forever" (Brown, 1989, p. 13). But their enduring popularity and appeal suggest that many women still believe (or want to believe) that love conquers all.

In romance novels, the heroine attracts the hero without planning or plotting on her part. In fact, she often fights her attraction, which she experiences as overwhelming, both physically and emotionally—her knees go weak, her head spins, her heart pounds, and her pulse quickens. The hero is often cold, insensitive, and rejecting, but by the end of the novel the reader learns that his coldness has merely been a cover for his love. The independent, rebellious heroine is swept away and finally gives in to the power of love and desire.

What do young women learn from reading teen romances? A close analysis of a sample of thirty-four teen romances showed that the novels portrayed girls' sexuality as dangerous until it was channeled into heterosexual pairing. Readers also learn that their bodies are the site of a struggle for control among boyfriends, themselves, and their parents, and that they should appear passive. Girls respond to boys' cues but never take the lead themselves (Christian-Smith, 1998). In these novels, the lives of the heroines are made meaningful only by their heterosexual relationships.

Unfortunately, these relationships rarely include safe sex. Romance novels almost never depict the use of condoms in first sexual encounters. And in a study of female college students, those who read the most romance novels had the most negative attitudes and intentions about condom use (Diekman, McDonald, & Gardner, 2000). This study also showed that including safe-sex scripts in romance stories led to more positive attitudes towards condoms.

Why do so many women enjoy these fantasies? For adolescent girls, they provide a way to make sense of their emerging sexuality (Christian-Smith, 1998). Unfortunately, belief in a "fairy-tale ending" can encourage girls to tolerate abusive relationships (Jackson, 2001). Reading romances is an escape from humdrum reality and a time when hardworking wives and mothers can treat themselves to solitude and leisure (Radway, 1984). They also provide a reassuring fable of women transforming men. Although the hero is initially cold, patronizing, sometimes even brutal, he actually loves the heroine, and it is the power of her love that transforms him into a sensitive, passionate, and caring lover. In reading the romance, women may learn to interpret the insensitivity of their own boyfriends and lovers as "evidence" that underneath the gruff exterior is a manly heart of gold (Radway, 1984). Some feminists argue that romance novels may even encourage women to accept relationship violence and abuse. Others maintain that one should not blame the novels or their readers: "an understanding of Harlequin romances should lead one not to condemn the novels but the conditions which have made them necessary" (Modleski, 1980, p. 448).

Romance novels are one of the many ways that women learn the cultural script that love defines a woman's existence. From earliest childhood, girls are encouraged to identify with heroines who are rescued by a handsome prince (Cinderella, Rapunzel), who are awakened from the coma of virginity by the love of a good man (Sleeping Beauty), or who transform an extremely unpromising prospect into a good catch through their unselfish devotion (Beauty and the Beast).

What meanings do romantic scripts have for women who read romance novels in other cultural contexts? In India, dating is usually unacceptable, and women are expected to be virgins when they marry. Romantic love has little or nothing to do with choosing a life partner; most marriages are arranged by the couples' families. Yet India, where many middle-class women read English, may be the world's largest sales outlet for romance novels. A study of more than 100 young, single, middle-class Indian women suggested that reading romance novels is a form of cultural resistance. In them, women explored alternative, more "liberated" kinds of relationships with men. They also admired the spunky, feminine-but-strong heroines. And they gained information about sexuality. As one woman said, she had learned about the biology of sex at school, but it was from romance novels that she learned there is nothing wrong with sex—indeed, that it is pleasurable. For better and for worse, romance novels are part of the globalization of Western culture (Puri, 1997).

The Experience of Romantic Love

Given that the ideology of romance is directed largely at women, it might be expected that women are more romantic in their beliefs about relationships than men. The opposite seems to be true (see Figure 8.3). Studies (reviewed by

FIGURE 8.3. Not what she bargained for.
Source: Sylvia. © 1987 by Nicole Hollander. Used by permission of Nicole Hollander.

Peplau and Gordon, 1985) show that, at least among the young, predominantly white college students studied by most researchers, men are more likely to believe that true love comes only once, lasts forever, and overcomes obstacles such as religious differences. They are more likely to believe in love at first sight and to be "game players," enjoying flirtation and pursuit. Consistent with their beliefs, men report falling in love earlier in a new relationship. They also feel more depressed, lonely, and unhappy after a breakup and are less likely to initiate the breakup than their female partners. Women are more likely to report feeling joy or relief after breaking up (Choo, Levine, & Hatfield, 1997).

Women, on the other hand, report more emotional symptoms of falling in love—feeling giddy and carefree, "floating on a cloud," and being unable to concentrate. And after a relationship has moved beyond its first stages, they may become more emotionally involved in it than their male partners.

The reasons for these differences in the experience of romantic love are unclear (Peplau & Gordon, 1985). Men may fall in love more readily because they rely more on physical attractiveness to decide whom to love—a characteristic that is easy to see at the start of a relationship. They may also react more quickly because the cultural script says that men should initiate a dating relationship. Women traditionally may have been more pragmatic because, in choosing a mate, they were choosing a provider as well as a romantic partner. Yet they may be more "emotional" because cultural norms allow them to admit to having feelings.

Gender-related differences in the experience of romantic love are not large, and there is a great deal of overlap in the beliefs and self-reported behaviors of women and men. But the differences are interesting because they do not always fit stereotypical expectations. Perhaps future researchers will examine them in more detail.

Do Romantic Scripts Affect Women's Sexual Experiences?

Young women, especially those of the dominant white culture, are exposed to many messages that tell them love is everything to a woman. At the same time, they learn that finding fulfillment and self in the love of a man is outside their control. In the romantic script, it is always the man who actively initiates and pursues; the woman passively offers token resistance but finally gives in to his desire.

These beliefs inform the sexual scripts of teens and young adults. Research on college students, other dating couples, and marital partners shows that men are more likely than women to initiate sex. People are especially vulnerable in sexual encounters; the woman who wants to initiate sex and the man who wants to say no may fear being rejected as future dates and labeled as deviants. It feels more comfortable and secure to follow familiar patterns, as expressed by this British 16-year-old being interviewed by a researcher:

INTERVIEWER: Do you think boys always take the lead?
RESPONDENT: Yeh.
I: Yeh? And do you want them to or—
R: Yeh! Definitely! It's tradition (laughs).
I: Yeh? Why? Does it feel better or does it—
R: I don't know? I just think they should.
I: Yeh.
R: 'Cause I wouldn't, so I would expect them to, really.
I.: So why wouldn't you?
R: I don't know? "Cause I am the girl? (both laugh) (Sieg, 2000, p. 501).

When the woman in a dating situation wants to respond positively to a man's sexual initiative, she may still feel that she ought to offer *token resistance*—in other words, to say no when she actually intends to have sex. Both women and men engage in token resistance for a variety of reasons: they want to test their partner's response, add interest to a boring relationship, or prevent being taken for granted (Muehlenhard & Rodgers, 1998). However, saying no when they really mean yes may have serious negative consequences for women. It discourages honest communication and perpetuates restrictive gender stereotypes. Most important, it may teach men to disregard women's refusals. If men learn from experience that no is often only a prelude to yes, they may become more aggressive with dates. Token resistance may provide a context of ambiguity that encourages date and acquaintance rape (Muehlenhard & Hollabough, 1988). Of course, some men are sexually aggressive despite a woman's clear, unambiguous no (see Chapter 13).

Romantic scripts also encourage people to think of lovemaking as something that "just happens." However, although sex may seem "perfectly natural," it is not naturally perfect (Tevlin & Leiblum, 1983). Women who take responsibility for their own pleasure and who take an active role in sex are much more likely to experience pleasure than those who are passive. Satisfying sex depends on communication, learning, and initiative on the part of both partners.

Women are encouraged to view sex in rosy, romantic terms, focusing on candlelight dinners, courtship, and soft caresses. Because many men do not require a romantic context for arousal, they may initiate intercourse with little romantic prologue. Romance novels portray men as the "experts" who make "their" women come alive sexually. But men are likely to be expert only in the techniques and behaviors that bring them pleasure. Though men could benefit from learning about women's desires, sexual scripts can impede their development. Women who have not learned to acknowledge their own arousal and who do not feel entitled to initiate or direct sex are not in a good position to teach their male partners how to give them pleasure.

Do Romantic Scripts Lead to Sexual Dysfunction?

Because our society does not give women the same permission to be fully sexual that it gives men, women may experience less sexual joy. A meta-analysis showed that women express somewhat more anxiety, fear, and guilt about sex than men and are less accepting of casual and extramarital sex (Oliver & Hyde, 1993). However, the women and men did not report any overall difference in sexual satisfaction. Most of the participants in these studies were college-age students. Other research suggests that adult women in heterosexual relationships experience less pleasure in sexual activity than their partners. In the NHSLS study, women were much more likely than men to report lack of interest or pleasure in sex (Laumann, Paik, & Rosen, 2001), and men reported more emotional and physical satisfaction in their relationships (Waite & Joyner, 2001).

Acceptance of traditional sexual scripts is implicated in women's sexual dysfunction and suppression of desire. Sexual pleasure and orgasm require an awareness of one's own needs plus a feeling that one is entitled to express those needs and have them met. Women's recognition of themselves as sexual beings is blocked in many ways by cultural influences. Women are more likely to feel guilty and ashamed about their bodies ("I look too fat in this position"; "I shouldn't ask my partner for oral sex or to touch my 'dirty' genitals"; "I don't smell good"). They may feel guilty about having needs and fear their partners' disapproval if they express their needs ("I shouldn't be taking so long to climax"; "He'll get angry if I suggest a new position") (Tevlin & Leiblum, 1983, p. 134).

Another script is that women are sexually passive, men sexually aggressive. Adolescents and college students believe that males almost always want to have sex and females almost always want to avoid it. The effect of accepting this script is that sexual activity may proceed on his, not her, timetable, and the woman's pleasure is reduced. Because both sexes believe that it is natural for the man to initiate a sexual encounter and take the lead throughout, it is he who decides what activities the couple will (and will not) try, the duration of intercourse, and the sequence of events. With such little control, it is unlikely that the woman will have her needs met. If the man prefers only brief foreplay, the couple may proceed to penile penetration before the woman is aroused, making intercourse painful and unpleasant for her. (The term *foreplay* itself implies that penis-in-vagina is the main event, with hugging, kissing, talking, genital touching, and all other sexual activities merely a prologue.) Women typically need more stimulation to have an orgasm than men do. If intercourse seems to be over almost before it has begun, the woman who has accepted a passive role may be reluctant to ask for more stimulation. Repeatedly engaging in sex when one is not aroused and not satisfied may lead to clinical sexual problems (Tevlin & Leiblum, 1983).

That passivity is a learned script rather than a natural mode for women is shown by comparing the behavior of the same women with both female and male partners. When bisexual women were with a male partner, they were much less active and initiating than when they were with a female partner (Masters & Johnson, 1979). Women who take an active, autonomous, and assertive part in sexual expression are more likely to be orgasmic (and multiorgasmic) (Radlove, 1983).

Another aspect of sexual scripts is the idea that women should be oriented primarily toward their partner's pleasure. *The Surrendered Wife* says that no woman should refuse to have sex with her partner just because she doesn't feel like it. Some sex manuals instruct women to fake orgasm, act like prostitutes, or perform strip routines for their partners. To feminists, advice like this raises troubling questions of where consent ends and coercion starts. Faking arousal, pleasure, and orgasm may become so ingrained that the woman may not be able to distinguish between her own sexual desire and her desire to please, and her sex life may come to feel like a part she is acting or a service she must perform.

SEXUALITY IN SOCIAL CONTEXT

Controlling Women's Sexuality

Radical feminist perspectives suggest that male dominance is fundamentally sexual. In other words, the power of men over women in society is expressed and acted out not only in sexual violence (see Chapter 13) but also in male control of the very definition and meaning of sexuality (MacKinnon, 1994).

Genital Mutilation

An example of overt control of women's sexuality is the practice of *female genital mutilation* (also termed *female circumcision,* although it involves much more drastic procedures than male circumcision). Female genital mutilation is a common practice in at least twenty-eight African countries, as well as parts of Asia and the Middle East. It is usually done to young girls between the ages of 4 and 12. It may involve removal of part or all of the clitoris (*clitoridectomy*), cutting away the clitoris plus part or all of the inner lips of the vulva (*excision*), or in addition to excision, sewing the outer lips of the vulva together to cover the urinary and vaginal entrances, leaving only a small opening for the passage of urine and menstrual blood (*infibulation*). A woman who has undergone infibulation must be cut open for childbirth and resewn afterward (Abusharaf, 1998).

The genital surgery is usually done by a midwife with no medical training under unsanitary conditions. Complications such as infection and hemorrhaging are common; the presence of open wounds makes women extremely vulnerable to HIV infection. Other long-term health consequences, especially for infibulated women, include chronic pelvic and urinary tract infections, childbirth complications, and depression. Because the clitoris is damaged or removed, circumcised women feel little or no sexual pleasure and do not have orgasms. "Circumcision is intended to dull women's sexual enjoyment, and to that end it is chillingly effective" (Abusharaf, 1998, p. 25).

According to Amnesty International, which has investigated genital mutilation as a human rights issue, 135 million women living today have been subjected to the process, and each year another 2 million girls are cut. Genital mutilation is spreading to countries where there are large numbers of refugees from Africa, Asia, and the Middle East. Great Britain outlawed the practice in 1985 when three girls bled to death after the procedure, but no one has ever been prosecuted under the law (Laurance, 2001).

Why does this custom persist? It is believed to purify women and control their sexuality, making them more docile and obedient. Women who remain uncut are disrespected, considered promiscuous, and may become social outcasts. The practice of genital surgery has been very resistant to change. However, studies show that the more educated women are, the less willing they are to allow their daughters to be cut. As women in developing countries make gains toward social equality, becoming less dependent on marriage for survival, their attitudes may change.

The custom of genital mutilation is the result of a cultural construction of sexuality that may seem barbaric to outsiders. However, it was actually a common practice in England and the United States only a century ago, when clitoridectomies were done by physicians to cure upper-class women of too much interest in sex, and one health expert advised parents of girls who masturbated to "apply pure carbolic acid to the clitoris" (Michael et al., 1994). And some current Western practices seem barbaric to outsiders, too. What counts as normal depends on one's cultural standpoint:

> Today, some girls and women in the West starve themselves obsessively. Others undergo painful and potentially dangerous medical procedures—face-lifts, liposuction, breast implants, and the like—to conform to cultural standards of beauty and femininity . . . people in the industrialized world must recognize that they too are influenced, often destructively, by traditional gender roles and demands. (Abusharaf, 1998, p. 24)

Clearly, each culture exerts its own pressures.

Cultural Variations in the United States

Even within the United States, Western (European) ideas about sexuality and love are not shared by people from all ethnic backgrounds. Because almost all psychological research on romantic beliefs and behavior has relied on white

Making a Difference

Fauziya (Fah-ZEE-ya) Kassindja fled the West African country of Togo alone at age 17, to avoid her aunt's plans for her—marriage to a 45-year-old stranger and female genital mutilation (FGM). Girls and women in the Middle East, Africa, Southeast Asia, and elsewhere have been subjected to FGM, which often results in deadly infection, problems in childbirth, and lifelong pain. Kassindja, with the support of her sister and mother, fled Togo hours before she was to undergo FGM. She reached the United States only to be imprisoned with other refugees for more than a year, at times with murderers and other violent criminals. She finally gained political asylum in 1996, when due to her lawsuit, it was ruled that the Immigration and Naturalization Service must recognize FGM as a form of persecution. Kassindja has since coauthored a book, *Do They Hear You When You Cry?*, which not only exposes the horrors of FGM, but also reveals the poor treatment of refugees in the United States. She says of her homeland, "I love my people, but this is a part of my culture I don't like." She dreams that some day no girl will have to fear the horrors of female genital mutilation.

Source: Associated Press.

heterosexual college students, there is much more to learn about the experiences of other groups of people.

Religion and social class separate cultural groups within the United States. Like their white peers, African-American girls learn different lessons about sex and love, depending on their social class and religion. They may be brought up in strict homes, receiving explicit warnings from their mothers about men and sex, or in quite permissive ones where sexual activity is regarded as good and pleasurable (Joseph & Lewis, 1981). In several studies, African-American teenage girls have reported strong conflicts between their sexuality and their plans for an education (Tolman, 2001). African-American girls, who are disproportionately poorer and living in urban areas, may experience their sexuality as more of a threat than white middle-class girls do because they have fewer social safety nets such as access to abortion and contraception (see Chapter 10). Behaviorally, African-American women are more conservative in some ways than white women—less likely to masturbate or to engage in oral sex (Hyde & DeLamater, 2003). Attitudes may differ, too; some writers have suggested that black women may be less likely than their white counterparts to believe in romantic love as a woman's reason for living and more likely to maintain strong feelings of independence (Williams, 1997).

Like black women, Latinas in the United States are a diverse group with respect to social class. In addition, their families come from many countries, including Cuba, Puerto Rico, Guatemala, and Mexico. Despite this diversity, there are some commonalities affecting romantic and sexual attitudes and behaviors. Because of historical influences and the Catholic religion, virginity is an important concept. In Hispanic cultures, the honor of a family depends on the sexual purity of its women. The Virgin Mary is presented as an important model for young women, and abstaining from sex before marriage is stressed (Castaneda, 2000: Espin, 1986).

The traditional Hispanic ideal for men is one of *machismo*—men are expected to show their manhood by being strong, demonstrating sexual prowess, and asserting their authority and control over women. Women's complementary role of *marianismo* (named after the Virgin Mary) is to be not only sexually pure and controlled but also submissive and subservient. Their main sources of power and influence are in their roles as mothers. These traditional roles vary widely with social class, urban versus rural locations, and generational differences (Castaneda, 2000). Nevertheless, the cultural imperatives of virginity, martyrdom, and subordination continue to exert influence over the experience of love for Hispanic women. This socialization pattern can create difficulties in sexual expression and increase vulnerability to partner violence and HIV infection (Espin, 1986; Raffaelli & Ontai, 2001; Salgado de Snyder, Acevedo, Diaz-Perez, & Saldivar-Garduno, 2000).

In Asian cultures the public expression of sexuality is suppressed, and sexual matters are rarely discussed. Yet sexuality is viewed as a healthy and normal part of life. The Confucian and Buddhist roots of Asian cultures stress women's roles as wives, mothers, and daughters and place strong importance on maintaining family harmony. Influenced by these traditions, Asian-Americans tend to be more sexually conservative than people of other ethnic groups; for example, Asian-American college students are less likely to be sexually active than their white peers (Chan, 2000). However, their views about abortion are liberal. Although their backgrounds differ, the majority are of Chinese origin and from non-Christian religions, and they view abortion as a socially responsible decision to avoid overpopulation and poverty (Hyde & DeLamater, 2003).

Cross-cultural and ethnic group differences in attitudes toward sexuality and sexual practices remind us that there is no "right" way to think about sexuality. Rather, sexuality, including beliefs, values, and behavior, is always expressed in cultural context. It is social, emergent, and dynamic (White, Bondurant, & Travis, 2000).

Attractiveness and Sexual Desirability

In Chapter 2 we discussed how physical attractiveness triggers stereotypes and affects judgments about others. Attractiveness is an important factor in romantic relationships as well (Sprecher & Regan, 2000). Good looks are especially important to men choosing a prospective sexual partner or mate, as shown by research in many cultures. When college students in the U.S. (Nevid, 1984) and in India (Basu & Ray, 2001) were asked to rate physical, personal, and background characteristics they consider important in a sexual relationship, males tended to emphasize their partners' physical characteristics and females to emphasize personal qualities (see Figure 8.4). However, when rating characteristics they considered important in a long-term, meaningful relationship, both men and women emphasized personal qualities more than looks. And in both studies there was considerable overlap between the traits desired by women and men.

Because attractiveness is more important to men, variations from attractiveness norms are more stigmatizing for women. In one study, college students received a description of an obese or normal-weight person and then evaluated the person on aspects of sexuality. Students believed that an obese and a normal-weight man would have about the same sexual experiences and desirability; however, they viewed an obese woman as less sexually attractive and likable, and less likely to have pleasurable sexual experiences (Regan, 1996). Clearly, women's sexuality, more than men's, was being evaluated in terms of physical attractiveness.

FIGURE 8.4.
Source: For Better or For Worse by Lynn Johnston, 1999. © Lynn Johnston Productions, Inc./Distributed by United Feature Syndicate, Inc. Reprinted by permission.

Once a girl starts to develop a mature female body, she becomes vulnerable to sexual objectification and its effects. She learns that she will be treated as a collection of body parts—breasts, thighs, butt—and valued primarily by how she measures up on unrealistic standards of beauty (Fredrickson & Roberts, 1997). In many studies, girls of diverse ethnic backgrounds have described this ideal girl: she is "reminiscent of a Barbie doll . . . blonde, blue-eyed, large-breasted, tall, and thin." And, because people tend to associate looks with personality, she is also "always sweet, popular, and smart (but not too smart)" (Tolman, 2001, p. 144). Of course, very few women can match the ideal image of femininity, and no woman can do so as she grows older. Increasingly, women are resorting to cosmetic surgery, seeking "cures" for aging and perceived defects through techniques such as liposuction, breast implants, collagen and botox injections, and face-lifts. Although cosmetic surgery is marketed as a choice to make the most of one's unique looks, the result is to make people look more alike—and to enforce a white beauty norm (Haiken, 1997; Morgan, 1998). The objectification of women is implicated in a variety of psychological problems such as anxiety, depression, and eating disorders (see Chapter 14).

Disability and Sexuality

Disabled girls and women, like nondisabled women, are judged by their attractiveness. Additionally, they are judged against an ideal of the physically perfect person who is free from weakness, pain, and physical limitations. In a study of attitudes about the sexuality of disabled and nondisabled women, Australian college students expressed much more negative attitudes about disabled women's sexuality, and men were more negative than women (Chandani, McKenna, & Maas, 1989). Interviews with women who had cerebral palsy showed that one of the psychological tasks they faced was reconciling their bodies and experiences with society's norms for women (Tighe, 2001).

Women with disabilities confront stereotypes that sexual activity is inappropriate for them; that people with disabilities need caretakers, not lovers; that they cannot cope with sexual relationships; that they are all heterosexual and should feel grateful if they find any man who wants them; and that they are too fragile to have a sex life. When people around them express these stereotypical beliefs, it is difficult for women with disabilities to see themselves as potential sexual and romantic partners. These beliefs can interfere with disabled women's sexual expression and their chances for finding loving relationships. In a national survey that compared women aged 18 to 83 with and without disabilities, the disabled women were less satisfied with the frequency of dating and perceived personal and societal barriers to dating relationships (Rintala et al., 1997). Indeed, disabled women are less likely to be married than disabled men, and more likely to be abandoned by their partners when a disability like multiple sclerosis is diagnosed (Chrisler, 2001; Fine & Asch, 1988).

Parental attitudes and expectations for daughters with disabilities can have important effects on daughters' sexual development. In a study of forty-three women with physical and sensory disabilities (including cerebral palsy and spinal cord injury), many of the parents had low expectations of heterosexual involvement for their daughters because they saw them as unable to fulfill the typical role of wife and mother. Some of these daughters became sexually active partly out of rebellion and a desire to prove their parents wrong, whereas others remained sexually and socially isolated. In contrast, other parents saw their daughters as normal young women, with the disability only one of many unique characteristics. These young women became socially and sexually active as a matter of normal growing up. One interviewee reported:

> In childhood, I was led to believe that the same social performance was expected of me as of my cousins who had no disabilities. I was a social success in part because my mother expected me to succeed. In fact, she gave me no choice. (Rousso, 1988, p. 156)

Is Sex Talk Sexist?

A negative evaluation of female sexuality is deeply embedded in language, as Chapter 2 discussed. Linguists agree that languages develop an abundance of terms for concepts that are of particular interest or importance to a society. English has many terms describing women and their genitals in specifically sexual ways, and most of these are negative (Adams & Ware, 1989)—*whore (ho), bitch, cunt,* and *gash* are a few examples. One analysis found more than 200 terms for *prostitute* in English novels (Stanley, 1977). Absences in language are also revealing. For men, *virile* and *potent* connote positive masculine sexuality, as do other, more colloquial terms such as *stud, macho man,* and *hunk.* However, there is no English word for a sexually active woman that is not negative in connotation.

Slang words for sexual intercourse (*ramming, banging, nailing*) suggest that it is something violent and mechanical done to women rather than a reciprocal pleasure. The same verb can even be used to describe harm and sex—as in "she got screwed." One anthropologist who studied college students in their natural habitat (the dorm) reported that about one-third of the young men talked of women, among themselves, as "chicks, broads, and sluts." Their "locker-room style" was characterized by "its focus on the starkest physicalities of sex itself, stripped of any stereotypically feminine sensibilities such as romance, and by its objectifying, often predatory attitudes toward women" (Moffat, 1989, p. 183). Sexist humor abounds too, with women as the butt of jokes that represent them as sexual prey (Crawford, 2000).

In one study, New Zealand psychology students observed talk about sex in their daily life settings for a week and then analyzed the metaphors used. The four most common kinds of metaphor were food and eating (*munching rug; tasty; fresh muffin; meat market*); sport and games (*muff diving, getting to first base, chasing, scoring*); animals (*pussy, spanking the monkey, hung like a horse*); and war and violence (*whacking it in, sticking, pussy whipped, launching his missile*). Males were two and a half times more likely to be the actor (*"He scored her sister"*) than females (*"She turns my crank"*) or both partners (*"They've been bonking away"*), reflecting a tendency to objectify women and portray men as active agents (Weatherall & Walton,1999). In a study of American college students, men (particularly fraternity members) were more likely than women to use degrading and aggressive terms to describe genitals and intercourse than women were. Most disturbing, a person who was described in degrading terms was judged to be less intelligent and moral than a person whose behavior was the same but was described in more neutral terms (Murnen, 2000). Clearly, women who are the objects of sexually degrading language pay a price in more than one way: they can develop negative attitudes toward their sexuality, and others' evaluation of them is lowered.

It is easy to see how women might become ambivalent about sexual pleasure when the very language of sex suggests that the female role is synonymous with being exploited, cheated, or harmed and the female body is dirty and disgusting. Negative language about women and sexual acts probably encourages both women and men to view women and their sexuality negatively. By making it hard to imagine alternatives, sexist language also inhibits social change. However, feminists have added new terms to the language, naming women's experiences (date rape, sexual harassment, girl power). Gay activists, too, have added to the language of sexuality (gay, straight, bi, coming out). Language change is an ongoing process (Crawford, 2001).

Studs and Sluts: Is There Still a Double Standard?

Traditionally, a double standard of sexual behavior was widely endorsed: Women were severely sanctioned for any sexual activity outside of heterosexual marriage, whereas for men such activity was expected and tolerated. Boys had to "sow their wild oats," but girls were warned that a future husband "won't buy the cow if he can get milk for free." Because sexual activity before marriage was viewed as wrong for women, fewer young women than young men were sexually active (Laumann & Michael, 2001).

For women, the double standard was often connected with a Madonna/whore dichotomy. Women were either "the pure, virginal, 'good' woman on her pedestal, unspoiled by sex or sin" or "her counterpart, the whore . . . consumed by desires of the flesh . . . dangerous and inherently bad" (Ussher, 1989, p. 14). A woman could not belong to both categories, and women who enjoyed sex were relegated to the "bad." Oliva Espin (1986) describes this dichotomy in Latin culture:

> To enjoy sexual pleasure, even in marriage, may indicate lack of virtue. To shun sexual pleasure and to regard sexual behavior exclusively as an unwelcome obligation toward her husband and a necessary evil in order to have children may be seen as a manifestation of virtue. In fact, some women even express pride at their own lack of sexual pleasure or desire. (p. 279)

By the 1970s, the double standard had decreased. Access to contraception, the sexual revolution, and women's liberation were said to have made women and men equally free to express themselves sexually outside of heterosexual marriage. Today, when people are asked to judge the sexual behavior of a hypothetical or average woman/man, the results may show little evidence of a double standard (Crawford & Popp, 2003).

However, although people may reject the double standard when asked about it hypothetically, they do not always behave that way in their daily lives. Researchers who have done their studies by interviewing their participants, meeting with them in small groups, or just "hanging out" with them find that the double standard is still used to control girls and women's sexual autonomy (Crawford & Popp, 2003). Behaviors that are acceptable for boys and men—having many partners, taking the sexual initiative, openly talking about sex—are less acceptable for girls and women. Sexual labels are still used to control and harass. For example, when middle-school students (ages 11–14) were observed in their daily interactions, the researchers reported that girls were often labeled whores, bitches, and sluts:

> Joe and Hank walked over to a girl sitting at a table and repeatedly called her "slut-face" and "whore." They asked if her rates had gone down, or if they were still a quarter. They also told her they knew she'd "fuck any guy in the school" . . . She finally said, "Fuck you," at which point Hank and Joe backed off and left her alone. (Eder, Evans, & Parker, 1995, p. 130)

Hite's surveys of college students in the 1980s revealed a double standard among men (see Box 8.3). Do you think that today's male college students would express similar or different attitudes?

WHERE IS THE VOICE OF WOMEN'S DESIRE?

As we learned earlier in this chapter, American attitudes toward girls' sexuality are mixed. Coupled with the attention given to girls' appearance is a relative silence about the normal physical aspects of being female. For girls, this mixed message means that normal bodily desires may be denied because they conflict with the pressure to monitor and control the body. And girls learn to

Box 8.3 College Men Vote on the Double Standard

Between 1983 and 1987, more than 2,500 college men were asked the following series of questions by sex researcher Shere Hite, with the following responses:

1. Do you believe the double standard is fair? *No, according to 92 percent of men.*
2. If you met a woman you liked and wanted to date, but then found out she had had sex with ten to twenty men during the preceding year, would you still like her and take her seriously? *Most men were quite doubtful they could take her seriously; only 35 percent could.*
3. If one of your best male friends had sex with ten to twenty women in one year, would you stop taking him seriously and see it as a character flaw? *Definitely not—according to 95 percent of the men.*
4. Isn't this a double standard? And to equalize it, what should be done? Do you believe (a) men should stop being so "promiscuous" or (b) women should have as much sex as men do, with no negative feedback? *Most men found this a very difficult choice, but could see the logic of the question; the majority, approximately two-thirds, voted for (b), preferring giving women "equal rights" to changing their own view regarding sex. But many men also commented that of course the woman they would marry would probably not be one of those women who had chosen to have sex with that many men!*

Source: From *Women and Love: A Cultural Revolution in Progress* by Shere Hite.

experience their sexuality through others' eyes. Lily, a 17-year-old Latina interviewed in a study of girls' sexual desire, was asked what makes her feel sexy. Her reply referred to her boyfriend: "When he says that I look sexy, that's one of my sexy days." Though the interviewer repeatedly asked her how she herself felt, she continued to describe what her boyfriend thought (Tolman, 2001, p. 143).

What role do parents play in educating girls about their sexuality? Unfortunately, many parents are uncomfortable discussing sexuality with their adolescents or do not know enough about its physiological aspects to be of much help (Hockenberry-Eaton, Richman, DiIorio, Rivero, & Maibach, 1996). Parents may mislabel sexually important parts of the body or simply give them no names at all—especially for girls. Mothers are more reluctant to name the sexual parts of their daughters' anatomy than their sons' and do it at a later age. Few girls know they have a clitoris or that it is a separate organ from the vagina; many confuse the urinary opening with the vagina. Boys learn to personify their penises with names like *johnson* or *dick,* to ascribe power and strength with names like *cock* and *tool,* or to make everyday comparisons (testicles are *nuts* or *balls*). Girls learn to talk about their genitals, if at all, with terms such as *down there, privates, between your legs, nasty,* or *bottom.* It is not surprising that after years of societal attention to their looks and shamed silence about their sexual embodiment, many young women are far more prepared to look sexy than to be sexual.

Can schools fill the education gap? Sex education does not seem to help girls and women give voice to their own desire. Nearly three-quarters of the African-American and white women participating in one community study reported that they had wanted more sex education when they were growing up (Wyatt & Riederle, 1994). In a British study, only 44 percent of a sample of more than 3,000 high school students considered their school sex education satisfactory. The majority thought it should start earlier, be taught in mixed-sex groups, and provide information on STDs and contraception. They did not want sex education left up to parents (Mellanby, Phelps, Crichton, & Tripp, 1996).

In many U.S. schools, sex education has been shaped by pressures from some conservative parents and religious groups who believe that knowledge about sexuality encourages sexual activity. There is a "behind-the-scenes war" being waged between conservatives and liberals (Hyde & Jafee, 2000, p. 292), and adolescents are in the line of fire. Many schools have adopted federally funded programs, such as *Sex Respect,* which teach that abstinence is the only safe and moral approach to sexuality. Middle-school children are taught to chant slogans such as "Don't be a louse, wait for your spouse," and take chastity pledges in class (Hyde & Jafee, 2000).

These programs present heterosexual marriage as the sole place for sexual expression. They encode gender stereotypes of boys as sexually insatiable aggressors and girls as defenders of virginity (Hyde & Jafee, 2000). At best, girls are taught that they should avoid being victims—of teen pregnancy, STDs, or selfish males. They also learn that "good girls just say no" to sex. But nowhere do they hear the suggestion that girls and women might like, want, need, seek out, or enjoy sexual activity (outside of heterosexual marriage). Even in the more enlightened programs, girls see educational videos only about menstruation, whereas boys are seeing films about wet dreams, erections, and penis size. And lesbian, gay, and bisexual students' need for information may be ignored altogether.

This kind of sex education does not allow young women to come to terms with their own feelings of sexuality. It "allows girls one primary decision—to say yes or no—to a question not necessarily their own" (Fine, 1988, p. 34). By emphasizing to girls the many ways that they can be victimized, it may also convey the idea that women are always weak and vulnerable, undermining their self-confidence (Marecek, 1986). Suddenly, a young girl's male companions, with whom she previously may have played freely, are transformed into slightly dangerous strangers. The neighborhood itself is no longer safe for her. bell hooks (1989) has poignantly described the consequences of this fear:

> I no longer felt the intimate sweet companionship with strange black men and even the old familiar faces. They were the enemies of one's virginity. They had the power to transform women's reality—to turn her from a good woman into a bad woman, to make her a whore, a slut. (p. 149)

This social construction of sexuality gives young women little opportunity to learn how to say no at whatever stage of sexual activity suits them, and no chance to learn when they would rather say yes. And it leaves no room for them to become initiators of sexual activity. Because society constructs sexuality in terms of the presumably dangerous and uncontrollable urges of boys and men, girls and women are assigned the role of keeping everything under control by wanting only romance, never sex (Tolman, 2001). By assuming that girls and women are not active agents in their own sexuality, sex education contributes to muting women's desires:

> The naming of desire, pleasure, or sexual entitlement, particularly for females, barely exists in the formal agenda of public schooling on sexuality. When spoken, it is tagged with reminders of "consequences"—emotional, physical, moral, reproductive, and/or financial. . . . A genuine discourse of desire would invite adolescents to explore what feels good and bad, desirable and undesirable, grounded in experiences, needs, and limits. (Fine, 1988, p. 33)

There is resistance to this silencing. Some girls mock scripts about love and sexuality when they are around boys (Eder et al., 1995). Among some African-American and Puerto Rican girls in one study, their comments often combined a sense of danger and desire. As one of them explained to the researcher: "Boys always be trying to get into my panties. . . . I don't be needin' a man who won't give me no pleasure but takes my money and expect me to take care of him" (Fine, 1988, p. 35).

Women's sexual agency and desire also have been relatively invisible in sex education materials for adults. The sex manuals available up to the 1950s "purported to be objective and scientific but in fact reflected and promoted the interests of men in a sexually divided society" (Jackson, 1987, p. 52). Women were characterized as slow to become aroused and capable of being sexually awakened only by the skill of their husbands in the security of marriage. Musical metaphors abounded, with women characterized as harps or violins that the male master musician could cause to give forth beautiful melodies. The sex manuals of the 1960s and 1970s urged women to be sexually free, but still on others' terms. After analyzing their contents, one feminist researcher asked, "Clearly, the new liberated woman is 'sensuous' and sexy—but is she sexual, on her own behalf?" (Altman, 1984, p. 123). Today, books such as *The Surrendered Wife* advise women to service their husbands sexually without question.

Even in feminist theorizing, it is hard to find positive accounts of erotic experiences. A large proportion of feminist writing about sexuality has come from a radical perspective that views men and heterosexuality as oppressive. These writers explore sexual domination by focusing on graphic depictions of sexual violence against women and making connections among forms of violence from pornography to rape. At the extreme, heterosexual intercourse is seen as inherently coercive, the prototype of male domination (Dworkin, 1987). This approach implies that women who experience heterosexual desire and pleasure are suffering a kind of false consciousness (Joseph & Lewis, 1981).

In the midst of the pressures to experience sex on others' terms, it is well to remember that in spite of social pressures from all sides, some women, some of the time, do manage to have good sex! Where can the missing discourse of women's sexual desire, action, and pleasure be found? Women's accounts of their sexual experiences, relationships, adventures, and fantasies offer possibilities (Friday, 1973; Hite, 1976, 1987; Vida, 1978). Celebrities such as Dr. Ruth and Susie Sexbright speak openly of the joys of sex; feminist therapists provide workshops on self-pleasuring and interventions to increase sexual pleasure (Dodson, 1987; Palace, 1999). Guides to women's health and sexuality such as *Our Bodies, Ourselves* have been written by women. Works of fiction and poetry by women explore their naming and claiming of desire. Powerful and playful voices emerge from women's music, too, from the blues (Bessie Smith singing "You've Been a Good Ole Wagon") to Janis Joplin ("One Night Stand") and Ani DiFranco ("In or Out").

Such records of women's experiences remind us that the terms of sexual attraction and erotic arousal are not merely programmed into us. Often, they may even contradict the cultural stereotypes that surround us, as shown when some women develop healthy lesbian and bisexual identities. Future research on heterosexuality needs to explore how, "in spite of the patriarchal contours separating and opposing men and women, women do still desire and even celebrate sexual pleasure with men, and men still can renounce some of the . . . oppressive sexual practices which the sexual power divisions of our society produce and encourage in them" (Joseph & Lewis, 1981, pp. 238–239).

CONNECTING THEMES

- *Gender is more than just sex.* In the study of sexuality and relationships, it is important to view the "facts of life" as socially and politically constructed. What appears to be natural and normal—female passivity, male aggression, the suppression of female desire—may be neither. Human sexuality is constructed within the gender system.
- *Language and naming are sources of power.* Women are defined negatively by their sexuality. The language of sex portrays women as objects and sexual activity as something aggressive done to a female. Women are viewed in terms of a Madonna/whore dichotomy. Their sexual body parts and their

sexual agency remain unnamed, leading to shame and suppression of desire. But names can change. One of the clearest examples of the power of a label is the reclassification of lesbianism from a psychiatric disorder to a normal sexual orientation.

- *Women are not all alike.* Sexuality and relationship norms are shaped by culture. How important is virginity before marriage? How will a family react to a daughter coming out as a lesbian? What is a woman's risk of HIV infection? The answers to all these questions depend on the social class, ethnicity, religious background, and disability status of individual women. Moreover, women's sexual identity is fluid and changeable across the life span, adding to the diversity of ways that women experience their sexual selves.
- *Psychological research can foster social change.* Sexual norms are changing rapidly in Western societies, and these changes have global impact. The increasing acceptance of same-sex and extramarital sexual behavior have been liberating in some ways, but a sexual double standard remains, and women's sexuality is still suppressed, both overtly (genital mutilation) and covertly (the double standard). Social change efforts should focus on developing nonsexist sex education, enlarging cultural images of women's sexuality, and empowering women to make sexual choices without coercion and shame.

SUGGESTED READINGS

BOSTON WOMEN'S HEALTH BOOK COLLECTIVE (1998). *Our bodies, ourselves for a new century: A book by and for women.* Boston: Boston Women's Health Book Collective. This is newest edition of the book that started a feminist revolution in women's health by critically examining the gaps and misconceptions in knowledge and establishing women as the experts on women's bodies. The diversity of women's sexual identities and expression is respected here.

D'EMILIO, JOHN D., & FRIEDMAN, ESTELLE B. (1988). *Intimate matters: A history of sexuality in America.* New York: Harper & Row. Changing values and practices throughout the history of American society. Reading about the meanings of sexuality (including homosexuality) over time shows how individual desire and social judgment interact.

HYDE, JANET S., & DELAMATER, JOHN. (2003). *Understanding human sexuality* (8th ed.) New York: McGraw-Hill. A matter-of-fact, nonsexist college text on human sexuality. This book, written with wisdom and humor, provides a great deal of factual information.

CHAPTER 9

Commitments: Women and Close Relationships

She gave a gasp as he slid her underneath him. . . . By now Merril didn't want to talk any more. She simply wanted to fly, wherever Torrin chose to pilot her into the upper reaches of the seventh heaven.

But he lifted his head one last time. "Now will you tell me what it is I haven't asked you yet?"

"It's all right, I think you already have—" she breathed.

"And will you? Marry me, I mean?" he asked tenderly.

"Torrin, what are you doing?"

His voice was husky. "I'm giving you a lesson in love."

"Let it last forever, my dream lover," she whispered, moving sensually beneath his touch. "Like our marriage."

"And like my love for you," he murmured in velvet tones beside her head.

And as she moved against him, all notion of holding back now gone, she knew that, like love, their dream would last forever—because it was the real thing.

—The ending of *Fantasy Lover,* a Harlequin Romance (Heywood, 1989, p. 187).

Happy endings like the ones in romance novels appeal to women's hopes of finding the "real thing" and settling down to a lifetime of happiness. Romantic relationships lead—at least sometimes—to a desire to make a commitment to one partner. In our society, that commitment often leads to marriage, and when people marry they almost always hope it will last a lifetime. Not all enduring commitments to a partner take the form of marriage. Some lesbian couples choose long-term commitment, although they do not have the right to legal marriage. Some heterosexual couples choose to live together without formal marriage.

What do women want from these relationships? Research on close relationships shows that women want and need intimacy and equality. However, they may have difficulty meeting those needs within heterosexual relationships and may settle for less than they would prefer (Worell, 1988). But women (as a group) are not in any way deficient in relationship skills. On the contrary, they often give much more social support to others, especially boys and men, than they receive in return (Canetto, 2001; Steil, 2001). They communicate clearly and listen to others. (Gender differences in communication skills are small, but they are in favor of women.) However, satisfaction in close relationships depends on *both* partners and also on social structural factors that couples cannot control. In this chapter we explore the kinds of commitments couples make to each other and the consequences of these commitments for women.

MARRIAGE

As a very old joke puts it, "Marriage is an institution—but who wants to live in an institution?" This joke recognizes that marriage is a way that societies regulate private relationships between couples. Laws and statutes stipulate who may marry whom—for example, same-sex couples and some biological relatives are prohibited from marrying. In the past, interracial marriages were forbidden. Laws also regulate the minimum age for marriage, the division of property when marriages dissolve (indeed, whether they are permitted to dissolve), and the responsibilities of each partner within the marriage (what behaviors constitute grounds for divorce).

In cultures in which written law is less important, religious codes or social norms may serve the same regulatory function. For example, cross-cultural studies of preindustrial hunter-gatherer societies show that 79 percent of these societies allow men to have more than one wife. Few prohibit divorce and remarriage, but most punish married people for having sexual relations outside the marriage (Gough, 1984).

As an institution, marriage has a strong patriarchal heritage (Grana, 2002). Historically, wealth and titles were passed on only through male heirs. In many countries, married women are still regarded as the property of their husbands.

In the United States most women still give up their own name and take their husband's name upon marriage.

Although people in Western societies are aware that marriage is a legal contract subject to regulation by the state, they rarely think of it that way in relation to themselves. Rather, they are influenced by the ideology of romance, choosing their partners as individuals and expecting to live out their married lives according to their own needs and wishes. Nevertheless, the rights and responsibilities imposed by the state may have consequences for both partners, especially when the marriage ends.

The institutional aspects of marriage shape behaviors and attitudes through cultural scripts:

> An institution is a way of life that is very resistant to change. People know about it; they can describe it; and they have spent a lifetime learning how to react to it. The idea of marriage is larger than any individual marriage. The role of husband or wife is greater than any individual who takes on that role. (Blumstein & Schwartz, 1983, p. 318)

Marriage, then, is both a personal relationship and a scripted social institution.

Who Marries and When?

The great majority—more than 90 percent—of people in Western societies marry at some time in their lives. However, marital patterns are diverging among ethnic groups. For example, African-American women are the least likely of any group to be married (Dickson, 1993; Steil, 1997).

In general, women marry at younger ages than men do. Women in developing areas of the world marry very young. In many parts of Africa and Asia, the average age at first marriage is under 18 (United Nations, 1995). In contrast, the typical first-time bride in the United States now is about 25 years old; just one generation ago, she was 20 (Michael, et al., 1994). A similar trend is occurring in other industrialized countries. Scandinavian countries lead the way in the trend to later marriage; for example, only 15 percent of 24-year-old Swedish women are married (Bianchi & Spain, 1986; Norton & Moorman, 1987).

Why are American women marrying later? The idea that women can have goals other than being a wife and mother is now widely accepted. Advances in contraception have made premarital sex and living-together arrangements less risky. For black women, there is a shortage of marriageable men, due to a number of socioeconomic forces (see Chapter 10 for more on African-American family patterns). Economic factors may play a part, too; some young people find it difficult to become financially independent of their parents (Bianchi & Spain, 1986; Taylor, 1997).

Whatever the causes, the tendency to marry later has important implications for women because the increased time between high school and marriage offers opportunities to broaden experience. A woman who enters her first marriage at an older age is less likely to exchange dependence on her parents for dependence on a husband. She is likely to have had some experience of independent living; has probably held jobs and supported herself; and has had time to get more education, which exposes her to a variety of viewpoints and experiences and also increases her employment opportunities. All in all, she is more likely than a younger woman to enter marriage with a well-developed sense of self and broad horizons for her life.

Who Marries Whom?

In a cross-cultural study, more than 9,000 people from thirty-seven nations representing every part of the world were asked to assess the importance of thirty-one characteristics in a potential mate (Buss et al., 1990). The characteristics included good health, chastity, dependability, intelligence, social status, religious background, neatness, ambition, and sociability. The participants were young (their average age was 23) and typically urban, well educated, and prosperous—in other words, they are not representative samples from their countries. Nevertheless, their answers give an interesting picture of what women and men from diverse cultures look for in a potential marriage partner.

No two samples ordered the characteristics in exactly the same way. The biggest difference across cultures was in a cluster of characteristics that reflect traditional values such as chastity (the potential husband or wife should not have had previous sexual intercourse), being a good cook and housekeeper, and having a desire for a home and children. Samples from China, Indonesia, India, and Iran, for example, placed great importance on chastity, whereas those from Scandinavia considered it irrelevant.

Overall, cultural differences were much more important than gender differences. Men and women from the same culture were more similar in their mate preferences than were men from different cultures or women from different cultures. In fact, men's and women's rankings were virtually identical overall, with a correlation of +.95. This gender similarity suggests that each culture—whether Bulgarian, Irish, Japanese, Zambian, Venezuelan, or whatever—socializes men and women to know and accept its particular script for marriage.

There were some gender differences, however. Women were similar to each other across cultures in being more likely to emphasize a mate's earning capacity and ambition, and men were more likely to emphasize good looks and physical attractiveness, a pattern also observed in dating preferences (Chapter 8). Do these differences reflect optimal mating strategies determined by evolution? Probably not. A later study found that women's preferences for men with material resources was greatest in countries where women had least ability to gain power on their own through access to education and jobs (Eagly & Wood, 1999). Clearly, there is more to choosing a mate than innate mating preferences (Miller, Putcha-Bhagavatula, & Pederson, 2002).

When all thirty-seven cultures were considered, an overall picture of an ideal mate emerged. Women and men agreed, rating mutual attraction and love, dependable character, emotional stability, and pleasing disposition as the four most important characteristics in a potential marriage partner. The U.S. women and men also agreed on the importance of education and intelligence.

Many other studies have focused on spouse choices in the United States. In general, these studies, like the cross-cultural one just described, show that the desires of men and women are more similar than different. However, men remain somewhat more traditional in their thinking about marital scripts and roles. They are more likely than their wives to believe that traditional gender roles are innate and unchangeable (Mirowsky & Ross, 1987). In a study of college students, the men were more conservative than the women on issues such as whether a mother should stay at home with an infant and whether they would be willing to move for a spouse's career (Novack & Novack, 1996). Overall, women appear to expect and desire more flexible marital patterns than men.

"Marrying Up" and "Marrying Down": The Marriage Gradient

Individual couples usually end up being closely matched on social class and ethnicity as well as on characteristics such as height, SAT scores, attractiveness, and age. Couples are similar in values, too: Religious people tend to marry other religious people, conservatives marry other conservatives, and feminists marry other feminists (Michael et al, 1994). When there are differences within a couple, it is usually the man who is older, is better educated, and has a more prestigious occupation, and this is true cross-culturally (United Nations, 1995).

The tendency for women to "marry up" and men to "marry down" by sorting themselves into couples in which the man has higher prestige and income potential is called the *marriage gradient* (Bernard, 1972). The marriage gradient probably came about because women had little access to education and high-status occupations and could achieve economic security only through marriage. In the United States, women's tendency to marry up has decreased as women have become more equal to men in earning power and educational opportunity. It also varies among groups of women. Black women, for example, are less likely than white women to marry up with respect to education (Schoen & Wooldredge, 1989).

Will the marriage gradient continue to exist, even though women have more equality today? Recent studies of U.S. college students suggest that both women and men value such attributes as intelligence, desire for children, and a pleasing personality most when choosing a mate—but that wealth and status are still important attributes for men (Regan, Levin, Sprecher, Christopher, & Cate, 2000; Stewart, Stinnett, & Rosenfeld, 2000). When playing a game in which they "designed" an ideal long-term mate by purchasing desirable characteristics, female students were willing to pay the most for status and resources when designing a man, and male students were willing to pay the most for physical attractiveness when designing a woman. As in other studies, intelligence and kindness were valued for both male and female mates (Li, Kenrick, & Linsenmeier, 2002). Even when young women are relatively empowered on their own, it seems that many still prefer men with status and wealth.

Varieties of Marriage

In the United States, many marriage patterns coexist (Blumstein & Schwartz, 1983). We classify these patterns into three types (traditional, modern, and egalitarian) based on three important characteristics: the division of authority, how spousal roles are defined, and the amount of companionship and shared activities they provide (Peplau, 1983; Peplau & Gordon, 1985; Scanzoni & Scanzoni, 1976; Schwartz, 1994).

Traditional Marriage

In a *traditional marriage,* both husband and wife agree that the husband has (and should have) greater authority; he is "the head of the family," or "the boss." Even in areas in which the wife has some decision-making responsibility (such as household shopping), he retains veto power over her decisions. The wife is a full-time homemaker who does not work for pay. Clear distinctions are made between the husband's and wife's responsibilities. She is responsible for home and child care, and he is the breadwinner. Couples in these marriages may not expect to be "best friends"; rather, the wife finds companionship with other women—neighbors, sisters and other kin, or members of her church. The husband's friendship networks are with male kin and co-workers, and his leisure activities take place apart from his wife. Attitudes toward traditional marriage have changed a great deal in the past few decades (Steil, 2001). In national opinion polls in the 1970s and 1980s, about half of the population said that traditional marriage was the best lifestyle and that working mothers were bad for children. By 1996, 85% of married people thought that both partners should be earning income, and two-thirds endorsed sharing housework equally (Steil, 2001).

These changes do not mean that marriages based on traditional beliefs and values are entirely a thing of the past. Even in the late 1990s, 30 percent of survey respondents agreed that "it is better for everyone if men are the achievers and women take care of the home" (Steil, 2001). Furthermore, certain religious groups strongly endorse the traditional marriage. For example, Orthodox Jews, Mormons, the Promise Keepers, and Nation of Islam insist that distinct gender roles and submission by the wife to her husband are necessary for marital and societal stability (Hewlett & West, 1998; Mathews, 1996). And women may find their marriages becoming more traditional than they expected if they temporarily leave paid employment to take care of young children. About 38 percent of women with children under the age of 6 and 28 percent of those with children under 18 are not employed (Gilbert & Rader, 2001; Steil, 2000).

Modern Marriage

In *modern marriage,* the spouses have a "senior partner-junior partner" or "near-peer" relationship. Modern wives work outside the home, but by mutual agreement, the wife's job is less important than the husband's. He is the breadwinner, and she is working to "help out" or to provide "extras." Moreover, it is expected that her paid employment will not interfere with her responsibilities for housework and child care. Within modern marriage, husbands and wives may spend an equal amount of time on paid work, but that work has different meanings because of the belief that the man is the real provider (Steil, 2001).

Modern couples emphasize companionship and expect to share leisure activities. They value "togetherness" and may discuss husband/wife roles rather than taking them for granted as more traditional couples do.

Modern marriage may seem to be a relationship of equality when compared with traditional marriage, but the equality is relative. Husbands still have more financial responsibility, and wives have more responsibility for the home and the children (see Figure 9.1). Modern wives do a *second shift* every day—they put in a day's work for pay and yet another day's work when they get home (Hochschild, 1989). Men are considerably more satisfied than women with this

FIGURE 9.1. Let's make a deal . . .
Source: Sylvia. © 1997 by Nicole Hollander. Used by permission of Nicole Hollander.

arrangement (Baker, Kiger, & Riley, 1996). As one marital researcher put it, the men in these couples "support female equality but only up to the point it collides with their privilege" (Schwartz, 1994, p. 9). Women may be content with this arrangement because they want to be closely involved with their children, or they may put up with it because they do not know how to change it.

Egalitarian Marriage

Egalitarian marriage, once relatively rare, is becoming more common (Schwartz, 1994). In *egalitarian marriages,* the partners have equal power and authority. They also share responsibilities equally without respect to gender roles. For example, one partner's paid job is not allowed to take precedence over the other's. In practical terms, this means that either the husband or the wife might relocate to accommodate the other's promotion; either would be equally likely to miss work to care for a sick child. The ever-present tasks of running a household—cleaning, cooking, bill paying, errands—are allocated by interest and ability, not because certain jobs are supposed to be women's work and others men's work. Although partners may be very involved in their careers, they may make career sacrifices to meet each other's and their children's needs because they believe in equity (Risman & Johnson-Sumerford, 1998). Such marriages are *postgender* relationships; the partners have moved beyond using gender to define their marital roles.

More than any other type of marriage, an egalitarian relationship provides the couple with profound intimacy, intense companionship, and mutual respect. Egalitarian couples put their relationship first, ahead of work and other relationships (even family and children). Because they share a great deal, they understand each other, communicate well, and choose to spend a lot of time together. Often, each says that the other is their "best friend," believes that the other is precious and irreplaceable, and says that their relationship is unique (Risman & Johnson-Sumerford, 1998; Schwartz, 1994).

Biases in Research on Varieties of Marriage

Marriages in which both spouses work for pay (termed *dual-earner* marriages) have been around for a long time. Especially among working-class, immigrant, and rural couples, two jobs were often necessary for economic survival. Farm wives sold butter, eggs, and homemade foods; immigrant women earned money in garment factories and textile mills or worked alongside their husbands in small mom-and-pop stores and businesses. Wives also took in boarders and did laundry, sewing, and cleaning for wealthier families (Aldous, 1982). During World War II, women held factory and industrial jobs of all kinds. These patterns are not just a matter of history; rural, immigrant, and working-class women continue to contribute to their families' economic survival in these ways.

However, working-class families like these have not been studied systematically by social scientists; neither have Asian-American, Puerto Rican immigrant, or African-American dual-earner families. Instead, research has focused on white, upper-middle-class professional couples, those with *dual-career* marriages. One reason for this bias may be that the values of both partners in dual-career couples resemble the male ideal in our society. Also, many researchers who study dual-career couples are themselves part of similar marriages (Aldous, 1982). These observations serve as a reminder of how social norms and values can influence a research agenda.

Power in Marriage

Different marriage types reflect different beliefs about what the duties of husband and wife should be and how they should view each other. Completely egalitarian marriages are still relatively rare. Although Americans like to think of marriage as an equal partnership, men end up having more power. Why is it that the result of a stroll down the aisle and saying the words "I do" is often a long-term state of inequality?

Studying marriages in terms of power is not an easy task. Many people do not like to think or talk about their relationships in such "crass" terms. Couples may construct a *myth of equality,* refusing to acknowledge how gender socialization and social forces have steered them toward traditional roles (Knudson-Martin & Mahoney, 1996). Marital privacy, the myths of equality constructed by couples, and the fact that power differences can mask conflict all make it difficult for researchers to see the power dynamics involved in a couple's life together. In spite of these difficulties, psychologists and sociologists have conducted studies of marital power for at least the past thirty years.

One definition of power is "the ability to get one's way, to influence important decisions" (Blumstein & Schwartz, 1983, p. 62). Accordingly, researchers have often compiled lists of types of decisions and asked one or both partners who usually makes the final decision about each type. In the best known of these studies (Blood & Wolfe, 1960), more than 900 wives were asked who had the final say on whether the husband should change jobs (90% said husbands always did) and on how much to spend on food (41% reported that wives always did). Only 39 percent of the wives had decision-making power over whether or not they themselves should hold a paying job. Note that the decision with the most far-reaching consequences, the husband's job, is one on which husbands had virtually uncontested power.

Another approach is to ask couples who is the "real boss" in the family. In a sample of Canadian households, 76 percent of wives said that the husband was the boss and only 13 percent said both had equal power (Turk & Bell, 1972). More recent research confirms that norms have not changed very much. Even in dual-earner and dual-career marriages, there is still a consistent pattern of inequality; the roles and responsibilities are more balanced than in traditional marriages, but both partners seem to accept some level of male dominance. Even though women and men agree that women do far more housework and child care in most marriages, the majority of wives, both employed and stay-at-home, say that this imbalance is fair (Steil, 2001). In another study, couples reported that decisions about work and family issues were made together, but in fact, husbands were far more likely to get their way. "Agreement" seemed to mean agreeing that the husband was right (Zvonkovic, Greaves, Schmiege, & Hall, 1996).

How Do Couples Justify Marital Inequality?

These studies, and others like them, show that couples make meaning of their lives in the context of overall inequality. Power in marriage is both structural and ideological—it is related to societal structures that give men greater status and earning power and also to beliefs about who is better at nurturing or more suited to doing housework (Dallos & Dallos, 1997). How is marital power exerted and justified? How do couples explain away inequalities in their own marriages?

When a sample of highly educated, dual-career couples were asked about other couples' relationships, they defined equality in terms of task sharing. However, when asked about their own relationships, they talked less about who did the cooking and cleaning than about mutual respect and commitment (Rosenbluth et al., 1998). In fact, most of the couples had not achieved their ideal of equality: the women did more household work and their careers were secondary to their husbands' careers. But they did not focus on adding up who did what around the house, perhaps because it would make inequality painfully apparent. Redefining the situation is a common way to avoid perceiving injustice of all kinds (Steil, 2001).

In an in-depth study of seventeen British couples, wives and husbands were interviewed together and then, 18 months later, separately (Dryden, 1999). The researcher was aware that married women are frequently in "Catch-

22," or double-bind situations. Ideologically, they believe that marriage is supposed to be about love, sharing, and mutual respect. Practically, they might be unable to challenge inequalities in their own marriages because of being dependent on a husband's income or having very young children. Therefore, openly admitting their dissatisfactions might be emotionally almost "too hard to bear" (p. 58). For husbands, admitting inequality might lead to a loss of power and privilege. Therefore, the researcher analyzed the interview data for subtle ways that the women and men justified the status quo.

The women used distancing, talking about equality in vague, hypothetical terms rather than challenging their husbands openly (*Some* men sit around watching TV all day. . . .) They minimized conflict or blamed themselves when it happened (It's only silly little things we fight about, and maybe I take them too seriously). And they made positive comparisons between their husbands and other people's (Some women have it really bad, with husbands who don't do a thing, so I'm in a fairly equal situation). These strategies helped the women create a vision of relative marital fairness for themselves as well as for the interviewer.

Although the women's challenges were indirect, minimal, and hedged with self-blame, the men often tried to deflect them, without actually mentioning inequality. Their strategies included describing their wives as inadequate (If she were better organized, she could get all her work done with time left over) and themselves as "hard done by" (having to work long hours and needing more time out with the boys). The researcher noted that the husbands participated in reflecting back to their wives a negative identity that the wives had already created through self blame—a "subtle undermining process that had the power to exacerbate in women a sense of lack of confidence, low self-esteem, and in some cases, depression" (p. 86). Clearly, these couples were "doing gender" in their marriages in ways that preserved and perpetuated marital inequality.

What Are the Sources of Men's Greater Power?

Many factors are associated with husband dominance in marriage (Steil, 1997). Social class and ethnicity make a difference: Black and working-class couples have less of a power differential than white middle- and upper-class couples do. Wives who are employed have more power than those who work only at home. White middle-class women in traditional marriages may have less marital power than any other group of women.

One reason the power balance in marriage is weighted in favor of men is the influence of traditional beliefs and social norms. In a major study of American couples (Blumstein & Schwartz, 1983), couples were asked whether they agreed or disagreed that it is better if the man works to support the household and the woman stays home. In couples where either spouse agreed, the husband was more powerful, regardless of how much money each partner actually earned. For example, Marlene and Art have been married for thirty years. She is an executive with the telephone company and he is a farm-equipment dealer; their incomes are about equal, although sometimes she earns more:

MARLENE: Art makes the major economic decisions in our household. We are as consulting of one another as possible, but I realize that in the final push comes to shove that he is the one who shoulders the responsibility for this family . . .

ART: I would say that I make the decision when it comes to money and I guess I would also say that if there is an argument and we cannot totally work it out so that we both agree, then I have more to say . . . someone has to finally make a decision and we have always done it this way. (Blumstein & Schwartz, 1983, pp. 57–58)

Another explanation for greater male power in marriage comes from *social exchange theory* (Thibault & Kelley, 1959). This theory proposes that the partner who brings greater outside resources to the relationship will have the greater influence in it. The partner who has less to offer, be it status, money, or knowledge, will inevitably take a back seat. Money establishes the balance of power in heterosexual relationships, even though this reality conflicts with American beliefs about equality:

> Most people like to think that the right to affect decisions is based on the demands of daily events, on which partner is wiser on a certain issue, or on special gifts of persuasion. They do not like to think that income, something that comes into the relationship from the outside, imposes a hierarchy on the couple. But it does. (Blumstein & Schwartz, 1983, p. 53)

In American marriages, husbands usually bring more of three very important resources: money, education, and prestige. Husbands usually earn more than wives, even when both are employed full time, and husbands are likely to have higher-status jobs. (This is true for a variety of reasons that we look at more closely in Chapter 11.) As already noted, wives who have no income or employment of their own have the least power of any group of married women. Moreover, because of the marriage gradient, the husband in most marriages has a higher level of education than the wife. In American society, educational attainment brings status and prestige in itself and is also associated with higher income.

When the husband earns more, couples agree that he automatically has the right to make important financial decisions for the family. But the money he brings in also may give the husband the right to make other important decisions that have nothing to do with money. In a British study, one wife described how a husband can dominate a wife by appealing to his earning power, and another described how things changed when she began to earn money on her own:

> He uses it all the time to get at me, if I try to bring up various issues and he doesn't want to talk about them, especially if I ask him to do something or other he just says I earn all the money so why should I do that as well. He uses it as an excuse for all sorts of things . . . I have to be careful about rocking the boat.
>
> Before, I had five children and was very vulnerable, I avoided raising some issues because I was worried that he would stop giving me any money . . . he threatened it a couple of times and that was enough. . . now I'm earning things have changed, I'm not so quiet about things I don't like now. (Dallos & Dallos, 1999, p. 58)

Social exchange theory implies that if husband and wife have equal external resources, marital interaction will also be equal. But even in dual-career families, where the resources are fairly well matched, husbands still have more weight. For example, in a national sample of more than 1,500 dual-career, dual-earner, and traditional couples, wives in all three categories spent considerably more time in housework each week than their husbands. Dual-career husbands did not spend any more time each week doing housework than other men (Berardo, Shehen, & Leslie, 1987). Dual-career marriages also often fall short of being truly egalitarian in the relative importance attached to each partner's career. Which spouse, husband or wife, is more likely to move to a different location for career advancement or to relocate because the spouse had a job offer in a different place? When male and female members of the American Psychological Association were surveyed, 42 percent of the men and only 19 percent of the women said they had moved for an increase in salary. However, 25 percent of the women and only 7 percent of the men had moved because of their partners' relocation (Gutek, 1989).

Social exchange theory is too limited; it has focused on economic exchange while ignoring the symbolic value of gender roles. For example, the provider role, still more important for men than for women, means that men's capacity to earn money is more highly valued than their capacity to nurture children. For women, on the other hand, "being there" to provide emotional nurturance to husband and children is more valued than the ability to earn money. Even if a wife brings in as much money as her husband, she may not have equal power because her success is seen as undermining his provider role and interfering with her nurturing role. In other words, the same resource (in this case, earned income) may function differently for husband and wife (Howard & Hollander, 1997; Steil, 1994; Steil & Weltman, 1991).

Just how central is earning power to marital equality? And does its influence work the same way for husbands and wives? To answer these questions, it is necessary to study couples in which the wives earn as much or more than their husbands. Couples like these used to be very rare, but today 20 percent of wives earn more than their husbands (Gilbert & Rader, 2001).

In one intriguing study, thirty couples in which the wife earned at least 33 percent more than the husband were compared with an equal number of couples in which the husbands earned at least 33 percent more than the wives (Steil & Weltman, 1991). Respondents were asked questions about the relative importance of careers ("Whose career is more important in the relationship?") and decision-making power ("Who has more say about household/financial issues?"). Consistent with social exchange theory, spouses who earned more saw their careers as more important and also had more say at home than spouses who earned less. Nevertheless, wives overall had less say in financial decisions, had more responsibility for children and housework, and felt that their husbands' careers were more important than their own. In another recent study, status-reversed couples in which the wives earned more or were in higher-status occupations than their husbands, or both, showed a similar pattern (Tichenor, 1999).

In other words, equal access to money can be an equalizer of power in marriage—but even when wives earn more money than their husbands, beliefs about the appropriate roles of women and men still influence the balance of power in favor of men. This implies that in order to change power imbalances in marriage, both women's economic power and couples' gender ideology will have to change. Such shifts are occurring, and not only in the United States. A national study in Taiwan recently showed that Taiwanese wives' bargaining power in marriage has increased as their economic opportunities rise and traditional gender ideology falls (Xu & Lai, 2002).

Happily Ever After? Marital Satisfaction and Psychological Adjustment

"Happily ever after" is our society's romantic ideal of marriage. However, in *The Future of Marriage* (1972), Jessie Bernard maintained that marriage is not good for women. She suggested that every marriage is really two marriages, "his" and "hers"—and "his" is much more advantageous.

Which is closer to reality, the romantic ideal or the social scientists' seemingly cynical view? Does marriage bring happiness and fulfillment? We can examine the issue by looking at research on whether women (and men) are generally satisfied with the marriages they make and whether marriage has any relationship to psychological adjustment.

Does Marital Happiness Change Over Time?

The happiness and satisfaction of married women (and men) varies greatly across the life course of a marriage. Almost all studies of marital satisfaction over time show an initial "honeymoon period" followed by a substantial decline in happiness with the birth of the first child. Wives are more likely than husbands to become dissatisfied with the marriage over time. Satisfaction often hits its lowest point when the children are school-aged or adolescents. Some studies have shown that the happiness of the early years is regained or even surpassed in later life, when the children have grown and left home. In other studies, the happiness trend has been all downhill (Feeney, Peterson, & Noller, 1994; Schlesinger, 1982; Steinberg & Silverberg, 1987).

What accounts for the changes in marital happiness after the birth of children? When more than 700 women were studied during pregnancy and three months after the birth of their first child, they reported doing much more of the housework and child care than they had expected. Their negative feelings about their marriages were related to the violation of their expectancies of equal sharing. In other words, it was not the domestic chores that made these new mothers less happy than they had been, but their feeling that the new division of labor was unfair. The more they had expected equality, the more dissatisfied they were (Ruble, Fleming, Hackel, & Stangor, 1988).

You might expect that happiness would decline less among women who feel respected and appreciated by their husbands, and this is just what was found in a study that followed couples for six years. Women whose marital satisfaction stayed the same or increased after giving birth were those who said that their husbands expressed love and were "tuned in" to their wives and their relationships. Those women whose marital satisfaction declined were those who perceived their husbands as negative or their lives as out of control and chaotic (Shapiro, Gottman, & Carrere, 2000).

Even when couples have been married thirty years or more, they look back at the child-rearing years as their least happy (Finkel & Hanson, 1992). When children leave home, couples have fewer demands on their money and time.

Many couples experience this stage of their marriage as a time of greater freedom and flexibility and, therefore, of increased marital happiness (Schlesinger, 1982).

Is Marriage Linked to Psychological Well-Being?

Studies in the 1970s showed that married women were more likely than married men to have psychological disorders and problems. Single women, on the other hand, had fewer disorders and problems than single men. In fact, for every type of unmarried person (ever-single, divorced, and widowed), most studies showed higher rates of psychological adjustment disorders for men than women. Only married women had more disorders than their male counterparts (Bernard, 1972; Gove, 1972; Steil & Turetsky, 1987b). Is marriage bad for women's mental health?

Recent research shows that marriage seems to be good for both women and men. People who are married or living together in a sexually exclusive relationship report greater emotional satisfaction and physical pleasure from sex than single people do (Waite & Joyner, 2001). Marriage is also associated with better psychological adjustment in both women and men. However, the benefits are unequally distributed: men are more satisfied than women with their marriages and receive greater mental health benefits from being married (Fowers, 1991; Steil, 1997).

Why do husbands enjoy better psychological adjustment and well-being than wives? To answer this question we need to consider the different types of marriage. Several studies have shown that full-time homemakers have the poorest psychological adjustment, employed husbands have the best, and employed wives are intermediate (Steil, 1997; Steil & Turetsky, 1987b)—suggesting that something about being a homemaker is related to the occurrence of psychological disorders. (Of course, it is also possible that women with poorer adjustment are less likely to be in paid employment.)

We will look at women's work in homemaking and child care more closely in Chapters 10 and 11 and at psychological disorders in Chapter 14. For now, it is important to note that some of the unpaid work that women do in marriage is low status and boring. It may provide valuable social and emotional resources for others, while the woman herself has less support (Peplau & Gordon, 1985). Wives usually keep up contacts with friends and relatives, care for family members when they are ill, and encourage their husbands and children to take good care of themselves. They are likely to be available to listen to their husbands' troubles and problems.

In one study of more than 4,000 married persons aged 55 and over, husbands said they were most likely to confide in their wives, whereas wives were less likely to confide in their husbands and more likely to turn to a friend, sister, or daughter. Both men and women who confided in their spouses had markedly higher marital satisfaction and overall psychological well-being than those who did not (Lee, 1988). The work of caring and emotional support that married women do is an important resource for others' well-being and may partly account for their husbands' better psychological adjustment.

Is Equality Linked to Well-Being in Marriage?

A great deal of research suggests that equality is beneficial for relationships (Steil, 1997). Couples who see their marriage as equal are more satisfied than more traditional couples, report better sexual adjustment and communication, and are less likely to use manipulative and indirect influence tactics with each other (Aida & Falbo, 1991; Steil, 1994, 1997). Perhaps it is not marriage per se that is bad for women's mental health, but marriages in which women have little power and status (Dallos & Dallos, 1999).

A study of more than 800 dual-career professional couples tested the hypothesis that marital power is related to psychological well-being (Steil and Turetsky, 1987a). The researchers gathered information on each woman's earned income, her influence and responsibilities within the marriage, and her symptoms of psychological disorders. Because of earlier research connecting the presence of children to lowered marital happiness, they also compared childless women and mothers.

For childless women, the more equal a woman's marital relationship, the more satisfied she was with her marriage—and marital satisfaction was an important factor in overall psychological well-being. The mothers experienced their marriages as significantly less equal than the childless women did, and the perceived inequality was directly related to psychological symptoms. Although the dual-career professional couples in this sample are not representative of all married couples, this study suggests that relative power and equality play an important role in married women's well-being.

What Makes a Marriage Last?

What are the "secrets of success" of husbands and wives in enduring marriages? There is little research on long-lasting marriages, but as you might expect, these studies suggest that love, friendship, intimacy, and shared interests are important factors in long-term marriages (Bachand & Caron, 2001; Goodman, 1999).

Lasting marriages also change over time. In one study of 581 adults who had been married an average of eighteen years, participants were asked to remember how they had felt about their partner at the beginning of their love relationship and to describe how they felt now. They reported less erotic feelings and game-playing, an equal amount of friendship-based love, and (among the men) an increase in selfless, nurturing love (Grote & Frieze, 1998).

In a study of Canadian couples who had been married an average of twenty-five years and had at least one child, more than half the women said that they had started out their married lives with traditional role expectations, but only 20 percent still had such expectations at the time of the study. Over the course of their marriages, their expectations had evolved to an ideal of shared responsibilities and more independence for themselves. Wives and husbands were asked to indicate the factors that had contributed to their staying together. Although they were interviewed separately, spouses agreed almost perfectly (Schlesinger, 1982). More recently, 147 U.S. couples who had been married at least twenty years were asked similar questions (Fenell, 1993). Table 9.1 shows the factors that both sets of couples thought were most important.

Of course, not all marriages that last a long time are happy marriages. In the Canadian study, about 10 percent of women and men indicated dissatisfactions with their relationships; for women, the dissatisfactions centered around sexual relations, finances, the husband's workload, and children (Schlesinger, 1982). Chronic marital dissatisfaction is related to problems of mental and

TABLE 9.1. Longtime Married Couples Cite Factors That Make Marriage Last

Canadian Couples	U.S. Couples
Respect for each other	Lifetime commitment to marriage
Trusting each other	Loyalty to spouse
Loyalty	Strong moral values
Loving each other	Respect spouse as best friend
Counting on each other	Commitment to sexual fidelity
Considering each others' needs	Desire to be a good parent
Providing each other with emotional support	Faith in God and spiritual commitment
Commitment to make marriage last	Desire to please and support spouse
Fidelity	Good companion to spouse
Give and take in marriage	Willingness to forgive and be forgiven

Source: Fenell, 1993; Schlesinger, 1982.

physical health for older women (Levenson, Carstensen, & Gottman, 1993). Social norms may keep some unhappy marriages together. One major study of couples found that those who were living together (but not legally married) were likely to break up when there was a pattern of inequality in the relationship; however, for married couples, inequality had no effect on whether the couple stayed together (Blumstein & Schwartz, 1983).

Psychological research on happiness in marriage points up some interesting discrepancies between the romantic ideal and the realities. Our society tells us that marriage and parenthood are more important routes to fulfillment for women than for men. Women are thought to be eager to catch a husband and men are thought to be caught reluctantly. Women may invest a great deal of energy in planning their weddings (have you ever seen a Grooms magazine on the newsstand?). Yet research suggests that Jessie Bernard was right when she proposed that there are two marriages in every marital union, his and hers, and that his is better than hers.

LESBIAN COUPLES

Lesbian couples have been an almost invisible minority. However, lesbian and gay relationships are increasingly becoming visible. This change is due to many factors, including the civil rights movement for lesbian, gay, and bisexual people and the destigmatization of homosexuality by the APA (Allen, 1997). In surveys of lesbians conducted over the last several decades, the great majority of respondents were currently in a steady relationship (Peplau & Spalding, 2000). Not all these relationships involve living with the partner.

Lesbian and Heterosexual Couples Compared

When two women make a commitment to live together as lovers and friends, their relationship has some similarities to conventional marriage—but without the institutional aspects or the label. Lesbians (and gay men) do not have access to the predictable features of marriage that make it seem desirable to become a couple and difficult to break up. For example, there is no standard way for them to have a public wedding ceremony or to establish reciprocal legal rights and responsibilities. There are no tax advantages or spousal insurance benefits. Lesbian partners may even be legally forbidden to see each other in the event of serious accident or hospitalization if their families of origin do not approve. Ending the relationship is not hampered by complicated divorce laws; nor does society urge same-sex couples to work at their relationships and remain loyal through the hard times.

This lack of institutional and societal support can give people the freedom to make their own rules, but it can also lead to instability. Some lesbian couples write their own wedding ceremonies, and some ask a minister or rabbi to perform a ceremony of union to bless their relationship. Occasionally one partner legally adopts the other or the other's children. Many include each other in their wills and insurance policies, buy homes together, or draw up contracts delineating rights and responsibilities to each other. All these are ways of giving the relationship some legal and institutional status (Blumstein & Schwartz, 1983; Cabaj & Purcell, 1998). Gay-rights activists are working for legal recognition of same-sex unions. The impact of these efforts has not yet been studied (Peplau & Spalding, 2000).

Making a Difference

Ninia Baehr and ***Genora Dancel*** met in 1990 and have been trying to get married ever since. What started as a private romantic relationship, however, soon turned public. When the couple inquired at the local gay community center about domestic partnership options, they were asked to join two other same-sex couples applying for marriage licenses in the state of Hawaii. The couples were denied licenses, but despite fears of job loss and other repercussions, Baehr and Dancel fought for same-sex marriage rights alongside gay and lesbian activists for the next seven years. In 1993, a Hawaiian court ruled that denial of marriage licenses to the three couples constituted gender discrimination and declared that Hawaii must allow same-sex marriage or show compelling reason not to. It seemed that Hawaii would become the first state to marry same-sex couples. At this point, conservatives, led by a group called "Save Traditional Marriage," campaigned aggressively and finally derailed the issue in Hawaii. In November of 1998, Hawaiian voters ratified a constitutional amendment permitting the legislature to restrict marriage to male-female couples. The Hawaiian Supreme Court may ultimately rule in favor of same-sex marriage, but most gay activists believe that the battle has been lost in Hawaii, and they plan to focus their efforts in other states. Dancel and Baehr are not defeated, however, declaring that even if they find they can never be legally married, at that point, "we'll just accept that we know we are married, and live our lives."

Sources: Ness, C. (1995, April 27). Lesbian couple leads fight for right to marry, http://polyamory.org/~howard/Poly/news/lesbian_couple.html. Davis, N. (1996). Love's Labors Won, http://bi.org /~ndavis/ninia.htm.

For many years, researchers and the public alike assumed that lesbian couples mimic traditional heterosexual roles, with one partner being the "husband" ("butch") and the other the "wife" ("femme"). This belief applied a heterosexual script to lesbian relationships. Most research shows no clear preference for masculine/feminine roles among lesbians (Peplau & Spalding, 2000).

When lesbians do endorse butch/femme roles, it may be with different meanings than heterosexuals might assume. When a researcher asked a sample of 235 self-identified lesbians to define these concepts for themselves, the majority did identify as butch (26%) or femme (34%), with 40 percent of the sample being neutral. The higher a woman's education and income, the more likely she was to have an independent (not butch/femme) gender identity (Weber, 1996).

However, these women did not use butch/femme to represent husband/wife roles. To them, "butch" signified that they did not enjoy "girly" things such as makeup, dresses, and elaborate hairdos. "Femme" signified the freedom to enjoy makeup and other feminine aspects of personal style, while still being committed to loving women. They stressed that butch did not mean they were dominant, acted like men, or disliked being women, and femme had nothing to do with being submissive. In summary, the butch/femme dimension is important to some lesbians, and it is linked to social class, but it is not about relationship dominance.

What Are the Characteristics of Enduring Lesbian Relationships?

Lesbian relationships can be described on the same dimensions as heterosexual marriages: roles and the division of labor, companionship and communication, power and authority, and satisfaction. Most lesbians reject gender roles (Peplau & Spalding, 2000). When looking for a long-term partner, they prefer characteristics such as intelligence and interpersonal sensitivity (Regan, Medina, & Joshi, 2001).

Because same-sex couples cannot assign the breadwinner role on the basis of gender and because they tend to value independence, the importance of the work interests of each partner is much more likely to be fairly equal than in heterosexual marriages. In one study of more than 1,500 lesbian couples, 75 percent expressed the belief that both should work for pay (Blumstein & Schwartz, 1983). Fewer than 1 percent of these couples lived in a one-earner situation.

Just as they balance work roles, lesbians are highly likely to share household duties (Kurdek, 1993). They assign housekeeping chores on the basis of preference and ability, rather than roles. The basic principle is fairness. In the following interview, the speaker is an investment officer at a bank and her partner is a medical student:

> She feels very strongly about having an equitable situation and I think that comes from her having lived with men and feeling taken advantage of in the past, so she definitely feels it ought to be equitable. It's easy to slip into something where she does more because I am the only one working full time . . . but we see the dangers of that and we are keeping things in line so she doesn't get stuck with too much. (Blumstein & Schwartz, 1983, p. 150)

Same-sex couples tend to share more leisure activities than heterosexual couples. They are more likely to socialize with friends together, belong to the same clubs, and share hobbies and sports interests. Perhaps, due to socialization, two women are more likely to have interests in common than a woman and a man; or perhaps most people need same-sex "best friends," and lesbians can find a same-sex friend and a spouse in the same person. The majority of lesbian couples say they want their relationship to be central to their lives, and they value companionship and communication (Blumstein & Schwartz, 1983).

Power in Lesbian Relationships

In general, most lesbians (like most heterosexuals) desire egalitarian relationships. In a study using matched samples of lesbians, gay men, and heterosexuals, all groups (and especially women, both lesbian and heterosexual) said that having an equal-power relationship was very important. However, only 59 percent of lesbians (and even fewer heterosexual women) reported that their current relationship was exactly equal (Peplau & Cochran, 1990). Power differences in a lesbian relationship are usually due to the same factors that influence power in heterosexual relationships, such as one partner having greater resources of money, status, or education, or one partner being more committed than the other. However, the egalitarian ideal may be more important than status and money in determining power relations among lesbians. Unlike heterosexual couples, many of whom believe that the man should be the head of the family, the lesbian ideal is a relationship "where two strong women come together in total equality" (Blumstein & Schwartz, 1983, p. 310). Some studies suggest that lesbians may be more likely to establish egalitarian relationships than heterosexual women (Caldwell & Peplau, 1984; Schneider, 1986; Steil, 1994). Other studies show no differences. Further research is needed on factors affecting the balance of power in lesbian couples (Peplau & Spalding, 2000).

Satisfaction in Lesbian Relationships

Studies that compared the self-reported satisfaction and happiness of lesbian and heterosexual committed couples show few differences between the two types of couples (Peplau & Spalding, 2000). For example, when matched samples of lesbians and heterosexuals were compared, the lesbians, like the heterosexual women, reported that they both loved and liked their partners (Peplau & Cochran, 1980). Like heterosexual women, lesbians may be more likely than men to have a relational orientation toward sexuality, enjoying sex in committed relationships more than transient ones (Peplau & Garnets, 2000). Lesbian relationships tend to decline in satisfaction over time at about the same rate as those of married people (Peplau & Spalding, 2000). When partners have different levels of commitment to their careers, satisfaction is lower (Eldridge & Gilbert, 1990).

Some subtle differences exist between lesbian and heterosexual couples, however. In a study of women in lesbian and heterosexual couples, the two groups were similar in their capacity for intimacy. In lesbian couples, a woman's capacity for intimacy was related to having a more intimate relationship and using more direct communication strategies. In heterosexual couples, however, the woman's capacity for intimacy had no connection with the intimacy of the relationship, probably because men's greater power allows them to set the limits on intimacy (Rosenbluth & Steil, 1995).

External pressures affect relationships, too. Women who love women have to cope with prejudice and discrimination. Parents and other family members may reject or disown a lesbian daughter, remove her from a will, refuse to acknowledge the partner or the relationship, exclude the couple from family gatherings, encourage them to break up, or forbid all contact between them.

One important factor in relationship satisfaction for lesbians is having a social support network. Receiving social support from friends and family is related to individual psychological adjustment as well as happiness in the relationship for both lesbian and gay male couples (Berger, 1990; Kurdek, 1988). This suggests that gay activists are right in encouraging lesbians to "come out" to friends and family despite the risk of rejection. However, the evidence is mixed. Although some studies show that women who are "out" to significant others in their lives (family, friends, employers) report more satisfaction with their partners, others find that relationship satisfaction is unrelated to disclosure about being a lesbian (Jordan & Deluty, 2000; Beals & Peplau, 2001).

Biases in Research on Lesbian Couples

Although psychology has come a long way in studying lesbian relationships, the research is limited in several important ways. Like research on heterosexual couples, it frequently relies on self-reports (interviews or questionnaires), which may be biased because people want to look well adjusted to researchers or because they lack insight into their relationships. The pressure to appear normal may be greater for lesbians, and some may want to present a rosy picture of their relationships to make their sexual orientation more acceptable to others.

Research has also depended heavily on samples of volunteers that are not representative of the general population of gay and lesbian people. Lesbians who have volunteered for research tend to be young, white, and middle class. Therefore, comparing them with more heterogeneous heterosexual couples may involve hidden race, class, and age biases. Much more research is needed on older couples, women of color, working-class women, and relationships that cross barriers of class, color, and ethnicity (Garcia, Kennedy, Pearlman, & Perez, 1987; Weber, 1996). Yet it may be all but impossible to study a truly representative sample of lesbians as long as the dominant culture stigmatizes lesbianism (Peplau & Spalding, 2000).

COHABITING COUPLES

Today many heterosexual couples choose to live together without being legally married. Sociologists give this arrangement the unromantic name *cohabitation.* Couples who do it usually call it "living together"—not a very good distinguishing term because roommates or parents and children can be said to live together, too. The absence of a suitable everyday term is one clue that the cohabitation relationship is not yet an institution in society.

Who Cohabits and Why?

Whatever the label, the practice of heterosexual couples living together without being officially married is more popular than ever in the United States. One of the most striking social changes of the past forty years has been the rise in cohabitation. According to the NHSLS, among women born in the decade up to 1942, only about 6 percent lived with a man before getting married (Michael et al., 1994). By the 1990s, about half of all first marriages were preceded by living together (Forste & Tanfer, 1996). By the end of the 1990s, about 25 percent of American women under the age of 39 were cohabiting (Popenoe & Whitehead, 1999). Black and Hispanic women are more likely than white women to cohabit, but there are differences among subgroups of Hispanic women. Mexican-Americans, for example, are more disapproving of living together without planning to marry than are Puerto Ricans (Oropesa, 1996).

Although the increase in cohabitation is dramatic, the United States still has a lower proportion of cohabiting couples than many other industrialized countries. For example, virtually all Swedes cohabit before marriage, and a growing number never marry at all. Cohabitation is accepted both legally and morally even for couples who have children. As a result, half of all Swedish children are born to unmarried women (Trost, 1996). A common attitude is, "Why marry? It's our love that counts" (Popenoe, 1987).

In the United States, people choose to cohabit for a variety of reasons (Popenoe & Whitehead, 1999). For some, it is a prelude to marriage or a "trial marriage" in which the couple assesses its compatibility. Some cohabitants are divorced and not yet ready to remarry. Some young people cohabit to show their independence from their parents. Some cohabit more as a matter of convenience than deep commitment; it's easier for two to pay the rent.

People who choose cohabitation tend to be liberal in attitudes about gender roles. They are more sexually experienced and sexually active than noncohabitors, and their relationships are less likely than married relationships to be monogamous. In a national sample of more than 1,200 women aged 20 to 37, cohabitors were five times more likely than married women to have sex with someone other than their partner—about one in five had sex with someone else while cohabiting. This was true for all ethnic groups studied (Forste & Tanfer, 1996).

Cohabiting couples usually have a division of labor similar to modern marriage. They almost always expect that both partners will work outside the home. However, as with most married couples, women do more housework than men (Blumstein & Schwartz, 1983). Liberal attitudes about gender roles do not always lead to liberated behavior.

Though many cohabiting women have egalitarian ideals (and choose to cohabit rather than marry partly because of those ideals), their goals of independence and autonomy within a relationship are usually only partly fulfilled. As with married couples, issues of money, power, and the division of labor inside and outside the home can be sources of conflict. Nevertheless, most cohabitants report high satisfaction with their arrangement, and a large majority plan to marry someday, though not necessarily their current partner (Murstein, 1986).

Does Living Together Affect Later Marriage?

One obvious potential outcome of living together is that the woman becomes pregnant. Cohabitation is associated with premarital pregnancy among all ethnic groups, and the likelihood of pregnancy during cohabitation is greater for Puerto Rican than white or African-American women. Does pregnancy push cohabitors toward marriage? This, too, depends on ethnic group. White women who get pregnant while cohabiting are very likely to marry; there is no effect for African-American women; and for Puerto Rican women, pregnancy lowers the odds of marrying before the birth of the child. There is a long tradition of cohabiting in Puerto Rico, and having a child may solidify the union without leading to marriage. The data show that cohabiting has different meanings to different ethnic groups (Manning & Landale, 1996).

Is cohabitation related to later marital satisfaction? It would seem that if people use living together as a trial marriage, those who do go on to marry should be better adjusted and less likely to divorce. However, in the United States, Sweden, and Canada, studies show a greater tendency for former cohabitants to divorce, though their total time together is as long as the average married couple spends before divorcing (Teachman & Polenko, 1990). There may be ethnic and racial differences, too. In a study of about 200 black and 175 white couples in their first year of marriage, living together before marriage was unrelated to marital happiness for whites, but negatively related for blacks (Crohan & Veroff, 1989). Of course, a higher divorce rate for people who had previously cohabited is not necessarily an indication that cohabitation is a social problem. Because women who cohabit (and their partners) are more unconventional, independent, and autonomous than those who do not, they may be more likely to leave a marriage that does not meet their expectations (Murstein, 1986).

NEVER-MARRIED WOMEN

At any time, about one-third of the adult women in the United States are single. Widows, divorced women, and single mothers are discussed elsewhere; here we focus on never-married women without children. Although the proportion of women who remain single throughout their lives is small (according to U.S. Census data, about 5% of all women), it is probably increasing.

The "Old Maid": Still a Stereotype?

Negative judgments of never-married women are easy to document. The goal of a perennial children's card game is to avoid being stuck with the "Old Maid" card. Poets and authors write of "maidens withering on the stalk" or belittle a male character by comparing him to a fussy old maid. In advertising, spinsters are symbols of penny-pinching, prissiness, and timidity. Barbara Levy Simon (from whose book these examples are taken) concludes that "In Anglo-American culture, the never-married old woman is a stock character, a bundle of negative personal characteristics, and a metaphor for barrenness, ugliness, and death" (p. 2). Never-married men, or bachelors, are rarely the targets of such negative assessments.

One legacy of patriarchy is that women are still to some degree expected to be under the control of a father or husband and to fulfill their destiny by having children. Women who deviate from this ideal may be stigmatized. At a minimum, their choice will be questioned by others. When a woman says she is single by choice, she may be accused of rationalization or denial.

Who Stays Single and Why?

In contrast to the negative stereotypes and social judgments, it is generally true that women who remain unmarried have better physical health and greater economic resources than those who marry. Earlier, we discussed research showing that unmarried women have fewer serious psychological disorders than married women. Single women are better educated, are more intelligent, and achieve greater occupational success than their married counterparts.

The marriage gradient discussed earlier may explain the lower marriage rate of highly capable women. Because men prefer to marry women who are slightly below them in education, occupational status, and income (and women prefer to "marry up"), the women who are at the top of the social scale are likely to be the "leftovers," with nobody sufficiently "superior" to them to want to marry them! (The marriage gradient idea also implies that men who do not marry are more likely to be those at the very bottom of the social scale.) However, data about who marries whom are correlational, and causation cannot be determined. Whether highly educated, intelligent women are unattractive to men, whether they are less likely to marry because they have alternatives that are more appealing, or whether other factors not yet analyzed are involved is an open question.

Rewards of the Single Life

What are the advantages and disadvantages of a permanently single way of life? Because never-married women have seldom been studied, the evidence is scarce. In the largest study of single women, 50 elderly women reflected on their lives in in-depth interviews in their homes (Simon, 1987). All these women had supported themselves, and many had helped support their parents in old age. Work and financial independence were important aspects of their lives.

Sixty-eight percent of the women stressed the importance of autonomy and freedom from the role expectations of marriage: "You see, dear, it's *marriage* I avoid, not men. Why would I ever want to be a wife? . . . A wife is someone's servant; a woman is someone's friend" (Simon, 1987, pp. 31–32). More than three-fourths of the group had deliberately chosen to be single:

> I dated four men over the years who wanted me as a wife. They were darlings, each of them. I spent huge amounts of time with them. But I never for a mo-

ment considered marrying one. Well, why would I? I had their company and their attention without all the headaches a wife bears. (Simon, 1987, pp. 41–42)

These women were closely involved with their families and had many friendships with both women and men. They were of an era that did not tolerate discussion of sexuality, and they refused to answer questions about lesbianism. However, many spontaneously described their friendships with women as especially rewarding, and some had intimate relationships with female life partners:

> There is nothing I did that Joyce didn't know about . . . I shared everything with her. She did the same with me . . . We stayed roommates for fifty-seven years, until her heart gave out suddenly six years ago . . . I'm still reeling from that loss. She leaned on me all those years just like I relied on her. Now I come home to silence and to memories. (Simon, 1987, p. 92)

Of course, people looking back on their lives in retrospect may remember selectively. Nevertheless, the voices of these never-married women give reason to challenge the stereotype of the frustrated, unfulfilled "old maid." In an era when marriage was very restrictive for middle-class women, they rejected it for largely positive reasons and led active, fulfilling lives.

ENDING THE COMMITMENT: DIVORCE AND SEPARATION

The rise in divorces has probably gained more attention and caused more concern than any other social trend of our times. The United States has the highest divorce rate of any industrialized nation, a rate that more than doubled between 1960 and 1980 and has only recently leveled off or, in some groups, declined slightly (Taylor, 1997). Divorce is an everyday occurrence—even in the funnies (see Figure 9.2). Between 40 percent and 50 percent of American marriages end within less time than it takes to bring up a family (see Figure 9.3), and the Department of the Census predicts that the U.S. divorce rate will continue to be among the world's highest. Black women are considerably more likely than white women to end a marriage through divorce or prolonged separation, and

FIGURE 9.2.
Source: Blondie. © 1997. Reprinted with Special Permission of King Features Syndicate.

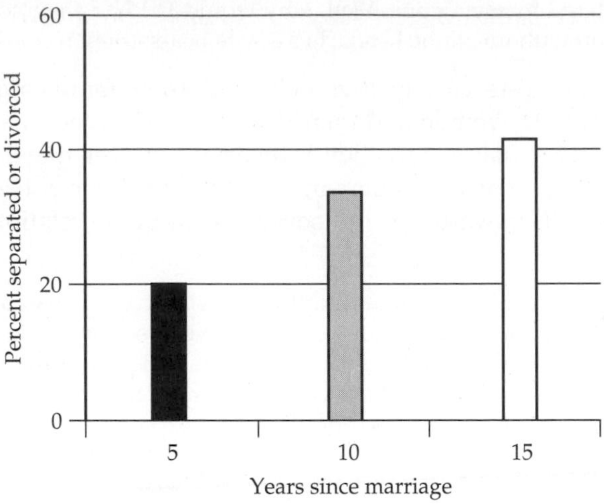

FIGURE 9.3. In the U.S. a large proportion of first marriages end within 15 years.
Source: First Marriage Dissolution, Divorce, and Remarriage: United States. (2001). National Center for Health Statistics.

Hispanic women less likely. Other countries have experienced similar increases in divorce rate, though none as extreme as the United States (Bianchi & Spain, 1986; McKelvey & McHenry, 2000; Norton & Moorman, 1987; Price & McKenry, 1988; Taylor, 1997).

What Are the Causes and Consequences of Divorce?

At the societal level, several factors have been correlated with rising divorce rates. Divorce rates rise along with women's participation in the paid workforce, both in the United States and in many other countries (Trent & South, 1989). Wives' paid employment is not usually a direct cause of divorce. Rather, it seems that when women have alternatives for economic survival other than dependence on a husband's income, they are less likely to stay in unsatisfactory marriages (Bianchi & Spain, 1986; Price & McKenry, 1988). Age at first marriage is also highly correlated with later divorce: The younger the man and woman are when they marry, the more likely they are to divorce (CDC, 2001). Other factors related to the rising divorce rate are changes in laws and attitudes; divorce is no longer the social disgrace it once was, and "no-fault" laws make it easier.

At the personal level, women and men tend to give somewhat different reasons for the breakup of their marriages. In one study (Cleek & Pearson, 1985), more than 600 divorcing persons were asked to indicate which of eighteen possible causes of divorce applied to their own situation. (The eighteen causes had been derived from counseling sessions with other divorcing spouses.) Table 9.2 shows the causes and the percentage of people who perceived each as applicable. Women were more likely than men to stress basic unhappiness, incompatibility, emotional and physical abuse, and their husbands' alcohol abuse and infidelity as causes of their divorce. Men were more likely to indicate that their own alcohol abuse and "women's lib" were responsible for their divorce.

TABLE 9.2. Perceived Causes of Divorce: Women's and Men's Accounts

Cause	Women (%)	Men (%)
Mentioned significantly more often by women:		
Basic unhappiness	60	47
Incompatibility	56	45
Emotional abuse	55	25
Alcohol abuse (spouse)	30	6
Infidelity (spouse)	25	10
Physical abuse	22	4
Children	9	4
Mentioned significantly more often by men:		
Women's lib	3	14
Alcohol abuse (self)	1	9
No significant difference between men and women:		
Communication problems	70	59
Financial problems	33	29
Sexual problems	32	30
In-laws	11	12
Religious differences	9	6
Mental illness	5	7
Drug abuse (spouse)	4	1
Infidelity (self)	4	6
Drug abuse (self)	—	1

Source: Adapted from *Journal of Marriage and Family, 47,* Table 3, p. 181. Percentages have been rounded to nearest whole number.

Very little research has looked at how events and feelings early in a marriage predict later divorce. In one recent study, those who were disillusioned within the first two years (as reflected in decreased love and affection and increased ambivalence) were more likely to end up divorced several years later (Huston, Caughlin, Houts, Smith & George, 2001).

Whatever the reasons for divorce, it has serious and long-lasting consequences for women. We examine three types of consequences, each intertwined with the others in its effects: psychological adjustment, economic effects, and responsibility for children.

How Do People Psychologically Adjust to Divorce?

A considerable number of divorcing women (from 17% to 33% in different samples) describe their divorces as causing little or no psychological disturbance or pain. These women view their divorces as ending a stressful or unbearable situation (e.g., abuse) and leading to increased feelings of freedom and competence. For most women, however, adjustment to divorce includes feelings of anger, helplessness, and ambivalence. Stress during divorce is related to a variety of physical health problems. (As with all correlational research, it is not possible to determine cause and effect in these studies.) Compared with married people, divorced people of both sexes have higher rates of illness, death, alcoholism, and serious accidents.

Displaced Homemakers. Older women who entered marriage with the expectation that they would be lifelong homemakers, their husbands the family providers—are especially likely to view divorce as a personal failure and a negation of all they have worked for. The divorce rate for older couples continues to rise (Taylor, 1997). When homemakers are divorced in middle or later life, they lose their source of financial support, have few marketable skills, and may view their divorce as a personal failure (Greenwood-Audant, 1984).

The adjustment to divorce seems to be more difficult for men than for women. Although both divorced men and women are more likely to commit suicide than their married counterparts, divorced men are 50 percent more likely to do so than divorced women. They are also more likely to show serious psychological disturbances (Price & McKenry, 1988). Women appear to be better at building and maintaining networks of close friends and family during and following divorce (Gerstel, 1988), and men may miss their partner's caretaking more (see Figure 9.4). However, women and men are quite similar in

"That's right, Phil. A separation will mean—among other things—watching your own cholesterol."

FIGURE 9.4.
Source: © The New Yorker Collection 1992 Michael Maslin from cartoonbank.com. All rights reserved.

their responses to divorce in many other ways (Gove & Shin, 1989). The question of whose divorce is worse, his or hers, is not easily resolved. Some researchers have suggested that men are more negatively affected in the short term, whereas women have more long-term problems to resolve (Price & McKenry, 1988).

Women's adjustment to divorce depends on the social support they receive, and this may differ for different groups of women. In a study using a national sample of divorced or separated women with at least one child, black women felt more positive about their personal ability to master their lives and their economic situation and were more likely than white women to receive support from a spiritual advisor such as a minister. White women were more likely to receive their support from friends and family and to start dating again sooner (McKelvey & McHenry, 2000).

Divorce is usually discussed as a personal and social tragedy. But divorce may be an important way that women counter marital inequality, a way out of an oppressive situation (Rice, 1994). In a study of successful egalitarian marriages, almost half were not first marriages, and most of the women said they had left their first marriage because of inequitable treatment (Schwartz, 1994). Divorce is a painful family transformation, but also a potential opportunity for growth and change (Stewart, Copeland, Chester, Malley, & Barenbaum, 1997).

What Are the Economic Effects of Divorce?

Divorce in the United States has been characterized as an economic disaster for women. The economic status of men improves upon divorce, whereas the economic status of women deteriorates (Price & McKenry, 1988). And "no-fault" divorce laws, designed to ensure equitable division of assets, have actually made the situation worse for women.

Why do women lose out financially with divorce? There are several reasons, but structural factors are probably more important than individual ones. The majority of state property laws assume that property belongs to the spouse who earned it. Because husbands usually have had greater earning power during the marriage, these laws result in men being awarded more of the couple's assets. The economic value of the wife's unpaid labor may not be considered.

In other states, attempts to make divorce fairer for women have led to laws that order equal division of property. However, most divorcing couples (especially younger ones) have very little in the way of valuable property—perhaps a car (complete with loan payments), household furnishings, and a modest bank account, offset by credit card debt. Fewer than half have equity in a house. The biggest assets for the large majority of couples are the husband's education, pension benefits, and future earning power.

As we discussed earlier, the husband's career usually takes priority in both single-earner and dual-earner marriages. Couples invest their time, money, and energy in his advancement; frequently the wife will postpone her education or career plans in order to put her husband through school, and she will do the unpaid work at home that allows him to concentrate on his paid job. Courts have been slow to recognize that the benefits husbands gain from traditional and modern marriage patterns translate into economic advantages upon divorce.

Only about 15 percent of all divorced women in the United States are awarded spousal support. Most awards are for a period of about two years, and in the past, less than half of the men ordered to provide such support have actually complied (Faludi, 1991; Price & McKenry, 1988).

Who Is Responsible for the Children?

The presence of children is an important factor in adjustment to divorce for women. Women of all social classes and marriage types are likely to be left with the financial responsibility and the day-to-day care of children when a marriage ends. The benefit of awarding custody to women is that most divorced women stay connected with their children and receive the emotional rewards of parenting more than most divorced men do. However, current custody arrangements also have costs for women.

Two-thirds of divorces involve children. More than half of all children in the United States will experience their parents' divorce before the age of 18, and they will then spend an average of about five years in a single-parent home, the great majority with their mothers (Arendell, 1997). Being a single parent is not easy. The single mother may feel overwhelmed with responsibility, guilty at having separated the children from their father, and compelled to be a "supermom" (L'Hommedieu, 1984).

The lack of a husband's income is a big handicap for divorced women and their children. About 60 percent of divorced mothers with custody of their children are awarded child support (Steil, 2001). However, the average amount paid as of the early 1990s was only about $3,600 a year (Arendell, 1997). Child support payments clearly do not cover the actual costs of bringing up a child.

Moreover, the majority of women entitled to child support do not receive it. Several national studies from the 1970s to the 1990s have shown that only 25 percent to 50 percent of men ordered to pay child support did so. No study has ever found that more than half of the fathers complied; many who comply do it irregularly and pay less than the designated amount; and one-fourth to one-third of fathers never make a single payment despite court orders. Black women are half as likely as white women to receive support, and the poorest, least-educated women are the least likely of all. Only 10 percent of welfare clients with children receive child support (Arendell, 1997; Costello & Stone, 1994; Price & McKenry, 1988).

Divorced women and their children must adjust to a lower standard of living. A woman's standard of living declines by about 30 percent to 40 percent on average (Duncan & Hoffman, 1991; Morgan, 1991). More than 25 percent of divorced women fall into poverty for some time within five years of divorce. Many more "balance on the brink of poverty" (Morgan, 1991, p. 96). For many women with children, the financial hardship that comes with divorce becomes the central focus of their lives, dictating where they can live, determining whether they and their children can afford health care, and affecting their psychological well-being (Arendell, 1997).

Breaking Up: When Relationships End without Divorce

In contrast to the large amount of research on divorce, few studies have examined the process or consequences when relationships end without a formal divorce. This can happen in several ways. Some spouses simply desert their families, leaving them without a division of assets or child support. Little is known about how these families fare. In others, partners agree to separate but do not get a divorce, a pattern that is more common in black than in white communities (McKelvey & McHenry, 2000).

The ending of relationships between cohabiting men and women or between lesbian couples has not been studied much. The breakup rate for cohabitors is higher than the divorce rate for married couples, and this is true cross-culturally—for example, in the United States, Australia (Sarantakos, 1991), and Sweden. One study of Swedish couples attempted to sample only highly committed cohabiting couples by selecting only those who had had a child. Still, their breakup rate was three times the rate for comparable married couples (Popenoe, 1987).

For U.S. couples, the best comparisons of breakup rates come from a study in which couples were contacted a year and a half after participating in the original study and asked if they were still together (Blumstein & Schwartz, 1983). Figure 9.5 shows the percentage of married, cohabiting, and lesbian couples who had separated. Lesbians were the most likely to break up, a surprising finding given their emphasis on commitment and equality, but not so surprising when lack of social support for lesbian relationships is considered. When gay, lesbian, and heterosexual individuals who had broken up with a partner were asked why their relationship ended and how they felt about it, they gave similar reasons and reported similar levels of distress (Kurdek, 1997). People rarely talked about a breakup without sadness, anger, or regret.

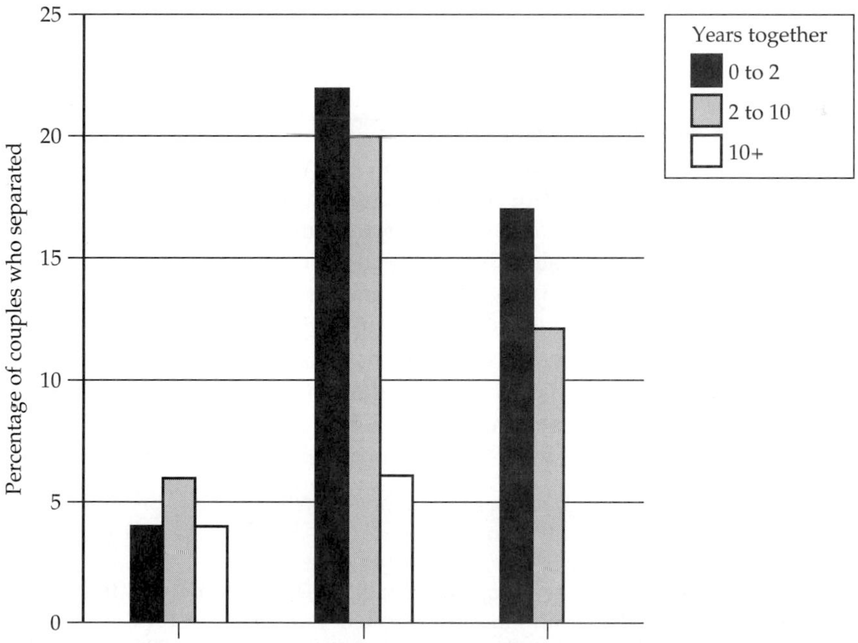

FIGURE 9.5. Separations over an 18-month period.
Source: Blumstein & Schwartz, 1983. Adapted from Figure 53, p. 308, and Figure 54, p. 315.

REMARRIAGE

About two-thirds of women who get divorced remarry, about half of them within three years of the divorce. White women are more likely to remarry than black or Hispanic women. In the United States, about half of all marriages involve at least one partner who was previously divorced (Ganong & Coleman, 2000). A cynic might say that remarriages represent a triumph of belief over experience; women (and men, who are even more likely to remarry) do not question the institution of marriage after they have been divorced. Rather, they believe that they chose the wrong partner last time and now know how to choose the right one.

Women may remarry partly to escape divorce-induced poverty. Women with lower levels of education and income are more likely to remarry than those with more economic options. However, given the importance of power relations in marriage, the consequences of entering a new marriage from an impoverished "one-down" position are unlikely to be positive. Economic discrepancies may be related to the higher rate of spouse abuse in remarried families (Crosbie-Burnett & Giles-Sims, 1991).

Are second marriages more successful? In general, the level of satisfaction in second marriages is about the same as in first marriages; as in first marriages, husbands are more satisfied than their wives (Ihinger-Tallman & Pasley, 1987). Decision-making may be more equal than in first marriages, but remarried women still do more housework than their partners (Ganong & Coleman, 2000). A Norwegian study of blended families showed that women did more housework and child care regardless of whether they were the mother or the stepmother of the children in the family (Levin, 1997). Second marriages are even more likely to end in divorce than first marriages (Ganong & Coleman, 2000), with the result that well over half of women who remarry go on to experience a second divorce.

The complex family structures and dynamics of second marriages ("his," "hers," and "their" children, stepparents, ex-spouses, in-laws, and ex-in-laws) may be a source of stress. Financial problems may be increased by lack of support payments from former husbands, and many families have conflicts over how to allocate money to various household members (Ganong & Coleman, 2000; Ihinger-Tallman & Pasley, 1987). (Who should pay Tiffany's college tuition—mother, father, or stepparent?) Second marriages may also be less stable because, having once violated the societal and religious ideal of lifelong marriage, people are even less inclined to stay in unsatisfying relationships.

Some of the special problems of remarried couples—and the unshaken belief in the ideal—can be seen in the words of one couple, married less than two years at the time of the interview. She is a homemaker and he is a carpenter:

WIFE: I feel anyone thinking about marrying a person who has been previously married should think very seriously about it. There are definitely special problems that accompany this type of marriage. . . . I feel my husband and I will always have his previous marriage overshadowing our marriage. My husband also feels guilty for not having his children with him. I in turn feel guilty and feel if it wasn't for me, maybe my husband would get back with his ex-wife and kids and live happily ever after.

HUSBAND: I think everyone should find the right spouse the first time. I found mine the second time and the only thing that stops it from being perfect is my previous marriage. (Ihinger-Tallman & Pasley, 1987, p. 60)

EQUALITY AND COMMITMENT: ARE THEY INCOMPATIBLE IDEALS?

Throughout this chapter we have focused on women in long-term relationships. A recurrent theme has been that close relationships are important and beneficial to both women and men. Another theme has been that women in relationships with men almost always have less power than their partners. Even when both partners believe in equality and want to work toward it, and even when both take on paid employment, the division of labor in the home remains relatively traditional, his job or career is given more importance than hers, and he has greater decision-making power.

This pattern seems to suggest that commitment and equality are incompatible, at least in heterosexual relationships. But studies of power in marriage have consistently found that a small number of couples do manage to have long-term egalitarian relationships. Although their numbers may be small, their existence tells us that the ideal is not beyond human power to achieve. Egalitarian marriage may be emerging as a new way to be married—a life pattern of the future (Risman & Johnson-Sumerford, 1998; Schwartz, 1994) (see Figure 9.6 on p. 314). The voices of women and men in relatively egalitarian relationships tell us that these relationships can work. Here, the speaker is a man married for sixteen years:

> I started out pretty traditional. But over the years it made sense to change. We both work, and so we had to help each other with the kids, and pretty soon they start asking for you—so only you will do, so you do some of that. And we worked together at church, and we both went whole hog into the peace program. So that got shared. I don't know; you can't design these things. You play fair, and you do what needs doing, and pretty soon you find the old ways don't work and the new ways do. (Schwartz, 1994, p. 31)

It is tempting to believe that equality in marriage or long-term cohabitation can be achieved simply by being willing to work at it. This belief is a variation of "Love conquers all." How many times have you heard people express the belief that "If two people love each other enough, and if they're both willing to compromise, they can have a good marriage"? A related belief is that if the husband does not *intend* to oppress or dominate the wife, oppression and domination will not occur. Happy marriage, then, should be mainly (or entirely) a matter of picking the right person. But one major conclusion that can be drawn from the research reviewed in this chapter is that power differentials between husbands and wives are *not* solely the result of individual differences. Rather, the institution of marriage has been organized around gender inequality, and attempts to change it have been only partially successful. Even couples who try very hard to change their own behavior have problems achieving gender balance in marriage. To understand how equality in marriage might become the

FIGURE 9.6. Life in an egalitarian family.
Source: Sally Forth by Greg Howard. © 1995. Reprinted with Special Permission of King Features Syndicate.

rule rather than the exception, we need to look at both personal and structural factors.

To have an egalitarian marriage, both wife and husband must be willing to integrate their work and family responsibilities despite social pressures to conform to more traditional roles (Gilbert, 1987). Women who value their work outside the home and set limits on the sacrifices they make for husbands and children may be perceived as cold, unfeminine, and selfish; men who do housework and child care and set limits on their career involvement may be perceived as weak and unmasculine. (One of our children once begged his father not to wear an apron in front of the child's friends!) Fortunately, attitudes toward the work and family roles of women and men have changed a great deal in the past thirty years and continue to become more flexible.

Women must lead the way to more egalitarian relationships because men are unlikely to fight a status quo that gives them many benefits. However, only when women perceive gender roles in relationships as unequal and unjust can they begin to change them. To recognize their position as unjust, women must be aware that other possibilities exist, must want such possibilities for themselves, must believe they are entitled to them, and must not feel personally to blame for not having them (Crosby, 1982; Steil, 1997).

Change involves negotiation. Roles are not engraved in stone, nor are they totally defined by society. Rather, they are expressed in day-to-day activities and can be negotiated between partners:

> Human beings are not just robots programmed by society. They are also willful actors, capable of choosing nonconformity and altering social structure if they so wish. . . . [There are] enormous possibilities for negotiation, compromise, and innovation [in marriage]. Individuals can construct their own realities to a surprising extent. (Thoits, 1987, p. 12)

What social factors give women more negotiating power in relationships with men? If society allows more flexible commitments to paid work by both women and men, there will be less likelihood that the man's job or career will take precedence. (The interaction of work and family life will be discussed further in Chapter 11.) Economic power is a key factor. The single biggest obstacle to egalitarian marriage and cohabiting relationships is men's greater earning power, which steers couples into investing in his career and leaving the work at home to her (Schwartz, 1994).

It is important for couples who are trying to find new postgender ways to live together to build networks of like-minded people. Couples who spend time with other nontraditional couples can learn from each other, provide havens from the criticism that more traditional people may aim their way, and provide role models of healthy alternatives to male dominance for themselves and their children. As the number of couples who are consciously trying to build egalitarian relationships increases, it should be easier for them to find each other and build supportive networks. Nontraditional arrangements are coming to be seen as legitimate, normal, and even routine (Thoits, 1987). Similar needs can be met for lesbian couples by being part of a lesbian community (Krieger, 1982).

The movement toward egalitarian relationships will bring benefits for both women and men. Men will be relieved of some of the economic burdens of traditional marriage and be freer to become involved with their children's growth and development. Women will experience better psychological adjustment. For both men and women, equality is linked to more satisfying relationships and greater intimacy (Schwartz, 1994; Steil, 2000, 2001). Equality and role flexibility in committed long-term relationships offer both women and men a chance to become more fully human.

CONNECTING THEMES

- *Gender is more than just sex.* Women and men in enduring relationships often have "his" and "her" experiences, such as differential workloads and roles, relationship satisfaction, and psychological adjustment. This is not because women and men are fundamentally different in needs and goals, but because differences in power and status structure different roles for them.
- *Language and naming are sources of power.* Marriage is an institution with a name and a script. The life paths of lesbians, unmarried women, and heterosexual cohabitants are either not named or given negative labels. Within marriage, inequality is so much the norm that it may be invisible.
- *Women are not all alike.* Women who do not enter heterosexual marriages are a diverse group. Lesbian couples form a largely invisible minority, and ever-single women are rarely studied. Even within heterosexual marriage, there is great diversity along lines of ethnicity, social class, and marriage type (traditional, modern, egalitarian).
- *Psychological research can foster social change.* The disadvantages women suffer in long-term relationships—and when those relationships end through death or divorce—cannot be remedied by individual efforts. Restructuring

the gendered domain of relationships requires restructuring the domains of work and public power that support it. However, individual couples can develop strategies to support egalitarian relationships.

SUGGESTED READINGS

BOSTON LESBIAN PSYCHOLOGIES COLLECTIVE (Eds.). (1987). *Lesbian psychologies: Explorations and challenges.* Urbana: University of Illinois Press. This book, winner of an award from the Association for Women in Psychology, has sections on lesbian identity, psychological adjustment, and community. Of special interest to this chapter is a section on lesbian relationships and families.

LERNER, HARRIET G. (1985). *The dance of anger.* New York: Harper & Row. Subtitled *A woman's guide to changing the patterns of intimate relationships,* this book encourages the reader to recognize that anger and dissatisfaction are signals that something is wrong in a relationship and can provide a starting point for the renegotiation of roles.

SCHWARTZ, P. (1994). *Peer marriage: How love between equals really works.* New York: Free Press. A sociologist reports on interviews with couples in egalitarian marriages and suggests that this kind of relationship is becoming more widespread.

CHAPTER 10

Mothering

Mother is one of the most fundamental archetypes of woman, and motherhood has been regarded as women's ultimate source of power—"the hand that rocks the cradle rules the world." In most societies, motherhood is viewed as central to a woman's identity and fulfillment. Indeed, mothering can be intensely satisfying:

> The day my husband and I took our newborn son home from the hospital I sat on my bed with him in my arms. All of a sudden, I realized I was in love. It is an indescribable love, comparable to nothing else in life. I never would have believed it before becoming a parent . . . Now twelve, he knows exactly how to

exasperate me, yet the love I feel for him today is as intense and passionate as when I held him in my arms on that beautiful fall day over a decade ago (Deutsch, 1999, p. 228).

Motherhood may seem the most natural thing in the world, a biological privilege accorded only to women. However, those aspects of society that seem most natural often are the ones most in need of critical examination. Like marriage, motherhood is an institution. Its meaning goes beyond the biological process of reproduction, encompassing many customs, beliefs, attitudes, rules, and laws. Like other institutions, it also has a powerful symbolic component. Yet women who become mothers are individuals. "Mother is a role; women are human beings" (Bernard, 1974, p. 7).

Motherhood raises troubling questions for feminist analysis. It is a key topic in debates between feminists who want to pursue equality on the basis of gender similarity and those who want to claim the value of women's bodies and women's work (see Chapter 4). Liberal feminists have stressed that the institution of motherhood has been used to exclude women from public life , and they have shown how the myths and mystique of motherhood keep women in their place. Some radical and cultural feminists, on the other hand, have pointed out that motherhood is a woman-centered model of how people can be connected and caring (McMahon, 1995).

Just as there is no single meaning of motherhood, there is no unified feminist position on it. But the diversity of feminist opinion on motherhood need not be a problem. In this chapter, we ask many questions about mothering, using a variety of feminist perspectives. What are the images and scripts that define mothers and motherhood? How do women go about choosing whether or not to have children, and to what extent are they allowed to choose? How does the transition to motherhood change women? What are women's experiences of birth and mothering? We also examine mother-blaming and explore fathering as a feminist issue.

IMAGES OF MOTHERS AND MOTHERHOOD

Western society has strong beliefs about motherhood. The ideology of motherhood has been termed the *motherhood mystique.* It includes the following myths (Hays, 1996; Hoffnung, 1989; Johnston-Robledo, 2000; Oakley, 1974):

1. Motherhood is the ultimate fulfillment of a woman. It is a natural and necessary experience for all women. Those who do not want to mother are psychologically disturbed, and those who want to but cannot are fundamentally deprived.
2. Women are instinctively good at caregiving and should be responsible for infants, children, elderly parents, home, and husband. Good mothers enjoy this kind of work; a woman who doesn't is maladjusted or poorly organized.
3. A mother has infinite patience and the willingness to sacrifice herself to her children. If she does not put her own needs last, she is an inadequate mother.

4. A woman's intense, full-time devotion to mothering is best for her children. Women who work are inferior mothers.

Although these beliefs may seem outdated, the motherhood mystique lives on (see Figure 10.1). It permeates advice to mothers, even from experts. An analysis of three best-selling child-rearing manuals showed that they held mothers primarily responsible for child care, prescribed intensive mothering, and glorified self-sacrifice (Hays, 1996).

The motherhood mystique may be a form of benevolent sexism in which women and men are seen as naturally having different roles and naturally being happy in them (Dallos & Dallos, 1997). It persists because it has important functions for *men* (Hays, 1996; Lorber, 1993b). Women are encouraged to sacrifice other parts of their lives for motherhood, which then creates economic dependence on men and is used to justify women's lower status and pay at work. "The social order that elevates men over women is legitimated by women's devotion to child care, since it takes them out of the running for top-level jobs and political positions and defuses their consciousness of oppression" (Lorber, 1993b, p. 170). The mystique may persist also because it is the one area in which Western society values connectedness and caring over individual achievement. But glorifying motherhood, and defining it in ways that make many women feel guilty and burdened by it, benefits groups that have the most power economically and politically.

THE DECISION TO HAVE A CHILD

Having a child profoundly changes a woman's life, and in our society, children are not expected to produce much useful work or income for their parents or to support them financially in their old age. The cost of bringing up even one child is high. Yet the great majority of women have children.

Why Do Women Choose to Have Children?

There are practical reasons for having children, particularly in traditional societies. Children are necessary as a source of family income, as domestic workers, as a path for passing on property and a customary way of life, and sometimes

FIGURE 10.1. The motherhood mystique internalized!
Source: Bringing Up Father. © 1989. Reprinted with Special Permission of King Features Syndicate.

as a form of personal immortality. In postcolonial and underdeveloped societies, many children are lost to disease and malnutrition. Five or more children may have to be conceived for two to live to adulthood; these children may provide the only economic support available in their parents' old age.

As third-world countries adopt industrialized ways of life, the birthrate drops. The best predictor of smaller families is not modernization itself, but attitudes toward modern science and medicine. As people begin to believe that science and medicine can deal with social problems, they may feel that it is not necessary to bear many children in order to have a few grow up. Nevertheless, attitudes change more slowly than material conditions, so that there is a considerable lag between the development of better medical conditions and a drop in family size.

In industrialized societies, children have little economic value—in fact, they are a big liability—and psychological reasons for having children are given more weight. One traditional explanation for childbearing is the existence of a "maternal instinct" (Bernard, 1974). But if wanting children is instinctive, why are so many powerful socialization forces directed at instilling this "instinct" in girls? (For example, recall the girl-toys discussed in Chapter 6.) And why have abortion and infanticide been features of so many human societies throughout history? There are no inherent physiological benefits of motherhood for women, and there is no instinctive drive for pregnancy.

Another theory is that women have a psychological need to care for a child and men do not. In Chapter 4, we discussed the ideas of Nancy Chodorow (1978): Because girls' separation from their mothers differs from boys', girls grow up defining the self in terms of relationship and connectedness. Having babies satisfies deep relational needs. Unfortunately, it also leads to dependence on and subordination to men.

Chodorow's theory has been criticized on several grounds. First, it takes white middle-class family patterns as the norm. In the African-American community, motherhood and self-sufficiency are seen as compatible (Joseph, 1991). Second, even among white middle-class mothers, many women feel isolated and unfulfilled by mothering (Kaplan, 1992; Wolf, 2000).

A third criticism is that men can mother very well when they have to. Virtually all studies of single fathers show that when men cannot depend on women for child care (because of death, desertion, or divorce), they develop skills and behaviors very much like those of women. In addition, they come to see themselves as nurturing, compassionate, and sensitive to the needs of others, all stereotypically feminine traits (Risman, 1998). Biological theories assume that women are "programmed" to care for children; socialization theories assume that women are more nurturing because of early learning. But it is just as likely that a "nurturing personality" is created by being put into a nurturing role as an adult. The process of mothering is a kind of "doing gender" that produces womanly persons (McMahon, 1995).

The reasons for choosing to become a mother are different for women of different social classes. In an in-depth study of fifty-nine white Canadian women, all employed full time and mothers of preschool children, the middle-class women talked about being ready to have a child only *after* they had met certain goals: maturity, the right relationship with a man, and career achievement. In contrast, the working-class women saw themselves as achieving adulthood *through* having a child. Their pregnancies, typically not planned, provided the opportunity to claim an identity as a mature, loving, and responsible person (McMahon, 1995).

Among the reasons our students mention when we discuss motherhood are the desire to experience pregnancy and birth, to participate in the growth of another human being, to please a husband or partner, to strengthen a relationship, to prove oneself an adult, to be needed and loved, and to pass on a family name or one's genes or one's values. Which of these reasons seems most compelling to you?

The Motherhood Mandate

There is considerable social pressure on women to have children, pressure that has been called the *motherhood mandate* (Russo, 1979) (see Figure 10.2). Ninety years ago, one of the first women psychologists, Leta Hollingworth, analyzed the social techniques used to persuade women to have babies (see Box 10.1). Americans surveyed in the 1950s through 1970s endorsed a strong norm against childlessness and one-child families (Baruch, Barnett, & Rivers, 1983; Unger, 1979a). Deliberately choosing not to have children was viewed as a sign of maladjustment in women. Stereotypes portrayed the "only child" as socially inadequate, self-centered, unhappy, and unlikable. (There is no evidence that "only" children actually are maladjusted.)

FIGURE 10.2.
Source: Cathy. Copyright © 1996 Cathy Guisewite. Reprinted with permission of Universal Press Syndicate. All rights reserved.

Box 10.1 Mothers Are Made, Not Born

In 1916, Leta Hollingworth wrote a powerful article titled "Social Devices for Impelling Women to Bear and Rear Children." Asserting that it is necessary to "clear our minds of the sentimental conception of motherhood and to look at facts," she went on:

> The facts, shorn of sentiment, then, are: (1) The bearing and rearing of children is necessary for tribal or national existence and aggrandizement. (2) The bearing and rearing of children is painful, dangerous to life, and involves long years of exacting labor and self-sacrifice. (3) There is no verifiable evidence to show that a maternal instinct exists in women of such all-consuming strength and fervor as to impel them voluntarily to seek the pain, danger, and exacting labor involved in maintaining a high birth rate.

Hollingworth described ways in which societies ensure that women will choose to have and care for children.

Leta Hollingworth

Personal Ideals. The "normal," or "womanly," woman is proclaimed by experts to be one who enthusiastically engages in maternity. Citing medical and psychological authorities, Hollingworth shows how women are told that "only abnormal women want no babies."

Law. Child rearing is ensured by restrictions on abortion. "There could be no better proof of the insufficiency of maternal instinct as a guaranty of population than the drastic laws which we have against birth control, abortion, infanticide, and infant desertion."

Belief. Religions, for example, may "regard family limitation as a sin, punishable in the hereafter."

Art. "The mother, with children at her breast, is the favorite theme of artists. Poetry abounds in allusion to the sacredness and charm of motherhood . . . fiction is replete with happy and adoring mothers. Art holds up to view only the compensations of motherhood, leaving the other half of the theme in obscurity."

Illusion. "One of the most effective ways of creating the desired illusion about any matter is by concealing and tabooing the mention of all the painful and disagreeable circumstances connected with it. Thus there is a very stern social taboo on conversation about the processes of birth. . . . The drudgery, the monotonous labor . . . are minimized."

Education. Women's education is aimed at making them better wives and mothers, not at enabling them to achieve independence or public achievement.

"Bugaboos." Women are told by experts that they must have their children before the age of 30 or they are highly likely to face grave complications. They are told that motherhood increases happiness and longevity. Finally, it is claimed that only children grow up selfish and disturbed.

Are the social devices described by Hollingworth valid today?

Source: Hollingworth, 1916.

Has the motherhood mandate decreased because of feminism? Surveys in the late 1970s began to show more tolerance for people who chose not to have children. However, in the 1980s, the media rediscovered motherhood. In a backlash against the gains of the women's movement, women were warned that equality comes at a terrible cost—home and family (Faludi, 1991). "Trend stories" abounded—there is a new baby boom; women are all giving up their careers for motherhood; day care is a pit of child abuse, and so on. The stories were based on biased anecdotes and sweeping generalizations, with little basis in reality. Each "trend" was a way of telling women that they must return to traditional roles or suffer dire consequences. "For women, the trend story was no news report; it was a moral reproach" (Faludi, 1991, p. 80).

In this social context, the decision to have a child may represent an inability to escape the pressure to conform. One feminist remembers her own decision in these words: "I had no idea of what *I* wanted, what *I* could or could not choose. I only knew that to have a child was to assume adult womanhood to the full, to prove myself, to be 'like other women'" (Rich, 1976, p. 25).

Childless by Choice or Circumstance?

Throughout history, the childless woman has been regarded as a failed woman (Phoenix, Woollett, & Lloyd, 1991; Rich, 1976). Traditionally, she was labeled *barren.* The more neutral term *childless* still defines her in terms of a lack. Recently, the term *child-free* has been suggested as a more positive alternative. Even in the 1990s, college students judged that women who remained childless by choice (even though they were happily employed) were less fulfilled, less acceptable role models, and more likely to be unhappy in later life (Mueller & Yoder, 1997).

Given the negative stereotype, why do some women choose not to have children? Reasons include financial considerations, a desire to pursue their education or career, the dangers of childbirth, the possibility of bearing a defective child, concerns about overpopulation, and a belief that they are not personally suited to nurturing and caring for children (Landa, 1990). Regardless of when the decision is made, it is common for women to have moments of doubt about it throughout their fertile years. Because the path of the childless woman has no clear map, "each woman seems to be travelling alone . . . unaware that others are on the same road ahead and behind her" (Morell, 2000, p. 321).

Of course, childlessness is not always a matter of choice. In a Canadian study of childless women and men over the age of 55, 72 percent attributed their childlessness to circumstance. Some people said they had not married because they had to take care of sick or elderly parents; others married late in life; others reported infertility or repeated miscarriages; and for others, it seemed to be simply fate: "It just didn't turn out that way" (Connidis & McMullin, 1996).

In the United States, about one woman in six experiences fertility problems, and only about half who seek medical treatment are able to conceive. Women who want to but cannot bear children may be stigmatized, leading to feelings of guilt and failure:

> His parents wouldn't leave me alone. They felt I wasn't trying. I was just feeling a failure—failure as a woman because you know this is what you are here for and

I actually felt as though I had failed my husband because I wasn't giving him an heir to the throne (Ulrich & Weatherall, 2001, p. 332).

Accepting childlessness is a gradual process. In a study of women who had given up trying to conceive a child after up to fifteen years of treatment, participants reported coming to a point where they realized that further efforts were futile. After years of treatment, they felt "exhausted" and "worn out." They felt profound grief and loss, and a sense of emptiness. At the same time, however, they felt relief at being out of the "medical machinery" and recognized an opportunity to take back their lives, moving on to other goals (Daniluk, 1996).

Does not having children (by choice or by chance) lead to unhappiness? As discussed in Chapter 9, marital satisfaction drops with the birth of the first child and may not return to its original level until children leave home. In a major study of American women at midlife, whether a woman had children had no relationship to her psychological well-being (Baruch et al., 1983). The women in this study grew up in an era when the motherhood mandate was in full force, yet their well-being at midlife did not suffer because of childlessness. These results contradict the belief that children are central to a woman's happiness. Unless motherhood *and* refusal of motherhood are equally validated as normal and desirable, women are not yet liberated (Morell, 2000).

How Does Society Restrict Women's Choices?

Women's choices about child rearing do not take place in a social vacuum. Most societies regulate women's rights to have—and to choose not to have—children. Moreover, practical and economic factors restrict women's options, especially those of poor and minority women. For example, a poor woman may have to choose a birth control method based on its cost. Women who receive government benefits are more vulnerable to government monitoring and control of their reproductive choices. Because they have less access to lawyers and less of a public voice, they may be less able to challenge government restrictions of their rights. And they are more likely to be coerced into having (or not having) children (Roberts, 1998).

Feminists advocate *reproductive freedom* for all women, an ideal that has not yet been achieved. This concept includes a range of issues, such as the right to comprehensive and unbiased sex education, access to safe and reliable contraception, an end to forced sterilization and forced birth control for poor and minority women, and access to safe and legal abortion (Baber & Allen, 1992; Bishop, 1989).

At the heart of the concept of reproductive freedom is the idea that all choices about reproduction should be made by the woman herself: it is her body and her right to choose. For this reason, feminist perspectives on reproductive freedom are often termed *pro-choice.* Because reproductive freedom affects every aspect of a woman's life, it has been a key component of every feminist movement throughout history. "Without the ability to determine their reproductive destinies, women will never achieve an equal role in social, economic, and political life and will continue to be politically subordinate to and economically dependent on men" (Roberts, 1998).

Contraception

Accidental pregnancies can be the result of a number of factors: contraceptive failure, lack of contraceptive knowledge or skill, lack of access to contraceptives, failure to use contraception, and unplanned or coerced sexual activity. Moreover, although women are expected to take most of the responsibility for safer sex, psychological factors, lack of power within heterosexual relationships, and sexual scripts make it difficult for many women, particularly young ones, to take control in this area.

Every form of contraception has drawbacks. Some methods are messy, inconvenient, and interfere with spontaneity (foam, condoms, diaphragms). Some may cause nausea and weight gain, require daily remembering, or have the potential for long-term side effects (the pill). Some offer no protection against STDs (see Chapter 8). Some are expensive and not covered by insurance (see Box 10.2). Hormonal contraceptives such as Norplant and Norplant 2 can be implanted under the skin to ensure infertility for up to five years, but the up-front cost is high (more than $500).

Problems with using contraceptives effectively are compounded for poor women and women in developing countries. For example, some methods cannot be used by women who are breastfeeding; but in countries without hygienic water supplies, breastfeeding is the only safe way to nourish an infant. Other contraceptive methods require supervision by medical professionals, which is prohibitive for the majority of the world's women (Owen & Caudill, 1996).

Information about contraception is widely available to middle-class U.S. women, everywhere from *Glamour* magazine to the *New York Times*. However, some groups of women are much less likely to get the information they need

Box 10.2 Viagra Bias

Viagra bias? The initial rush of some insurers to pay for Viagra, the so-called erection pill, is leaving women (and their doctors) crying foul. Nearly 40 years after the advent of the birth control pill, only 56 percent of Pill prescriptions are covered by insurers. Why the disparity? The American College of Obstetricians and Gynecologists (ACOG) says the fact that the financial burden of birth control is borne by women, not insurers, is a clear case of gender discrimination. In fact, the cost of covering contraception would more than pay for itself in savings on abortion, prenatal care and delivery. "Contraception isn't optional," says Anita Nelson, an associate professor of obstetrics and gynecology at UCLA School of Medicine. "Women need it to protect their health and quality of life, and the prohibitive cost is partly to blame for the high number of unintended pregnancies in this country."

The Equal Employment Opportunity Commission has ruled that excluding contraceptives from health insurance coverage is sex discrimination. Twenty states now require equal coverage for contraceptives. But federal legislation is needed, because not all states are complying with the ruling. The Equity in Prescription Insurance and Contraceptive Coverage Act (EPICC), introduced in Congress in 1997, would require insurers who pay for prescription drugs to cover all FDA-approved contraceptives, as well as related doctor visits. It still has not been made law.

Source: Courtesy of *Glamour*, Conde Nast Publications, Inc., *Glamour*, September 1998; and The Center for Reproductive Rights, www.crlp.org/pub_fac_epicc.html

and want. Young women just beginning to be sexually active are disadvantaged: only twenty states mandate school sex education at all, and only sixteen require education about contraception. Virtually no information is available in diverse languages, even in areas with large numbers of recent immigrants and ethnically diverse populations (Watson, Trasciatti, & King, 1996).

Family Health International's field studies have found that controlling one's fertility is often a "mixed blessing" in developing countries (Waszak, Severy, Kafafi, & Badawi, 2001). For example, in Egypt, family-planning services are easily accessible, and public acceptance is high. However, if a wife does not conceive a child soon after marriage, her husband's family may start looking for a replacement wife and encourage her husband to divorce her. Family planning empowers women, but it may also increase their anxiety and psychological distress when they live in contexts of gender inequality. For contraception services to be effective, women's psychological needs and cultural contexts must be taken into account.

Abortion

Of the world's estimated 210 million pregnancies annually, about 40 percent are unplanned. In the United States, about 1.3 million abortions take place each year, representing about 30 percent of pregnancies. Eighty-eight percent of these abortions take place within the first twelve weeks of pregnancy.

Women choosing abortion tend to be young, poor, and unmarried. The percentage of pregnancies that are aborted varies greatly by race/ethnicity: 16 percent for white women, 22 percent for Hispanic women, and 38 percent for black women. These differences suggest that women of color are experiencing more unwanted pregnancies than white women do—perhaps because they have less access to contraception or less sexual and contraceptive decision-making power (Alan Guttmacher Institute, 2002; Hyde & Delamater, 2003; Travis & Compton, 2001).

Abortion has been legal in the United States since 1973, when the Supreme Court, ruling in *Roe v. Wade,* affirmed that women have a right to decide whether to terminate their pregnancies on the basis of the constitutional right to privacy. Abortion, the court ruled, is a matter to be decided between a woman and her physician. Although the principle of choice was affirmed by this ruling, in practice there are many limitations and legal restrictions on women's choices.

How is abortion restricted? The Hyde Amendment, in effect since 1976, prohibits the use of federal Medicaid money for abortions except when the mother's life is (medically) endangered. Because Medicaid provides health care for low-income families, many poor women were forced to choose between paying for an abortion out of their own inadequate incomes or carrying an unwanted fetus to term. The Medicaid restriction has resulted in some poor women delaying abortion until they can afford to pay for it or resorting to illegal abortion, thus increasing the risk of complications (Bishop, 1989; Miller, 1996). Today, 99 percent of the money spent on abortions for poor women must come from state (rather than federal) funds. But states may do little to provide for poor women, even those who are victims of incest or rape (Daley & Gold, 1993). Many states have enacted restrictive laws directed at all women seeking abortions. These laws may require the consent of a husband or partner, mandatory waiting periods, and "educational" requirements that are designed to discourage women from seeking abortions (Lublin, 1998). Parental notification and consent for minors is now mandatory in thirty-two states (Alan Guttmacher Institute, 2002). Abortion is safest when it is performed early in the pregnancy; laws that delay it affect women's health (Miller, 1996).

A new and effective nonsurgical abortion procedure, developed in Europe in the 1980s, is *mifepristone* (Mifeprex), formerly known as RU-486. This drug safely induces abortion early in pregnancy by causing the uterine lining to slough off. Antiabortion groups prevented legalization of RU-486 in the United States for more than a decade because they believed that it would make abortions more private (the patient simply goes to her doctor's office for the pill, not to an abortion clinic) and therefore less vulnerable to political pressure (Hyde & Delamater, 2003). After a long campaign by women's health advocates, Mifeprex was finally, in 2000, made available to American women. However, the Bush administration restricted its availability to poor women (NOW, 2001).

A different kind of restriction comes from harassment and violence at abortion clinics. The number of doctors who perform abortions has dropped 18 percent since 1982, partly because of stalking, death threats, internet "hit lists," and murders of physicians and clinic staff (Cozzarelli & Major, 1998; Vobejda, 1994). Picketing, bomb threats, and demonstrations affect clients, too. Studies of women who encountered antiabortion protesters as they went to a clinic show that the encounters made women feel angry, intruded on, and guilty. However, they had no effect on the women's decision to have an abortion (Cozzarelli & Major, 1998).

Each year, about 46 million abortions occur worldwide, about 20 million of them illegally. In many developing countries in Africa and Asia, safe abortion is unavailable because medical facilities are scarce. When a developing country has restrictive laws, wealthy women can obtain abortions under medical supervision, but poor women may attempt self-induced abortion by taking caustic drugs or inserting objects into the vagina. In these countries, abortion mortality rates are hundreds of times higher than in the United States (Alan Guttmacher Institute, 2002).

Women in some European countries face restrictions on their abortion options. Poland had readily available abortions until 1994, when the legislature passed one of the most restrictive policies in Europe, largely as a result of pressure from Polish Catholic Church leaders. Other European countries have high fees, waiting periods, and requirements for women to have two doctors' opinions before obtaining an abortion (Darnton, 1993). Ireland has a complete ban on abortions as well as contraceptives.

The politics of abortion in the United States affect women around the world. U.S. law forbids using U.S. tax dollars to fund abortions abroad. On his first day in office in 2001, President George W. Bush extended that restriction by signing an order banning U.S. aid to global organizations that use their own funds to provide abortions or abortion counseling to poor women in developing countries. In 2002, he eliminated U.S. contributions to U.N. family planning programs. These programs provide not only abortion counseling but also contraceptive education, HIV and AIDS prevention, and general health education to women and children in more than 140 poor and developing countries (Helmore, 2002).

Does Abortion Have Psychological Effects?

One argument used in efforts to restrict abortion is that it has harmful psychological consequences—a "postabortion syndrome" (Miller, 1996; Russo, 2000). Although psychology cannot resolve moral differences of opinion about abortion, empirical research can answer questions of psychological well-being. Does abortion cause psychological damage and decreased psychological well-being for women?

To determine the effects of abortion on women's mental health, the American Psychological Association commissioned a study of all the scientific research published in the United States since abortion was legalized in 1973. This research review established that the legal termination of an unwanted pregnancy does not have major negative effects on most women. Measurements of psychological distress usually drop immediately following the abortion and remain low in follow-ups after several weeks (Public Interest Directorate, 1987). When a woman freely chooses a legal abortion, the typical emotion that follows is relief. In fact, abortion may be a milestone for a woman, as she takes control over her own life (Travis & Compton, 2001). In sum, there is no scientific evidence for "postabortion syndrome" (Russo, 2000).

This does not mean that women are always perfectly well-adjusted following abortion. Pregnancy, planned or not, is a life stressor. But the most important factor in adjustment after abortion is the woman's adjustment prior to the abortion (Russo, 2000). Research studies assessing psychological problems over a range from one week to ten years following abortion show negative effects for anywhere between 0.5 percent and 15 percent of clients. A woman is more likely to have postabortion psychological problems if she has a history of prior emotional problems, has received little support from her family or friends, felt pressured into the abortion decision, has strong religious beliefs that abortion is immoral, or believed in advance that she would have problems in coping (Public Interest Directorate, 1987). Women obtaining abortions have a much higher rate of past physical, sexual, and emotional abuse than other women, a factor that strongly affects their pre-abortion well-being (Russo, 2000). When a woman obtaining an abortion had a partner who did not support her choice, her likelihood of psychological problems was higher only if she did not firmly believe in the integrity of her own decision (Major, Cozzarelli, Testa, & Mueller, 1992). Encounters with antiabortion demonstrators at the time of the abortion also have negative effects. The more intense the protest outside the clinic when a woman tried to enter, the more depressed she was after the abortion (Cozzarelli & Major, 1998).

Most women contemplating an abortion have mixed feelings about it (recall Carol Gilligan's research, discussed in Chapter 4). Women who experience severe distress following abortion may want to obtain psychological counseling. However, women should not have to deny their conflicts for fear of being labeled emotionally disturbed:

> Abortion, like other moral dilemmas, does cause suffering in the individuals whose lives are impacted. That suffering does not make the choice wrong or harmful to the individual who must make the choice, nor should the individual be pathologized for having feelings of distress. In fact, the shouldering of such suffering and of responsibility for moral choices contributes to psychological growth. (Elkind, 1991, p. 3)

Choices about whether, when, and how often to bear children are complex ones. Although our society expects women to accept most of the responsibility for caring for children, it has been less willing to entrust them with the freedom to make responsible reproductive choices. Steeped in the motherhood mystique, many people still view reproductive rights as unnatural and maternal sacrifice as women's lot in life.

Technology and Choice

Controversies about contraception and abortion show that the development of new reproductive technology does not always increase choices for women. The reality is that reproductive technology has introduced many troublesome questions of ethics, morality, power, and choice. Indeed, the body may be the major battleground of women's rights for decades to come. The most difficult issues include the following.

Selective Abortion

Blood tests, amniocentesis, and other new technologies allow selective abortion of "defective" fetuses. The great majority of women who find that they are carrying a Down syndrome fetus, for example, choose to abort, and a majority of Americans endorse that choice (Wertz, 1992). Is abortion justified for disorders that cause mental retardation? What about those that may cause social (but not cognitive) problems, such as the sex chromosomal variations discussed in Chapter 5?

Some people believe that pregnant women do not have the right to end a potential life simply because the child will be less than perfect (Lee, 2000). On the other hand, it is women who bear the burden of child rearing. Disability activists argue that if social supports were available, parenting a disabled child would not involve the sacrifices it now does. And what counts as a "disability?" In a study in the U.K., many students expressed fears about widening the definition of disability. (Recall the selective abortion of female fetuses discussed in Chapter 6.) As one student said, "The danger is that choice can end up being unlimited. . . . It would mean that people could act out their prejudices about what makes a good person such as white children or straight children" (Lee, 2000, p. 398).

Fetal "Rights"

Under the U.S. constitution, legal rights for individuals begin at birth. However, there is increasing political pressure from conservatives to define fetuses as persons and endow them with rights. In 2002, the Bush administration proposed to change health insurance regulations in order to define "children" to include fetuses from conception onward. The administration claimed that this would allow health coverage for low-income pregnant women, but pro-choice advocates claimed it was a ploy to undermine women's right to choose. Abortion rights advocates fear that a federal court might rule that the rights of a fetus take precedence over the rights of a pregnant woman (Kemper, 2002).

Because of political pressures, the monitoring of women's behavior during pregnancy is increasing (Baber & Allen, 1992; Kline, 1996; Pollit, 1998). In at least seventeen states, women have been charged with child abuse for using drugs or alcohol during pregnancy, although fetuses are not children under the law. Meanwhile, media reports typically ignore the fact that there are almost no treatment programs available for pregnant women who are addicted to drugs. This form of social control falls more heavily on poor women; those who can afford private health care are not monitored or tested against their will. (One physician pointed out that if these were middle-class women, they would be referred to the Betty Ford Clinic, not sent to jail.)

Feminist health-care activists are concerned about the "slippery slope": Will women soon be jailed for smoking, failing to take their medication, or not getting enough exercise during pregnancy? And they point out that the concept of fetal rights places responsibility solely on women instead of on both parents and their community. The best way to foster infant health is to help pregnant women by providing low-cost prenatal care, drug treatment programs, and social support services—not by punishing women for being less than perfect incubators.

In Vitro Fertilization

Some couples who are unable to conceive a child use technologies such as *in vitro fertilization*, or *IVF*, commonly known as the "test-tube baby" procedure. A woman's ovaries are stimulated with strong fertility drugs so that they produce multiple eggs, which are then surgically removed. Her partner's sperm (obtained by masturbation) is combined with the eggs in a glass dish. If fertilization occurs, the embryos are inserted into the woman's uterus to develop (Williams, 1992).

IVF carries many risks. The fertility drugs and surgeries can lead to unpleasant and dangerous side effects and complications. The emotional costs are high, as women put their lives and careers on hold to concentrate on getting pregnant, and the success rate is low.

Women who choose to undergo IVF describe themselves as desperate to have children at any cost. Their strong desire to become biological mothers is usually seen as natural. The media frequently feature heart-rending stories of a woman's quest for a child, but rarely do these stories analyze how the need to have children is socially constructed. In an analysis of 133 news articles on IVF, 64 explicitly endorsed the belief that bearing children is the single most important accomplishment of adult life, and only 2 articles countered that belief (Condit, 1996). "To what extent does our society *create* a market for IVF by placing so many important meanings on fertility that to be infertile indeed becomes an unbearable problem?" (Williams, 1992, p. 262).

Studies exploring women's motivations for seeking IVF suggest that these women have been strongly influenced by the motherhood mandate: the majority believe that parenthood is an essential part of a woman's life. Moreover, they report having experienced strong external pressures to bear children (Williams, 1992). Indeed, some women may undergo IVF partly because only after IVF fails can they be accepted by others as childless due to fate, not choice (Koch, 1990).On the other hand, those who succeed in having a child through IVF or other medically assisted methods generally report more positive relationships between mother, father, and child than comparison mothers who conceived naturally, and IVF children are as well-adjusted as others (Hahn, 2001).

Other Methods of Conception

IVF is only one of the reproductive technologies being used to allow couples to have children. Some methods are decidedly low-tech, with the kitchen turkey-baster the favored means of insemination and the couples themselves in control of the technology. In one case, two longtime lesbian partners, D. and B., were approached by a cousin of B.'s with a request to bear a child for her and her husband. (The cousin was unable to conceive.) Using sperm donated by B.'s adult son, D. became pregnant and gave birth to a healthy baby daughter. D. described the process as deeply satisfying. In another case, a lesbian couple had a child with sperm donated by one partner's father to the other partner. Both genetic and social ties of grandparent to grandchild were thus created.

Some couples use reproductive technologies to employ others to breed children for them. Many feminists believe that this practice exploits women (Baber & Allen, 1992; Raymond, 1993); others argue that contract pregnancy can have substantial benefits to all parties if it is stringently regulated (Purdy, 1992). As currently practiced, contract pregnancy raises seemingly insoluble ethical dilemmas. The following are descriptions of actual cases:

> Robert M. contracts for a baby with Elvira J. without telling her that he is considering divorcing his wife, Cynthia M. On learning of the coming divorce, Elvira refuses to give up the baby for adoption, although she allows the Ms to take the baby home with them on the condition that they seek marriage counseling. Six months later, Robert M. files for divorce, triggering a three-way custody battle between biological father, biological mother, and caretaker mother. Who is being exploited here? Does the fact that Elvira is a Latina with only a seventh grade education make a difference? (Nelson, 1992)

> Mark C. and Cristina C. hire Anna J. to gestate an embryo grown from their sperm and egg. Finding herself attached to the child, Anna seeks visitation rights. A judge rules that Anna is not the child's mother (although it is she who has given birth), but merely a temporary foster mother, and denies her request. Anna is a black single mother; the Cs' are white and Asian-American, respectively. (Purdy, 1992)

These cases illustrate the ethical and social dilemmas created by reproductive technologies. Many feminists argue that women are at risk for exploitation by technologies that separate the genetic and physiological aspects of pregnancy. It is women's bodies that are manipulated and experimented on. More than ever, women may be viewed solely as egg providers and incubators, and motherhood defined only in biological terms (Baber & Allen, 1992; Raymond, 1993; Ulrich & Weatherall, 2000).

THE TRANSITION TO MOTHERHOOD

Becoming a mother changes a woman's life perhaps more than any other single life transition. Pregnancy, birth, and the transition to motherhood include both biological and social events. These events interact to produce changes in life circumstances, lifestyle, and involvement in paid work, as well as changes in relationships with partners, parents, and others. Once a woman becomes a mother, the role is hers for life, and she will be defined largely through that role, much more than men are defined through their roles as fathers. It is not surprising that motherhood profoundly affects a woman's sense of self (Ussher, 1989). Let's look more closely at some of the changes that occur with pregnancy and motherhood and their effects on women's identities.

How Does Motherhood Change Work and Marital Roles?

More than twenty longitudinal studies have shown that the birth of a child can negatively affect family relationships, reducing psychological well-being and marital satisfaction (Walzer, 1998). Husbands and wives become more different from each other; studies using large national samples show that parenthood results in bigger changes in women's lives than in men's, as women take on more child care and housework (Sanchez & Thomson, 1997) (see Figure 10.3).

Many women experience the change from paid worker to unpaid at-home mother as stressful. The changes from a nine-to-five schedule to being on call twenty-four hours a day, from adult company to isolation with an infant, from feeling competent to feeling overwhelmed with new tasks, all require adjustments. The difficulties may be offset by the rewards of getting to know one's growing baby, the belief that caring for one's children is worthwhile and important, and the sense of mastery that comes from learning how to do it well. Women who return to paid work have their own stresses, juggling many demands. For both groups, conflicts occur.

A major source of conflict is the discrepancy between women's expectations of their partners' involvement and men's actual behavior after the child is born. Studies suggest that although many men are positive about the idea of becoming a father, they do not follow through with a fair share of the work (Nicolson, 1990). In one study, new mothers kept time-use diaries and were also interviewed twice. Their workdays ranged from eleven to seventeen and a half hours a day, and they spent an average of six hours a day alone with their babies. Although they cited the babies' fathers as their main source of support, fathers actually contributed only zero to two hours a day of primary care (Croghan, 1991). In another study women described the kinds of help they received: "If I'm at the end of the rope, he'll step in and take over." "At dinner time he pitches in . . . entertains the baby" (Rhoades, 1989, pp. 131–141).

FIGURE 10.3.
Source: Sylvia. © 1991 by Nicole Hollander. Used by permission of Nicole Hollander.

These studies suggest that new mothers are stressed by inequality in marital roles. Women may enter motherhood with expectations of equality in parenting, but these expectations collide with reality (Ruble et al., 1988). It is difficult for women and men to change parenting relationships because cultural images and social structures constantly reinforce the idea that mothers, not fathers, should have day-to-day responsibility for children (Walzer, 1998). Myths of motherhood still imply that women should be fulfilled through self-sacrifice and grateful for any small contribution their husbands might make (Croghan, 1991).

Do Mothers Face Impossible Ideals?

Mothers are encouraged to evaluate themselves against images of ideal mothers such as the radiant, serene "Madonna" and the "superwoman" who juggles the demands of house, children, husband, and job while providing her children with unfailing love and plenty of quality time (Ussher, 1989). Women often are not prepared for negative and ambivalent feelings and may feel like failures when they occur. It is likely that a majority of women experience decreased emotional well-being at some point during pregnancy and early motherhood (Condon, 1987; Ruble et al., 1988; Ussher, 1989; Wells, Hobfall, & Lavin, 1997). Some women have described the conflicts that come from experiencing negative feelings they knew did not live up to the ideals:

> Motherhood wasn't what I expected—unadulterated wonder. The shock of the isolation and much of the sheer slog and boredom were exacerbated by the fact that I felt I wasn't supposed to feel dissatisfied. (Wandor, 1980, cited in Ussher, 1989, p. 84)

> Being brought up in the traditional way, I always feared something terrible would happen if I went away, like the house would burn down. I felt I would be punished for leaving the children, even to go to work. Especially to go to work. (A single mother; Hall, 1984, pp. 17–18)

> I couldn't seem to do anything right; I felt so tired, the baby kept crying, and I kept thinking that this was supposed to be the most fulfilling experience of my whole life. It felt like the most lonely, miserable experience. (A mother three weeks after the birth of her first child, cited in Ussher, 1989, p. 82)

The best strategies for coping with role changes during pregnancy seem to be active assertion and seeking communal relationships with other women. In a study of white, employed, pregnant women, these were associated with reduced depression and anger (Wells et al., 1997). In another study, women who received social support during pregnancy showed many beneficial physical and psychological outcomes that persisted through the first year of motherhood (Oakley, 1992).

Are Sexuality and Motherhood Incompatible?

When women become pregnant, they are confronted with many of the contradictions about sexuality that characterize Western society. The Madonna ideal—pure and serene—exists at the cost of desire: the Madonna must be a virgin (Young, 1998). The idea of a mother who has sexual desires and acts on them conflicts with the ideal of maternal selflessness. Becoming pregnant and giving birth highlight a woman's sexuality; at the same time, society denies the sexuality of pregnant women and mothers; this perpetuates a split between body and self (Ussher, 1989).

One example of this split is the disconnection between desire and behavior during pregnancy. Many women experience increased sexual desire while pregnant, especially in the middle three months (Kitzinger, 1983). This may reflect physical changes such as an increased blood supply to the pelvic area, as well as psychological factors. (For one thing, the woman and her partner needn't worry about contraception!) Yet women may engage in sexual activities less often, out of fear of harming the fetus, feeling unattractive, or physical awkwardness.

In a normal pregnancy, intercourse and orgasm are safe until four weeks before the due date; these activities do not harm the fetus or cause miscarriage (Masters & Johnson, 1966). When women were surveyed about their physicians' advice, however, 60 percent had received no information at all, and another 10 percent were told they should not have intercourse after their seventh month (Gauna-Trujillo & Higgins, 1989). Perhaps the medical profession perpetuates the myth of the asexual mother because doctors, themselves influenced by the myth, are reluctant and embarrassed to discuss sex with pregnant women (Ussher, 1989).

What Are the Psychological Effects of Bodily Changes During Pregnancy?

The hormonal changes of pregnancy are much greater than those of the menstrual cycle. The levels of progesterone and estrogen in pregnant women are many times higher than in nonpregnant women, and many of the physical experiences of early pregnancy may be related to rapid increases in these hormones. These include breast tenderness, fatigue, and "morning sickness" (which can actually occur at any time of the day): nausea, revulsion at the sight or odor of food, and sometimes vomiting.

In addition, other physiological changes may alter the functioning of the central nervous system. The level of the neurotransmitter norepinephrine drops during pregnancy while the levels of stress-associated hormones rise (Treadway, Kane, Jarrahi-Zadeh, & Lipton, 1969). Norepinephrine and progesterone have both been related to depression. In a study of mood changes during pregnancy, women were interviewed both before and during their pregnancies and compared with a control group of women who did not become pregnant. For the pregnant group, changes in mood increased compared with both their prepregnancy baseline and the control group, mainly during the first third of the pregnancy (Striegel-Moore, Goldman, Garvin, & Rodin, 1996).

Pregnancy is also a time of dramatic weight gain and changes in body shape. Many women feel extremely ambivalent about these changes (Ussher, 1989). Reactions include feeling temporarily free from cultural demands to be slim, feeling awe and wonder, feeling afraid and disgusted by their size, and feeling alienated and out of control (see Box 10.3). In a study of more than 200 women, changes in body image were among the most frequently reported stressors of pregnancy and early motherhood, second only to physical symptoms (Affonso & Mayberry, 1989). Recent research suggests that body image concerns are increasing; some women are choosing not to become pregnant because of fears about how it would change their bodies (Garner, 1997).

Indeed, the pregnant woman does lose some control over her body. Changes will occur no matter what she does (see Figure 10.4). She is helpless (short of terminating the pregnancy) to govern her own body. And yet, as we have discussed throughout this book, society defines her largely in terms of her body. Thus it should not be surprising if pregnant women feel unfeminine, moody, or insecure, even apart from hormonal causes.

Box 10.3 "A Brand New Body": One Woman's Account of Pregnancy

Suzanne Arms (1973) kept a journal during her first pregnancy. Her reactions to her changing body are captured in these journal entries, ranging from early to late in her pregnancy.

> I have the feeling that I brought a brand new body home from the doctor's office. I'm a new me. Nobody else would look at me and call me pregnant, but it's wonderful to know that I really am, and I look for every tiny sign to prove it's true. My developing breasts are encouraging, and my nipples have become much larger. My nipples stand erect at times, and they're at least three shades darker. (p. 13)
>
> I have never felt beautiful but I've always liked my face and filled-out body. . . . But looking at pictures of me crying last week really hurt. They're so un-me. Just a pudgy woman. Today I don't feel like that at all. I've tied my hair back, vowed not to wear those baggy farmer jeans till after the baby comes, and put on a dress; I really do feel beautiful. In fact, I feel like I'm a pretty good place for a baby to stay and grow in. Nice, round, firm, with just enough fat all over to make it really soft and safe for the baby. (p. 29)
>
> . . . I've been getting more and more pleasure from my sensual feelings. There's some old tightness in me that seems to be losing its hold at last, and I feel all of me expanding. (p. 35)
>
> I rub cocoa butter on my tummy and breasts every morning after showering. The skin has become pink and smooth and I can't help feeling it all the time. The other day we were in the bookstore, and I was absent-mindedly rubbing myself and staring into space. A young woman with a child called to me from across the store, "That's a lovely belly you have there!" (p. 40)
>
> . . . I've begun to feel huge. I remember hearing other pregnant women hassle themselves about getting fat. I never could figure it out. To me they looked beautiful, round and blooming. I assured myself that I would never feel that way, and I would love my tummy and all the extra pounds. Well, that's great in theory—but suddenly the day comes when I look in the mirror and my face is round and I really do look like an orange! even holding my stomach in. So yesterday I spent the whole day feeling fat, ugly, and unlovable. Despite every nice thing John has said, I knew he would soon see how unappealing I am. (p. 44)
>
> A very full feeling today, I'm thick and stuffed like a bulging cabbage. (p. 59)
>
> I never thought it would come to this. I can't reach over my stomach to get to my feet. John has to lace up my hiking boots! (p. 63)
>
> Sometimes it seems as though I've been pregnant all my life. I can't remember being unpregnant. (p. 64)

Suzanne Arms' pregnancy was planned and wanted, and she was in a stable relationship with a supportive male partner. How might the reactions of women to their changing bodies differ in differing social circumstances?

Source: "A Brand New Body" from Suzanne Arms, *A Season to Be Born.*

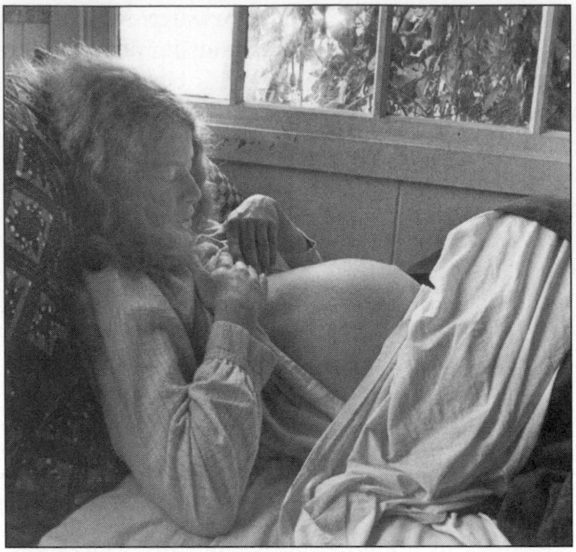

FIGURE 10.4. Suzanne Arms, pregnant.

How Do Others React to Pregnant Women?

Pregnant women are powerful stimuli for the behavior of others. "A woman begins to assume the identity of mother in the eyes of society almost as soon as she is visibly pregnant, ceasing to be a single unit long before the birth of her child" (Ussher, 1989, p. 81). Her body symbolizes the eternal power of women:

> As soon as I was visibly and clearly pregnant, I felt, for the first time in my adolescent and adult life, not-guilty. The atmosphere of approval in which I was bathed—even by strangers on the street, it seemed—was like an aura I carried with me, in which doubts, fears, misgivings, met with absolute denial. This is what women have always done. (Rich, 1976, p. 26)

Pregnant women may be genuinely cherished. One woman, who married into a Puerto Rican family, was delighted by her special status when she became pregnant:

> I'm treated like a precious, fragile person by my in-laws. I . . . get the best seat on the couch and am served dinner first. When my mother-in-law found out I was pregnant with my first child, she created a special ritual for me that involved a warm, scented candle-lit bath. She placed my husband's baby picture on the mirror and told me all about her experiences with pregnancy and birth (Johnston-Robledo, 2000, pp. 132–133).

On the other hand, pregnancy may elicit benevolent sexism because pregnant women are seen as fragile and dependent, and therefore less threatening. Pregnancy may even be a kind of stigma: people react very differently to pregnant and nonpregnant women, and their reactions may lead to change in the women's behavior in return. This was illustrated in an intriguing experiment in which two female experimenters alternated between appearing pregnant (with the help of a little padding) or carrying a box the same size as the "pregnancy"

(Taylor & Langer, 1977). The women stood in elevators and measured the distance that other passengers stood from them. Both men and women stood closer to the "nonpregnant" woman. Men, especially, avoided the "pregnant" woman. She was also stared at more; both men and women spent considerable time furtively looking at her stomach, so much so that both experimenters felt very uncomfortable when playing the pregnant role.

The public presence of pregnant women has since become more acceptable. Actress Demi Moore even appeared nude and very pregnant on the cover of *Vanity Fair* in 1991. Are pregnant women still stigmatized? With the help of a little padding, perhaps some intrepid female researchers will conduct another study.

Does Motherhood Change Women's Identity?

Pregnancy and mothering affect women's sense of self. In a Canadian study, for example, the women experienced themselves as profoundly changed. Middle-class women described the changes in terms of personal growth and self-actualization; working-class women described a process of "settling down." For both groups, motherhood involved a moral transformation in which they became deeply connected to their babies. However, the flip side of such connectedness—feeling responsible for the child—was described as one of the hardest things about motherhood (McMahon, 1995).

In another study that followed newly married couples over a three-year period, the birth of a child changed both parents' identities: men became more masculine and women more feminine on dimensions that defined masculinity and femininity for themselves. In other words, the changes in marital roles and activities following the birth of a child affected their sense of themselves as feminine women and masculine men (Burke & Cast, 1997).

An intensive case study of one woman's pregnancy illustrates the experience of change (Smith, 1991). Clare's identity change during early pregnancy involved imagining the child-to-be:

> In one respect, it's—it's a person, a whole person that just happens to be in there, and in another way, it's something different. (p. 231)

In the middle phase, Clare experienced a growing sense of psychological relatedness with others—partner, mother, sister. Near the end of the pregnancy, Clare sees herself as very changed:

> I'm one of two and I'm one of three. . . . An irrevocable decision, the steps have been made that mean that my other identities, if you like as a mother and a partner, make up that essential me now. (p. 236)

The transition to motherhood involves losses as well as gains. The woman ceases to be seen as an autonomous individual and is instead viewed as an "expectant mother" and then "mother." It is not surprising that feelings of loss are experienced. It is hard to change from being "Joy Williams, secretary/jogger/painter/daughter/spouse and more" to being "Timmy's mom." One of the authors remembers her feelings of sadness and loneliness when the nurses in the hospital following the birth of her first child referred to all the women in the obstetric unit as "Mother" ("Mother, are you ready for your lunch tray?") rather than by our names. It seemed as if everything that had gone before was now to be put aside for the all-encompassing identity and job of Mother.

Because feelings of loss conflict with the motherhood mystique, women may be ashamed of them, label themselves as ill or abnormal, or believe that "baby blues" are inevitable and biologically determined. One of the ways cultural constructions of motherhood may oppress women is that they are not allowed to mourn or grieve the old, lost self (Nicolson, 1993). Rather than pathologize women's experiences, feminist psychology looks for explanations in the sociopolitical context of mothering (Ussher, 1989).

So far, we have been talking about the transition to motherhood mainly as it has been constructed for white, middle-class women exposed to the motherhood mystique. What does the identity of mother mean for poor women? An eloquent expression of class and color differences in ideals of womanhood and motherhood comes from a famous speech attributed to Sojourner Truth, a crusader for abolition and suffrage and an ex-slave, to the Akron Convention for Women's Rights in 1852:

> That man over there says that women need to be helped into carriages, and lifted over ditches and have the best place everywhere. Nobody ever helps me into carriages, or over mud puddles or gives me any best place, and ain't I a woman? Look at me! Look at my arm! I have ploughed, and planted, and gathered into barns, and no man could head me! And ain't I a woman? I could work as much and eat as much as a man—when I could get it—and bear the lash as

FIGURE 10.5.
Source: Cartoon by David Horsey. Copyright 2003 Tribune Media Services, Inc. All rights reserved. Reprinted with permission.

> well! And ain't I a woman? I have borne thirteen children, and seen them most all sold off to slavery, and when I cried out with my mother's grief, none but Jesus heard me. And ain't I a woman? (Adapted from Ruth, 1990, pp. 463–464)

Attitudes toward pregnant women still vary by social class. Middle-class women in heterosexual marriages may be treated as delicate and special, but poor single women are labeled "welfare moms," undeserving of respect. Middle-class mothers are urged to stay home with their children, but poor mothers are forced to look for paid employment (see Figure 10.5). Heterosexual women's connectedness with their children is seen as positive, but lesbians' connectedness with theirs is seen as pathological. Identity is affected not only from within, but also by the social context of mothering.

THE EVENT OF CHILDBIRTH

If a woman were training to run a marathon, climb a cliff, or go on an "Outward Bound" trek, she would probably think of the upcoming event as a challenge. She would acknowledge that her body would be worked hard and stressed, her courage tested, and her life put at some risk. Yet she could feel in control and prepare for the challenge. She might undertake the experience as a way of knowing her own self or of developing her strengths and resources. Childbirth is a normal physical process with some of the same potential for empowerment, yet women are rarely encouraged to think of it in this way (Rich, 1976). Instead, they are taught to think of it as an event in which they will be dependent, passive, subject to authority, and in need of expert medical intervention.

How Is the Meaning of Childbirth Socially Constructed?

In virtually all cultures, birth is associated with fear, pain, awe, and wonder; it is viewed as both "the worst pain anyone could suffer" and as "peak experience." Yet there are surprisingly few accounts of childbirth by women, and women's experiences of childbirth are invisible in Western art. Images of war and death are innumerable, but images of birth are nonexistent (Chicago, 1990). Artist Judy Chicago's Birth Project is a collective effort by women artists and crafters to represent images of birth (see Figure 10.6).

Popular culture gives us its own version: many prime-time situation comedies have shown their stars giving birth. A study of books, magazines, newspaper articles, TV shows, and movies in the 1980s and early 1990s showed that these media usually portrayed a woman giving birth as a passive patient, not an active agent, and showed a very strong preference for hospital births over birthing centers or home births (Sterk, 1996). It seems that women are in charge of childbirth only when they write science-fiction novels (see Box 10.4).

Is Childbirth a Medical Crisis?

In some countries, birth is considered a natural phenomenon that needs no medical intervention in the majority of cases. For example, in the Netherlands the laboring woman is believed to need only "close observation, moral support,

FIGURE 10.6. Judy Chicago's image "Crowning" represents the moment the baby's head first becomes visible at the vaginal opening.

and protection against human meddling." A healthy woman can best accomplish her task of birthing her baby if she is self-confident, in familiar surroundings—preferably her own home—and attended by a birth specialist such as a midwife. Women at risk of complications are hospitalized, but most babies are born at home (MacFarlane, 1977, p. 29).

In contrast, virtually all U.S. births take place in hospitals. As recently as 1935, the majority of babies were born at home, but by the end of the 1970s, 99 percent of births took place in hospitals (Nelson, 1996). Today, nurse-midwives attend about 7 percent of U.S. births, with the rest attended by physicians (NCHS, 1999). Even the language of childbirth reflects the centrality of the physician: People routinely speak of babies being *delivered* by doctors instead of birthed by women.

Is the medical model of birth best for women? On the one hand, basic health care and education for pregnant women can save lives and improve infant health. On the other hand, the medical monopoly may lead to women being regarded as incompetent and passive patients, depriving them of control during one of life's most awesome experiences. Many of the customary procedures surrounding birth in the United States are virtually unknown in other societies and are not necessarily in the best interest of mother or baby. For example, in hospital births the woman lies on her back during delivery, whereas in most cultures women give birth in a squatting or semi-seated position. The supine position puts pressure on the spine, may slow labor, works against gravity, increases the risk of vaginal tearing, and makes it more difficult for the woman to push actively during the process. Why, then, do hospitals insist on this position? It is easier for the physician, who can view the birth more conveniently.

Box 10.4. Takver Gives Birth

In this passage from her novel *The Dispossessed,* acclaimed science-fiction writer Ursula LeGuin movingly describes the work and the triumph of giving birth.

Takver got very big in the belly and walked like a person carrying a large, heavy basket of laundry. She stayed at work at the fish labs till she had found and trained an adequate replacement for herself, then she came home and began labor. Shevek arrived home in midafternoon. "You might go fetch the midwife," Takver said. "Tell her the contractions are four or five minutes apart, but they're not speeding up much, so don't hurry very much."

He ran to the block clinic, arriving so out of breath and unsteady on his legs that they thought he was having a heart attack. He explained. They sent a message off to another midwife and told him to go home, the partner would be wanting company. He went home, and at every stride the panic in him grew, the terror, the certainty of loss. . . .

Takver had no time for emotional scenes; she was busy. She had cleared the bed platform except for a clean sheet, and she was at work bearing a child. She did not howl or scream, as she was not in pain, but when each contraction came she managed it by muscle and breath control, and then let out a great *houff* of breath, like one who makes a terrific effort to lift a heavy weight. Shevek had never seen any work that so used all the strength of the body.

He could not look on such work without trying to help in it. He could serve as handhold and brace when she needed leverage. They found this arrangement very quickly by trial and error, and kept to it after the midwife had come in. Takver gave birth afoot, squatting, her face against Shevek's thigh, her hands gripping his braced arms. "There you are," the midwife said quietly under the hard, engine-like pounding of Takver's breathing, and she took the slimy but recognizably human creature that had appeared. A gush of blood followed, and an amorphous mass of something not human, not alive. The terror he had forgotten came back into Shevek redoubled. It was death he saw. Takver had let go of his arms and was huddled down quite limp at his feet. He bent over her, stiff with horror and grief.

"That's it," said the midwife, "help her move aside so I can clean this up."

"I want to wash," Takver said feebly.

"Here, help her wash up. Those are sterile cloths—there."

"Waw, waw, waw," said another voice.

The room seemed to be full of people. . . .

Somehow in this extreme rush of events the midwife had found time to clean the infant and even put a gown on it, so that it was not so fishlike and slippery as when he had seen it first. The afternoon had got dark, with the same peculiar rapidity and lack of time lapse. The lamp was on. Shevek picked up the baby to take it to Takver. Its face was incredibly small, with large, fragile-looking, closed eyelids. "Give it here," Takver was saying. "Oh, do hurry up, please give it to me."

He brought it across the room and very cautiously lowered it onto Takver's stomach. "Ah!" she said softly, a call of pure triumph.

"What is it?" she asked after a while, sleepily.

Shevek was sitting beside her on the edge of the bed platform. He carefully investigated, somewhat taken aback by the length of gown as contrasted with the extreme shortness of limb. "Girl."

The midwife came back, went around putting things to rights. "You did a first-rate job," she remarked, to both of them. They assented mildly. "I'll look in in the morning," she said leaving. The baby and Takver were already asleep. Shevek put his head down near Takver's. He was accustomed to the pleasant musky smell of her skin. This had changed; it had become a perfume, heavy and faint, heavy with sleep. Very gently he put one arm over her as she lay on her side with the baby against her breast. In the room heavy with life he slept.

Source: "Takver Gives Birth" from *The Dispossessed* by Ursula K. LeGuin.

American women have experienced childbirth with feet in the air, drugged, shaved, purged with an enema, denied food and water, hooked up to machines and sensors, and psychologically isolated to a degree that is virtually unknown in other parts of the world (Nelson, 1996). Research shows that giving birth in an unfamiliar environment, being surrounded by strangers, and being moved from one room to another late in labor affect the birth process adversely even in nonhuman animals, yet these practices are routine in medicalized childbirth (MacFarlane, 1977; Newton, 1970).

In the United States, women have also been routinely taught that they will need pain relief during normal birth. The use of tranquilizers, barbiturates, and anesthetics during childbirth has become routine, but it is also controversial. On the one hand, drugs can spare women unnecessary pain. On the other hand, there are "a number of well-documented dangerous effects on both mother and infant" (Hyde & DeLamater, 2003, p. 165). For example, anesthetics in the mother's bloodstream are passed to the infant and may slow development for up to four weeks. Anesthetics may prolong labor by inhibiting contractions and making the mother unable to help push the baby through the birth canal. Psychologically, they reduce the woman's awareness and her ability to control one of the most meaningful events of her life.

The medical model of birth encourages physicians and pregnant women to focus on possible complications and emergencies and may cause them to react to even remote possibilities with drastic medical interventions. In the past twenty-five years, there has been a dramatic increase in the number of cesarean births in the United States, from about 4 percent to more than 24 percent of all births (Martin, Park, & Sutton, 2002). This rate is much higher than in other developed countries such as Great Britain (where it is about 10%) and is *not* associated with lower infant mortality. Other medical procedures such as fetal monitoring, ultrasound, and artificial induction of labor are also rising dramatically in the United States (NCHS, 1999).

The reasons for the epidemic of medical intervention are unclear. Some critics have rather cynically suggested that scheduled surgical births are more convenient and profitable for physicians. Others have attributed the increase to physicians' fear of malpractice suits. When birth is defined as a medical event, helping and supporting the laboring woman seems inadequate, and heroic medical measures seem desirable. It has also been suggested that the high rate of surgical deliveries is an attempt by the medical profession to keep its dominant role in childbirth, despite women's increasing insistence on viewing birth as a normal process.

Family-Centered Childbirth

The medicalization of birth reached its height in the United States in the 1950s and 1960s. After undergoing male-managed childbirth, many women began to write about their experiences and work toward more woman- and family-centered birthing practices. Women organizers founded the International Childbirth Education Association in 1960. Widely read books such as *Our Bodies, Ourselves; Immaculate Deception; Of Woman Born;* and *The Great American Birth Rite* helped change public attitudes in the 1970s.

At about the same time, methods of *prepared or natural childbirth* were introduced to the American public. The most popular type of prepared childbirth is the *Lamaze method,* named after a French obstetrician. Women who use this approach learn techniques of relaxation and controlled breathing. Relaxation helps to reduce tension and the perception of pain and conserves energy during labor. Controlled breathing helps the woman work with, not against, the strength of each uterine contraction. The Lamaze method does not rule out the use of pain-relieving drugs, but it emphasizes that with proper preparation they may not be needed, and it leaves the choice to the laboring woman.

Another part of the Lamaze technique is the help of a "coach," or trusted partner—usually the baby's father—during labor and birth. The coach helps the mother with relaxation and controlled breathing and provides emotional support and encouragement. Men had been banished from the delivery room at the heyday of the medical model because they were regarded as unhygienic, superfluous, and likely to get in the way (MacFarlane, 1977). Today, many men feel that participating in the birth of their child is an important part of being a father.

Studies comparing women who used Lamaze and other methods of childbirth education and training with women who had no special preparation have shown benefits associated with prepared childbirth. These include shorter labor, fewer complications, less use of anesthetics, less reported pain, and increased feelings of self-esteem and control (Hyde & DeLamater, 2003). These studies must be interpreted carefully. Perhaps women who sign up for Lamaze training are largely those who are motivated to experience childbirth positively under any circumstances. In other words, the studies do not rule out *self-selection.*

One study of support during childbirth does rule out self-selection effects (Kennell, Klaus, McGrath, Robertson, & Hinkley, 1991). More than 600 pregnant women, mostly Hispanic, poor, and unmarried, were randomly assigned to one of three groups. One group received emotional support during labor from a specially trained woman helper. The helpers, who were recruited from the local community, stayed with the laboring women to provide encouragement, explain the birth process, and offer soothing touch and handholding. A second group had a noninteractive female observer present, and the third group had standard hospital care.

Women in the emotional support group had a cesarean rate of 8 percent, compared with 13 percent in the observed group and 18 percent in the standard procedure group. They experienced less pain in labor: the standard group were almost seven times as likely to need anesthesia as the emotional support group. Moreover, their labor time was shorter, and they and their babies spent less time in the hospital. Clearly, emotional support made a large difference. The study's director estimated that investing small amounts of money in providing this kind of support would save $2 billion a year in hospital costs.

Women's efforts to regain control of the event of birth have resulted in many changes from the extreme medical model of thirty years ago. Today, fathers are more likely to be with the birthing woman. More births are taking place in homelike birth centers, attended by nurse-midwives. Women and their partners are far more likely to be educated about the normal processes and events of pregnancy and birth. Such knowledge reduces fear and helplessness, and thus reduces discomfort. Learning techniques to use during labor can replace passive suffering with active involvement and coping. However, new technology is continually being introduced, and each new intervention can readily be overused.

Women's struggle for choice and control in childbirth parallels the struggle for self-determination in general and is part of a social revolution that is not yet complete. The medical model of birth illustrates the way social institutions can decrease the power of women. When real control is lacking, women perceive themselves as helpless and passive, and this perception in turn contributes to powerlessness. Treating birth as a normal, woman- and family-centered event, rather than a medical one, could prove very beneficial to women, their partners, and their children.

Depression Following Childbirth: Why?

The first weeks following childbirth (the *postnatal period*) are often characterized as a time of mood swings and depression. For the first few days after giving birth, most women feel elated: the labor is over and the baby has arrived. Soon, however, they experience depression and crying spells. Between 50 percent and 80 percent of women experience mood swings for only a day or two. Longer-lasting depression (six to eight weeks) occurs in about 13 percent of women; it includes feelings of inadequacy and inability to cope, fatigue, tearfulness, and insomnia. The most severe form, a clinical psychosis, affects one-tenth of 1 percent of new mothers (Hyde & DeLamater, 2003; Mauthner, 1998).

Are postnatal mood disorders due to hormonal changes? Birth is followed by dramatic decreases in the high levels of estrogen and progesterone that characterize pregnancy. However, hormone changes have not been shown to *cause* depression; in fact, there is no direct link between postnatal hormone levels and mood (Johnston-Robledo, 2000; Treadway et al., 1969). The hormonal changes of pregnancy and the postnatal period are real. They give rise to bodily changes and sensations that must be interpreted by the woman who is experiencing them. But the social context of interpretation is crucial; postnatal depression may be more of a social construction than a medical condition. It is virtually unknown in many countries, including India, China, Mexico, and Kenya, suggesting that the causes are at least partly cultural (Mauthner, 1998).

Many social and interpersonal factors may contribute to depression and mood swings among new mothers: dissatisfaction with body size and shape, feeling incompetent to care for a newborn, a sense that one's real self is lost in the role of mother, disappointment with a partner's lack of support, and so on. In an intensive study of a small sample of Englishwomen experiencing postnatal depression, a key factor was conflicts between their expectations of motherhood and their actual experiences. Different mothers resolved these conflicts in different ways, but in all cases recovery was a process of accepting themselves and rejecting the impossible ideals of motherhood. Often, this came about through talking with other women (Mauthner, 1998). Women who find it difficult to relate to others because of their personality styles or past experiences may experience more depressive symptoms (Lutz & Hock, 1998).

One often overlooked factor obvious to the authors of this book, both mothers, is sleep deprivation. During the last weeks of pregnancy, a woman may not sleep well due to the discomfort caused by the heavy, restless fetus.

Next, the hard physical work and stress of birthing a child are followed by many consecutive nights of disturbed sleep. Babies rarely sleep for an unbroken 6- to 7-hour period before they are 6 weeks old, and some take much longer to "settle down." We know of no studies of postnatal depression that have examined sleep deprivation as a factor or compared moodiness in new mothers with moodiness in a sleep-deprived comparison group. The lack of attention to this possibility is a striking example of how sociocultural influences are often overlooked in studying women's lives.

Countries in which postnatal depression is rare offer a period of rest and special care for the new mother, practical and emotional support from other women, and positive attention to the mother, not just the baby (Johnston-Robledo, 2000; Mauthner, 1998). For example, in Guatemala, a new mother gets a herbal bath and a massage. In Nigeria, she and her baby are secluded in a "fattening room" where her meals are prepared by others. Customs like these may help the new mother interpret her bodily changes and sensations more positively and ease her adjustment to motherhood. One U.S. psychologist who studied new mothers suggests, "Next time a friend or relative has a baby, in addition to a gift for the baby, bring her a meal and offer to help around the house" (Johnston-Robledo, 2000, p. 139). And maybe somebody else could get up with the baby so she can get a good night's sleep.

EXPERIENCES OF MOTHERING

The realities of mothering are as different as the social circumstances of women who mother. In this section, let's look at what motherhood involves for diverse groups of women.

Teen Mothers

Each year in the United States, more than a million young women under the age of 20 become pregnant. Most of these teens are unmarried. Over half of teen pregnancies result in the birth of a child; about 30 percent are terminated by abortion; and the rest end in miscarriage (Hyde & DeLamater, 2003). The rate of births to teen mothers is much higher for Hispanic and black groups than for whites (Martin et al., 2002).

The rate of teen pregnancy dropped dramatically throughout the 1990s for all ethnic groups (Martin et al., 2002). However, the teen pregnancy rate in the United States is still much higher than in comparable countries (see Figure 10.7). U.S. teens are not more sexually active than their European counterparts, but they are much less likely to use contraception reliably and effectively (Alan Guttmacher Institute, 2002).

What factors put girls at risk for early pregnancy? First and foremost, teen pregnancy and childbearing are related to social class disadvantages. Living in a poor or dangerous neighborhood, growing up in a poor family with a single parent, and being sexually abused are all linked to teen pregnancy. Parents who supervise and regulate their teens' activities and teach them to avoid unprotected sex may lower the risk to some extent (Miller, Benson, & Galbraith, 2001).

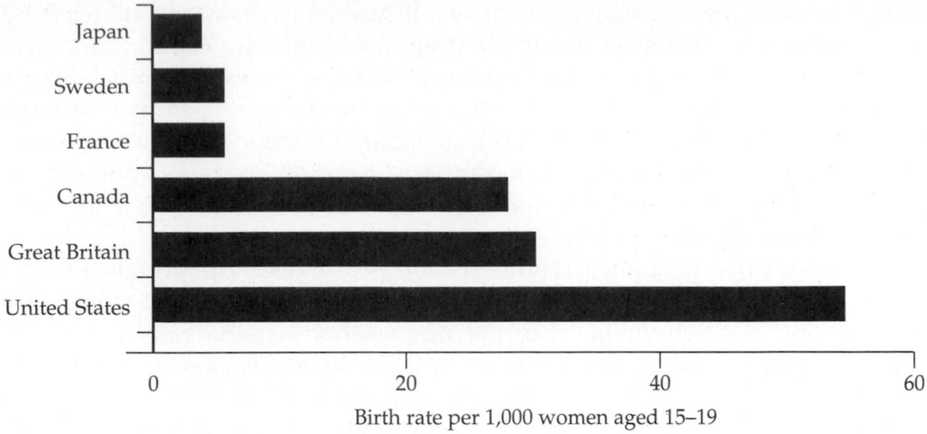

FIGURE 10.7. U.S. teenagers have higher birthrates than adolescents in other developed countries.
Source: "Teenagers' sexual and reproductive health," Facts in Brief (2002). New York: The Alan Guttmacher Institute.

Adolescent motherhood has serious consequences for the young women involved, their children, and society as a whole. These include interrupted education and lowered job opportunities for the mothers, health problems for the babies, and the costs of public assistance and interventions (Elise, 1995). In one major study, 281 teen mothers in Indiana were followed through pregnancy and when their children were 3, 5, and 8 years old. The average age of the mothers at the time of childbirth was 17; almost two-thirds were African-American, one-third white, and 4 percent Hispanic. Although most of the children were of normal weight and health at birth, they suffered increasing physical, emotional, and behavioral problems. By the age of 8, more than 70 percent were having problems in school. The mothers were suffering disadvantages, too. They did not know very much about taking care of children and did not have the cognitive maturity to be skilled parents. Five years after their child's birth, most remained undereducated, underemployed, and weighed down by depression, anxiety, and stress.

However, there was a great deal of variability in the group. About 18 percent of the mother-child pairs were thriving: The mothers were working, had continued their education, and showed high self-esteem and little depression or anxiety. Their children were developmentally normal. Another 20 percent of the women were also doing well, although their children were struggling with developmental or behavioral problems. The women who had managed to overcome the disadvantages of early motherhood were those who started off with more advantages in the first place (for example, they had more education before they got pregnant), those who received emotional support from a partner, and those whose coping skills and cognitive readiness for parenthood were high (Whitman, Borkowski, Keogh, & Weed, 2001).

Another study focused on a group of very disadvantaged inner-city teens from New York. These women ranged in age from 14 to 19; most were African-American or Puerto Rican; two-thirds came from families on welfare. The young mothers who were doing best at a 5-year follow-up had active lives that typically involved working, going to school, spending time with their partner and families, and taking care of their children. What contributed to their strengths? In-depth interviews revealed themes of having been raised in a strict home environment, receiving support from their family with the expectation that they would "make something of themselves," having role models and support for education, and having confidence, a strong will, and a "passion to succeed" (Leadbetter & Way, 2001).

These research findings show that statistics alone do not convey the meaning of teen pregnancy. Teen pregnancy is often used as a symbol of moral and social decay, and teen mothers are castigated for undermining family values. Research shows that adolescent mothers are a diverse group who are often struggling to overcome disadvantages that go far beyond just having a baby. Many teen mothers show resilience and courage in overcoming the obstacles they face. Surprisingly, adolescent motherhood does not always result in permanent disadvantage. The majority of teen mothers eventually finish high school, get stable jobs, move into their own apartments or houses, and raise children who do not go on to become teen parents themselves (Leadbetter & Way, 2001).

We are not arguing that early childbearing is desirable. But its meaning and consequences depend on its cultural context. Though teen pregnancy is seen as a huge social problem today, rates were actually higher in the 1950s than now (Nettles & Scott-Jones, 1987). It was less of an issue then because most teen mothers were married, or hastily got married on becoming pregnant.

Today, there are ethnic and cultural differences in the acceptance of teen pregnancy. Most African-American teen mothers live with and receive support from their own mothers. Among Hispanic families, teen pregnancy may not be seen as problematic as long as it results in marriage. Some young women see any child as a gift from God, no matter how unfortunate the circumstances of its birth (Leadbetter & Way, 2001; Whitman, et al., 2001). And some teen mothers become inspired to better their lives for the sake of their child (Leadbetter & Way, 2001).

Young mothers need access to programs to help them learn parenting skills, complete their education, and take control of their contraceptive use. Moreover, they need support from their families, their communities, and the educational system. There is also a great need for programs that help fathers take responsibility for birth control, family planning, and their children's economic and social support. With help, the negative effects of early childbearing can be overcome (Elise, 1995; Furstenberg et al., 1989; Henly, 1997; Leadbetter & Way, 2001; Whitman et al., 2001).

Single Mothers

The number of families headed by single women has increased dramatically over the past twenty-five years. Minority children are more likely to grow up in single-parent families; 23 percent of white, 31 percent of Hispanic, and 55 percent of African-American children are in single-parent households, the great majority headed by women (only 4% of children in single-parent families live with their fathers). The reasons for this increase are diverse, too. For whites, the primary reason for single parenthood is the high separation and divorce rate (see Chapter 9). For Hispanic and black women, the primary reason is a rise in births to single women (Steil, 2001; U.S. Census Bureau, 2000).

Single mothers, whether they are unmarried, separated, or divorced, are more likely to be holding down jobs than women with husbands present in the home. Yet families headed by women are far more likely to be poor than other families. More than half of all black and Hispanic woman-headed families and more than one-third of white woman-headed families are living in poverty. Poverty among women and children is one of the most serious social problems in the United States today (Polakow, 1993; Steil, 2001).

Why are women-headed households so likely to be poor? Some of the reasons for women's poverty are the same as men's: they may lack education or job skills or live in an area in which there are few jobs. But women are poor for gender-related reasons as well: because they receive little economic support from absentee fathers after divorce (Chapter 9) and because they are underpaid and underemployed (see Chapter 11). Perhaps most important, public policy does not reflect the needs of women and children.

Even women who have full-time employment may not be able to earn enough to keep themselves and their families out of poverty. The story of one single working mother illustrates the dilemmas of being both nurturer and provider. Lori P. worked full time as a secretary at a university, earning about $800 a month. When her partner left her and their 4-year-old son, she was unable to pay her monthly bills, which included $500 for child care. Although Lori started out with advantages—health care coverage, good child care, safe housing, occasional child-support contributions from the absent partner, and middle-class respectability—she barely manages to survive:

> I don't know what I'm going to do. My dad helped last month, but rent's due next Wednesday and I don't have any money. I mean I don't. I just paid all my bills. It's the end of the month now and I don't get paid for two more weeks. I have $2.50 in my account; two dollars and fifty cents! Rent's $545—I get paid in two weeks again, but that will only be $400 . . . I need help—I feel like I'm sinking. (Polakow, 1993, pp. 82–83)

Ashamed to be on welfare, Lori wants to get her college degree so that she can get a better job, but she cannot afford to pay for child care while she attends night classes. For now, she is relying on another poor single mother, who babysits for $2.00 an hour.

As Lori's story shows, men's failure to provide financial support is a major source of single mothers' economic burdens. In addition, the lack of publicly subsidized child care makes it impossible for a single working mother to get ahead. Even if she works full time at minimum wage, child care for one child will consume between 37 percent and 78 percent of her income (Polakow, 1993). Of all the Western industrialized nations, only the United States fails to provide family support benefits as a matter of public policy (Lorber, 1993b).

Most single mothers want to work, and most do have jobs (Youngblut, Singer, Madigan, Swegart, & Rodgers, 1997; Steil, 2001). But finding good child care is a worry. Many low-income mothers are raising their children in high-risk environments where the need for quality care is crucial. In a study of low-income African-American single mothers who were former welfare recipients, concerns about child care were linked with mothers' depression and negative feelings about their children (Jackson, 1997).

The primary response to the feminization of poverty in the United States seems to be to blame the victims. Women who accept welfare benefits are accused of causing the very problems they are trying to cope with. Since the 1980s, public aid programs to help people help themselves out of poverty have been repeatedly cut (Polakow, 1993; Sapiro, 1994). In 1996, welfare reform legislation mandated that mothers of young children who receive benefits find paid employment, and the current political climate is even more harsh. Consider that many middle-class mothers with safe homes, good child care, decent jobs, and husbands at home find it difficult or impossible to manage full-time employment when they have babies or toddlers—then think about doing it alone, poor, at a minimum-wage job, and in a dangerous neighborhood.

Many conservative policymakers assume that marriage is the answer to poverty among women and children. However, the majority of women who have children outside of marriage are poor before they become pregnant. Even if these women married the fathers of their babies, they would still be poor because the fathers are likely to be unemployed and living in economically depressed areas (Dickerson, 1995). And many of the fathers are simply not available or have so many problems of their own that they cannot help support a family. For example, in a major study of inner-city young mothers, by the time their first child was 6 years old, 10 percent of the fathers were dead, 25 percent were in jail, and 24 percent were selling or using drugs. Others were irresponsible, abusive, or involved in a new relationship. Only a few couples managed to stay together (Leadbetter & Way, 2001). Even among middle-class divorced women, remarriage is not always an option for mothers of small children, and second marriages are more likely than first marriages to end in divorce (Chapter 9).

But there is more to single-mother families than poverty and despair. Studies show that single mothers are proud that they are handling a difficult job well. They are just as satisfied with motherhood as married mothers are (Smith, 1997). Among white families, single-parent homes seem to be less gender-typed than two-parent homes. They encourage more gender-neutral play in children and create more flexible attitudes about gender roles (Smith, 1997). This result makes sense when we consider that fathers are more prone than mothers to treating children in gender-stereotypical ways (Chapter 6) and that children of single mothers see their moms as both the provider and nurturer. Among African-American single-parent families, strengths include role flexibility (many adults may "mother" a child), spirituality (relying on inner strength rather than material possessions for happiness), and a sense of community ("It takes a village to raise a child") (Randolph, 1995).

Little research has been done on single parents in other countries. In a recent study of single parents in China, one-third were men; the majority had arrived at single parenthood through divorce, and the others through the death or desertion of a spouse. (Parenthood outside of marriage is extremely rare in China.) Virtually all were employed, and they had an average of one child. In this sample, the psychological adjustment of both single mothers and fathers was positively related to the amount of emotional and practical support they received. This study shows that the social context of single parenthood differs across cultures and suggests that the same factors influence psychological well-being in single moms and dads when they are in comparable situations (Cheung & Liu, 1997).

Black Mothers and the Matriarchal Myth

African women were brought to the United States to work as slaves and to produce more slaves, sometimes through rape and forced breeding. If they were given a few days off from slave labor after childbirth, it was more to protect the owner's investment than to allow them to rest and recover. They were able to care for their own children only after all their other work was done and, as Sojourner Truth eloquently testified, were likely to see their children sold away from them (Almquist, 1989).

African-Americans are the only minority group in the United States to have had the experience of systematic, widespread destruction of their families through the institution of slavery. In addition to this legacy, there has since been a scarcity of black men to be providers and husbands. The causes for this scarcity include migration from the South, high death rates from poor health care, and the effects of poverty and discrimination, which lead to drug use, imprisonment, and violent death. Thus, black women have been (and still are) more likely than white women to be raising families without a resident father/husband. For African-American women, motherhood is not equated with being dependent on a man (Collins, 1991; Dickerson, 1995).

Black women have coped with oppression in many ways. They often form extended households, with two or three generations living together and sharing resources. Grandmothers, sisters, cousins, and aunts care for the children of young mothers. Black families are less likely than white ones to give children up for adoption by strangers and are more likely to take in the children of friends and relatives. In the black community, these informal adoptions are seen as better than stranger adoption because children can stay in contact with their mothers and live with people they know and trust (Almquist, 1989). This collective, cooperative child rearing may reflect a West African heritage (Collins, 1991; George & Dickerson, 1995; Greene, 1990).

Unfortunately, black women have been judged against a white middle-class norm of female submission and traditional marriage arrangements (Collins, 1991). Sociologists and psychiatrists have accused them of castrating their husbands and sons by being unfeminine and domineering (Giddings, 1984). The infamous *Moynihan Report* (Moynihan, 1965) attributed the problems of the urban black community to the "matriarchal" social organization of black families.

But blaming black women for social problems avoids confronting the real problems of racism, classism, and sexism. Moreover, it obscures the unique contributions of African-American family patterns. Black women's involvement in social activism often stems from their definition of motherhood: A good mother does not just take care of her own offspring, she works to meet the needs of her entire community (Collins, 1991; Naples, 1992).

Lesbian Mothers

Not all mothers are heterosexual; about one lesbian in six is a mother (Strommen, 1993). Some women who marry or cohabit with men and have children within these relationships later identify as lesbian and bring up their children in lesbian households. Other lesbians have a child through adoption or artificial insemination. What are the special issues and stresses that confront lesbian mothers?

One of the biggest potential problems is negotiating the marginalized identity of lesbian with the mainstream identity of mother (Hequembourg & Farrell, 1999). Although there is increasing acceptance of lesbians, many people consider a lesbian family unnatural:

> Vicky's parents had a party to introduce their grandchild to the family, but they refused to acknowledge me as the other parent; rather, they chose to identify me as a very good friend who is helping Vicky raise the baby. I wept for hours and knew that I would never again hide the nature of our relationship. (Mercer, 1990, p. 233)

Economic strains also exist. Like single mothers, lesbian mothers have to manage without a man's greater earning power. Their income is often so low that lack of money is a source of daily stress. If the mother has to deal with a welfare department, there is the added strain of a state agency making judgments about her lesbian lifestyle (Crawford, 1987).

Lesbian families may experience isolation. Lesbian mothers may feel little in common with the heterosexual families of their children's friends. Turning to the lesbian community for support, they may find that the lives of their child-free lesbian friends are very different from their own. As more lesbians decide to have children, support groups and networks of lesbian families are growing

Finally, lesbian mothers may confront problems of internalized homophobia:

> Lesbians should not be surprised or ashamed to find themselves grappling with questions such as: Is this natural? Is it okay for lesbians to have kids? Am I hurting my children . . . is it unfair to bring them into a homophobic world? Am I a woman who is able to mother like other women? These . . . are questions that have been answered in positive ways by many lesbian mothers over the years (Crawford, 1987, p. 197).

Do lesbians raise children differently than heterosexual mothers, and do their children turn out differently? Research suggests that the children of lesbian families are remarkably similar to those of heterosexual families.

One study of African-American women compared the attitudes of twenty-six heterosexual and twenty-six lesbian mothers. The two groups were similar in the value they placed on independence and self-sufficiency for their children. The lesbian mothers, however, were more tolerant about rules, less restrictive of sex play, less concerned with modesty, and more open in providing sex education. They also viewed boys and girls as more similar to each other than the heterosexual mothers did and expected more traditionally masculine activities from their daughters (Hill, 1987). Given the costs of feminine socialization for girls, these may be healthy attitudes.

In the United Kingdom, a unique study followed seventy-eight children, half raised by lesbian mothers and half by heterosexual single mothers, from middle childhood to young adulthood (Tasker & Golombok, 1997). As young adults, these participants were asked to look back on their family life. Children of lesbians were more positive about their family life than children of heterosexuals, especially if their mother was open about her sexual orientation and active in lesbian politics. Children of lesbians were no more likely to identify as gay or lesbian, but those who did were more likely to be involved in a relationship than were gay children of heterosexuals. Children raised by lesbians reported that their mothers had been more open and comfortable communicating with them about sexual development and sexuality as they were growing up. There was no difference in psychological adjustment in the two groups.

On the whole, it seems that lesbian family life produces children who are very much like children from heterosexual families. Research reviews (Falk, 1993; Tasker, 1999) have found no detrimental effects of lesbian parenting on children's psychological adjustment or gender-role development. Despite this evidence, courts have often assumed that lesbians are unfit mothers. In 1993, the American Psychological Association argued for a lesbian mother in a Virginia case in which the court had awarded custody of a 2-year-old boy to his grandmother. There was no evidence that Sharon Bottoms was a poor mother or that her son Tyler was suffering any problems; her relationship with another woman was the only custody issue. Typically, lesbians stand a fifty-fifty chance of losing their children in custody disputes (Falk, 1993). In this case, an appeals court, influenced by the APA brief and psychologists' expert testimony, overturned the earlier verdict and returned Tyler to his mother and her partner (Sleek, 1994).

Commonalities

The experiences of women who mother are shaped by social class, sexual orientation, economic status, and many other factors. Are there any overall similarities? In writing this chapter, we read many accounts by mothers of their feelings and thoughts about motherhood. Several themes emerged in these accounts. Here, we illustrate each of five themes we perceived in the words of mothers who told their stories in *Balancing Acts*, a book edited by Katherine Gieve (1989).

1. *Becoming a mother results in large, significant, and permanent changes in identity and life circumstances.*

   > Daniel is seven, Matthew, five, and when I think about the past seven years I feel like a person watching the dust begin to settle after an earthquake. (p. 41)

   > I did not imagine the force or the excitement—nor how I would willingly be taken over by my children. . . . I look at the world with different eyes and inward with a new vision. I feel riven, torn apart, and made again. (p. 51)

   > I am not where I was before—not in a single detail. I have learned to pride myself on new abilities, some I had never considered of value. I was blown wide open by motherhood and by the emotions that came with it. . . . I had no idea that I could love that well. . . . Conversely, other abilities by which I had set great store, producing words on time, selling an idea, keeping myself fired up . . . seem useful but little more than that. (pp. 127–128)

2. *Motherhood can involve feelings of intense love, competence, and achievement.*

   The rewards of motherhood were immediate and lasting. I have established a relaxed physical intimacy with both my children which tolerates anger and laughter, built up over a decade of washing them, reading to them, and tumbling about with them. (p. 114)

   Pregnancy had suited me, I enjoyed giving birth, but nothing prepared me for the reality of the new baby. I was almost paralyzed by the joy that shot through me as I looked through the plastic (hospital crib) that morning . . . it's just impossible to put into words . . . I was transported. (p. 124)

   She's brought into a room. . . . Not much hair, toothless, a fat bald child in a scratchy pink dress. It is love at first sight. . . . I feel as if I've been waiting all my life for this moment, for this child. . . . The "I" who adopts this four-month-old baby is forced to recognize that, physically and symbolically, she is another being, formed by other bodies, in relationships I know nothing of. But in my imagination, she is the missing part of myself, at last returned. I am complete. (pp. 138–139)

3. *Motherhood is a constantly changing relationship, as both child and mother grow and develop. Mothers and children move from a relationship of profound inequality to one of (ideally) equality. Throughout the process, the mother moves from meeting physical needs to meeting intellectual ones; emotional demands remain a constant.*

   It was not the hard work of child care that I found so difficult (probably because I shared it with others) but the constantly changing relationship which continued in terms not chosen by me at an unpredictable and changeable pace. It required constant reassessment and with it pain, anger, and remorse, as well as excitement and pleasure. Daniel elicited from me both my greatest love and generosity and my darkest anger and frustration. (p. 45)

   As our children grow and change, and new pleasures, new battles, take the place of the early ones, I feel I live in a constant state of surprise and suspense. It is like reading the best of novels, combined with being in love; I want things to stand still yet can't wait to see what will happen next. And, above all, I don't want the story to end. (p. 159)

4. *Both child and mother must confront the limitations of love and care.*

   With all my love, I cannot be everything she wants and needs any more than I can shield her from pain . . . indeed I must add to her pain. . . . My fantasy, that if I love her enough nothing else matters, has to give way. (p. 140)

   "You are not my real mother," says my daughter to me. I did not feel either that my mother was my real mother, perhaps every daughter, every child, has this doubt. . . . The gap between the ideal Mother, and the mother we actually have, is perhaps always there. If the Mother is the fixed perfect image of the ideal, a mother (small m) is always what falls short of that image. (pp. 143–144)

5. *Mothers and children must adapt to a society that is structured as though children did not exist and does not provide necessary support for those who care for the young* (see Figure 10.8).

> The world suddenly became a much more dangerous place once I had a baby dependent on me for his very life. For the first time I was thrown into a world that did not recognize my physical, emotional, social, and political needs. This applied to design, architecture, roads, public transport, dangerous machinery; not to mention lack of community child care facilities. . . . it isn't the child that makes your life hard, it is the adult world and the powers that be. Usually, it is the very people who sentimentalize and idealize motherhood who stop listening. (pp. 53–54)

> Motherhood . . . has made me aware of time in many different ways. In particular how women's time is taken for granted so that there is little concordance between the way time is structured in the so-called public world and the rhythm of time associated with caring for a young child. (p. 77)

These five commonalities emerged for us as we read the writings of diverse women about their experiences of motherhood. Perhaps you can think of others.

THE FUTURE OF MOTHERING

Bringing up children is an awesome responsibility. Traditionally, in Western societies it has been divided into a nurturing role, assigned to women, and a provider role, assigned to men. We have seen that this arrangement has many limitations. It does not allow for individual differences in personality and ability—some men might make better nurturers than providers, and some women better providers than nurturers. It keeps women and children economically dependent on men; when men default, families live in poverty. It keeps children dependent solely on their mothers for love and care. It overlooks the diversity of families. Single-parent families, gay and lesbian families, and families from

Making a Difference

Candy Lightner has suffered more sadness and anger than any mother should ever have to. Her daughter Serena was cut and bruised at age 6 when a drunk driver rear-ended Lightner's mother's car. Her son Travis was run over by a drugged driver when he was 4. And her 13-year-old daughter Cari was thrown 120 feet and killed when she was hit by a drunk driver. Police told Lightner Cari's killer was unlikely to serve time, even though he had a long record of drunk driving convictions. Lightner fought back. She founded Mothers Against Drunk Drivers (MADD), a group she headed until 1985, and she continues to speak out against driving under the influence of alcohol and drugs. In fact, Lightner has probably been the strongest individual force behind the 30 percent decline in drunk driving since the 1960s, behind the fact that every state raised the drinking age to 21 by the time she left MADD, and behind the drop in drunk driving–related deaths from 25,000 in 1980 to under 18,000 in 1992. Lightner was able to turn a mother's love and grief into an irresistible force. MADD now has over 3 million members, a staff of 300 plus, and a budget of $53 million. Thanks to Lightner's courage and determination, the United States continues to make progress against this deadly behavior, drunk driving.

Sources: Encyclopedia of Associations (32nd ed.) Vol. 1, Part 2, entry # 11710. Griffin, K. (1994, July). MADD again. *Health,* 62. *Time,* 1–7–85, p. 41.

FIGURE 10. 8. After security guards ordered a woman to leave the premises when she was discovered discreetly nursing her baby, mothers staged a "nurse-in" at a New York shopping mall.

different cultural traditions do not conform to the patriarchal ideal. In most families, women now participate in the provider role much more than men participate in nurturing. It also leads to blaming mothers for just about everything that can go wrong and overlooking fathers' potential for involvement with their children.

Why Blame Mom?

Our society has myths about both the Perfect Mother and the Bad Mother (Caplan, 1989). The Perfect Mother is an endless fount of nurturance, she naturally knows how to raise children and never gets angry. Bad Mother myths (see Figure 10.9) exaggerate mothers' limitations or faults and transform them into monstrous flaws; in these myths, mothers are bottomless pits of neediness, their power is dangerous, and closeness between mother and adult children is unhealthy.

"Mother-blaming is like air pollution"—so pervasive that it often goes unnoticed (Caplan, 1989, p. 39). A review of 125 articles published in major mental-health journals between 1970 and 1982 found that mothers were blamed for seventy-two different kinds of problems in their offspring (Caplan & Hall-McCorquodale, 1985). The list included aggressiveness, agoraphobia, anorexia, anxiety, arson, bad dreams, bedwetting, chronic vomiting, delinquency, delusions, depression, frigidity, hyperactivity, incest, loneliness, marijuana use, minimal brain damage, moodiness, schizophrenia, sexual dysfunction, sibling jealousy, sleepwalking, tantrums, truancy, an inability to deal with color blindness, and self-induced television epilepsy!

FIGURE 10.9
Source: Momma by Mel Lazarus, 3/3/99. By permission of Mel Lazarus and Creators Syndicate, Inc.

Our society has assigned mothers responsibility for their children's psychological well-being to an extent that few other cultures around the world or throughout history have done. It has asked them to fulfill their responsibilities in relative isolation, often without the support they need. Moreover, it has created myths that disguise the realities of parenting. Perhaps for each of us, one task of growing up is to look beyond the myths of motherhood at the human being who is our mother, to see her as a complex, multifaceted individual, and to stop blaming her for being only human (Caplan, 1989; Howe, 1989).

Fathering Is a Feminist Issue

Where are the fathers when blame is handed out? They seem to be invisible. Psychology has contributed more than its share to the father-invisibility problem. A review of 544 empirical research studies of children's psychological disorders published between 1984 and 1991 found that only 1 percent focused exclusively on fathers, whereas 48 percent focused exclusively on mothers. Another 25 percent included both parents but did not analyze for sex differences or interactions (Phares & Compas, 1993). When the studies including fathers were examined separately, clear effects were found: Fathers do play a role in children's psychopathology. The evidence is clearest in children whose fathers sexually molest them, abuse alcohol, or are depressed.

Fathering is being recognized as a feminist issue. There is more to being a father than providing a paycheck. Good fathers are those who are responsive and emotionally available to their children (Silverstein, 2002). As long as a good father is defined simply as a good provider, men will have more privilege both at home and in public life and will continue to be deprived of intimacy and emotional connection with their families. At present, many women are performing double roles as nurturers and providers, but men are less likely to do so. There is a need for social programs for men who father children and then fail to take care of them. Rather than condemn these men as "deadbeat dads," our society could consider them "dads in training" (Leadbetter & Way, 2001). Only when men, too, play dual roles, will public policy wake up to the needs of families.

What kind of changes would be beneficial to families? At present, public life is structured for the convenience of adults without children. Food and clothing stores, which depend on the business provided by women who shop for their families, rarely provide play areas for children. Commuter trains and airports make special provisions for smoking and dining but provide no facilities for children's play or rest. Although women's breasts can be seen exposed on magazine covers at every newsstand, there are very few places where women can comfortably nurse their babies outside their homes, and seeing women breast-feed in public is widely considered disgusting. Public institutions plan schedules as though all women were available for full-time child care; for example, nursery schools and kindergartens with half-day programs assume a mother will be free at midday to retrieve her child, and day-care hours frequently are inadequate for women on shift work. If men took care of children, too, these things would change.

Public policy on families in the United States lags behind policies in every other industrialized country in the world (Lorber, 1993b). The United States needs better paid parental leave, subsidized child care, and flexible working hours. The political activism to bring about these changes is unlikely to be effective until the changes are as relevant to men as to women (Silverstein, 1996).

What are the payoffs for redefining parenthood? Research reviews have shown that a father's love and involvement are good for children; they show better cognitive and emotional development when their fathers are involved in their lives (Rohner & Veneziano, 2001; Silverstein, 1996). It is good for couples, leading to greater marital satisfaction, and for mothers, who report decreased stress. And it is good for fathers themselves, who report higher self-esteem and satisfaction with their role as parent (Deutsch, 1999). Redefining parenting is a revolution that is past due. What is needed is a postgender definition that allows for flexibility and diversity of family patterns (Silverstein & Auerbach, 1999).

CONNECTING THEMES

- *Gender is more than just sex.* The ability to bear children is a biological capacity unique to women. However, birth, child rearing, and motherhood occur within a gender system that controls and regulates women's sexuality and fertility.
- *Language and naming are sources of power.* The motherhood mandate decrees that all women should be mothers, and the motherhood mystique defines the approved way to do it. Deviant mothers are stigmatized by labels such as "welfare mom." Accounts of motherhood in women's own language and images have been conspicuously absent from art, literature, and history.
- *Women are not all alike.* Experiences of mothering are shaped by social class, ethnicity, sexual orientation, and many other factors. Rather than generalize about a mythical motherhood, we should recognize the diverse experiences of women who mother.
- *Psychological research can foster social change.* The United States is virtually alone among industrialized nations in its failure to develop public policy that recognizes the needs of today's families. Poverty among women and children is a major social issue. Women's reproductive rights are contested, and new medical technologies complicate issues of ethics, choice, and power. Redefining fatherhood would benefit families.

SUGGESTED READINGS

CUSK, RACHEL (2002). *Life's Work: On Becoming a Mother.* NY: Picador. An intense introspection on the transition to motherhood by a gifted writer. It's not always a pretty story, but it has the raw edge of truth.

LUBLIN, NANCY (1998). *Pandora's box: Feminism confronts reproductive technology.* New York: Rowman & Littlefield. Is reproductive freedom furthered or hampered by technological advances? This book unites feminist theory and activism in an original analysis.

REDDY, MAUREEN T., ROTH, MARTHA, & SHELDON, AMY (1994). *Mother journeys: Feminists write about mothering.* Minneapolis: Spinster Ink. Poetry, art, and essays on the experience of mothering by an ethnically and culturally diverse group of women.

CHAPTER 11

Work and Achievement

Work is a part of almost every woman's life, but the world of work is a gendered world. Often, women and men do different kinds of work, face different obstacles to satisfaction and achievement, and receive unequal rewards. In this chapter we examine the unpaid and paid work of women, women's values about work and achievement, explanations for the differing work patterns of women and men, and factors affecting women's achievement. We listen to the voices of women as they talk about their work: its problems, its satisfactions, and its place in their lives.

IF SHE ISN'T PAID, IS IT STILL WORK?

Much of the work women do is unpaid and not formally defined as work. When women's work caring for their homes, children, and husbands is taken into account, virtually everywhere in the world women work longer hours than men and have less leisure time (United Nations, 2000). Because women's work in the home is invisible to the larger society, there are many misconceptions about it (Vanek, 1984). Let's look first at this invisible work: women's contributions in housework, meeting others' emotional needs, and enhancing the status of their male partners.

The Double Day: Housework

Scrubbing floors and toilets, shopping for food and cooking meals, changing beds, washing, ironing, and mending clothes, doing household planning and record keeping, driving children to activities—all the chores required to keep a household functioning—are classified as housework. Though fewer women today than in the past make housework a full-time job, it is still a part of life for most women around the world.

Women's work in the home demands more hours each day than many paid jobs. In developing countries, housework may include gathering firewood, carrying water over long distances, and grinding grain for cooking. In industrialized countries, technology (household electricity, running water, appliances) has made the work less dirty and arduous than it used to be, and the smaller size of modern families means less work, but new tasks have taken the place of old ones. Traveling for errands, shopping, and transporting children takes up hours each week. Having bigger houses and more possessions means that there is more "stuff" to take care of. And standards have risen, as icons of domesticity like Martha Stewart encourage women to cook gourmet meals, grow their own vegetables, and obsess over decorating details.

Is Housework Shared?

Chapters 9 and 10 documented that equality in the domestic realm is rare. Housework and child care remain largely the responsibility of women (Phillips & Imhoff, 1997) (see Figure 11.1). Chores tend to be assigned by gender: men do outside work, women do inside work, and women tend to do the chores that come up most often. A survey of more than 1,200 U.S. households showed that 93 percent of the women usually did the meal planning, 88 percent usually did the food shopping, and 90 percent usually did the cooking—percentages that had not changed much since the 1970s (Harnack, Story, Martinson, Neumark-Sztainer, & Stang, 1998). Women's chores are more stressful because often they have to be done on a tighter schedule—you can put off washing the car until it's convenient, but it's not so easy to put off making dinner (Barnett & Shen, 1997). In a random sample of married or cohabiting couples in which both partners worked for pay, women still did about twice as much housework (14.89 hours) as men (6.81) (Stevens, Kiger, & Riley, 2001). A survey of more than 2,700 U.S. couples showed that only when both husbands and wives share egalitarian beliefs do husbands do more than the minimum (Greenstein, 1996).

FIGURE 11.1.
Source: Baby Blues. © Baby Blues Partnership. Reprinted with Special Permission of King Features Syndicate.

In short, for most women, work outside the home is followed each day by another round of work at home. This has been termed the *double day* or *second shift* (Hochschild, 1989).

The prevailing pattern—overworked women and resistant men—is quite consistent across cultures and ethnic groups, including African-American (Hossain & Roopmarine, 1993) and Mexican-American families (Hartzler & Franco, 1985; Williams, 1990). In an Australian study of 128 wives' attempts to get their husbands more involved in housework, only 4 wives experienced any lasting success (Dempsey, 1997). U.N. studies of daily time use in developing countries consistently show that, compared with men, women are doing less paid work, more unpaid work, and working longer hours overall (United Nations, 2000).

Is Housework Trivial?

Within individual families the unpaid domestic work of women is often accorded very little value:

> The garbage could overflow and no one would dump it, or the dog may need to be fed . . . and everybody relies on mother to do it . . . some days I feel that they're taking me for granted. They know I'm not going out into the work force, and every once in a while I hear one of my sons say, "Well, you don't do anything all day long." . . . If they didn't have clean clothes or their beds weren't changed or something like that they might realize that their mother does do something. But most of the time they don't. I don't think men feel that a woman does a day's work. (Whitbourne, 1986, p. 165)

The devaluation of housework is also apparent at the societal level. The phrases *working woman* and *working mother* suggest that a woman is not really a worker unless she is in the paid workforce. Unpaid housework is not listed in the U.S. Department of Labor's *Dictionary of Occupational Titles.* Its monetary value is not computed into the gross national product—an "official denial that this work is socially necessary" (Ciancanelli & Berch, 1987).

Obviously, families could not thrive without the unpaid work of women. But exactly how much is her work "worth"? Its monetary value is difficult to compute. One way is to estimate the cost of replacing her services with paid workers—cook, chauffeur, babysitter, dishwasher, janitor, and so forth. But many women feel that their services could not be replaced with paid workers because the work demands loving care and an intimate knowledge of the family. Who could calculate the appropriate pay for planning a small child's birthday party or the "overtime" involved when a woman takes charge of children, pets, house, bills, and yard work while her husband travels on business? Women's homemaking responsibilities involve not only skills but also personal involvement.

Another method is to calculate the wages the homemaker loses by working at home instead of at a paid job. If she could earn $250 a week as a bank clerk, for example, that is the value of 40 hours of housework. By this method, however, housework done by a woman who could earn $140 an hour as an attorney is worth twenty times as much as the identical chores done by a woman who could only earn $7 an hour as a food server (Vanek, 1984).

Neither method of calculating the value of housework really captures the unique characteristics of homemaking, because it does not fit androcentric definitions of work.. Imagine how a "help wanted" ad for a homemaker might look:

> WANTED: Full-time employee for small family firm. DUTIES: Including but not limited to general cleaning, cooking, gardening, laundry, ironing and mending, purchasing, bookkeeping, and money management. Child care may also be required. HOURS: Avg. 55/wk but standby duty required 24 hours/day, 7 days/wk. Extra workload on holidays. SALARY AND BENEFITS: No salary, but food, clothing, and shelter provided at employer's discretion; job security and benefits depend on continued goodwill of employer. No vacation. No retirement plan. No opportunities for advancement. REQUIREMENTS: No previous experience necessary, can learn on the job. Only women need apply.

The homemaker's job looks unattractive indeed in this description. Women do find it unsatisfying in many ways. They dislike the boring, repetitive, and unchallenging nature of much of the work. On the other hand, full-time homemakers say they enjoy the rewards that come from taking care of their children and husbands (Baruch et al., 1983). In the rare cases in which men take primary responsibility for housework and child care, their feelings about the job are similar to women's—they like the emotional involvement with their families and dislike the housework (Rosenwasser & Patterson, 1984–1985).

Relational Work: Keeping Everybody Happy

Women are largely responsible for caring for others' emotional needs. Keeping harmony in the family has long been defined as women's work (Parsons & Bales, 1955). In a study of marital interaction in which more than 100 couples kept diaries about their communication patterns, wives did more relational work than did husbands. They focused on their husbands, friends, and family; spent time talking and listening with them; talked about relationships more; and worked to keep harmony in the family (Ragsdale, 1996). In another study of dual-earner couples, both partners were asked about how much time they and their spouse spent confiding thoughts and feelings, trying to help the partner get out of a bad mood, trying to talk things over when there was a problem, and so on. Women reported doing more of this "emotion work" than men did

FIGURE 11.2.
Source: Jump Start by Robb Armstrong. Reprinted by permission of United Feature Syndicate, Inc.

and were less satisfied with the division of emotion work between the partners (Stevens, Kiger, & Riley, 2001). The time and energy necessary for this work may be considerable, as everyone relies on "Mom" to smooth emotional crises.

Part of the reason mothers do more child care than fathers may be because they are believed to be the "relationship specialists" (see Figure 11.2). And this does not change when mothers work for pay. When full-time homemakers and full-time paid workers were surveyed, the employed women were doing just as many child-care activities as the homemakers, except for watching TV with their children. Working mothers were equally likely to read to their child, play games, offer praise, and stop their own activity to play with the child (DeMeis & Perkins, 1996).

Relational work goes beyond a woman's immediate family to a wider network of relatives (Baruch et al., 1983; Di Leonardo, 1987). Women are in charge of visits, letters, and phone calls to distant family members. They buy the presents and remember to send the card for Aunt Anna's birthday. They organize weddings, family reunions, and holiday celebrations, negotiating conflicts and allocating tasks. Although the specifics of the family rituals vary according to social class and ethnic group, families' dependence on women's labor is similar, whether they are upper-class Mexican, working-class African-American, middle-class Italian-American, migrant Chicano farm workers, or immigrants to America from rural Japan (research reviewed in Di Leonardo, 1987).

Like housework, the relational work of women is largely ignored in traditional definitions of work. But it requires time, energy, and skill, and it has economic and social value. Exchanging outgrown children's clothes with a sister-in-law or sending potential customers to a cousin's business firm are ways of strengthening relationships that also help families maximize financial resources (Di Leonardo, 1987).

Perhaps most important, relational work fosters marital satisfaction and happiness. But women do not want to do it all. Couples who balance emotional work, with each partner doing about the same amount, are more satisfied with their marriages than couples in which one person is responsible for doing it all (Holm, Werner, Cook, & Berger, 2001; Stevens, Kiger & Riley, 2001).

Status Work: The Two-Person Career

Women's unpaid work benefits the careers of their husbands. The terms *status-enhancing work* and *two-person career* describe situations in which wives serve as unofficial (and often unacknowledged) contributors to their husbands' work

(Papanek, 1973; Stevens et al., 2001). The most studied example is the corporate wife (e.g., Kanter, 1977); the wives of clergymen and college presidents are other very visible examples. The male graduate student whose wife supports him by working for pay, typing his papers, and keeping household problems out of his way so he can study is also receiving the benefits of a two-person career. So is the politician, whose wife must be able to "give the speech when he can't make it but to shut her mouth and listen adoringly when he is there" (Kanter, 1977, p. 122).

The role of helper to a prominent man may be rewarding, but it restricts a woman's freedom of action and ties her fate to her spouse's. Consider that Hillary Rodham Clinton, who did not take her husband's name when she married, was later pressured into doing so for political reasons (Marshall, 1997). When she took on the important task of health care reform, the press seemed more interested in her hairstyle than her health care plan. As First Lady, she was subjected to hostile jokes and public humiliation over her husband's sexual activities. Only when her husband left public office was Rodham Clinton able to build her own political career.

What kinds of work do women do in the service of their husbands' careers? The specific tasks vary, depending on the husband's job and career stage (Kanter, 1977). She may entertain clients in her home and make friends with people who can be useful in advancing her husband's career. She is expected to be available at any time for complete care of their children so that he can travel or work evenings and weekends. She often participates in volunteer or community service related to his position. She may also contribute direct services in place of a paid employee—typing, taking sales calls, keeping books or tax records for his small business, or scheduling his travel. Finally, she provides emotional support. She is expected to listen to his complaints, help him work through problems at work, cheerfully accept his absences and work pressures, avoid burdening him with domestic trivia, and motivate him to achieve to his fullest potential. She is, indeed, "the woman behind the man."

What Are the Costs and Benefits of Invisible Work?

Obviously, housework, relational work, and the ladies' auxiliary do not provide a paycheck. Traditionally, women were supposed to be rewarded by a sense of *vicarious achievement* (Lipman-Blumen & Leavitt, 1976). In other words, a woman is supposed to identify with her husband and feel gratified by his successes. Many women do report this kind of gratification; others feel exploited. One corporate wife complained to an interviewer, "I am paid neither in job satisfaction nor in cash for my work. I did not choose the job of executive wife, and I am heartily sick of it" (Kanter, 1977, p. 111).

Women who achieve through their husbands are vulnerable. If the marriage ends through the husband's death or divorce or if he does not achieve fame and glory, she may have little to put on a résumé and few skills that prospective employers would regard as valuable. Increasingly, women are insisting that divorce courts recognize that their unpaid work is vital to their husband's success (see Box 11.1).

The availability of some women as unofficial employees for their husbands' companies also has implications for women who are employed and competing with men. There is no "corporate husband" position to match that

Box 11.1 What Is a Wife Worth?

ONCE UPON A TIME, A GOOD CORPORATE WIFE was to be seen and not heard. She was to make sure nothing, but nothing, came between her man and his work. She was to shield him from the tedious and distracting details of domestic life. She was to raise beautiful, well-mannered children and maintain a beautiful, well-appointed home, making it look effortless. She was to work the charity circuit—to be the belle of the charity ball and also its unpaid CEO. She was to smile through scores of business dinners. And she was never, ever, to make a stink. Even in the worst of times, even when things unraveled, she was expected to know her place and, if need be, to slip quietly offstage. Lorna Wendt did all of these things except the last. When her 32-year marriage to GE Capital CEO Gary Wendt came apart two years ago, she raised a big ruckus. She wanted half of the $100 million she estimated he was worth. She wanted to tap what she considered her rightful share of the treasure-trove of stock options and pension benefits accumulated during the marriage but not due until later in his career. She wanted respect. She wanted acknowledgment, just once and writ large, that society valued all those things she'd done on the home front. As with executive pay, the amount one needs to live on wasn't the issue. The money was merely a way of keeping score.

And Lorna Wendt did score. . . . She came away with $20 million—far less than the $50 million she'd sought, but far more than the $8 million plus alimony that Wendt had originally offered. She got half the hard assets—breaking the glass ceiling that often exists in uppercrust divorces, where wives are more likely to get what the judge thinks they need according to a practice known in the divorce bar as "enough is enough."

The Wendt case has launched a thousand cocktail-party conversations and struck fear in the hearts of primary breadwinners everywhere. A lot of men are still incredulous of her demands. In a big-bucks case like hers, "the question becomes, Is the person who is making the money—is that person's contribution greater than the person who stays at home and runs the house?" says Robert Stephan Cohen, a New York divorce lawyer. "I'll tell you, having represented a number of high-net-worth individuals—they think the contribution of the at-home spouse is important, but not equal." Yet Lorna Wendt has elicited cheers from lots of career women and stay-at-home women alike. No matter the unlikelihood of this very proper, soft-spoken, 51-year-old woman straight out of another era becoming a feminist symbol. Her case has struck a chord.

Lorna Wendt: If marriage isn't a partnership between equals, why get married?

Lorna Wendt is rich, privileged, hardly Everywoman. But as the woman behind the success story, she has come to stand for the many things that wives still mostly end up doing and that society seems mostly to take for granted: child rearing, tending a family's emotional and spiritual needs, and the unglamorous stuff like car pools, doctor's appointments, sympathy notes. Lorna Wendt has become a lightning rod for the tensions that swirl around what has traditionally been called women's work. "I complemented him by keeping the home fires burning and by raising a family and by being the CEO of the Wendt corporation and by running the household and grounds and social and emotional ties so he could go out and work very hard at what he was good at," she says. "If marriage isn't a partnership between equals, then why get married? If you knew that some husband or judge down the road was going to say, 'You're a 30% part of this marriage, and he's a 70% part,' would you get married?"

Source: From "It's Her Job Too," by Betsy Morris, *Fortune,* February 2, 1998, pp. 65–67.

of the corporate wife. Indeed, the world of work assumes that workers are men and that these men have wives to take care of them (Wajcman, 1998). The female employee may appear less talented and motivated than her male colleague because she lacks his invisible support staff. If she is married, her husband is unlikely to invest his future in vicarious achievement. A study of more than 1,600 U.S. corporate employees showed that men at the highest executive levels were significantly more likely to have spouses who were full-time homemakers than men at lower levels and women at all levels (Burke, 1997). Similar results were found in a U.K. study of high-level managers: 88 percent of the married women, and only 27 percent of the married men, had partners who were employed full-time. In other words, the career success of men is given an invisible boost by their at-home support staff. Corporations know this very well; men are seen as bringing two people to their jobs, and women, because of their family duties, as bringing less than one (Wajcman, 1998).

Gay men and lesbians also are disadvantaged in the workplace by the expectation that everyone has a wife at home. A gay friend of ours in graduate school shared the feelings of many career-oriented women, lesbian and heterosexual, single and married, when he observed, "I need a wife!"

WORKING HARD FOR A LIVING: WOMEN IN THE PAID WORKFORCE

More women are working outside the home than ever before, a worldwide social change (United Nations, 2000). A majority of American women, including most mothers of young children, now work for a living. According to U.S. census data, about 62 percent of white women, 59 percent of black women, and 53 percent of Hispanic women are working for pay (Gutek, 2001). Women's and men's employment rates are converging. By 2005, the percentage of all American women who engage in paid work is expected to rise to nearly 62 percent, compared with a projected decline from 75 percent to 73 percent for men (Gutek, 2001; National Association of Working Women, 2000).

Sex Segregation

In 1900, the three main occupations available to women were schoolteacher, factory worker, and household servant (Perun & Bielby, 1981). Though women's job options have expanded a great deal, the workplace is still characterized by sex segregation. The workforce separation of women and men "extends to all regions and countries irrespective of the level of economic development, the political system, or the religious, social or cultural environment" (United Nations, 2000, p. 128). We will look at two varieties: *horizontal sex segregation,* the tendency for women and men to hold different jobs, and *vertical sex segregation,* the tendency for women to be clustered at the bottom of the hierarchy within occupations.

Horizontal Segregation

There are few occupations in which the proportion of women and men is about equal. Instead, there are women's jobs and men's jobs (Lorber, 1993b). Ninety-eight percent of all secretaries, 93 percent of nurses, and 84 percent of elementary schoolteachers are women. Ninety-nine percent of auto mechanics, more than 90 percent of engineers, and 70 percent of computer scientists are men (Gilbert & Rader, 2000). As Figure 11.3 shows, nearly 60 percent of all employed women work in service, clerical, administrative support, technician, and sales fields. Fewer than one-third of employed women are in the higher-paying managerial and professional occupations. Some occupations have an overall equal ratio of women and men but remain segregated at the level of the individual workplace or task (Lorber, 1993b; Gutek, 2001). For example, in retail sales, men sell appliances, computers, and cars (the "big-ticket items"), whereas women sell clothing. Women are more likely to work in fast-food chains and diners; men are more likely to be waiters and chefs in expensive restaurants.

The fact that workplaces tend to be "his" or "hers" is a product of the gender system. The jobs where women are clustered tend to be relatively low in pay and status, with little job security and few opportunities for career advancement. Most are service oriented and associated with stereotypical feminine characteristics such as caring (United Nations, 2000). In 1990 "for every one woman lawyer, there were 101 women doing clerical work, 33 women operating factory machines, 30 sales clerks, 9 nurses aides, and 8 waitresses" (Yoder, 2002).

The sex-segregated world of women clerical and service workers has been termed *pink-collar employment* (Howe, 1977.) Often, it is monotonous and unchallenging. Moreover, the worker has little decision-making power or autonomy; her task is to follow directions. Pink-collar jobs do have some positive aspects. Many women report that they enjoy the company of co-workers and develop close friendships with them (Ferree, 1987).

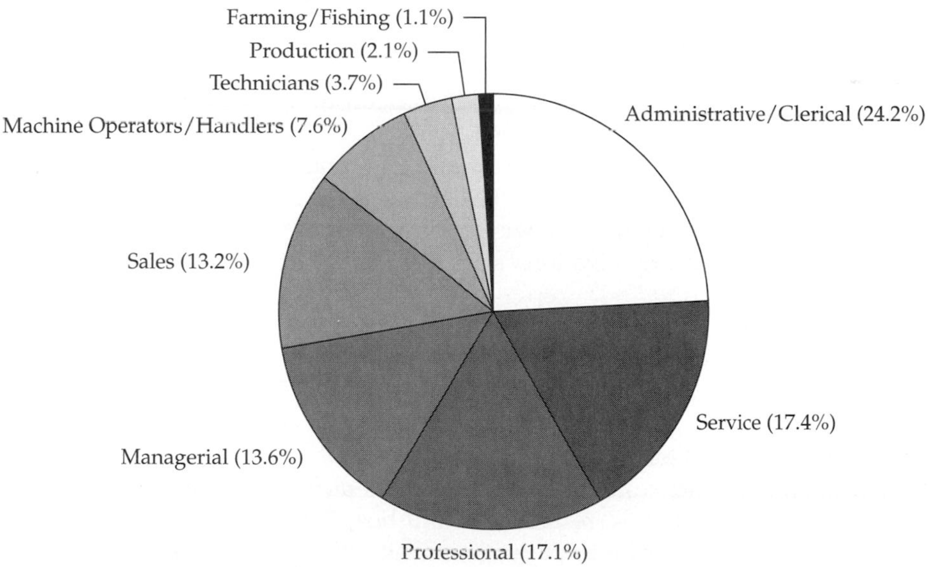

FIGURE 11.3. Women by occupation, 1997. Women are clustered in low-wage service, clerical, and sales jobs.
Source: National Committee on Pay Equity.

Unlike pink-collar jobs, the female-dominated fields of nursing, social work, and teaching offer intellectual challenge and the rewards of doing socially valued work. However, their educational requirements do not lead to high pay; they are characterized by "learning without earning." Moreover, like other occupations with a high proportion of women, they tend to lack clear avenues for advancement and autonomous working conditions (Betz & Fitzgerald, 1987).

The good news is that horizontal sex segregation has declined considerably since the 1970s. Most of the decline has been in professional and management areas. Sex segregation has been more persistent in jobs held by high-school graduates. Overall, horizontal sex segregation is still substantial, and women made fewer gains in the 1990s relative to the 1970s and 1980s (Gutek, 2001).

Vertical Segregation

Vertical sex segregation is present when men tend to hold positions that have higher status and better pay than the jobs women hold within an organization or occupation (Gutek, 2001; Lorber, 1993b). For example, in the health care industry the nurses' aides, abortion clinic workers, social workers, laboratory technicians, and nurses are likely to be women; physicians and hospital administrators are more likely to be men. The closer to the top of the hierarchy, the fewer women there are. In a recent study of more than 500 companies in the United Kingdom, 92 percent of top executives were male; in the United States, only about 5 percent of senior executives are women, and this hardly changed during the 1990s (Gilbert & Rader, 2000; Valian, 1998; Wajcman, 1998). Women hold between one and five percent of top executive positions in Canada, Brazil, and Germany (United Nations, 2000). In fact, there is not a single field open to both women and men in which there are more women than men at the top, in any country in the world.

The pervasive phenomenon of women being blocked from advancement has been called the *glass ceiling:* The woman can see her goal, but she bumps into a barrier that is both invisible and impenetrable (Lorber, 1993b). Women are not totally excluded, but they find it difficult to move past midlevel positions in business and the professions. Women on their way up perceive the glass ceiling as very real, but men in power do not agree. In one survey of women corporate vice presidents, 71 percent said there was a glass ceiling for women in their organization. However, 73 percent of the male chief executive officers in the same organizations said there was not (Federal Glass Ceiling Commission, 1998).

Women's Work as Extension of Family Roles: "It's Only Natural"

Many women's paid jobs are characterized by service to others in ways that are similar to the unpaid work wives and mothers do. Women provide food and cleaning services in hotels, restaurants, and hospitals. Nurses are expected to provide tender loving care to patients, manage the unit like good housekeepers, and serve as handmaidens to physicians (Cassell, 1997; Corley & Mauksch, 1988). Teachers provide emotional nurturance to young children, and social workers care for the poor and needy.

Even when women and men are in equivalent jobs, such as corporate management, women are expected to be more caring and supportive than men, creating extra demands on their time and energy (Wajcman, 1998). Though it is expected, their caring is simultaneously devalued. For example, one psychologist who received excellent teaching evaluations was described by her department chair as being "mama-ish" and "charming" in the classroom—hardly the qualities valued by the tenure and promotion committee (Benokraitis, 1997).

Because caring fits into a feminine stereotype, it is often seen as a natural by-product of being female rather than an aspect of job competence. This contributes to the devaluation of women's work: If women perform certain functions "naturally," the reasoning goes, virtually any woman can do them, and the woman who does so deserves no special recognition. Recently, *The New York Times* described new customer-service software that can detect an irate caller, suggesting that the software could be used to route "an angry man on the line" to "a soothing female operator" ("Press 1 If You're Steamed," July 7, 2002). We wonder if the female operators will get bonuses or raises for their "soothing" skills. Somehow, we doubt it. After all, women just naturally know how to calm down angry men.

The devaluation of caring is not trivial. People who take care of zoo animals earn, on average, $2,500 a year more than those who take care of children in child-care centers. Ninety-five percent of child-care workers are women, and 33 percent are women of color (Murray, 1997; Noble, 1993). Because child care

Making a Difference

Dolores Huerta (b. 1930) has been an activist in the farm workers' movement since 1955, fighting for the rights of California's migrant workers. With César Chavez in 1962, she founded a group now called the United Farm Workers (UFW), famous for their grape boycott and other strikes and political actions. Huerta has incredible stamina—she gave birth to eleven children, the first when she was 20 and the last at age 46, while carrying on a punishing schedule of union activities. And she rarely felt she had to make a choice between work and family. She loaded up her kids and took them with her whenever possible. Huerta's strength was never tested more than in 1988 when a 6'7" police officer brutally beat her at a political demonstration. She lost so much blood she was expected to die.

Largely because she is female, Huerta's role in the founding and success of the UFW has never been acknowledged in history books. Nevertheless, Huerta continues to struggle for workers' rights, bringing women's issues to the forefront now. In the early days of the UFW, Huerta kept a tally of the number of sexist remarks and jokes made by the male leaders at meetings. "At the end of the meeting, I'd say, 'During the course of this meeting you men have made 58 sexist remarks.' Pretty soon I'd have them down to 25, then 10, then 5." While there is still far to go, both men and women workers' rights have made substantial progress in the last thirty-five years, due in no small part to Huerta's efforts.

Source: Woman of the Year: For a lifetime of labor championing the rights of farmworkers. (1998, January/February) *Ms.,* 46–49.

is seen as natural for women, and unnatural for men, male child-care workers are frequently suspected of being gay (Murray, 1997). But excluding men contributes to the continuing devaluation of caring.

The Wage Gap

Women earn less money than men. Indeed, as Figure 11.4 shows, no group of women has a median income that comes close to the median income of white men. Journalist Barbara Ehrenreich has documented just how hard it is to get by on the jobs available to ordinary working women (see Box 11.2), and the difference between men's and women's wages holds for every level of education. Although young people are urged to get a college education to increase lifetime earnings, the financial payoff of education is much greater for men (see Figure 11.5).

The gender gap in wages has decreased slightly over the past forty years. As shown in Figure 11.6, this is partly because women are earning more and partly because men are earning less. Women now earn about 76 cents for every dollar of men's earnings, and the earnings of African-American women are catching up to those of white women. But the gap between all women's earnings and those of white men is still very large. And 24 cents out of every dollar has huge lifetime costs to women. If the current wage gap continues, a woman who is now 25 and works full-time for the next forty years will earn a lifetime total of $523,000 less than the average 25-year-old man. Around the world, the wage gap is even greater, with women earning about 66 cents for every dollar earned by men (United Nations, 2000).

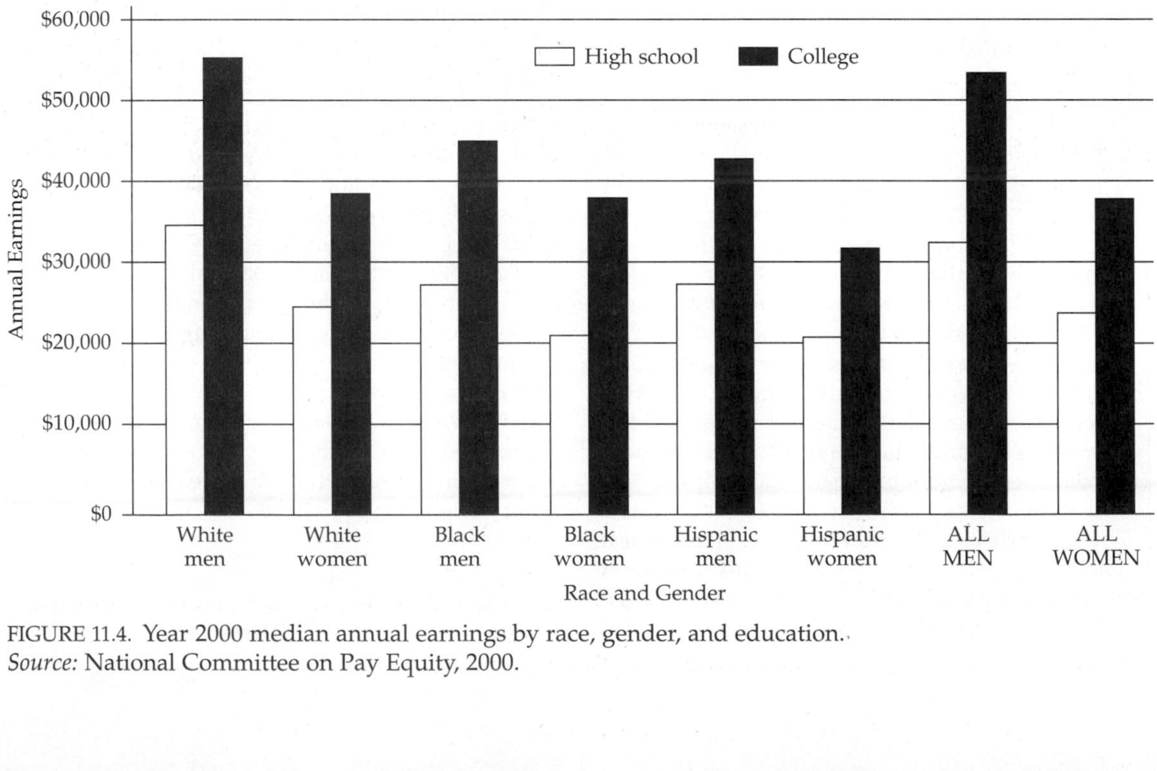

FIGURE 11.4. Year 2000 median annual earnings by race, gender, and education.
Source: National Committee on Pay Equity, 2000.

Why this large and persistent inequity in earnings? One traditional explanation is that women invest less in their work roles than men—they are less committed to their work, less likely to obtain extra training and education, more likely to be absent or to quit a job. However, little evidence exists to support these claims. On the contrary, the gender gap in earnings remains substantial when variables such as education, absences, number of hours worked, and years on the job are controlled (Gutek, 2001; Tsui, 1998; Valian, 1998; Wajcman, 1998). The individual investment hypothesis also does not explain why women's jobs that require high levels of education and skill (such as preschool teacher) pay less than men's jobs with lower requirements (such as drywall installer).

Another explanation focuses on the jobs rather than the gender of the worker—secretaries and clerks are paid less than electricians and truck drivers, and since more women choose to be secretaries and clerks, they earn less on

Box 11.2 Undercover at Wal-Mart: Life as a Low-Wage Worker

Can America's low-wage workers survive on their weekly paychecks? This is the question journalist Barbara Ehrenreich set out to answer when she went undercover as a minimally skilled laborer. Shedding the privileges of her education and social class, Ehrenreich took on the identity of a homemaker of modest education and job skills attempting to reenter the job market. Ehrenreich traveled to several states, spending approximately one month in each location and working at jobs such as housecleaner, waitress, and sales clerk. Using only the money she earned from her jobs, Ehrenreich attempted to pay for housing, food, transportation, and other living expenses.

Ehrenreich soon learned that minimum wage does not equate to living wage. Although she was physically fit, a native English speaker, and had no dependents, she had difficulty financially sustaining her simple needs on her earnings. Even working two jobs, seven days a week did little to help. Additionally, being short of money created many unforeseen problems for Ehrenreich, who found it difficult to obtain safe, inexpensive housing and reliable transportation and maintain a healthy diet. For example, because she could not afford security deposits for an apartment, Ehrenreich had to live in a motel, which cost more and was less safe. Living in a motel room created additional hardships. Lacking a refrigerator or stove, Ehrenreich had to make do with fast food, an expense she had not anticipated.

Ehrenreich's experience makes it clear that those who fill the low-wage rung on America's economic ladder are greatly disadvantaged. This includes especially the millions of women forced into the workforce because of welfare reform. The American dream of attaining wealth through hard work does not take into account the reality of the working poor, whose hard labor is not even enough to pay the bills.

Sources: Barbara Ehrenreich, *Nickel and Dimed: On (Not) Getting By in America.* Contributed by Roxanne Donovan, University of Connecticut.

FIGURE 11.5.
Source: Reprinted by permission. Steve Kelley © 2003.

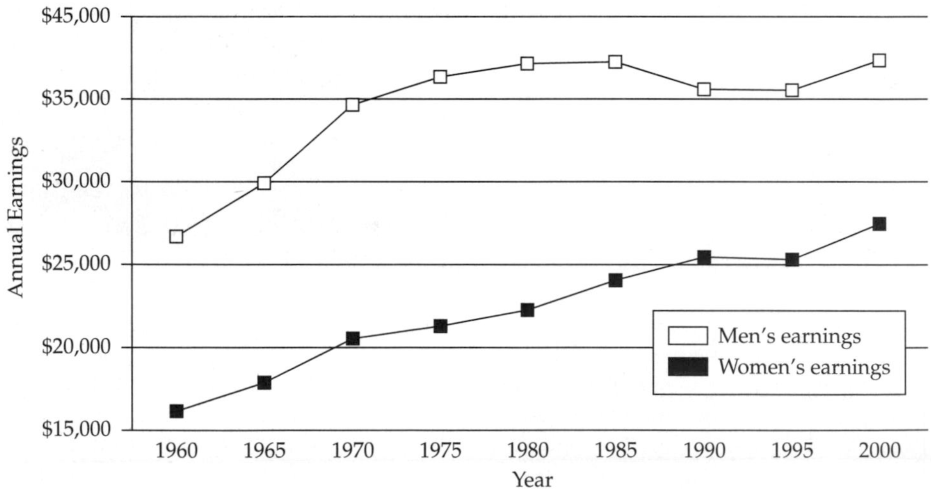

FIGURE 11.6. Median earnings of year-round full-time workers by sex, 1960–2000.
Source: National Committee on Pay Equity, 2001.

average. It is certainly true that women are clustered in a few low-paying job sectors, but is this entirely a matter of choice? Moreover, there are substantial wage differences when women and men do exactly the same jobs. Female truck drivers earn 76 percent, and female computer programmers and engineers 89 percent, of what their male counterparts earn (U.S. Department of Labor, 2002).

It is hard to escape the conclusion that men are paid more for whatever they do simply because they are men (Betz and Fitzgerald, 1987). The income discrepancy between women and men is part of a larger pattern of overvaluing whatever is male and undervaluing whatever is female (see Figure 11.7). A U.N. study (cited in Landrine & Klonoff, 1997) of 140 people who had sex-change operations found that all the women who changed to men had higher salaries after the change, whereas all but two of the men who changed to women received much lower salaries.

What Are the Costs of Underemploying Women?

Workers are classified as *underemployed* when they are in jobs that do not fully use their education, skills, and abilities (Feldman, 1996). Most of the top ten occupations for women are low in status, are poorly paid, and offer few opportunities for advancement. This lack of opportunity translates into lower pensions and Social Security income for women in later life and contributes to a high poverty rate for older women (see Chapter 12).

When women (and people of color) are underemployed, there is loss both to individuals and to society (Betz & Fitzgerald, 1987). Underemployment leads to poor job attitudes and lowered psychological well-being. Individuals may come to believe that the job they are "stuck" in is all they deserve, and their work motivation declines (Feldman, 1996; Kanter, 1977). Society comes to accept the clustering of women into a few occupations as natural and inevitable, making future change difficult. And society loses much-needed talent.

One of the most poignant examples of underemployment of women comes from a well-known study of gifted children (Terman & Oden, 1959). More than 1,500 children with measured IQs over 135 were followed as they grew into

FIGURE 11.7. Sex discrimination—the power of a good allegory.
Source: Sally Forth by Greg Howard. © 1993. Reprinted with Special Permission of King Features Syndicate.

adulthood. The boys almost invariably became prominent professionals. The girls were most likely to become full-time homemakers; only about half held paid jobs, and most of these were schoolteachers and secretaries. The researcher, Louis Terman, recognized the waste of talent that his results demonstrated:

> The woman who is a potential poet, novelist, lawyer, physician, or scientist usually gives up any professional ambition she may have had and devotes herself to home, husband, and children . . . robbing the arts and sciences of a large fraction of the genius that might otherwise be dedicated to them. My data strongly suggest that this loss must be debited to motivational causes and limited opportunity rather than to lack of ability. (Seagoe, 1975)

Terman's sample reached adulthood in the 1950s. Would gifted girls growing up today still be less likely than gifted boys to achieve their fullest potential? Unfortunately, research done in the 1980s and 1990s showed that substantial numbers of gifted and talented young women underrate their own ability, lower their career goals during high school and college, and are less likely to achieve a high-status professional career than gifted boys (Reddin, 1997).

DOING GENDER IN THE WORKPLACE

Women's position in the workplace is not just a static aspect of social structure. Rather, it is continually re-created as people make workplace decisions influenced by gender. Chapter 3 discussed how men and women "do gender" within groups, describing some of the cognitive and social processes that sustain inequality. Here we take a closer look at how sexism operates in the world of work. In particular, how does gender influence explanations and evaluations of behavior at work? How does it influence hiring and advancement within the workplace?

Attributions for Success and Failure

When faced with an example of a woman or a man who has succeeded at some achievement, people very often come up with different reasons to explain her or his success. Men's success is more likely to be seen as the result of high ability ("He succeeded because he's talented or smart"). Women's success is more likely to be attributed to luck (Deaux & Emswiller, 1974). When the task cannot be attributed entirely to luck (such as becoming a physician), people are still reluctant to judge women equal to men in ability. Instead, they attribute the woman's success more to hard work (Feldman-Summers & Kiesler, 1974).

How do people explain situations in which a male or female attempts achievement but fails? Several studies show that they are likely to blame a woman's failure on lack of ability and a man's failure on bad luck or the quirks of the situation, such as an unusually difficult task (Cash, Gillen, & Burns, 1977; Etaugh & Brown, 1975).

It is easy to see how the typical pattern of attributing males' successes to ability and females' to luck disadvantages women in the workplace. A manager is probably far more likely to hire or promote someone who is perceived as very able than someone who just got lucky. Similarly, an employer might view an isolated failure as confirmation of a woman's lack of ability, but as only a temporary setback for a man. The assumption behind the typical pattern of attribution seems to be that men are basically competent; whether they succeed or fail, that belief remains intact. Women, on the other hand, are basically incompetent, and that belief, too, can be maintained whether they succeed or fail.

Devaluing Women's Performance

"Are women prejudiced against women?" is a question asked in a study that set off a wave of research on how people judge the performance of women versus men (Goldberg, 1968). Female college students were asked to rate the quality and importance of several professional articles. Some of the articles were from stereotypically female professions, such as dietetics; others from stereotypically male professions, such as city planning; and others from relatively gender-neutral areas. Each article was prepared in two versions, as though written either by "John MacKay" or "Joan MacKay." Except for the authors' names, the two versions of each article were identical. The students rated the articles more highly when they thought they had been written by a man, including the articles from "feminine" fields. Other researchers found that male raters showed similar prejudice (Paludi & Bauer, 1983; Paludi & Strayer, 1985).

Sometimes highly competent performance by a woman is actually evaluated more positively than comparable performance by a man—as though female competence has more value because it is unexpected (Abramson, Goldberg, Greenberg, & Abramson, 1977). In general, though, many laboratory studies from the 1960s to the present made a convincing case that work attributed to a woman is often devalued. For example, a classic study used psychologists as the participants. Fictitious sets of credentials for psychologists were sent to psychology department chairpersons; the credentials were identical except for the gender of the applicant. The chairpersons were asked how likely they would be to hire the individual described and what level of job they might offer. When the chairpersons thought they were evaluating a female psychologist, "she" was rated less favorably and considered qualified for a lower-level position than when "he" was evaluated (Fidell, 1970).

Are these experimental studies relevant to real job settings today? A meta-analysis of supervisors' ratings of employees showed little overall bias. In other words, controlling for employees' education, experience, and other relevant variables, supervisors did not typically devalue female employees. However, pro-male biases did show up when the raters were all male and when the rating dimensions were masculine (e.g., leadership ability). Pro-female bias showed up when the rating dimensions were feminine (e.g., concern for others) (Bowe, Swim, & Jacobs, 2000). These results suggest that traditional gender attitudes held by many men may affect their evaluations of women's work and that gender stereotypes associated with the measures used to rate employees may produce bias.

Women's own stories about their experiences at work suggest that evaluation bias affects how they are treated on a daily basis. "Women report that their comments and suggestions are ignored or ridiculed; that men making the identical comments receive praise whereas they do not, and that they are excluded from meetings, networks, lunches and other activities that are part of the 'old boy' network and of the road to career advancement" (Landrine & Klonoff, 1997, p. 11). As Chapter 3 described, women whose jobs defy gender norms may be stigmatized: those who work as professors, surgeons, attorneys, police officers, and firefighters may face hostile and dismissive treatment (Cassell, 1997; Haslett & Lipman, 1997; Lott & Rocchio, 1997). For women of color, sexism may be compounded by racism. In a study of a matched sample of 200 African-American and white women in professional and managerial positions, the majority of both groups reported differential treatment at work due to their gender, and a majority of the African-American women also perceived differential treatment due to their race (Weber & Higginbotham, 1997).

Discrimination in Hiring and Promotion

Sex discrimination in employment has been illegal since 1964, when the Civil Rights Act was passed. Before that time, many employers discriminated as a matter of policy. For example, AT&T allowed women to work only up to certain levels and in a limited range of tasks (Gutek & Larwood, 1987). Many states had laws that "protected" women by excluding them from certain jobs. For example, women were forbidden to take jobs that required them to work at night, work around chemicals, serve drinks, or lift more than thirty pounds (McCormick, 2002). (And just how much does the average 3-year old weigh?)

Although employers today cannot directly refuse to hire or promote applicants because of race or gender, a great deal of discrimination still occurs. One source of evidence comes from studies of evaluation bias that used simulated job resumés or applications. A recent meta-analysis of forty-nine such studies showed a strong preference for men when the job was seen as masculine and a somewhat weaker preference for women when the job was seen as feminine (Davison & Burke, 2000). Unfortunately, leadership roles are still usually perceived as masculine (Eagly & Karau, 2002).

More direct evidence of discrimination comes from reports from women themselves. For example, 37 percent of women in a recent Australian study said they had been discriminated against in promotion decisions (Snizek & Neil, 1992). In a U.S. sample of more than 1,200 women, over 40 percent said that at some time in their lives they had been denied a raise, a promotion, or some other deserved reward at work because they were women. One in five (and more women of color than white women) had experienced such discrimination within the past year (Landrine & Klonoff, 1997).

Many other studies indicate that equally qualified women are less likely than men to be hired or are offered lower-paying, less desirable jobs (Betz & Fitzgerald, 1987; Eagly & Karau, 2002; Fassinger, 2002). Sexism today is unfortunately alive and well; however, unlike sexism of the past, it is more likely to be subtle than blatant. Often, it is not even intentional (Benokraitis, 1997).

In addition to gender discrimination, lesbians may also face discrimination on the basis of sexual orientation. They may be fired, not hired, or not promoted due to stereotypes about lesbians being maladjusted, mentally ill, or child molesters. In a survey of 203 lesbians in a metropolitan area (mainly white-collar, middle-class, and highly educated women), 25 percent reported specific instances of formal or informal discrimination, including being fired or forced to resign when their personal life became known. Others were denied raises or promotions. Informal discrimination included taunts, gossip, ridicule, social rejection, and even physical violence (Levine & Leonard, 1984). In several large-sample surveys, between 13 percent and 62 percent of lesbian and gay adults reported that they had experienced employment discrimination (Badgett, 1996).

Lesbians may try to remain "in the closet" at work. The "out or not" decision is a classic double bind. Being out in the workplace is linked to greater satisfaction with the job and with interpersonal relationships at work (Driscoll, Kelley, & Fassinger, 1996; Ellis, 1996). On the other hand, it may lead to increased discrimination (Croteau, 1996; Fassinger, 1996). Staying closeted also constrains gays and lesbians from speaking out against heterosexual privilege in the workplace.

Unfortunately, patterns of discrimination are often very hard to see. For example, if you are a woman with a bachelor's degree who has been with a company for five years and you are not promoted, you might compare yourself with a male coworker who was promoted. Suppose this man has been with the company for only three years but he has a master's degree: It's hard to decide whether you have been discriminated against. But suppose you look further in the company and find a man who was promoted with only a high school diploma and ten years of service and a woman who was not promoted with two years of college and eight years of service. A pattern begins to form. But that pattern is apparent only when many cases are averaged, and discrimination is usually examined one case at a time (Crosby, Clayton, Alksnis, & Hemker, 1986). One important function of affirmative action programs is to keep records so that patterns of discrimination become evident over time. You can't fix a problem if nobody knows the problem exists (Crosby, in press).

Discrimination is not inevitable or invariable. By showing how discrimination works, psychological research can help point the way to change. How can gender bias in hiring and promotion be eliminated? Both individuals and organizations must change (Valian, 1998):

- Ensure that women's performance is accurately evaluated by teaching people about attributional biases.
- Develop clear, specific criteria for performance evaluation and make people responsible for meeting the criteria.
- Allow enough time and attention for performance evaluations. The quicker and more automatic the decision making, the more people rely on cognitive biases that disadvantage women.
- Increase the number of women in the pool, which reduces the salience of gender.
- Appoint leaders who are committed to gender equity.
- Develop clear institutional policies about gender equity and make sure they are consistently implemented.

Parallel changes are also needed to eliminate bias due to race, ethnic group, sexual orientation, age, disability, and other dimensions of disadvantage.

Social Reactions to Token Women

From the local fire department or welding shop to the U.S. Senate, the corporate boardroom, and everywhere in between, women in nontraditional careers are likely to work mostly with men. They are a minority in workplaces where the environment is highly masculine. Just by being numerically rare, a woman in a male-dominated field is sure to "stick out." (see Figure 11.8). This is true for other disadvantaged groups, too. The "odd person," whether black, Hispanic, disabled, or female, becomes a *token.*

Generally, researchers define a token as a member of a group that is less than about 15 percent of the larger group. Female firefighters and male nurses, for example, are usually tokens in their workplaces.

Tokens are highly visible and may feel as though they are on display. Marian Pour-El, a mathematician, described her reception as a graduate student in the math department at Harvard in the 1970s:

> My first colloquium at Harvard University was a memorable event. The tea, which preceded the actual lecture, was held in the library and was a rather formal affair. As I entered, all eyes sank lower into the teacups in a great effort not

FIGURE 11.8. Affirmative distraction.
Source: Signe Wilkinson, as found in *NOW Times,* March 1998. © 1998 The Washington Post Writers Group. Reprinted with permission.

to seem to notice me. Needless to say, no one talked to me at all. At the end of the tea the chairman . . . turned to me and said with a twinkle in his eye, "Your presence is noted here." (Pour-El, 1974, p. 36)

Because of this visibility, tokens feel a great deal of performance pressure. When a white male employee makes a mistake, it is interpreted as an individual error and no more; if the token woman or minority makes a similar mistake, it may be taken as evidence that "those people" should not have been hired and are bound to fail. Paradoxically, the token must also worry about being too successful. Because all eyes are on her, if she performs well enough to "show up" members of the dominant group, she will be criticized for being a workaholic or "too aggressive." Visibility is heightened when the token woman or black employee is displayed to prove that the company is complying with affirmative-action policies or asked to give speeches about the progress made by women and blacks. As one woman commented, "If it seems good to be noticed, wait until you make your first major mistake" (Kanter, 1977, p. 213).

Tokens are also socially isolated. Often, members of the dominant group avoid them. The very presence of a token may remind dominant group members of what they have in common. For example, when a lone female engineer joins the working group, men may actually spend more time talking about topics that exclude her, such as their military experiences (Gutek, 2001). This isolation adds to the stress of the token position (see Box 11.3).

Finally, tokens are often stereotyped by those in the majority. They get pigeonholed into familiar roles such as mother, wife, or sex object. One female commercial pilot reported that her co-pilot questioned whether she was following the directions from air traffic control, saying "Oh well my wife gets lost when she goes to the supermarket" (Davey & Davidson, 2000, p. 213).

When the token does not play along with stereotyped roles, she may be cast as the archetypal unfeminine "iron maiden" or "bitch" (Gutek, 2001). A corporate training program, "Bully Broads," is aimed at women executives who are perceived as too aggressive. Its goal is to help them re-learn indirect and manipulative techniques such as crying, wearing more provocative clothing, and pretending to be incompetent. Tokens are usually eager to fit in and may choose not to challenge the values and practices of the men in power—indeed, they may outdo the men in enforcing the status quo (Lorber, 1993b). Or they may want to support other women and make the workplace more welcoming but are so stressed by their own token status that they cannot (Yoder, 2002).

Women and minorities are much more likely than white men to experience token status. However, when white men are the tokens, they suffer no disadvantages. In a field study of workers in a zoo park, new employees were randomly assigned to work groups in which they were tokens (for example, a man assigned to a gift shop staffed by women) or to gender-balanced groups. Only female tokens were negatively evaluated. In fact, male tokens advanced more quickly than men in gender balanced groups (Yoder & Sinnett, 1985).

Moreover, men earn more than women whether they are in male-dominated, female-dominated, or gender-balanced occupations (Budig, 2002). Men in female-dominated occupations (nurse, librarian, elementary teacher, and social worker) fare better than women in the same occupations in several ways—they are more satisfied with their jobs, get better evaluations, and advance faster. This has been dubbed the *glass escalator* to contrast with the glass ceiling experienced by women (Williams, 1992).

Comparisons of male and female tokens show that the negative effects of being a token are not due just to numbers. Rather, they reflect differences in status and power. When women or ethnic minorities enter a group that was formerly all white and male, it is perceived as a kind of infiltration by less-desirable people. The negative effects of tokenism for women and ethnic minorities decrease after the formerly tokenized group is about 35 percent of the larger group (Yoder, 2002). But numbers alone are not the answer, because tokens are still lower in status.

How can women tokens become more respected and effective? A recent study reaffirms that just getting the job and having the expertise to do it are not enough. When women were appointed leaders of all-male task groups and supplied with

BOX 11.3 *The Effects of Tokenism: A Case Study*

Social psychologist Janice Yoder has written a moving description of her experiences as a visiting faculty member at a U.S. military academy. Yoder's token status was extreme on several dimensions: She was one of sixteen women among 545 faculty members, 97 percent of whom were military officers. Her visibility, isolation, and relegation to negative roles were correspondingly extreme:

> My differences as a civilian, a researcher, and a woman created uncertainty among my colleagues and threatened to disrupt the team. . . . I frequently was isolated from group discussions. . . . One subgroup (of the department) dubbed itself the "Wolf Gang," used "We eat sheep!" as their motto, and howled when called upon to make group presentations. The departmental theme song chosen was "Macho Man," hardly appropriate for an academic department that included two female officers and myself. The gossip about my sexuality ranged from lesbian to heterosexually promiscuous. . . .
>
> I was assigned to one of two female roles: "wife" or "feminist/libber." In the former role, I was invited to a luncheon for wives. . . . While this was mildly amusing, the effects of my second label as "feminist/libber" were not. . . . I watched as my colleagues began to get restless when I raised my hand, rolled their eyes as I spoke, and concluded by ignoring. . . . I became totally ineffectual, yet unwilling to keep quiet and thus implicitly condone these actions. My role as a deviate became predictable, unwelcome, and ignored. (pp. 64–65)

Yoder described the psychological effects of token treatment in a journal entry made after only three months of such treatment:

> What does happen to the deviate? The deviate can convert, but short of a sex-change operation . . . and a personality overhaul, conversion seems out of the question for me. . . . What can I do? Yet, the failure is placed squarely on my shoulders. "What's wrong with you?" "Why can't you get along?" These questions haunt me, undermining my self-image to a point where I am reduced to crying at home alone at night. . . . I feel impotent, I can't sleep, but I am never clear-headed and fully awake. I have an eye infection. Daily problems have become insurmountable difficulties. . . . I can't work. I can't go out and have fun. . . . I have become bad in my eyes; the attributions of blame have been internalized. (p. 66)

Janice Yoder resigned from her visiting professorship after one semester.

Source: From Janice Yoder, "An Academic Woman as a Token: A Case Study," *Journal of Social Issues, 41,* 1985, pp. 61–72. Plenum Publishing. Reprinted by permission of the publisher, Blackwell Science.

task-relevant expertise to help them lead the groups, they still were not very successful or appreciated as leaders. Only when a male experimenter specifically told group members that the woman leader had special training and useful information for their task was the woman able to be effective (Yoder, Schleicher, & McDonald, 1998). Although it is worrisome that women's leadership still needs to be given legitimacy by high-status men, this study suggests one way that fair-minded men can use their organizational power on behalf of competent women.

Mentors and Role Models

Role models are members of one's own reference group who are visibly successful (Yoder, Adams, Grove, & Priest, 1985). Just knowing that other women have managed to overcome the obstacles to success may help the newcomer (Basow & Howe, 1980; O'Connell & Russo, 1980). For example, female graduate students who had female professors as role models described themselves as more career-oriented, confident, instrumental, and satisfied than those who had male role models (Gilbert, Galessich, & Evans, 1983). In a recent study of more than 400 undergraduate psychology students, having a good relationship with a supportive role model was an important factor in helping the students decide their future career goals (Perrone et al., 2002).

Unlike white men, women and minority men have had few role models. Lack of role models probably contributes to loneliness and feelings of deviance. Adding a few token women to the workplace does not solve the role model problem. In fact, pressure to be a role model adds to the pressures on the token.

Role models may be admired from afar; *mentors* are people who take a personal interest in the newcomer (Yoder et al., 1985). Knowing the formal rules in a workplace is rarely enough. Whether you are working in a corporation, factory, hospital, or office, there is inside knowledge that is never written down in the employee manual. Instead, workers rely on informal social networks to work "the system" to their advantage (Lorber, 1993b). Successful older men frequently serve as mentors to young men on their way up, providing them with introductions to important people, special training, and hints about office politics. They may also stand up for the young man if he makes a controversial decision and raise his status simply by associating with him.

Having a mentor increases job satisfaction and career advancement for both women and men. The beneficial effects of mentoring have been shown for many groups, including African-American students from urban high schools, who showed improved grades and attendance after being in a mentor program (Linnehan, 2001), and adults from diverse ethnic backgrounds in professional careers (Gutek, 2001). A study of 231 female attorneys showed that those who had had mentors earned more money, were more successful, and were more satisfied in their careers than those who had not (Wallace, 2001). A study of women psychologists showed that those who had a research mentor were more likely to do research (a masculine-typed activity) and also to become research mentors for others (Dohm & Cummings, 2002).

Having a white man as mentor may be especially beneficial to future income. In one study, graduates of business administration (MBA) programs who had established a mentoring relationship with a white man earned $16,840 more annually than those who did not. Having a woman or a minority man for a mentor had no effect on salary. African-American and Hispanic graduates of both sexes, and white women, were less likely to have white male mentors (Dreher & Cox, 1996). For attorneys, too, those with male mentors end up earning more than those with female mentors (Wallace, 2001).

Why do women have more difficulty finding a mentor than men do? One reason is that women lack access to the *old-boy network,* with its "bands of brothers" who look out for each other's interests (Lorber, 1993b). As one female corporate executive put it: "It's always been men at the top of this company and the top of the company I was in before. They all know each other. They've all come up the same route together, all boys together" (Wajcman, 1998, p. 97).

Often, high-status men are reluctant to mentor women. Quite simply, they feel more comfortable with people they perceive as more similar to themselves. Also, young women may not always realize the importance of finding mentors (Kanter, 1977; Nieva & Gutek, 1981). Or they may be reluctant to ask senior men for mentoring because they fear the relationship would be misinterpreted as sexual (Gutek, 2001).

What about women mentoring other women? In the past, only a few women were in positions that would enable them to mentor other women, and the pressures of their token status may have prevented them from reaching out (Yoder, 2002). The scarcity of mentors is probably easing, as old-girl networks have grown. For example, the Psychology of Women Division of the American Psychological Association matches beginning researchers with accomplished ones for mentoring. And MentorNet, a national e-mail network, offers opportunities for women in engineering, math, and science to connect with supportive experts in their fields (www.mentornet.net). Women may be better mentors for women in creating a professional self-image, empowerment, and supportive personal counseling (Burke & McKeen, 1997; Gaskill, 1991; Gilbert & Rossman, 1992). Among a sample of female attorneys, those mentored by men earned more; but those mentored by women reported less conflict between work and family and greater career satisfaction, and they were more likely to intend to continue practicing law (Wallace, 2001).

Leadership: Do Women Do It Differently?

Clearly, there are barriers that prevent many women from achieving positions of leadership. But despite the many obstacles discussed here and in Chapter 3, more women are moving into positions of leadership. When they are in leadership positions, do women lead differently from men?

Contrary to stereotype, there are no dramatic gender differences in leadership style. In a meta-analysis of 370 previous comparisons, women were somewhat more democratic and participative leaders than men. However, the difference depended on the situation—for example, it was larger in laboratory studies than real-life settings (Eagly & Johnson, 1990). In laboratory studies, people are usually strangers to each other and the manager role is simulated; gender roles may be salient. In actual workplaces, people have clear job titles and roles and long-term relationships; the demands of the manager role may be more important than gender roles (Eagly & Johannesen-Schmidt, 2001).

Are women more effective as leaders? Effectiveness is usually defined as how well the leader helps the group reach its stated goals. A meta-analysis of seventy-six studies of leadership effectiveness showed that there were no gender differences except in the military, where men were more effective (Eagly et al., 1995). Again, the effect of situation is apparent—military leadership takes place in an extremely masculine realm where women are a small minority of each work group. In another measure of effectiveness, studies of woman-owned businesses (reviewed by Hooijberg & DiTomaso, 1996) show that they are equally likely to survive and thrive as businesses owned by men.

In contrast to these findings of overall similarity, a recent study of managers from the United States and eight other countries found some significant gender differences. Women were rated higher on several positive attributes such as motivating others, showing optimism about goals, mentoring others, being considerate, and rewarding others for good performance. Men were more likely to be critical about others' mistakes, to be absent or uninvolved during a crisis, and to wait until problems were severe before trying to solve them. Overall, in this study the women were perceived as more effective managers (Eagly & Johannesen-Schmidt, 2001).

In summary, the evidence suggests that when women are seen as legitimate leaders, they behave similarly to men in the same kinds of positions and they are equally likely to succeed. Where there are differences in leadership style, the styles that women are more likely to use may enhance the effectiveness of their organizations. But any advantage that women may have in leadership style may be offset by the resistance of men in power to accepting women's leadership. As more women enter formerly masculine domains, however, the salience of gender will diminish in leadership contexts.

WOMEN'S CAREER DEVELOPMENT: ARE THERE OBSTACLES FROM WITHIN?

So far our discussion of obstacles to women's job and career satisfaction has focused on forces in the social environment. We now turn to psychological factors—individual differences in beliefs, values, motives, and choices.

Do Women Have Limited Expectations?

In 1991, pro tennis player Monica Seles suggested that the prize money in tennis tournaments should be the same for women and men. Tennis pro Steffi Graf responded, "We make enough, we don't need more," and Mary Jo Fernandez agreed, "I'm happy with what we have; I don't think we should be greedy" (Bailey, 1991, cited in Valian, 1998). In Chapter 3, we noted that women often do not feel entitled to equality. They know that gender discrimination is pervasive but deny that it has ever happened to them (Crosby, 1984). They pay themselves less than men in laboratory experiments, even though they do equal or better work (Jost, 1997; Major, 1994). When they achieve positions of power, they may continue to question the legitimacy of their authority even though they know they are competent (Apfelbaum, 1993). And, like Graf and Fernandez, they may say that they don't need or want equality.

Why do women not expect equality? The answer may lie partly in early gender socialization. The good news is that gender-linked perceptions about jobs are decreasing and can be reduced by educational programs for children and teens (Phillips & Imhoff, 1997). Low expectations for equality also may occur because women are aware of the social obstacles described earlier. If a woman suspects that her attempt at a career may lead to devaluation of her competence, the stresses of being a token, and social rejection, she may give up her high aspirations. These effects are compounded for women of color, who also may experience racism (Mays, Coleman, & Jackson, 1996). If women sometimes do not feel entitled to equality, it is because they are responding to pervasive cultural norms.

Do Women Have Different Values and Interests?

Do women workers want and need different rewards than men? Do they end up in feminized occupations because these occupations fit with their personal values? A great deal of research has attempted to answer these questions: a recent meta-analysis found 242 different samples totaling well over half a million people (Konrad, Ritchie, Lieb, & Corrigall, 2000). Aggregating these many studies has provided a clearer picture of what women and men value in their jobs.

In general, sex differences were small. Women tended to value intrinsic rewards more highly—those rewards that come from actually doing the job, such as intellectual stimulation, a chance for creativity, a sense of accomplishment, and feeling that the work is meaningful. Men tended to value different intrinsic rewards, such as freedom, challenge, and power. They also valued extrinsic rewards more highly—those that come after the job is done or as a by-product of the job, such as pay and promotion, fringe benefits, and job security. Women placed higher value on a pleasant working environment—friendly co-workers, comfortable surroundings, commuting ease, and convenient hours. Perhaps women value comfort and friendliness on the job more than men because many women leave paid work at the end of the day for a second full-time job of homemaking and child care.

Women's and men's values seem to be converging, especially when they occupy similar positions. In the meta-analysis just described, job attributes such as "wanting responsibility" became more important to women in the 1980s and 1990s, and many sex differences found in the 1970s disappeared, suggesting that women's aspirations have risen with their opportunities (Konrad et al., 2000). In a recent study of senior managers of multinational corporations, women and men agreed that "a sense of achievement" and "enjoying the job" were their most important motives. In fact, they agreed on every motive they were asked about—respect from colleagues, developing other people, meeting goals, and so on. The only gender differences were that women were slightly more likely than men to care about having power and slightly less likely to care about money (Wajcman, 1998). Thus, it is highly unlikely that the wage gap or the glass ceiling can be attributed to differences in values (Gutek, 2001).

While values may help determine one's occupational setting, the occupational setting may also affect one's values. When a person is given opportunities to advance, he or she is likely to develop a strong work commitment and aspirations for promotions and raises. A person placed in a job with little upward mobility tends to become indifferent, to complain, and to look for extrinsic satisfactions. Thus, the social structure of the workplace is a powerful force in shaping values and behavior. But its effects are often overlooked. When women in dead-end jobs develop poor attitudes, these attitudes are sometimes seen as characteristic of women as a group instead of a human response to blocked opportunities. As one organizational researcher put it, "What the clerical worker with low motivation to be promoted might need is a promotion; what the chronic complainer might need is a growthful challenge. But who would be likely to give it to them?" (Kanter, 1977, p. 158).

Math and Computing: Still Barriers

Many of the best career opportunities in American society today require a background in mathematics and computer technology. People who lack a math/technology background tend to be limited to a small range of potential career fields. Those people are still predominantly female.

In Chapters 3–6 we discussed various processes that contribute to this important gender difference. Mathematics has been stereotyped as a male domain, and many girls lose confidence and interest in doing it. Girls are also socialized to like computers less than boys do. Their actual performance, however, may depend on the situation, as a study of more than 700 workers in university faculty, clerical, and administrative jobs that required computer and technology-related skills demonstrated. The male faculty had more computer experience, used more applications, and were less anxious and intimidated by computers than female faculty. However, among the clerical workers, these gender differences were reversed: the women were more competent and confident than the men. It is not computer use in itself but the gendered meaning of computers that creates difficulties for women (Harrison, Rainer, & Hochwarter, 1997).

Fortunately, research has demonstrated effective ways for improving the math/technology background of girls (Betz & Fitzgerald, 1987; Eccles, 1989; Hyde & Kling, 2001; Sadker & Sadker, 1994):

- Create a positive classroom climate for girls.
- Educate girls to understand that math is necessary to many high-paying and exciting careers.
- Require four years of math in high school for all students.
- Eliminate gender bias in standardized testing and over-reliance on test scores.
- Offer special math, science, and computer conferences for junior high and high school girls.

- Provide opportunities for single-sex education through girls' schools and women's colleges.
- Provide girls with stories and pictures of female role models in math, science, computing, and engineering
- Create mentoring programs for girls and women in these areas.

Are Women Less Motivated to Achieve?

For more than 50 years, psychologists have explored the question of why some people strive for success. *Achievement motivation* is the desire to accomplish something valuable and important and to meet high standards of excellence. Starting in the 1950s, researchers devised tests for measuring achievement motivation and predicting achievement-oriented behavior (McClelland, Atkinson, Clark, & Lowell, 1953). Achievement behaviors of any sort—from running a marathon to winning a beauty contest—could theoretically be predicted by one's score on an achievement-motivation measure. For research purposes, however, scores were used to predict performance in academic settings and competitive games in the laboratory.

Early research showed that achievement-motivation scores predicted the achievement behavior of men but not of women. Reflecting the strong gender bias of research at that time, the intriguing question of why women behaved less predictably than men was not explored. Instead, researchers just excluded women from their studies, concluding that they must lack achievement motivation (Unger, 1979a; Veroff, Wilcox, & Atkinson, 1953).

Today, it is recognized that women and men have similar motivation to achieve, but that motivation may be channeled in different directions. As they are growing up, girls and boys continually make choices, both consciously and unconsciously, about how they will spend their time and efforts. This decision making is complex and multi-dimensional (Hyde & Kling, 2001). The most important current theory for understanding these choices and their relationship to achievement motivation is the *expectancy X value model* (Eccles, 1994).

The expectancy part of the theory involves the individual's *expectations of success.* Research shows that junior high and high school students consistently have gender-linked expectations for success: boys are more confident in math, and girls in English. But even if a girl believes she can succeed at a task, she is unlikely to attempt it unless it is important to her—this is where the value part of the theory comes in. The *subjective value* of various options (Do I enjoy English more than math? Will I really need math for my chosen career?) strongly affects decision making; for example, girls typically view math as less useful and important to them than boys do.

Expectancies and values are shaped by parental attributions (My daughter got an A in math because she works hard, my son because he's bright), gender-role beliefs (Scientists are nerdy guys), and self-perceptions (I can't do physics). Because gender socialization affects values, definitions of success, and the kinds of activities seen as crucial to one's identity, it affects virtually every aspect of achievement-related decision making.

One example of differently socialized values is the importance placed on being a parent. Gender differences in the subjective value of having children, and its effects on career planning, were demonstrated in an interesting study of college students (Stone & McKee, 2000). When they responded to surveys, both women and men were strongly career-oriented. However, interviews with the same students gave a different picture. Men consistently planned to put their career first, whereas most of the women planned to cut back or stop their careers after they had children. As one said, "Once I'm a parent, my career is on hold." Perhaps because of these differences in the value attached to parenthood, women had much less knowledge than men did about the fields they planned to enter (the graduate training needed, how much they could earn) and were gaining much less relevant work experience while in college. Although they expected to work and to be successful, the women's values were affecting the attention they gave to their career future. Do you think that results would be similar or different on your campus?

EXCEPTIONAL WORK LIVES

Achievement in the Professions

Until recently, women professionals worked mostly in education, social work, and nursing. Today, many women continue to enter these professions. Meanwhile, others are entering formerly male-dominated professions—law, medicine, psychology, science and engineering, the military, and business management. For example, women went from 3 percent of all attorneys in the 1970s to about 25 percent in the 1990s (Valian, 1998). It is still the case that relatively few women achieve professional success. Yet despite the many obstacles, some women do. How are these women different? What factors in their personalities and backgrounds make the difference between them and their nonachieving peers?

What Factors Affect Women's Career Development?

Although high-achieving women in the professions are few in number, they provide potential role models for other women. Their backgrounds suggest ways to bring up girls without limiting their aspirations and development, and their achievements represent the possibility of breaking down sex segregation in the workplace. If a few women can "make it," a world of equal power and status for all women and men becomes easier to imagine.

In general, high-achieving women come from backgrounds that provide them with a relatively unconstricted sense of self and an enriched view of women's capabilities (Lemkau, 1979, 1983). Their families and their upbringing are unusual in positive ways (see Table 11.1). As social-learning theory would predict, girls who are exposed to less gender-stereotyped expectations are more likely to become high achievers. Attending all-girls' schools and women's colleges can provide role models and opportunities for leadership. Not surprisingly, parents play an important role. Employed mothers—especially when they enjoy their work and are successful at it—provide an important model for achievement. Because fathers usually encourage gender typing in their children more than mothers do and usually have more family power, a father who supports and encourages his daughter's achievements may be especially influential (Weitzman, 1979). One black woman who became a distinguished physician has provided an eloquent description of her parents' belief in her:

TABLE 11.1. Characteristics Associated with Achievement in Women

Individual variables	*Background variables*
High ability	Working mother
Liberated sex role values	Supportive father
Instrumentality	Highly educated parents
Androgynous personality	Female role models
High self-esteem	Work experience as adolescent
Strong academic self-concept	Androgynous upbringing
Educational variables	*Adult lifestyles variables*
Higher education	Late marriage or single
Continuation in mathematics	No or few children
Girls' schools and women's colleges	

Source: From Betz & Fitzgerald, *The Career Psychology of Women,* p. 143.

> As a woman, I was told, I would be able to do whatever I wanted. I was taught that my skin had a beautiful color. This constant, implicit reinforcement of positive self-image was my parents' most valuable gift to me. I grew up loving my color and enjoying the fact that I was a woman. . . . In school, I performed well because my mother and father expected it of me. When I entered high school, I elected the college preparatory program as a matter of course. (Hunter, 1974, pp. 58–59)

Setting high goals and persisting despite setbacks are important factors in women's career development. In a survey of more than 200 African-American women attorneys, 80 percent said that their families and teachers had encouraged them to work hard and set high goals. They also said they had benefited from having access to black women role models and to equal opportunity programs (Simpson, 1996). In a longitudinal study, an ethnically diverse group of high school girls who expressed interest in math/science careers in 1980 were followed up to thirteen years later. Those who had achieved their goals had taken more elective math and science in high school, set high standards for themselves, and stressed how important it is to "hang in there" when difficulties arise. Those who had experienced their parents' divorce were especially motivated to be financially independent because they had seen what happens to women who have to support their children on their own. Among the group that had not achieved their goals, some were stopped by family socialization (they were taught that the most important goal for a woman is marriage) or critical life events such as an unplanned pregnancy (Farmer et al., 1997).

Variations among Successful Women

The research summarized in Table 11.1 has been very useful in helping psychologists understand the dynamics of achievement in women, but it does have limitations. Obviously, all these characteristics are not true of all high-achieving women. Some women who do not have any of them manage to succeed anyway, and some even report having been spurred on by a disapproving parent or an attempt to hold them back (Weitzman, 1979). In one study, black women and white women who came from poor families in which neither parent had finished high school were extensively interviewed. Despite their disadvantaged backgrounds, these women had achieved extraordinary success in business, academia, or government service. The "odds-defying" achievers had an unusually strong belief in their ability to control their lives. They believed that "You can do anything if you put your mind to it" (Boardman, Harrington, & Horowitz, 1987).

Research on high-achieving women has been done mostly on white women. More research is needed on diverse groups of women achievers to give a complete profile of successful women. Family background and socialization probably affect Hispanic, Asian-American, and African-American women differently. For example, black women generally grow up expecting to support themselves; traditional Asian-American culture discourages women from independence and rewards subservience.

It is likely that racism and sexism interact to impede the career development of women of color. Black women, for example, have higher aspirations than black men or white women during high school, but, like white women, their career goals decline during college. Black women are more likely than black men, but less likely than white women, to achieve success in a profession. Compared with white women, they are more likely to be in a traditional "woman's" profession, especially teaching (Betz & Fitzgerald, 1987).

Models of career development based on heterosexuals may have limited applicability to lesbian and bisexual women. Recent research suggests that the process of coming out and accepting a lesbian identity (see Chapter 8) is personally demanding and, in some cases, may delay career development. However, coming out is a normal phase for lesbian and bisexual women, one that should be taken into account in career counseling (Boatwright, Gilbert, Forrest, & Ketzenberger, 1996).

Cause—or Effect?

Studying the factors leading to success by looking at successful women is an example of *retrospective research* in which participants look back at factors influencing them at an earlier time. It can show us what characteristics successful women tend to share. However, it can also lead us to assume that we know the causes of success when we may be observing its results.

In other words, women who—for whatever reason—have the opportunity to test themselves in a demanding career may develop high self-esteem, assertiveness, independence, and achievement motivation as a consequence of their success. From this perspective, opportunity creates a "successful" personality, rather than vice versa (Kanter, 1977). Retrospective memory is not always accurate, either. Successful women may remember more achievement emphasis in their backgrounds than less successful women simply because this dimension is relevant to them as adults (Nieva & Gutek, 1981).

Nontraditional Occupations: From Pink Collar to Blue

During the 1970s and 1980s, federal affirmative-action guidelines, discrimination suits from workers, and unions all pressured employers to open opportunities for women in blue-collar fields (Harlan & O'Farrell, 1982). Women began to enroll in apprentice programs in the skilled trades and to take jobs as coal miners, police officers, truck drivers, welders, carpenters, and steelworkers (Braden, 1986; Deaux & Ullman, 1983; Hammond & Mahoney, 1983; Martin, 1988). Blue-collar women are an important group because they challenge stereotypes and because they represent one way that women break out of the pattern of low earnings.

Most women who became skilled blue-collar workers in male-dominated areas did not plan to do so (Deaux & Ullman, 1983; Martin, 1988). Rather, they often started out in other occupations and changed to meet perceived opportunities. Those who pioneered in entering the trades before affirmative-action mandates have been described by themselves and their co-workers as "fighters": brave, rugged, tough, aggressive, confident, and willing to take risks (Harlan & O'Farrell, 1982). Even today, women entering blue-collar work are more assertive, less gender-typed, and more likely to use active, direct problem-solving strategies than women in pink-collar work (Nash & Chrisler, 2000). They have a strong sense of self and a desire to be independent (Greene & Stitt-Gohdes, 1997).

In one study, 470 African-American, white, and Hispanic women who entered programs in which more than 80 percent of the students were male were compared with women who entered programs with a preponderance of female students. The biggest difference between the two groups was that women in the nontraditional group (regardless of ethnic background) had received more support and encouragement from female and male friends, family, teachers, and counselors. They were also more instrumentally oriented (Houser & Garvey, 1985). Another study showed that economic need was the biggest factor in women's decision to move to blue-collar jobs, and this was especially true for black women (Padavic, 1991). Thus, individual background, personality factors, and current contexts may interact to influence women's employment choices.

Blue-collar women generally report a high level of satisfaction with their jobs. They like the variety and challenge of the work. They are proud of their competence and autonomy, have high levels of self-esteem, and often aspire to promotion and advancement (Deaux & Ullman, 1983; Ferree, 1987; Hammond & Mahoney, 1983; O'Farrell & Harlan, 1982). Being well paid is an important part of job satisfaction for blue-collar women because they need to provide for their families. In one study, two-thirds of a sample of black, white, and Hispanic women steelworkers had children at home, and 61 percent of these were the sole wage earners for their families (Deaux & Ullman, 1983). One woman coal miner remembered her experience as a waitress: "I thought there must be a better way—here I am making $1.45 an hour and $1.00 an hour in tips. Jesus, there's gotta be another way." She described her decision to become a coal miner in vivid terms: "I can wash off coal black but I can't wash off those damn bill collectors" (Hammond & Mahoney, 1983, p. 19).

Of course, we do not know whether the woman shapes the job or the job shapes the woman—a problem with retrospective research discussed earlier. It does seem that proving oneself in a job that requires physical strength and endurance is empowering. One woman mechanic/shipfitter described her early fears but also reported how she learned to deal with "static" from male co-workers, one of whom told her "This is no place for a woman, you ought to be outside taking care of your kids."

> I got angry one day, and I told one of the guys that I had to feed my damn kids just like he did, that's why I was there, and I never had too much trouble after that. (Braden, 1986, p. 75)

Blue-collar women do face some disadvantages. They are workplace tokens, few in number and low in status. Male co-workers and supervisors may feel threatened by their presence. Physical strength, endurance, and courage are central components of manhood. If mere women can handle their jobs, how are these men to distinguish themselves as men? Women may be taunted and ridiculed, subjected to hazing, threatened with physical injury, deliberately given unsafe equipment, and exposed to hostile, violent pornography on the job (Fitzgerald, 1993). A survey of blue-collar women (compared with school secretaries) showed that they experienced more sexual harassment and gender discrimination, more adverse working conditions, higher stress, and lower satisfaction. The black women in the sample also reported more racial discrimination than their counterparts who were secretaries (Mansfield et al., 1991). On-the-job stress creates psychological symptoms for blue-collar women (Goldenhar, Swanson, Hurrell, Ruder, & Deddens, 1998). Clearly, the satisfaction of doing a tough job and getting paid well for it can be offset by the burden of working in a hostile environment. (For more on workplace sexual harassment, see Chapter 13.)

Other job disadvantages include the often dirty and dangerous working conditions and the fact that as the "last hired, first fired," women are subject to layoffs and plant closings (Deaux & Ullman, 1983; Ferree, 1987). Despite these obstacles, research suggests that women perform similarly to blue-collar men and are no more likely to quit their jobs (Deaux & Ullman, 1983).

PUTTING IT ALL TOGETHER: WORK AND FAMILY

Women's increasing involvement in paid work has been one of the strongest social trends of the past 30 years. According to U.S. Census data, in 1970 only 30 percent of married women with children under the age of 6 worked outside the home; by the mid-1990s, 63 percent of these women were working, along with 71 percent of married women with school-age children (Gilbert, 2001). Moreover, as we discussed in Chapters 9 and 10, many mothers are single and must provide all or most of the financial support of their children.

It is interesting that women's work became a research issue only in the 1970s, when middle-class white women began entering the workforce in greater numbers. The fact that working-class, black, and some Hispanic women had always held paid jobs had not been considered worthy of psychological research. Unlike most research on work, which focuses on men, research on the problems of combining work and family has focused almost exclusively on women, especially on white, upper-middle-class women who are pursuing careers in business and the professions.

When psychologists first began studying working women, they emphasized the social and personal costs of multiple roles, rather than their rewards (Crawford, 1982; Gilbert, 2001). For example, researchers investigated whether women's work was detrimental to their mental health or their marriages. They were much less likely to ask whether family involvement or a happy marriage may make one a better and more productive worker. Researchers are now examining work and family from a broader perspective, looking at how women's and men's activities at work and at home converge.

Although people sometimes say that "You shouldn't bring your work home from the office" or "You shouldn't let personal problems affect your work," they do affect each other. Men's and women's work and family roles function as a system, with each component affecting every other (Gilbert, 2001; Lorber, 1993b). A woman's involvement in her paid work may depend not only on whether she has young children but also on whether she has a partner. If so, can her partner stay home from work with a sick child? How do both partners define housework responsibilities? Each partner's involvement in paid work depends on the other. If one earns a high salary, the other may feel less tied to a particular job; if one job is only part time, the other may put in overtime. Combining the multiple obligations of spouse, parent, and worker has often been described as a "balancing act." Here we look at some costs and benefits of the balancing act for working women and their families.

What Are the Costs of the Balancing Act?

There is no doubt that combining work and family is hard for both women and men and that the "double day" of paid and unpaid work done by many women is particularly demanding. *Role conflict* refers to the psychological effects of being faced with sets of incompatible expectations or demands; *role overload* describes the difficulties of meeting these expectations. The secretary who is asked to work overtime on short notice and must scramble to find child care may experience both conflict (feeling guilty and torn between her two obligations) and overload (as she calls baby-sitters while typing the overdue report). Because her mother and worker roles are incompatible, there is no really satisfactory resolution of the conflict, and it may lead to guilt, anxiety, and depression. Chronic overload may lead to fatigue, short temper, and lowered resistance to physical illness.

Research has consistently shown that women workers experience role conflict (Crosby, 1991; Gilbert, 1993; Wajcman, 1998). In some studies, men also report role conflict. However, women are much more likely than men to adjust their jobs around their family responsibilities (Mennino & Brayfield, 2002). For example, women are more likely than men to arrange flextime schedules, to work only part time, to turn down opportunities for promotion or overtime, or to use their own sick days to care for others. Women also adjust their family lives around their paid work, by limiting the number of children they have, cutting back on housework, hiring live-in child-care workers, and so on. Of course, these trade-offs affect their partners, too. Some couples work out mutual strategies such as sharing child care and housework or hiring someone else to do chores.

Though both women and men make trade-offs to keep up with the balancing act, their choices may be shaped more by sociocultural aspects of gender than by their own attitudes and beliefs. When more than 900 men and women in a national survey were asked about the trade-offs they made and their gender-role attitudes, individual attitudes had little effect. In other words, more traditionally oriented people did not make different choices than more egalitarian people. However, both women and men in male-dominated occupations made more trade-offs that put family needs second to work needs. For example, they were more likely to take on extra work and to miss a family event. These results suggest that "male-typed occupations, regardless of whether they are held by women or men, are less accommodating to job-family balance" (Mennino & Brayfield, 2002, p. 251).

There is very little research on the costs of the balancing act among people who are not heterosexual, economically privileged, or white. In a study of lesbians, most of whom currently had a partner, 41 percent reported conflicts between their relationship and work roles—usually problems in allocating time and energy. Moreover, 33 percent reported conflicts at work in feeling socially unacceptable. They felt unable to "be themselves" or to discuss their partner or home life, and they reported pressure to dress and act in stereotyped heterosexual ways (Shachar & Gilbert, 1983).

What Are the Benefits of the Balancing Act?

Effects on Women and Men

Side by side with research showing widespread problems with role conflict and overload is a great deal of research showing *benefits* associated with multiple roles. Indeed, study after study shows that involvement as a spouse, parent, and worker is beneficial for both women and men. The value of the balancing act is reflected in better mental health, physical health, and relationship quality (Barnett & Hyde, 2001).

Why does involvement in many roles benefit well-being? One reason may be that paid work in itself is generally a source of increased self-esteem, more social involvement, and an independent identity (Steil, 1997). When women make paid work part of their lives, they gain more than just an income. Another reason is that success in one domain may help people keep a sense of perspective about the other domains (Crosby, 1982, 1991). In a study of more than 200 managers, both women and men believed that their roles as parents and active members of their community had more positive than negative effects on their performance at work (Kirchmeyer, 1993). Being passed over for promotion might seem less of a disaster if one is happily involved in leading a Girl Scout troop; dealing with a difficult teenager at home may be made easier by being respected at the office. Women who juggle home and work develop good coping strategies, such as choosing the most rewarding aspects of each job and delegating the others. Having a paid job can provide a handy excuse for a woman not to do things she didn't want to do in the first place (Baruch et al., 1983). Employment also increases women's power in the family (see Chapter 9). And it provides families with higher incomes, which benefits everyone and reduces the pressure on husbands (Barnett & Hyde, 2001). Men who get involved with the care of their children are often surprised to find how deeply rewarding this can be and say that they would never give it up (Deutsch, 1999).

However, multiple roles may be beneficial only up to a point, after which overload and psychological distress may prevail. Role quality is important, too. A woman's job is unlikely to bring her satisfaction if she is subject to sexual harassment or discrimination (Barnett & Hyde, 2001).

There are some limitations to the research in this area. Research samples are *self-selected*—people have sorted themselves into employed and nonemployed groups before being studied. It is possible that multiple roles and happiness go together simply because better-adjusted people are more likely to attempt multiple roles in the first place. Furthermore, most of the research on the benefits of multiple roles has been done on people who have the advantages of high income and professional status. Role conflict and overload may contribute to "burnout" in jobs such as nursing and teaching (Greenglass & Burke, 1988; Statham, Miller, & Mauksch, 1988).

Effects on Children

What about the children? Do they suffer when both parents work outside the home? It's easy to find conservative commentators and "experts" who claim that working mothers (but never working fathers) contribute to juvenile delinquency, behavior problems, and poor adjustment in children. Day-care scare articles tell parents that their children will be abused and neglected if they are not home with mom. And employed mothers are still viewed as second-class mothers.

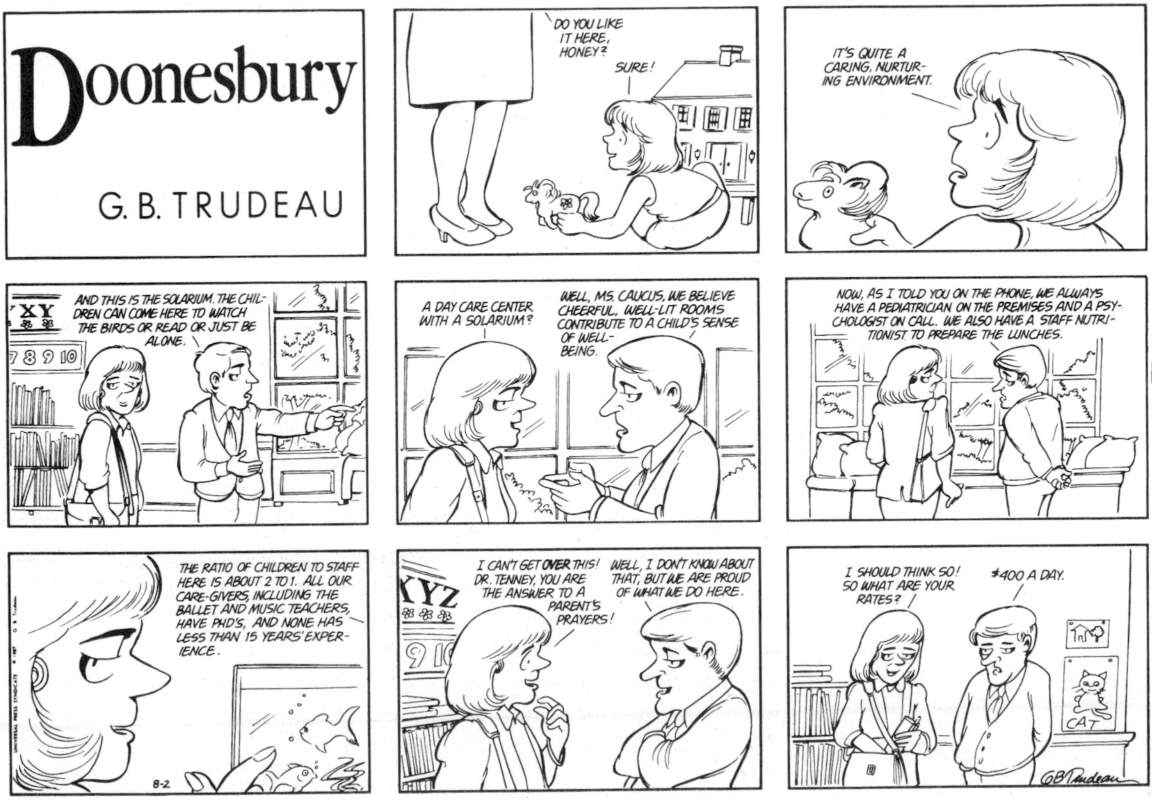

FIGURE 11.9. Day-care fantasies and realities.
Source: Doonesbury. Copyright © G. B. Trudeau. Reprinted by permission of Universal Press Syndicate. All rights reserved.

However, research does not confirm the popular wisdom. A recent meta-analysis of 59 studies confirmed that children cared for by their mothers did not differ developmentally in any important way from those cared for by other adult caretakers (Erel, Oberman, & Yirmiya, 2000). In general, children in day care do not suffer from disruption of their bond with their mothers; they may experience increased intellectual growth and development, especially if they come from low-income homes that cannot provide an enriched environment; and they are at least as socially skilled as other children (Scarr, 1998; Scarr, Phillips, & McCartney, 1990). And as for juvenile delinquency, a study of more than 700 adolescents showed that mothers' work status (both when the teens were preschoolers and currently) was unrelated to the teens' delinquency (Vander et al., 2001). For many families today, the issue is not whether mom and dad should both work, but how to find affordable, good-quality child care (see Figure 11.9).

Researchers may have overlooked potential benefits associated with working mothers—an example of bias in the framing of research questions. Child care can provide enrichment and foster intellectual and social development. In some cases, good child care may help offset poor parenting (Scarr, 1998; Silverstein, 1991). Furthermore, in many families, mothers' incomes are a matter of necessity. Two-thirds of mothers are working to keep their families out of poverty, and with welfare reform, this proportion is increasing (Scarr, 1998).

Employed mothers also provide alternative role models for their children. Several studies have shown that daughters of employed women are more independent and self-confident. Both daughters and sons of employed women hold more egalitarian attitudes about women and view women (including their own mothers) as more competent (Steil, 1997). The benefits of a mother who models many areas of competence may be especially great for girls. As adults, daughters of employed women are more likely to become high achievers (Betz & Fitzgerald, 1987). As yet, there is no research on how fathers who care for their children and do a fair share of housework affect their children's attitudes or behavior.

WOMEN, WORK, AND SOCIAL POLICY: MODELS FOR CHANGE

Clearly, the world of work presents women with many problems. Alexis Herman eloquently expressed some of the needs of working women:

> They want decent wages and benefits; they want affordable child care . . . ; they want training and education for advancement in their jobs; and they want decent and dignified working conditions. They have said it over and over again—with different accents and in different ways, but it is always the same. As Bella Abzug says, "It is shocking that as women, we have to beg . . . for family support systems, decent wages, and the dignity to do what men have always done." (Herman, 1988, p. x)

The problems may seem large and unsolvable, but equity for women workers, whether pink collar, blue collar, or professional, is not an impossible dream. How to go about achieving that dream is, however, an open question. Different ideas about the causes of inequity lead to different proposed solutions. Some researchers and policymakers focus on the individual level, others on the interpersonal or intergroup level, and still others on the structural level.

At the individual level, there is an emphasis on problems within women themselves: Women may lack the skills or motivation to succeed. According to this model, the best way to change women's work situation is to provide self-improvement and training programs to help women overcome their deficiencies. Examples are assertiveness training and time-management courses for women (Crawford, 1995). Individual change may be helpful for some women, but as we have seen, there is little evidence that women as a group lack ability or motivation. The individual-deficit model runs the risk of blaming the victim by ignoring social factors that are beyond the control of the individual (Fassinger, 2002). It leaves the work of change to women, without questioning the masculine values that underlie both corporate culture and the double day at home.

A structural-level approach focuses on the impact of organizations on the people in them. It proposes that the situation a person is placed in shapes behavior. From this perspective, low expectations and lack of ambition may be adaptive adjustments to reality and will change if real opportunities for advancement become available. The system, not the individual, must change for equity to be achieved. Rather than viewing women as unique, it sees their problems as similar to problems faced by other disadvantaged groups such as racial and ethnic minorities. Legislation for equal opportunity and affirmative action is one route to change (Crosby, in press). However, affirmative action is currently being undermined and eliminated. According to the structural approach, equal opportunity leads to equal performance. Family-leave policies and affordable, high-quality child care are important structural changes, too.

A final approach is based on intergroup power, which has been stressed throughout this book and is the focus of Chapter 3. From this perspective, when men have more social power, women inevitably become the outgroup. This model explains why women's work is devalued, why male career patterns and definitions of work and achievement are taken as the norm, and why occupations so frequently end up segregated by sex. Stereotypes about differences between women and men reinforce the in-group–out-group distinction.

The intergroup perspective views change in the workplace as dependent on societal change. Educating people about stereotyping might help in the short run, but fundamental change depends on altering the power structure. Power-oriented strategies include passing and enforcing equal-opportunity legislation, increasing women's political power, and forming women's organizations and networks to exert pressure for social change. Many women today are engaged in these strategies.

The information and analysis in Chapters 9 to 11 show that women's and men's experiences in relationships, families, and workplaces are interdependent. Women who cannot achieve economic parity at work are disadvantaged by having less power in their marriages. Much of the work women do is unpaid and undervalued. Sex discrimination at work affects productivity and quality of life. If women are to have the same career opportunities as men, they must be able to decide if and when they will bear children. Families suffer when social policy is based on myths of motherhood instead of the realities of contemporary life. These are just a few examples of the complex relationships among family roles and workplace issues. Models of change that focus on gendered social structures and power inequities are more useful than those that stress changing women's attitudes and values.

CONNECTING THEMES

- *Gender is more than just sex.* Women and men have very different experiences in the workplace, and these differences both reflect and perpetuate the gender system. The gendered world of work encompasses structural factors (such as horizontal and vertical sex segregation), interactional factors (such as tokenism), and individual-level differences (such as feelings of entitlement).
- *Language and naming are sources of power.* Because work has been defined in terms of a male norm, much of the work that women do—housework, child care, emotional maintenance of families, and building the careers of their male partners—has remained largely invisible. A feminist perspective names all the work women do and focuses on its benefits, not just its costs.
- *Women are not all alike.* Most research on women and work has focused on upper-middle-class women who have professional careers. However, the majority of women are underemployed in low-paying clerical and service jobs. Discrimination is based not only on sex/gender but also on race/ethnicity, social class, and sexual orientation.
- *Psychological research can foster social change.* Women and their partners are engaged in a complex balancing act as they try to integrate work and family. However, solutions depend not only on individual efforts but also on developing public policy that recognizes the realities of work/family roles for both women and men. Women and their families need social supports such as child-care options, paid parental leave, wage equity, and effective sanctions against sex/gender discrimination.

SUGGESTED READINGS

CROSBY, FAYE (2003). *Affirmative action is dead: Long live affirmative action.* New Haven: Yale University Press. Affirmative action is probably the most misunderstood social policy of our times. Crosby's clear thinking and lively writing clear up misconceptions and show why affirmative action is still needed.

EHRENREICH, BARBARA (2001). *Nickel and dimed: On (not) getting by in America.* New York: Henry Holt. An inside expose of low-wage jobs. Ehrenreich worked as a nursing aide, a Wal-Mart clerk, a waitress, and a housecleaner to experience the realities of life for low-wage working women. Despite her best efforts, she found it was almost impossible to survive. The author goes beyond simple reporting to place working women's struggles in the context of broader social policies.

HAYS, SHARON (2003). *Flat broke with children.* New York: Oxford University Press. The impact of welfare reform seen through the eyes of welfare recipients, most of whom are poor women forced onto the labor market in low-wage jobs with few benefits. Hays's study is based on interactions with both welfare recipients and caseworkers.

CHAPTER 12

Midlife and Beyond

What is age? If someone asks a person's age, he or she will have little difficulty in providing a number. Does this number mean that a person is young, middle aged, or old? The answer depends not only on who is giving the answer but also on the gender of the person being talked about, among other factors. Age is often treated as a simple biological variable, but it is a social construction, and its meaning varies at different times and in different societies.

Like gender, age is also a social classification system that organizes identity and social roles. *Roles* are clusters of expectations placed on people who occupy a position in the social structure. Many roles carry assumptions about the gender, traits, behavior, and age of the person occupying them. As people age, their roles change.

A society's beliefs and attitudes about aging shape these roles and provide a powerful cultural context for growing older. In a society where the old are seen as wise elders or keepers of valued traditions, the stress of aging is less than in a society where they are seen as mentally slow and socially useless. In the United States, *ageism*—negative attitudes and behaviors targeting older people—has been the rule. Ageism tends to make all old people seem alike. But as a result of the accumulation of differences in power, prestige, and opportunities, older people are more different from each other (and more unequal) than are middle-aged or younger individuals.

Ageism shapes and distorts the lives of many women. Because women live longer than men, the majority of old persons are women. In 1990, for example, there were 149 women for every 100 men over age 65 and 259 women for every 100 men over age 85 in the United States (Hatch, 1995). The majority of those caring for old people were also women. How does society view women as they age, and what are their lives actually like?

THE SOCIAL CONSTRUCTION OF AGE

The significance of age as a number is relatively new. In northern Europe, for example, it was not until the mid-sixteenth century that numerical age had any social significance. Indeed, few people knew their age (Cole, 1992).

Stating a number implies that age can be objectively measured. However, the meaning of this number is relative, especially when one applies labels, such as midlife or old, to an age. People define these boundaries differently depending on their own age. Thus, people in their twenties see middle age as beginning at 35, but two decades later they see it as beginning at 50. Age boundaries also depend on how long people expect to live in a given time and place. In the United States, what used to be considered old age is now the realm of midlife (Lachman & James, 1997).

In many societies there is also a double standard for aging that depicts women as older than men of the same age. For Freud, women as young as 30 were unfit for analysis because of what he perceived as their psychological rigidity and inability to change. He saw men of the same age as youthful and pliable (Markson, 1997). To understand the meaning of age and aging for women in contemporary Western societies, we start by examining stereotypes about the old in general and old women in particular.

Images of Age and Aging

In Western cultures, aging has long been viewed negatively or, at best, ambivalently. One of the authors' mother-in-law, who is over 90, was very upset when a sign appeared outside her apartment building indicating that it had been bought by the Hebrew Home for the Aged. Even the word *old* is avoided, as though to be old is so terrible that it should not be mentioned in polite company. In some senior centers, members who use the word *old* are fined (Cruikshank, 2003). Instead, people are encouraged to use euphemisms such as "senior citizen" or "golden ager."

When college students and adults were asked to list the characteristics of 35-year-old and 65-year-old women and men, age stereotypes were more pronounced than gender stereotypes (Kite, Deaux, & Miele, 1991). Like other stereotypes discussed in Chapter 2, stereotypes of old people vary in the dimensions of competence and warmth. Elderly people are seen as "doddering but dear" (Cuddy & Fiske, 2002). (This combination of incompetence and warmth is also characteristic of perceptions about disabled and retarded people.) Viewed through slang, old people are weak, foolish, and pathetic (see Table 12.1).

People form not only global stereotypes of the aged, but also stereotypes of subtypes. Grandmothers, for example, are seen as nurturing but low in traits such as independence and intelligence. In contrast, senior citizens are seen as both incompetent and lacking in warmth.

Grandmothers aside, the image of aged women in Western society is decidedly unappealing. Although some terms for old men connote respect (an "old salt," for example, refers to an experienced sailor), terms for old women—such as "old hag"—are less kind. Older women are often portrayed as the wicked witch, the bad mother who is needy and neurotic, or the comical, powerless little old lady. Such archetypes are regularly found in Disney movies in

TABLE 12.1 Terms for Old People from the Late Eighteenth Century to the Present

Male or Gender-Neutral	Female
Old buzzard	Little old lady
Old coot	Granny
Old salt	Old hag
Old duffer	Old maid
Gay old dog	Old bag
Old crock	Old biddy
Old fogey	Old crow
Dirty old man	Old cow
Gramps	Old bird
Grandpa	Crone
Old codger	Old hen
Fuddy-duddy	
Fossil	

Source: From Rosalie A. Kane, "Historical Terminology Used to Represent Older People," *Gerontologist, 28,* 1988, 291–297, and conveyed through Copyright Clearance Center, Inc.

which old women are depicted as ugly, evil, and power hungry as well as greedy and crazy (Perry, 1999). Fear and dislike of older women can also be found in folklore, as in the saying "If the devil can't come himself, he sends an old woman" (Cruikshank, 2003).

Sexism and Ageism

As they age, women are subject not to only to ageism but also to continued sexism. Both ageism and sexism involve the negative categorization of people on the basis of their membership in a group. Both are reflected and perpetuated in language about the devalued groups. Both are pervasive in our society (see Figure 12.1). Finally, both are frequently shared by members of the devalued groups themselves.

The combination of subtle ageism and sexism can be seen in expressions of surprise that an old woman retains her competence or assertiveness, as in phrases that begin "still creative at . . . ." or "still attractive at . . . ." (Williams & Giles, 1998). "Feisty" is especially likely to be used to express surprise that an older woman can be vigorous or assertive. A pamphlet from Old Lesbians Organizing for Change asked, "Would you call Superman feisty?" (Cruikshank, 2003).

FIGURE 12.1. This cover manages to be sexist and ageist at the same time. Note the contrast between the young postfeminist, Ally McBeal (whose fictional name is used rather than that of the actress, Calista Flockheart) and the three real feminists who are portrayed as both aging and literally colorless. Only Ally McBeal was pictured in color; the others were in black, white, and tones of grey.

An absence of images is also significant because it indicates that people have lost their perceived value. Older women are almost invisible in public life. When elderly women filled a political rally in Iowa, a journalist described them this way: "a blizzard of blue-gray permanent waves, they radiated the starched, sweet propriety of a Temperance union meeting" (*New Yorker*, July 26, 1999, p.30). The women were depicted as out of place at a political rally and figures of fun. They lost their individuality by being reduced to one part of themselves—their hair.

Ageism, like sexism, includes not only beliefs and attitudes, but also discriminatory practices that follow from prejudice (Butler, 1980). Discrimination based on sex adds to discrimination based on age to put older women in double jeopardy. For example, a study of a large geriatric center in England found that the nurses treated male residents better than female residents. They knew more about the lives of the men and were more likely to describe the women as difficult (Bernard, 1998). Ageism is particularly destructive when it is combined with sexism.

The Double Standard of Aging

Feminists have long argued that images of old women are a logical extension of sexist beliefs that "women are only valuable when they are attractive and useful to men" (Healy, 1986, p. 59). Men are perceived as becoming old later than women (Hummert, Gartska, & Shaner, 1997). In the United States today, women are perceived as reaching middle and old age about five years earlier than men (Kite & Wagner, 2002).

The double standard for aging takes many forms. For example, the physical changes of age are viewed very differently in men and women: The middle-aged man's wrinkles and gray hair are seen as evidence of character and distinction, whereas the middle-aged woman is urged to conceal all signs of growing older with makeup, hair dye, and cosmetic surgery. Jokes about older women are more frequent and negative than those about either younger women or older men. Most of the jokes about age concealment involve women. One such joke says, "It's terrible to grow old alone—my wife hasn't had a birthday in six years" (Palmore, 1997). Jokes like this reinforce the idea that all older women are ashamed of their age but older men are not.

Women are also seen as losing their sexual attractiveness at a younger age than men. Men's sexual value is defined mainly in terms of personality, intelligence, and social status. Women's sexual value is defined almost entirely as physical attractiveness. The double standard is obvious when middle-aged and older men remarry following divorce or widowhood. It is socially acceptable for men to marry women as much as twenty years younger than themselves, but older women/younger men combinations are still rather rare.

Ageism and Sexism in the Media

The gendered double standard is also evident in the movies and on TV, where male actors play romantic leads into their fifties and sixties and are often paired with females a generation younger. Some recent romantic pairings include Harrison Ford (age 56) and Anne Heche (age 29), Robert Redford (age 61) and Kristin Scott Thomas (age 31), Michael Douglas (age 53) and Gwyneth Paltrow (age 25), and Jack Nicholson (age 60) and Helen Hunt (age 34) (Taylor, Lambert, Perry, & Tobin, 1999). One movie critic commented that he wasn't sure whether the men were going to adopt these women or make love to them.

Film is an insidiously powerful tool for telling women what they are not and what they should be. Romantic leading roles for middle-aged women are almost nonexistent. At age 40, Jane Fonda told an interviewer that she could find no good roles because "Who wants to look at a 40-year-old woman?" Other middle-aged actresses opt to play older parts. Sally Field was Tom Hanks's lover in *Punchline* in 1988 and his mother in *Forrest Gump*, six years later (Weinraub, 1994).

An analysis of the Academy Awards illustrates the differential impact of aging on women and men. From 1927 through 1990, women over the age of 39 accounted for 27 percent of the nominations for best actress, whereas men over the age of 39 accounted for 67 percent of the nominations for best actor (Markson & Taylor, 1993). Katherine Hepburn was the recipient of half the awards made to women over 60.

Ageist images are not limited to starring roles. One analysis of 100 top-grossing movies from the 1940s through the 1980s charged that aging women in popular movies were "underrepresented, unattractive, unfriendly, and unintelligent" (Bazzini, McIntosh, Smith, Cook, & Harris, 1997, p. 531). Female characters were consistently younger than male characters. Older women were almost invisible. Only 19 percent of the characters over the age of 35 were female. Although both men and women were seen to be less attractive as they aged, the effect was stronger for women than for men. A well-worn male face is thought to convey maturity, character, and experience. In contrast, a female face is valued only if it stays the same (Cruikshank, 2003).

Well-worn female faces rarely appear on TV. Only 2 percent of new season characters on network TV from 1960 to 1992 were older than 65 years of age. Only 3 percent of characters on daytime soap operas could be classified as seniors (Pasupathi & Lockenhoff, 2002). Most older performers had minor roles and were more likely than any other age group to be targets for comic relief. They were exploited through stereotypes about their physical, cognitive, and sexual ineffectiveness (Zebrowtiz & Montepare, 2000). Under these circumstances, it may be positive that older women are underrepresented and that elderly women of color are almost invisible on television (Hajjar, 1997)!

Women in the media are permitted to be middle aged only if they look 30. Lucille Ball starred in *I Love Lucy* (a TV show that has been on the air for 45 years and has been shown in every country in the world) when she was in her forties, but she played a 29-year-old woman. A famous cinematographer lit the stage to eliminate her wrinkles and sags (Mellencamp, 2002).

In the print media, too, ageism and sexism reign. Editors of women's magazines admit that signs of age are routinely airbrushed from photographs through computer imaging so that 60-year-old women can be made to look 45 (Chrisler & Ghiz, 1993). *Lear's*—a now defunct magazine that portrayed itself as being "for the woman who wasn't born yesterday"—rarely published photographs of gray-haired women (see Figure 12.2). In recent years, the pressure

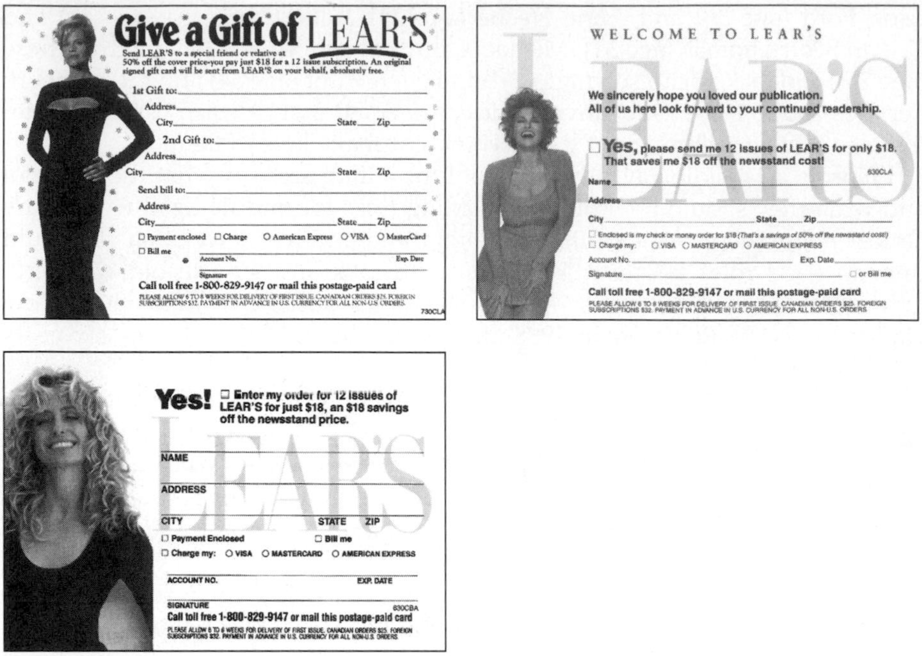

FIGURE 12.2. Do you know many women over 40 who look like these women?

on men to remain youthful has also increased. *Modern Maturity*—the magazine of the American Association for Retired Persons (AARP)—used to feature vigorous-looking, middle-aged heterosexual couples in their early fifties on their covers. Now young celebrities appear on the covers with an occasional middle-aged star. One critic quipped, "If you look old enough to join AARP, you can't be on the cover" (Cruikshank, 2003, p. 143).

The absence of women over 40 in advertising is also striking. One recent analysis of TV commercials found that only 12 percent featured people over 50, and three quarters of them were men (Quadagno, 1999). When older women appear on TV commercials, they are likely to pitch food, health, and hygiene products.

> Old women vanish from ads when they lose their sex appeal for men, appearing only to sell food they can cook and medications they can take, or being foolish in a modern female version of Uncle Tom. (Reinharz, 1997, p. 78)

Cultural Differences in the Images of the Aging Woman

Powerful as they are, the modern media did not originate the negative stereotype of aging women. In European folklore, barren or powerful old women were likely to be transformed into witches by way of a false logic that argued that because good power is fertile, unfertile power must be evil. Other archetypes of older females were recast in similar ways. For example, the term *crone* once meant a wise elder woman, but it changed to mean a malevolent old woman (Mantecon, 1993). Feminists have reclaimed the term as a symbol of experience and wisdom. The goddess Kali in India was once seen as a source of transformation. Although her image implied both creation and destruction, she is generally portrayed to Western eyes as an image of chaos and death.

Non-Western cultural images of old women can be quite positive. Native American legends include many powerful old women. The Navajo's "Changing Woman" is responsible for all new life and successful crop growth. In the Cheyenne legend the "Old Woman of the Spring," it is the old woman who has the knowledge and power to restore the buffalo. "Grandmother Spider," despite her infirmities, succeeds in bringing fire to the world after the young men had failed, and she teaches the art of pottery making and weaving to many American Indian tribes (John, Blanchard, & Hennessy, 1997). Such figures help create strong self-images for Indian women and enhance their position in Native American society. For example, only older women can perform certain kinds of medicine work (Cypress, 1993).

In traditional Japanese culture, age denotes wisdom, authority, and a hard-won freedom to be flexible and creative (Lock, 1998). Even in the entertainment media, older Japanese women are often portrayed as respected and admired, not only for their artistic skills, but for their beauty. When asked about aging, several older Japanese women said that they were looking forward to old age because they would no longer have to "keep a low profile" and display feminine reserve (Lock, 1993).

In contrast, traditional Indian views of old women may be even more negative than those found in Western Europe and the United States. One popular saying about aging in Hindi uses "teesi-kheesi" to describe women. This means that when a woman reaches age 30 (*tees*), her face caves in and teeth fall out (*khees*). Men, on the other hand, are described as "satha-patha," which means that even at age 60 (*sath*), a man remains a virile youth (*patha*) (Kakar, 1998). Hindu movies portray middle-aged women (who are now mothers-in-law) as witches, snakes in human form, or malevolent female ghosts. Although older women are given power and authority by this role, it is shadowed by the resentment of their daughters-in-law.

Our own culture gives women few reasons to celebrate their age. Birthday cards for older women allude to failing memory, decreased sexual abilities, and diminished vigor and attractiveness, all in the guise of humor (Adolph, 1993). Clearly our culture views getting older to be a cause for mourning.

Internalized Ageism

The double standard of aging encourages women to deny their age to themselves and others. Even professional women, for whom age represents professional experience and maturity, are rarely candid about it. In the official membership directory of the American Psychological Association, women are ten times as likely as men not to list their age (Bell, 1989). Recent books by Betty Friedan and Madeline Albright showed photos of them thirty years younger than they were when the books were written. The photo on a book by one California therapist in her 60s made her look 25 (Cruikshank, 2003). This may be a tactic to enhance the marketability of the books, but it is also a sign of internalized ageism.

Whatever their age, women never seem to escape cultural demands about their appearance. A recent survey that compared women between 50 and 65 years of age with an older group of women found that both groups had similar body size preferences and levels of body dissatisfaction. Disordered eating was associated with fear of aging for both groups (Lewis & Cachelin, 2001).

The need to appear younger has spawned a large empire advocating multiple cosmetic surgeries and, more recently, botox injections. One prominent media critic described her best friend's secret (and expensive) face-lift:

> Having achieved a seamless face, my best friend has lost her voice. She cannot speak of the time and labor it took to transform her. The whole point is that for the "magic" to work, the "seams"—both the lines traced by age and the scars traced by surgery—must not show. (Sobchack, 1999, p. 205)

Sobchack also points out the irreversible costs of these procedures:

> four hours on the operating table, one night of hell, a week of limited jaw motion, time for her hair to grow back, a few months for her upper and lower jaws to "relax," three years before she will do her eyelids, seven years before the surgeon's work is undone again by time and gravity. The "magic" of plastic surgery . . . . costs always an irrecoverable part of a mortal life. (p. 207)

Her friend's delight with the results illustrates the intimate connection between a woman's appearance and her power in our society:

> the response has been terrific—everyone is dazzled, but they can't quite tell why. It must be the color I'm wearing, they say, or my hair, or that I am rested. At any rate, I feel empowered again. (p. 209)

The Meanings of Midlife

Before people are considered old in today's culture, they pass through a period called *midlife*—usually defined as the years from 45 to 65. Midlife appears to be a twentieth-century invention; the term cannot be found in older dictionaries (Gullette, 1997).

The transition to midlife can be particularly problematic for women because they "age" sooner than men and are more dependent on appearance for social success. Based on her clinical practice, one psychologist described a phenomenon she termed "late midlife astonishment" (Pearlman, 1993). She found that between the ages of 50 and 60, many women suddenly become aware of an acceleration of aging and an increasing stigmatization based on its visible signs. They can no longer pass as younger. They fear being discriminated against in the workplace and rejected or abandoned by romantic partners or mates.

These fears are realistic. Women have a shorter period of presentability in the labor market than men do. For example, one manager was quoted as saying, "We have two good secretaries with first-rate skills who cannot move up because they dress like grandmothers" (Rodeheaver, 1990, p. 57). The most frequent compliment given to older women is: "You don't look your age." Think about the unstated assumptions in this remark! "If you looked your age, you would look ugly" (Healy, 1993).

Do most middle-aged women see midlife as a time of decline? On the contrary, research indicates that middle age is a very positive part of the life cycle for women. For example, longitudinal studies of college-educated women by Abigail Stewart and her students found that certainty about one's identity and confidence in one's power were higher among women in their forties than among women in their twenties and higher still among women in their sixties (Zucker, Ostrove, & Stewart, 2002). *Generativity* (defined as the ability to care for and contribute to the next generation and to the larger world outside of oneself) was higher for women in their forties than in their twenties and leveled off among women in their sixties. Personal distress was also highest among women in their twenties. The only negative characteristic that increased with age was concern with aging.

Interviews with university-educated Canadian women also indicated that most of these 45- to 65-year-old women were optimistic about aging. They expected overall stability in themselves, their financial situation, and their relationships, with an improvement in the area of leisure. These positive expectations were associated with satisfaction with themselves and their past accomplishments (Quirouette & Pushkar, 1999). Because of ageist stereotypes, however, it is often difficult for middle-aged women to reconcile their sense of well-being, self-confidence, achievement, and pleasure at the richness of their lives with the socially devalued image they see in their mirrors (Sobchack, 1999).

MENOPAUSE

Although many women view middle age as positive, they must deal with the way Western culture equates middle age with menopause. The equation of aging and menopause has no parallel in men. The language of loss tells women that all midlife changes are negative, inevitable, and debilitating (Ussher, 1989).

This focus on menopause as the major feature of midlife women is an example of how women are defined by their reproductive functions (see Chapters 7 and 10). This approach has a long history, as the following quotations illustrate:

> Women are treated for diseases of the stomach, liver, kidneys, heart, lungs, etc.; yet, in most instances, these diseases will be found on due investigation, to be . . . merely the sympathetic reactions or the symptoms of one disease, namely, a disease of the womb. (Dirix, 1869; cited in Zimmerman, 1987, p. 448)

> A woman is a uterus surrounded by a supporting organism and a directing personality. In advancing this proposition I am neither facetious nor deprecatory of womankind. I am biologically objective. (Galdston, 1958; cited in Zimmerman, 1987, p. 448)

Beliefs about biological causality have led to the neglect of other psychological and social events that occur at the same stage of life—such as children leaving home; changes in relationships; changes in identity and body image; possible divorce or widowhood; the anticipation or experiences of retirement; increasing anxiety about aging, dying, and losing friends, loved ones, and financial security.

Rather than analyzing women's responses to these events, menopause is portrayed as a fundamental cause of women's loss of prestige, status, visibility, and value during their last quarter century of life (Zita, 1993).

What Is Menopause?

What do we know about menopause? The word did not exist in English until the last quarter of the nineteenth century (Sommer, 2001). *Menopause* is defined as having occurred when a woman has not menstruated in a year. It is caused by a decrease in the production of estrogen and progesterone by the ovaries; this is a gradual process.

Menopause—or what is sometimes known as the "change of life"—occurs in most women between the ages of 45 and 55. The average age of menopause (around 50) has not changed since the medieval period. This average age is constant across cultures despite a wide range in levels of nutrition and health.

The only symptom of menopause that is found in *all* women is the end of menstruation. However, bleeding is irregular for a number of years before menstrual periods finally cease. Therefore, women can define their own menopause only after it has occurred.

Many women are unsure about their menopausal status. One recent survey of more than 13,000 women aged 40 to 55 years found that for women with an intact uterus, at least one ovary, and not using hormones, menstrual patterns predicted only half the variation in the self-definition of menopause (Harlow, Crawford, Sommer, & Greendale, 2000). The vagueness in menopausal timing is one of the reasons it causes anxiety among middle-aged women.

In a study of thousands of women, researchers found that 80.8 percent reported no limitation in physical functioning due to menopause. Only 9.2 percent indicated substantial limitations, and these women had twice the rate of having had a surgical menopause than other participants (Sowers, Pope, Welch, Sternfeld, & Albrecht, 2001). Surgical menopause (removal of the uterus and, sometimes, the ovaries) produces a precipitous drop in hormones rather than the gradual decrease found during normal menopause.

For some women, menstrual irregularity is the *only* sign of menopause (Sommer, 2001). Other signals of the end of menstrual life occur in some women—for example, hot flashes, night sweats, anxiety, moodiness, and insomnia. Although all these effects have been attributed to a decline in ovarian hormones, no relationship has been found between hormone levels and the number and severity of symptoms (Derry, 2002).

The Aging Woman's Body and Its Social Meaning

Menopause is not treated as a normal life event in our society. Instead it is used as a metaphor for disparaging the aging female body (see Figure 12.3). Although media descriptions of women during menopause have changed over the past three decades, they continue to accentuate the negative.

The symptoms stressed during each decade document changes in cultural attitudes toward women. In the 1960s, for example, the focus of articles on menopause in popular magazines was on beauty and femininity. Symptoms such as weight gain, sagging breasts, wrinkles, loss of femininity, and loss of

FOR BETTER OR FOR WORSE by Lynn Johnston

FIGURE 12.3. Elly's husband is certainly expecting the worst from menopause. *Source:* For Better or For Worse by Lynn Johnston, 1998. © Lynn Johnston Productions, Inc./Distributed by United Feature Syndicate, Inc. Reprinted by permission.

sexuality were noted frequently. In succeeding years, comments on emotional symptoms and psychiatric conditions declined. The 1980s woman was not warned to fear for her sanity. Instead, she was told to worry about such health issues as osteoporosis and heart disease (Chrisler, Torrey, & Matthes, 1990). The major trend in the 1990s was to portray menopausal symptoms as occurring at an earlier age. For example, a special issue of *Newsweek* on women's health featured an article on *perimenopause* (defined as the ten years before menopause), which was said to cause physical problems for women early in their fourth decade. In large bold type, the article began:

> It can masquerade as insomnia, moodiness, or depression. But physicians now understand that in the years before menopause, women ride a hormonal roller coaster. The grab bag of symptoms that it brings has a single underlying cause, so you don't have to take it lying down. (Begley, 1999, p. 31)

Social and cultural factors contribute to fears about menopause. For example, European-American women in focus groups were primarily concerned about menopause as a harbinger of physical aging and the ensuing disadvantages that accompany deviation from society's ideal of a youthful appearance. In contrast, African-American women viewed menopause as a normal, even welcome, part of life. Awareness of gender bias against aging women was prominent in the stories of both groups of women (Sampselle, Harris, Harlow, & Sowers, 2002). In a much larger cross-national survey, African-American women were also found to be significantly more positive toward menopause and aging than were members of other groups. In general, women's attitudes toward menopause ranged from neutral to positive (Sommer, Avis, Meyer, et al., 1999).

A woman's attitudes about her life influence her experience of menopause. Researchers have found, for example, that women who were satisfied with their physical appearance reported fewer menopausal symptoms. There was also a significant association between high self-esteem and fewer symptoms, but no relationship between estrogen levels or menopausal status and depression, misery, or headaches (Bloch, 2002). Women who were least satisfied with their marriage had significantly more negative symptoms during menopause

(Kurpius, Nicpon, & Maresh, 2001). Stress has also been found to be a better predictor of negative health outcomes among middle-aged women than menopausal status (Glazer, Zeller, Delumba, et al., 2002).

The Physical Signs of Menopause: Myths and Facts

There is a great deal of variation in the physical signs of menopause. A cross-national survey of nearly 15,000 40- to 55-year-old women found that symptoms could be separated into two groups: *vasomotor symptoms* (hot flashes and night sweats) and psychological and *psychosomatic symptoms* (anxiety, mood disturbances, and insomnia). Controlling for age, education, health, and economic status, European-American women reported more psychosomatic symptoms than other groups. African-American women reported more vasomotor symptoms (Avis, Stellato, Crawford, et al., 2001). The researchers used these data to argue that there is no such thing as a universal menopausal syndrome.

The idea that there is no such thing as a universal menopausal syndrome is supported by evidence from many cultures. In Japan, for example, typical symptoms include shoulder stiffness, headaches, and dizziness. These symptoms are considered part of the normal aging process and women are expected to "ride over" their physical distress. Mayan women in the Yucatan did not report any symptoms at menopause except menstrual-cycle irregularities (Beyene, 1989). In general, women in non-Western societies suffer fewer physical and psychological problems during menopause than do women in the United States. For example, no evidence of depression in menopausal women was found in fifteen non-Western cultures (Kaiser, 1990).

The Medical Model of Menopause: Myths and Facts

According to the medical model, menopausal symptoms are the result of a malfunction in which the ovaries stop working. From this point of view, menopause is a deficiency disease similar to the pancreatic failure that produces diabetes (Derry, 2002).

> By defining menopause as an illness, all middle-aged and old women are characterized as ill, a Y chromosome has become a necessity for well-being. (Gannon, 1998, p. 296)

Feminist scholars have criticized the medical model of menopause for many years. They have criticized the idea that normal aging is a disease, the confusion between aging and women's health issues, the assumption that women are a homogenous group with universal bodily signals of middle age, the lack of research on the connection between individual differences among women and so-called menopausal symptoms, the neglect of cross-cultural studies on middle age, and the idea that there is a "magic bullet" (estrogen) that can solve all the problems of aging women.

Recent research in medicine as well as in psychology has endorsed these criticisms. For years, doctors urged women in the United States to use first estrogen and then *hormone replacement therapy (HRT)*—a combination of estrogen and progestin, a form of progesterone—to avoid the symptoms of menopause and aging. But ovarian hormones such as estrogen and progesterone are potent substances that carry a number of risks. Although physicians believed that the benefits outweighed the risks, recent studies have indicated that this is not the case.

While women were being urged to take HRT to prevent heart disease, depression, sagging breasts, wrinkled skin, loss of sexual desire, and marital discord, similar symptoms in men were said to be due to natural aging rather than decreased levels of testosterone. General signs of women's aging have been confused with more specific effects of the decrease in ovarian hormones. Because these issues are so important to midlife women, we will discuss separately some of the signs of midlife change in terms of social and cultural factors as well as biology.

The Hot Flash

The most consistently found symptom during menopause is the hot flash. *Hot flashes* are usually described as sensations of heat, often limited to the face and upper torso, that can last from 30 seconds to 12 minutes. They are often accompanied by sweating (Sommer, 2001). Hot flashes are among the few menopausal symptoms that are successfully treated with estrogen (Gannon, 1998).

Hot flashes appear to be caused by fluctuations of the temperature-regulating center in the hypothalamus triggered by a decrease in the level of estrogen in the brain. Evidence suggests, however, that hot flashes are not completely controlled by hormones. For example, hot flashes begin before menopause in many women—frequently before their level of estrogen has declined to a critical level (Kronenberg, 1990). Moreover, although women vary enormously in the severity of this symptom, no relationship has been found between hormone levels and the number or intensity of hot flashes reported (Derry, 2002). Researchers do not know why hot flashes last only a few months in some women, whereas in others they persist for years or never occur at all. They are unrelated to employment status, social class, age, marital status, domestic workload, and number of children (Kronenberg, 1990).

The prevalence rate of hot flashes varies widely from culture to culture. For instance, Japanese and Indonesian women report far fewer than women from Western societies do (Flint & Samil, 1990; Kaufert, 1990). One study, using comparable data-gathering techniques, found that 69.2 percent of Caucasian women reported having experienced a hot flash at some time, whereas only 20 percent of a sample of Japanese women reported having had one (Lock, 1986). Women from cultures whose diet includes plants that contain natural estrogens (yams in the Yucatan and soy products in the Far East) report fewer hot flashes.

These cross-cultural findings illustrate how biological determinism can produce overly simplistic causal explanations. Hot flashes may be partly a function of a reduction in female hormones during menopause, but other factors also play a role. Hot flashes have been successfully treated using stress reduction techniques (Freedman & Woodward, 1992) and are also influenced by weight and diet.

Osteoporosis

A decrease in skeletal mass or in the quantity of bone characterizes *osteoporosis.* This reduction in mass is a major factor in the bone fractures found in older people. Some physicians believe that menopause is at least a contributing factor, and possibly the primary factor, in the development of osteoporosis, but this view may be another example of the confusion between menopause and the normal processes of aging.

Loss of skeletal mass with age is not found only in women. Both men and women begin to lose bone mass after age 35. Women are usually more prone to fractures resulting from bone thinning because they have less massive skeletons to begin with. However, men who live long enough for their skeletons to reach a critically thin level are also prone to osteoporotic fractures.

There is also no evidence that loss of estrogen is directly associated with the development of osteoporosis. Loss of bone mass in women normally begins during the fourth decade of life, well before menopause. No difference has been found in the level of estrogen in the blood between postmenopausal women with osteoporotic fractures and age-matched women without fractures (Edman, 1983b).

Weight, ethnicity, and diet are important in the development of osteoporosis. For example, the risk of osteoporosis is five times greater in thin than in obese women (Gannon, 1999). Women who have been anorexic are particularly prone to this problem. Ethnic differences are also significant. Black and Puerto Rican women in the United States have a lower incidence of vertebral atrophy and fractures than white women (Gannon, 1999). The less-affected women had a higher level of calcium in their diet. Asian women also appear to have a lower rate of osteoporosis than white North American women. In fact, risk for this disorder appears to be related to skin color—the fairer the complexion, the greater the risk (Doress-Worters & Siegal, 1994). In the last twenty years, osteoporetic fractures have increased in urban areas of Scandinavia to the highest rate in the world (Johansson, Mellstrom, Lerner, & Osterberg, 1992). Other factors associated with osteoporosis include low lifetime calcium intake, consumption of alcohol and caffeine, and smoking.

Exercise can reduce the loss of bone mass (Doress-Worters & Siegal, 1994). In fact, traditional gender-role differences in levels of physical activity may account for the greater risk of osteoporosis in women. Women from a lower socioeconomic bracket, with jobs that are more physically demanding, have lower amounts of bone loss than other women. Furthermore, men begin to lose bone mass in their sixties, the age at which men retire and drastically reduce their level of physical activity. An equivalent reduction in physical activity for women may take place in their forties, when their children leave home. Thus the connection between osteoporosis and menopause may reflect traditional gender roles rather than biology.

Individuals most at risk for osteoporosis are thin, small-framed, white women who smoke and who weigh less than 120 pounds (Edman, 1983b). Calcium supplements and daily exercise are less risky treatments than estrogen.

Coronary Heart Disease

Loss of ovarian hormones has also been assumed to increase the risk of coronary heart disease. Some physicians argued that because death from coronary heart disease is rare in premenopausal women and relatively high in men under 50, estrogens must protect women before menopause. The incidence of cardiovascular disease appears to increase disproportionately in women following menopause. However, the logic of this argument is flawed. The gender reversal is not due to a rapid acceleration of death among women after menopause but to a decline in male deaths with age. The drop may be due, in part, to a high incidence of early death in men who are genetically predisposed to fatal coronary heart disease. In fact, women never catch up to men in risk for coronary heart disease. Women in their forties and fifties have disease rates approximately 45 percent lower than men of the same age. This same 45 percent difference is found for people in their sixties and seventies.

It would seem to be a contradiction that more women die from coronary heart disease than men, although they have a lower rate of risk. The contradiction is explained by the fact that women, on the average, develop the disease seven to eight years later than men. Because there are substantially more older women than men, more women die of coronary heart disease, but always at a lower rate (Bush, 1990).

The erroneous connection proposed between hormones and heart disease in women illustrates the extent to which health problems in women are overly attributed to their reproductive functions. This emphasis on reproductive events leads researchers to ignore important social and cultural factors. For example, the ratios of males to females who die from coronary heart disease at ages 45 to 54 are two to one in Italy and one to one in Japan (Edman, 1983b).

Excessive attention to biology leads to less attention to other important risk factors. For example, smoking increases the rate of coronary heart disease for women as much as it does for men. It has been said that "women who smoke like men die like men who smoke" (Bush, 1990, p. 226). In the United States, the wives of men who develop coronary heart disease are twice as likely to suffer from heart disease as women whose husbands are free of heart disease. Unless coronary heart disease is contagious, this suggests a powerful role for environmental influences (Strickland, 1988).

The Myth of Emotional Instability

The stereotype of menopausal women contributes to an overestimation of the extent to which menopausal women experience bad moods (Marcus-Newhall, Thompson, & Thomas, 2001). Little evidence supports a connection between menopause and psychological disorders (Doress, et al., 1987; Gannon, 1998a). There is also little evidence that postmenopausal women are more depressed than younger women. In one study of nearly 600 women aged 45–54 years, menopausal status was not directly associated with depression (Bosworth, Bastian, et al., 2001). Longitudinal epidemiological studies indicate that depression during midlife is predicted by psychosocial variables, physical distress, and a previous history of depression—not by menopausal status (Dennerstein, Lehert, Burger, & Dudley, 1999).

Although no relationship between measures of mood and the level of ovarian hormones has been found, popular culture (as interpreted in comic strips) supports the use of estrogen for a variety of disturbances (see Figure 12.4). The media take their cue from medical and scientific "experts." One survey of medical and science-based journal articles on menopause from 1984 to 1994 found that both the presence and absence of women's hormones are assumed to make them crazy (Rostosky & Travis, 1996)! Estrogens are useless in dealing with

FIGURE 12.4. Estrogen is stressed for all kinds of women's disorders—real and unreal. *Source:* Us & Them by Wiley Miller & Susan Dewar. © Susan Dewar. Reprinted with permission.

anxiety, irritability, depression, or other negative moods. But women have been socialized to attribute their midlife feelings to menopause and aging, rather than to other stressful life events.

Consequences of the Medical Model

Overgeneralization of Pathology

Medical personnel encounter only 10 percent to 30 percent of all menopausal women. These women probably have more severe symptoms than most women do. Thus it is not surprising that physicians and nurses see menopausal symptoms as more severe and pathological than menopausal women see them (Cowan, Warren, & Young, 1985).

Women who seek treatment have more negative attitudes about menopause than other women. They complain about its unpredictability, their inability to control symptoms, and the loss of a sense of continuity in their lives. In one study conducted in England, women patients at menopausal clinics saw themselves as having completely changed with the onset of menopause—both physically and in terms of their personalities. They viewed their symptoms as some sort of mystery over which they had little control (Ussher, 1989).

Physiological signs and symptoms can be interpreted in a number of ways. Symptoms can also be experienced differently, depending on how medical authorities react to them. Physicians do not create physiological symptoms, but they can define which symptoms are important, which are to be disregarded, which should be treated, and which should not. The creation of a diagnostic category such as "menopausal syndrome" can lead physicians as well as women themselves to assign symptoms of stress to menopause rather than to social causes.

Hormone Replacement Therapy

Defining the normal changes of midlife as a hormone deficiency disease has serious consequences for women.

> Convincing women that their normal and natural development is flawed and requires intervention—that they should have large breasts, be safe sex partners, and have premenopausal levels of estrogen at the age of 70—engenders feelings of inadequacy and low self-esteem. When women internalize this negative self-image, they become vulnerable to a quick fix or fountain of youth. (Gannon, 1997, p. 262)

One consequence of applying the medical model to menopause was the widespread use of hormone replacement therapy (HRT). More than 20 million women over the age of 65 represented a lucrative market for hormones if women and their physicians could be convinced that hormones were a way of treating the ills of aging and staying feminine forever. And for years, many women and physicians were persuaded that hormone replacement therapy made sense.

In 2002, however, "The end of the age of estrogen" arrived, as a cover story in *Newsweek* proclaimed (Cowley & Springer, 2002). The article reported on a study of more than 16,000 healthy volunteers, ages 50 to 79, who were randomly assigned to receive either a hormone replacement pill once a day or a placebo. The study was cut short because those receiving HRT were more likely to suffer heart attacks and other cerebral-vascular accidents than those women who had received placebos (see Figure 12.5). The risk to any one individual was small, but small risks can have large consequences when a large number of people take them. Physicians now recommend that estrogen should be taken at the smallest possible dosage for the shortest possible time to treat a specific set of symptoms experienced by a minority of women, primarily for women who experience severe hot flashes.

It took too long for large-scale, solid research on HRT's actual long-term effects to be done (see Figure 12.6), but there was an earlier report of the World Health Organization that challenged the use of estrogens in treating

The Study

Among 10,000 users of hormone replacement therapy there were:

MORE
+7 Heart attacks
+8 Strokes
+8 Breast cancers
+8 Blood clots

FEWER
–6 Colon cancers
–5 Hip fractures

BOTTOM LINE
20 Extra adverse outcomes per year for every 10,000 users

FIGURE 12.5. Do you like these odds?
Source: Newsweek, July 22, 2002, p. 38.

FIGURE 12.6. The consequences of the androcentric bias in medical research.
Source: Rob Rogers. Reprinted by permission of United Features Syndicate, Inc.

menopausal symptoms. This report stated that in 70 percent to 80 percent of postmenopausal women, the level of circulating estrogens is sufficient (Ussher, 1989). The excessive use of hormones continued anyway. One important area for investigation is how the medical establishment came to endorse HRT, why its use continued, and how to prevent this kind of overmedication from occurring again.

Ironically, low income women of color may have been protected from HRT because they are more positive toward aging than white middle-class women and because they lacked access to a healthcare provider who would prescribe it (Appling, Allen, et al., 2000).

Other Voices: Nonclinical Views of the Menopausal Experience

Studies that examine women's accounts of their experiences of menopause find relatively little distress. Over and over, women described menopause by saying, "It was nothing"; "Nothing. Never had any problem. It just stopped, it slowed up"; and "Nothing. Just stopped and that's about it" (Martin, 1987, p. 173). The vast majority of older women respondents saw menopause in a positive light. They felt pleasure at avoiding whatever discomfort they had felt during menstruation and relief from the nuisance of dealing with bleeding, pads, or tampons. For those women who were sexually active with men, menopause meant delight in freedom from the fear of pregnancy.

Another study that asked women between the ages of 40 and 60 to write about menopause found similar results. The women's unconstrained responses were overwhelmingly positive (Logothetis, 1993). Women did not appear to experience menopause as if it were a separate episode in life similar to a major illness. Instead, interviewers had difficulty keeping older women respondents on the topic because they wanted to wander off from menopause to talk about many other aspects of their lives. (Martin, 1987)

Women's negative reports about menopause may be influenced by the kinds of questions they are asked. In a creative study of how both women and men may be influenced by the social setting in which questions are asked, attitudes were examined in the context of medical problems, life transitions, or symbols of aging (Gannon & Ekstrom, 1993). For example, one group of people expressed their attitudes toward a broken leg, a stomach ulcer, and menopause. Another group expressed their attitudes about menopause in the context of discussing puberty and leaving the parental home, and a third group responded to questions that included attitudes toward gray hair and retirement. The researchers found that the medical context elicited significantly more negative attitudes than the other two contexts. In general, women's attitudes were more positive than those of men, and their attitudes became increasingly positive with age and experience.

Attitudes about menopause have many similarities to other gender-related stereotypes (see Chapter 2). For example, women believe others have more problems than they themselves do. Attitudes are most negative among those women who have not yet experienced the event. Negative views of menopause may be a response to popular stereotypes or to what is perceived as the expectations of others about this life stage.

THE SOCIAL CONTEXT OF MIDDLE AND LATER LIFE

In the United States, women are typically identified by an adjective referring to the menopause—menopausal, postmenopausal, or premenopausal (Parlee, 1990). Physical symptoms are stressed, but women's own accounts are ignored. The reliance on biomedical causes leads researchers to neglect social context and to exaggerate differences between women and men. Gender differences are seen as important because other differences, such as ethnicity, class, and culture, are ignored (Unger, 1990).

Midlife, Power, and Status

Women who have the most positive attitudes about menopause perceive that it has given them more power to direct their own lives. In general, however, U.S. women lose power and status as they age. This loss of power appears to be a result, not of menopause per se, but of U.S. society's attitude toward aging. Women in all societies go through menopause, but cultures vary in their response to aging women.

For example, a study of fifteen non-Western societies found that older women in these societies enjoyed enhanced social status and political power. They were freed from taboos involving menstrual pollution; they gained seniority in their domestic unit, new role opportunities, permission to participate in traditional male domains of power, greater decision-making authority, and the respect and responsibility accorded to the elderly. As noted earlier, these women also suffered fewer problems during menopause than U.S. women typically do (Kaiser, 1990).

TABLE 12.2. The Structural Arrangements and Cultural Values Associated with Increases and Decreases in Women's Status after Childbearing Years

Increased Status	Decreased Status
Strong tie to family of orientation (origin) and kin	Marital tie stronger than tie to family of orientation (origin)
Extended family system	Nuclear family system
Reproduction important	Sex an end in itself
Strong mother–child relationship reciprocal in later life	Weak maternal bond; adult-oriented culture
Institutionalized grandmother role	Noninstitutionalized grandmother role; grandmother role not important
Institutionalized mother-in-law role	Noninstitutionalized mother-in-law role; mother-in-law doesn't train daughter-in-law
Extensive menstrual taboos	Minimal menstrual taboos
Age valued over youth	Youth valued over age

Source: From P. B. Bart & M. Grossman (1978), "Menopause." In M. T. Notman & C. C. Nadelson (Eds.). *The Woman Patient: Medical and Psychological Interfaces*, pp. 351–352.

Table 12.2 lists some structural arrangements and cultural values that appear to be associated with an increase in women's status after the childbearing years (Bart & Grossman, 1978). This increased status with the end of fertility or responsibility for child rearing may take the form of greater opportunity for geographic mobility, for example, or the right to exert authority over daughters or daughters-in-law, or recognition beyond the household unit (Menon, 2001). Studies conducted in Israel, Kenya, and the United States, however, indicated that only women with high economic and social status gain greater power with age (Todd, Friedman, & Kariuki, 1990).

Cultural Context and Midlife Transitions

> Irrevocable decisions of childhood, adolescence, and young adulthood shape the social context of middle age determining whether a woman will be surrounded by many children or one or two; whether she will be surrounded by grandchildren while she still has small children of her own at home; whether her family will be her primary concern or if she is likely to seek an outside job; if she does seek work outside the home whether she can hope for white-collar work or will be restricted by illiteracy to menial jobs. (Datan, Antonovsky, & Maoz, 1981, pp. 2B3)

The preceding quotation is from a pioneering study of midlife transitions for women in five subcultures in Israel. The participants ranged from a modern city-living population, similar to most women in the United States, to women living in a traditional nomadic tribal society. Other groups of women in the study were in various stages of the process of modernization; that is, they had been born or raised in a traditional society but were now living in a more modern one.

The basic question asked by the researchers was, "How is a woman's response to the changes of middle age shaped by the culture in which she has grown?" The researchers had expected that attitudes about the end of fertility would be shaped by the value placed on childbearing in a woman's cultural group. They hypothesized that middle age would be perceived most negatively by women in the most traditional groups, because their cultural role is defined largely by their reproductive and mothering roles.

Surprisingly, the study found that few of the women in any of the groups mourned their loss of fertility. Menopause was welcomed by women of all five subcultures, regardless of whether they had borne fifteen children or one. Psychological well-being at middle age was found to be highest for the most modern and the most traditional subcultures. Women in the transitional groups were least satisfied because they saw no choices for themselves among possible roles, although they recognized the broadened horizons open to other women. Women in the most traditional group appeared to gain power after menopause.

The researchers suggested that Western biases may have led some previous researchers to confuse tradition for passivity. For example, one traditional Arab woman described the measures she took to deal with menopause: She made use of free medical help in Israeli clinics, traveled to a gynecologist for the sake of the excursion, and consulted a faith healer.

All Older Women Are Not Alike

Cohort Effects

Sometimes women change cultures through the passage of time rather than by moving from one place to another. Women who grew up during different historical periods differ in their response to midlife and aging. An examination of cohort effects allows researchers to explore the interaction between biological changes and social roles. A *cohort* is a group of persons born in the same close time period—for example, within the same year or the same decade. Individuals of the same cohort tend to be exposed to the same broad societal events, which shape their life prospects and values similarly.

Consider the following cohorts of U.S. women:

- Women now in their 80s were born earlier than 1920. They were infants during World War I and young adults during the Great Depression. Their educational attainment is considerably lower than that of younger cohorts. Many probably never expected to live as long as they have. When they were born, life expectancy was 49. They are usually widowed, living alone or with relatives, and typically have insufficient incomes.
- Women born in the 1920s were adults during World War II. They might have enlisted in the military or worked in war industries, filling traditionally male jobs. Many returned to their homes after the war, but some juggled jobs, homemaking, and children. Many experienced drastic changes in

family structures and social networks as a result of mass migration from rural areas to northern cities. They are likely to have limited access to pension programs as a result of interrupted and uneven work histories.

- Women born in the 1930s are a privileged group who benefited from a booming postwar economy. Many entered professions, reaching maturity at a time when women had begun to combine work with families. Feminist ideas were discussed, if not realized. Having now reached retirement age, some plan to continue working outside the home. Others are caring for husbands or parents with chronic illnesses (Crose, Leventhal, Haug, & Burns, 1997).
- The most recent cohort of women to enter middle age are the so-called baby boomers (born 1944–1959). They were the first cohort legally able to control childbearing through effective contraception and legal abortion. Thus, they are the first generation of women who could plan a career without a high probability that it would be disrupted by an unplanned pregnancy (Grambs, 1989). The great majority of this cohort are high school graduates, and a substantial number have college degrees. For women of earlier cohorts, divorce was a shame and a scandal; for this cohort it has been an acceptable personal decision. Earlier generations of women were also much less likely to have lived alone or been financially independent as young adults than today's women.

Would you expect these cohorts to respond in the same way to life changes? It should not be surprising that a person's cohort provides a better prediction of beliefs, values, and behavior than chronological age does. A 40-year-old woman in 1940 cannot be readily compared with a 40-year-old woman in 2002.

Research on women is particularly influenced by cohort effects because women's roles in the past few generations have changed more dramatically than men's roles. For example, baby-boom women who adjusted work schedules to accommodate family demands had poorer self-esteem than their peers who had worked continuously. In contrast, older women (born 1931–1942) who had adjusted their work schedules had higher self-esteem than did their peers (Carr, 2002). These differences between different cohorts of women are probably due to changes in role expectations over time.

Differences between cohorts demonstrate that old age is not an isolated stage of life. The resources available to older women derive from the opportunities and constraints they have experienced over a lifetime. As women grow older, their lives diverge and they become more different from each other. Besides historical era, variables such as class and race or ethnicity also have major impacts on women's lives.

Older Women and Poverty

Thirteen percent of adults 65 or older are poor, and nearly three-quarters of this group are women. Nearly one-third of all older women have incomes near the poverty line (Browne, 1998). What accounts for these gender disparities?

Much of women's poverty is due to discontinuities in their participation in the workforce, lower salaries and pensions compared with those of men, and rural residence. Many groups of ever-poor women find themselves in poverty for more than half of their old age (Vartaman & McNamara, 2002).

However, relative affluence in middle age does not necessarily insulate women from poverty in later life. Nearly half of all widowed and divorced women over 65 had incomes below or near the poverty line. Widows have the lowest income of any demographic group in the United States (Rubin, 1997). More than one-half of poor widows were not poor before the death of their husband (Browne, 1998). Furthermore, older lesbian couples are often unprotected by policies that provide heterosexual couples with a safety net through social security, pensions, and health insurance (Motenko & Greenberg, 1995).

Because recent cohorts of women have had more years of work experience than the currently retired, one might expect that poverty in old age will be less likely for them. But little has changed since the data shown in Figure 12.7 were compiled. The income gap for retired men and women has actually widened in the last two decades because of gender inequities in income from pensions and financial investments. "Midlife women need to be vigilant lest when they reach old age they will be no better off than their mothers and grandmothers before them" (Grambs, 1989, p. 179).

Race and Ethnicity

Women from ethnic minority groups have shorter life spans and may be functionally old well before age 65. The burden of poverty is also greater for aging women of color. Black women make up 5 percent of the elderly population, but they account for 16 percent of the poor elderly. The poverty rates for Latinas is double that for white women (Browne, 1998). The median income for older Asian-American women is also less than that of older Euro-American women (Yee, 1997).

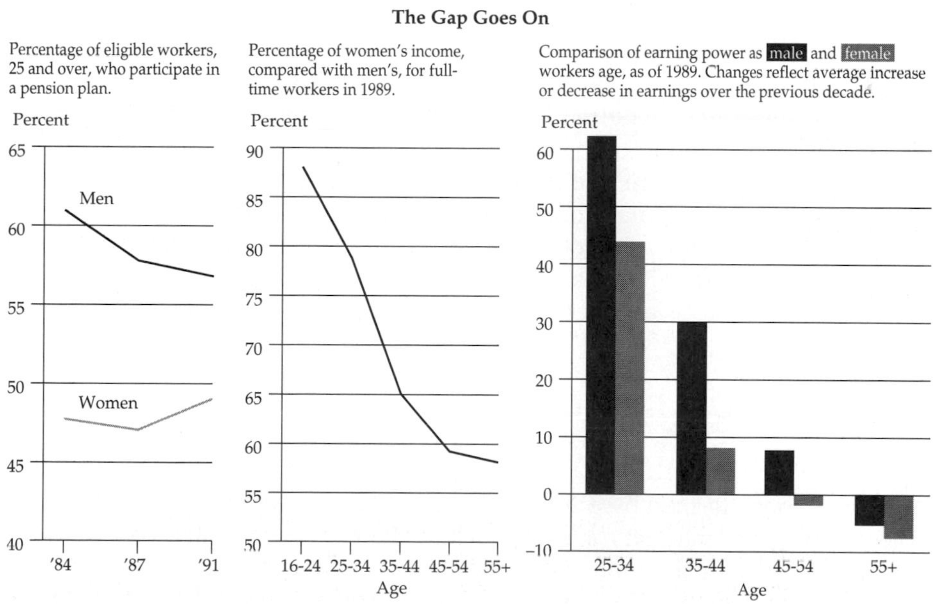

FIGURE 12.7. Women's financial well-being declines more than men's with age.
Source: The New York Times.

Although older women of color suffer a greater relative decline in health as they age than other American women, their relative deprivation in income and health is not necessarily linked to less satisfaction in life. Black women actually report greater life satisfaction than white women during their late middle age (Carlson & Videka-Sherman, 1990). African-American women have consistently been found to have the lowest rate of suicide of all age/ethnic categories (Canetto, 2001). Despite a lifetime of racism and poverty, they seem to view old age as a reward. Older women of color may be survivors who expect less than older women from more privileged groups.

These ethnic differences may also reflect the fact that social networks within minority communities play an important role in life satisfaction. Investigators conducting an in-depth examination of aging African-Americans living in low-income high-rise public housing found, for example, that almost everyone had received help from family, friends, or neighbors (Faulkner & Heisel, 1987). Women were significantly more likely to both give and receive favors than men.

Much of this support occurred in the context of religious activity. Older Native-American women were more likely to attend church and perform volunteer activities than were either Anglo or Latina women (Harris, Begay, & Page, 1989). Researchers often overlook religion as an important source of support for older women of all ethnicities and races. For example, church activities provided white widows with a supportive community as well as opportunities to overcome hardships, maintain friendships, and contribute to the community (Neill & Kahn, 1999).

Ethnic minority families place great importance on interdependence and the needs of the family over the needs of the individual. These values mean that increasing dependency in old age is not viewed as negatively as it is within dominant cultures (Yee, 1990). The majority of Asian-American women over age 65 are widowed, but they are less likely to live alone than non-Asian women. Like Mexican-American women, they are likely to share housing and receive help from an adult child (Yee, 1997).

Social support can be both a comfort and a burden. Black single women who have dependent children or other relatives living with them are more likely to have economic problems than those who live alone (Ralston, 1997). Nevertheless, families are also the most dependable source of aid.

Communal values may contribute to a feeling of entitlement among older individuals so that they do not lose their sense of self-worth when their needs are met by others (Faulkner & Heisel, 1987). This sharing of limited economic and social resources is a positive adaptation to the pressures of poverty.

HOW DO ROLES CHANGE IN MIDDLE AND LATER LIFE?

Midlife is characterized by a series of role transitions. Most people have many roles. These roles may be *relational*, such as the role of daughter, mother, wife, or grandmother, or they may be work related, such as the role of nurse, truck driver, or salesperson. During midlife, many roles begin to be redefined, resulting in permanent changes in an individual's life.

The Complex Nature of Midlife Role Transitions

Roles are not acted out in isolation from each other. For the midlife woman, the departure of her last child from home; loss of a spouse or other longtime companion; entry into, reentry into, or departure from the labor market; or acquisition of a college degree is not an isolated event. All these role transitions influence one another and interact with other events such as the aging of one's parents, the birth of grandchildren, and the new freedom to explore alternative lifestyles offered by retirement.

The consequences of life transitions are also influenced by their timing. Individuals are judged as being *on time* if their role behavior accords with cultural prescriptions for their age and sex and *off time* if it does not. Ironically, for a midlife woman, a lifetime of on-time events such as marriage and childbearing in early adulthood means being vulnerable to economic declines throughout the latter half of the life span. Being off time, as in entering an occupation early in one's work life and postponing marriage and childbearing so as to advance in one's career, usually predicts more economic security in later years (Long & Porter, 1984). Because psychologists have tended to focus on women who are on time in their roles, they may have developed an overly negative image of women at midlife. Little attention has been paid to older women in off-time roles. The next part of this chapter looks at both traditional and nontraditional midlife roles.

The Empty-Nest Syndrome: Is It Real?

For women who have followed a traditional lifestyle of early marriage and childbearing, midlife is usually the time when their last child leaves home. This period had been thought to be characterized by the *empty-nest syndrome*—depression after the youngest child leaves home, when a mother may feel that she is no longer needed by her family. This reaction, however, may reflect the expectations of particular cohorts of women. The concept of an empty-nest syndrome seems to have been the result of psychologists' focus on women who had been socialized in traditional beliefs about motherhood.

This conclusion was suggested by an interesting study that illustrated how changes in early socialization can influence role transitions much later in life. Researchers compared samples of women twenty years apart, so that the women were the same age when they were surveyed. They found that an "empty nest" was more likely to be a negative experience among the cohort of women who had reached adulthood during a time when society strongly emphasized women's maternal role. Women who came of age during the 1950s reacted more negatively to the empty nest than women who came of age during World War II, when many women were encouraged to enter the labor market. These results demonstrate that the empty-nest syndrome is more an effect of socialization during young adulthood than an inevitable response. In fact, the researchers argued that the current group of midlife women—who reached their young adulthood during the feminist movement—should experience the departure of their last child from home as positively as their grandmothers did (Adelmann, Antonucci, Crohan, & Coleman, 1989)!

This prediction appears to be confirmed by more recent research. In one study of women between the ages of 40 and 60, there was no indication of the empty-nest syndrome; instead, the women frequently communicated a sense of freedom from the responsibility of bearing and nurturing children (Logothetis, 1993). More recently, more than 400 women in Australia were followed for nine years during midlife. In the first year after the last child departed, women's moods and sense of well-being improved and the number of daily hassles dropped. The return of adult children did not have any impact on mood, but did reduce the frequency of sexual activity (Dennerstein, Dudley, & Guthrie, 2002).

The empty-nest syndrome may depend not only on early socialization but also on class. For example, in two successive samples of the alumnae of a private women's college, women in their early fifties often described their lives as "first-rate" and rated their quality of life as high (Mitchell & Helson, 1990). Empty nests, better health, and higher incomes were correlated with a positive quality of life. These women reported that after the children left home, life at home became simpler, they felt a greater sense of control over their lives, and they redirected their energy to their partners, work, the community, or self-development. These women were, however, in an economic position to make use of the opportunities that became open to them when their children left home.

Her and His Retirement

Retirement is a major life transition. Stereotypes of retired people include both positive images—of freedom, travel, hobbies, and leisure—and negative ones of boredom, withdrawal, and feelings of uselessness. The norm has been a male one. When people think of retirement, what comes to mind is the stereotypical male pattern of leaving at the top of a lifelong career. For women, whose work patterns and life goals may be different, this stereotype does not always fit.

Until recently, few women had enough years of continuous employment to afford the luxury of retirement. Many women of color remain in the work force after age 65 because they cannot afford to stop working. A majority of nonemployed older women did not describe themselves as retired, even up to age 74 (Bernard, Itzin, Phillipson, & Skucha, 1995). They have good reason not to do so. A recent study in Berlin found, for example, that women in their seventies spent more time working in the household than men of the same age. For older men, living with a partner was associated with having more leisure time; the reverse was true for older women (Klumb & Baltes, 1999). Older women continue to have domestic and family responsibilities so that "retirement," with its implication of freedom from the obligation to work, does not describe the reality of their lives.

Women are likely to retire at an earlier age than men and for different reasons. Men are likely to leave for work-related reasons, whereas women are more likely to leave for family reasons, often involving the care of a spouse or parent. One study found that wives caring for their husbands were five times more likely to retire than women who were not caregivers. In contrast, men caring for their wives were substantially slower to retire than those with able-bodied wives (Denninger & Clarkberg, 2002).

Married women are also sometimes pressured to retire at the same time as their usually older husbands (Carp, 1997). When the wife works and the husband does not, traditional gender roles are threatened. The woman's employment enhances her status and power and may put pressure on her husband to take on some of her household tasks. Women still in their primary jobs reported higher marital conflict if their husbands were no longer employed. Marital quality improved once couples settled into retirement (Moen, Kim, & Hofmeister, 2001).

Other women are forced into retirement by employers. Compared with men, black, Latino, and elderly women are more likely to lose their jobs in the years prior to retirement. The resulting periods of joblessness often become "retirement" (Flippen & Tienda, 2000).

In general, women do not plan for retirement. For example, interviews with 275 Canadian women over age 45 found that although family caregiving responsibilities and health stress affect the timing of retirement, pre-retirees did not perceive these factors to be important for the timing of their own expected retirement (Zimmerman, Mitchell, Wister, & Gutman, 2000). Women do less financial planning and less adequate planning than men do (Carp, 1997). This pattern might reflect women's traditional reliance on their husbands' income, but studies have also found deficiencies in financial planning among divorced and newly widowed women (Hayes & Anderson, 1993) and female same-sex couples (Mock, 2001). Money matters remain the domain of men.

The experience of retirement varies greatly among different groups of women. Homemakers often find their husbands' retirement problematic. They complain about the men's intrusion into their domain at home (Vinick & Ekerdt, 1992). As one joke puts it, "I married him for better and for worse, but not for lunch." Women who worked at jobs with low salaries had more adjustment problems after retirement than women in more highly paid occupations. The loss of the work role often resulted in poor self-esteem, and feelings of uselessness, loneliness, and isolation (Perkins, 1992). For working class and low-income women, psychological distress after retirement also reflects financial concerns (Choi, 2001).

Widowhood

Women are more likely to be widowed than are men, in part because of differences in the life expectancies of women and men and because women tend to marry men older than themselves. One study in the United States found that almost half of all the women over age 65 were widows. In contrast, only 14 percent of all men over 65 were widowers (Bradsher, 1997). Men who lost their wives were more likely to remarry than women who lost their husbands.

Responses to the loss of a spouse do not seem to vary much in terms of age, but they do vary with gender. Widows must acquire new roles beyond that of wife and learn to make their own decisions. Widowers do not seem to have trouble abandoning the role of husband (which may not have been fundamental to their identity), but they do need to learn domestic routines and to nurture relationships (which had been the responsibility of their wives). In some ways, "the women who have been disadvantaged over the life course compared to men have an edge in bereavement" because "elderly widowed women are adept at housekeeping and kinkeeping but elderly widowed men are inexperienced at these tasks" (Blieszner, 1993, p.178).

There are also gender differences in psychological distress. For men, depression was associated with the strain of household management (Umberson, Wortman, & Kessler, 1992). Depression in widows was associated with financial strain. These financial difficulties are not minor. One study found that, on average, widowhood reduced women's living standards by 18 percent and pushed 10 percent of the women whose pre-widowhood income was above the poverty line below it (Bound, Duncan, Laren, & Oleiniek, 1991).

Despite these economic disadavantages, women cope better with the loss of a spouse than men do. Compared with widowed men, widowed women report higher levels of happiness, life satisfaction, and home-life satisfaction (Gove & Shin, 1989). These data are consistent with findings showing that widowhood is a much higher predictor of suicide for older men than for older women (Canetto, 2001).

Loss of a Lesbian Life Partner

Lesbians who have lost their companions may suffer additional stress because the relationship is not publicly acknowledged. Women who have lost a lover may have to carry on without the usual social supports offered to widows. Even when the relationship is an open one, friends may not be aware of the depth of the loss. As one woman recounted:

> Recently, I vacationed with friends who had been friends also with my deceased partner-in-life. A guest arrived with slides of earlier vacations, including pictures of my lover. I objected that if I had been a man who had been recently widowed, they surely would have asked if I would object to showing the pictures. One friend responded that she wanted very much to see them. She blanched when I suggested she might feel differently after the death of her husband. Clearly, she thought that my relationship with Karen differed from her marriage; she evidently also thought my love differed from her friendship with Karen only by degree. Heterosexuals really do not understand what lesbians feel for their partners, even when they know us well. (In Doress et al., 1987, p. 139)

The loss of a significant other—female or male—to whom a woman has not been married is multiplied by the lack of any legal acknowledgment of the relationship. The lover of the departed person may find herself deprived of economic resources she has long shared. And, of course, she receives no spousal benefits of any kind.

CAREGIVING IN MIDDLE AND LATER LIFE

Being a Grandmother

A woman who has led a traditional on-time lifestyle of early marriage and motherhood is likely to become a grandmother during her fifties. This is a positive event for most women; they may look forward to having a less stressful relationship with their grandchildren than they had with their own children.

> Our three-year-old granddaughter has just left after a four-week visit. As the wildflowers in the juice glass fade, I try to decide which of the twenty-one crayon and watercolor pictures to keep taped to the banister. I rescue a 1950 miniature trailer truck her father used to play with from under the bed and hear her say proudly, "I'm bigging!" I see the world anew through her eyes and hope I'm still bigging too. (A woman in her seventies, in Doress et al., 1987, p. 133)

Recent evidence from the first international conference on grandmothers indicates that the benefits go both ways. Studies conducted in subsistence societies (with high levels of manual work done by women, with low income, and with little access to modern medical care) in Africa and Asia indicate that the presence of the maternal grandmother in the home increases the survival rate of her grandchildren. Surprisingly, the presence of a paternal grandmother had either no effect or a negative impact on children's level of mortality (Angier, 2002).

In a study of U.S. grandparents, only 8 percent of grandparents of either sex indicated dissatisfaction with their grandparenting role. Frequent contact with grandchildren predicted high levels of satisfaction. Opportunities to observe grandchildren's development and share in activities were considered the best features of grandparenting (Peterson, 1999). Lesbian grandmothers also take satisfaction from providing emotional support and varied experiences to their grandchildren and from providing support for the parent of their grandchildren (Whalen, Bigner, & Barber, 2000).

An increasing number of midlife women have taken on responsibility for the care of grandchildren because of the illness, incapacity, or death of the child's parents. Many of these custodial grandmothers report that they gain satisfaction from this role (Waldrop & Weber, 2001). However, grandparents who are primary caretakers also reported more physical and mental health problems than noncustodial grandmothers or those who provide supplementary care (Fuller-Thomson & Minkler, 2000; Musil & Ahmad, 2002).

In some ethnic groups, active grandmothering is common and considered normal. For example, black grandmothers are more likely than white grandmothers to have peers who also live with their grandchildren, to come from families in which multiple generations lived together, and to be receiving financial support. These differences may account for findings that suggest that white grandmothers experience more burden from their caretaking role than black grandmothers do (Pruchno, 1999).

Little attention has been paid to subcultures in the United States that value the wisdom and support of older women. Grandmothers are seen as the center of the Native American family and as the people who hold it together. The children are often cared for by their grandmothers (John et al., 1997). Similarly, in most Hispanic cultures, grandmothers are ever present and highly involved in family affairs. Chicana grandmothers are usually considered to be the backbone of family endurance and the symbol of cultural survival (Facio, 1997). They are presumed to have a great deal of practical knowledge and are seen as the family's advice giver and chief storyteller.

Lack of involvement in an extended family appears to be peculiar to white middle-class culture. In one survey of women over 60 in the American Southwest, only 14 percent of Anglo respondents, but 50 percent of Native American and 32 percent of Latina respondents, reported taking care of children (Harris et al., 1989).

Gender and Caregiving

Although the role of caregiver (especially being a grandmother) has many rewards, it is frequently invisible and usually devalued. It is also generally assigned to women. Women make up 75 percent of caregivers in the United States (Browne, 1998), and older women care for the most disabled persons (Canetto, 2001).

Our society assumes that wives will care for their incapacitated husbands (see Figure 12.8). Indeed, they may have little choice about the matter, and little attention has been paid to their emotional or physical needs.

> I cry a lot because I never thought it would be this way. I didn't expect to be mopping up the bathroom, changing him, doing laundry all the time. I was taking care of babies at twenty; now I'm taking care of my husband.
>
> People tell me he deserves all the care I can give him because he's such a nice person and was always so good to me. Well, I'm a nice person and have always been good to him—what do I deserve? (Doress et al., 1987, pp. 199–200)

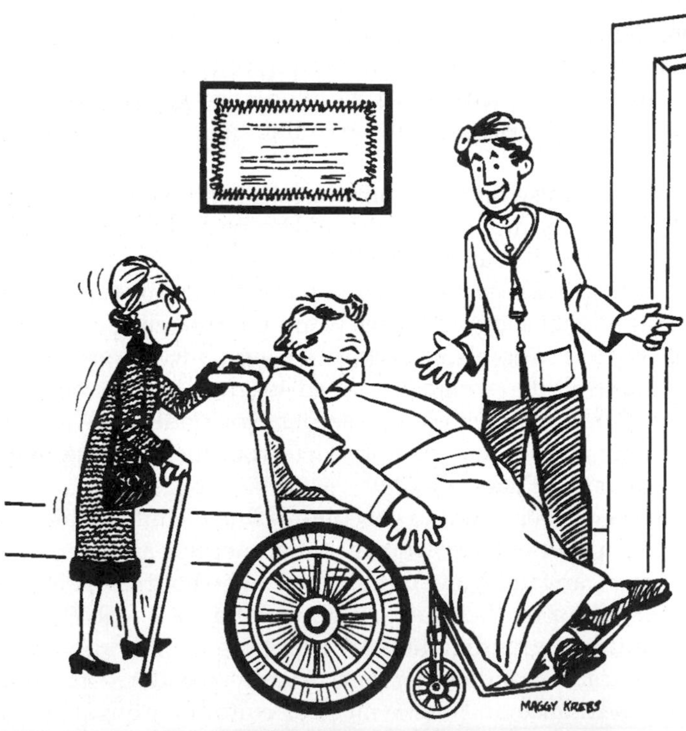

FIGURE 12.8. "Your husband is lucky to have you to take care of him at home, Mrs. Jacobs."
Source: Maggy Krebs from Paula B. Doress-Worters and Diana Laskin Siegal. *The New Ourselves Growing Older: Women Aging with Knowledge and Power* (NY: Simon & Schuster, 1994). Copyright © Paula B. Doress-Worters and Diana Laskin Siegal. Used by permission of the authors.

Women are also expected to tend to their elderly parents when they are ill, provide transportation to the doctor's office, and be on call for any emergency. A phone survey of 315 adults in western Alabama confirmed these gender-stereotypic assumptions. Both women and men agreed that it was more appropriate for an employed son to help his infirm parent with yard work, whereas it was more appropriate for a similarly employed daughter to assist with housework and to bring meals to her mother's home (Roff & Klemmack, 1986). When there are no daughters, sons do not necessarily step in. Daughters who were only children were found to be twice as likely as only sons to become caregivers (Coward & Dwyer, 1990). When sons did involve themselves in the care of their elderly parents, they were likely to wind up as care managers (Montgomery & Kamo, 1989).

In a study in Quebec, daughters also had more contact than sons with formal authorities on behalf of the elderly. Employed women provided as much care as unemployed women. The group that spent the least time on caregiving were single men with children and married men without children (Jutras & Veilleux, 1991).

Women may be unaware of the amount of elder care they are providing:

> Nora Dubchek lives two miles away from her widowed father. She works part time as a hairdresser, and her husband is a self-employed gardener. When she was first asked if her father had come to rely on her, she replied, "No, no. Only when he doesn't feel well. You know, I will sometimes take him to the post office, or drive him here, or go over and do a few things in the house." When asked how often she saw her father, however, she went on to say, "Oh, I see him every day. I was there this morning. This morning I did the dishes for him because he has a bad hand. And I just talked to him." Later in the conversation, it came out that Mrs. Dubchek did many other things for her father—she tends to home repairs, makes sure his house is properly cleaned, takes him places in bad weather, and nudges her brothers and children to make regular visits. (Stueve & O'Donnell, 1984, p. 217)

Another study found that male caregivers provided fewer hours of personal care than their female counterparts, but only about one hour less per week. Both men and women caregivers reported lost opportunities for promotion and career advancement (Mathews & Campbell, 1995).

Elder care takes an emotional as well as an economic toll. A meta-analysis found that caregiving had a greater impact on women than on men. The effect was not explained by how well the dependent individual functioned nor by the caregiver's degree of involvement (Miller & Cafasso, 1992). In another study, women felt much more burdened than men and had more health complaints despite being younger than the male caregivers (Pushkar-Gold, Franz, Reis, & Senneville, 1994). Caregivers have twice the depression rate of the general population, and depression is greatest for those taking care of a cognitively impaired relative (Tennstedt, Cafferata, & Sullivan, 1992).

The Woman in the Middle: Myths and Realities

Cultural demands that women serve others have become increasingly problematic for today's middle-aged women. Longer life spans have made it increasingly likely that adult children will need to care for aging parents. Only 45 percent of the oldest group of women surveyed (born between 1905 and 1917) had ever been caregivers. For the youngest group surveyed (born between 1927 and 1934), 64 percent were caregivers (Moen, Robison, & Fields, 1994). Because of smaller families, the number of daughters per mother has also decreased.

A new version of the problems associated with women's involvement in multiple caregiving roles is the conception of the *woman in the middle* (Brody, 1981)—the middle-aged woman who must cope simultaneously with the needs of elderly parents and teenaged children. Mary Pipher, a noted psychotherapist whose work with adolescent girls was discussed in Chapter 7, described her experiences during the year she was responsible for the care of her dying mother:

> That year, no matter where I was, I felt guilty. If I was with my mother, I wasn't caring for my own kids or my clients. If I was working, I was ignoring my family. When I was with my children, I thought of my mother alone in a faraway hospital. I got depressed and crabby. My husband and I fought more and my children didn't get the supervision and nurturing they needed. I got a speeding ticket. (Pipher, 1999, p. 9)

The burdens of the "woman in the middle" have been richly detailed by the popular media (see Figure 12.9), but this view may be a construction of mainstream society's preoccupation with autonomy and independence. Ethnic minority groups seem to have a more interdependent view of relationships between the generations. African-American women take relatives into their

FIGURE 12.9. An example of negative images of the caretaking role.

homes at twice the rate of their Anglo-American age peers (Beck & Beck, 1989). Black middle-aged women provide both economic and social support for older and younger relatives. Black elders are also likely to be supported by a variety of helpers rather than just one, as in white elder care (Doress-Worters, 1994). Although these practices are probably partly a result of economic necessity, they also provide psychological benefits for the elderly that help explain why older African-Americans are more satisfied with their lives than are their white peers.

Feelings about the personal costs of caregiving differ greatly from one woman to another. It is important that society permit women to have as many choices as possible, including the availability of support systems to relieve the primary caregiver. Caregiving can be rewarding, but also frustrating and alienating. Caregiving when a woman resents it or is overwhelmed by economic and social responsibilities is a great burden—one that our society has preferred to ignore. It may interfere with financial independence, personal development, and self care. Most of these negative outcomes result from societal assumptions that only women should and can provide care. Some researchers have charged that differences in the amount of caregiving are responsible for much of the gender inequality associated with aging (Browne, 1998).

PSYCHOLOGICAL WELL-BEING IN THE SECOND HALF OF LIFE

Growing older is neither all good nor all bad. Social scientists tend to do their research on the problematic areas of life, but life at midlife and beyond should not be considered merely a catalog of woes.

The Reentry Woman

Middle age may be a time during which women review their lives, examine their regrets about the family and career choices they have made, and, in some cases, make "midlife corrections." According to one study, women who transformed their regrets into life changes had as great a sense of well-being in subsequent years as women who had no regrets about their lives. Women who had regrets but failed to make changes during this period were more discontented. Their inability to make positive changes was not the result of external barriers. Instead, these women were impeded by a tendency to ruminate about their experiences (see Chapter 14) as well as a relative lack of instrumental traits (Stewart & Vandewater, 1999).

"Women's history is filled with stories about women for whom life began at 40 or thereabouts. Grandma Moses's late start was somewhat excessive—at age 78—but the fact that her serious work began late is not atypical for her sex: (Alington & Troll, 1984, p. 196). In some cases, misfortune serves as a catalyst for new kinds of achievement. Midlife achievement may also reflect a reduction in family responsibilities or other changes that give women a new opportunity to indulge their passions for personal achievement. Two-thirds of all adults who have returned to school (the majority of whom are women) reported that they had wanted to enroll sooner than they did (Schlossberg, 1984). They were impeded by institutional barriers, such as requirements that students take at least twelve credits during a semester or the lack of evening courses. Divorced women are disproportionately represented among the ranks of adult students (Alington & Troll, 1984).

Gender differences in interest in learning appear at midlife. For example, more women than men attend classes at the University of the Third Age, an international movement designed to help people engage in new endeavors during their last three decades of life (the third age). The so-called feminization of this institution prompted one disgruntled male scholar to complain that older women want to learn while older men want to "sit" (Williamson, 2000).

Many older women choose to do new things and expose themselves to new experiences. An exciting catalog of achievements was provided by one group of fifty-six women between the ages of 60 and 70:

> Emalu has published a book of her newly written poems; Betty and Laura took a study tour to Antarctica; Charlotte and her husband attend a different Elder Hostel every year; Bev gave herself a cruise in Norwegian waters for her 60th birthday; Laci is taking piano lessons and has given two recitals; Carol learned Italian before taking a sabbatical year in Rome. . . . Lydia Peyton tutors children in her granddaughter's elementary school. Lucille Parker, an African-American civil service retiree, helped create new projects at her senior center. (Siegel, 1993, p. 181)

Midlife can bring with it a sense that there is still much to do and options are diminishing; it is now or never, but not yet too late. Many women become more assertive and independent at this time (Lachman & James, 1997). As life expectancies increase and the health of people in their fifties and beyond improves, we can expect that the ranks of women who are off-time in their years of peak achievement will continue to grow. For economically advantaged women, midlife may indeed be prime time.

Sexuality at Midlife and Beyond

As they grow older, sexual activity decreases both for women and men. However, it is difficult to predict what sexuality at middle and old age will be like for the current generation of young women because they have grown up with different values and less restrictive norms than today's older women. A woman's past sexual patterns of desire and behavior appear to be the best predictors of sexual patterns as she grows older. For women who never, or rarely, enjoyed sex, menopause may be experienced as relief from having to be sexually available and active (Barbach, 1993).

Changes in sexual activity thought to be a result of aging may also reflect women's difficulty in finding a suitable partner or lack of privacy in living arrangements (Daniluk, 1998). Good sex for women over 70 has been linked to having good health and an interesting and interested partner. It is also linked to financial well-being: "For some elderly women who are struggling to survive, sexuality is simply irrelevant" (Gannon, 1994, p. 121).

The equation of youth and sexuality may also contribute to women's lessening sexual activities. Middle-aged women see themselves as less attractive than any other age group (Stevens-Long & Commons, 1992). It is not uncommon for middle-aged men to blame their diminishing sexual drive or problems in sexual functioning on their partners. Women may accept the blame, believing that their aging bodies are no longer sexually desirable (Daniluk, 1998). Older women find no validation of their erotic desires in the media. Sean Connery, a man in his midsixties, was recently voted the "Sexiest Man Alive" by readers of *People* magazine. The media may offer photos of Sophia Loren and Elizabeth Taylor, but it is difficult to imagine either of these women, or others of their cohort, receiving the designation of "Sexiest Woman Alive" (Daniluk, 1998).

Although midlife lesbians are less influenced by cultural pressures than heterosexual women, they are not free from them. They reported to one interviewer that their ability to be comfortable with the changes of age involved a conscious process of rejecting cultural messages that blame women for their failure to retain the appearance of youth. The changes of midlife also enabled some women to recognize their attraction to women. Almost half the sample of more than 100 midlife lesbians had heterosexual relationships at some point in their lives and had one or more children (Sang, 1991).

Friendship and Social Support

Perhaps the most important psychological factor in satisfaction during later life is connections with other people. Loneliness is one of the most feared consequences of aging. It is a major problem for women who live alone, especially if they live in small towns or rural areas (Adams, 1997). Nevertheless, older women seem to have an advantage over men in creating and sustaining networks of friends. Women of all ages are more likely than men to have close friends, to confide intimate matters to their friends, and to have a varied circle of friends (Adams, 1997). Their friendships help to maintain physical health, increase psychological adjustment and satisfaction, and contribute to psychological growth in old age. Women have closer networks of relatives as well (Antonucci & Akiyama, 1997).

Making a Difference

Maggie Kuhn (1905–1995), a lifelong social activist, was forced to retire at age 65 in 1970, but her most important work was about to begin. She met with five friends in similar circumstances and together they began an alliance called Consultation of Older and Younger Adults for Social Change, later renamed the Gray Panthers. Kuhn was a Gray Panthers leader until her death in 1995 at age 89. She and her organization took on issues ranging from pension rights and the hearing aid industry to the Vietnam War. Kuhn's charisma and speaking ability—she gave thousands of speeches around the country including several on Capitol Hill—attracted media attention and helped the Panthers achieve "a contemporary cultural revolution" in the form of nursing home and health-care reform and ending forced retirement provisions. Two weeks before her death, Kuhn picketed with striking transit workers. In her own words, "Well-aimed slingshots can topple giants."

Sources: Mority, C. (Ed.) (1978). *Current biography.* New York: The H. W. Wilson Co.; Graham, J. (Ed.) (1995). *Current biography yearbook.* New York: The H. W. Wilson Co.

Friends appear to be more important than relatives for many groups of elderly women. For example, elderly widows' contact with their adult children was found to be unrelated to morale, whereas contact with friends and neighbors was correlated with decreased loneliness, less worrying, and feeling useful and respected (Grambs, 1989). Ever-single elderly women are healthier than their widowed, divorced, or separated counterparts probably because they have maintained relationships with a supportive peer group of friends. Those who have been married report that their spouse is their preferred provider of most types of informal social support, followed by adult children. The effect of this dependency may be a less-effective support system for the formerly married at a time when it is needed (Newtson & Keith, 1997).

Relationships with friends may be important because they are voluntarily chosen and based on common interests. Interacting with friends is a boost to one's sense of efficacy and self-esteem in old age. Women maintain and widen their friendship networks even when they are limited in their mobility. In a study of elderly residents in a retirement home, the women relied on the telephone to keep in touch with old friends and made new friends in nearby rooms (Hochschild, 1978).

Women are probably being socialized for affiliation no less today than they ever were. We can predict that younger cohorts of women will continue to rely on their connectedness with friends as they grow older, and we can speculate that they will find keeping in touch easier with advances in communication technology. If it seems far-fetched to imagine Great-Grandma logging on to her computer network from her bedside chair in a retirement home, remember that future cohorts of elderly women will have grown up with such technology.

ACTIVISM AND FEMINISM AMONG OLDER WOMEN

Midlife is a time when many women feel freed from the constraints of femininity. Just at they outgrow their early roles, midlife women may also outgrow a need to conform to social pressures to be passive and self-sacrificing (see Figure 12.10). One study found that, in general, women in their early 50s saw themselves as assured, oriented in the present rather than the future, cognitively broad and complex, well adjusted and smooth in relationships (Helson & Wink, 1992). Women physicians reported some of the same changes as professional men, such as a greater sense of their leadership potential and better judgment and impulse control. These women also reported less concern for validation from others (Cartwright & Wink, 1994).

Another view of the freedom of middle and later life for women is shown in Figure 12.11. It is a work by Elizabeth Layton, who began her life as an artist at the age of 68 and won many honors. In this radiant self-portrait titled *Her Strength Is In Her Convictions,* Layton shows off a chestful of political buttons (Lippard, 1986).

As family and job pressures recede for midlife women, activism and political involvement of all kinds may increase. This will probably be especially true of cohorts of women now entering middle and later life, because they grew up with social movements such as the civil rights movement, the women's movement, the antinuclear and antiwar movements, and environmental activism.

FIGURE 12.10. These photos appeared with an article in *The New York Times* about women in New York City who want to retire, but remain part of its life. They are unusual because they portray older women who are neither frail nor anonymous. They are, however, economically well-off. Clockwise from the upper left, these women are Helen Iglesias (a founder of Thea) at her summer home in Maine; Nora Eisenberg; Nancy Biberman; Vivian Gornick (a writer who edited one of the first anthologies of women's studies) in her Greenwich Village apartment; and Vera S. Williams in her studio on West 12th Street.

Among women who became activists against social injustice, many connect their activism to their feminism (Duncan, 1999). Interviews have chronicled the activism of women leaders on issues such as toxic waste, neighborhood community life, education for disadvantaged children, auto safety, and nuclear

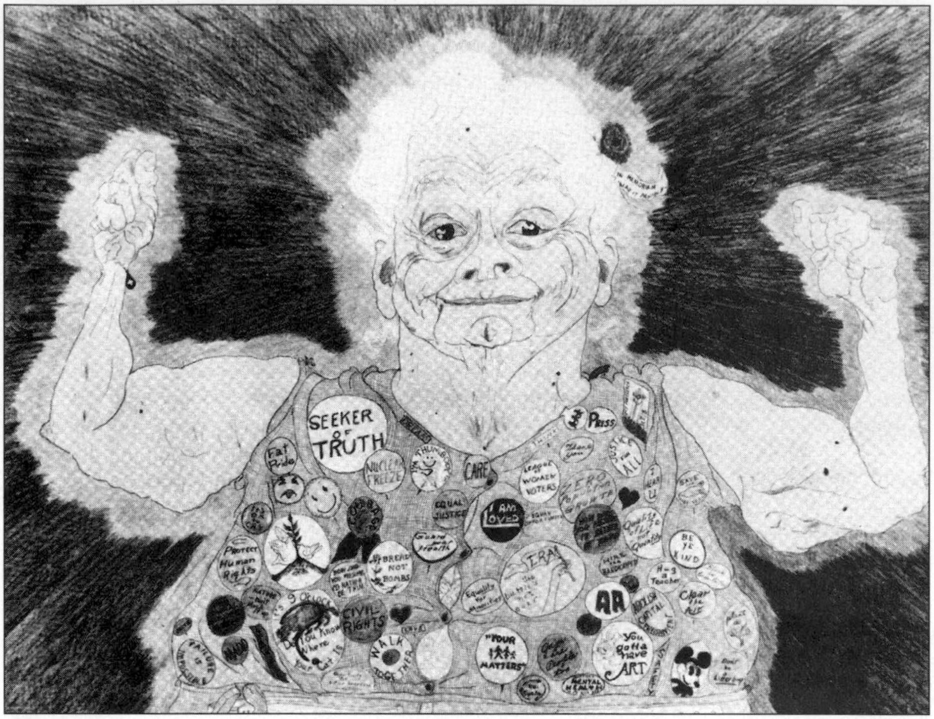

FIGURE 12.11. Older women as activists: an alternative view.

weapons. They conceived of their feminism broadly, believing that "everything is connected," and that social activism is a form of nurturing others. One reported that she had started seeing the nuclear issue in terms of her children; another said that she had never thought of herself as a feminist, but

> when I have to fight for my children, I do, and I guess I've always been a feminist in my own way; I've always fought for what I think is important. To me, that's what it means to be a feminist—being able to fight for your rights, your community, your children, and other women (Garland, 1988, p. xxi).

To begin understanding the meaning that political and social events have for women, feminist psychologists recommend the use of intensive case studies. In one such study of three women who graduated from college in 1964, several factors seemed to have influenced political consciousness in later life (Stewart & Gold-Steinberg, 1990). These included growing up in a politically aware family; political activity in adolescence and young adulthood; the desire to make a contribution to the world; experiences as a parent; and access at midlife to time, energy, and resources.

The political activism of older people is often focused on the position of the elderly in society. Activist Maggie Kuhn founded the Gray Panthers after she was forced to retire at the age of 65. The Older Women's League (OWL) lobbies effectively on policy issues affecting older women. Senior Action in a Gay Environment (SAGE) provides services and information for older gay men and lesbians (Macdonald & Rich, 1983). As women become more sensitive to their vulnerability in old age and more educated in public affairs, more participation and more leadership from older women can be expected.

In a powerful message to feminists of all ages who want to be active on behalf of older women, one older feminist cautioned that activism must be based on a real knowledge of women in all their diversity, not on stereotypes or a person's own fears of aging (Macdonald & Rich, 1983). She advised women not to talk about "the woman's movement" until all the invisible women are present, all races and cultures, and all ages of all races and cultures. She reminded her readers that an old woman has not always been old. She is in the process of discovering what 70, 80, and 90 mean. As more and more old women talk and write about the reality of this process in a world that tries to make them invisible, we will all discover how revolutionary that is.

CONNECTING THEMES

- *Gender is more than just sex.* Women's and men's lives are different because of sexism rather than sex. It is more difficult to make generalizations about people as they age because the cumulative effect of biological, social, and cultural forces creates differences within groups as well as between them. Both the timing and kind of roles available differ greatly, so that aging has very different implications for women and men. The gendered nature of these roles accounts for most of the inequalities between women and men found in later life.
- *Language and naming are sources of power.* The power to name is particularly clear in the identification of menopause as synonymous for aging. This has made aging appear to be more destructive for women than for men and has put women at risk for many medical procedures that cannot cure aging.
- *Women are not all alike.* Models of aging are based almost entirely on white middle-class women in the United States. Studies that look at aging across class, ethnicity, and culture indicate that gender differences in aging are not biologically determined but are constructed by a variety of social forces.
- *Psychological research can foster social change.* Social change is impeded by U.S. views of individualism and independence. Successful transitions from midlife to beyond are facilitated by social support systems and collectivistic philosophies. Middle-aged women's renewed sense of personal freedom and defiance of societal constraints can provide an important source of energy for effective social change.

SUGGESTED READINGS

COYLE, JEAN M. (Ed.). (1997). *Handbook of women and aging.* Westport, CT.: Greenwood Press. An excellent source book for information on diverse populations of women. Chapters are written by experts in each area and include many citations for further reading.

CRUIKSHANK, MARGARET (2003). *Learning to be old: Gender, culture, and aging.* New York: Rowman and Littlefield. This new book does a wonderful job of exposing ageism and showing how women internalize ageist ideology. Its feminist critique of aging studies ranges across many disciplines and provides much to think about for women of all ages.

DATAN, NANCY, ANTONOVSKY, AARON, & MAOZ, BENJAMIN (1981). *A time to reap: The middle age of women in five Israeli subcultures.* Baltimore: Johns Hopkins. Although we usually recommend much more current books, this book is a classic that was way ahead of its time. In analyzing how the meaning of the empty nest is socially and culturally constructed, this book goes beyond the particular cultures studied to show how researchers' beliefs about women influence the questions they can ask and the answers they can find. A wise blend of anthropology, sociology, and psychology.

GULLETTE, MARGARET M. (1997). *Declining to decline: Cultural combat and the politics of midlife.* Charlottesville, VA: The University Press of Virginia. Although this prize-winning book is about midlife for men and women, it is important reading nevertheless. This book wittily exposes the cultural construction of midlife and moves attention away from "midlife crisis" as a private psychological condition to a collective problem.

CHAPTER 13

Violence Against Women

This chapter was contributed by Jacquelyn Weygandt White, Barrie Bondurant, and Patricia L. N. Donat

Note: Chapter contributors are Jacquelyn Weygandt White (University of North Carolina at Greensboro), Barrie Bondurant (Radford, Virginia), and Patricia L. N. Donat (Mississippi University for Women).

- Analyzing and Ending Violence
- Connecting Themes
- Suggested Readings

Reading this chapter may be a distressing experience. You may realize, perhaps for the first time, that you or someone you know has been a victim of violence. Feelings of despair and anger may arise. This is natural. We, too, have experienced frustration, sadness, and anger while researching and teaching this material. But we are learning to turn our emotions into activism. You can learn to do likewise.

Though the magnitude of violence against women is alarming, awareness of the problem is the first step toward prevention. We cannot stop something we cannot see. Once named, violence against women, in its various forms, is no longer socially and culturally invisible. As noted in Chapter 1, naming is power.

One devastating consequence of gender inequality is violence toward women. Women are victimized by criminal violence (robbery, burglary, aggravated assault, forcible rape, and murder) and by intimate violence (child abuse, incest, stalking, courtship violence, acquaintance rape, battering, marital rape, and elder abuse). For many reasons, the risk of intimate victimization is significantly greater for women than men. Although strangers victimize women, women are much more likely to be victimized by someone they know. The consequences are psychological and physical, short term and long term. Assaults committed by someone known to the woman are often more violent and result in more physical trauma than those committed by strangers (Stermac, DuMont, & Dunn, 1998). Until recently, women shunned reporting incidents of intimate violence.

> Although most intimate violence qualifies as crime, a historical tradition that has condoned violence within the family has created strong forces toward secrecy. . . . The small proportion of victims who informed authorities attests that victims were silent. In fact, only 2% of intrafamilial child sexual abuse, 6% of extrafamilial sexual abuse, and 5% to 8% of adult sexual assault cases were reported to police according to recent victimization studies. (Koss, 1990, pp. 374–375)

Many experts have suggested that nations worldwide are experiencing an epidemic of violence against women. (World Health Organization, 2002).

A FRAMEWORK FOR UNDERSTANDING VIOLENCE AGAINST WOMEN

Jacquelyn White and Robin Kowalski (1996) proposed a model that integrates a wide range of factors that underlie violence against women and puts individual behavior in context. Their model describes five levels of interacting factors: sociocultural, social, dyadic, situational, and intrapersonal (see Figure 13.1).

The sociocultural level includes historical and cultural values. These values have been patriarchal, giving men a higher value than women and assuming that men should dominate in politics, economics, and the social world. The

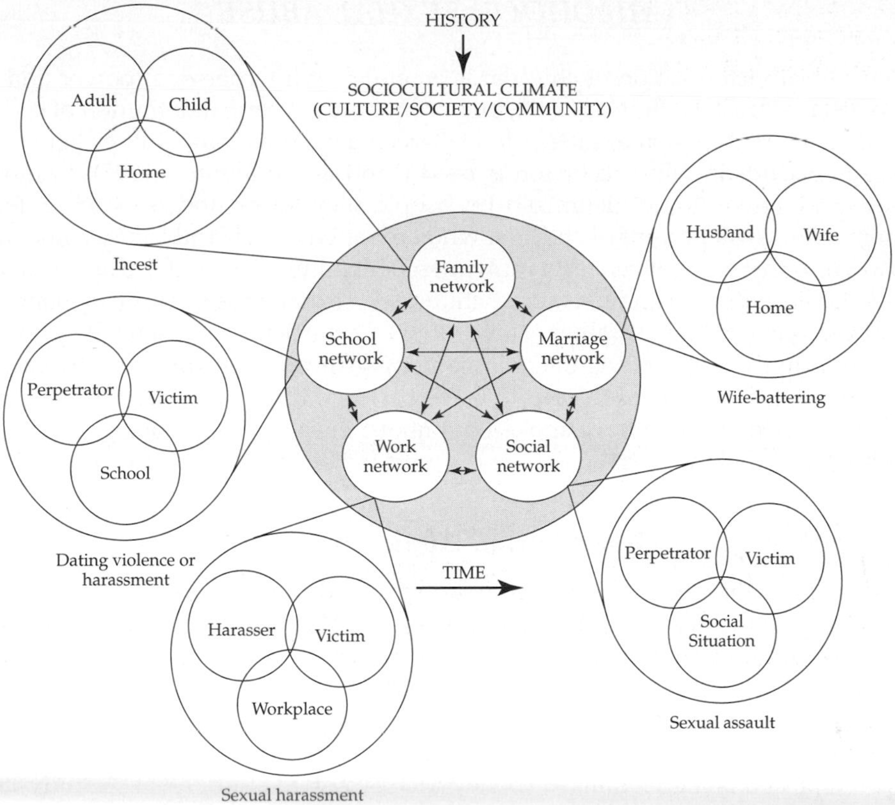

FIGURE 13.1. An integrative contextual developmental model of violence against women.

model assumes that patriarchy operating at the historical/sociocultural level affects the power dynamics of all relationships. Shared patterns of ideas and beliefs passed down from generation to generation define social networks, the second level of the framework. Historical and sociocultural factors create an environment in which children learn rules and expectations, first in the family network, and later in peer, intimate, and work relationships. Early experiences define the context for later experiences (Huesmann & Eron, 1995; Olweus, 1993; White & Bondurant, 1995). Individual violence is embedded in these gendered contexts. Power dynamics become enacted at the interpersonal level and result in the internalization of gendered values, expectations, and behaviors. Thus, cultural norms governing the use of aggression as a tool of the powerful to subdue the weaker combine with gender inequalities to create a climate conducive to violence against women. Violence against women is an assertion of patriarchal power and control that operates simultaneously at all five levels of the model.

Using this model as an organizing framework, we begin this chapter with a discussion of childhood sexual abuse, followed by discussions of courtship violence, acquaintance rape, sexual harassment, and wife battering.

The sexual victimization of children is an abuse of interpersonal power and a violation of trust. Definitions vary, but a commonly accepted definition of *childhood sexual abuse* is sexual interaction between a child and an adult or between two nonadults in which coercion is used (Rind & Tromovitch, 1997). In most cases, the children are victimized by people they know and trust to protect them. Almost 90 percent of children who are raped are victimized by someone known to them, 43 percent by family members (Greenfeld, 1997). The betrayal of trust is central to understanding childhood sexual abuse, its consequences, and the systems that sustain it (Freyd, 1997). In particular, patriarchal systems result in higher rates of victimization among girls and contribute to the barriers to disclosure of abuse. Despite these barriers, increasing numbers of survivors of sexual abuse have spoken out about their victimization. By refusing to be silent, these women challenge the patriarchal system (Brown, 1996).

Frequency of Childhood Sexual Abuse

Estimates of the frequency of childhood sexual abuse vary, depending on the sampling method and definition used. The best information to date comes from three national samples. One found that 27 percent of women and 16 percent of men, in a telephone interview, reported childhood sexual abuse (Finkelhor, Hotaling, Lewis, & Smith, 1990). In a telephone survey of children between the ages of 10 and 16, researchers found that 15 percent of girls and 6 percent of boys reported being victimized (Boney-McCoy & Finkelhor, 1995). A study using face-to-face interviews and a more restrictive definition, requiring physical contact, found similar results: 17 percent of women and 12 percent of men reported childhood sexual abuse (Laumann et al., 1994).

Making a Difference

In 1990, ***Katie Koestner*** was raped by a young man she was dating at the College of William and Mary. After an unsuccessful attempt to bring the man to justice, Koestner began speaking out publicly against this crime of silence. She presents her program, "He Said She Said," at campuses and conferences around the country, spotlighting the little understood crime of date/acquaintance rape. Koestner has appeared on "Oprah," "Larry King," and dozens of other television shows. She graced the cover of *Time* magazine in June of 1991. In 1993, HBO produced the docudrama, "No Visible Bruises: The Katie Koestner Story." Koestner coauthored the book *Sexual Assault on Campus: What Every College Needs to Know About Protecting Victims, Providing for Just Adjudication, and Complying with Federal Laws* (1995). Her lobbying efforts on Capitol Hill helped convince Congress and President Bush to pass the 1992 Victim's Bill of Rights. Since Koestner's graduation from William and Mary in 1994, her message has been heard by hundreds of thousands of students at almost 700 colleges. Through her activism, Katie Koestner has made, and continues to make, great progress in raising awareness about the damage of sexual violence and what we can all do to prevent it.

Sources: Profile: Katie Koestner, Founder of COS, www.campusoutreachservices.com/katie.htm., *Time,* June 3, 1991.

White women were more likely to have experienced sexual abuse earlier in their childhood than black women (Wyatt, 1985), but the rates of victimization by childhood sexual abuse are similar for black and white women, for Hispanic and non-Hispanic women (Arroyo, Simpson, & Aragon, 1997; Arroyo et al., 1997), and for Native American women (Robin, Chester, Rasmussen, Jaranson, & Goldman, 1997). Rates of reported child sexual abuse in the Asian American community appear to be lower (Futa, Hsu, & Hansen, 2001). It is not clear whether this difference is due to actual differences in prevalence or to underreporting. Researchers, however, have suggested that underreporting may be a particular problem in the Asian American community (Futa, Hsu, & Hansen, 2001; Hong & Hong, 1991; Wong, 1987).

Disclosure of child sexual abuse may be difficult for many reasons (Paine & Hansen, 2002). The perpetrator may threaten the child or warn that disclosure will result in devastating consequences. Children may fear that they will not be believed or that the perpetrator, perhaps a member of the family, will be incarcerated. The victim of incestuous abuse tends to feel overwhelmed by her father's authority and unable to resist. A conspiracy of silence within the family may develop. The family refuses to see the abuse, and the daughter may feel she cannot talk about the abuse for fear of betraying the family secret. The perpetrator also may convince the child that she is a co-conspirator and that the abuse is her fault. These barriers to disclosure may be further intensified among recent immigrants because of differences in cultural values and concerns (Tyagi, 2001).

Who Commits Childhood Sexual Abuse?

Most sexual abuse of girls (91 percent) involves men as sole perpetrators; 4 percent of abuse involves women as co-perpetrators with a male partner (Laumann et al., 1994). Only 7 percent of sexual contacts between adults and children involve strangers. The most commonly identified perpetrators are family friends and relatives. Within the family, 7 percent of women reported incestuous contact by a father, 7 percent by a stepfather, 9 percent by an older brother, and 29 percent by another relative (e.g., cousin, uncle) (Laumann et al., 1994). Asian American victims, in particular, are more likely to be abused by a male relative (Rao et al., 1992).

In addition, Asian American and Hispanic American children are more likely to be living in the same home as the perpetrator (Rao et al., 1992). The privacy of the home allows incestuous contact to be of longer duration, greater frequency, and greater severity; as a result, the consequences tend to be more serious than those of child sexual abuse outside the home (Estes & Tidwell, 2002). Hispanic children more often report abuse of a year or longer by a parent (Feiring, Coates, & Taska, 2001). Under these circumstances, the child is more likely to be entrapped in a continuing cycle of abuse and to be reluctant to disclose the abuse (Arata, 1998).

What are the preconditions for abuse? For abuse to occur, the individual must possess the motivation to offend and an ability to overcome internal barriers, external barriers, and the resistance of the child (Finkelhor, 1984). Incestuous relationships may show a cyclical pattern (Wolf, 1985; Simon-Roper, 1996). The perpetrator may gradually engage in increasingly inappropriate comments and behavior so that the child may not label the behavior abusive until substantial violations have occurred (Conte et al., 1989). Moreover, the perpetrator may use many strategies to induce compliance (e.g., purchasing gifts, attention, privileges). After the abusive incident, the perpetrator may experience transitory guilt and promise to himself and to the child that he will not victimize her again. This pattern of violation mixed with contrite, loving behavior perpetuates the cycle of abuse.

Who Are the Victims?

The risk factors for becoming a victim of child abuse are situational, not characteristics of the victim. Any child may be victimized by an adult family member, but several studies have identified family variables associated with childhood sexual abuse (Carson, Gertz, Donaldson, & Wonderlich, 1990; Edwards & Alexander, 1992; Jackson, Calhoun, Amick, Maddever, & Habif, 1990; Yama, Tovey, & Fogas, 1993).

Three key factors have been identified in sexually abusive families (Draucker, 1996; Whealin, Davies, Shaffer, Jackson, & Love, 2002). First, incest is more common in families in which members are emotionally distant—without intimacy, cohesion, or open displays of affection. Second, incest is more common in families with a rigid, traditional family structure. Fathers are the heads of the household, women are subordinate to their husbands, and children are subordinate to their parents. Obedience and control permeate all aspects of the parent-child relationship. Third, incest is more common in families with a number of conflictual relationships, particularly between parents.

Several risk factors relate specifically to the father or stepfather in the family. Children living without a father or with a stepfather are more likely to become the victims of incest (Finkelhor, 1984). Not only are girls who have stepfathers more likely to be abused by the stepfather himself, but also they are more vulnerable to abuse by other men if there is no father in the home. Before and after the mother's remarriage, girls may face increased risk from a variety of unfamiliar men as the new spouse introduces his friends to the family.

Until recently, mothers were often blamed for colluding in their children's abuse (Green, 1996). Recent studies do not support the concept of collusion (e.g., Deblinger, Hathaway, Lippman, & Steer, 1993; Peterson, Basta, & Dykstra, 1993). Mothers of children who have been sexually abused do not display higher levels of psychopathology and often are proactive in responding. Most mothers believe their children's reports of abuse and take action to protect them (Joyce, 1997). Future research may need to consider social and cultural factors that enhance or limit a mother's ability to believe and protect her child from abuse.

Consequences for the Survivor

Children who are victimized often feel powerless to stop the abuse and feel they have nowhere to turn for help, comfort, and support. The child's ability to confront and refuse sexual contact is overwhelmed by loyalty and trust. The adult is in a position of authority and has a great deal of control over the child's life. Perpetrators often select emotionally vulnerable children and establish a trusting relationship with them (Paine & Hansen, 2002). They communicate to the child that the behavior is part of an exclusive, secret relationship. The perpetrator may even come to believe and attempt to convince the child that the relationship is a mutually loving and caring one (Gilgun, 1995). For children who may otherwise be neglected and emotionally isolated, the special attention and inappropriate sexual contact with the adult may be confusing. (See Box 13.1.)

Responses to sexual abuse vary. Some children develop very successful coping strategies for isolating the abuse; other children develop self-destructive strategies to cope with their pain. The immediate effects of sexual abuse may be seen in children's emotional, social, cognitive, and physical functioning (Kendall-Tackett, 2001). For example, children who are victims of sexual abuse may have difficulty in school. They may fear going to bed at night, wet the bed, and may have nightmares. They may fear being alone and may cry hysterically when left with the perpetrator. As adolescents, they may be more likely to exhibit signs of depression and social withdrawal. They also may be more likely to run away from home, to be sexually active, and to contemplate suicide (Johnson, 2001).

Although survivors may remain silent as children, the abuse may resurface in adulthood. Adult survivors may be reminded of their abuse when seeing a family member again, looking at pictures, watching a movie about incest, being sexually victimized again, or having children reach the same age they were when they were abused. "Abuse is not destiny, but it does make progress toward successful social, interpersonal, and intrapsychic functioning in adult life more difficult" (Mullen, 1993, p. 431).

Box 13.1 Recovery of Repressed Memories

Recently, controversy has flared in the media regarding whether repressed memories of childhood sexual abuse can be recovered years after the abuse. On one side of the debate, reports of childhood sexual abuse uncovered during the course of psychotherapy are accepted as truth. On the other side of the debate, accused abusers are claiming that these recovered memories are, in fact, false memories created by highly suggestive therapeutic techniques, such as hypnotism and age regression, and that the clients of therapists who used these techniques are suffering from a false memory syndrome.

Unfortunately, there has not been enough research to date to resolve the controversy. Moreover, real cases of childhood sexual abuse may be discounted amid the controversy. Laboratory studies show that, depending on the circumstances, memories can be recalled accurately, memories can be distorted, or memories can be created. However, for ethical reasons, laboratory research cannot deal with memories of the same traumatic nature as childhood sexual abuse. Before the possibility of false memory syndrome can be accepted, further research is needed to

- determine whether a distinction between repression and ordinary forgetting is meaningful and what the nature of the differences is;
- clarify the diagnostic criteria for a "false memory syndrome" and determine its clinical usefulness; at present, such a syndrome does not exist in the *Diagnostic and Statistical Manual of the American Psychiatric Association;*
- evaluate the legal criteria for establishing the validity of repressed memories; for example, a therapist may be more interested in how a person interprets what has happened while the legal system is more interested in observable, verifiable behaviors;
- explore repression and ordinary forgetting in accused perpetrators as well as abuse survivors; and
- explore the effects of an unequal distribution of power in child abuse relationships on memory.

Many women (70%) report that childhood abuse significantly affected the rest of their lives (Laumann et al., 1994). The most commonly reported psychological effects include shame and guilt, fear, disgust, distrust, feelings of isolation, hostile and aggressive feelings toward the perpetrator, and anxiety (Rind & Tromovitch, 1997). Some studies have found that childhood sexual abuse can impair adult relationships and sexual functioning (Davis & Petretic-Jackson, 2000; DiLillo, 2001). Rates of mental health symptoms also are greater among women who experienced childhood sexual abuse (Banyard, Williams, & Siegel, 2001; Paolucci, Genuis, & Violato, 2001; Smolak & Murnen, 2002). In addition, victimization as a child is related to increased risk of victimization as an adult (Humphrey & White, 2000; Messman-Moore & Long, 2000). The effects of abuse for some survivors remain part of their lives:

> People have said to me, "Why are you dragging this up now?" Why? WHY? Because it has controlled every facet of my life. It has damaged me in every possible way. It has destroyed everything in my life that has been of value . . . It's prevented me from being able to love clearly . . . I don't care if it happened 500 years ago! It's influenced me all the time, and it does matter. It matters very much. (Lavender in Bass & Davis, 1988, p. 33)

Although the psychological impact can be very serious, many victims of incest use coping strategies that allow them to protect their personal integrity (DiPalma, 1994). During in-depth interviews, many incest survivors demonstrated great inner strength and determination. As child victims, these women used realistic, future-oriented fantasies to find relief from their pain and to escape their identity as a victim. Some focused their energy toward academic achievements. Others used creative outlets (e.g., writing, drama, music, dance) to enhance their ability to cope. Their strategies demonstrate that survivors have strengths as well as vulnerabilities.

Steps to Protect Children and Treat Victims

Protection of children from abuse has been a focus of national attention in recent years. Schools are educating teachers about the signs of physical and sexual abuse. They also are teaching children to distinguish appropriate and inappropriate touch and to say no to someone who is abusive, and they are encouraging children to tell a teacher, parent, or adult friend when someone touches them inappropriately (Wurtele, 2002). Doctors also are being trained to identify signs of child sexual abuse and to conduct the necessary tests to verify sexual abuse.

Many adult survivors are becoming aware of their victimization and seeking help from therapists, support groups of other survivors, and books. Survivors report that others can help by believing their stories and by allowing them to talk about what happened and their feelings (Nelson-Gardell, 2001). Group therapy, in particular, may be helpful for survivors. Many women find ways to heal.

> I don't know if I will ever be completely healed. It's like there was a wound and it healed over, but it was still infected in there. It needed to be lanced and cleaned out so that a good healthy scar tissue could grow over it. I knew

> that once that scar tissue grew, it wouldn't be very pleasant to look at, but it wouldn't hurt anymore. It would be raised, and you would know it was there, but you could touch it and it wouldn't be painful. And I think that's how it is. I have scars, but they don't hurt. They're cleaned out now. (Bass & Davis, 1988, p. 167)

COURTSHIP VIOLENCE

Young people usually begin dating in high school, although children as young as kindergartners talk about having boyfriends and girlfriends. The idea of being paired with a member of the other sex is pervasive in our society. Dating offers opportunities for companionship, status, sexual experimentation, and conflict resolution. Ideally, a pattern of healthy relationships emerges. However, courtship has a different meaning for young women and men (Lloyd, 1991). See Box 13.2. Whereas for men courtship involves themes of "staying in control," for women, themes involve "dependence on the relationship." Inevitably, as a relationship develops, conflicts arise. How do young people deal with conflicts?

Unfortunately, the research evidence is clear. Violence is a frequent reaction to the confusion and anger young people experience in heterosexual conflicts. Violence is also a tactic used to gain control in a relationship.

> When I was 16 my boyfriend of two years began to hit me . . . I spent most of my time covering up for him—putting make-up on my bruises, going into the hospital under an assumed name (for a cracked rib). I was afraid to tell my friends because I was embarrassed. I didn't want to tell my father because I

Box 13.2 Teenager Glad She's Rid of Abusive Boyfriend

Dear Ann Landers: I know you've written a lot about battered women, but most people aren't aware that teenage girls can be battered, too.

I began dating a terrific-looking guy when I was 16. He was really cool and had his own car. A year later, I was scared to death of him. I didn't dare tell my family for fear they'd make me stop seeing him, and I didn't want to. If I broke one of his rules, he would beat me up. Once, when I wore my jeans too tight (according to him), he locked me in the trunk of his car. I thought I would suffocate to death. It was a horrible experience.

My family knew nothing of the hell he put me through. He made an effort to put the bruises where no one would see them. On the rare occasion when they were visible (like a black eye), I would tell people I had had an accident.

I was the ideal child—I had straight As, got home on time, did all my household chores, and never gave my parents any trouble. It wasn't until I attempted suicide at the age of 18, and then got some great counseling, that I began to understand how he had taken control of my life.

Ann, please print this letter and alert teenage girls and their parents to this potentially dangerous situation. No one would have guessed such a thing was going on in my life. I realized that I wasn't alone when I met other girls in the support group who were just like me.—Lucky to Be Out of It.

Dear Lucky: This is not the first letter I've printed from a teenager who was battered by her boyfriend. My advice has been to get out at once. No guy is worth it.

Since this was published, many resources for teens are now available at local domestic violence services and on the Web.

Source: By permission of Esther P. Lederer and Creators Syndicate, Inc.

knew he would fight violence with violence. I couldn't tell my mother because she was beaten by my father when she was younger. I felt helpless and alone. (Anonymous student).

Courtship violence, dating violence, and *premarital violence* are all terms that refer to aggression between unmarried adolescents or young adults in dating-like relationships. Researchers have studied the gamut of aggression, from verbal aggression, such as screaming and name-calling, to stalking and physical violence involving the use of weapons.

Frequency of Courtship Violence

Depending on the definition used, rates of courtship violence range from a low of 6 percent, when the definition includes only severe physical aggression, to a high of almost 90 percent, when the definition includes all forms of aggression. Over the past decade, rates of verbal and physical aggression in dating relationships have remained fairly constant. *Verbal aggression,* which includes screaming and name-calling, is a common experience. A national survey of approximately 2,600 college women and 2,100 college men in 1991 revealed that within the year prior to the survey, 81 percent of the men and 88 percent of the women had engaged in some form of verbal aggression, either as perpetrator or victim (White & Koss, 1991). A decade later the rates were similar (Shook et al., 2000). *Psychological abuse,* which is similar to verbal aggression and involves intimidation, is frequently experienced by women and men (Jackson, Cran, Seymour, 2000). Rates of *physical aggression*—which includes hitting, pushing, shoving, and more serious aggression—remain around 30–40 percent (White & Koss, 1991; Hall, 2002).

Studies also indicate that courtship violence during the teen years is pervasive, with as many as 35 percent of female and male students surveyed reporting at least one episode (O'Keeffe, Brickopp, & Chew, 1986). Fewer experience recurring violence (Burcky, Reuterman, & Kopsky, 1988). Courtship violence is also evident across regions (Spencer & Bryant, 2000), types of schools (White & Koss, 1991; Clark, Beckett, Wells, & Dungee-Anderson, 1994), and ethnic groups (Agbayani-Siewert & Flanagan, 2001; Coker et al, 2000; Baldassano, 2001).

Who Inflicts and Sustains Courtship Violence?

Just as many women as men report that they engage in physical aggression toward a dating partner. These findings are fueling ardent debate. Some suggest that women are just as aggressive as men (Archer, 2000); others argue that comparable frequencies in reported aggression do not mean that there are no gender-related differences in aggression (White, Smith, Koss, & Figueredo, 2000).

When the motives for violence and consequences are considered, gender-related differences are clear. Although both women and men initiate violence, women are more likely than men to sustain serious injury. Men are two to four times more likely to use the severe forms of violence, and women are three to four times more likely to report injuries (Makepeace, 1983; Sugarman & Hotaling, 1989). Women are much more likely to experience fear than men as a result of a partner's aggressive behavior. Although both women and men report self-defense as a motive (Harned, 2001), men's motives for violence also often involve a desire to intimidate and control the relationship, whereas women report being aggressive as a result of loss of control (Campbell, 1992). Anger and jealousy are reported more often by women than men (Harned, 2001).

Studies of the underlying processes involved in courtship violence also show that they are different for women and men. The most recent work identifies different types of perpetrators of courtship violence and different psychological mechanisms linking childhood experiences to courtship violence.

Three types of perpetrators of dating violence are relationship-only, violent/antisocial, and histrionic/preoccupied. *Relationship-only* perpetrators appear the most "normal"; they engage in only mild psychological and physical abuse and are not aggressive outside the dating relationship (Monson & Langhinrichsen-Rohling, 2002). About half of the cases of dating violence can be ascribed to relationship-only perpetrators.

In contrast, the *violent/antisocial* type is responsible for about 20 percent of all cases and is most likely to be a male. These individuals are likely to be aggressive inside as well as outside the dating relationship and to have witnessed domestic violence and parental physical punishment. They are likely to have an arrest record for acting out: they also are likely to abuse alcohol and to show patterns of antisocial behavior and deficits in ability to form social relationships.

Finally, the *histrionic/preoccupied* type is responsible for about 30 percent of all cases of dating violence and is likely to be female. This type is likely to have experienced childhood sexual abuse and parental physical punishment. In relationships, this type also tends to be intensely expressive, reactive, and dependent.

In the past five years, there has been an explosion of research on how developmental experiences differentially affect women's and men's likelihood of engaging in dating violence. Summarizing this body of work is complicated by the fact that studies use different variables. They may examine only males or only females, high school students, college students, or high-risk groups such as bullies or students in drop-out-prevention programs. Some examine only one form of dating violence. In spite of these variations, some tentative conclusions are possible.

The best predictor of being aggressive is having an aggressive partner (Bookwala & Frieze, 1992; White, Merrill, & Koss, 1999). Violence begets violence. Growing up in a dysfunctional family increases young people's risk of becoming involved with delinquent peers and developing unhealthy understandings of gender, relationships, and strategies for resolving conflicts. Learning about violence in the home and associating with peers who endorse the use of violence may provide a backdrop of social norms that legitimate violence. Violence is learned as a tactic of dealing with interpersonal conflict (White & Kowalski, 1998; Wolfe & Feiring, 2000).

For men in particular, dating violence is associated with being quick to react to anger, believing that violence will aid in winning an argument, and having successfully used violence in other situations (Riggs & Caufield, 1997;

White, Koss, & Kissling, 1991). Other predictors of dating violence include drug use, divorced parents, stressful life events, beliefs that violence between intimates is justifiable, and less-traditional gender-role attitudes (Bookwala & Frieze, 1992; Tontodonato & Crew, 1992). Similarities between men who engage in courtship violence and wife-batterers have been found (Ryan, 1995).

For women, anxiety, depression (White et al., 1991), and drug use (Tontodonato & Crew, 1992), as well as drinking within three hours of the violent episode (Shook et. al., 2000) have been related to courtship violence. Childhood maltreatment may result in increased *rejection sensitivity (RS)* in women—the tendency to expect, readily perceive, and intensely react to rejection (Purdie & Downey, 2000). Rejection sensitivity, in turn, has been associated with insecurity and hostility in relationships. For females, parental abuse is a stronger predictor of dating violence than sibling abuse (and vice versa for males) (Simonelli, Mullis, Elliott, & Pierce, 2002).

Romantic relationships may become "destructive traps" for women when they feel they must put maintenance of the relationship above their own self-interests (Carey & Mongeau, 1996). Women who experience ongoing victimization are often more committed and in love with their partner, less likely to end the relationship because of abuse, and also allow their partner to control them, compared to nonvictimized women. These women also report more traditional attitudes toward women's roles, justify their abuse, and tend to romanticize relationships and love (Follingstad et al., 1992).

When Does Courtship Violence Occur?

Courtship violence is most likely to occur in private settings (Laner, 1983; Roscoe & Kelsey, 1986) and on weekends (Olday & Wesley, 1983). Violence is more likely to occur in serious than in casual relationships (Pedersen & Thomas, 1992). Violence in committed relationships may reflect the acceptance of violence as a legitimate mode of conflict resolution (Billingham, 1983). In contrast, violence in a developing relationship may be a way of "testing the relative safety of a relationship before movement to greater commitment is risked" (Billingham, 1983, p. 288). In a large percentage of committed, violent relationships, the violence occurs more than once, the couples stay together, and some even feel the relationship improved as a result of the violence. Some interpret violence as a sign of love (Cate, Henton, Koval, Christopher, & Lloyd, 1982). Although students believe that courtship violence is less acceptable than peer violence (Cauffman, Feldman, Arnett-Jensen, & Arnett-Jensen, 2000), many believe that violence is more acceptable in serious than in casual relationships and is not sufficient grounds for ending the relationship (Bethke & DeJoy, 1993). Violence is more likely in relationships plagued by problems that result in confusion and anger (Sugarman & Hotaling, 1989). These problems include jealousy, fighting, interference from friends, lack of time together, breakdown of the relationship, and difficulties outside the relationship (Riggs, 1993), as well as disagreements about drinking and sexual denial (Roscoe & Kelsey, 1986).

One recent model of courtship aggression includes background factors and situational factors (Riggs & O'Leary, 1989; 1996). Background factors that increase the likelihood of courtship aggression include the observation of physical aggression by parents and the experience of childhood physical abuse. These experiences contribute to the establishment of a pattern of aggressive behavior, to the acceptance of aggression, and to the development of an impulsive, aggressive personality style. Situational factors that influence courtship violence include characteristics of the relationship (such as relationship satisfaction and communication patterns), expectations about the outcome of aggression, stress, alcohol use, and the partner's use of aggression. Situational factors increase the likelihood of conflict in relationships, which in turn increases the likelihood that aggression will be used to resolve the conflict. Personal history may be more important for women than for men because women need more life experiences with violence to overcome traditional sanctions against female violence (O'Leary, Malone, & Tyree, 1994).

Consequences of Courtship Violence

There is no doubt that the consequences of courtship violence tend to be more severe for women. Women are three times as likely as men to experience a major emotional trauma (Makepeace, 1986). Victims are most likely to experience anger, fear, or surprise (Matthews, 1984), whereas offenders experience sorrow.

Being a victim of courtship violence may disrupt normal adolescent development (Hanson, 2002). Many problems have been associated with victimization: lack of motivation, low energy, poor concentration, poor academic performance, hyperarousal, substance abuse, post-traumatic stress disorder, depression, low self-esteem, and eating disorders, as well as sexually risky behaviors, unwanted pregnancy, and suicidality (Silverman, Raj, Mucci, & Hathaway, 2001).

In addition, courtship violence might increase the risk of marital violence either with the same or a different partner. Little systematic research on this has been conducted. For example, it is not known what percentage of women who were victimized during courtship also are victimized in marriage, but in 25 percent of violent marriages, the violence began before marriage (Gayford, 1975). More recently, interviews with eighty-two clients at domestic violence shelters found that 51 percent of the clients had experienced previous physical abuse in a dating relationship (Roscoe & Benaske, 1985). Interviews with battered women revealed that the key factor linking marital battering with earlier courtship violence was the women's acceptance of traditional gender roles (Avni, 1991).

What Is Being Done?

Until recently, courtship violence did not receive the public attention that has been given to other forms of violence against women. There have been calls to prevent child maltreatment as a form of primary prevention (Wekerle & Wall, 2002) and to emphasize interventions across the life span (Schewe, 2002). There is no one solution nor any one point of entry. Programs should include sexual abuse prevention and education about peer aggression and courtship violence. Programs are needed for young children as well as for adolescents. See Fig. 13.2.

Unfortunately, most programs so far have been more effective at changing attitudes than at changing behavior (Foshee, Bauman, Greene, Koch, Linder & MacDougall, 2001; Silverman, 2001). In contrast, an evaluation after three years

FIGURE 13.2. Information table at the Port Authority Bus Terminal in New York City, educating the public about violence against women.

found that The Youth Relationships Program significantly reduced physical and psychological violence. This 18-week program targets at-risk 14- to 17-year-olds; "at risk" was defined as experiencing maltreatment and witnessing domestic violence. The program stressed education and awareness, skill development, and social action (Pittman & Wolfe, 2002).

ACQUAINTANCE SEXUAL ASSAULT AND RAPE

> At age 17 I lost my virginity on a squeaky hotel bed—against my will. It scared the hell out of me. I didn't want to be touched by any man for months. Worse yet, it was my boyfriend—someone I had trusted. I got pregnant—a scared 17-year-old who couldn't even afford a pregnancy test. I confided in only one person, my best friend. I told her that if I really was pregnant I was going to kill myself. My period was about one month and a half late already—a week later I miscarried (anonymous student).

Defining Sexual Assault

Sexual assault, sexual coercion, and *sexual aggression* are all terms used to refer to instances in which one person engages in sexual behavior against another's will. These terms encompass acts that range from unwanted sexual contact, such as forced kissing or fondling, to attempted rape and rape. *Rape* is often taken to mean oral, vaginal, or anal penetration by the penis or other objects.

Amnesty International (1992) defines rape to include forced female genital examinations, child rapes occurring as part of arranged marriages, and unwanted genital contact related to cultural rituals (such as genital mutilation). Researchers often use the term *sexual assault* rather than *rape.* Tactics in sexual assaults include psychological pressure (such as threatening to end the relationship or professing love), verbal persuasion ("if you loved me, you'd let me"), verbal threats of harm, use of alcohol and drugs, physical intimidation, mild physical force, severe physical force, and displaying or using a weapon.

The term *rape* has different meanings for women and men, as well as for different segments of the population (Chasteen, 2001). Some people are hesitant to label forced sex between acquaintances as rape, particularly if any of the following circumstances were present: the man initiated the date; he spent a great deal of money; the couple went to his place; there had been drinking, kissing, and petting; the couple had been sexually intimate on previous occasions; the woman had sex with other men (Goodchilds, Zellman, Johnson, & Giarrusso, 1989); or "no" was not explicitly verbalized (Sawyer, Pinciaro, & Jessell, 1998; Chasteen, 2001). College students in general, and sexually aggressive men in particular, believe that *sexual precedence* (a past history of sexual intercourse) reduces the legitimacy of sexual refusal. Some people suggest that if women do not label their experiences as rape, then they are not victims. Of course, this is illogical. Although a woman may not realize that forced sexual intercourse by an acquaintance during a date is rape, this does not change the legal definition of the act as rape, nor does it reduce the culpability of the perpetrator (Koss, 1994).

Frequency of Sexual Assault

Rape is the crime least likely to be reported and, if reported, the least likely to result in a conviction, particularly if committed by an acquaintance. Not only do many women not report their assault to the authorities, many never tell anyone. Thus, crime statistics greatly underestimate the frequency of rape.

Researchers rely on large-scale surveys of women to obtain accurate estimates of victimization rates. Women are asked about sexual experiences that may have involved force or threat of force, some of which meet the legal criteria for rape, rather than being asked directly, "Have your ever been raped?" This is important because many victimized women (73%) never label forced sexual intercourse as rape. This approach has suggested that the actual rape victimization rate is ten to fifteen times greater than FBI estimates (Koss, 1992). Because most of these unlabeled, unreported rape experiences are perpetrated by acquaintances, acquaintance rape has been called a "hidden crime" (Koss, 1985).

There has been remarkable consistency in the reported rates of rape during the past two decades. The most reliable estimates come from the United States (Koss & Kilpatrick, 2001). A 14–15 percent prevalence is estimated worldwide, with perpetrators most likely to be known to the women and the majority of female victims being adolescents and children (Koss, Heise, & Russo, 1994).

A comprehensive survey of more than 3,000 college women from institutions of higher education across the United States in 1987 remains the standard against which other surveys are compared (Koss et al., 1987). Of those surveyed, more than half (53.7%) had experienced some form of sexual victimization; 15.4

percent had experienced acts by a man that met the legal definition of rape (though only 27 percent labeled the experience rape), and 12.1 percent, attempted rape. An additional 11.9 percent had been verbally pressured into sexual intercourse, and the remaining 14.4 percent had experienced some other form of unwanted sexual contact, such as forced kissing or fondling.

More recent studies confirm these high numbers among Canadians (DeKeseredy, 1997) and Navy recruits (Merrill et al., 1998), as well as among U.S. women (Tjaden & Thoennes, 1998). Although the rates of completed rapes were similar for blacks (18%), Asians (19%), Hispanics (21%), and whites (24%), Hispanics reported considerably more attempted rapes (22%) than did the other groups, and blacks reported the most verbal coercion (24%) (Kalof, 2000). High school women also appear to be at greater risk for rape than previously thought. A recent survey of 834 first-year college students found that 13 percent reported being raped between the ages of 14 and 18, and an additional 16 percent reported being victims of an attempted rape (Humphrey & White, 2000).

Who Is at Risk?

The greatest risk factor for sexual victimization is being female. Adolescence is the period of greatest vulnerability. The risk of being victimized increases steadily from ages 14 to 18 and declines thereafter (Humphrey & White, 2000). Frequency of dating and number of sexual partners have also been associated with an increased risk of sexual victimization (Abbey et al., 1996; Testa & Dermen, 1999). This is probably because of the increased likelihood of being involved with a perpetrator or because of some men's belief that women who "get around" are fair targets (Abbey et al., 1996; Testa & Dermen, 1999).

Box 13.3 Gang Rape

Most research on acquaintance rape has focused on instances involving a single attacker. However, gang rape is a phenomenon that is beginning to receive attention (O'Sullivan, 1991). Looking at police records, Amir (1971) found that 26 percent of the reported rapes had involved three or more perpetrators, and that 55 percent of convicted rapists had been involved in a gang rape. The rate of conviction for gang rape is probably higher than the rate for rapes by single perpetrators because a victim of a gang rape is more likely to label the rape as a crime and report it than a victim of a single perpetrator, especially if he is an acquaintance. However, because not all gang rapes are reported, we need to consider data sources that assess unreported gang rapes. On the Koss survey described earlier (Koss et al., 1987), data revealed that multiple offenders were involved for 5 percent of the women who had been raped. The survey also revealed that for 16 percent of the men who reported having committed rape, at least one other male was involved. O'Sullivan (1991) noted that, "Of the twenty-three documented cases of alleged gang-rape by college students in the last ten years, thirteen were perpetrated by fraternity men, four by groups of basketball players, four by groups of football players, and only two men unaffiliated with a formal organization" (p. 11). She feels that the cohesiveness of all-male groups that promote macho values of sex as adventure may challenge men to perform in a group situation to prove they belong. According to O'Sullivan, victims of gang rape are usually first-year students who are naive, but have a reputation among the men for being promiscuous.

Other risk factors have been difficult to determine. Several researchers have confirmed that the best predictor of victimization is past victimization. Typically, childhood victimization increases the risk of adolescent victimization, which in turn increases the risk of victimization as a young adult (Collins, 1998; Gidycz, Latham, Coble, & Layman, 1992; Mills & Granoff, 1992; Humphrey & White, 2000; Wyatt, Guthrie, & Notgrass, 1992). In addition, childhood victimization has been related to early menarche and sexual activity (Vicary, Klingman, & Harkness, 1995), which are also associated with an increased likelihood of victimization. Experiencing other forms of victimization, such as psychological abuse or physical abuse by a dating partner, is associated with sexual assault (Smith, White, & Holland, 2003). Alcohol is also implicated as a risk factor in several direct and indirect ways. Victimization increases the likelihood of alcohol and drug use, and drug use increases the odds of a sexual assault (Kilpatrick, et al, 1997). Women with a history of victimization may turn to alcohol as a means of coping.

Unfortunately, in spite of all the research, we cannot do a very good job of predicting victimization. "No matter what researchers discover about vulnerability, and in spite of how well potential victims are trained in avoidance techniques, women will still be susceptible to rape and sexual assault to the extent that men commit these acts of sexual violence" (Bachar & Koss, 2001, pp. 124–125.).

Who Does This?

The vast majority of sexual perpetrators are men. The Koss survey (Koss et al., 1987) described earlier also examined the sexual experiences of more than 2,900 college men and found that that 25.1 percent of the college men admitted to some form of sexual aggression. Of this group, 4.4 percent admitted to behaviors meeting the legal definition of rape, 3.3 percent admitted to attempted rape, 7.2 percent to sexual coercion, and 10.2 percent to forced or coerced sexual contact. Four percent of the white men, 10 percent of the black men, 7 percent of Hispanic men, and 2 percent of Asian men reported rape.

Similar rates have been reported more recently in college samples (Abbey et al., 2001; Calhoun, 1997; White & Smith, in press) and in a community college sample (White, Holland, Mazurek, Lyndon, et al., 1998). Of the 34.5 percent (13.8% were attempted/completed rapes) of the men who had committed at least one form of sexual assault by the end of the fourth year of college, 22 percent had committed their first assault while in high school (6.3% were attempted/completed rapes) (White & Smith, in press). In this sample there were no differences related to ethnicity. See Box 13.3.

The typical acquaintance rapist appears to be a "normal" guy, but he may display tendencies suggestive of a personality disorder (Kosson, Kelly, & White, 1997). Among college students, alcohol use (Abbey et al., 2001; Koss & Gaines, 1993), athletic affiliation (Jackson, 1991; Frintner & Rubinson, 1993; Koss & Gaines, 1993), and fraternity membership (Frintner & Rubinson, 1993, but not Koss & Gaines, 1993) have been associated with sexual aggression toward women. Other significant correlates of sexual assault include a history of family violence; an early and varied sexual history, including many sexual partners; a history of delinquency; acceptance of rape myths; an impulsive personality; hedonistic and dominance motives for sex; lower than average sense of self-worth; and lower religiosity; as well as peers who condone and encourage sexual conquests (Abbey et al., 2001; White & Koss, 1993). Among men already predisposed to sexually offend, exposure to pornography tends to increase the risk of sexual perpetration (Seto et al., 2001). Finally, sexually aggressive men are more likely than other men to perceive a wide range of behaviors as indicating sexual interest (Bondurant & Donat, 1999) and are attracted to sexual aggression (Calhoun, Bernat, Clum, & Frame, 1997). See Box 13.4.

Box 13.4 Acquaintance Sexual Assault a Result of Miscommunication?

Miscommunication has been put forth as a way of understanding the social process that results in a young woman being forced into sexual activity by her date. The term *miscommunication* implies that the problem lies in the communication skills of the two people involved, particularly the woman. Many young women on college campuses across the nation are admonished in "rape awareness workshops" to communicate more clearly their refusal to have sex; the implication is that if the woman believes she has communicated her nonconsent and sexual intercourse occurs, the failure is hers. Researchers frequently study women's verbal and nonverbal cues that may suggest sexual interest on the assumptions that the man's motive is sexual, and he is looking for cues from the woman that may communicate sexual interest. This work also assumes that if these cues are present, any man would interpret them as indicators of a woman's willingness to engage in sex with him. However, these assumptions are incorrect.

Men who self-report sexually aggressive behaviors have been found to perceive nonverbal cues, especially cues that others perceive as reflecting little sexual interest, as connoting more sexual interest than nonaggressive men (Bondurant & Donat, 1999). Furthermore, sexually aggressive men claim that their victims were more sexually interested in them than sexually nonaggressive men involved in consensual sex do, and they base this perception on the presence of behaviors that previous research has found to indicate low sexual interest (Kowalski, 1992). These behaviors include eye contact, smiling, accepting a date, and slow dancing. In contrast, sexually nonaggressive men base their inferences of their partner's sexual interest on the presence of behaviors such as kissing the man, undressing him, removing her top, and suggesting they spend the night (White & Humphrey, 1994a).

Sexually aggressive men may also believe that a woman's no does not always mean no. The term *token resistance* has been used to describe the situation in which a woman says no but is really *game-playing*. In an early study, Charlene Muehlenhard and Lisa Hollabaugh (1988) found that about one-third of the women they surveyed indicated that they had said no at least once when they really wanted to have sex. Many people latched onto this finding as evidence that women are deceptive and that maybe men are justified in their belief that they ought to pursue sexual activity in spite of the no. However, in a follow-up study, Charlene Muehlenhard and Carrie Rodgers (1998) discovered that women who say no in spite of desiring sex genuinely meant no; they were not manipulating or teasing. Rather, although they were interested in sexual activity, they decided to refrain for a variety of reasons, including moral beliefs, fear of sexually transmitted diseases, or fear of pregnancy.

Whereas the language of miscommunication suggests that a sexual assault occurs because a normal guy understandably misunderstands his date's intentions on the basis of how she looks or what she does, the language of aggression and violence suggests a more negative view of men who commit acts of sexual aggression. It is sexually aggressive men's perception rather than a woman's actions that drives the inference of sexual interest. The language of miscommunication tends to reduce the culpability of the perpetrator and diverts attention from a study of perpetrator characteristics and factors that contribute to perpetrators' attitudes and behaviors, such as sexism and the glorification of violence in the media.

Compared with other men, sexually aggressive men also tend to be more domineering with women. In an unstructured, 5-minute get-to-know-each-other conversation, these men used more "one up" messages aimed at "gaining control of the exchange" (e.g., bragging about oneself and criticizing the other person) with a female confederate than with a male confederate (Malamuth & Thornhill, 1994). Being domineering in conversation may be a way for sexually aggressive men to identify vulnerable targets. A woman who resists the domination may be seen as unavailable, but a submissive response from a woman may indicate that she is a potential target.

Efforts to predict which men are most likely to be sexually aggressive have been relatively successful. Neil Malamuth (1998) has developed the most comprehensive model of sexual perpetration to date. Experiences with parental violence and child abuse combine to increase the likelihood of engaging in delinquent behavior. Sexual promiscuity is one consequence of a delinquent lifestyle. When these factors are combined with a hostile, dominating personality, sexually coercive behavior is likely. Furthermore, the combination of these factors is most likely to result in sexual aggression in men who tend to be self-centered and have little empathy (Dean & Malamuth, 1995).

Consequences for the Victim

Rape has short-term and long-term effects on most victims. The effects cut across all domains of functioning, including neurobiological, cognitive, psychological, physical, social, and economic (Koss & Kilpatrick, 2001). Emotional reactions to the assault include fear and anxiety, phobias, depression, diminished self-esteem, sexual dysfunctions, nightmares, and *post-traumatic stress disorder (PTSD)* (see Chapter 14). Behavioral reactions may include alcohol or drug use and dependency and behavioral deviancy, including sexual promiscuity, and an increased risk of future victimization. Even behaviors such as smoking, drug use, and failure to wear seat belts may increase after a rape. Physical difficulties can arise from injuries associated with the assault itself as well as from the emotional trauma. Chronic health problems are common, requiring significantly more physician visits and health-care dollars spent among rape victims compared with nonvictims in the years after the assault. Pregnancy (5%) and risks of contracting sexually transmitted diseases (3.6–30% rate), including AIDS (rate unknown), are also associated with rape. Among many rape victims, relationships with family members, friends, and intimate partners become severely strained. In some instances, the victim is blamed; in others, the assault is trivialized—often with the well-meaning intention of trying to make her feel better.

A trauma such as rape may render victims more physiologically reactive to environmental stimuli. This reactivity can affect sleep and other bodily systems, accounting for many of the negative health consequences of rape. Mary Koss and her colleagues (Koss & Kilpatrick, 2000) have suggested that rape affects mental, physical, and social health because of personal factors such as previous exposure to violence and social cognitions that include self-blame for the rape and maladaptive beliefs. The result is general distress and PTSD.

Victims go through various phases during their recovery. Initially, they struggle with the meaning of the assault (Taylor, 1983). Subsequently, they attempt to gain a sense of control, which can include self-blame ("What did I do wrong?" "How could I have avoided this situation?"). Following this, victims may tend to minimize the seriousness of the experience as a means of self-enhancement; for example, they are grateful they lived through the attack. As victims redefine the meaning of the assault and develop a greater sense of mastery, positive outcomes emerge; the victim progresses from being a victim to being a survivor (Koss & Burkhart, 1989).

In spite of the tendency for the public to consider stranger rape as "real rape" and acquaintance rape as less serious, mental health data clearly suggest otherwise. Several studies have shown that the psychological impact of nonstranger rape may be worse than that of stranger rape (Karp, Silber, Holmstrom, & Stock, 1995; Katz, 1991). It appears that a woman's strong negative reactions to acquaintance rape are due to feelings of betrayal by a trusted acquaintance and to uncertainty about her role in the assault (Frazier & Seales, 1997; Pitts & Schwartz, 1997).

Many victims cannot acknowledge their victimization for months or even years after the assault (Bondurant, 2001). A survey of women at three midwestern universities found that only 28 percent of the sexual assault victims sought any type of help, and of those who did, 75 percent turned to a friend (Ogletree, 1993). Whether the rape is acknowledged or not, however, symptoms develop, with 31 to 48 percent of rape victims eventually seeking professional help (Koss & Burkhart, 1990). Unfortunately, rapid recovery is not likely. Interviews with rape victims four to six years after the sexual assault revealed that only 37 percent felt they had recovered within a few months of the assault; 26 percent did not yet feel recovered. Although recovery is often slow, the good news is that recovery is possible.

What Is Being Done?

Key efforts to combat sexual assault involve the criminal justice system, campus programs, and male-based programs.

In the mid-1970s, most states began to revise their rape laws in the hope that changes in the definition of rape, the statutory age, and evidentiary rules (such as making a woman's past sexual history or manner of dress inadmissible) would produce increases in the reporting, prosecution, and conviction of rape cases, as well as improvement in the treatment of rape victims (Searles & Berger, 1987). However, analyses of the effects of these legal reforms provide little optimism that the plight of victimized women has improved. Continuing problems include victims' reluctance to report rape, the low likelihood that a report will result in a conviction, and few efforts to prevent reoffending (Koss, Bacher & Hopkins, 2002). Additionally, judicial reform has not changed attitudes about rape.

A new approach is needed, and fortunately one is on the horizon. Mary Koss and her colleagues (Koss et al., 2002) are developing and testing a *restorative justice program.* It holds the offender accountable through reparations and rehabilitation proposed by the victim and the community.

College campuses have been a second center of efforts to combat sexual assault. However, most efforts to develop sexual assault prevention programs on college campuses have not been very successful. Those that claim some success have been able to change attitudes, at least for a short time, but few have been effective in changing behavior.

Typical programs for women have provided general information about sexual assault, offered tips for day-to-day conduct that may reduce one's risk for sexual assault, and taught self-defense (Cummings, 1992). There are several problems with these programs. First, they may deter a perpetrator from assaulting a particular woman but will not prevent him from seeking another victim (Lonsway, 1996). Second, the recommendations offered result in a life full of restrictions (don't go out alone; watch what you wear; don't drink on dates; don't take any man for granted) and precautionary behaviors (walk with a friend or a dog; take a flashlight; dress for easy escape). Third, the research suggests that the best predictor of engaging in precautionary behaviors is fear and, paradoxically, women fear stranger assault far more than acquaintance assault (Hickman & Muehlenhard, 1997). Lastly, rape prevention programs may not work equally well for all women. Programs may be successful for women with no prior history of sexual assault but may be ineffective for women with a sexual assault history (Hanson & Gidycz, 1994). Resistance training that includes leaving the scene, forceful verbal strategies, and physical resistance, as well as self-defense, may be a useful alternative to the typical program because it emphasizes agency rather than victimization (Rozee & Koss, 2001).

A very promising trend is the development of rape prevention programs developed by men and run by men for men. Especially interesting are programs that focus on fraternities and athletic teams on college campuses (Mahlstedt, 1999). Northeastern University's Center for the Study of Sport in Society sponsors a multiracial, mixed-gender Mentors in Violence Prevention Program that is "the first large-scale attempt to enlist high school, collegiate, and professional athletes in the effort to prevent all forms of men's violence against women" (www.sportinsociety.org/mvp.html). It is unique in that it focuses on bystander behavior. The program

> views student-athletes and student leaders not as potential perpetrators or victims, but as empowered bystanders who can confront abusive peers. Program participants develop leadership skills and learn to mentor and educate younger boys and girls on these issues. By focusing on bystander behavior, MVP reduces the defensiveness and hopelessness that many men and women often feel when discussing men's violence against women. MVP aims to construct a new vision for society that does not equate strength in men with dominance over women. (www.sportinsociety.org/mvp.html)

Other community-based programs encourage men to take responsibility for violence against women. The White Ribbon Campaign (www.undp.org/rblac/gender/mens.htm), begun in Canada, is the largest worldwide effort of men to end men's violence against women. During White Ribbon Week, which begins on November 25, the International Day for the Eradication of Violence Against Women, men wear a white ribbon as a pledge to never commit violence nor to remain silent about other men's violence. See Figure 13.3.

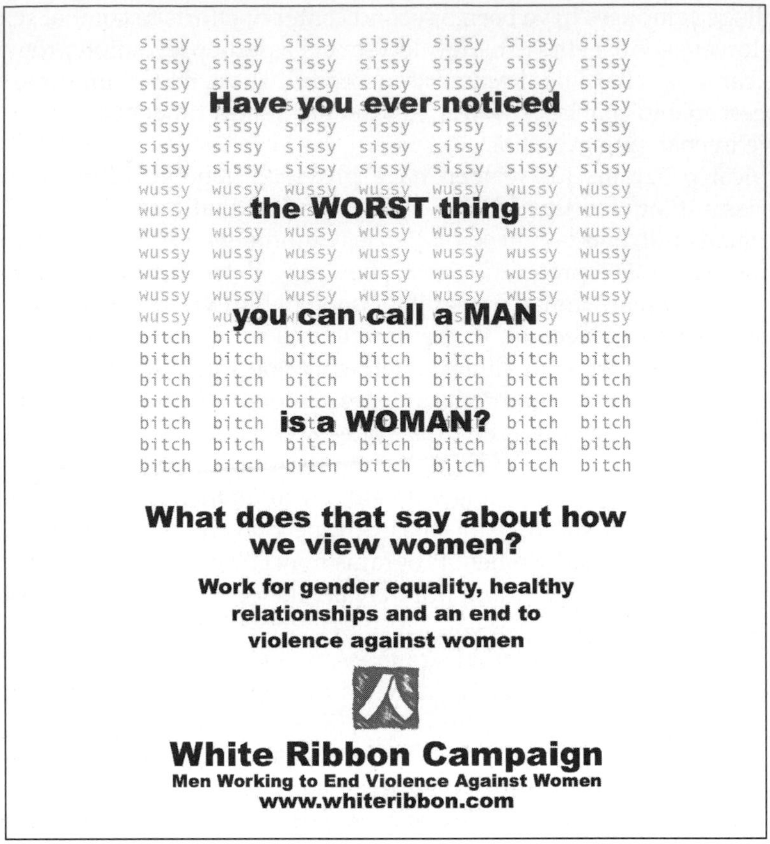

FIGURE 13.3.

SEXUAL HARASSMENT

Defining Sexual Harassment

A great deal of confusion surrounds the question of what constitutes sexual harassment. Although sexual harassment is an old problem, the term first appeared in the 1970s (Gutek & Done, 2001) and the first legal definition of sexual harassment did not appear until 1980 (EEOC, 1980). Many behaviors that are now defined as sexual harassment were once seen as socially acceptable. This redefinition of accepted social behavior as unacceptable and, in some cases, illegal has generated disagreement and confusion. The Supreme Court has complicated the situation by changing its decisions regarding the behaviors and circumstances that qualify as sexual harassment (Laabs, 1998). Furthermore, the definitions used by the legal system and those used by researchers don't always agree. Some research definitions are broader than legal definitions and rely on individuals' self-reports (Gutek & Done, 2001).

In the United States, sexual harassment is a form of sex discrimination that violates Title VII of the Civil Rights Act of 1964. It is legally defined as follows:

> Unwelcome sexual advances, requests for sexual favors, and other verbal or physical conduct of a sexual nature constitute sexual harassment when (1) submission to such conduct is made either explicitly or implicitly a term or condition of an individual's employment, (2) submission or rejection of such by an individual is used as a basis for employment decisions affecting such individual, or (3) such has the purpose or effect of substantially interfering with an individual's work performance or creating an intimidating, hostile or offensive work environment. (EEOC, 1980, p. 33)

Students who are sexually harassed by professors are protected under Title IX of the Education Amendment of 1972, which prohibits sex discrimination in higher education (Watts, 1996).

There are two broad categories of sexual harassment: quid pro quo and hostile environment. *Quid pro quo sexual harassment* (conditions 1 and 2 in the preceding definition) occurs when sexual conduct is implicitly or explicitly

Box 13.5 Organizational Climate Affects Experience of Sexual Harassment

Louise Fitzgerald and her colleagues (Fitzgerald, Swan & Magley, 1997) provide two examples, based on actual sexual harassment cases, to illustrate how the consequences of sexual harassment depend not only on the incident but upon the reactions of others to the harassment and the victim's past experiences.

Victim A works as a waitress in a popular restaurant where the manager and other male employees routinely engage in the crudest type of sexual commentary concerning the waitresses, the female busers, and the customers. This occurs virtually every day, all day, and has since the beginning of A's employment. A, who was raped as a young girl, was horrified to learn that the manager had recently forced one of the other waitresses to have oral sex. Although several women have complained to the owner about the behavior of the male employees, he seems unconcerned, saying "There are always two sides to every story." The restaurant has no sexual harassment policy. Victim A, who is the sole support of her two daughters and has no salable skills besides waitressing, has no option but to remain employed. At the time she was assessed, she was seriously depressed and had suffered a recurrence of the nightmares and flashbacks that followed her previous victimization.

In contrast, Victim B was employed as a secretary in a high-technology software firm. The firm, which had a well-developed human resources program, had an extensive sexual harassment policy and offered periodic training; the president made many public statements to the effect that harassment would not be tolerated, and the few problems that arose were dealt with immediately, usually informally, and effectively. B was thus caught off guard one night when, working late to finish a proposal, her new supervisor followed her into the women's restroom, turned out the light, locked the door, and attempted to have sex with her. Terrified, she managed to evade him, ran out of the building, and drove home; despite several frantic phone calls from her assailant protesting that he "didn't mean anything" and had thought she was interested in him, she filed a formal complaint with the director of human resources the following morning. After a brief investigation the manager was summarily fired; the company apologized to B, offered her time off with pay, and offered to pay for counseling. At the time of her assessment, B, who had never previously been victimized, was experiencing anxiety and mild phobic reactions to public restrooms. She was diagnosed with Adjustment Disorder, from which she subsequently recovered rapidly and fully.

required for a person to maintain or advance his or her position. *Hostile environment sexual harassment* (condition 3 in the preceding definition) occurs when one or more people create a noxious working environment—for example, by putting up sexual signs or posters, making sexist comments, making sexual comments, or singling a person out for negative remarks because of his or her sex.

A slip of the tongue, however, does not qualify as harassment. Hostile environment sexual harassment exists only if a number of incidents have occurred that demonstrate a pattern of behavior (Paetzold & O'Leary-Kelly, 1996). A person cannot charge hostile environment sexual harassment for one incident unless it is severe, such as a sexual assault. Furthermore, the conduct must meet a "reasonable person" standard of offensiveness (Paetzold & O'Leary-Kelly, 1996). Finally, the behavior must in some way interfere with the person's work.

Frequency of Sexual Harassment

Sexual harassment can happen to anyone, in any kind of job; it even happens to clergywomen (Cowen, 1993). Nationwide studies of federal employees found that over a fourteen-year period 42 percent to 44 percent of the women surveyed experienced some form of sexual harassment (USMSPB, 1981, 1987, 1995). Other studies suggest that 35 percent to 50 percent of working women will experience sexual harassment during their career (Gutek & Done, 2001). In about half the cases, the harasser is a supervisor but may also be a peer, coworker, or client (AAUW, 2001, Kalof et al., 2001, USMSPB, 1995).

Harassment is also widespread in high schools and colleges. On college campuses, 40 percent to 50 percent of female students experience sexual harassment (Cortina et al., 1998; Kalof et al., 2001). The rate is even higher for female medical school students (Shinsako, Richman, & Rospenda, 2001). A survey of eighth- to eleventh-graders across the United States found that 83 percent of girls and 79 percent of boys report having experienced harassment (AAUW, 2001). Furthermore, one in four students report that it happens often. Although boys and girls both experience sexual harassment, girls are more likely to fear harassment and to report negative effects. White girls reported the greatest sexual harassment, followed by African American and Latina girls.

Gender harassment—generalized sexist remarks and behavior that convey hostile or degrading attitudes about women—is the most frequent form of sexual harassment (AAUW, 2001; Gutek & Done 2001; Kalof et al., 2001). Sexual harassment against men happens much less often than harassment against women (USMSPB, 1981, 1987, 1995). Men are at least as likely to be harassed by a man as a woman and when harassed men report fewer negative reactions (Waldo, Berdahl, & Fitzgerald, 1998). Sexual harassment of schoolboys has received new attention after bullying became associated with several cases of school violence (AAUW, 2001).

The United States has somewhat higher rates of sexual harassment than European countries do (Gruber, 1997). Some Eastern European countries, however, lack the basic vocabulary and awareness to effectively name and deal with the problem (Duban, 2002; Johnson, 1999). A cross-cultural review concluded that sexual harassment is a problem in all cultures, although the form of sexual harassment may differ from culture to culture (Barak, 1997).

Who Is at Risk?

Sexual harassment can be seen as an abuse of power, a reflection of the low status of women, and a means of social control (Morgan, 2001). Because men have greater authority, status, and power, they can force their sexual attentions on women. Male-dominated organizations legitimize harassment by claiming that it is a minor problem and by treating women who complain as though they were crazy. (For example, a U.S. senator suggested that Anita Hill was schizophrenic for reporting sexual harassment by a Supreme Court nominee in 1991.) Both sociocultural power and organizational power influence who is sexually harassed (Gutek & Done, 2001).

People with less power are more likely to be harassed, and the greater the difference in power between two people at work, the more likely sexual harassment will occur (Gruber, 1997). Our culture marks women as having lower status than men and young, unmarried people as having lower status than older, married persons (Fain & Anderton, 1987). Thus, young women and women who are unattached to men (lesbians, single women, and divorced women) are more likely to be harassed than any other group (Fain & Anderton, 1987; Gruber, 1997). Within universities, African American and Latina women and lesbian and bisexual women are more likely to report sexually harassing experiences than are white heterosexual women (Cortina, Swan, Fitzgerald, & Waldo, 1998). Military women with less sociocultural and organizational power are more likely to be harassed (Harned, Ormerod, Palmieri, Collinsworth, & Reed, 2002).

Sexual harassment is not inevitable or natural. Lower rates of sexual harassment and less severe cases are reported when workplaces have clear, well-publicized policies on sexual harassment and when supervisors support sexual harassment policies, encourage women to report violations, and punish harassers (Fitzgerald, Drasgow, Hulin, Gefland, & Magley, 1997). A study of sexual harassment in the U.S. military found that reports of sexual harassment were highest when the commanding officer was perceived as encouraging or supporting sexual harassment and lowest when the commanding officer actively discouraged sexual harassment (cited in Pryor, Giedd, & Williams, 1995).

Clearly, social norms within an organization influence whether people are sexually harassed. Women in male-dominated jobs or workplaces encounter more sexual harassment than those in workplaces with an equal gender ratio (Gutek & Done, 2001). Workplaces that are male dominated are more likely to emphasize sexual aggression and sexual posturing and to belittle femininity (Morgan, 2001). A national survey of African-American women firefighters found that all but one had suffered sexual harassment; the harassment was prolonged, sometimes lasting years, and made the women feel excluded and less valued as employees. But these women did not let the harassment reduce the sense of commitment and accomplishment they felt in their job (Yoder & Aniakudo, 1996).

Who Sexually Harasses? The Interaction of Individual and Organizational Factors

Sexual harassment can be predicted by the presence of four factors (Sbraga & O'Donohue, 2000). For sexual harassment to occur, a person must be motivated to harass, overcome internal inhibitions not to harass, overcome external inhibitions, and overcome victim resistance.

Some men are more motivated to harass than others. Men who associate power with sexuality have a greater predisposition to sexually harass women (Pryor & Whalen, 1997). These men may be more likely to view women as objects.

Characteristics of a situation interact with personality factors in determining the likelihood of harassment. This interaction was demonstrated in a study in which male college students trained female college students either to play poker or to putt a golf ball (Pryor, 1987). The men believed that their evaluations of the women would influence how many credits they received. Men with a greater predisposition to sexually harass (as measured by a likelihood-to-harass scale) engaged in more sexual touching and sexual language than other men—but only when they were acting as the golf instructor. A boss who leans on a secretary when she is typing or a coach who touches players to explain how to improve their stance may be illustrating how specific situations can reduce the inhibitions on men who are motivated to harass.

One characteristic of situations is the climate set by supervisors. Consider a study in which male students taught a computer program to female students. The male students were exposed to a graduate student who modeled either professional behavior or sexually harassing behaviors, including flirting, leering, and touching. Men with a predisposition to sexually harass engaged in more touching, sexual comments, and nonverbal behaviors than other men when they were exposed to the harassing role model but did not do so when shown the professional role model (Pryor, La Vite, & Stoller, 1993). This research suggests that the tone set by leaders can either reduce or increase the inhibitions on potential sexual harassers.

Consequences of Sexual Harassment

Although research has documented that sexual harassment is widespread, many people are reluctant to label themselves as victims (Cortina et al., 1998; Kalof, Eby, Matheson, & Kroska 2001). Often, women do not label an event as sexually harassing because it involves behaviors that the culture has considered normal. Furthermore, women who report harassment risk being stigmatized as "being too fussy" or "uptight" (Kelly & Radford, 1996). Women may believe that their work conditions will suffer if they do not go along with the harassment (USMSPB, 1995). Indeed, a study of harassment in the U.S. military found that women who reported harassment faced retaliation (Bergman, Langhout, Palmieri, Cortina, & Fitzgerald, 2002). Women who do not label an event as sexual harassment, however, have psychological consequences just as serious as women who do name their experiences (Cortina et al., 1998; Munson, Miner, Hulin, 2001).

Women frequently describe the experience of harassment as degrading, disgusting, and humiliating. One woman described her experiences with workplace sexual harassment as follows:

> He was a gross man. That was his manner toward everyone in the office. He thought it was cute that he could have every woman in the office. He was executive vice president and he thought this would give him special privileges. I thought it was disgusting how he acted. He acted real macho, like he was God's gift to men. I quit. (Gutek, 1985, p. 80)

Women who are sexually harassed report psychological symptoms including anxiety, depression, decreased satisfaction with life, and symptoms of post-traumatic stress disorder (see Chapter 14) (Gutek & Done, 2001; Morgan, 2001). They may also suffer lowered self-esteem, self-blame, and impaired social relationships. Sexual harassment sometimes results in post-traumatic stress disorder (Avina & O'Donohue, 2002). Students in the eighth- to twelfth-grades reported feeling embarrassed, self-conscious, less confident, scared, confused about who they were, and less popular in response to sexual harassment (AAUW, 2001). Who does the harassing can make a difference. A study in the Netherlands found that high school students were more upset and showed more psychosomatic symptoms when harassed by a teacher than by a peer (Timmerman, 2002).

Even when it is not severe, sexual harassment may have negative consequences (Schneider et al., 1997). College women who were sexually harassed at "low levels" reported negative feelings about themselves, their peers, their professors, and the campus (Cortina et al., 1998). Significantly, women who were sexually harassed felt less competent academically and were more likely to leave school.

The economic costs of sexual harassment can be quite high. A study of a large West Coast utility company found that harassment was associated with higher levels of absenteeism and a greater desire to leave the company (Fitzgerald, Drasgow, Hulin, Gefland, & Magley, 1997). A study of sexual harassment of federal employees estimated that $327 million was lost over a two-year period due to job turnover, sick leave, and loss of productivity (USMSPB, 1995). Women who are sexually harassed have been found to be less satisfied with work, their co-workers, and their supervisors (Schneider, Swan, & Fitzgerald, 1997). More than 20 percent of women have quit a job, been transferred, been fired, or quit trying to get a job because of harassment (Gutek, 1985).

What Is Being Done?

To fight sexual harassment, schools and businesses are adopting clear policies on sexual harassment that are well publicized and easily accessible (AAUW, 2001; Bell, Cycyota, & Quick, 2002). Policies and educational programs need to encourage women to label incidents as offensive, provide support when they do report sexual harassment, and protect them from retribution by those accused (Sbraga & O'Donohue, 2000). Ethnic minority women may have different concerns from other women, and care should be taken to understand their perspectives (Paludi, 1997). It is important for organizations to recognize that those with little power, who cannot defend themselves from retribution, face the greatest risk of harassment.

Although many institutions have implemented polices and educational programs, none has been shown to reduce sexual harassment (Grundmann, O'Donohue, & Peterson, 1997). Education and prevention efforts should be designed and evaluated carefully. Presentations about sexual harassment may increase the negative attitudes of men, especially men with a propensity to sexually harass (Bingham & Scherer, 2001; Robb, & Doverspike, 2001).

The ineffectiveness of programs to reduce harassment may also be the result of institutions' adopting policies merely to reduce legal liability. Women are more likely to report harassment and feel satisfied with the process when they have faith in their organizations' efforts to stop harassment (Offermann & Malamut, 2002). If schools and businesses adopt sexual harassment policies "in name only," then important organizational factors that support sexual harassment may remain unchanged. To combat sexual harassment, those in power must be committed to creating an environment in which harassment is not tolerated.

PARTNER ABUSE AGAINST WOMEN

The maltreatment of one partner in an intimate relationship by the other constitutes *partner abuse.* It includes psychological abuse—such as intimidation, threats, public humiliation, and intense criticism—as well as physical force, which can range from a slap or a push to the use of a weapon. Although physical abuse is easier to define and more frequently studied (Smith et al., 1999), psychological abuse almost always occurs in these incidents. For many battered women, the psychological abuse is more traumatic than the physical abuse (Dutton, Goodman, & Bennett, 1999; O'Leary, 1999). Furthermore, the terror and control associated with battering can persist even after the physical abuse has stopped.

Wife Abuse, Partner Abuse, or Domestic Violence?

Partner abuse occurs between both married and unmarried partners, including lesbian and gay couples (Renzetti, 1997). See Box 13.6. The majority of cases, however, involve heterosexual couples, and the woman is at greater risk of physical injury and sexual abuse (Swan & Snow, 2002; Tjaden & Thoennes, 2000). Numerous studies have documented that women report inflicting approximately the same amount of violence against men as men inflict against

Box 13.6 Abuse in Same-Sex Relationships

Relationship abuse is not limited to heterosexual relationships. Although men engage in more violent acts against women (rape, attempted rape, courtship violence, or nonconsensual pain during sexual activities) than women do against men or women, this does not hold true for committed relationships (Tjaden, Thoennes, & Allison, 1999). For lesbian women and gay men, the rate of relationship abuse is equal or greater than for heterosexuals (Bernhard, 2000; Burke, Jordan, & Owen, 2002; Tjaden, Thoennes, & Allison, 1999). Apparently, violence in committed relationships is not simply a gender issue. Preliminary research suggests that issues of power and control may be less a factor in lesbian battering (Miller, Greene, Causby, White, & Lockhart, 2001). More research is needed to understand the similarities and differences between same-sex and opposite-sex abuse.

Lesbians and gay men face discrimination from police, counselors and shelters who assume an abused person is a heterosexual woman. Counselors and police officers may have heterosexist reactions when dealing with a same-sex abuse case (Bernhard, 2000).

women (Straus, 1999). In the majority of these cases, however, women do not cause as much physical damage as men; thus engage in less severe forms of violence and act in self-defense. Still, some argue that husband abuse is being ignored (Kimmel, 2002; DeKeseredy, 1999; Straus, 1999).

Although men are abused by women, the data do not support the idea that women and men abuse equally. Some political groups, however, misrepresent the data in order to further their goals. While this was being written, a case is before the courts arguing that the Minnesota Battered Women's Act discriminates against men and hence is unconstitutional (*Booth* v. *Hvass,* 2002). Ironically, the case erroneously cites research by one of this chapter's authors as supporting the claim that women abuse men as much as men abuse women. The evidence suggests that abuse of women in intimate relationships is a much more frequent and serious social problem than abuse of men.

Some people argue that terms such as *spouse abuse, partner abuse,* and *domestic violence* obscure the central issue of men physically harming women (Bograd, 1988). *Wife abuse* has been offered as an alternative label that highlights the economic, political, and social context in which the violence occurs, but this term has been criticized as heterosexist.

The Context of Domestic Violence

Whatever label is used, violence between intimate partners must be viewed within its context. Historically, women in the United States had fewer rights than men (Steil, 1989). Prior to the American Civil War, husbands had the right to control their wives' property, collect and spend their wages, and punish their wives for transgressions. The abuse of women was tolerated, if not accepted, by many men and women (Gordon, 1988).

Social acceptance of wife beating varies both within the United States and from country to country. People with more traditional attitudes toward gender roles tend to blame the victim more and the perpetrator less for wife assault. This has been found among U.S citizens (Hillier & Foddy, 1993), Chinese Americans (Yick, 2001), African Americans (Bell & Mattis, 2000), and Australians (Pavlou & Knowles, 2001). Clergy who counsel women often hold traditional attitudes that blame women for their abuse (Wood & McHugh, 1994). There is some evidence that attitudes that support wife abuse are declining in the United States (Straus, Kaufman Kantor, & Moore, 1997). The situation is not as promising in some other countries where patriarchal views are stronger. For example, in Israel, the West Bank, and the Gaza Strip, acceptance of patriarchal values is associated with acceptance of wife beating. Despite growth in opportunities for women in Arab countries, religious and family values condone wife abuse (Haj-Yahia, 1996, 1998 a, b).

Today, feminists point to the patriarchal structure of U.S. society as encouraging and supporting the abuse of women in relationships. A woman's second-class status in society makes her more likely to be economically dependent and unable to leave an abusive situation (Bograd, 1988; Browne, 1993). Social factors that may contribute to domestic violence against women include a general societal acceptance of violence, devaluation of women, and acceptance of men's right to dominate women.

Women who have been battered by a male partner often report that control is a major part of the violence (Eisikovits & Buchbinder, 1999). One battered woman, who eventually lost her unborn child in a battering incident, recounts the relationship between control and violence:

> I didn't even realize he was gaining control and I was too dumb to know any better. . . . He was gaining control bit by bit until he was checking my pantyhose when I'd come home from the supermarket to see if they were inside out . . . He'd time me. He'd check the mileage on the car. . . . I was living like a prisoner . . . (Yllo, 1993, p. 57)

The *power and control wheel* shown in Figure 13.4, developed by the Domestic Abuse Intervention Project in Duluth, Minnesota, has been used with batterers and women's support groups around the country because it clearly links power and control to violence. Each spoke of the wheel represents a different tactic used by abusive men to dominate their partner. In-depth interviews with male batterers confirm that abusive men connect masculinity with being able to control and dominate their partners (Anderson & Umberson, 2001). The power and control wheel, however, may not fit all cultures equally well. Samoan societies, for instance, do not have notions of family and the objectification of women comparable to those in U.S. society (Crichton-Hill, 2001).

Who Commits the Abuse?

Partner abuse against women is one of the most common causes of injury for women worldwide (United Nations Children's Fund, 2000). Estimates range from a "low" of 16 percent in South Africa and Cambodia to a high of 59 percent in Japan. Most researchers agree that abuse is probably underreported due to shame, guilt, and the belief that wife beating is a normal part of marriage (Browne, 1993; Ellsberg, Heise, Pena, Agurto, Winkvist, 2001). Women in many countries suffer high rates of abuse, including Ecuador, Sri Lanka, Tanzania, Mexico, and India (Neft & Levine, 1997). Russian women have the highest rates of spousal homicide in the industrialized world, four to five times the rate in the United States (Horne, 1999).

How are men who batter different from those who do not? Men who earn less than their wives are more likely to engage in wife abuse, a finding that supports the idea that battering is related to patriarchal beliefs (Anderson, 1997). Children, especially male and nonwhite children, are more likely to develop attitudes approving violence against spouses if they grow up witnessing violence against women in the home (Markowitz, 2001). Men who batter are more likely than those who do not to have been exposed to physical violence and shaming by a parent as children and to have developed insecure attachment early in life (Dutton, 2000). This early trauma is then associated with aggression, an externalizing attributional style, and problems in coping with emotions. Men who are rejected by their parents in childhood while suffering verbal and physical abuse are more likely to develop an abusive personality. A tendency toward anger and aggressiveness and a lack of coping skills may explain why some men are violent toward their partners (Date & Ronan, 2000).

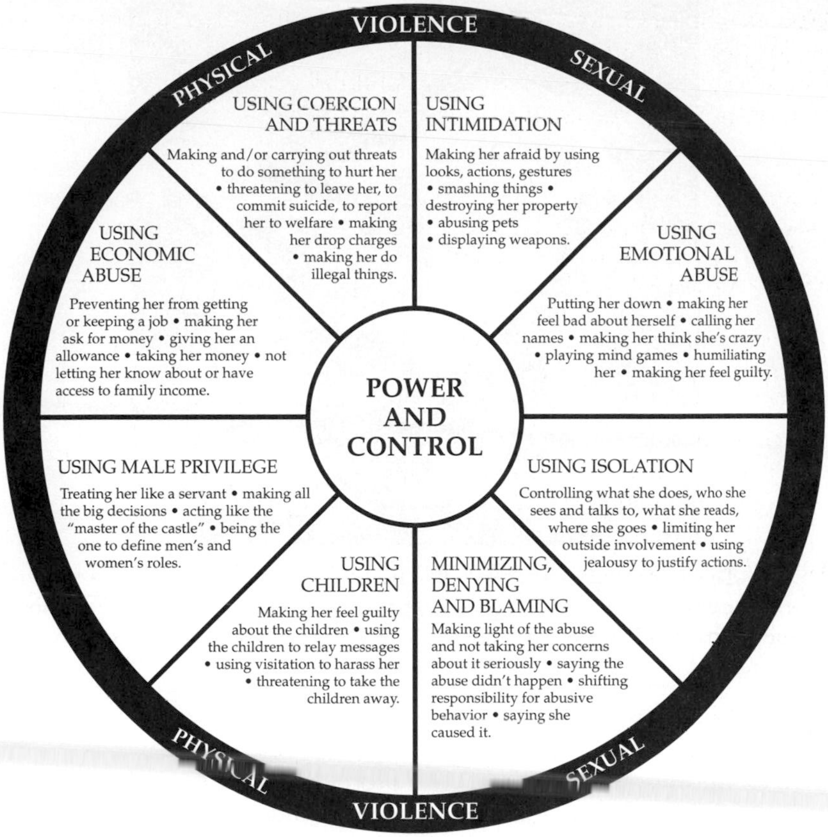

FIGURE 13.4. The power and control wheel.
Source: From R. J. Gelles & D. R. Loseke (eds.). *Current Controversies on Family Violence,* pp. 47–62.

Who Are the Victims, and What Are the Consequences?

When wife abuse was first widely publicized, the theory that women who enjoy pain are likely to seek out and stay in abusive relationships was offered as an explanation (Goldstein, 1983). This theory has found no support and is now seen as a way of blaming the victim. Furthermore, studies of abusive couples have found little evidence that battered women have certain personalities that put them at risk (Russell, Lipov, Phillips, & White, 1989).

Because research typically focuses on women who are married or in relationships with abusers, women who *do* leave abusive relationships often are not studied. A follow-up study of fifty-one battered women found that after 2.5 years, only 25 percent of the previously battered women were still in a violent relationship (Schwartz, 1989). Some women who leave a battering relationship may go back several times before they make a final separation (Campbell, Rose, Kub, & Nedd, 1998).

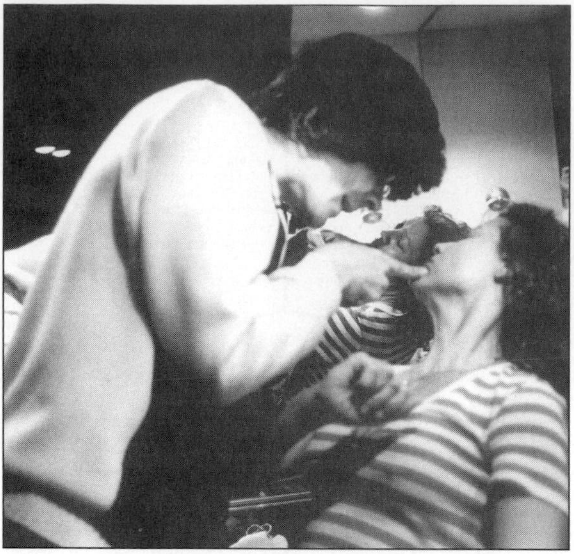

FIGURE 13.5. This photo, from a series taken by Donna Ferrato, shows one of many actual abusive episodes between Garth and Lisa. Their marriage, which had the appearance of being ideal, ended after many bouts of violence when Lisa divorced Garth and moved away with their children. Garth continued to deny that he ever hit Lisa (Ferrato, 1991).

Two contrasting theories have been proposed to explain why it is difficult for women to make a permanent break with an abuser: battered woman's syndrome and survivor theory. Both theories are useful.

Battered woman's syndrome is a special case of post-traumatic stress disorder (see Chapter 14) and explains how battering creates feelings of helplessness (Walker, 1984; 1993). A woman who lives with someone who abuses her develops a stress response when attacked. If the attack is repeated or the threat of attack is present, chronic symptoms develop. Many battered women suffer from depression and post-traumatic stress disorder (Stein & Kennedy, 2001). When repeatedly degraded and ridiculed by their husbands, wives can come to believe the husbands' accusations. Their self-esteem and confidence erode. They may come to believe that they deserve their husbands' abuse and that they are incapable of caring for themselves and their children.

In contrast, *survivor theory* emphasizes women's attempts to seek help and cope with violence (Gondolf & Fisher, 1998). Battered women seek help from family, clergy, police, lawyers, counselors, and social service agencies, but often their responses to abuse are undermined by the responses of others (Dutton, 1996).

Social and economic pressures frequently prevent battered women from taking effective action. African-American battered women who perceive themselves as having fewer options because of racism are less likely to call the police or use social services in part because they mistrust these institutions (Joseph, 1997; Sorenson, 1996). It is not unusual for abused women to be blamed for their husbands' behavior or have their stories discounted. Women are often told to "try and be a better wife," to "be thankful for what you have," or to "think of the children." Abusive men may threaten to fight for custody of the children or threaten to harm the children if the wife leaves or doesn't come back (Butts Stahly, 1999). Furthermore, many women lack the money or job skills to provide for themselves and their children. Women in abusive relationships who try to work outside the home or go back to school may risk increased violence and interference from their abusers (Rigor, Ahrens, & Blickenstaff, 2000). Battered women may accurately believe that they have nowhere to go.

Battered women are often afraid to leave their husbands because they fear that their husbands will follow them and intensify their abuse, perhaps killing them, their children, or other family members. Indeed, women who leave a relationship are at increased risk for battering (Wilson & Daly, 1994; Dearwater, Coben, Campbell, Nah et al., 1998) as the following cases illustrate:

> Sharon had been separated from Roy for over two years and was divorcing him, yet he continued to harass her. He broke into her home, destroyed her furniture, poured acid in the motor of her car, and slit the seats with a knife. He cut power and phone lines to her house, set small fires, and bragged to others about how he was going to kill her. He attacked and severely injured her at work, and she finally took a leave of absence from her job. She had unlisted phone numbers, but he always got them. She repeatedly called the police for protection. (Browne, 1987, pp. 120–121).

> Every time Karen would have ugly bruises on her face and neck. She would beg me for a divorce, and I would tell her, "I am sorry. I won't do it again. But as for divorce, absolutely not. If I can't have you for my wife, you will die. No one else will have you if you ever try to leave me" (Browne, 1987, p. 114).

The physical abuse of women through severe beating or use of a gun or knife sometimes does result in death. Two-thirds of partner homicides in the United States are women killed by their male partners (Browne & Williams, 1993) and 30 percent of all murders of women are committed by current or former partners (U.S. Department of Justice, 2000). In contrast, only 3 percent of male murder victims are killed by wives or girlfriends (U.S. Department of Justice, 2000).

What Is Being Done?

Today, some argue that our society still supports abuse with a male-dominated family structure and economic system. As discussed in Chapter 9, husbands usually have more power than wives in a society in which men make most of the money and many of the important family decisions. This unequal distribution of power leads men to feel entitled to dominate and leads women to feel vulnerable. From this perspective, the way to end battering is to change our social structure.

The battered women's movement over the past two decades has begun this process through public education, legal reform, and programs designed to aid battered women. The first battered women's shelter in the United States opened in 1974. Now there are shelters in most large cities and many small towns. These shelters, largely through volunteer effort, provide temporary emergency housing, emotional support, and information about legal and social services. Women often cite shelters as the most helpful intervention when dealing with abuse (Gordon, 1996). Battered women in South Africa reported that access to a shelter enabled them to escape abuse and transform their lives (Angless, Maconachie, & Van Zyl, 1998).

Historically, police have been reluctant to arrest male batterers and have discouraged women from pressing charges. Due to education programs, officers are now more likely to respond to calls and make arrests. Some localities have adopted programs to arrest an abusive person without waiting for the abused person to press charges.

It is not yet apparent whether these mandatory arrest policies are effective. Taking away a woman's choice may be disempowering (Hoyle & Sanders, 2000). Other studies suggest that mandatory arrest policies can be an effective deterrent (Garner & Maxwell, 2000). Offenders arrested and sentenced have lower recidivism rates than men who did not have formal charges filed (Wooldredge & Thistlewaite, 2002).

In addition, psychologists have designed programs targeted toward men who batter their partners. Batterers who are court mandated to attend a treatment program and who complete the program are less likely to be charged with future abuse (Shepard, Falk, & Elliott, 2002). Compared with men who drop out, men who complete treatment programs are more likely to be in more egalitarian relationships, to be younger and less stressed, and to have more court monitoring (Gerlock, 2001).

Some progress has been made against domestic violence. Unfortunately, many areas still need shelters for battered women, and many shelters have inadequate funds and space to meet the needs of battered women. In addition, programs that treat male batterers are still in their infancy, and it is difficult to attract participants unless a court orders them to attend. Clearly, the battle to end abuse is not over.

ANALYZING AND ENDING VIOLENCE

This brief review of violence against women makes clear that common themes underlie all these forms of violence. The levels-of-analysis approach described at the beginning of this chapter shows how these themes are related.

The sociocultural level includes sexual inequalities, gender role prescriptions, and cultural myths as well as scripts for enacting relationships. Whether discussing childhood sexual abuse, sexual harassment, courtship violence, sexual assault, or wife abuse, a common underlying theme is societal endorsement of male dominance. Cultural norms governing aggression as a tool of the powerful to subdue the weak interact with gender inequalities to create a context conducive to violence against women.

The social network level of analysis helps show how gendered norms and expectations are transmitted through the various social networks of which we are all a part, including the family, peer groups, school, faith communities, and work groups. Witnessing domestic violence or experiencing parental physical punishment as a child is related to the various forms of violence against women. Indeed, roughly a third of individuals who witness or experience violence as children become violent as adults. Many households in which violence occurs are characterized by patriarchal family structures in which traditional gender roles are encouraged.

The dyadic level of analysis calls attention to the power and status differences between the perpetrator and victim. According to historical and sociocultural traditions, women and children are weaker and more passive than men and thus should be dependent on men. Such culturally prescribed dependence affects communication patterns and other relationship dynamics to increase women's vulnerability to abuse.

However, for male violence against women to occur, the situation must be conducive to the violence. A number of situational variables have been examined, including time, place, and the presence of social inhibitors or disinhibitors (such as the presence of others or the presence of alcohol). Regardless of the type of violence under investigation, features of the situation influence the likelihood that violence will occur by affecting the opportunity for the violent acts (such as times when privacy is available) or by contributing to the ambiguity of the situation.

Finally, intrapersonal variables appear to underlie various forms of male violence against women. These characteristics include endorsement of traditional gender-role stereotypes, acceptance of cultural myths about violence, and a need for power, dominance, and control over women and children. Other characteristics include antisocial tendencies and nonconformity, as well as impulsivity, irresponsibility, hypermasculinity, affective dysregulation, and self-centeredness coupled with insensitivity to others. The extent to which these specific intrapersonal variables influence the incidence of violence against women depends on the degree to which cultural norms and the influence of social groups affect mental representations of the situation and the relationship with the woman.

Analysis of violence against women from a feminist perspective emphasizes the sociocultural level. Our culture teaches men to protect women and women to look to others for safety and security. Ironically, in a chivalrous society, men are both those who commit violence and those who protect. Chivalry promotes the man as the protector and the woman as the protected, the man as the aggressor and the woman as the victim.

A key aspect of chivalrous behavior by men is to protect women's chastity and vulnerability from involuntary defilement and violent attacks. The protection, however, has its costs for women by prescribing a code of appropriate behavior—femininity. The characteristics of traditional femininity may make women perfect victims and vulnerable to attack. If a woman is attacked, she may be accused of noncompliance with the traditional codes for feminine behavior and blamed for her victimization. The culture in general, and men specifically, may accuse her of teasing and dressing provocatively in a sexual attack or of nagging and being disrespectful in a physical attack. Within the patriarchal system, a woman is both bound by rules for feminine behavior and accused when she is attacked and cannot protect herself, even though it is the culture that discouraged her from learning how to defend herself.

"Each girl as she grows into womanhood is taught fear. Fear is the form in which the female internalizes both chivalry and the double standard" (Griffin, 1971, p. 33). Her fear results in a passive response to male aggression. She may become paralyzed with fear, restrict her behavior (i.e., not go out alone, not do anything without her partner's permission), or try to appease her attacker. "The passive woman is taught to regard herself as impotent, unable to act, unable even to perceive, in no way self-sufficient" (Griffin, 1971, p. 33). To confront violence in our patriarchal society, women must use their own strength as an energy source for reform:

> Social movements, feminism included, move toward a vision; they cannot operate solely on fear. It is not enough to move women away from danger and oppression; it is necessary to move toward something: toward pleasure, agency, and self-definition. Feminism must increase women's pleasure and joy, not just decrease our misery. (Vance, 1984, p. 24)

Men must be included in the fight to end violence against women. Men are secondary victims as their girlfriends, sisters, wives, mothers, and daughters face the threat of attack. Men are also the victims of the codes that demand accountability for protecting women in a society where it is impossible to do so. By recognizing women as equals, refusing patriarchal demands for men to be dominant and aggressive, and fighting for legal and societal reforms, men will be liberated and our society transformed.

Feminist analyses of patriarchy and violence have given women and men a basis for combating violence against women. Documenting the problem provides the first step toward eradication. Public demand for legal reforms, explicit institutional policies condemning sexual misconduct of all forms, treatment facilities, and educational programs for young people signal hope that future generations of women, in equal partnership with men, will enjoy a life free from the fear of violence.

CONNECTING THEMES

- *Gender is more than just sex.* The pattern of intimate violence, in which women are the victims and men are the perpetrators, is not due to biological destiny. Women are not born victims and men are not biologically predetermined to be aggressors. Rather, stereotypes of how women and men are supposed to behave, experiences that reinforce stereotypical behaviors, and a social structure that supports power inequities between women and men all contribute to violence against women.
- *Language and naming are sources of power.* Traditionally, secrecy and myths regarding male-female relationships trivialized or justified male violence against women. The women's movement has done much to bring to public awareness the extent of the harm done to women by men and has prompted redefinitions that acknowledge the violence. Thus, for example, no longer is rape defined as a sexual act, sexual harassment as standard working conditions, and wife abuse as a legitimate way to "show the little woman who is boss"; rather, each is seen as an act intended to dominate and control women.
- *Women are not all alike.* Violence against women is influenced by social and cultural factors that affect the occurrence of and responses to intimate violence. Although violence against women is a problem throughout the

world, the incidence of violence and the forms it takes, as well as societal attitudes, can vary greatly across cultures.

- *Psychological research can foster social change.* Violence against women in its various forms is now recognized as a public health and social problem. Hence, research has moved from focusing on individual psychopathology to identifying the sociocultural factors that contribute to such violence. Also, communities, institutions, and organizations are combating violence against women by developing interventions that not only help individuals but also promote change in values and attitudes at the societal level.

SUGGESTED READINGS

BERGEN, RAQUEL KENNEDY (1998). *Issues in intimate violence.* Thousand Oaks, CA: Sage Publications. This is a comprehensive and accessible anthology that prepares the foundation for understanding a wide range of violence that commonly occurs in families and between intimates. Many articles offer a feminist perspective that addresses the gendered nature of violence and the consequences of power inequality in our society.

KOSS, MARY; GOODMAN, LISA; FITZGERALD, LOUISE; RUSSO, NANCY; KEITA, GWENDOLYN; & BROWNE, ANGELA (1994). *No safe haven.* Washington, DC: American Psychological Association. A comprehensive review of psychological research on the prevalence, causes, and effects of forms of violence against adult women is presented. Recommendations for effective intervention, treatment, and public policy initiatives are given.

RENZETTI, C. M.; EDELSON, J. L.; & BERGEN, R. K. (Eds.). (2001). *Sourcebook on violence against women.* Thousand Oaks, CA: Sage Publications. This edited volume contains scholarly articles on theoretical and methodological issues in research, reviews of various types of violence, and suggestions for prevention, treatment and public policy.

SCHEWE, P. (2002). *Preventing violence in relationships: Interventions across the life span.* Washington DC: American Psychological Association. This edited book provides a developmental approach to examining violence. Each chapter covers relationship violence at a different stage of life and in different relationships, from child and partner abuse to rape and elder abuse.

WALKER, ALICE (1982). *The color purple.* New York: Washington Square Press. This novel, which won the Pulitzer Prize and American Book Award for fiction, follows an African-American woman's life as she deals with life, love, and interpersonal violence.

CHAPTER 14

Mental and Physical Health

Why is gender central to any discussion of mental and physical health? Gender differences seem to be evident in both areas. Women are more likely than men to seek psychotherapy, and despite their longer life span, they are more likely to seek medical help as well. Are women actually sicker than men? If not, what accounts for these gender differences?

In this chapter we will examine psychological and physical distress through a gender lens. This is very complex because women's and men's identities, roles, and life circumstances influence their physical and mental health. Moreover, age, race and ethnicity, sexual orientation, and social class interact with gender. Developmental factors (such as the way families socialize girls and boys and the influence of peers) and cultural factors, which vary over time as well across national borders, all play a role. Each person's experiences are unique.

The *prevalence rates* of different psychological disorders (how often they appear) seem to vary with sex. Women appear to be prone to disorders that involve *internalization* (anxiety, depression, eating disorders), whereas men are prone to disorders that *externalize* their distress (substance abuse and problems with violence and aggression). Feminists have raised many unresolved questions about these trends. Do women and men manifest different kinds of psychological disorders, or do they show different symptoms of the same disorders? If some disorders are more prevalent in women than in men, can this difference be explained by biological sex? How important are gender roles and situational context in producing gender differences in psychological and physical distress? Can a person's social environment create psychological disorders? Are traditional methods of diagnosis and treatment intrinsically sexist? And, finally, how can the psychological and medical treatment of women be improved? All these questions will be addressed in this chapter.

GENDER AND PSYCHOLOGICAL DISORDERS

Clinical researchers generally agree about the disorders that are more likely to be diagnosed in women than in men. These include depression, eating disorders, and various anxiety disorders, such as *agoraphobia* (fear of being outside of one's home or in a crowd or, sometimes, being on a bridge or traveling by train, bus, or automobile) and *panic disorder* (recurrent, unexpected bouts of intense fear). Most mental health surveys indicate that the incidence of anxiety and depression is two to two-and-a-half times greater among women than among men. Prevalence studies indicate that clinical eating disorders are ten times more common in women than in men (Piran, 2001). What should we make of these statistics?

Is There a Feminist View of Psychological Disorders?

Feminist researchers have explored the diagnosis and treatment of women for nearly thirty years. Beginning in the 1970s, feminist therapists charged that the social system makes women "mad" (Chesler, 1972). They viewed psychological distress as a social as well as a personal event. Feminists today offer several perspectives on gender differences in psychological disorders.

Some feminist theorists question whether gender differences exist at all (Marecek, 2001). They view psychological diagnoses as forms of social construction. Societal norms define what traits and behaviors are considered acceptable and unacceptable in women and men. When people violate these norms, they are seen as having a psychological disorder. The gender biases of mental health practitioners shape perceptions and practices so that women are overdiagnosed for some disorders and underdiagnosed for others. Women's perceptions of their personal and social reality also influence the ways in which they show their psychological distress.

Other feminist theorists stress differences between the sexes and the special properties of women that shape both their distress and their resilience (Miller & Stiver, 1997). These theorists see many forms of women's distress as due to disturbances in women's sense of connection with others.

Still other feminist theorists look at women's symptoms of distress in terms of everyday sexism (Klonoff, Landrine & Campbell, 2000). They argue that the social power and dominance of men are major contributors to women's health problems. Women are more vulnerable because they encounter more stress than men do.

Each of these feminist perspectives is in sharp contrast to earlier theories, which focused on women's psychological weaknesses, and they include the social context of women's lives. The research inspired by these perspectives helps us understand gender differences in the diagnosis of psychological disorders.

Gender and Problems of Psychological Diagnosis

Psychological diagnoses are much more problematic than diagnoses of physical illness because objective standards are few. How do you take a psychological temperature or do a psychological blood test? Therapists are usually limited to information given by the client or to observations by people in close contact with the client. From this limited information, therapists infer causes and offer a diagnostic label.

Most mental health professionals (psychiatrists, psychologists, and psychiatric social workers) currently use the fourth edition of the *Diagnostic and Statistical Manual of Mental Disorders,* or DSM-IV (1994), in making their diagnoses. This impressive-looking book is published by the American Psychiatric Association. It includes descriptions of the symptoms of disorders as they are currently defined by the psychiatric community and provides information on prevalence rates for males and females for 101 of these disorders (Hartung & Widiger, 1998). Relatively few disorders have equal rates for women and men, and many show large gender differences. What is the source of these differences? Sampling biases and stereotypes are among the possible answers.

Sampling Bias

Several potential sources of sampling bias have been identified. First, women and men may differ in their ability or willingness to acknowledge that they have a disorder and in their willingness to seek treatment. Even the same symptoms may provoke different reactions in women and men. For example, some disorders, such as depression, are incompatible with the traditional masculine role. Alcoholism is more socially acceptable for men than women and appears to mask their depression.

Considerable evidence suggests that gender is related to whether a person seeks help. For example, although surveys of health agencies indicate that phobias and alcoholism are the most often reported disorders, depression and anxiety (both more common in women) are the most often treated (Becker, 2001).

Both women and men seem to agree that women need more help. When college students listened to audiotapes of a male or female actor describing the same psychological problem, they recommended more intervention for the female than for the male (Mosher, 2002). This study also showed that men are less likely to see themselves as needing help. Although both male and female students recommended more intervention for an actor than for themselves (if they had similar problems), this difference was greater for men.

Gender Bias and the DSM

Therapists are taught to give individuals a psychological label based on how well their symptoms match the list of symptoms given for one of the diagnostic categories in the DSM-IV. Here are some descriptions of two disorders:

- This person is depressed most of the time, tending to feel sad, blue, down in the dumps, and "low."
- The person doesn't seem to be interested in his/her usual activities and doesn't get pleasure out of them anymore.
- The person passively allows others to assume responsibility for major areas of his/her life because of a lack of self-confidence and an inability to function independently.
- The person subordinates his/her own needs to those of others on whom he/she is dependent in order to avoid any possibility of having to be self-reliant.

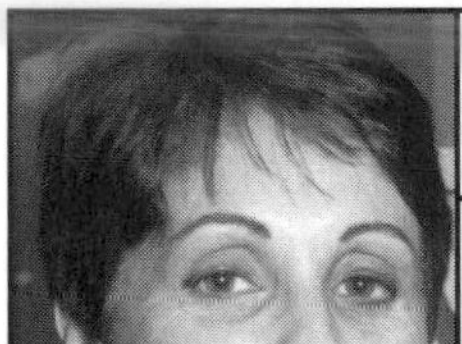

Making a Difference

Phyllis Chesler (b. 1935), psychotherapist, professor, public lecturer, and author, is best known for her 1972 book, *Women and Madness.* This volume, which has sold 2.5 million copies, told the world that women aren't crazy—they're oppressed—and their trauma is only increased when they are misdiagnosed and mistreated by the psychological and psychiatric professions. Chesler argued that a double standard of mental health exists for women and men; women are medicated, put in mental institutions, and pathologized for behaviors that would be considered normal in men. Women's status as second-class citizens and the frequency with which they are physically and psychologically abused add to their difficulties. Yet, when they respond assertively, they are deemed mentally ill. The twenty-fifth anniversary edition of *Women and Madness,* with its new introduction on the trauma of psychiatric labeling, is unfortunately still quite relevant to women's lives.

Since 1972, Chesler has written several other important books. These include *With Child: A Diary of Motherhood* (1979) and *Sacred Bond: The Legacy of Baby M* (1986). Chesler was also a founder, in 1969, of the Association for Women in Psychology. She was recently named the first research scholar to the International Institute for Research on Jewish Women at Brandeis University. Phyllis Chesler is a founding mother of feminist therapy, and it has been said that she enjoys "a reputation as one of America's most articulate and thoughtful feminist writers, [whose] activism in representing women who are marginalized by illness, poverty, and exploitation has not diminished despite personal hardship."

Source: About Dr. Chesler, www.phyllis-chesler.com/biography.htm. *Contemporary Authors.* (1998). New Revision Series, Volume 59, pp. 85–86.

- The person is unwilling to make demands on the people he/she depends on for fear of jeopardizing the relationships.
- The person tends to belittle his/her abilities and assets by constantly referring to himself/herself as "stupid."

The first three symptoms describe mild depression, and the last four describe a dependent personality.What kind of people do these descriptions bring to mind? Do you think they are male or female? Young or old? Rich or poor?

When lists including such descriptions were shown to students who were asked what kind of person was being described, they tended to agree on the individual's gender, ethnicity, and social class (Landrine, 1988, 1989). A large majority agreed that the individuals described above were white, middle class, and female. Psychological symptoms are not evaluated in a social vacuum. Perceptions of psychological symptoms are inextricably associated with social characteristics. They involve assumptions about social roles (married or single) as well as about class, race, age, and gender.

Although it is impossible to do a similar study with professionals (because they are familiar with DSM categories), research shows that diagnoses are linked to stereotypes. For example, clinicians labeled a stereotypical description of a single, middle-class white woman as a hysterical personality, and they labeled the stereotype of a married, middle-class woman as depressed (Landrine, 1987). Neither the therapists' gender nor their clinical orientation had any effect on the labels they chose.

Why are gender stereotypes and diagnostic categories connected? Some theorists conclude that actual differences in the incidence of various disorders create the link (Hartung & Widiger, 1998). Others argue that some disorders are identified in some people just because they are members of a particular gender, race, or class category (Landrine, 1987). In other words, under some circumstances, simply being a woman is a sufficient reason to be considered "crazy" (Caplan, 1995).

Questions about gender and psychological diagnosis have become more compelling as the number of labeled disorders has risen steadily in each edition of the DSM. The first edition in 1952 listed 198 disorders; the 1994 edition listed 340. The proliferation of disorders means that more areas of life can be brought under the scrutiny of mental health practitioners and subjected to judgments about normality and abnormality (Hare-Mustin & Marecek, 1997).

The proliferation of diagnostic categories is particularly problematic for women because the identification and treatment of gender-characteristic disorders are not value free. Many signs of psychological distress are both vague and highly subjective. Stereotypic beliefs can lead to different labels being attached to the same symptoms, different opinions about the severity of such symptoms, and different views about the nature of effective treatment for women and men. Women and men may internalize these beliefs so that they themselves view their symptoms differently and seek treatment at differing rates.

Gender biases in the DSM are particularly troubling because it is used by most therapists. DSM labels determine whether people will be reimbursed for their treatment. Feminists charge that the research base of this manual is weaker than the psychiatrists who constructed it claim (Caplan, 1995; Becker, 2001).

Gender Differences in Distress: A Review of Explanations

If we assume that diagnostic biases do not explain all the difference in the incidence of various disorders in men and women, what causes the difference? We will briefly review the major theories that aim to explain gender differences in psychological distress.

Medical Models

Medical models assert that women are biologically more vulnerable to certain disorders, especially depression. As discussed in Chapters 7, 10, and 12, women are regarded as being particularly at risk during periods of hormonal change such as menstruation, after childbirth, and during menopause. Thus, medical models define women almost entirely in terms of their reproductive functions. In effect, they see a direct connection between the uterus and the mind.

If biological vulnerability explains gender differences in disorders, however, one would expect these differences to remain fairly constant over time. In fact, a higher rate of mental illness in women appears to be a recent development in the United States. Before World War II, more men than women were admitted to mental hospitals. Moreover, although recent surveys report a higher incidence of psychological symptoms among women than men, the reverse was true in earlier studies (Unger, 1979a).

Gender differences in depression also vary with race and ethnicity and across cultures. For example, a study of various ethnic groups in Los Angeles County found no gender differences in depression among Asian Americans (Root, 1995). In developed countries such as the United States, Canada, the United Kingdom, Italy, and Germany, women have higher rates of depression than men, but the ratio varies from a low of 1.6: 1 to a high of 3.5:1. Gender differences are more inconsistent in developing countries (Whiffen, 2001). Such historical variations and ethnic and cultural differences suggest that biological vulnerability is too simplistic an explanation for gender differences.

Stereotypes and Gender Identity

An alternative explanation for gender differences in the prevalence of some psychological disorders is the idea that traditional gender roles increase the risks for some disorders. In other words, behaving like a feminine woman increases a woman's chance of developing depression, agoraphobia, panic disorder, or an eating disorder. High scores on passivity, dependency, and concern for pleasing others—all aspects of femininity—are associated with agoraphobia (Fodor & Epstein, 2001), depression (Bay-Cheng, Zucker, Stewart, & Pomerleau, 2002), and disordered eating (Murnen & Smolak, 1997). In contrast, men who score high on masculinity are more likely to suffer from alcoholism and aggressive acting-out disorders (Good & Sherrod, 2001). In other words, conforming to one's gender-role appears to be pathological for both women and men (Huselid & Cooper, 1994).

The Impact of Sexist Events

Living in a sexist society may contribute to women's psychological distress. A scale called "The Schedule of Sexist Events" measures women's experience with sex discrimination in four areas: their close relationships, their distant relationships, the workplace, and encounters involving sexual degradation (Klonoff & Landrine, 1995). The latter category includes, for example, having to listen to sexist jokes (reported by 94% of the women as having occurred at least once in their lives) and being sexually harassed (reported by 82%). Fifty-six percent of the women sampled reported that they had been picked on, hit, shoved, or threatened with harm because they were women. A woman's score on this scale was related to her level of psychological and physical distress—for example, to premenstrual discomfort; depression; obsessive, compulsive, and somatic symptoms; as well as the total number of psychiatric and physical symptoms (Landrine, Klonoff, Gibbs, Manning, & Lund, 1995). Sexist discrimination contributed more to women's symptoms than did other stressors such as family problems.

In a later study, these researchers found that college women who reported experiencing little sexism in their lives did not differ significantly from college men. However, compared with men and less-stressed women, those women who were exposed to a high level of sexist stress reported more symptoms of anxiety, depression, and *somatization* (body symptoms such as headaches or pain that are due, in part, to psychological causes) (Klonoff, Landrine, & Campbell, 2000). These data suggest that a sexist society can truly make some women "crazy."

Sexist discrimination does not occur randomly. For example, never-married women reported more sexist treatment in every domain but work. Women of color reported more incidents of sex discrimination than white women did. And younger women reported more sexism than older women. The prototypic woman who reported the fewest incidents was a 32-year-old married white woman (Klonoff & Landrine, 1995).

The Social Construction of Symptoms

Society not only makes women sick, it also tells them what the signs of their sickness should be. Stereotypes function as prescriptions for women's behavior rather than accurate descriptions of that behavior (see Chapter 2). Social systems can create many behaviors that are considered maladaptive.

A major mechanism in this process is the *double bind,* which exists when mutually contradictory assumptions exist within the same social context (see Chapter 3). For example, it is almost impossible for a woman to be seen as feminine and instrumentally competent at the same time because society's definition of competence excludes so-called feminine characteristics such as sensitivity and dependence. For a woman to gain the rewards of femininity, she must forgo rewards for competence, and vice versa. Because of contradictory demands, a woman is likely to incur some social penalty no matter how she behaves.

Double binds are the result of social definitions. They are more likely to be imposed on individuals who are relatively powerless. Many so-called female disorders may be a response to covert control mechanisms like the double bind. Whatever a woman does under such circumstances may be labeled "sick." Socially defined feminine illness may be the only way that some women can find to rebel against social constraints. Conversely, the label of psychological disorder can serve to control rebellious women as well.

Social construction theories emphasize the situational context of women's lives. They do not, however, explain why some women acquiesce in their roles, others develop effective coping mechanisms, and still others develop maladaptive behavioral patterns. But this weakness is not unique to social construction theories. More generally, although psychologists understand some of the risk factors for illness, they cannot explain why some individuals show symptoms of distress and others do not.

POWER ISSUES

Norms—including those that define what is mentally healthy—change over time, and they are not applied to everyone the same way. People who have little power are more likely than powerful people to be punished for engaging in undesirable behaviors. This is because the less powerful do not have the ability to define themselves. Power greatly influences how psychological diagnoses are created, applied, and treated.

The Case of Dora

In general, women have less power than men do. In clinical psychology, women have been the patients and men the practitioners. The effect of this power differential on diagnosis and treatment may be seen in the earliest psychoanalytic annals. One example that has been reconstructed by feminist scholars is the case of Dora (Hare-Mustin, 1983; Lakoff, 1990), an 18-year-old girl who was treated by Freud (see Box 14.1).

Freud did not see himself as Dora's advocate but as her father's (who was paying for the therapy). His task, as he saw it, was not to make Dora happy or productive but to "bring her to reason"—to make her stop pestering her father and his friends. Freud was able to define Dora, not her family, as the source of her problems. In his notes, he indicated that he "forced her to acknowledge" certain truths; that she "confessed that she had masturbated"; and that her objections to his interpretations were "easy to brush aside." In case histories of male patients, Freud noted that they "discovered" such facts together or that he "explained" his hypothesis. With Dora, in contrast, Freud used his interpretations as weapons to convince her to submit. His analysis of Dora represents therapy in its most adversarial form (Lakoff, 1990), and the case illustrates the abuse of therapeutic power.

The Social Construction of Female Disorders: The View from History

Much as Freud was able to define Dora's view of her reality as a fantasy, doctors through the decades have silenced patients' voices. Psychologist Gail Hornstein (2002) has a large collection of personal accounts of mental illness. The patients' narratives are filled with reports of their being locked in isolation rooms, deprived of writing materials, or having their letters censored. Women's accounts often mention sexual and physical abuse as sources of their symptoms, but biological theories dominate the medical accounts of women's disorders.

An Epidemic of Nervous Disorders

Scientific classification has often been used to legitimate biological explanations for women's distress. One example comes from the mid-nineteenth century, when an epidemic of nervous disorders raged among women in England and the United States.

Anorexia nervosa, hysteria, and neurasthenia were the labels given to these nervous disorders. *Anorexia nervosa*—identified in 1873 among adolescent girls in England and France—was characterized by extreme emaciation, loss of appetite, lack of menstruation, and restless activity (Showalter, 1987). Classic *hysteria* had two defining characteristics—seizures or fits and sensations of choking (the latter was believed to be caused by the rising of the uterus within the body). However, attention soon moved from these symptoms to traits, moods, and personality. By the end of the nineteenth century, "hysterical" had become almost interchangeable with "feminine" (Showalter, 1987). Hysterical women were described as highly impressionable, suggestible, and narcissistic (Smith-Rosenberg, 1985). *Neurasthenia,* like hysteria, had a wide range of symptoms, from blushing, vertigo, and headaches to insomnia, depression, and uterine irritability. It was seen as being caused by increased mental activity in women, which sapped their strength (Showalter, 1987).

Box 14.1 The Dora Case

In 1899, an acquaintance and former patient brought his 18-year-old daughter, known as Dora, to Freud. She suffered from a number of hysterical symptoms, which were making life annoying for her family and, in particular, for her father. The father requested that Freud "bring her to reason." Freud was acting on the father's behalf. He saw it as his job to persuade Dora that—however correctly she may have analyzed her family's situation—she had to admit that her neurosis was self-induced and that, in order to be "cured," she must renounce her own perceptions in favor of those of her father's and Freud's.

For many years, Dora's family had been friends with another family, the Ks. Herr K. was like Dora's father (and Freud): an ambitious and successful man in his forties. Frau K. and Dora, not yet out of childhood, became confidantes, and Dora came to realize that her father and Frau K. were having an affair and that the families were making vacation plans to facilitate it. Since no one wanted Dora's mother, Herr K. was the odd man out.

From the time Dora was 7 or 8, Herr K., the busy, successful businessman, found the time to take long walks with her and to buy her expensive gifts. At the age of 14, Dora went by invitation to Herr K.'s office to watch a festival from the window. Herr K.'s family was supposed to be there too. When she arrived, Herr K. was alone and the curtains were drawn. He grabbed the child when she went up the stairs and gave her a deep kiss. She felt his erection and pulled away in horror and disgust. Her symptoms began with this incident. There were a couple of similar, but more serious, incidents, and after each, her symptoms increased. Dora eventually tried to tell her father about the incidents. He confronted Herr K., who denied everything, and Dora was accused of creating fantasies in order to make trouble. Dora ultimately came to the conclusion that the two men were using her as an item of barter: my wife for your daughter. The only problem with the arrangement was that, although the other three were consenting adults, Dora's preferences were never consulted. Freud acknowledged that Dora's perceptions had validity but felt that it would be an error for him to tell her because it would just encourage her in her willful and disruptive ("neurotic") behavior.

Dora remained in analysis with Freud for only three months. Freud offered several reasons for her ending treatment. She was taking revenge on him for not responding sexually to her or she was incapable of relating to him because of her homosexual attraction to Frau K. There is no explicit evidence for either argument in Dora's own recollections or associations.

Source: From *Talking Power: The Politics of Language* by Robin Tolmach Lakoff. Copyright © by Robin Tolmach Lakoff. Reprinted by permission of Basic Books, a member of Perseus Books, L.L.C.

All these disorders were especially frequent among well-to-do, intellectual women. Physicians attributed them to the weakness of the female reproductive system and the strains put on that system by women's ambition. As late as 1900, one physician pictured the female reproductive cycle in the following melodramatic terms:

> Many a young life is battered and forever crippled in the breakers of puberty; if it crosses these unharmed and is still not dashed to pieces on the rock of childbirth, it may still ground on the ever-recurring shallows of menstruation, and lastly, upon the final bar of the menopause ere protection is found in the unruffled waters of the harbor beyond the reach of sexual storms. (Quoted in Smith-Rosenberg, 1985, p. 184)

Others declared that mental breakdown would occur when women defied their "nature" by competing with men instead of serving them or by seeking alternatives or additions to their maternal functions. One physician "concerned about 'the danger of solitary work' for girls 'of nervous family' studying at home, forbade the 15-year-old Virginia Woolf to continue her lessons and ordered her to spend four hours a day gardening" (Showalter, 1987, p. 126).

Many well-known women suffered from these disorders. Alice James, the sister of Henry and William James, began her career as an invalid at the age of 19. There is no way to know if Alice James's lifelong illness had a "real" organic basis. However, unlike her brothers, she was never encouraged to go to college or to develop her gift for writing (Ehrenreich & English, 1979).

Psychiatric treatment of nervous women has been described as ruthless. Physicians assumed that patients were shamming. Their goal "was to isolate the patient from her family support systems, unmask her deceitful stratagems, coerce her into surrendering her symptoms, and finally overcome her self-centeredness" (Showalter, 1987, p. 137). The standard treatment was a "rest cure" pioneered by a noted American neurologist, Silas Weir Mitchell. The patient was isolated from her family and friends for six weeks, confined to bed, and forbidden to sit up, sew, read, or write.

One of Mitchell's patients was Charlotte Perkins Gilman, who wrote a fictionalized account of her experiences in *The Yellow Wallpaper.* Gilman's heroine went mad, but Gilman herself recognized that she was being brainwashed and left treatment. Among Mitchell's other patients were Jane Addams and Edith Wharton. These women were exceptions in that they went on to live full and active lives. Most cases were more like that of Alice James—neither fatal nor curable (Ehrenreich & English, 1979).

Gender, Class, and Social Control

What created this epidemic of nervous diseases? Feminist scholars emphasize the limited roles that upper-class women were permitted during the Victorian era. These women had no serious productive work in the home; tasks such as housework, cooking, and child care were left as much as possible to domestic servants. Women were expected to exchange sexual and reproductive duties for financial support (Ehrenreich & English, 1979). Nervous disorders such as neurasthenia and hysteria provided a socially acceptable way for a woman to remove herself from her self-sacrificing role as a wife or mother. This escape from emotional and sexual demands was, however, purchased at the personal cost of pain and disability and the social cost of an intensification of stereotypes about women's passivity and dependence (Smith-Rosenberg, 1985).

These nervous disorders were constructed in terms of gender: similar symptoms in men and women were given different labels. The years between 1870 and World War I were the "golden age" of hysteria, but the diagnosis of hysteria was limited to women. When large numbers of men began to suffer from "shell shock" in response to the intolerable conditions of World War I, their "hysterical" behavior was labeled instead as a functional neurosis (Showalter, 1987).

The disorders were also constructed in terms of social class. Working-class women did not have the time nor money to be patients. Nineteenth-century experts blamed education for the greater weakness of affluent women. Their arguments were both sexist and racist:

> At war, or at play, the white man is superior to the savage, and his culture has continually improved his condition. But with woman the rule is reversed. Her squaw sister will endure effort, exposure, and hardship which will kill the white woman. Education which has resulted in developing and strengthening the physical nature of man has been perverted through folly and fashion to render women weaker and weaker. (Dr. Sylvanus Stall, in Ehrenreich & English, 1979, p. 114)

Social Construction Today

Social constructionism does not deny the reality of women's suffering; it does not claim that nineteenth-century women made up their symptoms. However, the social constructionist view does point out how some parts of women's experience may be expressed, whereas others may not. What is important is how women are taught to describe and label their experiences and how these labels fit socially acceptable roles. In the nineteenth century, educated women were permitted to be sick or mad, but they were not allowed to be angry or to protest their limited choices.

It is possible that some twentieth-century female disorders, such as PMS, involve social construction much as the nineteenth-century nervous disorders did. If the unacceptable parts of personality can be labeled PMS and be seen as the result of an unfortunate hormonal imbalance, a woman can retain her self-definition as a good woman and deny responsibility for violent, aggressive, or antisocial behavior (Laws, 1983).

The boom in PMS may be a response to the second wave of feminism (Laws, 1983). Like nineteenth-century nervous disorders, PMS defines women's consciousness of discontent in medical terms, and we look at it in detail later in this chapter.

Differences in power because of ethnicity and class also shape the social construction of psychological disorders and how clinicians treat disorders. Clinicians may be unaware of culturally diverse coping strategies and insensitive to the negative consequences of so-called healthy coping strategies under some circumstances. Following is a candid account of a rape-counseling session between a volunteer counselor, Michelle Fine, and a black woman who lived in poverty, Altamese Thomas. Altamese did not want to prosecute her attackers or talk with social workers or counselors. She disrupted the counselor's white, middle-class views about taking control in the face of injustice.

FINE: Altamese, the police will be here to speak with you. Are you interested in prosecuting? Do you want to take these guys to court?

THOMAS: No, I don't want to do nothin' but get over this. . . . When I'm pickin' the guy out of some line, who knows who's messing around with my momma, or my baby. Anyway nobody would believe me.

FINE: Do you think maybe you would like to talk with a counselor, in a few days, about some of your feelings?

THOMAS: I've been to one of them. It just made it worse. I just kept thinking about my problems too much. You feel better when you are talking, but then you got to go back home and they're still there. No good just talking when things ain't no better. (Fine, 1983–1984, pp. 253–254)

Altamese Thomas had little power to change the causes of her problems—racism, poverty, and violence. Individualistic strategies could have made matters worse for her family. They would do little to improve oppressive economic and social arrangements. Self-knowledge without the power to change her circumstances will do little for her.

Two recent studies show that any therapeutic system that looks at individual behavior in isolation from sociocultural circumstances is fundamentally flawed. In a sample of more than 2,400 adults, depression was significantly higher among residents of economically disadvantaged neighborhoods (Ross, 2000). Within those neighborhoods, however, average income had no effect on reported levels of psychological distress. Instead, the negative effect on mental health appeared to come from the social disorder of the neighborhood (measured by crime, dilapidated housing, and vagrancy). A similar study that focused on black women found similar results. Women who were already at risk for a psychological disorder reported more symptoms of distress if they lived in disordered rather than socially cohesive neighborhoods (Cutrona, Russell, Hessling, Brown, & Murry, 2000).

DEPRESSION

The Gender Gap in Depression

Depression is the disorder that has received the most attention in terms of gender issues. On the surface, depression appears to be an exaggeration of normal sadness. Although depressed individuals may have a sad facial expression, other signs are more serious. These include loss of appetite, insomnia, and fatigue, as well as indecisiveness, hopelessness, and feelings of inadequacy and guilt. Research shows that many factors in women's lives combine to make them more vulnerable than men to this form of psychological distress.

It has been estimated that as many as 28 percent of women in the United States and 14 percent of men will suffer from depression at some point in their lives (Hankin et al., 1998). The so-called gender gap in depression is not found at all ages. In a recent national survey of more than 12,000 Norwegian adolescents, no gender difference was found at age 12 (Wichstrom, 1999). However, more girls than boys became depressed between 13 and 14 years of age. A gender gap in depression in Norway is particularly disheartening because this country seems to have considerable social equality: it has had a female prime minister for a long time, half of the other ministers are also female, and more young women than young men pursue a university degree. Nevertheless, the gender differences found among Norwegian adolescents are very close to those found in the United States.

In the United States (as in other Western counties), the rate of depression for both boys and girls rises rapidly during adolescence, but the increase is much greater for girls. One study found that between the ages of 15 to 18, the rate of depression among girls rose from 4 percent to 23 percent, whereas the rate among boys rose from 1 percent to 11 percent (Hankin & Abramson, 2001). After the teenage years, the 2:1 difference in rate of depression for women and men remains unchanged until late middle age. After age 60, men show an increase in depression, but women do not (Barefoot, Mortensen, Helms, Avlund, & Schroll, 2001). Older men also have a much higher rate of suicide than older women do (Canetto, 2001).

Many researchers have attempted to explain developmental changes in the risk of depression for females and males. Explanations include gender differences in biology, in personality traits, in roles, in cognitive styles of perceiving and coping with stress, and in power. It is likely that all these factors play a role, and we will discuss each of them.

Blaming Women: Reproductive Function as a Source of Depression

Despite considerable evidence suggesting social causes for depression, medical texts give great weight to explanations based on women's body chemistry. Women are regarded as being particularly vulnerable during critical points in

FIGURE 14.1. If feminst researchers dispute one label, others can find another. *Source:* Six Chix. Reprinted with Special Permission of King Features Syndicate.

their reproductive cycle. Several forms of depression are labeled in terms of women's reproductive stages—for example, premenstrual syndrome (PMS), postpartum depression, and menopausal syndrome. But the *syndromes*—or constellations of symptoms—associated with women's reproductive stages are very poorly defined. For example, no single pattern of symptoms is required for a diagnosis of PMS (a disorder in which women become more emotionally erratic and hostile during the few days before menstruation). There is no agreed-upon test to determine its existence (Ussher, 1989). Nevertheless, claims have been made that from 25 percent to 100 percent of women suffer from some form of premenstrual or menstrual emotional disturbance (Laws, 1983).

The Example of PMS

In fact, empirical research has produced little evidence to support the idea that most women have a negative premenstrual phase. In one study, 10 percent of the women who said they had PMS and 10 percent of those who said they did not met the criteria for the diagnosis (McFarlane & Williams, 1994). Because most participants (men as well as women) experience a cyclic fluctuation of moods, the researchers suggested that those women who believe they have PMS are attending to actual physiological changes but mislabeling them.

Labels have an important impact on the way women view their bodily changes. In another recent study, female college students completed either a "Menstrual Joy Questionnaire" or a "Menstrual Distress Questionnaire" before responding to a measure of menstrual attitudes. Those who first encountered "menstrual joy" reported more positive attitudes and cyclic changes (Chrisler, Johnston, Champagne, & Preston, 1994). Participants also reported that they were surprised by these findings because they had never before considered positive aspects of the menstrual cycle.

More recently, researchers have demonstrated that "a little psychiatric knowledge may be a dangerous thing" (Nash & Chrisler, 1997). When participants read the description of "Premenstrual Dysphoric Disorder" with the label attached, they were more likely to perceive that premenstrual changes were a problem for women than if they read the same description with the label "Episodic Dysphoric Disorder." The premenstrual label did not influence women's perception of their own menstrual changes but made them more likely to attach a psychiatric label to women they knew who had symptoms. Men had a more negative response to symptoms when the symptoms were associated with the menstrual cycle than with a more gender-neutral label..

Medical and pharmaceutical interests have helped to create PMS (Parlee, 1989), and women's magazines have popularized the idea that PMS exists and is a hormonal problem (Markens, 1996). These magazines use women's experiences to show what is wrong with women's bodies, and this focus on women's bodies allows the structure of work organizations to go unchallenged. They endorse gender roles as "natural" just when inequities of power and privilege are being contested. Their stories about PMS focus on professional women. They have little to say about women who work in low-wage jobs. Even the self-help instructions for dealing with PMS—such as "changing jobs" or "closing the office door"—are class biased. There has been very little coverage of PMS in magazines aimed at African-American women (Markens, 1996).

Deconstructing the Reproductive Syndromes

Menopause and the period *after* pregnancy are also considered times when women are at high risk for depression (see Chapters 10 and 12). Why? Menstruation and menopause carry negative values in our society, but pregnancy is a more mixed event. Thus, it is not surprising that the postpartum period is presented as dangerous.

The reproductive syndromes help to justify beliefs in the biological inferiority of women. The notion that their reproductive cycle makes women vulnerable to psychological problems serves to limit women—to define them as dangerous and deviant and to exclude them from a role in society equal to that of men. Biological determinism—or anatomy as destiny—leads people to neglect the social sources of women's unhappiness. Rather than social change, unhappy women are offered chemicals in the form of hormones or psychotropic drugs. The use of such drugs to control women's emotions during periods of hormonal change is problematic. At best, these substances are ineffective and, at worst, they may be habit forming or medically harmful. Although there is little evidence to support the existence of hormonal imbalance syndromes, belief in them supports a thriving industry for physicians, psychiatrists, and drug companies.

Personality Characteristics and Depressive Symptoms

If biology cannot explain gender differences in depression, do personality traits provide the answer? Several studies have linked the likelihood of becoming depressed and identification with negative aspects of femininity. For example, in a national sample of women ages 18 to 45, women who placed a high value on *embodied femininity*—acceptance of mainstream criteria of what women should look like and the use of media standards for judging one's own body—had more depressive symptoms than those who were less accepting of such cultural demands (Bay-Cheng et al., 2002).

Instrumental traits (associated with traditional masculinity) may protect both men and women from depression. A meta-analysis of studies of the relationship between gender-role orientation, depression, and general adjustment found that "masculine" people (both females and males) showed higher adjustment and less depression than "feminine" people (Whitley, 1985).

Before everyone decides that women would be better adjusted if they were just like men, it is important to recognize the role that other characteristics associated with traditional masculinity play in mental health. For example, the inability to speak up for oneself is associated with depression (Smolak & Munstertieger, 2002). But the ability to speak up for oneself, or *assertiveness,* appears to be a function of status and roles rather than gender. In an ingenious meta-analysis that compared assertiveness scores of college women and men from 1931 to 1993, Jean Twenge (2001) found that women's assertiveness scores increased from 1931 to 1945, decreased from 1946 to 1967, and increased again from 1968 to 1993. Changes in assertiveness were closely associated with indicators of women's status, such as their educational attainment and their average age at first marriage. Men's roles have not changed much over the past sixty years, and their assertiveness scores exhibited neither a birth cohort effect nor any relationship to social indicators.

Self-esteem also plays a role in the association between gender and depression. Recent work indicates that the sources from which people derive their self-esteem are key. Both male and female college students who derived their self-worth from other people (for example, from being admired for academic achievement or appearance) paid a higher cost in stress than did students with largely internal sources of self-esteem (Crocker, 2002). External sources of self-worth are less stable than internal sources, and instability of self-esteem is a risk factor for depression (Crocker, 2002). Thus, women may be at increased risk for depression because they are socialized to rely on external sources of self-esteem (see Chapters 2 and 7).

Gender Roles and Depression

Other researchers have suggested that women's need for relationship is linked to their higher risk of depression. Women's sense of self is thought to be related to their need to be connected with others (Miller, 1991). When their relational needs are not met, women tend to see this as their own failure—they see themselves as not caring enough or not doing enough. A lack of mutuality in relationships has been found to be a significant predictor of depression in women (Genero, Miller, Surrey, & Baldwin, 1992).

Maintaining relationships with men is an important part of the socialization of Euro-American girls (see Chapter 8). To do so in a patriarchal society, they must silence their authentic self and deny that their needs are not being met. College women who reported a high level of self-silencing also reported speaking out less with parents, fellow students of both sexes, and with professors (Smolak & Munstertieger, 2002). Self-silencing has been linked to depression in young white women (Jack & Dill, 1992).

Do gender roles affect how women and men experience depression as well as whether they become depressed? Male and female college students with the same level of depression reported differing symptoms, and the differences were consistent with gender stereotypes. Depressed men reported physical symptoms, such as sleep disturbance and loss of sexual drive, as well as social withdrawal and suicidal thoughts. Depressed women were more likely to report emotional symptoms such as crying, sadness, and a sense of failure (Oliver & Toner, 1990). Similar stereotypic differences have also been reported in patients who have been hospitalized for severe depression (Vredenburg, Krames, & Flett, 1986).

Depression and Cognitive Styles of Perceiving and Coping with Distress

A number of researchers believe that the risk for depression is increased and periods of depression are prolonged by particular cognitive styles or ways of perceiving and dealing with negative events. One of the most important of these is *rumination*—a passive focus on one's symptoms of distress and on the possible causes and consequences of these symptoms (Nolen-Hoeksema & Jackson, 2001). Examples of rumination include sitting alone thinking about how tired and unmotivated you feel, worrying that your moods will interfere with your job or studies, and passively reviewing all the things that are wrong with your life.

People who believe they have little control are more likely than other people to ruminate (Nolen-Hoeksema & Jackson, 2001). Women ruminate more than men, and rumination is a significant predictor of future depression even after the current level of depression is taken into account (Nolen-Hoeksema, Larson, & Grayson, 1999). Depressed adolescent girls, like depressed women, report elevated use of rumination, less use of distraction, less effective and active problem solving, and fewer attempts to seek help from others (Broderick & Korteland, 2002).

Gender differences in rumination begin early. Early socialization encourages different ways of dealing with problems in girls and boys (Keenan & Shaw, 1997). Preschool girls are explicitly taught to take other's feelings into account when dealing with conflict. In retrospective reports, college men more than women reported that their parents punished or ignored their expressions of sadness (Garside & Klimes-Dougan, 2002). During middle school, girls' scores for rumination were significantly higher than boys' scores. By adolescence, both sexes believe that girls ruminated more than boys and that boys should not ruminate about their problems (Broderick & Korteland, 2002). Ironically, the fact that coping scripts are more rigid for boys than girls may help protect them from obvious signs of depression.

Power and Depression

The statistics on rates of depression suggest another factor behind the gender differences. Rates of depression are very high among less-privileged groups of women. For example, 35 percent of the Mexican-American women who came to a community health center were found to be clinically depressed (Tazeau & Gallagher-Thompson, 1993). And 83 percent of the women who used a domestic violence shelter were depressed (Campbell, Sullivan, & Davidson, 1995). Only 58 percent were still depressed ten weeks later, probably because the shelter experience reduced their sense of powerlessness and increased their sense of social support.

Depression is lower among women who are employed full time, have jobs that allow autonomy, and have little difficulty obtaining help with child care and housework (Mirowsky, 1996). Having multiple roles and being employed gives women more power, and power is linked to psychological well-being for both women and men.

In fact, a great deal of the gender gap in depression may be due to power differences. Individuals who are younger, are less educated, have lower incomes, or are unemployed are at high risk for depression, regardless of whether they are female or male (Golding, 1988). Many of these factors are associated with being female. When they are all taken into account, gender differences become insignificant.

A report of the Task Force on Women and Depression of the American Psychological Association highlights how women's place in the social structure depresses them. It found, for example, that the prototypic depressed individual was a woman with a young child who was living in poverty (McGrath, Keita, Strickland, & Russo, 1990) and that the victims of sexual and physical abuse were very vulnerable to depression. When one looks at social context, it is difficult to view the greater depression of women than men as an indicator of psychopathology unless it is the psychopathology of society rather than that of individuals.

The Demographics of Eating Disorders

Depression, we have shown, does not exist in isolation. Many factors linked to depression are also linked to eating disorders, and women who are depressed are also more likely than other women to display eating disorders. For example, in one recent survey, embodied femininity, weight concerns, and depression were positively associated for Latina and white women (Bay-Cheng et al., 2002). In another study, depression and binge eating were also significantly correlated for both groups (Fitzgibbon et al., 1998). Girls with high body-dissatisfaction scores at ages 13 to 16 were found to be much more likely to develop a major depression four years later (Stice, Haywood, Cameron, Killen, & Taylor, 2000). As Chapter 7 discussed, dieting is not consistently tied to eating disorders, but eating disorders have been linked to a concern with thinness and to body dissatisfaction.

Beginning in elementary school, girls are more dissatisfied with their weight and shape than boys. As Chapter 7 discussed, it takes a relatively greater degree of overweight for boys (or men) to be dissatisfied (see Figure 14.2). Significantly more girls than boys reported spending time dieting, wishing they were thinner, feeling pressured to eat, and feeling guilty after eating sweets (Keel, Fulkerson, & Leon, 1997).

Body dissatisfaction increases as girls move into adolescence. Middle school girls with high body dissatisfaction or weight concerns are likely to develop problematic eating attitudes and behaviors in later adolescence (Smolak & Striegel-Moore, 2001). Approximately two-thirds to three-quarters of high school girls in the United States report dieting to lose weight despite being of normal weight or underweight (Pike, 1995). Between 5 and 15 percent of adolescent girls engage in more extreme forms of weight control, such as vomiting and purging (Phelps, Andrea, Rizzo, Johnston, & Main, 1993).

Estimates of the incidence of eating disorders vary widely, but it is clear that the vast majority of people with anorexia and bulimia are women. In fact, the extent of dieting and concern about weight control among women is so high today that it has been termed a "normative discontent" (Rodin, Silberstein, & Striegel-

FIGURE 14.2. The media reinforces weight concerns in vulnerable teenage girls.
Source: Stone Soup. © 2001 Jan Eliot/Distributed by Universal Press Syndicate.

Moore, 1984). In contrast, male body concerns are focused around being bigger or more muscular. For males, lack of muscularity is associated with low self-esteem (Smolak & Striegel-Moore, 2001).

"Normal" Strategies for Weight Control

Many girls begin to monitor their food intake during the middle-school years. A girl's preoccupation with weight and body shape is correlated with that of her friends (Paxton et al., 1999). In-depth interviews with high school girls illustrate the collective nature of concern with weight and appearance. The girls engaged in a form of discourse that has been termed *fat talk* (Nichter & Vuckovic, 1994). Throughout the school day they frequently repeated the statement, "I'm so fat." It was not used, however, by girls who were actually overweight or who had attempted to change their weight over a sustained time. The phrase appeared to be a request for reassurance, not an actual statement about weight. Here is the response of one 14-year-old to the interviewer's question, "What usually happens when someone says I'm so fat?"

> JAMIE: About six or seven girls go "No, you're not!" Probably it's just because, you know, you like to hear that people don't think you're fat. And it's mostly like in gym, cuz when you change into your gym clothes those are so bunchy anyway they make you look fat. And, uh, but I'd say, I'd say that not very many of them mean that, mean it when they say it. They just want to hear "Oh no you're not." (Nichter & Vuckovic, 1994, p. 114)

Confusion between thinness and a perfect life is common among white adolescents. Researchers reported being struck by the uniformity of teenage girls' descriptions of the ideal girl (tall, thin, and usually with long blond hair) regardless of the girls' own physical characteristics (Nichter & Vuckovic, 1994). The responses of African-American adolescents were much more varied. They often began with a list of personality traits rather than physical attributes (Parker et al., 1995). They described the ideal girl as having it "going on." This meant having what they had work for them: long nails, pretty eyes, big lips, nice thighs, whatever.

By the time they reach university, women are judged by how well they regulate their eating behavior. In a study using videotapes of college women and men consuming the same large or small meal, the female who ate the smallest "feminine" meal (a salad) was rated as more socially appealing than the same woman when she ate the larger "masculine" hoagie (Basow & Kobrynowicz, 1993). College-age women appear to be aware of the effect that eating less has on perceptions of them. They have been found to eat a smaller snack during a "get-acquainted" study when they interacted with a desirable male confederate than when they interacted with an undesirable male or any female (Mori, Chaikin, & Pliner, 1987).

Weight Control and Health

Attempts to lose weight may endanger health and affect school performance. One of the most dangerous forms of weight control is smoking (see Figure 14.3). In a sample of college women, believing that smoking controls weight, exposure to thinness-depicting media, and low levels of skepticism about tobacco adver-

FIGURE 14.3. Dying to be thin.
Source: For Better or For Worse by Lynn Johnston, 1992. © Lynn Johnston Productions, Inc./Distributed by United Features Syndicate, Inc. Reprinted by permission.

tising were associated with being a smoker. Among smokers, smoking for weight control was associated with believing that smoking controls weight, internalizing pressure to be thin, and having low levels of feminist consciousness (Zucker, Harrell, Miner-Rubino, Stewart, Pomerleau, & Boyd, 2001). In a recent national sample of women smokers, 39 percent said they would be very concerned about gaining weight if they stopped smoking. Fourteen percent of the women who were very concerned about weight gain said they "would be very willing to risk their health in order to be slim" (Pomerleau, Zucker, & Stewart, 2001).

Although there is extensive documentation of the negative relationship between smoking and health, data on the relationship between being overweight and poor health are much less clear. Recent studies indicate that repeated cycles of weight loss and gain increase the risk of many disorders associated with obesity. Dieting is also unlikely to be successful over the long term and may be related to weight gain (Ernsberger & Koletsky, 1999). Experts in nutrition and health are beginning to shift toward a focus on a healthy lifestyle, a positive attitude toward health and self-care, and a disregard for predetermined weight standards. Of course, this perspective must confront the continued obsession of the media with thinness at the expense of health.

Disordered Eating as Pathology

It is unclear at what point the desire for thinness translates into pathological behaviors. DSM-IV includes criteria for diagnosing anorexia and bulimia.

Anorexia is currently defined as the refusal to maintain a weight that is minimally normal for an individual of that age and height, intense fears of gaining weight or becoming fat, body image disturbance, and a denial of the seriousness of the current low weight (Pike & Striegel-Moore, 1997). Anorexics may use dieting, fasting, and excessive exercise to lose weight, or they may induce vomiting and abuse laxatives and diuretics.

Anorexia usually emerges between puberty and 17 years of age. Girls and women account for the great majority of reported cases, although the disorder may be present in 1 percent of adolescent males (Walters & Kendler, 1995). It has been estimated that 40 percent of individuals with anorexia recover, 30 percent improve, and symptoms become chronic in 20 percent. As many as 10 percent may die (Pike & Striegel-Moore, 1997) (see Figure 14.4.).

Bulimia is characterized by episodes of binge eating that may last two hours or more, during which the person feels a loss of control. Bulimics feel that they cannot stop eating or control what or how much is eaten. Weight is regulated by excessive purging or use of laxatives and diuretics. Males account for about 10 percent of all bulimics. Between 1 to 2 percent of adult women have the disorder, with a greater incidence among those women born after 1960.

Binge eating disorder is defined by recurrent episodes of binge eating without regular attempts to control weight by the excessive use of laxatives or purging. People with this disorder also eat faster than normal, eat until they are uncomfortably full, eat a large amount of food when they are not physically hungry, and eat alone because they are embarrassed about the amount of food they eat. They feel disgusted, depressed, or guilty after overeating. About 2 percent of adult females in community surveys meet the criteria for binge-eating disorder, and about 30 percent of the obese individuals who participate in university weight control programs have the disorder (Yanovski, 1993). It is only slightly more common in women than it is in men.

Many women with eating disorders appear to be able to function reasonably well despite their extreme preoccupation with weight. Most anorexic women deny that they have any problem at all. Bulimic women are also unwilling to disclose their "disgusting and wasteful" food practices. Because our culture so highly values thinness, excessively low weight may be ignored or

FIGURE 14.4. The consequences of anorexia. Photographs of Karen Carpenter "before" and "after."

even socially rewarded. Women in treatment are often those who still live in their parents' home, where the abnormal food habits and excessive exercise cannot escape notice.

Ethnic Differences in Body Concerns

The "typical" anorexic woman is usually portrayed as upper or middle class and white. Recent evidence suggests, however, that eating disorders are increasing among girls and women of color (Ofosu, Lafreniere, & Senn, 1998; Striegel-Moore & Smolak, 1996). For example, both Euro- and Asian-American female college students were more concerned about their weight than their male counterparts were and believed that they were heavier than they actually were. However, Euro-American women reported more dieting and binging behavior than the Asian-American women did (Mintz & Kashubeck, 1999).

Recent generations of marginalized girls and women appear to be at greater risk for eating disorders because of acculturation into the middle class. Latina and Asian women who presented themselves at community health clinics with symptoms of anorexia, bulimia, or binge disorder were more likely than their peers with other symptoms to speak English and to have mothers and fathers who were born in the United States (Cachelin, Veisel, Barzegarnazani, & Striegel-Moore, 2000). Latina girls and women appear to be especially at risk for disordered eating (and depression) (Bay-Cheng et al., 2002).

Black women show a more complex picture of body dissatisfaction. For example, a recent sample of low-income African-American girls in sixth through eighth grade found that 50 percent reported that they would like to lose weight (Grant et al., 1999). Although low-income black girls may have better body esteem than their white or middle-class black counterparts, they had much lower esteem than comparable African-American boys. In another study, older urban black women were less likely than white women to use extremely restrictive dieting practices. However, a substantial percentage reported fasting (25%), use of diuretics (11.9%) and laxatives (8.8%), and self-induced vomiting (2%) for weight control (Thomas & James, 1988).

How can we explain these differences between ethnic groups, and what can they tell us about the causes of weight concern and eating disorders? Some studies suggest that black women are as concerned about their weight as women from other ethnic groups, but that their preferred weight is higher than that of white women (Pomerleau et al., 2001). A more intriguing theory is that different ethnic groups have different ideals of appearance, focusing on different aspects of their bodies. In one study, for example, women from all ethnic groups wished to be taller. White and Latina women wanted larger breasts, whereas neither Asian nor black women mentioned breast size as important. All groups of women except African-Americans indicated a desire for a darker complexion (Altabe, 1998). In another study, Asian-American women reported less satisfaction with their eyes and face than European-American women (Mintz & Kashabeck, 1999).

Skin color and hair texture are often issues for African-American women in therapy (Greene, White, & Whitten, 2000). Among women who attended an historically black college, those who were less satisfied with their skin color were also less satisfied with their overall appearance (Falconer & Neville, 2000).

Although for white women, ideals of thinness and body and weight concerns are centrally linked to mental health, the focus on white women has obscured issues important to women from other ethnic groups.

Prevailing stereotypes of the white, upper-middle-class victim may have conspired against the early recognition of eating disorders in people of color. Although there was no difference in the presenting symptoms of eating disorders of women from different ethnic groups, women of color were less likely to receive treatment at a community health center (Cachelin et al., 2000). Women of color who sought treatment for anorexia had lower weights at the start of their treatment, suggesting that the disorder may go undetected or untreated longer in ethnic-minority women (Pike & Striegel-Moore, 1997).

Obviously, some people are more susceptible to eating disorders than others. We have focused on social risk factors rather than on individual ones because it is important to keep individual behavior in cultural perspective. But individual traits are important. For example, compared with women with eating disorders, unaffected women were less vulnerable to self-objectification—they did not look at their bodies from another's perspective (Noll & Fredrickson, 1998). They were more likely to identify with feminist values such as commitment to nonsexist roles and personal empowerment (Snyder & Hasbrouck, 1996).

Several studies indicate that lesbians have less negative views of their bodies than heterosexual women (Bergeron & Senn, 1998; Lakkis, Ricciardelli, & Williams, 1999). A lesbian identity buffered them from the impact of social norms. It did not, however, completely protect them from pressure to be thin. For all groups of women, internalization of societal norms predicted negative attitudes about their bodies.

Feminist Perspectives on Eating Disorders

A feminist focus avoids blaming the victim and highlights issues of social and cultural change. Feminists ask: Why are standards for women's attractiveness under such tight social control, and who in society benefits from these standards? Young women's bodies are subject to unwanted scrutiny as soon as they begin to mature. Offensive comments and put-downs are certainly not good for women's mental health. Teasing about appearance has been connected to body dissatisfaction and eating restraint among young teenage girls in Sweden and Australia as well as in the United States (Lunner et al., 2000).

Sexual harassment has been more closely linked to signs of eating disorders among undergraduate women than to any other form of psychological distress (Harned, 2000). Feminist therapists argue that a person's behavior cannot be changed without considering her situational context. In the case of eating disorders, "situational" refers to cultural norms about male-female relationships as well as personal circumstances.

ISSUES IN TREATMENT

Most psychological therapy is designed to help change the individual. Beginning with Freud, therapy has been more often used to reconcile the powerless to their circumstances than to assist them in creating social change. Diagnosis and therapy have focused on biological or on intrapsychic factors, which leads to the neglect of social context and thus to pathologizing the individual (Becker, 2001). We turn now to the contributions of feminist theory, research, and practice in dealing with issues of personal and social change.

The Double Standard in Diagnostic Categories

Treatment begins with diagnosis. Therapists use DSM-IV to determine which individuals are worthy of treatment and how those individuals should be treated. But how are the diagnostic categories determined? More specifically, one feminist clinical psychologist's questions include: How is the boundary drawn between disorders on the one hand and crime, eccentricity, or alternative lifestyles on the other? Who is part of the negotiations that fix the boundaries? What kinds of activities surround the birth of new categories of disorders and the death of old ones? (Marecek, 1993).

The process that determines the diagnostic categories in DSM is in part political. When DSM III-R was being revised to create DSM-IV, feminist therapists realized that several categories that had negative implications for women were being considered for inclusion. For example, they objected to the proposed inclusion of "self-defeating personality disorder," which corresponds to what is popularly called masochism, and it is not in DSM-IV. Creating a label does not make ambiguous data stronger, but it can cause people to believe that a particular disorder really exists. The power to name has important consequences.

Androcentric biases have led to important omissions in DSM. For example, during the creation of DSM-IV, the proposal to add battered women's symptoms to DSM was not accepted. As Chapter 13 discussed, *battered women's syndrome* appears to be a special case of *post-traumatic stress disorder*, or *PTSD*, a diagnostic label that does appear in DSM-IV. The criteria for a diagnosis of PTSD include recurrent and intrusive memories and dreams, distressful experiences when exposed to events symbolizing the trauma, persistent avoidance of thoughts and feelings associated with the trauma, and persistent and heightened arousal symptoms such as irritability, hypervigilance, and exaggerated startle responses (American Psychiatric Association, 1994). If a battered woman comes to a therapist and her history of physical and psychological abuse is not considered, she is likely to be diagnosed as depressed or paranoid.

As DSM-IV currently defines it, however, PTSD does not fully describe the complexity of battered women's experience. This is because the diagnosis was originally conceptualized to deal with the traumatic impact of war on men. Unlike the abrupt ending of a war or act of terrorism, the ongoing and intimate nature of the violence that women experience in the home may lead to a different set of reactions. Moreover, the traumatic situation may still be present when battered women enter the mental health system seeking assistance.

Androcentric biases in DSM include the assumption that autonomy and individualism are healthier than dependency and concern with relationships. These assumptions may be flawed. What if gender-biased definitions of dependency were reversed? Here is one feminist's answer:

> Suppose dependency were defined as letting someone else choose one's underwear, clean one's clothing, cook one's meals, arrange details of one's vacation? Men who do not become competent in these spheres or exert energy in fulfilling these tasks are not perceived as dependent or having failed to separate.

> They are not thought to suffer psychologically or emotionally from the condition, nor perceived to be less developed as individuals. Rather men are thought to be exhibiting their independence of women and home by pursuing public activities. (Travis, 1988b, p. 20)

In a similar vein, another feminist therapist proposed a new diagnostic category called "delusional dominating personality disorder" (Caplan, 1991). This diagnostic category describes the pathology of men who conform to social norms for the "real man." Its behavioral criteria include the following:

> The presence of any one of the following delusions: (a) the delusion of personal entitlement to the services of (1) any woman with whom one is personally associated, (2) females in general for males in general, (3) both of the above; (b) the delusion that women like to suffer and be ordered around; (c) the delusion that physical force is the best method of solving interpersonal problems; (d) the delusion that sexual and aggressive impulses are uncontrollable in (1) oneself, (2) males in general, (3) both of the above; (e) the delusion that pornography and erotica are identical. . . .
>
> A pathological need to affirm one's social importance by displaying oneself in the company of females who meet any three of the following criteria: (a) are conventionally physically attractive; (b) are younger than oneself; (c) are shorter in stature than oneself; (d) weigh less than oneself; (e) appear to be lower on socioeconomic criteria than oneself; (f) are more submissive than oneself.
>
> A distorted approach to sexuality, displaying itself in one or both of these ways: (a) a pathological need for flattery about one's sexual performance and/or the size of one's genitalia; (b) an infantile tendency to equate large breasts on women with their sexual attractiveness. A tendency to feel inordinately threatened by women who fail to disguise their intelligence. (Caplan, 1991, p. 173)

Whether or not you take this new diagnostic category seriously, it demonstrates the extent to which social norms and individual pathology can be confused, as well as the effect values have on what is considered normal.

Gender Bias in Practice

Some of the earliest studies on gender stereotypes found that clinical practitioners shared popular beliefs about the appropriate characteristics of men and women (Broverman et al., 1972). Although clinical practitioners now see traits in less gender-biased ways, they still classify more stereotypically masculine than feminine characteristics as socially desirable (Phillips & Gilroy, 1985).

Furthermore, clinicians, whether female or male, are likely to view a female client more positively than a male with identical symptoms (Hansen & Reekie, 1990). In contrast, male physicians like male patients better than female patients even when the patients' education, income, and occupation are taken into account (Roter & Hall, 1997). These biases increase the likelihood that females will be treated for psychological disorders whereas medical causes will be explored for males.

Biases also influence decisions about appropriate treatment. In general, powerless individuals are more likely to be treated with drugs, electroshock, or medical hospitalization than with long-term individual psychotherapy. For example, therapists are likely to recommend more medication and less psychotherapy for elderly, depressed female clients than for younger women or for men of any age (Ray, McKinney, & Ford, 1987). In Great Britain, black women are more likely than white women to be diagnosed as having a chronic rather than an acute mental health problem and to be institutionalized for mental illness (Watson & Williams, 1992).

Perceptions about gender differences influence all aspects of treatment. When they violate norms of acceptable behavior, women are more likely to be defined as mentally ill and are treated by clinical practitioners. Men are more likely to be seen as engaging in antisocial activities and are dealt with by the criminal justice system. Thus, they are not counted as suffering from psychological disorders, which makes it appear that more women than men are mentally ill.

Is it better to be defined as ill or as a criminal? Unlike psychological treatment, a criminal's sentence has time limits or criteria for termination. The standards of what is criminal behavior are clearer than definitions of mental instability; every society has a set of laws and penalties for breaking them. Definitions of criminality are applied to behavior and hold the person responsible for it; mental illness is perceived as more internally based and less under the individual's control. Thus, society's gender-typed responses to deviance may contribute to myths about women's greater weakness and instability.

There are some interesting exceptions to society's beliefs about women's lack of control and need for psychological help. These exceptions occur when domestic affairs go awry. For example, the mothers of abused children are frequently punished severely by the law for failing to control the violence of their male partners. Women who kill their batterers often receive more severe penalties than men who kill their female partners. Implicit assumptions about women's responsibility for the family and home appear to underlie these legal double standards (Fine & Carney, 2001). In a recent well-publicized case, a mother was jailed for life for killing her five children. Her husband had failed to seek help despite clear evidence that she was severely depressed, but the media portrayed him as a hero because he stood by her in the courtroom and pleaded for her life.

The Feminist Critique of Traditional Treatment

The use of drugs instead of psychotherapy and support for social change is one of the most negative aspects of a medical model of women's mental health. More women than men are given prescription drugs by their physicians. Although most forms of substance abuse are more common among men, women are more likely to abuse prescription drugs (Kilbey & Burgermeister, 2001). Many of the chemical addictions of women over the past century are directly attributable to medical practices. Physicians and other practitioners provided women with opium-based patent medicines in the 1800s, amphetamine-based diet pills in the 1960s, and tranquilizers such as Librium and Valium in the 1970s (Kandall, 1999) (see Figure 14.5).

The medical model has also encouraged women to seek individual solutions to many problems that may not best be solved individually—or may not be responsive to individual remedies at all. It has discouraged women from

FIGURE 14.5. A cartoonist's view of gender-biased prescriptions.
Source: Rubes. Reprinted by permission of Leigh Rubin and Creator's Syndicate, Inc.

finding social or collective avenues of self-help. For people with less power—people whose emotional problems are most often rooted in social arrangements and practices that have severely restricted their life options—the medical model can be destructive. The belief that they can solve by themselves problems over which they have no control as individuals can have severely depressing consequences.

Feminist therapists have charged that traditional therapies often lead practitioners to make the *fundamental attribution error:* the locus of causality is placed within individuals rather than in their circumstances. Because of this perspective, traditional therapists are more likely to see pathology in normal behavior, especially when they are evaluating people whose life circumstances are most different from their own. Women are labeled as disordered when the true diagnosis should be that society is unjust. As one early feminist therapist pointed out:

> As long as basic structural inequities of power exist in society, large numbers of women will manifest symptoms of this inequality. Working to correct social inequities is, in the long run, the only final cure for most forms of female emotional distress. Therapy can help people cope with certain intolerable social conditions, but it cannot improve those conditions unless it contributes to raising the consciousness of patients so that they will be less likely to tolerate them. On the one hand, this points to the necessity to demystify therapy so that people are no longer encouraged to believe that only individual psychological

"treatment" can cure what ails them. On the other hand, this points to the by-and-large unexplored potential of therapy to be an instrument of social change. (Greenspan, 1983, p. 36)

Traditional therapy can be viewed as a form of social control because it focuses on personal rather than on social change. Feminist therapists aim to help clients understand the ways in which they collude with their own oppression and to recognize their own power, both as individuals and as members of a community of women.

Feminist therapists have criticized the process of therapy as well as its assumptions and goals. The myth of the detached and neutral expert has tended to cloud the fact that every therapist offers a worldview to his or her clients—the terms by which they are to understand themselves and their world. As is shown in the case of Dora, the therapist's choice of words, of what to analyze, what to stress, and what to ignore, are all political acts laden with meaning. There is nothing neutral about this process (Greenspan, 1983).

Feminist Therapy

What does feminist therapy offer as an alternative? Unlike many other schools of therapy, feminist therapy does not have a single "founding mother." Instead, a number of pioneering practitioners recognized the need to provide solutions for the practical problems facing women: discrimination, violence, oppression, and marginalization (Brabeck & Brown, 1997). Feminist therapy is a philosophy of therapy rather than a set of specific techniques (Marecek, 2001). Its basic principles include honoring the client's own perspective on her life, placing the person and her problems in a social context, attending to the power relationship in therapy, closely examining multiple sources of oppression in the client's life (in addition to gender), and fostering social change (Hill & Ballou, 1998).

One of the most important contributions of feminist therapy is its focus on power. Unlike other schools of therapy, feminist therapy is concerned about the world outside of people's heads. A key issue is how to devise ways to call attention to women's oppression and its debilitating effects without losing sight of women's agency (Marecek & Kravetz, 1998). Although they see gender as the primary focus for understanding oppression and power imbalances, feminist therapists also call attention to multiple sites of oppression. They see each individual as both oppressor and oppressed—as a part of dominant culture and marginal to it (Brabeck & Brown, 1997).

On a practical level, feminist therapists try to avoid using diagnostic labels as a means of stigmatizing women who do not conform to gender stereotypes. They call for a recognition that clients' behaviors are adaptive responses to an unhealthy society rather than forms of pathology for which they must be blamed (Wyche & Rice, 1997). They try to assist their clients' understanding that many personal problems are a result of social inequality and common to many women. But they also help their clients use their own personal resources to challenge and alter their circumstances in ways that are consistent with their own values (Greene, 1994).

The goal of feminist therapy is personal empowerment—defined as helping women to become more independent and assertive about attaining their goals and achieving psychological growth (Wyche & Rice, 1997). Empowerment is a complex phenomenon involving changes at the personal, interpersonal, and sociopolitical level (Morrow & Hawxhurst, 1998). To become empowered, individuals must seek permission, enablement, and information at each of these levels (see Table 14.1). They must determine, for example, what sources of power they have, whether it is all right for them to use power, whether they will be able to use it, and what will happen to themselves and others if they choose to use their power.

Notice that we have shifted from the word *patient* to the word *client* in describing feminist therapy. Because of their concerns about power and hierarchy, feminist therapists strive for an egalitarian relationship with their clients. They often disclose some aspects of their own lives. This helps to demystify the therapeutic process and helps the client to see herself as an adult who is responsible for the solution of her own problems.

A recent article looked at whether individuals who identify themselves as feminist therapists differ in their therapeutic practices from those who do not identify with this label (Moradi, Fischer, Hill, Jome, & Blum, 2000). Unlike other practitioners, feminist therapists used behaviors reflecting the idea that the personal is political and paid attention to issues of oppression (sexism, racism, and heterosexism). Feminist therapists agreed most with practices such as

- Educating clients regarding the inequity of power between the sexes.
- Raise sex-role issues whether or not the clients bring them up.
- Teach clients to negotiate a balance between their own needs and the needs of their significant other.

Putting principles into practice is not always easy. Using more open-ended interviews, Jeanne Marecek and Diane Kravetz (1998) found that nearly all the feminist therapists wrestled with dilemmas stemming from the backlash against feminism. For example, they worried about how openly they should

TABLE 14.1. Conditions and Dimensions of Empowerment in Feminist Therapy

Conditions for Empowerment	*Dimensions of Empowerment*: **Personal** *(Power within)*	**Interpersonal** *(Power with others)*	**Sociopolitical** *(Power in society)*
Permission (May I? Am I worthy?)	Individual rights and freedoms	Approval or permission from another	Legal rights
Enablement (Can I? Am I able?)	Personal resources	Support and advocacy from others	Access to resources
Information (What do I need to know?)	"Know thyself"	Sharing stories, breaking silences	Questioning "the truth"

Source: S. L. Morrow & D. M. Hawxhurst. (1998). Feminist therapy: Integrating political analysis in counseling and psychotherapy. *Women & Therapy, 21,* p. 43.

identify with feminism when it meant alienating and losing potential clients. Sometimes, two feminist principles were in conflict. One example involved respecting a client's right to self-determination even if she chooses a self-defeating or potentially dangerous course of action.

Sometimes clients are not comfortable with feminist practices. Some are relieved to receive a diagnosis because it acknowledges that others share their problem and that treatments are available (Marecek, 2001). Clients who respect authority may be uncomfortable when the therapist shifts power to them (Raja, 1998). Many feminist therapists have called for more outcome studies to determine if and how feminist therapy differs from other forms of good therapy (Worell & Johnson, 2001).

Relational-Cultural Therapy

Another major theoretical framework whose primary concern is women's lives is *relational-cultural therapy* (formerly known as the *self-in-relation* model). It focuses on women's inner lives as well as on their social situation. It argues that the childhood experience of girls—especially the mother-daughter relationship—produces a unique self-structure that seeks connection to others and that needs such connection to flourish (Jordan et al., 1991). Psychological difficulties such as depression, anger, and work inhibition occur when women's need for relationships is thwarted. The empathy of the therapist and her ability to form an emotional relationship with the client is seen as key to women's growth and well-being (Miller & Stiver, 1997). Box 14.2 gives a summary of relational-cultural therapy written for this text by Jean Baker Miller (2002).

The work of Miller and her colleagues has been criticized by feminist therapists because of their lack of dialogue with others interested in women's distress (Chodorow, 1999; Marecek, 2001). Recently, however, relational-cultural theorists have conducted empirical research on the effectiveness of their therapy and published articles in peer-refereed journals. They have developed an instrument designed to assess growth-fostering connections with peers, mentors, and communities (Liang, Tracey, Taylor, Williams, Jordan, & Miller, 2002). This scale measures qualities important to relationships such as mutual engagement, authenticity (the ability to be honest), empowerment/zest (feeling personally encouraged and inspired to take action), and the ability to deal with difference and conflict. Preliminary studies indicate that depression is related to poor connections with the college community but not to relationship problems with peers or mentors. Undergraduates who were lonely scored lower on all aspects of their relationships.

The Impact of Therapist Characteristics

Does the Gender or Sexual Orientation of the Therapist Matter?

Current research indicates no differences in therapeutic outcome based only on the sex of the therapist. However, one problematic aspect of therapy between a female client and a male therapist is the possibility of sexual involvement between them. Although female-female relationships among therapists and clients have become increasingly visible, sexual involvement is still overwhelmingly a problem of violations by male therapists with female clients. There is no difference in the rates at which psychiatrists, psychologists, and social workers report having engaged in sex with their clients (Pope, 2001).

Having a sexual relationship with a client is a major abuse of the relationship. Although the rate at which sex occurs between therapist and client has declined in recent years, the problem has not been eliminated. A therapist will be expelled from the APA if he is found to have had a sexual relationship with a client.

Box 14.2. Brief Summary of Relational-Cultural Theory Therapy

Relational-Cultural Theory (RCT) departs from traditional psychological theories by focusing on the development of growth-fostering relationships. As relationships grow, so grows each person in them. The theory describes the nature of growth-fostering connections and by contrast the nature of relationships that cause disconnections via empathic failure, hurt, violation, and the like. Disconnections are the underlying source of psychological problems. RCT theorists contend that traditional theories, following from the premises basic to Western patriarchal thinking, emphasize individualism and separation. Learning from women's experience, RCT theorists have incorporated the neglected, invisible, and more complicated aspects of human connections that can enlarge understanding of people of both sexes.

While the initial group of RCT theorists were white, middle-class, and heterosexual, the theory group now is led also by women of color and lesbian theorists, who are deepening the theory by incorporating the specific experience of women of color and lesbians. Most especially, they are elaborating on the more complex understanding of power and privilege based on the intersections of racism, classism, heterosexism, and sexism.

Following from these theoretical ideas, RCT has provided specific "guides" for therapy, emphasizing such features as mutual empathy, mutual empowerment, authenticity, relational competence, moving away from the therapeutic power differential, and therapy as "movement-in-relationship" toward more mutual connection. This approach also involves understanding strategies of disconnection, internalized relational images, and the central relational paradox, which asserts that all people desire connection but because of hurtful, sometimes terrifying relational experiences, we develop strategies for keeping parts of ourselves out of connection. Within an overarching framework encompassing all of our experience is the concept of controlling images, derived from the work of sociologist Patricia Hill Collins (2000). Society inflicts controlling images on all of us based on the societal groups to which we're assigned; these images define our identities and our possibilities, including our notions of what therapy is and what therapist and patient can be and do.

RCT has now created a growing body of literature on many topics, including depression, trauma, eating problems, substance abuse, chronic illness, mother-daughter relationships, boys' and males' development, lesbian relationships, racism, classism, heterosexism, as well as a multitude of other topics. It has also created Research Network of more than 70 researchers studying these and other subjects.

The group has published a series of working papers and project reports, now numbering over 100, and conducts an annual research forum and therapy training institutes for therapists of various levels. Information on these and other topics as well as sample working papers are available at the website, jbmti.org or by writing the Jean Baker Miller Training Institute, Stone Center, Wellesley College, 106 Central St., Wellesley, MA, 02481. Phone: 781-283-3800.

Sources: Collins, P. H. (2000). *Black feminist thought* (2nd ed.). NY: Routledge. Jordan, J. Kaplan, A., Miller, J. B., Stiver, I., & Surrey, J. (1991) *Women's growth in connection.* NY: Guilford.
Jordan, J. (Ed.) (1997). *Women's growth in diversity.* NY: Guilford.
Miller, J. B., & Stiver, I. (1997). *The healing connection.* Boston: Beacon Press.
Work in Progress, Nos. 1–99, Wellesley, MA: Stone Center Working Paper Series.

Lesbian clients may encounter dilemmas during psychotherapy if the therapist is heterosexual. Heterosexual therapists may have conscious or unconscious prejudices about a "homosexual lifestyle." They may be unaware of the extent of abuse and violence that lesbians experience, and they may lack knowledge of lesbian communities. Here are some questions designed to stimulate therapists' awareness of their attitudes toward lesbians (Rigby & Sophie, 1990):

1. Do I believe a heterosexual woman has a better chance at a happy life?
2. How do I respond to two women publicly showing affection in a manner that has obvious sexual overtones? How does this compare to the way I feel when a heterosexual couple shows similar public behavior?
3. How do I react when a female shows that she is sexually attracted to me?
4. Should a mother tell her children she is a lesbian? Why or why not?

You may want to answer these questions to explore your own level of awareness or discomfort about lesbians.

When both therapist and client are lesbian or bisexual, there is the possibility of sexual relationships between them. If sexual attraction exists, the therapist is likely to terminate the therapy, refer the client elsewhere, and then enter a long-term relationship with her that frequently involves their living together. Such actions have great potential harm for the client and are unethical. True informed consent for any kind of sexual relationship is not possible, regardless of the client's expressed wish, because of the carryover from unequal power in the therapist–client relationship (Lerman & Rigby, 1990). Despite these problems, many lesbians feel it is important to have a lesbian therapist.

Does the Race and Ethnicity of the Therapist Matter?

Racial and ethnic similarity between therapist and client is probably a positive feature in therapeutic relationships, but there has been little research in this area partly because of the low number of minority therapists. The likelihood that an African-American woman, for example, will find a therapist who is also black, a woman, and a feminist is extremely small. Two decades ago, fewer than 100 black women psychologists listed themselves as clinicians in an APA directory, and among these, fewer than ten mentioned women's issues as a psychological interest (Childs, 1990). The number of African-American therapists has grown enormously in the past decade, but it is still likely that a combination of white therapist–black client will occur, particularly in public health clinics and hospitals.

Most therapists have had little training in the treatment of patients of color. Frances Trotman (2000), who is the director of a psychotherapy institute in a socioeconomically and ethnically diverse area, has written about potential pitfalls for both black and white therapists working with black clients.

> Racial guilt may make the European American therapist reluctant to suggest that the African American client has to take responsibility for her own life. Other behaviors that are more readily seen in the European American therapist-African American client relationship is the therapist acting as the self-appointed advocate, as the client-controller, or as the self-effacing sympathizer . . . The therapist subtly implies an inequality in their humanity and a disrespect for the

client's judgment and abilities. Well-meaning, dedicated, and sympathetic European American therapists are often trapped by the symbolism of their white skin and the subtle pervasiveness of America's guilt. The self-effacing therapist is neither genuine nor completely available to the client. (Trotman, 2000, p. 259)

Potential dangers also exist when therapist and client are both African-American.

> One is the possibility that the African American therapist will become overidentified with the client as a "victim of the system" and will aid her in denial of responsibility for her own life. . . . He or she may attempt to raise the consciousness of any African American woman who is seemingly unaware of the circumstances, history, and implications of her blackness via intellectual discussion. Such interventions may be quite instructional and educational. They are not, however, always therapeutic and often lead to premature termination by a client who either may be uninterested in or defended against such information (Trotman, 2000, p. 259).

Diversity and Therapy

Psychotherapy is based on the philosophical assumption that all members of society deserve life, liberty, and happiness. However, therapy is not equally available to all members of society. A user of therapy is likely to be a middle-class person with discretionary income, and have values that include being able to spend money on oneself rather than on family or children (Faunce, 1990). But feminist therapists feel that it is particularly important that therapists from the dominant group sensitize themselves to the experiences and values of many diverse groups, including women who belong to several oppressed categories, such as disabled women of color or lesbians from ethnic minority groups (Greene & Sanchez-Hucles, 1997). The needs of poor, older white women have also been neglected.

Groups that are marginalized and stigmatized by society have special problems in therapeutic situations. Therapists may be unaware of norms in other communities. For example, they may have difficulty distinguishing between wanting to work and having to work. For many women of color, work is not a novelty; it is burdensome and inescapable (Greene & Sanchez-Hucles, 1997).

Problems in therapy often stem from therapists' inability to "get inside the skin" of individuals whose life circumstances are very different from their own. For example, for clients in poverty, the concern may not be so much how to express anger but whether to express it at all (Faunce, 1990). For women with little power, the expression of anger may have extremely negative consequences in terms of abuse (see Chapter 13). Sometimes therapists invent stories to explain behaviors they do not understand. One social worker reported the experience of one mother:

> [She] waited four hours with her children for a clinic appointment and then finally acceded to the demands of her youngest for a snack. When the doctor eventually appeared, the mother hadn't yet returned and her absence was taken as a sign of irresponsibility. Filing for neglect was initiated. (Schnitzer, 1996, p. 574)

African-American Clients

Black women live in a culture that frequently reminds them of their skin color. To ignore it is to fail to acknowledge the individual's complete experience (Greene, 1986). Women of color are likely to live in environments where racism is pervasive. Encounters with racism are stressful and potentially traumatic and may have long-term psychological effects (Henderson-Daniel, 1994).

White therapists may also lack awareness of the pervasive effects of internalized racism. *Colorism* (which is found among some Asian-American groups as well) is a consequence of the internalization of the dominant culture's standard of beauty. Skin-color variations can be a source of conflict even within African-American families, but a European-American therapist might not think to ask about the skin color of family members (Greene, 1992). Following is a vivid account of how family conflict may be driven by perceived color differences:

> When I was growing up, calling someone black was worse than calling them nigger. We sat on the porch steps, and in a terrible game of degradation, compared our colors. Who was the darkest? Who was "it"? I was, more times than not. I fought my sister and my brother because they called me black. I generally got beaten up in those fights, and then beaten up again by my light-skinned mother for my loud, violent, attention-getting behavior. (Harris, 1994, p. 10)

Although race and class are confounded in the United States, a substantial number of women of color are middle or upper class. Class does not have the same meaning, however, for black and white women. African-American women are more vulnerable to unemployment because they lack the accumulated assets that many European-American women possess (Wyche, 1996). They also suffer more stress than comparable white middle-class women because they are likely to be one of the few minority group members in their place of employment and because social class does not necessarily protect black Americans from the stress of racist encounters.

Asian-American Clients

If most therapists know little about African-American women, they know even less about Asian-American women. The Asian-American community has become much more diverse in recent years as large numbers of Vietnamese, Koreans, East Indians, Cambodians, Hmong, Thai, and Tibetans have joined the Chinese-, Japanese-, and Filipino-Americans who were the predominant Asian-American groups during the past fifty years.

These groups vary from one another as well as from dominant U.S. culture, but most share traditional values that relegate women to subordinate roles (Bradshaw, 1994). Some Asian-American women are especially oppressed. In the Khmer culture, for example, women are supposed to "stay in the shadows and in the home" (Ho, 1990). They are particularly at risk for domestic violence, which is considered acceptable if the woman refuses sexual overtures from her husband or refuses to tolerate his extramarital affairs.

Asian-American women may not seek therapy because silence is supposed to convey pain and suffering (Bradshaw, 1994). When they are seen in community clinics, they tend to have a high rate of depression (Homma-True, 1990).

Latina Clients

The U.S. Census Bureau reported that in 2000, Latinos became the largest minority group in the United States—a more than 50 percent increase since 1980. The largest group includes those of Mexican origin followed by South and Central Americans, Puerto Ricans, and Cubans. There is great diversity among the groups categorized by the single label "Latino." For example, Cuban Americans have achieved higher levels of education and occupational attainment than individuals from other Latin American countries. Puerto Ricans, Chicanas, and Cuban Americans also differ in terms of their acceptance of traditional values and gender roles (Ginorio, Gutierrez, Cauce, & Acosta, 1995). A major factor that contributes to differences between various Latina populations is the conditions under which they immigrated to the United States (Espin, 1987b; Ginorio et al., 1995).

Although it might appear that they are protected by their extended family networks, Latinas are at high risk for mental health problems, especially depression. Their families are a source of both strength and distress (see Chapter 12). Latinas usually come to therapy angry and discouraged and feeling that they have little control over their lives (Vasquez, 1994).

Immigrants

Immigration is probably more stressful to women than to men because women are held responsible for maintaining family ties and ethnic traditions. It is particularly stressful when migration has been forced by war or other forms of state-supported violence (Lykes, Brabeck, Ferns, & Radan, 1993). Many Native American groups have engaged in a kind of internal immigration because of the poverty and lack of opportunities available on their reservations (LaFromboise, Choney, James, & Running Wolf, 1995). Immigrant women may show symptoms of multiple loss.

Poor Women

Poor clients may have a very different set of priorities than their middle-class therapists. The words of one participant in a black woman's support group illustrate this point:

> When I heard about this group I asked my therapist (a white woman) if I could attend. It seemed like all she was concerned about was the fact that I got raped. Hell! I know that was important, but that bastard got my last twenty-five dollars. That was all the money I had, till payday. I can deal with the rape later, but I won't have a job if I can't get back and forth to work. (Boyd, 1990, p. 156)

Therapists must be attentive to clients' material as well as personal needs. For example, when those in charge complain that "they" don't come in for appointments, the statement indicates concern about personal irresponsibility rather than problems such as lack of transportation or money for child care. Social workers or therapists may label women "disorganized" if they are unwilling to offer information that is socially stigmatizing (e.g., different fathers for several children). It is easy to confuse dire social circumstances with personal pathology.

Invisible Women

Feminist research on ethnically diverse populations has increased in recent years (cf. Landrine, 1995), but many groups are still invisible. Some groups of women have been almost entirely ignored even by feminist psychologists. There are, for example, many different Native American cultures, with more than 200 indigenous languages (LaFromboise, Berman, & Sohi, 1994), and half of the Native American population lives in urban environments separated from their tribal communities.

Other invisible populations are not part of any particular ethnic group. They include homeless women, lesbians, and disabled women. Because the latter group is often denied both the traditional feminine nurturing role and the role of independent worker, disabled women may feel that they have no role in society (Prilleltensky, 1996). Minimizing a client's disability or overemphasizing its impact on her life are common therapeutic pitfalls (Esten & Willmott, 1993). Dealing with disabled women may be particularly difficult for feminist therapists when these women do not fit their ideal of strong, independent, self-sufficient women (Barshay, 1993).

When researchers do examine neglected populations such as homeless women, they often find surprising results. For example, a study of homeless women found that they did not differ psychologically from a population of women from the same neighborhood who were not homeless (Jackson-Wilson & Borgers, 1993). Neither group of women had a high rate of psychological or physical disability. Instead, women in both groups were likely to be black and single and to have a higher than average number of children, an educational level of less than twelve years, and severely limited work histories. Social rather than intrapsychic variables appear to be the source of the homeless women's situation. They had fewer sources of social support during a period of need.

Invisible Values

Psychologists are much more likely to focus on weaknesses rather than on strengths. Thus, the value of women's coping strategies may be ignored or their difference from strategies used by men seen as evidence of individual pathology. Similarly, differences from the dominant culture can be either unseen or misinterpreted.

For example, as discussed in Chapter 12, the mother-daughter bond and other close kin relationships are often more important among other racial and ethnic groups than they are among European-American women. Also, the role of religion and spirituality has been neglected or misunderstood. A spiritual woman can construct meaning for her life in a belief system that includes behavioral (attending a religious service) and cognitive (prayer) components. Clinicians, however, may be unaware of indigenous religions such as santeria and may view spirituality as a passive rather than an active form of coping; they may fail to use this area of strength to help women make meaningful changes in their lives (Wyche, 2001).

Because of psychology's biases, women who deviate from cultural stereotypes about their weakness and need may also be ignored. Not all women of color are poor, some old women make important contributions to society, and lesbians vary as much as heterosexual women in terms of their need for therapy. A focus on diversity should not be used to promote stereotyping.

THE RELATIONSHIP BETWEEN PHYSICAL AND MENTAL HEALTH

There are many differences in the life experiences of white women and women of color in the United States. For example, women of color have always worked outside the home in greater numbers than white women. They are also overrepresented in occupations that pay low wages, have inadequate or no health insurance, and carry high risks of occupational injuries (Chrisler & Hemstreet, 1995). These include injuries that result from exposure to dangerous chemicals (laundry workers and hairdressers) as well as from repetitive movement (factory workers). Even though unionized automotive workers and college professors may earn the same amount of money, they are exposed to very different levels of stress. Worrying about "How am I going to find the time to write that journal article?" is quite different from worrying, "Will I come home from work today with both my hands?" (Baker, 1996).

The ability of women of color to endure and survive has not left them unscarred. Survival has come at the cost of adaptation to high levels of stress and, not infrequently, moving from crisis to crisis with little respite (Greene, 1986). Women of color have a higher mortality rate from coronary heart disease than white women do (Chrisler, 2001). Their increased vulnerability to heart disease is probably due to a combination of physiological and behavioral factors. For example, coronary heart disease has a strong inverse relationship with socioeconomic status (Adler & Coriell, 1997). Higher mortality is also linked with smoking, little or no exercise, and a high-fat diet. African-American women are less likely to smoke than European-American women, but are more likely to eat a high-fat diet and to be overweight.

Both medical and psychological researchers are beginning to understand the enormous role that stress plays in women's lives. Earlier in this chapter we discussed the impact that sexism and racism have on women's likelihood of developing a psychological disorder. Recent research also suggests that sexism and racism contribute to women's physical distress as well (Landrine & Klonoff, 2001). The highest mortality rates are among women with the least amount of education who are exposed to more stress than well-educated women are. Interestingly, chronic harassment from peers higher on the social hierarchy has been found to produce stress in monkeys and build up fatty deposits in their arteries (Goode, 2002).

In general, women live longer than men, but they have many more chronic diseases. This is especially true for auto-immune disorders such as diabetes and rheumatoid arthritis. There are race/ethnic differences in these chronic diseases as well. Black women have higher rates of lupus (a form of arthritis) and diabetes as well as higher levels of heart disease and high blood pressures than white women do (Chrisler, 2001). Although these disorders are probably not caused by stress, stress makes them worse. Recent studies have tied psychological stress, either directly or indirectly, to diabetes, rheumatoid arthritis, fibromyalgia, and severe depression (Goode, 2002). These are all diseases more common to women than to men.

One researcher has argued that women's well-known advantage in longevity can be altered by stress (Sered, 2000). Using data from Israel, a country with a high level of medical care available to all, she found that in the past ten years, the life expectancy of Israeli women has ranked between thirteenth and seventeenth in the world, whereas the life expectancy of Israeli men remained among the highest—first or second after Japan and Sweden. Women in Israel are also sicker than men. Susan Sered argues that this difference is a response to the multiple stresses on Israeli women from the Israeli military and religious establishment as well as its public policies. She notes, for example, that because of religious laws prescribing modesty, women's bodies are scrutinized more closely than in most democracies. She also points out that although women are expected to serve in the military, they are put in subordinate positions and exposed to a great deal of sexism. And although most women in Israel work outside the home, their salaries are lower than those of men, and they are expected to do most of the domestic work as well. They have little power to control either governmental policies or their own lives.

WHEN IS A CULTURE HEALTHY FOR WOMEN?

We have discussed this information about Israeli culture in part because there are some recent intriguing and unexpected findings on the relationship between cultural factors and individual differences in mental health. For example, a meta-analysis found that levels of anxiety and neuroticism have increased greatly in the United States in recent decades (Twenge, 2000). The average American child in the 1980s reported more anxiety than had child psychiatric patients in the 1950s. Women's level of anxiety is higher than men's, but gender differences in anxiety have not increased since 1968. Anxiety was highly associated with measures of lack of connectedness in society (for example, divorce rate) and perceived societal threat. These variables, however, predicted anxiety with a lag of five to ten years. In other words, it was the level of these variables during childhood and adolescence, not their current level, that had an impact on anxiety.

Interestingly, statistics measuring women's status (labor force participation and rate of college graduation) were also consistently related to anxiety for both women and men. Jean Twenge suggests that the growing level of anxiety may be a result of the increasing individualism of U.S. society. Greater opportunities lead to greater expectations and thus more stress. Perceived freedom may also cause one to blame oneself if things do not go well.

Such beliefs may also explain a puzzling finding: societies that place a high premium on individualism also show larger gender differences in personality traits than do more traditional communal societies (Costa, Terraccianco, & McCrae, 2001). Women showed the greatest difference from men in components of neuroticism (anxiety, self-consciousness, and vulnerability) in prosperous and healthy countries with the greatest educational opportunities.

In other words, extremely individualistic societies are not necessarily good for women's mental health. There are a number of reasons why this may be true. First, the drive for personal achievement can produce stress, especially because the playing field for women and men is not level (see Chapter 11). Individualism is also associated with stereotypical masculine traits, including unwillingness to ask for social support (Reavy & Maslach, 2001). One longitudinal study of high achieving men and women (who were originally part of the Terman study on gifted children) found a significant relationship between masculine identification and earlier death in both sexes (Lippa, Martin, & Friedman, 2000). The relationship between gender-related traits and mortality was about as large as the relationship between mortality and hypertension or cholesterol level.

We have come full circle. Culture influences gender-related personality traits which, in turn, influence how one deals with various aspects of one's culture. Gender operates at intrapersonal, social, and structural levels; but age, class, sexual orientation, and ethnicity are all closely interwoven with gender. None of these categories is politically neutral or value free. Each (separately and in combination) can serve as a tool for oppression. But they can serve as sources of strength as well (see Chapter 15).

It is also important to remember that no woman (or man) is solely at the mercy of social forces. Individuals can be remarkably resilient in the face of adversity. It is easy to forget the meanings people make from their reality and the extent to which they create these realities. We can find these meanings only by listening to each woman's words. This is what clinical practitioners do. Unfortunately, we have had little space in this chapter to tell individual stories. But we invite you to listen to each other's stories as well as those of more diverse groups of girls and women.

CONNECTING THEMES

- *Gender is more than just sex.* Women's psychological disorders are more closely related to their identity, roles, and status (in other words, aspects of gender) than they are to their biological sex. Emphasis on gender differences in psychological disorders is a consequence of lack of attention to the social context of people's lives.
- *Language and naming are sources of power.* Diagnostic categories are clear examples of the power to name. Feminist critiques stress the need to question the economics and politics of diagnostic labels. Feminist therapists have been active in renaming. Terms such as *client* instead of *patient* or *coping strategies* rather than *symptoms* do much to break down traditional views that most women are either "sick" or "crazy."
- *Women are not all alike.* Mental and physical well-being largely depend on an interplay of social structures and individual experience. Women from many different groups respond to discrimination and subordination by developing similar psychological and physical disorders. However, the buffering effect of education and income reveals that women's so-called weaknesses are often the product of social construction.

- *Psychological research can foster social change.* Feminist theory stresses social change in addition to personal change. Because therapy is an individual process, the contradiction between theory and practice is an ongoing problem for feminist therapists. Nevertheless, feminist practitioners have made great strides in empowering women from many diverse groups to make constructive changes in their lives.

SUGGESTED READINGS

COMAS-DIAZ, LILLIAN, & GREENE, BEVERLY (Eds.). (1994). *Women of color: Integrating ethnic and gender identities in psychotherapy.* New York: Guilford Press. This book contains a wealth of information about the lives and needs of many groups of ethnic minority women. The contributors are mainly working therapists—many women of color—who interweave theory and practice.

GALLANT, SHERYLE, KEITA, GWENDOLYN, & ROYAK-SCHALER, RENEE (Eds.). (1997). *Health care for women: Psychological, social, and behavioral influences.* Washington DC: American Psychological Association. Psychologists have only begun to recognize the importance of integrating the mind and the body. The contributors to this book (also the result of an APA-sponsored conference) examine women's health in terms of their social context, lifestyle, and stage of life cycle.

UNGER, RHODA. K. (Ed). (2001). *Handbook of the psychology of women and gender.* Another recent resource that includes substantive chapters by experts on mental and physical health. It contains chapters on feminist and multicultural issues in therapy, and each chapter looks at the way race/ethnicity, class, and sexual orientation interact with gender.

WORELL, JUDITH (Ed.). (2001). *Encyclopedia of women and gender: Sex similarities and differences and the impact of society and gender.* San Diego, CA: Academic Press. It is unusual to recommend an encyclopedia, but this resource includes at least twenty-three sizeable entries on areas of mental and physical health written by recognized experts in the field. Some of the areas covered are anxiety, chronic illness, depression, diagnosis, disabilities, eating disorders, post-traumatic stress disorder, social support, and substance abuse.

CHAPTER 15

Making a Difference: Toward a Better Future for Women

What do women want? This is an especially important question to ask of young women, because they are the future. The first wave of feminist activists included the suffragists who achieved the vote for women in the early 1900s. The second wave, whose activism began in the 1960s, worked on issues such as reproductive rights, workplace equality, sexism in the media, and an end to violence against women. Despite media claims that feminism is dead, many young women identify as third-wave feminists who are defining their own goals for the next round of social change. Third-wave feminists are a diverse group (on dimensions of ethnicity, social class, religion, etc.), and they consider feminism as only one part of their identity—a part they try to integrate with other aspects of who they are:

> Young feminists are constantly told that we don't exist. It's a refrain heard from older feminists as well as in the popular media: "Young women don't consider themselves feminists." Actually a lot of us do. And many more of us have integrated feminist values into our lives, whether or not we choose to use the label "feminist." This is an important barometer of the impact of feminism, since feminism is a movement for social change—not an organization doing a membership drive. (Findlen, 1995, p. xv)

Other young women believe that feminism has failed because it did not allow women to "have it all":

> If there is a troublesome legacy from the feminism that has come before, it's the burden of high expectations—of both ourselves and the world. Many young feminists describe growing up with the expectation that "you can do anything," whether that message came directly from parents or just from seeing

> barriers falling. But there's a point where you realize that while you may indeed feel capable of doing anything, you can be stopped—because of sexism. Maybe you played Little League baseball but found yourself relegated to girls' softball at age thirteen. Maybe you were the smartest kid in your high school class, and were stunned the first time you heard a college professor say that women couldn't be great artists or mathematicians or athletes. Maybe your mother gave you *Our Bodies, Ourselves* and taught you to love your body, but that didn't stop you from being raped. (Findlen, 1995, pp. xv–xvi)

But is the message that "you can have it all" or "you can do anything" what feminism promised? There are many different kinds of feminism, and feminists have had different goals, as we described in Chapter 1, such as gaining equality for women in education and employment, achieving respect for women's traditional work of mothering, and exposing the systemic nature of violence against women. This diversity is a strength because it encourages people to work for social change in many areas and to use many strategies.

Despite their diversity, feminists also have shared values and goals. Feminists believe in the worth and value of women. As a 1970s bumper sticker proclaimed, "Feminism is the radical notion that women are people." Moreover, feminists recognize that social change is necessary and that no one can create social change by herself. And they believe that people should work together to change society so that women can lead more secure, satisfying, and fulfilling lives. This belief in collective action, or group solidarity toward social change, is part of what differentiates feminism from just individual women achieving success.

How can feminist goals be achieved? Four themes have been traced throughout this book:

- Gender is more than just sex.
- Language and naming are sources of power.
- Women are not all alike.
- Psychological research can foster social change.

Let's look at each of these themes one last time, with a focus on how they relate to making a difference for women.

TRANSFORMING GENDER

Gender is a system of power relations that affects individuals, relationships, and society. Changes can be fostered at each of these levels.

Transforming Ourselves

Most women have internalized at least some of the sexist messages of our culture. Some feel shame about their bodies, their sexuality, or the normal changes of aging. Some doubt their abilities or do not feel entitled to equal treatment, whether at work or at home. Many women feel guilty about not being perfect mothers or blame themselves for having been subjected to rape, incest, or sexual harassment. This self-hatred is fostered by exposure to media images, gender socialization in childhood and adolescence, and the experience of having lower status and power in everyday interactions and relationships.

What can women do to change these beliefs and attitudes? In the 1970s, second-wave feminists developed *consciousness-raising* (C-R) groups, in which women met informally to talk about their lives as women. Women who took part in these groups began to see that their problems were not just individual deficiencies but were related to society's devaluation of women. Consciousness-raising groups encouraged social action, leading to such activities as opening shelters for battered women and protesting against sexist advertising. However, as women made some social progress in the 1970s and 1980s, many of these groups became more individually focused and then disappeared altogether (Kahn & Yoder, 1989; Rosenthal, 1984). Nevertheless, many organizations working for social change have incorporated the values and norms of C-R groups into their process.

C-R groups often led to positive changes for the women in them, including an altered worldview, greater awareness of sexism, positive changes in self-image, increased self-acceptance, and increased awareness of anger (Kravetz, 1980). Consciousness-raising became a model for feminist therapy because it offered women an opportunity to share experiences without being treated as patients who needed expert psychiatric help and because C-R groups assumed that the environment plays a major role in women's problems and difficulties (Brodsky, 1973). Today, although C-R groups no longer exist, feminist counseling and therapy empower women who want to make changes in their lives. Nonsexist or feminist therapies may be particularly valuable for women who have a history of physical or sexual abuse, eating disorders, or depression—all of which are due in part to gender-related social influences.

Today, relatively few women take part in feminist therapy, but many develop political and personal values compatible with feminism. Some women develop feminist values after having personal experiences with sexism, such as sexual harassment. These negative experiences can lead to transformative moments in which women suddenly realize that they live in a sexist society and want to change it, not just for themselves but also for other women (Dole, Zucker, & Duncan, 2001).

Still another route to feminist consciousness and activism is education. The growth of women's studies programs may be filling some of the gap left by the disappearance of C-R groups (Cole et al., 2001; Davis, Crawford, & Sebrechts, 1999). Women's studies classes often provide powerful consciousness-raising (James, 1999). In one study, taking a single women's studies course led to a decrease in the passive acceptance of sexism, an increase in commitment to feminism, and plans for social activism (Bargad & Hyde, 1991).

Women's studies courses have a positive influence partly because they make women and gender their main focus, countering the androcentric bias of other courses. When students take these courses, they read about women's activism throughout history; study the work of women writers, artists, and scientists; and learn about women's lives across cultures. In addition, women's studies teachers often use feminist teaching principles: They encourage class participation, teach critical thinking, and help young women find their own voice and set their own goals (James, 1999; Kimmel, 1999). The combination of woman-centered topics and teaching can be both enlightening and empowering.

Do women's studies courses change men's attitudes? There has been less research on this question, and results are mixed. Men who are conservative and very gender typed when they enroll may change little (Vedovato & Vaughter, 1980). Changes may be subtle, becoming evident only through in-depth interviews (Crawford, McCullough & Arato, 1983). In one study, the attitudes of male students changed in a profeminist direction, but not as much as the attitudes of female students did (Steiger, 1981).

As women redefine gender expectations, other girls and women have more models of different ways to be a woman. The women in the "Making a Difference" boxes throughout this book can serve as models of women's strengths. Consider Jamie Lee Curtis (Chapter 2), who had the courage to step outside her movie-star image and allow the world to see her real body because she believed that unrealistic images of perfection are harmful to women.

Transforming Interpersonal Relations

Gender inequity is reproduced in everyday interactions with others. The cognitive processes that lead to devaluing women usually occur outside awareness. Even the most well-meaning people can make sexist attributions, and sexist patterns of interaction lead to self-fulfilling prophecies. The interactional level may be the most important one to change precisely because gender processes are largely invisible and taken for granted.

Stereotyping exerts control over people in several ways. First, stereotypes describe how people in a certain group supposedly behave: Women are emotional, Asian Americans are academically motivated, old people are always talking about the past, and so forth. These stereotypes exert pressure to conform among group members. They are prescriptive as well as descriptive—in other words, they tell members of stereotyped groups how they should behave. People who do not conform may be penalized. A woman who does not show much emotion, for example, may be judged as cold, unfeminine, and controlling.

"Doing gender" can be disrupted when people treat others as individuals, not as members of a stereotyped group. One important strategy for change is to become aware of how we often respond to others as members of a category. In general, people with more power engage in stereotyping of people with less power. Powerful people do not need to pay attention to the powerless, because their well-being does not depend on it. For example, a worker must pay more attention to the moods and demands of the boss than the boss must pay to the worker's, because the worker does not control important outcomes for the boss (Fiske, 1993). Knowing how power affects stereotyping can help change these processes. Psychological research on power and stereotyping was influential in the Supreme Court decision in the Price-Waterhouse v. Ann Hopkins case, in which Hopkins won a partnership that had been denied because of stereotyped judgments about her femininity (Fiske et al., 1991).

When awareness of sexism is raised, small acts of resistance can follow. Gloria Steinem, a founding editor of Ms. magazine, calls this kind of resistance "outrageous acts and everyday rebellions" (Steinem, 1983). For example, although not everyone can run for the Senate or aid battered women, each of us can give money or time to those who do. We can unite with others who may be devalued for their differences, just as Kelli Peterson supported lesbian and gay students by forming a student association at her school (Chapter 7). Both women and men can support others who work for change; in particular, women can choose to support and mentor each other. The motto of one feminist organization that provides leadership seminars for women is "Lift as you climb."

Doing gender is also disrupted when people refuse to be cooperative or silent in the face of sexism. Humor can be an effective tool. Not laughing at sexist jokes undermines their aggressiveness. And women often defuse hostile situations with their own take-charge humor. When Britain's former prime minister Margaret Thatcher received the backhanded compliment from a member of the opposing political party, "May I congratulate you for being the only man on your team?" she responded, "That's one more than you've got on yours." When a casting director was chasing actress Judy Holliday around the room, she reached into her bra, pulled out the foam rubber pads, and said calmly, "I believe it's these you're after" (Barreca, 1991). Women's self-aware use of humor can be an effective tool in challenging gender-based power plays (Crawford, 1995).

More seriously, activist Dolores Huerta effectively stopped sexist talk in farm workers' union meetings by counting how often it happened and speaking up about it (Chapter 11). Another effective "everyday rebellion" occurred at Cornell University. Four male students electronically posted a list of "Top 75 Reasons Why Women (Bitches) Should Not Have Freedom of Speech." The list included items such as "She doesn't need to talk to get me a beer"; "If my dick's in her mouth she can't talk"; and "If she can't speak she can't cry rape." When women protested, the men defended the list as "Humor, that's all." In response, a group of women students posted a list of "75 Reasons Why Angry Cornell Women (Your Worst Nightmare) Are Exercising Their Freedom of Speech." The list consisted of evidence about women's lives, such as "In the U.S. four women are killed every day by their husbands or boyfriends" and "45% of underweight women think they are too fat." By moving the dialogue to a more serious level, these women effectively showed how truly unfunny the men's "humor" was (Women's Action Collective, 1992).

Transforming Society

Transforming gender at the social structural level is linked with the individual and interactional transformations just described. When people are empowered as individuals, they can speak out against injustice, and they can begin to change the institutions, laws, customs, and norms that harm girls and women. The effect is reciprocal, as speaking out leads to increased feelings of self-efficacy and empowerment.

Feminist activists of the 1970s achieved many important goals, and third-wave feminist activists are building on them. For example, Amy Cohen (Chapter 4) thought of herself as "nonconfrontational" and "agreeable," but because 1970s feminists had achieved the passage of Title IX, she could use it to achieve more equitable resources for college women athletes. Dolores Huerta co-founded the United Farm Workers; Maggie Kuhn (Chapter 12) lobbied for the elderly; and Katie Koestner (Chapter 13) organized a movement to end acquaintance rape. All these women transformed personal hardship into powerful collective action so that others might not have to endure their pain. Their activism reflects women's traditional roles as nurturers of others and celebrates the power of connectedness and caring.

Social change is not easy; attempts to change power relations almost always provoke backlash. Certainly, there has been a strong backlash against each wave of feminist activism throughout history. Today, the backlash ranges from repeated media claims that "feminism is dead" to the murder of people connected with women's health clinics. Moreover, change does not always result in progress. Feminist activists worked for no-fault divorce laws, only to find that they worsened the economic consequences of divorce for women (Weitzman, 1985). When more women entered the workforce, one result was the "second shift" of paid work followed each day by child care and housework (Hochschild, 1989). When Title IX legislated equality in sports opportunity in schools and colleges, the number of coaching positions for women's sports rose—but men took 75 percent of the new jobs (Valian, 1998). Attempts to change society must be reevaluated periodically to judge whether they have had their intended effects and also whether they have had unanticipated negative effects. Fortunately, social science research can help find the answers.

TRANSFORMING LANGUAGE

Throughout history, women have struggled to have their voices heard, their injustices recognized and their contributions to society accepted. The women's movement has provided a powerful force for change in how women are talked about, what problems can be named, and who can speak and be heard. Consider the life of Mary Edwards Walker (Chapter 3), who lived during feminism's first wave in the mid-nineteenth century. Walker, a physician, was denied a commission as an army physician, despite the pressing need for doctors during the Civil War. Although she was awarded the Congressional Medal of Honor for her military service, it was later revoked. After Walker's death, her granddaughter spoke up for her and succeeded in having Walker's medal restored.

Mary Edwards Walker knew the power of language to change opinions and attitudes. After the Civil War, she lectured widely on equal rights for women. She also was attuned to the symbolic power of language. In defiance of social norms, she refused to change her name or to promise to obey her husband when she married.

Women in the United States are now free to keep their own names if they marry, to use Ms., and to assign gender-neutral names to their children. Textbooks and professional journals no longer refer to all humans as he, him, and man. Terms such as battered woman, date rape, and sexual harassment have entered the language. Victim (as in rape victim, breast cancer victim) has been replaced by survivor, a change that emphasizes women's strength and coping skills in adversity. In all these ways and more, women are claiming the right to name.

Even more important, women are speaking out about injustices that they used to suffer in silence and shame. Within psychology, Phyllis Chesler (Chapter 14) was among the first to draw attention to the misuse of psychiatric power; Paula Caplan (1989, 1991) fought mother blaming and the misuse of

DSM labels by mental health professionals; and Lenore Walker (1979) brought the experiences of battered women to public attention. When Fauziya Kassindja (Chapter 8) was threatened with forced marriage and genital mutilation, she had the courage not only to save herself by fleeing but also to write about these forms of control and to work for political change to protect women. Ninia Baehr and Genora Dancel (Chapter 9) dared to say that lesbian couples should have the right to marry, and Katie Koestner went public as a victim of acquaintance rape, educating thousands of people about the problem.

Along with positive language change, there is also a new language of backlash. Terms such as bra-burners and feminazis diminish women's rights activists. Unfortunately, even the word *feminist* has been tainted by the backlash. Activist Rebecca Walker is working to change the negative perception of feminism by encouraging young women to learn about the first and second waves of the women's movement. Although the accomplishments of our foremothers are important, each generation must define its own goals. With knowledge of past victories, backlash, and defeats, today's women can shape third-wave feminism to their own goals.

CELEBRATING DIVERSITY

Women are not all alike. The problems faced by a working-class woman such as Dolores Huerta are quite different from those faced by college students such as Amy Cohen or Katie Koestner. Older women experience different forms of sexism than younger women, as Maggie Kuhn showed. Anyone whose sexual

Making a Difference

Contemporary Authors says of ***Rebecca Walker,*** "Through both her activism and her writing, Rebecca Walker has become a role model for a new generation of feminists attempting to reinterpret the legacy of the women's movement as we approach the twenty-first century." Walker (b. 1970), daughter of novelist Alice Walker, graduated from Yale University in 1992 and soon thereafter cofounded Third Wave Direct Action Corporation, a group whose goal is to encourage activism among young women. In its first year of existence, TWDAC won the Feminist of the Year award from the Fund for the Feminist Majority for its efforts in registering young women to vote. In 1995, Walker edited a volume of essays by young writers, called *To Be Real: Telling the Truth and Changing the Face of Feminism.* In this inspiring volume, each writer answers the question, "Is there more than one way to be a feminist?" The answer is clearly yes, and Walker believes that there is therefore a need for a "third generation" feminist movement. Many young women have been misled by the media's narrow, negative stereotypes of feminism into believing that feminism has nothing to offer contemporary young women, and that they owe nothing to the women's movement of the 1960s through 1990s. Before young women disavow feminism altogether, Walker asserts, they should become better informed about the past feminist movement's contributions to their own lives and think about ways in which they can shape today's feminism to fit their own needs.

Sources: Rooney, T. M. (Ed.). (1997). *Contemporary Authors,* Vol. 154, pp. 455–457.
"Changing the Face of Feminism" (1996, January). *Essence,* p. 123.

orientation is different from the heterosexual norm may encounter prejudice and discrimination on that basis, as the stories of Baehr, Dancel, and Peterson testify. People whose bodies are marked by difference are beginning to claim a right to their own dimensions of diversity, as shown by Cheryl Chase's activism for the rights of intersex people to determine their own bodily form and gender label (see Chapter 5).

Making the women's movement, and feminist psychology, more inclusive is not an easy task. Much of feminist theory has assumed that gender is the primary source of oppression for all women. If this were true, being inclusive would consist simply of studying how sexism affects women of color, disabled women, and any other defined group of women. However, many women do not consider gender the primary source of oppression in their lives. They urge other women to become more aware of how sexism varies or interacts with other kinds of oppression and privilege (Greene & Sanchez-Hucles, 1997).

Women of color argue that feminist theory and research should go beyond analyzing the position of white women in relation to white men. It should also analyze the position of white women in relation to women of color, white women to men of color, and people of color to white men. These analyses would help white feminists confront and change their own unacknowledged racism and ethnocentrism. As a start, each white feminist might ask herself, "What privileges does my white skin give me?" (Fine, Weis, Powell, & Wong, 1997; McIntosh, 1988). Similarly, each heterosexual feminist might ask, "How has my heterosexuality affected my feminist politics?" (Wilkinson & Kitzinger, 1993).

The importance of women-of-color perspectives is eloquently stated by one Asian-American third-wave feminist, Jee Yeun Lee:

> Women of color do not struggle in feminist movements simply to add cultural diversity, to add the viewpoints of different kinds of women. Women of color feminist theories challenge the fundamental premises of feminism, such as the very definition of "women," and call for recognition of the constructed racial nature of all experiences of gender. . . . These days, whenever someone says the word "women" to me, my mind goes blank. What "women"? What is this "women" thing you're talking about? Does that mean me? Does that mean my mother, my roommates, the white woman next door, the checkout clerk at the supermarket, my aunts in Korea, half the world's population? . . . Sisterhood may be global, but who is in that sisterhood? None of us can afford to assume anything about anybody else. This thing called "feminism" takes a great deal of hard work, and I think this is one of the primary hallmarks of young feminists' activism today: We realize that coming together and working together are by no means natural and easy. (Lee, 1995)

The womanist perspective in feminism was articulated by women of color who believed that white women had omitted recognition of their issues. In response, white women have tried harder to overcome the racism that is part of our society and to work together with women of color. Similarly, lesbians and bisexual women criticized feminist organizations for focusing on straight women's issues, and older women wrote about ageism within the women's movement. As a result of these criticisms, the women's movement has made respect for differences a cornerstone of feminist philosophy and activism.

As feminism becomes a more global movement, the issues of women in other cultures become more visible. Many societies do not allow women to have access to sex education, contraception, and abortion. Medical activist Dr. Rebecca Gomperts (Chapter 10) has refused to accept this denial of basic human rights to women. Her floating medical clinic provides women with the basic health services their governments deny. Anuradha Koirala (Chapter 6) has intervened in the sexual slavery trade that takes Nepalese girls as young as nine to brothels in India. Her organization, Maiti Nepal, rescues these girls and provides them with education and medical care. Moreover, Koirala speaks up about the pervasive devaluing of females that underlies the slave trade in girls. Other activists are working on issues such as sweatshop labor in Asian countries, genital mutilation in African countries, and rape as a tactic of war around the world in the former Yugoslavia. Yet global feminism may bring troubling questions of who is entitled to define a problem and whose viewpoint should determine what constitutes a solution. For example, white Western feminists may be appalled by female genital surgery, but the women who perpetuate it may see themselves as protecting their daughters from social ostracism. Whose viewpoint should prevail?

New women's issues, reflecting the differences in women's positions in diverse cultures, continue to emerge. The Internet is a powerful tool for connecting activists around the world and creating dialogue among diverse groups of women. For example, organizations such as Feminist Majority and Women Leaders Online/Women Organizing for Change draw attention to human rights abuses and provide information on how women can make their voices heard in protest.

PSYCHOLOGY AND SOCIAL CHANGE

The second wave of the women's movement has had important effects on psychology. Only a few short years ago, psychologists who happened to be women could not get hired by high-status universities and were rarely taken seriously as scientists or theorists (Unger, 1998). Today, women earn the majority of higher degrees in psychology, lead well-established professional organizations, produce many books and journals, and participate in every aspect of psychological research, education, and practice.

One of the authors saw a good example of change recently. At our university, there are regular lunchtime talks for faculty and graduate students. At one recent meeting, the speakers were a married couple (with different last names) from a nearby college, who do their research jointly. With them were their two children: a 4-year-old son and a 1-month-old infant. The man in the couple started their research presentation while Mom took the children to play outside. Sexist? Not exactly. Halfway through the talk, she returned, Dad took the kids outside, and she concluded the presentation and discussion of their research. Afterward, another male professor arranged for the older child to join a playgroup with his own 4-year-old daughter. A lunchtime psychology program became an example of collaborative research, shared parenting, and the "balancing act" of multiple roles for both women and men.

Progress is uneven, however. It will probably be a while before such a scene occurs regularly enough that it is taken for granted, and even longer before it happens in business settings. And there are more subtle signs that women and feminist perspectives have not yet been fully integrated into psychology. Publishing one's research in a psychology of women journal still may have less impact than if it were published in a "mainstream" journal. Despite the wealth of feminist books and journals, college textbooks and course syllabi too often still exclude gender, women, ethnicity, and diversity (Chin & Russo, 1997).

The continued lack of integration of feminist scholarship is a serious problem because throughout history, women's contributions have often been curtailed by their exclusion from powerful positions and erased by their omission from the history books. The life and work of Mary Calkins, discussed in Chapter 1, is only one example.

What can a student do? Students can make a difference by contributing to research and by using their knowledge of women's issues to work for change. When you have a choice of topic, you can write term papers on women or gender in your psychology, history, and literature courses. You can do an independent study or thesis on women and gender. You can ask questions in class when women are excluded or trivialized in readings and lectures. These strategies enrich the time and effort you put into your education, and they can help raise consciousness for yourself and others.

You can join an organization for women or volunteer at the women's center on your campus. If your campus has no women's center or women's studies program, start asking why. By taking courses that focus on women and gender, you can show the administration that there is a demand for this knowledge.

In 1999, students at the University of Connecticut formed a group called the Coalition for Multicultural Undergraduate Education. Their goal was to enlarge the general education requirements to include more courses on diversity (gender, sexual orientation, ethnicity, and culture). Because of their persistent, informed leadership, the administration agreed to endorse their effort publicly and to form a long-term committee of supportive faculty and students who will continue their mission even after the original members graduate. Their success shows that student activism can bring about change that will continue to benefit the next generation of students.

If you are planning to apply to graduate schools in psychology (or any other area), look carefully at the number of women faculty in the programs you consider, and how many have tenure. Look for courses on women and gender in the catalog, and find out whether there are women's studies and ethnic studies programs and a women's center. When visiting, ask about the level of support for feminist scholarship on campus. Psychology students can find information and support on a variety of gender issues by joining the Association for Women in Psychology or Division 35 of APA as student affiliates. These organizations allow students to become part of networks of people with similar concerns. Such coalitions provide meaningful personal relationships as well as sites of social change (Unger, 1998).

If you are seeking employment after graduation, look carefully at the gender and family sensitivity of the companies you consider. Do they have flextime, on-site day care, parental leave, and benefits for same-sex partners? What proportion of management are women? How often do women get promoted from inside the company? Is there ethnic and racial diversity? What is the company's record on sexual harassment complaints? Ask questions based on your knowledge of the psychology of women and gender.

One of the most important things students can do is to educate themselves on the issues facing girls and women. Overcoming androcentrism in education helps people think critically about what they read and hear in their textbooks, classes, and from the popular media. It also helps them become effective employees and responsible citizens after graduation. The students who formed the Coalition for Multicultural Undergraduate Education were effective because they had "done their homework"—they presented evidence for their position logically and systematically. The Cornell women who responded to aggressive humor did the same. Like the women faculty who fought sex discrimination at MIT, discussed in Chapter 3, they knew that evidence and reason do count.

Psychological research and theory have provided a wealth of evidence and reason on why women want and deserve full human rights. We offer the research and theory in this book as a resource and a gift. This gift is unusual in that it can be made meaningful only by the recipient. How will you use psychology to make a difference?

SUGGESTED READINGS

FINDLEN, BARBARA (Ed.). (1995). *Listen up! Voices from the next feminist generation.* Seattle: Seal Press. This collection reflects the passion and vibrancy of third-wave feminists. It shows how they fight feminist struggles in their own creative and diverse ways. Plus, it is fun to read!

UNGER, RHODA. (1998). *Resisting gender.* London: Sage. The title says it all. A pioneer, second-wave feminist discusses the history of feminist psychology over the past twenty-five years and argues for feminist coalitions toward future social change.

VALIAN, VIRGINIA (1998). *Why so slow? The advancement of women.* Cambridge, MA: MIT Press. Studies from sociology and psychology document that equality in the professions has not yet been achieved. Most important, this book suggests practical, concrete ways to increase personal and social power.

References

Aarons, S. J., & Jenkins, R. R. (2002). Sex, pregnancy, and contraception-related motivators and barriers among Latino and African-American youth in Washington D.C. *Sex Education, 2,* 5–30.

Aaronson, I. A. (undated) The molecular basis for intersexuality. Part one: The developing testis. *Digital Urology Journal,* http://www.duj.com/Article/Aaronson.html.

Abortion rights now. (1999). Washington, DC: National Organization for Women.

Abrams, D., Sparkes, K., & Hogg, M. A. (1985). Gender salience and social identity: The impact of sex of siblings on educational and occupational aspirations. *British Journal of Educational Psychology, 55,* 224–232.

Abramson, P. E., Goldberg, P. A., Greenberg, J. H., & Abramson, L. M. (1977). The talking platypus phenomenon: Competency ratings as a function of sex and professional status. *Psychology of Women Quarterly, 2,* 114–124.

Abusharaf, R. M. (1998, March/April). Unmasking tradition. *The Sciences,* pp. 22–27.

Achte, K. (1970). Menopause from the psychiatrist's point of view. *Acta Obstetrica et Gynecologica* (Suppl.), 1, 3–17.

Adams, K. L., & Ware, N. C. (1989). Sexism and the English language: The linguistic implications of being a woman. In J. Freeman (Ed.), *Women: A feminist perspective* (4th ed., pp. 470–484). Mountain View, CA: Mayfield.

Adams, R. C. (1997). Friendship patterns among older women. In J. M. Coyle (Ed.), *Handbook on women and aging* (pp. 400–417). Westport, CT: Greenwood Press.

Adams, S., Kuebli, J., Boyle, P. A., & Fivush, R. (1995). Gender differences in parent-child conversations about past emotions: A longitudinal investigation. *Sex Roles, 33,* 309–323.

Addelston, J. (1998). *The pig award and other acts of gender terrorism.* Unpublished manuscript, Rollins College, Winterpark, FL.

Adelmann, P. K., Antonucci, T. C., Crohan, S. E., & Coleman, L. M. (1989). Empty nest, cohort, and employment in the well-being of midlife women. *Sex Roles, 20,* 173–189.

Ader, D. N., & Johnson, S. B. (1994). Sample description, reporting and analysis of sex in psychological research: A look at APA and APA division journals in 1990. *American Psychologist, 49,* 216–218.

Adler, N. E., & Coriell, M. (1997). Socioeconomic status and women's health. In S. J. Gallant, G. P. Keita, & R. Royak-Schaler (Eds.), *Health care for women: Psychological, social, and behavioral influences* (pp. 11–23). Washington, DC: American Psychological Association.

Adolph, M. A. (1993). The myth of the golden years: One older woman's perspective. In N. D. Davis, E. Cole, & E. D. Rothblum (Eds.), *Faces of women and aging* (pp. 55–66). Binghamton, NY: Harrington Park Press.

Affonso, D. D., & Mayberry, L. J. (1989). Common stressors reported by a group of childbearing American women. In P. N. Stern (Ed.), *Pregnancy and parenting* (pp. 41–55). New York: Hemisphere.

Agence-France Press. (1999). China reportedly has 20 percent more males than females. Media Resource Service, Sigma Xi home page (www.sigmaxi.org).

Aida, Y., & Falbo, T. (1991). Relationships between marital satisfaction, resources, and power strategies. *Sex Roles, 24,* 43–56.

Aizenman, M., & Kelley, G. (1988). The incidence of violence and acquaintance rape in dating relationships among college men and women. *Journal of College Student Development, 29,* 305–311.

Aldous, J. (Ed.). (1982). Two paychecks: *Life in dual-earner families.* Beverly Hills, CA: Sage.

Alexander, S., & Ryan, M. (1997). Social constructs of feminism: A study of undergraduates at a women's college. *College Student Journal, 31,* 555–567.

Alfieri, T., Ruble, D. M., & Higgins, E. T. (1996). Gender stereotypes during adolescence: Developmental changes and the transition to junior high school. *Developmental Psychology, 32,* 1139–1137.

Alington, D. E., & Troll, L. E. (1984). Social change and equality: The roles of women and economics. In G. Baruch & J. Brooks-Gunn (Eds.), *Women in midlife* (pp. 181–202). New York: Plenum Press.

Allan, J. S., Mayo, K., & Michel, Y. (1993). Body size values of White and Black women. *Research in Nursing and Health, 16,* 323–333.

Allan, K., & Coltrane, S. (1996). Gender displaying television commercials: A comparative study of television commercials in the 1950s and 1980s. *Sex Roles, 35,* 185–203.

Allen, I. L. (1984). Male sex roles and epithets for ethnic women in American slang. *Sex Roles, 11,* 43–50.

Allen, L. S., & Gorski, R. A. (1992). Sexual orientation and the size of the anterior commissure in the human brain. *Proceedings of the National Academy of Sciences, 89,* 7199–7202.

Allgood-Merten, B., & Stockard, J. (1991). Sex role identity and self-esteem: A comparison of children and adolescents. *Sex Roles, 25,* 129–139.

Allport, G. W. (1954). *The nature of prejudice.* Cambridge, MA: Addison-Wesley.

Almquist, E. M. (1989). The experiences of minority women in the United States: Intersections of race, gender, and class. In J. Freeman (Ed.), *Women: A feminist perspective* (4th ed., pp. 414–445). Mountain View, CA: Mayfield.

Alpert, D., & Culbertson, A. (1987). Daily hassles and coping strategies of dual-earner and nondual-earner women. *Psychology of Women Quarterly, 11,* 359–366.

Altabe, M. (1998). Ethnicity and body image: Quantitative and qualitative analysis. *International Journal of Eating Disorders, 23,* 153–159.

Altman, M. (1984). Everything they always wanted you to know. In C. S. Vance (Ed.) *Pleasure and danger: Exploring female sexuality* (pp. 115–130). Boston: Routledge & Kegan Paul.

Amaro, H. (1993). Reproductive choice in the age of AIDS: Policy and counselling issues. In C. Squire (Ed.), *Women and AIDS: Psychological perspectives* (pp. 20–41). London: Sage.

Amaro, H., Russo, N. F., & Johnson, J. (1987). Family and work predictors of psychological well-being among Hispanic women professionals. *Psychology of Women Quarterly, 11,* 523–532.

Amaro, H., Raj, A., & Reed, E. (2001). Women's sexual health: The need for feminist analyses in public health in the decade of behavior. *Psychology of Women Quarterly, 25,* 324–334.

American Academy of Pediatrics (July 3, 2000). Report on treatment of newborns with genital abnormalities.

American Association of University Women (AAUW). (1993). *Hostile hallways: The AAUW survey on sexual harassment in America's schools.* Washington, DC: The American Association of University Women Educational Foundation.

American Psychiatric Association (APA). (1994). *Diagnostic and statistical manual of mental disorders* (4th ed.). Washington, DC: American Psychiatric Association.

America's children 2000. (2000). Washington, DC: www.ChildStats.gov.

Amir, M. (1971). *Patterns of forcible rape.* Chicago, IL: University of Chicago Press.

Anderson, C. M., & Stewart, S. (1994). *Flying solo: Single women in midlife.* New York: Norton.

Anderson, J. V. (1973). Psychological determinants. In R. B. Kundsin (Ed.), *Successful women in the sciences: An analysis of determinants.* New York: New York Academy of Sciences.

Anderson, K. J., & Leaper, C. (1998). Meta-analysis of gender effects on conversational interruptions: Who, what, when, where, and how. *Sex Roles, 39,* 225–252.

Anderson, K. L. (1997). Gender, status, and domestic violence: An integration of feminist and family violence approaches. *Journal of Marriage and the Family, 59,* 655–670.

Anderssen, N. (2002). Does contact with lesbians and gays lead to friendlier attitudes?

A two year longitudinal study. *Journal of Community and Applied Social Psychology, 12,* 124–136.

Angier, N. (1994, May 3). Male hormone molds women, too, in mind and body. *New York Times,* pp. C1, 13.

Angier, N. (2002, September 5). Weighing the grandma factor. *The New York Times,* pp. F1, F4.

Angless, T., Maconachie, M., & Van Zyl, M. (1998). Battered women seeking solutions: A South African study. *Violence Against Women, 4,* 637–658.

Angrist, S., Dinitz, S., Lefton, M., & Pasamanick, B. (1968). *Women after treatment.* New York: Appleton-Century-Crofts.

Anson, O., Antonovsky, A., Sagy, S., & Adler, I. (1989). Family, gender, and attitudes toward retirement. *Sex Roles, 20,* 355–369.

Antonucci, T. C., & Akiyama, H. (1997). Concern with others at midlife: Care, comfort, or compromise. In M. E. Lachman & J. B. James (Eds.), *Multiple paths of midlife development* (pp. 147–169). Chicago: University of Chicago Press.

Apfelbaum, E. (1993). Norwegian and French women in high leadership positions: The importance of cultural contexts upon gendered relations. *Psychology of Women Quarterly, 17,* 409–429.

Appling, S. E., Allen, J. K., Van Zandt, S., Olsen, S., Berger, R., & Hallerdin, J. (2000). Knowledge of menopause and hormone replacement therapy use in low-income urban women. *Journal of Women's Health & Gender-Based Medicine, 9,* 57–64.

Araoye, M. O., & Adegoke, A. (1996). AIDS-related knowledge, attitude and behaviour among selected adolescents in Nigeria. *Journal of Adolescence, 19*(2), 179–181.

Arendell, T. (1997). A social constructionist approach to parenting. R. Arendell (Ed.), *Contemporary parenting: Challenges and issues* (pp. 1–44). Thousand Oaks, CA: Sage.

Arms, S. (1973). *A season to be born.* New York: Harper & Row.

Arnold, F., & Kuo, E. C. (1984). The value of daughters and sons: A comparative study of the gender preferences of parents. *Journal of Comparative Family Studies, 15,* 299–318.

Aronson, J., Lustina, M. J., Good, C., Keough, K., Steele, C. M., & Brown, J. L. (1999). When White men can't do math: Necessary and sufficient factors in stereotype threat. *Journal of Experimental Social Psychology, 35,* 29–46.

Arroyo, J. A., Simpson, T. L., & Aragon, A. S. (1997). Childhood sexual abuse among Hispanic and non-Hispanic White college women. *Hispanic Journal of Behavioral Sciences, 19,* 57–68.

Assunta, M., & Jalleh, M. (1995, April 16). Consumer organization calls for Barbie doll ban. Third World Network Features, PNEWS.

Atwood, J. D. (Ed.). (1997). *Challenging family therapy situations: Perspectives in social construction.* New York: Springer.

Auerbach, J., Blum, L., Smith, V., & Williams, C. (1985). On Gilligan's In a different voice. *Feminist Studies, 11,* 149–161.

Ault, A. (1996). Ambiguous identity in an unambiguous sex/gender structure: The case of bisexual women. *The Sociological Quarterly, 37*(3), 449–463.

Avis, N. E., Stellato, R., Crawford, S., Bromberger, J., Ganz, P., Cain, V., & Kigawa-Singer, M. (2001). Is there a menopausal syndrome? Menopausal status and symptoms across racial/ethnic groups. *Social Science & Medicine, 52,* 345–356.

Avni, Noga. (1991). Battered wives: characteristics of their courtship days. *Journal of Interpersonal Violence, 6*(2), 232–239.

Azocar, F., Miranda, J., & Dwyer, E. V. (1996). Treatment of depression in disadvantaged women. *Women & Therapy, 18,* 91–105.

Baber, K. M., & Allen, K. R. (1992). *Women and families: Feminist reconstructions.* New York: Guilford.

Bachand, L. L., & Caron, S. L. (2001). Ties that bind: A qualitative study of happy long-term marriages. *Contemporary Family Therapy: An International Journal, 23,* 105–121.

Badgett, M. V. L. (1996). Employment and sexual orientation: Disclosure and discrimination in the workplace. In A. L. Ellis and E. D. B. Riggle (Eds.), *Sexual identity on the job: Issues and services* (pp. 29–52). New York: Harrington Park Press.

Bailey, J. M., Bechtold, K. T., & Berenbaum, S. A. (2002). Who are tomboys and why should we study them? *Archives of Sexual Behavior, 31,* 333–341.

Bailey, M. J., Pillard, R., Neale, M., & Agyei, Y. (1993). Heritable factors influence sexual orientation in women. *Archives of General Psychiatry, 50,* 217–223.

Baker, N. L. (1996). Class as a construct in a "classless" society. *Women & Therapy, 18,* 13–23.

Baker, R., Kiger, G., & Riley, P. J. (1996). Time, dirt, and money: The effects of gender, gender ideology, and type of earner marriage on time, household-task, and economic satisfaction among couples with children. *Journal of Social Behavior and Personality, 11*(5), 161–177.

Ballie, R. (2001). *Where are new psychologists going?* APA's research office presents employment and salary data at the 2001 Annual Convention [Electronic Version]. *Monitor on Psychology, 32,* n.p.

Bandura, A. (1965). Influence of model's reinforcement contingencies on the acquisition of imitative responses. *Journal of Personality and Social Psychology, 1,* 589–595.

Bannon, L. (1998, October 13). Little big spenders: As children become more sophisticated, marketers think older. *The Wall Street Journal,* A1.

Bannon, L. (2000, March). More kids' marketers pitch number of single-sex products. *The Wall Street Journal,* B1, 4.

Barak, A. (1997). Cross-cultural perspectives on sexual harassment. In W. O'Donohue (Ed.), *Sexual harassment: Theory, research, and treatment* (pp. 263–300). Boston: Allyn & Bacon.

Barak, A., Feldman, S., & Noy, A. (1991). Traditionality of children's interests as related to their parents' gender stereotypes and traditionality of occupations. *Sex Roles, 24,* 511–524.

Barbach, L. (1993). *The pause: Positive approaches to menopause.* New York: Dutton.

Barber, M. E., Foley, L. A., & Jones, R. (1999). Evaluations of aggressive women: The effects of gender, socioeconomic status, and level of aggression. *Violence & Victims, 14,* 353–363.

Bardwell, J. R., Cochran, S. W., & Walker, S. (1986). Relationship of parental education, race, and gender to sex-role stereotyping in five-year-old kindergartners. *Sex Roles, 15,* 275–281.

Barefoot, J. C., Mortensen, E. L., Helms, M. J., Avlund, K., & Schroll, M. (2001). A longitudinal study of gender differences in depressive symptoms from age 50 to 80. *Psychology and Aging, 16,* 342–345.

Bargad, A., & Hyde, J. S. (1991). Women's studies: A study of feminist identity development in women. *Psychology of Women Quarterly, 15,* 181–201.

Bargh, J., & Raymond, P. (1995). The naive misuse of power: Nonconscious sources of sexual harassment. *Journal of Social Issues, 51,* 85–96.

Barnett, O. W., & Fagan, R. W. (1993). Alcohol use in male spouse abusers and their female partners. *Journal of Family Violence, 8,* 1–25.

Barnett, O. W., Lee, C. Y., & Thelen, R. E. (1997). Gender differences in attributions of self-defense and control in interpartner aggression. *Violence Against Women, 3,* 462–481.

Barnett, R. C. (1997). Gender, employment, and psychological well-being: Historical and life course perspectives. In M. E. Lachman & J. B. James (Eds.), *Multiple paths of midlife development* (pp. 323–344). Chicago: The University of Chicago Press.

Barnett, R. C., & Hyde, J. S. (2001). Women, men, work, and family: An expansionist theory. *American Psychologist, 56,* 78–96.

Barnett, R. C., & Shen, Y-C. (1997). Gender, high- and low-schedule-control housework tasks, and psychological distress: A study of dual-earner couples. *Journal of Family Issues, 18*(4), 403–428.

Barreca, G. (1991). *They used to call me Snow White . . . but I drifted: Women's strategic use of humor.* New York: Viking.

Barshay, J. M. (1993). Another strand of our diversity: Some thoughts from a feminist therapist with severe chronic illness. *Women & Therapy, 14,* 159–169.

Bart, P. B. (1971). Sexism and social science: From the gilded cage to the iron cage, or, the perils of Pauline. *Journal of Marriage and the Family, 33,* 734–735.

Bart, P. B., & Grossman, M. (1978). Menopause. In M. T. Notman & C. C. Nadelson (Eds.), *The woman patient: Medical and psychological interfaces* (pp. 337–354). New York: Plenum.

Bar-Tal, D., & Saxe, L. (1976). Perceptions of similarly and dissimilarly attractive couples and individuals. *Journal of Personality and Social Psychology, 33,* 772–781.

Baruch, G. K., Barnett, R. C., & Rivers, C. (1983). *Lifeprints: New patterns of love and work for today's women.* New York: New American Library.

Basow, S. A., & Howe, K. G. (1980). Role model influence: Effects of sex and sex-role attitude in college students. *Psychology of Women Quarterly, 4,* 558–572.

Basow, S. A., & Kobrynowicz, D. (1993). What is she eating? The effects of meal size on impressions of a female eater. *Sex Roles, 28,* 335–344.

Bass, E., & Davis, L. (1988). *The courage to heal: A guide for women survivors of child sexual abuse.* New York: Harper and Row.

Basu, J., & Ray, B. (2001). Friends and lovers: A study of human mate selection in India. *Psychologia: An International Journal of Psychology in the Orient, 44,* 281–291.

Bauer, P. J. (1993). Memory for gender-consistent and gender-inconsistent event sequences by twenty-five-month-old children. *Child Development, 64,* 285–297.

Baumeister, R. F. (2000). Gender differences in erotic plasticity: The female sex drive as socially flexible and responsive. *Psychological Bulletin, 126,* 347–374.

Baumgardner, J., & Richards, A. (2000). *Manifesta: Young women, feminism, and the future.* New York: Farrar, Straus and Giroux.

Bay-Cheng, L. Y., Zucker, A. N., Stewart, A. J., & Pomerleau, C. S. (2002). Linking femininity, weight concern, and mental health among Latina, Black, and White women. *Psychology of Women Quarterly, 26,* 36–45.

Bazzini, D. G., McIntosh, W. D., Smith, S. M., Cook, S., & Harris, C. (1997). The aging woman in popular film: Underrepresented, unattractive, unfriendly, and unintelligent. *Sex Roles, 36,* 531–543.

Beach, M. (2001). Abortion funds halted: Bush creates first rift. *Herald Sun,* Wednesday, January 24, p. 31.

Beals, K. P., & Peplau, L. A. (2001). Social involvement, disclosure of sexual orientation, and the quality of lesbian relationships. *Psychology of Women Quarterly, 25,* 10–19.

Beausang, C. C. & Razor, A. G. (2000). Young Western women's experiences of menarche and menstruation. *Health Care for Women International, 21,* 517–528.

Beck, R. W., & Beck, S. J. (1989). The incidence of extended households among middle-aged black and white women. *Journal of Family Issues, 10,* 147–168.

Becker, D. (2001). Diagnosis of psychological disorders: DSM and gender. In J. Worell (Editor), *Encyclopedia of Sex and Gender* (pp. 333–343). NY: Academic Press.

Becker, E., Rankin, E., & Rickel, A. U. (1998). *High-risk sexual behavior: Interventions with vulnerable populations.* New York: Plenum Press.

Beckstein, D., Dahlin, M., & Wiley, D. (1986). Overview of sexuality education for young men. In C. H. Gregg & S. Renner (Eds.), *Sexuality educational strategy and resource guide: Programs for young men.* Washington, DC: Center for Population Options.

Beckwith, B. (1984). How magazines cover sex differences research. *Science for the People, 16,* 18–23.

Begley, S. (1999, Spring/Summer). Understanding perimenopause. *Newsweek: Health for Life,* pp. 30–34.

Bell, C. S., & Chase, S. E. (1996). The gendered character of women superintendents' professional relationships. In K. D. Arnold & K. D. Noble (Eds.), *Remarkable women: Perspectives on female talent development. Perspectives on creativity* (pp. 117–131). Cresskill, NJ: Hampton Press.

Bell, I. P. (1989). The double standard: Age. In J. Freeman (Ed.), *Women: A feminist perspective* (4th ed., pp. 236–244). Mountain View, CA: Mayfield.

Bellaby, M. D. (2001, January 4). Teen's birthday gift causes concern in Britain. *The Associated Press* (website), London.

Bem, S. (1993). *The lenses of gender.* New Haven: Yale University Press.

Bem, S. L., & Bem, D. J. (1971). Training the woman to know her place: The power of a nonconscious ideology. In M. H. Garskof (Ed.), *Roles women play: Readings toward women's liberation* (pp. 84–96). Belmont, CA: Brooks Cole.

Bem, S. L., & Bem, D. J. (1973). Does sex-biased job advertising "aid and abet" sex discrimination? *Journal of Applied Social Psychology, 3,* 6–18.

Benbow, C. P. (1988). Sex differences in mathematical reasoning ability in intellectually talented preadolescents: Their nature, effects, and possible causes. *Behavioral and Brain Sciences, 11,* 169–132.

Benbow, C. P., Lubinski, D., Shea, D. L., & Eftekhari Sanjani, H. (2000). Sex differences in mathematical reasoning ability at age 13: Their status 20 years later. *Psychological Science, 11,* 474–480.

Benbow, C. P., & Stanley, J. C. (1980). Sex differences in mathematical ability: Fact or artifact? *Science, 210,* 1262–1264.

Benenson, J. F., Morash, D., & Petrakos, H. (1998). Gender differences in emotional closeness between preschool children and their mothers. *Sex Roles, 38,* 975–985.

Benjet, C., & Hernandez-Guzman, L. (2001). Gender differences in psychological well-being of Mexican early adolescents. *Adolescence, 36,* 47–65.

Benokraitis, N. V. (Ed.). (1997). *Subtle sexism: Current practice and prospects for change.* Thousand Oaks, CA: Sage.

Benokraitis, N. V., & Feagin, J. R. (1986). *Modern sexism: Blatant, subtle, and covert discrimination.* Englewood Cliffs, NJ: Prentice Hall.

Bequaert, L. (1976). *Single women alone and together.* Boston: Beacon.

Berardo, D. H., Shehen, C. L., & Leslie, G. R. (1987). A residue of tradition: Jobs, careers, and spouses' time in housework. *Journal of Marriage and the Family, 49,* 381–390.

Berenbaum, S. A., & Bailey, J. M. (1998). May. *Variations in female gender identity: Evidence from girls with congenital adrenal hyperphasia, tomboys, and typical girls.* Paper presented at the meeting of the Midwestern Psychological Association, Chicago.

Berenbaum, S. A., & Hines, M. (1992). Early androgens are related to childhood sex-typed toy preferences. *Psychological Science, 3,* 203–206.

Berger, P. L., & Luckmann, T. (1966). *The social construction of reality: A treatise in the sociology of knowledge.* Garden City, NY: Doubleday.

Berger, R. M. (1990). Passing: Impact of the quality of same-sex couple relationships. *Social Work, 35,* 328–332.

Bergeron, S. M., & Senn, C. Y. (1998). Body image and socio-cultural norms: A comparison of heterosexual and lesbian women. *Psychology of Women Quarterly, 22,* 385–401.

Bergman, L. (1992). Dating violence among high school students. *Social Work, 37,* 21–27.

Berk, R. A. (1993). What the evidence shows: On the average, we can do no better than arrest. In R. J. Gelles & D. R. Loseke (Eds.), *Current controversies on family violence* (pp. 323–336). Newbury Park, CA: Sage.

Berman, P. W. (1980). Are women more responsive than men to the young? A review of developmental and situational variables. *Psychological Bulletin, 88,* 668–695.

Bernard, C., & Schlaffer, E. (1983). The man in the street: Why he harasses. In L. Richardson & V. Taylor (Eds.), *Feminist frontiers: Rethinking sex, gender, and society.* New York: Random House.

Bernard, J. (1972). *The future of marriage.* New York: World.

Bernard, J. (1974). *The future of motherhood.* New York: Penguin.

Bernard, J. (1981). The good provider role: Its rise and fall. *American Psychologist, 36,* 1–12.

Bernard, M. (1998). Backs to the future: Reflections on women, aging, and nursing. *Journal of Advanced Nursing, 27,* 633–640.

Bernard, M. (1998). Backs to the future: Reflections on women, aging, and nursing. *Journal of Advanced Nursing, 27,* 633–640.

Bernard, M., Itzin, C., Phillipson, C., & Skucha, J. (1995). Gendered work, gendered retirement. In S. Arber & J. Ginn (Eds.), *Connecting gender and aging: A sociological approach* (pp. 56–68). Buckingham, UK: Open University Press.

Berryman-Fink, C., & Verderber, K. S. (1985). Attributions of the term feminist: A factor analytic development of a measuring instrument. *Psychology of Women Quarterly, 9,* 51–64.

Besnier, N. (1996). Polynesian gender liminality through time and space. In G. Herdt (Ed.), *Third sex, third gender: Beyond sexual dimorphism in culture and history* (pp. 285–328). New York: Zone Books.

Best, D. L. (2001). Cross-cultural gender roles. In J. Worell (Ed.), *Encyclopedia of Women and Gender* (pp. 279–290). San Diego, CA: Academic Press.

Bethke, T. M., & DeJoy, D. M. (1993). An experimental study of factors influencing the acceptability of dating violence. *Journal of Interpersonal Violence, 8,* 36–51.

Betz, N. E., & Fitzgerald, L. E. (1987). *The career psychology of women.* New York: Academic Press.

Beyene, Y. (1989). *From menarche to menopause: Reproductive lives of peasant women in two cultures.* Albany: State University of New York Press.

Biaggio, M., & Brownell, A. (1996). Addressing sexual harassment: Strategies for prevention and change. In M. A. Paludi (Ed.), *Sexual harassment on college campuses: Abusing the ivory power* (pp. 215–234). Albany: State University of New York Press.

Bianchi, S. M., & Spain, D. (1986). *American women in transition.* New York: Russell Sage Foundation.

Biernat, M., Crandall, C. S., Young, L. V., Kolbrynowicz, D., & Halpin, S. M. (1998). All that you can be: Stereotyping of self and others in a military context. *Journal of Personality & Social Psychology, 75,* 301–317.

Biernat, M., & Kobrynowicz, D. (1999). A shifting standards perspective on the complexity of gender stereotypes and gender stereotyping. In W. B. Swann, Jr., J. H. Langlois, & L. A. Gilbert (Eds.), *Sexism and stereotypes: The gender science of Janet Taylor Spence* (pp. 75–106). Washington, DC: American Psychological Association.

Biernat, M., Manis, M., & Nelson, T. E. (1991). Stereotyping and standards of judgment. *Journal of Personality and Social Psychology, 60,* 485–499.

Bigler, R. S. (1995). The role of classification skill in moderating environmental influences on children's gender stereotyping: A study of the functional use of gender in the classroom. *Child Development, 66,* 1072–1087.

Bigler, R. S. (1997). Conceptual and methodological issues in the measurement of children's sex typing. *Psychology of Women Quarterly, 21,* 53–69.

Bigler, R. S. (1999). Psychological interventions designed to counter sexism in children: Empirical limitations and theoretical foundations. In W. B. Swann Jr., J. H. Langlois, & L. A. Gilbert (Eds.), *Sexism and stereotypes in modern society: The gender science of Janet Taylor Spence* (pp. 129–151). Washington, DC: American Psychological Association.

Billingham, R. E. (1987). Courtship violence: The patterns of conflict resolution strategies across seven levels of emotional commitment. *Family Relations, 36,* 283–289.

Billingham, R. E., & Sack, A. R. (1986). Courtship violence and the interactive status of the relationship. *Journal of Adolescent Research, 1,* 315–325.

Bing, V. M., & Reid, P. T. (1996). Unknown women and unknowing research: Consequences of color and class in feminist psychology. In N. R. Goldberger & J. M. Tarule (Eds.), *Knowledge, difference, and power: Essays inspired by "Women's Ways of Knowing"* (pp. 175–202). New York: Basic Books.

Birrell, S. J., & Cole, S. L. (1990). Double fault: Renee Richards and the construction and naturalization of difference. *Sociology of Sport Journal, 7,* 1–21.

Bishop, K. M. & Wahlsten, D. (1997). Sex differences in the human corpus callosum: Myth or reality? *Neuroscience and Biobehavioral Reviews, 21*(5), pp. 581–601.

Bishop, N. (1989). Abortion: The controversial choice. In J. Freeman (Ed.), *Women: A feminist perspective* (4th ed., pp. 45–56). Mountain View, CA: Mayfield.

Black, J., & Underwood, J. (1998). Young, female, and gay: Lesbian students and the school environment. *Professional School Counseling, 1*(3), 15–20.

Blackless, M., Charuvastra, A., Derryck, A., Fausto-Sterling, A., Lauzanne, K., & Lee, E. (2000). How sexually dimorphic are we? Review and synthesis. *American Journal of Human Biology, 12,* 151–166.

Blair, S. L., & Lichter, D. T. (1991). Measuring the division of household labor: Gender segregation of housework among American couples. *Journal of Family Issues, 12,* 91–113.

Blanchard, R. (1985). Gender dysphoria and gender reorientation. In B. W. Steiner (Ed.), *Gender dysphoria: Development, research, management.* New York: Plenum.

Bleier, R. (Ed.). (1986). *Feminist approaches to science.* Elmsford, NY: Pergamon Press.

Blieszner, R. (1993). A socialist-feminist perspective on widowhood. *Journal of Aging Studies, 7,* 171–182.

Bloch, A. (2002). Self-awareness during menopause. *Maturitas. 41,* 61–68.

Blood, R. O., & Wolfe, D. M. (1960). *Husbands and wives.* New York: Free Press.

Blumstein, P., & Schwartz, P. (1983). *American couples.* New York: William Morrow.

Blumstein, P. W., & Schwartz, P. (1993). Bisexuality, Some social psychological issues. In L. D. Garnets & D. C. Kimmel (Eds.), *Psychological perspectives on lesbian and gay male experiences* (pp. 168–184). New York: Columbia University Press.

Boardman, S. K., Harrington, C. C., & Horowitz, S. V. (1987). Successful women: A psychological investigation of family class and education origins. In B. A. Gutek & L. Larwood (Eds.), *Women's career development* (pp. 66–85). Newbury Park, CA: Sage.

Boatwright, K. J., Gilbert, M. S., Forrest, L., & Ketzenberger, K. (1996). Impact of identity development upon career trajectory: Listening to the voices of lesbian women. *Journal of Vocational Behavior, 48,* 210–228.

Bogal-Allbritten, R. B., & Allbritten, W. L. (1987). Availability of community services to student victims of courtship violence. *Response to the Victimization of Women and Children, 10,* 22–24.

Bograd, M. (1988). Feminist perspectives on wife abuse: An introduction. In K. Yllo and M. Bograd (Eds.), *Feminist perspectives on wife abuse* (pp. 11–26). Berkeley, CA: Sage.

Bohan, J. (1990). Contextual history: A framework for re-placing women in the history of psychology. *Psychology of Women Quarterly, 14,* 213–227.

Bohan, J., & Russell. (1999). Support networks for lesbian, gay, and bisexual students. In S. Davis, M. Crawford, & J. Sebrechts (Eds.), *Coming into her own: Encouraging educational success in girls and women,* pp. 279–294. San Francisco: Jossey-Bass.

Bohan, J. S. (1996). *Psychology and sexual orientation: Coming to terms.* New York: Routledge.

Bolin, A. (1996). Transcending and transgendering: Male-to-female transsexuals, dichotomy, and diversity. In G. Herdt (Ed.), *Third sex, third gender: Beyond sexual dimorphism in culture and history* (pp. 447–485). New York: Zone Books.

Bond, M. (1991). Division 27 sexual harassment survey: Definitions impact and environmental context. In M. A. Paludi & R. B. Barickman (Eds.), *Academic and workplace sexual harassment: A resource manual.* Albany: State University of New York.

Bond, S., & Cash, T. F. (1992). Black beauty: Skin color and body images among African-American college women. *Journal of Applied Social Psychology, 22,* 874–888.

Bondurant, B. (1994, March). *Men's perceptions of women's sexual interest: Sexuality or sexual aggression?* Paper presented at Southeastern Psychological Association 40th Annual Meeting, New Orleans.

Bondurant, B., & Donat, P. L. N. (1999). Perceptions of women's sexual interest and acquaintance rape: The role of sexual overperception and affective attitudes. *Psychology of Women Quarterly, 23,* 691–705.

Boney-McCoy, S., & Finkelhor, D. (1995). Psychosocial sequelae of violent victimization in a national youth sample. *Journal of Consulting and Clinical Psychology, 63,* 726–736.

Bookwala, J., Frieze, I. H., Smith, C., & Ryan, K. (1992). Predictors of dating violence: A multivariate analysis. *Violence and Victims, 7,* 297–311.

Bordo, S. (1993). *Unbearable weight: Feminism, western culture and the body.* Berkeley, CA: University of California Press.

Bornstein, K. (1994). *Gender outlaw: On men, women, and the rest of us.* New York: Routledge.

Boswell, S. L. (1979). *Nice girls don't study mathematics: The perspective from elementary school.* Presented at the meeting of the American Educational Research Association, San Francisco.

Boswell, S. L. (1985). The influence of sex-role stereotyping on women's attitudes and achievement in mathematics. In S. F. Chipman, L. R. Brush, & D. M. Wilson (Eds.), *Women and mathematics: Balancing the equation* (pp. 175–198). Hillsdale, NJ: Erlbaum.

Bosworth, H. B., Bastian, L. A., Kuchibbhata, M. N., Steffens, D. C., McBride, C. M., Skinner, C. S., Rimer, B. K., & Siegler, I. C. (2001). Depressive symptoms, menopausal status, and climacteric symptoms in women at midlife. *Psychosomatic Medicine, 63,* 603–608.

Bound, J., Duncan, G. J., Laren, D. S., & Oleiniek, L. (1991). Poverty dynamics in widowhood. *Journal of Gerontology: Social Sciences, 46,* S115–S124.

Bowen, C. C., Swim, J. K., & Jacobs, R. R. (2000). Evaluating gender biases on actual job performance of real people: A meta-analysis. *Journal of Applied Social Psychology, 30,* 2194–2215.

Bowker, L. (1993). A battered woman's problems are social, not psychological. In R. J. Gelles & D. R. Loseke (Eds.), *Current controversies on family violence* (pp. 154–166). Newbury Park, CA: Sage.

Boxer, A. M., Cook, J. A., & Herdt, G. (1999). Experiences of coming out among gay and lesbian youth: Adolescents alone. In *The adolescent alone: Decision making in health care in the United States* (pp. 121–136). Cambridge, England: Cambridge University Press.

Boyatzis, C. J., Nallis, M., & Leon, I. (1999). Effects of game type on children's gender-based peer preferences: A naturalistic observational study. *Sex Roles, 40,* 93–105.

Boyd, B., & Wandersman, A. (1991). Predicting undergraduate condom use with the Fishbein and Ajzen and the Triandis attitude-behavior models: Implications for public health interventions. *Journal of Applied Social Psychology, 21,* 1810–1830.

Boyd, J. A. (1990). Ethnic and cultural diversity: Keys to power. In L. S. Brown & M. P. P. Root (Eds.), *Diversity and complexity in feminist therapy* (pp. 151–167). New York: Harrington Park Press.

Brabant, S., & Mooney, L. (1986). Sex role stereotyping in the Sunday comics: Ten years later. *Sex Roles, 14,* 141–148.

Brabant, S., & Mooney, L. A. (1997). Sex role stereotyping in the Sunday comics: A twenty year update. *Sex Roles, 37,* 269–281.

Brabeck, M., & Brown, L. (1997). Feminist theory and psychological practice. In J. Worell & N. G. Johnson (Eds.), *Shaping the future of feminist psychology: Education, research, and practice* (pp. 15–35). Washington, DC: American Psychological Association.

Bradbard, M. R., & Endsley, R. C. (1983). The effects of sex-typed labeling on preschool children's information-seeking and retention. *Sex Roles, 9,* 247–260.

Braden, A. (1986). Shoulder to shoulder. In J. B. Cole (Ed.), *All American women: Lines that divide, ties that bind* (pp. 74–80). New York: Macmillan.

Bradley, C. (1993). Women's power, children's labor. *Behavior Science Research, 27,* 70–96.

Bradshaw, C. K. (1994). Asian and Asian American women: Historical and political considerations in psychotherapy. In L. Comas-Diaz & B. Greene (Eds.), *Women of color: Integrating ethnic and gender identities in psychotherapy.* New York: Guilford.

Bradsher, J. E. (1997). Old women and widowhood. In J. M. Coyle (Ed.), *Handbook on women and aging* (pp. 418–429). Westport, CT: Greenwood Press.

Bramlet, M. D., & Mosher, W. D. (2001). *First marriage dissolution, divorce, and remarriage: United States.* Hyattsville, MD: National Center for Health Statistics.

Brand, P. A., & Kidd, A. H. (1986). Frequency of physical aggression in heterosexual and female homosexual dyads. *Psychological Reports, 59,* 1307–1313.

Branscombe, N. R. (1998). Thinking about one's gender group's privileges or disadvantages: Consequences for well-being in women and men. *British Journal of Social Psychology, 37,* 167–184.

Branscombe, N. R., Schmitt, M. T., & Harvey, R. D. (1999). Perceiving pervasive discrimination among African Americans: Implications for group identification and well-being. *Journal of Personality & Social Psychology, 77,* 135–149.

Breedlove, S. M. (1994). Sexual differentiation of the human nervous system. *Annual Review of Psychology, 45,* 389–418.

Breines, W., & Gordon, L. (1983). The new scholarship on family violence. *Signs, 8,* 490–531.

Brelis, M. (1999, February 7). The fading "gay gene." *The Boston Sunday Globe,* pp. C1, C5.

Brendgen, M., Vitaro, F., Doyle, A. B., Markiewicz, D., & Bukowski, W. M. (2002). Same-sex peer relations and romantic relationships during early adolescence: Interactive links to emotional, behavioral, and academic adjustment. *Merrill-Plamer Quarterly, 48,* 77–103.

Bridges, J. S. (1993). Pink or blue: Gender-stereotypic perceptions of infants as conveyed by birth congratulations cards. *Psychology of Women Quarterly, 17,* 193–205.

Bridges, J. S., & Orza, A. M. (1992). The effects of employment role and motive for employment on the perceptions of mothers. *Sex Roles, 27,* 331–343.

Briere, J., & Lanktree, C. (1983). Sex-role related effects of sex bias in language. *Sex Roles, 9,* 625–632.

Bringaze, T. B., & White, L. J. (2001). Living out proud: Factors contributing to healthy identity development in lesbian leaders. *Journal of Mental Health Counseling, 23,* 162–173.

Brinkerhoff, D. B., & Booth, A. (1984). Gender, dominance, and stress. *Journal of Social and Biological Structures, 7,* 159–177.

Broderick, P. C., & Korteland, C. (2002). Coping styles and depression in early adolescence: Relationships to gender, gender role, and implicit beliefs. *Sex Roles, 46,* 201–213.

Brodsky, A. (1973). The consciousness-raising group as a model for therapy with women. *Psychotherapy: Theory, Research, and Practice, 10,* 24–29.

Brody, E. (1981). "Women in the middle" and family help to older people. *Gerontologist, 21,* 471–485.

Brody, L. R., Lovas, G. S., & Hay, D. H. (1995). Gender differences in anger and fear as a function of situational context. *Sex Roles, 32,* 47–78.

Bromberg, J. J. (1997). *The body project: An intimate history of American girls.* New York: Random House.

Brooks, L., & Perot, A. (1991). Reporting sexual harassment: Exploring a predictive model. *Psychology of Women Quarterly, 15,* 31–47.

Brooks-Gunn, J. (1986). The relationship of maternal beliefs about sex typing to maternal and young children's behavior. *Sex Roles, 14,* 21–35.

Brooks-Gunn, J. (1987b). Pubertal processes and girls' psychological adaptation. In R. M. Lerner & T. T. Foch (Eds.), *Biological-psychosocial interactions in early adolescence* (pp. 123–153). Hillsdale NJ: Erlbaum.

Brooks-Gunn, J. (1988). Antecedents and consequences of variations in girls' maturational timing. *Journal of Adolescent Health Care, 9,* 365–373.

Brooks-Gunn, J., & Furstenberg, F. F., Jr. (1989). Adolescent sexual behavior. *American Psychologist, 44,* 249–257.

Brooks-Gunn, J., & Mathews, W. S. (1979). *He & she: How children develop their sex-role identity.* Englewood Cliffs, NJ: Prentice Hall.

Brooks-Gunn, J., & Petersen, A. C. (1983). (Eds.), *Girls at puberty: Biological and psychological perspectives.* New York: Plenum.

Brooks-Gunn, J., & Zehayhevich. (1989). Parent-daughter relationships in early adolescence: A developmental perspective. In K. Kreppner & R. Lerner (Eds.), *Family systems and life-span development.* Hillsdale, NJ: Erlbaum.

Broughton, J. M. (1983). Women's rationality and men's virtues: A critique of gender dualism in Gilligan's theory of moral development. *Social Research, 50,* 597–642.

Broverman, I. K., Vogel, S. R., Broverman, D. M., Clarkson, F. E., & Rosenkrantz, P. S. (1972). Sex-role stereotypes: A current appraisal. *Journal of Social Issues, 28,* 59–78.

Brown, B. A., Frankel, B. G., & Fennell, M. P. (1989). Hugs or shrugs: Parental and peer influence on continuity of involvement in sport by female adolescents. *Sex Roles, 20,* 397–409.

Brown, E. A. (1989, June 9). Happily ever after. *Christian Science Monitor,* p. 13.

Brown, J. K. (1982). A cross-cultural exploration of the end of the childbearing years. In A. M. Voda, M. Dinnerstein, & S. R. O'-Donnell (Eds.), *Changing perspectives on menopause* (pp. 51–59). Austin: University of Texas Press.

Brown, L. M. (1998). *Raising their voices: The politics of girls' anger.* Cambridge, MA: Harvard University Press.

Brown, L. M., & Gilligan, C. (1992). *Meeting at the crossroads: Women's psychology and girls' development.* Cambridge, MA: Harvard University Press.

Brown, L. M., & Gilligan, C. (1993). Meeting at the crossroads: Women's psychology and girls' development. *Feminism & Psychology, 3,* 11–35.

Brown, L. M., Way, N., & Duff, J. F. (2000). The others in my I: Adolescent girls' friendships and peer relations. In N. G. Johnson, M. C. Roberts, & J. Worell (Eds.), *Beyond appearance: A new look at adolescent girls* (pp. 205–225). Washington D.C.: American Psychological Association.

Brown, L. S. (1986). *Diagnosis and the Zeitgeist: The politics of masochism in the DSM-III-R.* Paper presented at the meeting of the American Psychological Association, Washington, DC.

Brown, L. S. (1994). *Subversive dialogues: Theory in feminist therapy.* New York: Basic Books.

Brown, L. S. (1996). Politics of memory, politics of incest: Doing therapy and politics that really matter. *Women & Therapy, 19,* 5–18.

Brown, L. S., & Burman, E. (1997). Feminist responses to the "false memory" debate. *Feminism & Psychology, 7,* 7–16.

Brown, R. P., Charnsangavej, T., Keough, K. A., Newman, M. L., & Renfrew, P. J. (2000). Putting the "affirm" into affirmative action: Preferential selection and academic performance. *Journal of Personality & Social Psychology, 79,* 736–747.

Brown, W. M., Finn, C. J., Cooke, B. M., & Breedlove, S. M. (2002). Differences in finger length ratios between self-identified "butch" and "femme" lesbians. *Archives of Sexual Behavior, 31,* 123–127.

Browne, A. (1987). *When battered women kill.* New York: Macmillan.

Browne, A. (1993). Violence against women by male partners: Prevalence, outcomes, and policy implications. *American Psychologist, 48,* 1077–1087.

Browne, A., & Finkelhor, D. (1986). Impact of sexual abuse: A review of the research. *Psychological Bulletin, 99,* 66–77.

Browne, A., & Williams, K. R. (1993). Gender, intimacy, and lethal violence: Trends from 1976 to 1987. *Gender & Society, 7,* 78–98.

Browne, C. V. (1998). *Women, feminism, and aging.* New York: Springer.

Brownmiller, S. (1975). *Against our will: Men, women, and rape.* New York: Simon & Schuster.

Buchman, D. D., & Funk, J. B. (1996). Video and computer games in the 90s: Children's time commitment and game preferences. *Children Today, 24,* 12–16, 31.

Buckner, J. P., & Fivush, R. (1998). Gender and self in children's autobiographical narratives. *Applied Cognitive Psychology, 12,* 455–473.

Budig, M. J. (2002). Male advantage and the gender composition of jobs: Who rides the glass elevator? *Social Problems, 49,* 258–277.

Buhl, M. (1989, September/October). The feminist mystique. *In View,* p. 16.

Bullock, H. E., Wyche, K. F., & Williams, W. R. (2001). Media images of the poor. *Journal of Social Issues, 57* (2), 229–246.

Bullough, V. L. (2002). Discrimination against gays, lesbians, and highly androgynous. In L. Diamant & J. A. Lee (Eds.), *The psychology of sex, gender, and jobs: Issues and resolutions* (pp. 145–154). Westport, CT: Praeger.

Bumagin, V. E. (1982). Growing old female. *Journal of Psychiatric Treatment and Evaluation, 4,* 155–159.

Buntaine, R. L., & Costenbader, V. K. (1997). Self-reported differences in the experience and expression of anger between girls and boys. *Sex Roles, 36,* 625–637.

Burcky, W., Reuterman, N., & Kopsky, S. (1988). Dating violence among high school students. *School Counselor, 35,* 353–358.

Burke, P. J., & Cast, A. D. (1997). Stability and change in the gender identities of newly married couples. *Social Psychology Quarterly, 60*(4), 277–290.

Burke, R. J. (1997). Alternate family structures: A career advantage? *Psychological Reports, 81*(3, Pt. 1), 812–814.

Burke, R. J., & McKeen, C. A. (1997). Gender effects in mentoring relationships. In R. Crandall (Ed.), *Handbook of gender research* (pp. 91–104). Corte Madera, CA: Select Press.

Burn, S. M., Aboud, R., & Moyles, C. (2000), The relationship between gender, social identity, and support for feminism. *Sex Roles, 42,* 1081–1089,

Burn, S. M., O'Neil, A. K., & Nederend, S. (1996). Childhood tomboyism and adult androgyny. *Sex Roles, 34,* 419–428.

Burns, D. (2000). Feminism, psychology and social policy: Constructing political boundaries at the grassroots. *Feminism and Psychology, 10,* 367–380.

Burns, J. (1992). Mad or just plain bad? Gender and the work of forensic clinical psychologists. In J. M. Ussher & P. Nicolson (Eds.), *Gender issues in clinical psychology* (pp. 106–128). London: Routledge.

Busby, L. J. (1975, Autumn). Sex-role research on the mass media. *Journal of Communication,* 107–131.

Busby, L. J., & Leichty, G. (1993). Feminism and advertising in traditional and nontraditional women's magazines, 1950s–1980s. *Journalism Quarterly, 70,* 247–264.

Buschman, J. K., & Lenart, S. (1996). "I am not a feminist but . . .": College women, feminism, and negative experiences. *Political Psychology, 17,* 59–75.

Bush, T. L. (1990). The epidemiology of cardiovascular disease in postmenopausal women. In M. Flint, F. Kronenberg, & W. Utian (Eds.), *Multidisciplinary perspectives on menopause. Annals of the New York Academy of Sciences, 592,* 263–271.

Buss, D. M. (1989). Sex differences in human mate preferences: Evolutionary hypotheses tested in 37 cultures. *Behavioral and Brain Sciences, 12,* 1–49.

Buss, D. M. (1995). Psychological sex differences: Origins through sexual selection. *American Psychologist, 50,* 164–168.

Buss, D. M., et al. (1990). International preferences in selecting mates: A study of 37 cultures. *Journal of Cross-Cultural Psychology, 21,* 5–47.

Bussey, K., & Bandura, A. (1999). Social cognitive theory and gender development and differentiation. *Psychological Review, 106,* 676–713.

Butler, D., & Geis, F. L. (1990). Nonverbal affect responses to male and female leaders: Implications for leadership evaluations. *Journal of Personality and Social Psychology, 58,* 48–59.

Butler, L. D., & Nolen-Hoeksema, S. (1994). Gender differences in responses to depressed mood in a college sample. *Sex Roles, 30,* 331–346.

Butler, R. N. (1980). Ageism: A foreword. *Journal of Social Issues, 36,* 8–11.

Butts, Stanley G. (1999). Women with children in violent relationships: The choice of leaving may bring the consequences of custodial challenge. *Journal of Aggression, Maltreatment, and Trauma, 2,* 239–251.

Buzawa, E. S., & Buzawa, C. G. (1993). The scientific is not conclusive: Arrest is no panacea. In R. J. Gelles & D. R. Loseke (Eds.), *Current controversies on family violence* (pp. 336–356). Newbury Park, CA: Sage.

Cabaj, R. P., & Purcell, D. W. (Eds.). (1998). *On the road to same-sex marriage: A supportive guide to psychological, political, and legal issues.* San Francisco: Josey-Bass.

Cabecinhas, R., & Amancio, L. (1999). Asymmetries in the perception of other as a function of social position and context. *Swiss Journal of Psychology, 58,* 40–50.

Cachelin, F. M., Veisel, C., Barzegarnazani, E., & Striegel-Moore, R. H. (2000). Disordered eating, acculturation, and treatment-seeking in a community sample of Hispanic, Asian, Black, and White women. *Psychology of Women Quarterly, 24,* 244–253.

Cahill, B., & Adams, E. (1997). An exploratory study of early childhood teachers' attitudes toward gender roles. *Sex Roles, 36,* 517–529.

Caldera, Y. M., Huston, A. C., & O'Brien, M. (1989). Social interactions and play patterns of parents and toddlers with feminine, masculine, and neutral toys. *Child Development, 60,* 70–76.

Caldera, Y. M., & Sciaraffa, A. (1998). Parent-toddler play with feminine toys: Are all dolls the same? *Sex Roles, 39,* 657–668.

Calderone, K. L. (1990). The influence of gender on the frequency of pain and sedative medication administered to postoperative patients. *Sex Roles, 23,* 713–725.

Calhoun, K. S., Bernat, J. A., Clum, G. A., & Frame, C. L. (1997). Sexual coercion and attraction to sexual aggression in a community sample of young men. *Journal of Interpersonal Violence, 12*(1), 392–406.

Califia, P. (1997). *Sex changes: The politics of transgenderism.* San Francisco, CA: Cleis Press.

Campbell, A., Shirley, L., Heywood, C., & Crook, C. (2000). Infants' visual preference for sex-congruent babies, children's toys, and activities: A longitudinal study. British *Journal of Developmental Psychology, 18,* 479–498.

Campbell, A., Shirley, L., & Cargill, L. (2002). Sex-typed preferences in three domains: do two-year-olds need cognitive variables? *British Journal of Psychology, 93,* 203–217.

Campbell, B., Schellenberg, E. G., & Senn, C. Y. (1997). Evaluating measures of contemporary sexism. *Psychology of Women Quarterly, 21,* 89–101.

Campbell, D. W., & Eaton, W. O. (1999). Sex differences in the activity level of infants. *Infant & Child Development, 8,* 1–17.

Campbell, E. K., & Campbell, P. G. (1997). Family size and sex preferences and eventual fertility in Botswana. *Journal of Biosocial Science, 29,* 191–204.

Campbell, R., Sullivan, C. M., & Davidson, W. S. II. (1995). Women who use domestic violence shelters: Changes in depression over time. *Psychology of Women Quarterly, 19,* 237–255.

Campenni, C. E. (1999). Gender stereotyping of children's toys: A comparison of parents and nonparents. *Sex Roles, 40,* 121–138.

Canetto, S. S. (1997). Meanings of gender and suicidal behavior during adolescence. *Suicide and Life Threatening Behavior, 27,* 339–351.

Canetto, S. S. (2001). Older adult women: Issues, resources, and challenges. In R. K. Unger (Ed.), *Handbook of the psychology of women and gender* (pp. 183–197). NY: Wiley.

Canetto, S. S., & Hollenshead, J. D. (1999). Gender and physician-assisted suicide: An analysis of the Kevorkian cases, 1990–1997. *Omega, 40,* 165–208.

Cano, M. A., & Kite, M. E. (1998, August). *Gender role violations: Perceived homosexuality as a mediating variable.* Paper presented at the annual meeting of the American Psychological Associaiton, San Francisco.

Cantor, J., & Nathanson, A. I. (1997). Predictors of children's interest in violent television programs. *Journal of Broadcasting and Electronic Media, 41,* 155–167.

Cantor, M. G. (1987). Popular culture and the portrayal of women: Content and control. In B. B. Hess & M. M. Ferree (Eds.), *Analyzing gender* (pp. 190–214). Newbury Park, CA: Sage.

Caplan, P. J. (1989). *Don't blame mother.* New York: Harper & Row.

Caplan, P. J. (1991). Delusional dominating personality disorder (DDPD). *Feminism & Psychology, 1,* 171–174.

Caplan, P. J. (1995). *They say you're crazy: How the most powerful psychiatrists decide who's normal.* Reading, MA: Addison-Wesley.

Caplan, P. J., & Hall-McCorquodale, I. (1985). Mother-blaming in major clinical journals. *American Journal of Orthopsychiatry, 55,* 345–353.

Carey, C. M., & Mongeau, P. A. (1996). Communication and violence in courtship relationships. In D. D. Cahn & S. A. Lloyd (Eds.), *Family violence from a communication perspective.* Thousand Oaks, CA: Sage.

Carli, L. L. (1990). Gender, language, and influence. *Journal of Personality and Social Psychology, 59,* 941–951.

Carli, L. L. (1999). Gender, interpersonal power, and social influence. *Journal of Social Issues, 55* (1), 81–99.

Carli, L. L. (2001). Gender and social influence. *Journal of Social Issues, 57* (4), 735–741.

Carlson, B. E., & Videka-Sherman, L. (1990). An empirical test of androgyny in the middle years: Evidence from a national survey. *Sex Roles, 23,* 305–324.

Carmen, E. H., Russo, N. F., & Miller, J. B. (1981). Women's inequality and women's mental health: An overview. *American Journal of Psychiatry, 138,* 1319–1330.

Carp, F. M. (1997). Retirement and women. In J. M. Coyle (Ed.), *Handbook on women and aging* (pp. 112–128). Westport, CT: Greenwood Press.

Carr, D. (2002). The psychological consequences of work-family tradeoffs for three cohorts of men and women. *Social Psychology Quarterly, 65,* 103–124.

Carr, J. G., Gilroy, F. D., & Sherman, M. F. (1996). Silencing the self and depression among women: The moderating role of race. *Psychology of Women Quarterly, 20,* 375–392.

Carson, D. K., Gertz, L. M., Donaldson, M. A., & Wonderlich, S. A. (1990). Family-of-origin characteristics and current family relationships of female adult incest victims. *Journal of Family Violence, 5,* 153–171.

Cartwright, L. K., & Wink, P. (1994). Personality change in women physicians from medical student year to mid 40s. *Psychology of Women Quarterly, 18,* 291–308.

Cash, T. F. (1995). Developmental teasing about physical appearance: Retrospective descriptions and relationships with body image. *Social Behavior & Personality, 25,* 123–130.

Cash, T. F., Ancis, J. R., & Strachan, M. D. (1997). Gender attitudes, feminist identity, and body images among college women. *Sex Roles, 36,* 433–448.

Cash, T. F., Gillen, B., & Burns, D. S. (1977). Sexism and "beautyism" in personnel consultant decision making. *Journal of Applied Psychology, 62,* 301–310.

Cassell, J. (1997). Doing gender, doing surgery: Women surgeons in a man's profession. *Human Organization, 56*(1), 47–52.

Castaneda, D. (2000). Gender issues among Latinas. In J. C. Chrisler, C. Golden, & P. D. Rozee (Eds.), *Lectures on the psychology of women* (pp. 193–208). Boston, MA: McGraw-Hill.

Cate, C. A., Henton, J. M., Koval, J., Christopher, F. S., & Lloyd, S. (1982). Premarital abuse: A social psychological perspective. *Journal of Family Issues, 3,* 79–90.

Cauce, A. M., Hiraga, Y., Graves, D., Gonzales, N., Ryan-Finn, K., & Grove, K. (1996). African American mothers and their adolescent daughters: Closeness, conflict, and control. In B. J. R. Leadbeater & N. Way (Eds.), *Urban girls: Resisting stereotypes, cre-*

ating identities (pp. 100–116). New York: New York University Press.

Chaikin, S., & Pliner, P. (1987). Women, but not men, are what they eat: The effect of meal size and gender on perceived femininity and masculinity. *Personality and Social Psychology Bulletin, 13,* 166–176.

Chan, C. S. (1993). Issues of identity development among Asian-American lesbians and gay men. In L. D. Garnets & D. C. Kimmel (Eds.), *Psychological perspectives on lesbian and gay male experiences* (pp. 376–388). New York: Columbia University Press.

Chan, C. S. (2000). Asian American women and adolescent girls: Sexuality and sexual expression. In J. C. Chrisler, C. Golden, & P. D. Rozee (Eds.), *Lectures on the psychology of women* (pp. 149–162). Boston, MA: McGraw-Hill.

Chandani, A. T., McKenna, K. T., & Maas, F. (1989). Attitudes of university students towards the sexuality of physically disabled people. *British Journal of Occupational Therapy, 52,* 233–236.

Charlesworth, W. R., & Dzur, C. (1987). Gender comparisons of preschoolers' behavior and resource utilization in group problem-solving. *Child Development, 58,* 191–200.

Charlesworth, W. R., & LaFreniere, P. (1983). Dominance, friendship utilization and resource utilization in preschool children's groups. *Ethology and Sociobiology, 4,* 175–186.

Chesler, P. (1972). *Women and madness.* New York: Doubleday.

Cheung, C., & Liu, E. S. (1997). Impacts of social pressure and social support on distress among single parents in China. *Journal of Divorce & Remarriage: International Studies, 26*(3/4), 65–82.

Chicago, J. (1990, March). *The birth project.* Women's History Month Lecture, Trenton State College, Trenton, NJ.

Childs, E. K. (1990). Therapy, feminist ethics, and the community of color with particular emphasis on the treatment of black women. In H. Lerman & N. Porter (Eds.), *Feminist ethics in psychotherapy* (pp. 195–203). New York: Springer.

Chilman, C. S. (1983). *Adolescent sexuality in a changing American society* (2nd ed.). New York: John Wiley & Sons.

Chin, J. L., & Russo, N. F. (1997). Feminist curriculum development: Principles and resources. In J. Worell & N. G. Johnson (Eds.), *Shaping the future of feminist psychology* (pp. 93–102). Washington, DC: American Psychological Association.

Chipman, S. F., & Thomas, V. G. (1985). Women's participation in mathematics: Outlining the problem. In S. F. Chipman, L. R. Brush, & D. M. Wilson (Eds.), *Women and mathematics: Balancing the equation* (pp. 1–24). Hillsdale, NJ: Erlbaum.

Chipman, S. F., & Wilson, D. M. (1985). Understanding mathematics course enrollment and mathematics achievement: A synthesis of the research. In S. F. Chipman, L. R. Brush, & D. M. Wilson (Eds.), *Women and mathematics: Balancing the equation* (pp. 275–328). Hillsdale, NJ: Erlbaum.

Chodorow, N. (1978). *The reproduction of mothering.* Berkeley, CA: University of California Press.

Chodorow, N. (1979). Feminism and difference: Gender relation and difference in psychoanalytic perspective. *Socialist Review, 46,* 42–64.

Chodorow, N. J. (1999). *The power of feelings.* New Haven, CT: Yale University Press.

Choi, N. G. (2001). Relationship between life satisfaction and postretirement employment among older women. *International Journal of Aging & Human Development, 52,* 45–70.

Choo, P., Levine, T., & Hatfield, E. (1997). Gender, love schemas, and reactions to romantic break-ups. In R. Crandall (Ed.), *Handbook of gender research* (pp. 143–160). Corte Madera, CA: Select Press.

Chow, E. N. (1987). The influence of sex-role identity and occupational attainment on the psychological well-being of Asian-American women. *Psychology of Women Quarterly, 11,* 69–82.

Chow, E. N-L. (1996). The development of feminist consciousness among Asian American women. In E. N-L Chow, D. Wilkinson, & M. B. Zinn (Eds.), *Race, class, & gender: Common bonds, different voices* (pp. 251–264). Thousand Oaks, CA: Sage.

Chrisler, J. C. (2001). Gendered bodies and physical health. In R. K. Unger (Editor), *Handbook of the psychology of women and gender* (pp. 289–302). NY: Wiley.

Chrisler, J. C., & Ghiz, L. (1993). Body image issues of older women. In N. D. Davis, E. Cole, & E. D. Rothblum (Eds.), *Faces of women and aging* (pp. 67–75). Binghamton, NY: Harrington Park Press.

Chrisler, J. C., & Hemstreet, A. H. (1995). The diversity of women's health needs. In J. C. Chrisler & A. H. Hemstreet (Eds.), *Variations on a theme: Diversity and the psychology of women* (pp. 1–28). Albany: State University of New York Press.

Chrisler, J. C., Johnston, I. K., Champagne, N. M., & Preston, K. E. (1994). Menstrual joy: The construct and its consequences. *Psychology of Women Quarterly, 18,* 375–387.

Chrisler, J. C., Torrey, J. W., & Matthes, M. A. (1990). Brittle bones and sagging breasts, loss of femininity and loss of sanity: The media describe the menopause. In A. M. Voda & R. Conover (Eds.), *Proceedings of the eighth conference of the Society for Menstrual Cycle Research* (pp. 23–35). Salt Lake City: Society for Menstrual Cycle Research.

Cialdini, R. B., Wosinska, W., Dabul, A. J., Wheatstone-Dion, R., & Heszen, I. (1998). When social role salience leads to social role rejection: Modest self-presentation among women in two countries. *Personality and Social Psychology Bulletin, 24,* 473–481.

Ciancanelli, P., & Berch, B. (1987). Gender and the GNP. In B. B. Hess and M. M. Ferree (Eds.), *Analyzing gender: A handbook of social science research* (pp. 244–266). Newbury Park, CA: Sage.

Clark, M. L., Beckett, J., Wells, M., & Dungee-Anderson, D. (1994). Courtship violence among African American college students. *Journal of Black Psychology, 20*(3), 264–281.

Cleek, M. G., & Pearson, T. A. (1985). Perceived causes of divorce: An analysis of interrelationships. *Journal of Marriage and the Family, 47,* 179–183.

Coates, E. J., & Feldman, R. S. (1996). Gender differences in nonverbal correlates of social status. *Personality and Social Psychology Bulletin, 22,* 1014–1022.

Code, L. B. (1983). Responsibility and the epistemic community: Woman's place. *Social Research, 50,* 537–555.

Cohen, B. P., Berger, J., & Zelditch, M. (1972). Status conceptions and interactions: A case study of developing cumulative knowledge. In C. McClintock (Ed.), *Experimental social psychology.* New York: Holt, Rinehart, & Winston.

Cohen, C. E. (1981). Person categories and social perception: Testing some boundaries of the processing effects of prior knowledge. *Journal of Personality and Social Psychology, 40,* 441–452.

Cohen, K. M. (2002). Relationships among childhood sex-atypical behavior, spatial ability, handedness, and sexual orientation in men. *Archives of Sexual Behavior, 31,* 129–143.

Cohen, L. L., & Swim, J. R. (1995). The differential impact of gender ratios on women and men: Tokenism, self-confidence, and expectations. *Personality and Social Psychology Bulletin, 21,* 876–884.

Colapinto, J. (1997, December 11). The true story of John/Joan. *Rolling Stone,* pp. 54–97.

Colapinto, J. (2000). *As nature made him: The boy who was raised as a girl.* NY: Harper/Collins.

Colby, A., & Damon, W. (1983). Listening to a different voice: A review of Gilligan's In a different voice. *Merrill-Palmer Quarterly, 29,* 473–481.

Cole, T. R. (1992). *The journey of life: A cultural history of aging in America.* New York: Cambridge University Press.

Coles, R. (1985). *Sex and the American teenager.* New York: Rolling Stone Press.

Coley, R. J. (2001). *Differences in the gender gap: Comparisons across racial/ethnic groups in education and work.* Princeton: Educational Testing Service.

Collaer, M. L., & Hines, M. (1995). Human behavioral sex differences: A role for gonadal hormones during early development? *Psychological Bulletin, 118,* 55–107.

Collins, M. E. (1998). Factors influencing sexual victimization and revictimization in a sample of adolescent mothers. *Journal of Interpersonal Violence, 13,* 3–24.

Collins, P. H. (1991). The meaning of motherhood in Black culture and Black mother-daughter relationships. In P. Bell-Scott, B. Guy-Sheftall, J. J. Royster, J. Sims-Wood, M. DiCosta-Willis, & L. P. Fultz (Eds.), *Double stitch: Black women write about mothers and daughters* (pp. 42–60). New York: HarperCollins.

Collins, P. H. (1993b). The sexual politics of Black womanhood. In P. B. Bart & E. G. Moran (Eds.), *Violence against women: The bloody footprints* (pp. 85–104). Newbury Park, CA: Sage.

Collins, R. K. L., & Skover, D. M. (1993). Commerce and communication. *Texas Law Review. 71,* 697–746.

Collins, S. K. (1988). Women at the top of women's fields: Social work, nursing, and education. In A. Statham, E. M. Miller, & H. O. Mauksch (Eds.), *The worth of women's work: A qualitative synthesis* (pp. 187–201). Albany, NY: State University of New York Press.

Collins-Standley, T., Gan, S., Yu, H. J., & Zillmann, D. (1996). Choice of romantic, violent, and scary fairy tale books by preschool girls and boys. *Child Study Journal, 26,* 279–302.

Condit, C. M. (1996). Media bias for reproductive technologies. In R. L. Parrott & C. M. Condit (Eds.), *Evaluating women's health messages* (pp. 341–355). Thousand Oaks: Sage.

Condon, J. (1987). Psychological and physical symptoms during pregnancy: A comparison of male and female expectant parents. *Journal of Infant and Reproductive Psychology, 5,* 207–220.

Condry, S. M., Condry, J. C., Jr., & Pogatshnik, L. W. (1983). Sex differences: A study of the ear of the beholder. *Sex Roles, 9,* 697–704.

Connidis, I. A., & McMullin, J. A. (1996). Reasons for and perceptions of childlessness among older persons: Exploring the impact of marital status and gender. *Journal of Aging Studies, 10*(3), 205–222.

Conway, M., Pizzamiglio, M. T., & Mount, L. (1996). Status, communality, and agency: Implications for stereotypes of gender and other groups. *Journal of Personality and Social Psychology, 71,* 25–38.

Conway, M., & Vartanian, L. R. (2000). A status account of gender stereotypes: Beyond communality and agency. *Sex Roles, 43,* 181–199.

Cook, S. (2000, October 3). Study finds women test better in math without men. *Christian Science Monitor,* p. 14.

Cooksey, E. C., Rindfuss, R. R., & Guilkey, D. K. (1996). The initiation of adolescent sexual and contraceptive behavior during changing times. *Journal of Health and Social Behavior, 37*(1), 59–74.

Corbett, K. (1987). The role of sexuality and sex equity in the education of disabled women. *Peabody Journal of Education, 64,* 198–212.

Corley, M. C., & Mauksch, H. O. (1988). Registered nurses, gender, and commitment. In A. Statham, E. M. Miller, & H. O. Mauksch (Eds.), *The worth of women's work: A qualitative synthesis* (pp. 135–150). Albany, NY: State University of New York Press.

Cortina, L. M., Swan, S., Fitzgerald, L. F., & Waldo, C. (1998). Sexual harassment and assault: Chilling the climate for women in academia. *Psychology of Women Quarterly, 22,* 419–441.

Costa, P. T., Terracciano, A., & McCrae, R. R. (2001). Gender differences in personality traits across cultures: Robust and surprising findings. *Journal of Personality and Social Psychology, 81,* 322–331.

Costello, C., & Stone, A. J. (Eds.). (1994). *The American woman 1994–1995: Where we stand–Women and health.* New York: Norton.

Costigan, C. L., & Cox, M. J. (2001). Fathers' participation in family research: Is there a self-selection bias? *Journal of Family Psychology, 15,* 706–720.

Costos, D., Ackerman, R., & Paradis, L. (2002). Recollections of menarche: Communication between mothers and daughters regarding menstruation. *Sex Roles, 46,* 49–59.

Courtois, C. A. (1988). *Healing the incest wound: Adult survivors in therapy.* New York: W. W. Norton.

Covey, H. C. (1988). Historical terminology used to represent older people. *Gerontologist, 28,* 291–297.

Cowan, G. (1995). Black and White (and blue): Ethnicity and pornography. In H. Landrine (Ed.), *Bringing cultural diversity to feminist psychology: Theory, research, practice* (pp. 397–411). Washington, DC: American Psychological Association.

Cowan, G., & O'Brien, M. (1990). Gender and survival vs. death in slasher films: A content analysis. *Sex Roles, 23,* 187–196.

Cowan, G., Warren, L. W., & Young, J. L. (1985). Medical perceptions of menopausal symptoms. *Psychology of Women Quarterly, 9,* 3–14.

Coward, R. T., & Dwyer, J. W. (1990). The association of gender, sibling network composition, and patterns of parent care by adult children. *Research on Aging, 12,* 158–181.

Cowen, J. R. (1993, October). *Survey finds that 70% of women rabbis sexually harassed.* Moment, 34–37.

Cowley, G., & Springer, K. (2002, July 22). The end of the age of estrogen. *Newsweek,* 38–45.

Cozzarelli, C., & Major, B. (1998). The impact of antiabortion activities on women seeking abortions. In L. J. Beckman & S. M. Harvey (Eds.), *The new civil war: The psychology, culture, and politics of abortion* (pp. 81–104). Washington, DC: American Psychological Association.

Craig, R. S. (1992). The effect of television day part on gender portrayals in television commercials: A content analysis. *Sex Roles, 26,* 197–211.

Crandall, C. S. (1994). Prejudice against fat people: Ideology and self interest. *Journal of Personality and Social Psychology, 66,* 882–894.

Crandall, C. S. (1995). Do parents discriminate against their heavyweight daughters? *Personality and Social Psychology Bulletin, 21,* 724–735.

Crandall, C. S., & Martinez, R. (1996). Culture, ideology, and anti-fat attitudes. *Personality and Social Psychology Bulletin, 22,* 1165–1176.

Crawford, M. (1978, November). Climbing the ivy-covered walls: How colleges deny tenure to women. *Ms.,* pp. 61–63, 91–94.

Crawford, M. (1981, August). Emmy Noether: She did Einstein's math. *Ms.,* pp. 86–89.

Crawford, M. (1982). In pursuit of the well-rounded life: Women scholars and the family. In M. Kehoe (Ed.), *Handbook for women scholars* (pp. 89–96). San Francisco: Americas Behavioral Research.

Crawford, M. (1989). Agreeing to differ: Feminist epistemologies and women's ways of knowing. In M. Crawford & M. Gentry (Eds.), *Gender and thought* (pp. 128–145). New York: Springer Verlag.

Crawford, M. (1995). *Talking difference: On gender and language.* London: Sage.

Crawford, M., & Chaffin, R. (1997). The meanings of difference: Cognition in social and cultural context. In P. J. Caplan, M. Crawford, J. S. Hyde, & J. T. E. Richardson, *Gender differences in human cognition* (pp. 81–130). New York: Oxford.

Crawford, M., & English, L. (1984). Generic versus specific inclusion of women in language: Effects on recall. *Journal of Psycholinguistic Research, 13,* 373–381.

Crawford, M., & Kimmel, E. (1999). Promoting methodological diversity in feminist research (pp. 1–6). In M. Crawford & E. Kimmel (Eds.), *Innovations in feminist research* (special issue). *Psychology of Women Quarterly, 23,* 1.

Crawford, M., & Marecek, J. (1989). Psychology reconstructs the female. *Psychology of Women Quarterly, 13,* 147–166.

Crawford, M., McCullough, M., & Arato, H. (1983, June). *Do women's studies classes change attitudes in women but not men?* Paper presented at the annual meeting of the National Women's Studies Association, Bloomington, Indiana.

Crawford, S. (1987). Lesbian families: Psychosocial stress and the family-building process. In Boston Lesbian Psychologies Collective, *Lesbian psychologies* (pp. 195–214). Urbana, IL: University of Illinois Press.

Crewdson, J. (1988). *By silence betrayed: Sexual abuse of children in America.* New York: Harper and Row.

Crews, D. (1987a). Diversity and evolution of behavioral controlling mechanisms. In D. Crews (Ed.), *Psychobiology of reproductive behavior: An evolutionary perspective* (pp. 89–119). Englewood Cliffs, NJ: Prentice Hall.

Crick, N. R., & Bigbee, M. A. (1998). Relational and overt forms of peer victimization: A multi-informant approach. *Journal of Consulting and Clinical Psychology, 66,* 337–347.

Crick, N. R., & Rose, A. J. (2000). Toward a gender-balanced approach to the study of social-emotional development: A look at relational aggression. In P. H. Miller & E. K. Scholnick (Editors), *Toward a feminist developmental psychology* (pp. 153–168). NY: Routledge.

Crick, N. R., Casas, J. F., & Ku, H. (1999). Physical and relational peer-victimization in preschool. *Developmental Psychology, 33,* 376–385.

Crisp, A., Sedgwick, P., Halik, C., Joughin, N., & Humphrey, H. (1999). Why may teenage girls persist in smoking? *Journal of Adolescence, 22,* 657–672.

Crittenden, D. (1995, January 25). Sisterhood vs. new-wave thought. *The Wall Street Journal, 225,* A14.

Crocker, J. (2002). The costs of seeking self esteem. *Journal of Social Issues, 58* (3), 597–615.

Crocker, J., Cornwell, B., & Major, B. (1993). The stigma of overweight: Affective consequences of attitudinal ambiguity. *Journal of Personality and Social Psychology, 64,* 60–70.

Crocker, J., & McGraw, K. M. (1984). What's good for the goose is not good for the gander: Solo status as an obstacle to occupational achievement for males and females. *American Behavioral Scientist, 27,* 357–369.

Croghan, R. (1991). First-time mothers' accounts of inequality in the division of labour. *Feminism & Psychology, 1,* 221–246.

Crohan, S. E., & Veroff, J. (1989). Dimensions of marital well-being among white and black newlyweds. *Journal of Marriage and the Family, 51,* 373–383.

Crosbie-Burnett, M., & Giles-Sims, J. (1991). Marital power in stepfather families: A test of normative-resource theory. *Journal of Family Psychology, 4,* 484–496.

Crosby, F. (1982). *Relative deprivation and working women.* New York: Oxford University Press.

Crosby, F. (1984). The denial of personal discrimination. *American Behavioral Scientist, 27,* 371–386.

Crosby, F. J. (1991). *Juggling: The unexpected advantages of balancing career and home for women and their families.* New York: Free Press.

Crosby, F. J., Clayton, S., Alksnis, O., & Hemker, K. (1986). Cognitive biases in the perception of discrimination: The importance of format. *Sex Roles, 14,* 637–646.

Crosby, F. J., Pufall, A., Snyder, R. C., O'Connell, M., & Whalen, P. (1989). The denial of personal disadvantage among you, me, and all the other ostriches. In M. Crawford and M. Gentry (Eds.), *Gender and thought: Psychological perspectives* (pp. 79–99). New York: Springer-Verlag.

Crose, R., Leventhal, E. A., Haug, M. R., & Burns, E. A. (1997). The challenges of aging. In S. J. Gallant, G. P. Keita, & R. Royak-Schaller (Eds.), *Health care for women: Psychological, social and behavioral influences* (pp. 221–234). Washington, DC: American Psychological Association.

Croteau, J. M. (1996). Research on the work experiences of lesbian, gay, and bisexual people: An integrative review of methodology and findings. *Journal of Vocational Behavior, 48,* 195–209.

Crovitz, E., & Steinmann, A. (1980). A decade later: Black-white attitudes toward women's familial role. *Psychology of Women Quarterly, 5,* 171–176.

Cruikshank, M. (2003). *Learning to be old: Gender, culture, and aging.* Lanham, MD: Rowman & Littlefield, Publishers.

Cuddy, A. J. C., & Fiske, S. T. (2002). Doddering but dear: Process, content, and function in stereotyping of older persons. In T. D. Nelson (Ed.), *Ageism: Stereotyping and prejudice against older persons* (pp. 3–26). Cambridge, MA: MIT Press.

Cummings, N. (1992). Self-defense training for college women. *Journal of American College Health, 40,* 183–188.

Cunningham, M. R., Roberts, A. R., Barbee, A. P., Druen, P. B., & Wu, C. (1995). Their ideas of beauty are on the whole the same as ours: Consistency and variability in the cross-cultural perception of female physical attractiveness. *Journal of Personality and Social Psychology, 68,* 261–279.

Cusick, T. (1987). Sexism and early parenting: Cause and effect? *Peabody Journal of Education, 64,* 113–131.

Cusk, R. (2002). *Life's work: On becoming a mother.* New York: Picador.

Cutrona, C. E., Russell, D. W., Hessling, R. M., Brown, P. A., & Murry, V. (2000). Direct and moderating effects of community context on the psychological well-being of African American women. *Journal of Personality and Social Psychology, 79,* 1988–1101.

Cypress, A. (1993). Men were taught more than women. In S. Wall (Ed.), *Wisdom's daughters: Conversations with women elders of Native America* (pp. 85–90). New York: HarperCollins.

Daley, D., & Gold, R. B. (1993). Public funding for contraceptive, sterilization, and abortion services, fiscal year 1992. *Family Planning Perspectives, 25,* 244–251.

Dall'Ara, E., & Maass, A. (1999). Studying sexual harassment in the laboratory: Are egalitarian women at higher risk? *Sex Roles, 44,* 681–704.

Dallos, S., & Dallos, R. (1997). *Couples, sex, and power: The politics of desire.* Philadelphia: Open University Press.

D'Amico, R. (1986). Authority in the workplace: Differences among mature women. In L. B. Shaw (Ed.), *Midlife women at work: A fifteen-year perspective.* Lexington, MA: D. C. Heath.

Dancer, L. S., & Gilbert, L. A. (1993). Spouses' family work participation and its relation to wives' occupational level. *Sex Roles, 28,* 127–145.

Daniluk, J. C. (1996). When treatment fails: The transition to biological childlessness for infertile women. *Women & Therapy, 19*(2), 81–98.

Daniluk, J. C. (1998). *Women's sexuality across the life span: Challenging myths, creating meaning.* New York: Guilford.

Dansky, B. S., & Kilpatrick, D. G. (1997). Effects of sexual harassment. In W. O'Donohue (Ed.), *Sexual harassment: Theory, research and treatment* (pp. 152–174). Boston: Allyn & Bacon.

Darnton, J. (1993, March 11). Tough abortion law provokes dismay in Poland. *The New York Times,* p. A13.

Datan, N., Antonovsky, A., & Maoz, B. (1981). *A time to reap: The middle age of women in five Israeli subcultures.* Baltimore: Johns Hopkins Press.

Daubman, K. A., & Lehman, T. C. (1993). The effects of receiving help: Gender differences in motivation and performance. *Sex Roles, 28,* 693–707.

Davey, C. L., & Davidson, M. J. (2000). The right of passage? The experiences of female pilots in aviation. *Feminism and Psychology, 10,* 195–225.

Davis, D. M. (1990). Portrayal of women in prime-time network television: Some demographic characteristics. *Sex Roles, 23,* 325–332.

Davis, S., Crawford, M., & Sebrechts, J. (Eds.). (1999). *Coming into her own: Encouraging educational success in girls and women.* San Francisco: Jossey-Bass.

Davison, H. K., & Burke, M. J. (2000). Sex discrimination in simulated employment contexts: A meta-analytic investigation. *Journal of Vocational Behavior, 56,* 225–248.

Dean, K. E., & Malamuth, N. (1997). Characteristics of men who aggress sexually and of men who imagine aggressing: Risk and moderating variables. *Journal of Personality and Social Psychology, 72,* 449–455.

Dear, G. C., & Roberts, C. M. (2002). The relationship between codependency and femininity and masculinity. *Sex Roles, 46,* 159–165.

Dearwater, S. R., Coben, J. H., Campbell, J. C., Nah, G., et al. (1998, August 5). Prevalence of intimate partner abuse in women treated at community hospital emergency departments. *Journal of the American Medical Association, 280,* 433–438.

Deaux, K., (1984). From individual differences to social categories: Analysis of a decade's research on gender. *American Psychologist, 39,* 105–116.

Deaux, K. (1993). Commentary: Sorry, wrong number–A reply to Gentile's call. *Psychological Science, 4,* 125–126.

Deaux, K., & Emswiller, T. (1974). Explanations of successful performance on sex-linked tasks: What's skill for the male is luck for the female. *Journal of Personality and Social Psychology, 29,* 80–85.

Deaux, K., & Hanna, R. (1984). Courtship in the personals column: The influence of gender and sexual orientation. *Sex Roles, 11,* 363–375.

Deaux, K., & Kite, M. E. (1985). Gender stereotypes: Some thoughts on the cognitive organization of gender-related information. *Academic Psychology Bulletin, 7,* 123–144.

Deaux, K., & Lewis, L. L. (1984). The structure of gender stereotypes: Interrelationships among components and gender labels. *Journal of Personality and Social Psychology, 46,* 991–1004.

Deaux, K., & Stewart, A. J. (2001). Framing gendered identities. In R. K. Unger (Ed.), *Handbook of the psychology of women and gender* (pp. 84–97). New York: McGraw Hill.

Deaux, K., & Ullman, J. C. (1983). *Women of steel.* New York: Praeger.

Deaux, K. Winton, W., Crowley, M., & Lewis, L. L. (1985). Level of categorization and content of gender stereotypes. *Social Cognition, 3,* 145–167.

DeBlasio, C. L., Argiro, L. G., Orbin, J. A., & Ellyson, S. L. (1993, April). *Gender strategies in displaying power and attractiveness.* Paper presented at the annual meeting of the Eastern Psychological Association, Arlington, VA.

Deblinger, E., Hathaway, C. R., Lippman, J., & Steer, R. (1993). Psychosocial characteristics and correlates of symptom distress in nonoffending mothers of sexually abused children. *Journal of Interpersonal Violence, 8,* 155–168.

DeBold, E., Brown, L. M., Weseen, S., & Brookins, G. K. (2000). Cultivating hardiness zones for adolescent girls: A reconceptualization of resilience in relationships with caring adults. In N. G. Johnson, M. C. Roberts, & J. Worell (Eds.), *Beyond appearance: A new look at adolescent girls* (pp. 187–204). Washington D.C.: American Psychological Association.

DeKeseredy, W. S. (1997). Measuring sexual abuse in Canadian university/college dating relationships: the contribution of a national representative sample survey. In M. D. Schwartz (Ed.), *Researching sexual violence against women: Methodological and personal perspectives* (pp. 43–53). Thousand Oaks, CA: Sage.

Delaney, J., Lupton, M. J., & Toth, E. (1988). *The curse: A cultural history of menstruation* (rev. ed.). Urbana, IL: University of Illinois Press.

DeLisi, R., & McGillicuddy-DeLisi, A. (2002). Sex differences in mathematical abilities and achievement. In A. McGillicuddy-DeLisi & R. DeLisi (Eds.), *Biology, Society, and Behavior: The development of sex differences in cognition* (pp. 155–181). Westport, CT: Ablex.

DeMaris, A. (1992). Male versus female initiation of aggression: The case of courtship violence. In E. C. Viano (Ed.), *Intimate violence: Interdisciplinary perspectives* (pp. 111–120). New York: Hemisphere Publishing Corp.

DeMeis, D. K., & Perkins, H. W. (1996). "Supermoms" of the nineties: Homemaker and employed mothers' performance and perceptions of the motherhood role. *Journal of Family Issues, 17*(6), 776–792.

D'Emilio, J., & Freedman, E. B. (1988). *Intimate matters: A history of sexuality in America.* New York: Harper & Row.

Dempsey, K. (1997). Trying to get husbands to do more work at home. *Australian and New Zealand Journal of Sociology, 33*(2), 216–225.

Denmark, F. L. (1980). Psyche: From rocking the cradle to rocking the boat. *American Psychologist, 35,* 1057–1065.

Denmark, F. L., Russo, N. F., Frieze, I. H., & Sechzer, J. A. (1988). Guidelines for avoiding sexism in psychological research: A report of the ad hoc committee on nonsexist research. *American Psychologist, 43,* 582–585.

Dennerstein, L., Dudley, E., & Guthrie, J. (2002). Empty nest or revolving door? A prospective study of women's quality of life in midlife during the phase of children leaving and reentering the home. *Psychological Medicine, 32,* 545–550.

Dennerstein, L., Lehert, P., Burger, H., & Dudley, E. (1999). Mood and the menopausal transition. *Journal of Nervous and Mental Disease, 187,* 685–691.

Denniger, E., & Clarkberg, M. (2002). Informal caregiving and retirement timing among men and women: Gender and caregiving relationships in late midlife. *Journal of Family Issues, 23,* 857–879.

Derry, P. S. (2002). What do we mean by "the biology of menopause?" *Sex Roles, 46,* 13–23.

Deutsch, F. M., LeBaron, D., & Fryer, M. M. (1987). What is in a smile? *Psychology of Women Quarterly, 11,* 341–351.

Devor, H. (1987). Gender blending females: Women and sometimes men. *American Behavioral Scientist, 31,* 12–40.

Devor, H. (1996). Female gender disphoria in context: Social problem or personal problem? *Annual Review of Sex Research, 6.*

Devor, H. (1997). *MTF: Female-to-male transsexuals in society.* Bloomington, IN: University of Indiana Press.

Dew, M. A. (1985). The effect of attitudes on inferences of homosexuality and perceived physical attractiveness in women. *Sex Roles, 12,* 143–155.

Dewhurst, A. M., Moore, R. J., & Alfano, D. P. (1992). Aggression against women by men: Sexual and spousal assault. *Journal of Offender Rehabilitation, 18,* 39–47.

De Witt, K. (1997, June 23). Girl games on computers, where shoot 'em up simply won't do. *The New York Times,* p. D3.

DeZolt, D. M., & Hull, S. H. (2001). Classroom and school climate. In J. Worell (Ed.), *Encyclopedia of Women and Gender* (pp. 257–264). San Diego, CA: Academic Press.

Diamond, L. M. (2000). Sexual identity, attractions, and behavior among young sexual-minority women over a 2-year period. *Developmental Psychology, 36,* 241–250.

Diamond, M. (1995). Biological aspects of sexual orientation and identity. In L. Diamant & R. McAnulty (Eds.), *The psychology of sexual orientation, behavior, and identity: A handbook* (pp. 45–80). Westport, CT: Greenwood Press.

Diamond, M. (in press). Pediatric management of ambiguous and traumatized genitalia. *Journal of Urology.*

Diamond, M., & Sigmundson, H. K. (1997). Management of intersexuality: Guidelines for dealing with persons with ambiguous genitalia. *Archives of Pediatric and Adolescent Medicine, 151,* 1046.

Diamond, M. A. (1982). Sexual identity, monozygotic twins reared in discordant sex roles and a BBC follow-up. *Archives of Sexual Behavior, 11,* 181–186.

Diamond, M. A. (1993). Some genetic considerations in the development of sexual orientation. In M. Haug, R. E. Whalen, C. Aron, & K. L. Olsen (Eds.), *The development of sex differences and similarities in behavior* (pp. 291–309). Dordrecht: Kluwer Publishing Company.

DiBlasio, F. A., & Benda, B. B. (1992). Gender differences in theories of adolescent sexual activity. *Sex Roles, 27,* 221–239.

Dickerson, B. J. (Ed.). (1995). *African-American single mothers.* Thousand Oaks, CA: Sage.

Dickman, A. B., & Eagly, A. H. (2000). Stereotypes as dynamic constructs: Women and men of the past, present, and future. *Personality and Social Psychology Bulletin, 26,* 1171–1188.

Dickson, L. (1993). The future of marriage and family in Black America. *Journal of Black Studies, 23,* 472–491.

Diekman, A. B., McDonald, M., & Gardner, W. L. (2000). Love means never having to be careful: The relationship between reading romance novels and safe sex behavior. *Psychology of Women Quarterly, 24,* 179–188.

Dietz, T. L. (1998). An examination of violence and gender role portrayals in video games: Implications for gender socialization of aggressive behavior. *Sex Roles, 38,* 425–442.

Dijker, A. J., Koomen, W., van der Heuvel, H., & Frijda, N. H. (1996). Perceived antecedents of emotional reactions in inter-ethnic relations. *British Journal of Social Psychology, 35,* 313–329.

Di Leonardo, M. (1987). The female world of cards and holidays: Women, families, and the work of kinship. *Signs, 12,* 440–453.

Dion, K. K., Berscheid, E., & Walster, E. (1972). What is beautiful is good. *Journal of Personality and Social Psychology, 24,* 285–290.

DiPalma, L. M. (1994). Patterns of coping and characteristics of high-functioning incest survivors. *Archives of Psychiatric Nursing, 8*(2), 82–90.

Discover Magazine. (April, 1996). Laws of Physiques, p. 22.

Dittmann, R. W., Kappes, M. E., & Kappes, M. H. (1992). Sexual behavior in adolescent and adult-females with congenital adrenal hyperplasia. *Psychoneuroendocrinology, 17,* 153–170.

Dittmar, H., Lloyd, B., Dugan, S., Hallwell, E., Jacobs, N., & Cramer, H. (2000). The "body beautiful": English adolescents' images of ideal bodies. *Sex Roles, 42,* 887–915.

Dixon, D. A., Antoni, M., Peters, M., & Saul, J. (2001). Employment, social support, and

HIV sexual-risk behavior in Puerto Rican women. *AIDS and Behavior, 5,* 331–342.

Dodd, E. H., Giuliano, T. A., Boutell, J. M., & Moran, B. E. (2001). Respected or rejected: Perception of women who confront sexist remarks. *Sex Roles, 45,* 567–577.

Dodson, B. (1987). *Sex for one: The joy of self-loving.* New York: Crown.

Dohm, F. A., & Cummings, W. (2002). Research mentoring and women in clinical psychology. *Psychology of Women Quarterly, 26,* 163–167.

Doress, P. B., Siegal, D. L., & the Midlife and Old Women Book Project (1987). *Ourselves, growing older.* New York: Simon & Schuster.

Doress-Worters, P. B. (1994). Adding elder care to women's multiple roles: A critical review of the caregiver stress and multiple roles literature. *Sex Roles, 31,* 597–616.

Doress-Worters, P. B., & Siegal, D. L. (1994). *The new ourselves growing older.* New York: Simon & Schuster.

Douglas, S. J. (1994). *Where the girls are: Growing up female with the mass media.* New York: Times Books/Random House.

Dovidio, J. F., & Gaertner, S. L. (1981). The effects of race, status, and ability on helping behavior. *Social Psychology Quarterly, 44,* 192–203.

Dovidio, J. F., & Gaertner, S. L. (1983). The effects of sex, status, and ability on helping behavior. *Journal of Applied Social Psychology, 13,* 191–205.

Draucker, C. B. (1996). Family-of-origin variables and adult female survivors of childhood sexual abuse: A review of the research. *Journal of Child Sexual Abuse, 5,* 35–63.

Dreger, A. D. (1998). "Ambiguous sex"—or ambivalent medicine? *The Hastings Center Report, 28,* 24–35.

Dreher, G. F., & Cox, T. H., Jr. (1996). Race, gender, and opportunity: A study of compensation attainment and the establishment of mentoring relationships. *Journal of Applied Psychology, 81*(3), 297–308.

Driscoll, J. M., Kelley, F. A., & Fassinger, R. E. (1996). Lesbian identity and disclosure in the workplace: Relation to occupational stress and satisfaction. *Journal of Vocational Behavior, 48,* 229–242.

Dryden, C. (1999). *Being married, doing gender.* New York: Routledge.

Dugger, C. W. (2001, April 22). Abortions in India spurred by sex test skew the ratio against girls. *The New York Times, 12.*

Duncan, G. J., & Hoffman, S. D. (1991). A reconsideration of the economic consequences of marital dissolution. *Demography, 22,* 485.

Duncan, L. E. (1999). Motivation for collective action: Group consciousness as mediators of personality, life experiences, and women's rights activism. *Political Psychology, 20,* 611–635.

Duncan, L. E., Peterson, B. E., & Winter, D. G. (1997). Authoritarian and gender roles: Toward a psychological analysis of hegemonic relationships. *Personality and Social Psychology Bulletin, 23,* 41–49.

Dunkin, K., & Nugent, B. (1998). Kindergarten children's gender role expectations for television actors. *Sex Roles, 38,* 387–402.

Dunlop, E. (1968). Emotional imbalances in the premenopausal woman. *Psychosomatics, 9,* 44–47.

Dutton, D. G. (1996). Patriarchy and wife assault: The ecological fallacy. In L. K. Hamberger, & C. Renzetti (Eds.), *Domestic partner abuse* (pp. 125–151). Springer.

Dutton, D. G., Starzomski, A., & Ryan, L. (1996). Antecedents of abusive personality and abusive behavior in wife assaulters. *Journal of Family Violence, 11,* 113–132.

Dutton, M. A. (1996). Battered women's strategic response to violence. The role of context. In J. L. Edleson, & Z. C. Eisikovits (Eds.), *Future interventions with battered women and their families* (pp. 105–124). Thousand Oaks, CA: Sage.

Dworkin, A. (1987). *Intercourse.* New York: Free Press.

Dwyer, C. A. (1979). The role of tests and their construction in producing apparent sex-related differences. In M. A. Wittig & A. C. Petersen (Eds.), *Sex-related differences in cognitive functioning: Developmental issues* (pp. 335–353). New York: Academic Press.

Eagly, A. H. (1987). *Sex differences in social behavior: A social role interpretation.* Hillsdale, NJ: Erlbaum.

Eagly, A. H., & Johnson, B. T. (1990). Gender and leadership style: A meta-analysis. *Psychological Bulletin, 108,* 233–256.

Eagly, A. H., & Karau, S. J. (1991). Gender and the emergence of leaders: A meta-analysis. *Journal of Personality and Social Psychology, 60,* 685–710.

Eagly, A. H., & Karau, S. J. (2002). Role congruity theory of prejudice toward female leaders. *Psychological Review, 109,* 573–598.

Eagly, A. H., Karau, S. J., & Makhijani, M. (1995). Gender and the effectiveness of leaders: A meta-analysis. *Psychological Bulletin, 117,* 125–145.

Eagly, A. H., & Mladinic, A. (1989). Gender stereotypes and attitudes toward women and men. *Personality and Social Psychology Bulletin, 15,* 543–558.

Eagly, A. H., & Mladinic, A. (1993). Are people prejudiced against women? Some answers from research on attitudes, gender stereotypes, and judgments of competence. In W. Strobe & M. Hewstone (Eds.). *European review of social psychology* (pp. 1–35). NY: Wiley.

Eagly, A. H., & Wood, W. (1999). The origins of sex differences in human behavior: Evolved dispositions versus social roles. *American Psychologist, 54,* 408–423.

East, P. L. (1998). Racial and ethnic differences in girls' sexual, marital, and birth expectations. *Journal of Marriage and the Family, 60,* 150–162.

Eastman, S. T., & Billings, A. C. (1999). Gender parity in the Olympics: Hyping women athletes, favoring men athletes. *Journal of Physical Education, Recreation, and Dance, 69,* 37–45.

Eccles, J. S. (1989). Bringing young women to math and science. In M. Crawford and M. Gentry (Eds.), *Gender and thought: Psychological perspectives* (pp. 36–58). New York: Springer-Verlag.

Eccles, J. S. (1994). Understanding women's educational and occupational choices: Applying the Eccles et al. model of achievement-related choices. *Psychology of Women Quarterly, 18,* 585–610.

Eccles, J. S., Adler, T. F., Futterman, R., Goff, S. B., Kaczala, C. M., Meece, J. L., & Midgley, C. (1985). Self-perceptions, task perceptions, socializing influences, and the decision to enroll in mathematics. In S. F. Chipman, L. R. Brush, & D. M. Wilson (Eds.), *Women and mathematics: Balancing the equation* (pp. 95–122). Hillsdale, NJ: Erlbaum.

Eccles, J. S., Barber, B., Jozefowicz, D., Malenchuk, D., & Vida, M. (2000). Self-evaluations of competence, task values, and self-esteem. In N. G. Johnson, M. C. Roberts, & J. Worell (Eds.), *Beyond appearance: A new look at adolescent girls* (pp. 53–83). Washington D.C.: American Psychological Association.

Eccles, J. S., & Jacobs, J. E. (1986). Social forces shape math attitudes and performance. *Signs, 11,* 367–389.

Eckes, T. (1994). Features of men, features of women: Assessing stereotypic beliefs about gender subtypes. *British Journal of Social Psychology, 33,* 107–123.

Eder, D., Evans, C. C., & Parker, S. (1995). *Gender and adolescent culture.* Rutgers: Rutgers University Press.

Eder, D., Evans, C., & Parker, S. (1995). *School talk: Gender and adolescent culture.* New Brunswick, NJ: Rutgers University Press.

Edleson, J. L. (1996). Controversy and change in batterer's programs. In J. L. Edleson & Z. C. Eisikovits (Eds.), *Future interventions with battered women and their families* (pp. 154–169). Thousand Oaks, CA: Sage.

Edman, C. D. (1983a). The climacteric. In H. J. Buchsbaum (Ed.), *The menopause* (pp. 23–33). New York: Springer-Verlag.

Edman, C. D. (1983b). Estrogen replacement therapy. In H. J. Buchsbaum (Ed.), *The menopause* (pp. 77–84). New York: Springer-Verlag.

Edwards, C. P., Knoche, L., & Kumru, A. (2001). Play patterns and gender. In J. Worell (Ed.), *Encyclopedia of women and gender* (pp. 809–815). San Diego, CA: Academic Press.

Edwards, C. P., & Whiting, B. B. (1988). *Children of different worlds.* Cambridge, MA: Harvard University Press.

Edwards, J. J., & Alexander, P. C. (1992). The contribution of family background to long-term adjustment of women sexually abused as children. *Journal of Interpersonal Violence, 7,* 306–320.

Ehrenreich, B., & English, D. (1979). *For her own good: 150 years of the experts' advice to women.* Garden City, NY: Anchor Books.

Eichler, M. (1988). *Nonsexist research methods.* Boston: Allen & Unwin.

Eisenberg, A. R. (1996). The conflict talk of mothers and children: Patterns related to culture, SES, and gender of child. *Merrill-Palmer Quarterly 42,* 438–458.

Eldridge, N. S., & Gilbert, L. A. (1990). Correlates of relationship satisfaction in lesbian couples. *Psychology of Women Quarterly, 14,* 43–62.

Elise, S. (1995). Teenaged mothers: A sense of self. In B. J. Dickerson (Ed.), *African American single mothers* (pp. 53–79). Thousand Oaks: Sage.

Elkind, S. N. (1991, Winter). Letter to the editor. *Psychology of Women, 18,* 3.

Elliot, R. (1989). *Song of love.* New York: Harlequin.

Ellis, A. L. (1996). Sexual identity issues in the workplace: Past and present. In A. L. Ellis & E. D. B. Riggle (Eds.), *Sexual identity on the job: Issues and services* (pp. 1–16). New York: Harrington Park Press.

Ellis, J., & Fox, P. (2001). The effect of self-identified sexual orientation on helping behavior in a British sample: Are lesbians and gay men treated differently? *Journal of Applied Social Psychology, 31,* 1238–1247.

Ellis, P., & Murphy, B. C. (1994). The impact of misogyny and homophobia on therapy with women. In M. P. Mirkin (Ed.), *Women in context: Toward a feminist reconstruction of psychotherapy* (pp. 48–73). New York: Guilford.

Ellyson, S. L., Dovidio, J. F., & Brown, C. E. (1992). The look of power: Gender differences and similarities in visual dominance behavior. In C. L. Ridgeway (Ed.), *Gender, interaction, and inequality* (pp. 50–80). New York: Springer-Verlag.

England, P., & McCreary, L. (1987). Gender inequality in paid employment. In B. B. Hess and M. M. Ferree (Eds.), *Analyzing gender: A handbook of social science research* (pp. 286–320). Newbury Park, CA: Sage.

Epel, E. S., Spanakos, A., Kasl-Godley, J., & Brownell, K. D. (1996). Body shape ideals across gender, sexual orientation, socioeconomic status, race, and age in personal advertisements. *International Journal of Eating Disorders, 19,* 265–273.

Equal Employment Opportunity Commission (EEOC). (1980). Guidelines on discrimination because of sex. *Federal Register, 45,* 74676–77.

Erel, O., Oberman, Y., & Yirmiya, N. (2000). Maternal versus nonmaternal care and seven domains of children's development. *Psychological Bulletin, 126,* 727–747.

Erkut, S., Fields, J. P., Sing, R., & Marks, F. (1997). Diversity in girls' experiences: Feeling good about who you are. In B. J. R. Leadbeater & N. Way (Eds.), *Urban girls: Resisting stereotypes, creating identities* (pp. 53–64). New York: New York University Press.

Ernsberger, P., & Koletsky, R. J. (1999). Biomedical rationale for a wellness approach to obesity: An alternative to a focus on weight loss. *Journal of Social Issues, 55* (2), 221–260.

Espin, O. M. (1987a). Issues of identity in the psychology of Latina lesbians. In Boston Lesbian Psychologies Collective (Ed.), *Lesbian psychologies: Explorations and challenges* (pp. 35–55). Urbana: University of Illinois Press.

Espin, O. M. (1987b). Psychological impact of migration on Latinas: Implications of psychotherapeutic practice. *Psychology of Women Quarterly, 11,* 489–503.

Esten, G., & Willmott, L. (1993). Double bind messages: The effects of attitude toward disability on therapy. *Women & Therapy, 14,* 29–41.

Etaugh, C., & Brown, B. (1975). Perceiving the causes of success and failure of male and female performers. *Developmental Psychology, 11,* 103.

Etaugh, C., & Liss, M. B. (1992). Home, school, and playroom: Training grounds for adult gender roles. *Sex Roles, 26,* 129–147.

Etcoff, N. (1999). *Survival of the prettiest: The science of beauty.* New York: Anchor Books.

Etter-Lewis, G. (1988). *Power and social change: Images of Afro-American women in the print media.* Paper presented at the annual meeting of the National Women's Studies Association, Minneapolis, MN.

Evans, L., & Davies, K. (2000). No sissy boys here: A content analysis of the representation of masculinity in elementary school reading textbooks. *Sex Roles, 42,* 255–270.

Fabes, R. A. (1994). Physiological, emotional, and behavioral correlates of gender segregation. In C. Leaper (Ed.), *The development of gender and relationships* (pp. 19–34). San Francisco: Jossey-Bass.

Fabes, R. A., Shepard, S. A., Guthrie, I. K., & Martin, C. L. (1997). Roles of temperamental arousal and gender-segregated play in young children's social adjustment. *Developmental Psychology, 33,* 693–702.

Facio, E. (1997). Chicanas and aging: Toward definitions of womanhood. In J. M. Coyle (Ed.), *Handbook on women and aging* (pp. 335–350). Westport, CT: Greenwood Press.

Facts in brief: Induced abortion worldwide. (1999). New York: The Alan Guttmacher Institute.

Facts in brief: Induced abortion. (2002). New York: The Alan Guttmacher Institute.

Facts in brief: Teenagers' sexual and reproductive health. (2002). New York: The Alan Guttmacher Institute.

Faderman, L. (1981). *Surpassing the love of men: Romantic friendship and love between women from the Renaissance to the present.* New York: William Morrow.

Fagot, B. I. (1985a). Beyond the reinforcement principle: Another step toward understanding sex role development. *Developmental Psychology, 21,* 1097–1104.

Fagot, B. I. (1985b). Changes in thinking about early sex role development. *Developmental Review, 5,* 83–98.

Fagot, B. I., & Leinbach, M. D. (1987). Socialization of sex roles within the family. In D. B. Carter (Ed.), *Current conceptions of sex roles and sex typing: Theory and research* (pp. 89–100). New York: Praeger.

Fagot, B. I., & Leinbach, M. D. (1995). Gender knowledge in egalitarian and traditional families. *Sex Roles, 32,* 513–526.

Fain, T. C., & Anderton, D. L. (1987). Sexual harassment: Organizational context and diffuse status. *Sex Roles, 17,* 291–311.

Falconer, J. W., & Neville, H. A. (2000). African American college women's body image. *Psychology of Women Quarterly, 24,* 236–243.

Falk, P. J. (1993). Lesbian mothers: Psychosocial assumptions in family law. In L. D. Garnets & D. C. Kimmel (Eds.), *Psychological perspectives on lesbian and gay male experiences* (pp. 420–436). New York: Columbia University Press.

Faludi, S. (1991). *Backlash: The undeclared war against American women.* New York: Doubleday.

Farmer, H. S., et al. (Eds.). (1997). *Diversity & women's career development: From adolescence to adulthood.* Thousand Oaks, CA: Sage.

Fassinger, R. E. (1996). Notes from the margins: Integrating lesbian experience into the vocational psychology of women. *Journal of Vocational Behavior, 48,* 160–175.

Fassinger, R. E. (2002). Hitting the ceiling: Gendered barriers to occupational entry, advancements, and achievement. In L. Diamant & J. A. Lee (Eds.), *The psychology of sex, gender, and jobs: Issues and resolutions* (pp. 21–46). Westport, CT: Praeger.

Faulkner, A. O., & Heisel, M. A. (1987). Giving, receiving, and exchanging: Social transactions among inner-city black aged. In H. Strange & M. Teitelbaum (Eds.), *Aging and cultural diversity* (pp. 117–130). South Hadley, MA: Bergin & Garvin.

Faunce, P. S. (1990). Women in poverty: Ethical dimensions in therapy. In H. Lerman & N. Porter (Eds.), *Feminist ethics in psychotherapy* (pp. 185–194). New York: Springer.

Fausto-Sterling, A. (1992). *Myths of gender: Biological theories about women and men* (rev. ed.). New York: Basic Books.

Fausto-Sterling, A. (1997). Beyond difference: A biologist's perspective. *Journal of Social Issues, 53,* 233–258.

Fausto-Sterling, A. (2000). *Sexing the body: Gender politics and the construction of sexuality.* NY: Basic Books.

Favreau, O. E. (1997). Sex and gender comparisons: Does null hypothesis testing create a false dichotomy? *Feminism and Psychology,* 7(1), 63–81.

Federal Bureau of Investigation. (1985). *Uniform crime report.* Washington, DC: U.S. Department of Justice.

Federal Glass Ceiling Commission. (1998). Working women face barriers to advancement. In M. E. Williams (Ed.), *Working women: Opposing viewpoints* (pp. 64–72). San Diego: Greenhaven Press.

Feeney, J., Peterson, C., & Noller, P. (1994). Equality and marital satisfaction in the family life cycle. *Personal Relationships, 1,* 83–99.

Feinman, S. (1981). Why is cross-sex-role behavior more approved for girls than for boys? A status characteristic approach. *Sex Roles, 7,* 289–300.

Feldman, D. C. (1996). The nature, antecedents and consequences of underemployment. *Journal of Management, 22*(3), 385–407.

Feldman-Summers, S., & Kiesler, S. J. (1974). Those who are number two try harder: The effects of sex on attributions of causality. *Journal of Personality and Social Psychology, 30,* 846–855.

Fenell, D. L. (1993). Characteristics of long-term first marriages. *Journal of Mental Health Counseling, 15,* 446–460.

Ferguson, S. J. (2000). Challenging traditional marriage: Never married Chinese American and Japanese American women. *Gender and Society, 14,* 136–159.

Fernandez, M. (1997). Domestic violence by extended family members in India. Interplay of gender and generation. *Journal of Interpersonal Violence, 12,* 433–455.

Fernberger, S. W. (1948). Persistence of stereotypes concerning sex differences. *Journal of Abnormal and Social Psychology, 43,* 97–101.

Ferree, M. M. (1987). She works hard for a living: Gender and class on the job. In B. B. Hess & M. M. Ferree (Eds.), *Analyzing gender: A handbook of social science research* (pp. 322–347). Newbury Park, CA: Sage.

Fidell, L. S. (1970). Empirical verification of sex discrimination in hiring practices in psychology. *American Psychologist, 25,* 1094–1098.

Fidell, L. S. (1982). Gender and drug use and abuse. In I. Al-Issa (Ed.), *Gender and psychopathology* (pp. 221–236). New York: Academic Press.

Fiese, B. H. & Skillman, G. (2000). Gender differences in family stories: Moderating influence of parent gender role and child gender. *Sex Roles, 43,* 267–283.

"Finding the inner swine." *Newsweek,* February 1, 1999, p. 51–52.

Findlen, B. (Ed.). (1995). *Listen up! Voices from the next feminist generation.* Seattle: Seal Press.

Fine, M. (1983–1984). Coping with rape: Critical perspectives on consciousness. *Imagination, Cognition, and Personality, 3,* 249–267.

Fine, M. (1985). Reflections on a feminist psychology of women: Paradoxes and prospects. *Psychology of Women Quarterly, 9,* 167–183.

Fine, M. (1988). Sexuality, schooling, and adolescent females: The missing discourse of desire. *Harvard Educational Review, 58,* 29–53.

Fine, M. A. (2000). Divorce and single parenting. In C. Hendrick & S. S. Hendrick (Eds.), *Close relationships: A sourcebook* (pp. 139–154). Thousand Oaks, CA: Sage Publications, Inc.

Fine, M., & Asch, A. (1988). *Women with disabilities: Essays in psychology, culture, and politics.* Philadelphia: Temple University Press.

Fine, M. & Carney, S. (2001). Women, gender, and the law: Toward a feminist rethinking of responsibility. In R. K. Unger (Ed.), *Handbook of the psychology of women and gender* (pp. 388–409). NY: Wiley.

Fine, M., & Gordon, S. M. (1989). Feminist transformations of/despite psychology. In M. Crawford & M. Gentry (Eds.), *Gender and thought* (pp. 146–174). New York: Springer-Verlag.

Fine, M., & Macpherson, P. (1992). Over dinner: Feminism and adolescent female bodies. In M. Fine (Ed.), *Disruptive voices: The possibilities of feminist research* (pp. 175–203). Ann Arbor: University of Michigan Press.

Fine, M., Weis, L., Powell, L. C., & Wong, L. M. (Eds.). (1997). *Off white: Readings on race, power, and society.* New York: Routledge.

Finkel, J. S., & Hanson, F. J. (1992). Correlates of retrospective marital satisfaction in long-lived marriages: A social constructivist approach. *Family Therapy, 19,* 1–16.

Finkelhor, D. (1984). *Child sexual abuse: New theory and research.* New York: Free Press.

Finkelhor, D., Hotaling, G. T., Lewis, I. A., & Smith, C. (1989). Sexual abuse and its relationship to later sexual satisfaction, marital status, religion, and attitudes. *Journal of Interpersonal Violence, 4,* 379–399.

Finkelhor, D., Hotaling, G., Lewis, I. A., & Smith, C. (1990). Sexual abuse in a national survey of adult men and women: Prevalence, characteristics, and risk factors. *Child Abuse and Neglect, 14,* 533–542.

Firestein, B. A. (1998, March 7). *Bisexuality: A feminist vision of choice and change.* Paper presented at the annual meeting of the Association for Women in Psychology, Baltimore, MD.

Fisher, J. D., & Fisher, W. A. (2000). Theoretical approaches to individual-level change in HIV risk behavior. In J. L. Peterson, R. J. DiClemente (Eds.), *Handbook of HIV prevention, AIDS prevention and mental health* (pp. 3–55). New York: Kluwer Academic/Plenum.

Fisher, J. D., Fisher, W. A., Misovich, S. J., Kimble, D. L., & Malloy, T. E. (1996).Changing AIDS risk behavior: Effects of an intervention emphasizing AIDS risk reduction information, motivation, and behavioral skills in a college student population. *Health Psychology, 15*(2), 114–123.

Fisher, J. D., Nadler, A., & Whitcher-Alagna, S. (1982). Recipient reactions to aid. *Psychological Bulletin, 91,* 27–54.

Fisher, W. A., Williams, S. S., Fisher, J. D., & Malloy, T. E. (1999). Understanding AIDS risk behavior among sexually active urban adolescents: An empirical test of the information-motivation-behavioral skills model. *AIDS and Behavior, 3,* 13–23.

Fiske, A. P., Haslam, N., & Fiske, S. T. (1991). Confusing one person with another: What errors reveal about the elementary forms of social relations. *Journal of Personality and Social Psychology, 60,* 656–674.

Fiske, S. T. (1993). Controlling other people: The impact of power on stereotyping. *American Psychologist, 48,* 621–628.

Fiske, S. T., Bersoff, D. N., Borgida, E., Deaux, K., & Heilman, M. E. (1991). Social science research on trial: Use of sex stereotyping research in Price Waterhouse v. Hopkins. *American Psychologist, 46,* 1049–1060.

Fiske, S. T., & Stevens, L. E. (1993). What's so special about sex? Gender stereotyping and discrimination. In S. Oskamp & M. Constanzo (Eds.), *Gender issues in contemporary society* (pp. 173–196). Newbury Park, CA: Sage.

Fiske, S. T., Xu, J., & Cuddy, A. C. (1999). (Dis)respecting versus (dis)liking: Status and interdependence predict ambivalent stereotypes of competence and warmth. *Journal of Social Issues, 55,* 473–489.

Fitch, R. H., & Denenberg, V. H. (1998). A role for ovarian hormones in sexual differentiation of the brain. *Behavior and Brain Science, 21,* 311–352.

Fitzgerald, L. F. (1993). Sexual harassment: Violence against women in the workplace. *American Psychologist, 48,* 1070–1076.

Fitzgerald, L. F. (1996). Sexual harassment: The definition and measurement of a construct. In M. A. Paludi (Ed.), *Sexual harassment on college campuses: Abusing the ivory power* (pp. 25–47). Albany: State University of New York Press.

Fitzgerald, L. F., & Betz, N. E. (1983). Issues in the vocational psychology of women. In W. B. Walsh & S. H. Osipow (Eds.), *Handbook of vocational psychology, Vol. 1.* Hillsdale, NJ: Erlbaum.

Fitzgerald, L. F., Drasgow, F., Hulin, C. L., Gelfland, M. J., & Magley, V. J. (1997). Antecedents and consequences of sexual harassment in organizations: A test of an integrated model. *Journal of Applied Psychology, 82,* 578–589.

Fitzgerald, L. F., Swan, S., & Magley, V. J. (1997). But was it really sexual harassment? Legal, behavioral, and psychological definitions of the workplace victimization of women. In W. O'Donohue (Ed.), *Sexual harassment: Theory, research, and treatment* (pp. 5–28). Boston: Allyn & Bacon.

Fitzgibbon, M. L., Spring, B., Avellone, M. E., Blackman, L. R., Pingitore, R., & Stolley, M. R. (1998). Correlates of binge eating in Hispanic, Black, and White women. *International Journal of Eating Disorders, 24,* 43–52.

Fivush, R., Brotman, M. A., Buckner, J. P., & Goodman, S. H. (2000). Gender differences in parent-child emotion narratives. *Sex Roles, 42,* 233–253.

Flanagan, D., Baker-Ward, L., & Graham, L. (1995). Talk about preschool: Patterns of topic discussion and elaboration related to gender and ethnicity. *Sex Roles, 32,* 1–15.

Flanagan, D., & Perese, S. (1998). Emotional references in mother-daughter and mother-son dyadic conversations about school. *Sex Roles, 39,* 353–367.

Flint, M., & Samil, R. S. (1990). Cultural and subcultural meanings of the menopause. In M. Flint, F. Kronenberg, & W. Utian (Eds.), Multidisciplinary perspectives on menopause. *Annals of the New York Academy of Sciences, 592,* 134–155.

Flippen, C., & Tienda, M. (2000). Pathways to retirement: Patterns of labor force participation and labor market exit among preretirement population by race, Hispanic origin, and sex. *Journals of Gerontology: Series B: Psychological Sciences & Social Sciences, 55B,* S14–S27.

Foa, E. B., Olasov, B., & Steketee, G. S. (1987). *Treatment of rape victims.* Paper presented at the conference, State of the Art in Sexual Assault, Charleston, SC.

Foddy, M., & Smithson, M. (1999). Can gender inequalities be eliminated? *Social Psychology Quarterly, 62,* 307–324.

Fodor, I., & Epstein, J. (2001). Agoraphobia, panic disorders, and gender. In J. Worell (Ed.), *Encyclopedia of sex and gender* (pp. 109–123). NY: Academic Press.

Follingstad, D. R., Rutledge, L. L., McNeill-Hawkins, K., & Polek, D. S. (1992). Factors related to physical violence in dating relationships. In E. C. Viano (Ed.), *Intimate violence: Interdisciplinary perspectives* (pp. 121–135). New York: Hemisphere.

Ford, M. R., & Lowery, C. R. (1986). Gender differences in moral reasoning: A comparison of the use of justice and care orientations. *Journal of Personality and Social Psychology, 50,* 777–783.

Ford, T. E. (2000). Effects of sexist humor on tolerance of sexist events. *Personality & Social Psychology Bulletin, 26,* 1094–1107.

Fordham, S. (1993). "Those loud black girls": (Black) women, silence, and gender "passing" in the academy. *Anthropology and Education Quarterly, 24,* 3–32.

Foreit, K. G., Agor, A. T., Byers, J., Larue, J., Lokey, H., Palazzini, M., Patterson, M., & Smith, L. (1980). Sex bias in the newspaper treatment of male-centered and female-centered news stories. *Sex Roles, 6,* 475–480.

Forste, R., & Tanfer, K. (1996). Sexual exclusivity among dating, cohabiting, and married women. *Journal of Marriage and Family, 58,* 33–47.

Foschi, M., & Freeman, S. (1991). Inferior performance, standards, and influence in same-sex dyads. *Canadian Journal of Behavioral Sciences, 23,* 99–113.

Foster, M. D. (2001). The motivational quality of global attributions in hypothetical and experienced situations of gender discrimination. *Psychology of Women Quarterly, 25,* 242–253.

Foucault, M. (1978). *The history of sexuality.* New York: Pantheon.

Fouts, G., & Burggraf, K. (2000). Television situation comedies, female weight, male negative comments, and audience reactions. *Sex Roles, 42,* 925–932.

Fowers, B. J. (1991). His and her marriages: A multivariate study of gender and marital satisfaction. *Sex Roles, 24,* 209–221.

Fox, D., & Prilleltensky, I. (1997). *Critical psychology: An introduction.* London: Sage Publications.

Frank, E., Anderson, C., & Rubenstein, D. (1978). Frequency of sexual dysfunction in "normal" couples. *New England Journal of Medicine, 299,* 111–115.

Franzoi, S. L. (2001). Is female body esteem shaped by benevolent sexism? *Sex Roles, 44,* 177–188.

Frazier, P. A., & Seales, L. M. (1997). Acquaintance rape is real rape. In M. D. Schwartz (Ed.), *Researching sexual violence against women: methodological and personal perspectives* (pp. 54–64). Thousand Oaks, CA: Sage.

Fredrickson, B. L., & Roberts, T. (1997). Objectification theory: Toward understanding women's lived experiences and mental health risks. *Psychology of Women Quarterly, 21*(2), 173–206.

Freedman, R. (1986). *Beauty bound.* Lexington, MA: D. C. Heath.

Freedman, R., & Woodward, S. (1992). Behavioral treatment of menopausal hot flushes: Evaluation of ambulatory monitoring. *American Journal of Obstetrics and Gynecology, 167,* 439–449.

Freud, S. (1933/1965). *New introductory lectures on psychoanalysis.* New York: Norton.

Freyd, J. (1997). Violations of power, adaptive blindness and betrayal trauma theory. *Feminism & Psychology, 7,* 22–32.

Friday, N. (1973). *My secret garden: Women's sexual fantasies.* New York: Simon & Schuster.

Fridell, S. R., Zucker, K. J., Bradley, S. J., & Maing, D. M. (1996). Physical attractiveness of girls with gender identity disorder. *Archives of Sexual Behavior, 25,* 17–31.

Friedman, A., & Pines, A. M. (1992). Increase in Arab women's perceived power in the second half of life. *Sex Roles, 26,* 1–9.

Frintner, M. P., & Rubinson, L. (1993). Acquaintance rape: The influence of alcohol, fraternity membership, and sports team membership. *Journal of Sex Education and Therapy, 19,* 272–284.

Frisch, R. E. (1983a). Fatness, menarche, and fertility. In S. Golub (Ed.), *Menarche: The transition from girl to woman* (pp. 5–20). Lexington, MA: Lexington Books.

Frisch, R. E. (1983b). Fatness, puberty, and fertility: The effects of nutrition and physical training on menarche and ovulation. In J. Brooks-Gunn & A. C. Petersen (Eds.), *Girls at puberty* (pp. 29–49). New York: Plenum.

Fuegen, K., & Biernat, M. (2002). Reexamining the effects of solo status for women and men. *Personality and Social Psychology Bulletin, 28,* 113–125.

Funk, J. B., & Buchman, D. D. (1996). Children's perceptions of gender differences in social approval for playing electronic games. *Sex Roles, 35,* 219–231.

Furnham, A., & Bitar, N. (1993). The stereotyped portrayal of men and women in British television advertisements. *Sex Roles, 29,* 297–310.

Furnham, A., & Mak, T. (1999). Sex-role stereotyping in television commercials: A review and compendium of fourteen studies done on five continents over twenty-five years. *Sex Roles, 41,* 413–437.

Furumoto, L. (1979). Mary Whiton Calkins (1863–1930): Fourteenth president of the American Psychological Association. *Journal of the History of the Behavioral Sciences, 15,* 346–356.

Gagnon, J. H., & Simon, W. (1973). *Sexual conduct: The social sources of human sexuality.* Chicago: Aldine.

Gaiter, D. (1994, March 8). The gender divide: Black women's gains in corporate America outstrip Black men's. *The Wall Street Journal, 223,* 1.

Galambos, N. L., Petersen, A. C., Richards, M., & Gitelson, I. B. (1985). The Attitudes toward Women Scale for Adolescents (AWSA): A study of reliability and validity. *Sex Roles, 13,* 343–356.

Galler, R. (1984). The myth of the perfect body. In C. S. Vance (Ed.), *Pleasure and danger: Exploring female sexuality* (pp. 165–172). Boston: Routledge & Kegan Paul.

Galligan, R. F., & Terry, D. J. (1993). Romantic ideals, fear of negative implications, and the practice of safe sex. *Journal of Applied Social Psychology, 23,* 1685–1711.

Gannon, L. (1994). Sexuality and menopause. In P. Y. L. Choi & P. Nicolson (Eds.), *Female sexuality: Psychology, biology, and social context* (pp. 100–124). New York: Harvester/Wheatsheaf.

Gannon, L. (1997). Perspectives on biological, sociological, and psychological phenomena in middle- and old-age women: Interference or intervention? In S. M. C. Dollenger & L. F. DiLalla (Eds.), *Assessment and interventions issues across the life span* (pp. 239–266). Mahwah, NJ: Erlbaum.

Gannon, L. (1998). The impact of medical and sexual politics on women's health. *Feminism & Psychology, 8,* 285–302.

Gannon, L. R. (1999). *Women and aging: Transcending the myth.* NY: Routledge.

Gannon, L. R., & Ekstrom, B. (1993). Attitudes toward menopause: The influence of sociocultural paradigms. *Psychology of Women Quarterly, 17,* 275–288.

Gannon, L. R., Luchetta, T., Rhodes, K., Pardie, L., & Segrist, D. (1992). Sex bias in psychological research: Progress or complacency? *American Psychologist, 47,* 389–396.

Ganong, L. H., & Coleman, M. (2000). Remarried families. In C. Hendrick & S. S. Hendrick (Eds.), *Close relationships: A sourcebook* (pp. 155–170). Thousand Oaks, CA: Sage Publications, Inc.

Garcia, N., Kennedy, C., Pearlman, S. F., & Perez, J. (1987). The impact of race and culture differences: Challenges to intimacy in lesbian relationships. In Boston Lesbian Psychologies Collective (Ed.), *Lesbian psychologies: Explorations and challenges* (pp. 161–174). Urbana: University of Illinois.

Gardner, C. B. (1995). *Passing by: Gender and public harassment.* Berkeley, CA: University of California Press.

Garland, A. W. (1988). *Women activists: Challenging the abuse of power.* New York: Feminist Press.

Garland, H., Hale, K. F., & Burnson, M. (1982). Attributions for the success and failure of female managers: A replication and extension. *Psychology of Women Quarterly, 7,* 155–162.

Garner, D. M. (1997, February). The 1997 body image survey results. *Psychology Today,* pp. 30–44.

Garside, R. B., & Klimes-Dougan, B. (2002). Socialization of discrete negative emotions: Gender differences and links to psychological distress. *Sex Roles, 47,* 115–128.

Garst, J., & Bodenhausen, G. V. (1997). Advertising's effect on men's gender role attitudes. *Sex Roles, 36,* 551–572.

Gaskill, L. R. (1991). Same-sex and cross-sex mentoring of female proteges: A comparative analysis. *Career Development Quarterly, 40,* 48–63.

Gastil, J. (1990). Generic pronouns and sexist language: The oxymoronic character of masculine generics. *Sex Roles, 23,* 629–643.

Gauna-Trujillo, B., & Higgins, P. G. (1989). Sexual intercourse and pregnancy. In P. N. Stern (Ed.), *Pregnancy and parenting* (pp. 31–40). New York: Hemisphere.

Gayford, J. J. (1975). Wife-battering: A preliminary survey of 100 cases. *British Medical Journal, 1,* 194–197.

Ge, X., Conger, R. D., & Elder, G. H., Jr. (2001). Pubertal transition, stressful life events, and the emergence of gender differences in adolescent depressive symptoms. *Developmental Psychology, 37,* 404–417.

Ge, X., Elder, G. H., Jr., Regnerus, M., & Cox, C. (2001). Pubertal transitions, perceptions of being overweight, and adolescents' maladjustment: Gender and ethnic differences. *Social Psychology Quarterly, 64,* 363–375.

Geary, D. C. (1996). Sexual selection and sex differences in mathematical abilities. *Behavioral and Brain Sciences, 19,* 229–284.

Geis, F. L., Brown, V., Jennings, J., & Porter, N. (1984). TV commercials as achievement scripts for women. *Sex Roles, 10,* 513–525.

Gelles, R. J., & Straus, M. A. (1988). *Intimate violence: The definitive study of the causes and consequences of abuse in the American family.* New York: Simon & Schuster.

Gelwick, B. P. (1984, September). Lifestyles of six professional women engaged in college student development careers. *Journal of College Student Personnel,* 418–429.

Genero, N. P., Miller, J. B., Surrey, J., & Baldwin, L. M. (1992). Measuring perceived mutuality in close relationships: Validation of the Mutual Psychological Development Questionnaire. *Journal of Family Psychology, 6,* 36–48.

Gentile, D. A. (1993). Just what are sex and gender, anyway?: A call for a new terminological standard. *Psychological Science, 4,* 120–122.

Gentry, M. (1989). Introduction: Feminist perspectives on gender and thought: Paradox and potential. In M. Crawford & M. Gentry (Eds.), *Gender and thought* (pp. 1–16). New York: Springer-Verlag.

George, S. M., & Dickerson, B. J. (1995). The role of the grandmother in poor single-mother families and households. In B. J. Dickerson (Ed.), *African American single mothers* (pp. 146–163). Thousand Oaks: Sage.

Gergen, M. M. (1990). Finished at 40: Women's development within the patriarchy. *Psychology of Women Quarterly, 14,* 471–493.

Gerstel, N. (1988). Divorce, gender, and social integration. *Gender & Society, 2,* 343–367.

Gibber, J. R. (1981). Infant-directed behaviors in male and female rhesus monkeys. Unpublished doctoral dissertation. Department of Psychology, University of Wisconsin–Madison.

Gibbons, J. L., Stiles, D. A., & Shkodriani, G. M. (1991). Adolescents' attitudes toward family and gender roles: An international comparison. *Sex Roles, 25,* 625–643.

Giddings, P. (1984). *When and where I enter: The impact of black women on race and sex in America.* New York: Morrow.

Gidycz, C. A., Coble, C. N., Latham, L., & Layman, M. J. (1992). Relation of a sexual assault experience on adulthood to prior victimization experiences: A prospective analysis. *Psychology of Women Quarterly, 7,* 151–168.

Gieve, K. (1989). *Balancing acts: On being a mother.* London: Virago.

Gilbert, L. A. (1987). What makes dual-career marriages tick? ERIC Document Reproduction Service No. ED 289 135.

Gilbert, L. A. (1993). *Two careers/One family: The promise of gender equality.* London: Sage.

Gilbert, L. A. (1994). Reclaiming and returning gender to context: Examples from studies of heterosexual dual-earner families. *Psychology of Women Quarterly, 18,* 539–558.

Gilbert, L. A., Galessich, J. M., & Evans, S. L. (1983). Sex of faculty role model and students' self-perceptions of competency. *Sex Roles, 9,* 597–607.

Gilbert, L. A., & Rader, J. (2001). Current perspectives on women's adult roles: Work, family, and life. In R. Unger (Ed.), *Handbook of the psychology of women and gender* (pp. 156–170). New York: Wiley.

Gilbert, L. A., & Rossman, K. M. (1992). Gender and the mentoring process for women: Implications for professional development. *Professional Psychology: Research and Practice, 23,* 233–238.

Gilgun, J. F. (1995). We shared something special: The moral discourse of incest perpetrators. *Journal of Marriage and the Family, 57,* 265–281.

Gill, D. L. (2001). Sport and athletics. In J. Worell (Ed.), *Encyclopedia of women and gender* (pp. 1091–1100). San Diego, CA: Academic Press.

Gilligan, C. (1982). *In a different voice.* Cambridge, MA: Harvard University Press.

Gilmore, D. D. (1990). *Mankind in the making: Cultural concepts of masculinity.* New Haven: Yale University Press.

Ginorio, A., Gutierrez, L., Cauce, A. M., & Acosta, M. (1995). Psychological issues for Latinas. In H. Landrine (Ed.), *Bringing cultural diversity to feminist psychology* (pp. 241–263). Washington, DC: American Psychological Association.

Giroux, H. A. (1998). Stealing innocence: The politics of child beauty pageants. In H. Jenkins (Ed.), *The children's culture reader* (pp. 265–282). New York: New York University Press.

Giuffre, P. A., & Williams, C. L. (1994). Boundary lines: Labeling sexual harassment in restaurants. *Gender and Society, 8,* 379–401.

Gjerberg, E., & Kjolsrod, L. (2001). The doctor-nurse relationship: How easy is it to be a female doctor cooperating with a female nurse. *Social Science & Medicine, 52,* 189–202.

Glazer, G., Zeller, R., Delumba, L., Kalinyak, C., Hobfoll, S., Winchell, J., & Hartman, P. (2002). The Ohio midlife women's study. *Health Care for Women International, 23,* 612–630.

Glick, P., Diebold, J., Bailey-Werner, B., & Zhu, L. (1997). The two faces of Adam: Ambivalent sexism and polarized attitudes toward women. *Personality and Social Psychology Bulletin, 23,* 1323–1334.

Glick, P., & Fiske, S. T. (1996). The ambivalent sexism inventory: Differentiating hostile and benevolent sexism. *Journal of Personality and Social Psychology, 70,* 491–512.

Glick, P., & Fiske, S. T. (1999). Sexism and other "isms": Interdependence, status, and the ambivalent content of stereotypes. In W. B. Swann, Jr., J. H. Langlois, & L. A. Gilbert (Eds.), *Sexism and stereotypes: The gender science of Janet Taylor Spence* (pp. 193–221). Washington, DC: American Psychological Association.

Glick, P., & Fiske, S. T. (2001). An ambivalent alliance: Hostile and benevolent sexism as complementary justifications for gender inequality. *American Psychologist, 56,* 109–118.

Glick, P. et al. (2000). Beyond prejudice as simple antipathy: Hostile and benevolent sexism across cultures. *Journal of Personality & Social Psychology, 79,* 763–775.

Glick, P., Fiske, S. T., Mladnic, A., Salz, J., Abrams, D., et al. (2000). Beyond prejudice as simply antipathy: Hostile sexism across cultures. *Journal of Personality and Social Psychology, 79* (5), 763–775.

Goffman, E. (1963). *Stigma.* Englewood Cliffs, NJ: Prentice Hall.

Goldberg, C. (1999, March 23). M.I.T. acknowledges bias against female professors. *The New York Times,* pp. A1, A16.

Goldberg, P. A. (1968). Are women prejudiced against women? *Transaction, 5,* 28–30.

Golden, C. (1987). Diversity and variability in women's sexual identities. In Boston Lesbian Psychologies Collective (Eds.), *Lesbian psychologies* (pp. 18–34). Urbana: University of Illinois Press.

Goldenhar, L. M., Swanson, N. G., Hurrell, J. J., Ruder, A., & Deddens, J. (1998). Stressors and adverse outcomes for female construction workers. *Journal of Occupational Health Psychology, 3*(1), 19–32.

Golding, J. M. (1988). Gender differences in depressive symptoms: Statistical considerations. *Psychology of Women Quarterly, 12,* 61–74.

Goldman, R., & Goldman, J. (1982). *Children's sexual thinking.* London: Routledge & Kegan Paul.

Goldstein, D. (1983). Spouse abuse. In A. Goldstein (Ed.), *Prevention and Control of Aggression* (pp. 37–65). New York: Pergamon Press.

Golombok, S., & Fivush, R. (1994). *Gender development.* New York: Cambridge University Press.

Gomez, C. A., & Vanoss-Marin, B. (1996). Gender, culture, and power: Barriers to HIV-prevention strategies for women. *Journal of Sex Research, 33*(4), 355–362.

Gondolf, E. W. (1998). *Assessing women battering in mental health services.* Thousand Oaks, CA: Sage.

Gondolf, E. W., & Fisher, E. R. (1998). *Battered women as survivors: An alternative to treating learned helplessness.* Lexington, MA: Lexington.

Gondolf, E. W., & Shestakov, D. (1997). Spousal homicide in Russia versus the United States: Preliminary findings and implications. *Journal of Family Violence, 12,* 63–74.

Gonzales, P. M., Blanton, H., & Williams, K. J. (2002). The effects of stereotype threat and double-minority status on the test performance of Latino women. *Personality & Social Psychology Bulletin, 28,* 659–670.

Good, G. E., & Sherrod, N. B. (2001). The psychology of men and masculinity: Research status and future directions. In R. K. Unger (Ed.), *Handbook of the psychology of women and gender* (pp. 201–214). NY: Wiley.

Good news in the fight for contraceptive coverage (2001, February). NOW Legislative Update. Retrieved from the World Wide Web: http://www.fight4choice.com/betrayal/roe.asp.

Goodchilds, J. D., Zellman, G. L., Johnson, P. B., & Giarrusso, R. (1988). Adolescents and their perceptions of sexual interactions. In A. W. Burgess (Ed.), *Rape and sexual assault,* Vol. II (pp. 245–270). New York: Garland.

Goode, E. (2002, December 17). The high cost of chronic stress. *The New York Times,* F1.

Gooden, A. M., & Gooden, M. A. (2001). Gender representations in notable children's picture books: 1995–1999. *Sex Roles, 45,* 89–101.

Goodman, C. (1999). Intimacy and autonomy in long term marriage. *Journal of Gerontological Social Work, 32,* 83–97.

Goodwin, S. A., & Fiske, S. T. (2001). Power and gender: The double-edged sword of ambivalence. In R. K. Unger (Ed.), *Handbook of the psychology of women and gender* (pp. 358–366). New York: McGraw Hill.

Goos, L. M., & Silverman, I. (2002). Sex-related factors in the perception of threatening facial expressions. *Journal of Nonverbal Behavior, 26,* 27–41.

Gordon, C. (1968). Self-conceptions: Configurations of content. In C. Gordon & K. Gergen (Eds.), *The self in social interaction.* New York: Wiley.

Gordon, J. S. (1996). Community services of abused women: A review of perceived usefulness and efficacy. *Journal of Family Violence, 11,* 315–329.

Gordon, L. (1988). *Heroes of their own lives: The politics and history of family violence.* New York: Penguin.

Gorski, R. A. (1999). Development of the cerebral cortex: XV. Sexual differentiation of the central nervous system. *Journal of the American Academy of Child and Adolescent Psychiatry, 37,* 1337–1339.

Gottman, J. M., & Parker, J. G. (Eds.). (1987). *Conversations of friends: Speculations in affective development.* New York: Cambridge University Press.

Gough, K. (1984). The origin of the family. In J. Freeman (Ed.), *Women: A feminist perspective* (3rd ed., pp. 83–99). Palo Alto, CA: Mayfield.

Gould, S. J. (1980). *The panda's thumb.* New York: Norton.

Gould, S. J. (1981). *The mismeasure of man.* New York: Norton.

Gove, W. R. (1972). The relationship between sex roles, marital status, and mental illness. *Social Forces, 51,* 34–44.

Gove, W. R., & Shin, H-C. (1989). The psychological well-being of divorced and widowed men and women: An empirical analysis. *Journal of Family Issues, 10,* 122–144.

Gowaty, P. A. (2001). Women, psychology, and evolution. In R. K. Unger (Ed.), *Handbook of the psychology of women and gender.* N.Y.: Wiley & Sons (pp. 53–65).

Grady, K. E. (1977, April). *The belief in sex differences.* Paper presented at the meeting of the Eastern Psychological Association, Boston.

Grady, K. E. (1979). Androgyny reconsidered. In J. H. Williams (Ed.), *Psychology of women: Selected readings* (pp. 172–177). New York: Norton.

Grady, K. E. (1981). Sex bias in research design. *Psychology of Women Quarterly, 5,* 628–636.

Graham, A. (1975). The making of a nonsexist dictionary. In B. Thorne & N. Henley (Eds.), *Language and sex: Difference and dominance.* Rowley, MA: Newbury House.

Graham, J. A., & Cohen, R. (1997). Race and sex as factors in children's sociometric ratings and friendship choices. *Social Development, 6,* 355–372.

Grambs, J. D. (1989). *Women over forty: Visions and realities.* New York: Springer.

Grant, K., Lyons, A., Landis, D., Cho, M. H., Scudiero, M., Reynolds, L., Murphy, J., & Bryant, H. (1999). Gender, body image, and depressive symptoms among low-income

African American adolescents. *Journal of Social Issues, 55* (2), 299–316.

Gravenkemper, S. A., & Paludi, M. A. (1983). Fear of success revisited: Introducing an ambiguous cue. *Sex Roles, 9,* 897–900.

Gray, J. D. (1983). The married professional woman: An examination of her role conflicts and coping strategies. *Psychology of Women Quarterly, 7,* 235–243.

Green, J. (1996). Mothers in "incest families": A critique of blame and its destructive sequels. *Violence Against Women, 2,* 322–348.

Greene, B. (1994). Diversity and difference: The issue of race in feminist theory. In M. P. Mirkin (Ed.), *Women in context: Toward a feminist reconstruction of psychotherapy* (pp. 333–351). New York: Guilford.

Greene, B. (2000). African American lesbian and bisexual women. *Journal of Social Issues, 56,* 239–250.

Greene, B., & Sanchez-Hucles, J. (1997). Diversity: Advancing an inclusive feminist psychology. In J. Worell & N. G. Johnson (Eds.), *Shaping the future of feminist psychology: Education, research, and practice* (pp. 173–202). Washington, DC: American Psychological Association.

Greene, B., White, J. C., & Whitten, L. (2000). Hair texture, length, and style as a metaphor in the African American mother-daughter relationship: Considerations in psychodynamic psychotherapy. In L. C. Jackson & B. Greene (Eds.), *Psychotherapy with African American Women* (pp. 166–193). NY: Guilford Press.

Greene, B. A. (1986). When the therapist is white and the patient is black: Considerations for psychotherapy in the feminist heterosexual and lesbian communities. In D. Howard (Ed.), *The dynamics of feminist therapy* (pp. 41–65). New York: Haworth Press.

Greene, B. A. (1990). Sturdy bridges: The role of African-American mothers in the socialization of African-American children. In J. P. Knowles & E. Cole (Eds.), *Motherhood: A feminist perspective* (pp. 205–225). New York: Haworth.

Greene, B. A. (1992). Still here: A perspective on psychotherapy with African American women. In J. C. Chrisler & D. Howard (Eds.), *New directions in feminist psychology: Practice, theory, and research* (pp. 13–25). New York: Springer.

Greene, C. K., & Stitt-Gohdes, W. L. (1997). Factors that influence women's choices to work in the trades. *Journal of Career Development, 23*(4), 265–278.

Greenfeld, L. A. (1997, February). *Sex offenses and offenders: An analysis of data on rape and sexual assault.* U.S. Department of Justice. Office of Justice Programs. Bureau of Justice Statistics. (NJC-163392). www.ojp.usdoj.gov/bjs.

Greenglass, E. R., & Burke, R. J. (1988). Work and family precursors of burnout in teachers: Sex differences. *Sex Roles, 18,* 215–229.

Greenspan, M. (1983). *A new approach to women and therapy.* New York: McGraw-Hill.

Greenspan, M. (1986). Should therapists be personal? Self-disclosure and therapeutic distance in feminist therapy. In D. Howard (Ed.), *The dynamics of feminist therapy* (pp. 5–17). New York: Haworth Press.

Greenstein, T. N. (1996). Husbands' participation in domestic labor: Interactive effects of wives' and husbands' gender ideologies. *Journal of Marriage and the Family, 58*(3), 585–595.

Greenwald, A. G., & Banaji, M. R. (1995). Implicit social cognition: Attitudes, self-esteem, and stereotypes. *Psychological Review, 102,* 4–27.

Greenwood-Audant, L. M. (1984). The internalization of powerlessness: A case study of the displaced homemaker. In J. Freeman (Ed.), *Women: A feminist perspective* (3rd ed., pp. 264–281). New York: Mayfield.

Gremaux, R. (1996). Woman becoming man in the Balkans. In G. Herdt (Ed.), *Third sex, third gender: Beyond sexual dimorphism in culture and history* (pp. 241–281). New York: Zone Books.

Griffin, S. (1971). Rape: The all-American crime. *Ramparts, 10,* 26–35.

Grimm, D. E. (1987). Toward a theory of gender: Transsexualism, gender, sexuality, and relationships. *American Behavioral Scientist, 31,* 66–85.

Grogan, S., Knott, J. A., & Gaze, C. E. (1996). The effects of viewing same gender photographic models on body esteem. *Psychology of Women Quarterly, 20,* 569–575.

Grossman, A. L., & Tucker, J. S. (1997). Gender differences and sexism in the knowledge and use of slang. *Sex Roles, 37,* 101–110.

Grossman, F. K., Gilbert, L. A., Genero, N. P., Hawes, S. E., Hyde, J. S., & Marecek, J. (1997). Feminist research: Practice and problems. In J. Worell & N. G. Johnson (Eds.), *Shaping the future of feminist psychology: Education, research, and practice* (pp. 73–91). Washington, DC: American Psychological Association.

Grote, N. K., & Frieze, I. H. (1998). 'Remembrance of things past': Perceptions of marital love from its beginnings to the present. *Journal of Social and Personal Relationships, 15*(1), 91–109.

Gruber, J. E. (1997). An epidemology of sexual harassment: Evidence from North America and Europe. In W. O'Donohue (Ed.), *Sexual harassment: Theory, research and treatment* (pp. 84–98). Boston: Allyn and Bacon.

Gruber, J. E., & Bjorn, L. (1982). Blue-collar blues: The sexual harassment of women autoworkers. *Work and Occupations, 9,* 271–298.

Grundman, E. O., O'Donohue, W., & Peterson, S. H. (1997). The prevention of sexual harassment. In W. O'Donohue (Ed.), *Sexual harassment: Theory, research and treatment* (pp. 175–184). Boston: Allyn & Bacon.

Gruppuso, P. A. (1999, August 18). Point/counterpoint: Should cosmetic surgery be performed on the genitals of children born with ambiguous genitals? *Physician's Weekly, XVI, 31.*

Guiliano, T. A., Ropp, K. E., & Knight, J. L. (2000). Footballs vs Barbies: Childhood play activities as predictors of sports participation by women. *Sex Roles, 42,* 159–181.

Guinier, L., Fine, M., & Balin, J. (1997). *Becoming gentlemen: Women, law school, and institutional change.* Boston: Beacon Press.

Guinn, S., & Russell, L. G. (1987). Personnel decisions and the dual-earner couple. *Employment Relations Today, 14,* 83–90.

Gullette, M. M. (1997). *Declining to decline: Cultural combat and the politics of the midlife.* Charlottesville: University Press of Virginia.

Gutek, B. A. (1985). *Sex and the workplace.* San Francisco: Jossey-Bass.

Gutek, B. A. (1989). Relocation, family, and the bottom line: Results from the Division 35 survey. *Psychology of Women Quarterly, 16,* 5–7.

Gutek, B. A. (2001a). Change and stability in work and family experiences. *Psychology of Women Quarterly, 25,* 259–260.

Gutek, B. A. (2001b). Women and paid work. *Psychology of Women Quarterly, 25,* 379–393.

Gutek, B. A. (2001c). Working environments. In J. Worell (Ed.), *Encyclopedia of women and gender,* pp. 1191–1204. New York: Academic Press.

Gutek, B. A., & Larwood, L. (Eds.). (1987). *Women's career development.* Newbury Park, CA: Sage.

Guthrie, R. V. (1976). *Even the rat was white: A historical view of psychology.* New York: Harper & Row.

Gwartney-Gibbs, P. A., Stockard, J., & Brohmer, S. (1983). Learning courtship violence: The influence of parents, peers and personal experiences. *Family Relations, 36,* 276–282.

Haavind, H. (1983). Love and power in marriage. In H. Holter (Ed.), *Patriarchy in a welfare society* (pp. 136–167). Oxford, England: Oxford University Press.

Haddock, G., & Zanna, M. P. (1994). Preferring "housewives" to "feminists": Categorization and the favorability of attitudes toward women. *Psychology of Women Quarterly, 18,* 25–52.

Hahn, C. S. (2001). Review: Psychosocial wellbeing of parents and their children born after assisted reproduction. *Journal of Pediatric Psychology, 26,* 525–538.

Haiken, E. (1997). *Venus envy: A history of cosmetic surgery.* Baltimore: Johns Hopkins University Press.

Haj-Yahia, M. M. (1996). Wife abuse in the Arab society in Israel. Challenges for future changes. In J. L. Edleson & Z. C. Eisikovits (Eds.), *Future interventions with battered women and their families* (pp. 87–101). Thousand Oaks: Sage.

Haj-Yahia, M. M. (1998). *Beliefs about wife beating among Palestinian women: The influence of their patriarchal ideology.* Violence Against Women, 4, 533–558.

Hajjar, W. J. (1997). The image of aging in television commercials: An update for the 1990s. In H. S. Nor Al-Deen (Ed.), *Cross-cultural communication and aging in the United States.* Mahway, NJ: Erlbaum.

Hale, G., Duckworth, J., Zimostrad, S., & Nicholas, D. (1988). Abusive partners: MMPI profiles of male batterers. *Journal of Mental Health Counseling, 10* (4), 214–224.

Hall, J. A. (1985). *Nonverbal sex differences: Communication accuracy and expressive style.* Baltimore: Johns Hopkins University Press.

Hall, J. A., LeBeau, L. S., Reinoso, J. G., & Thayer, F. (2001). Status, gender, and nonverbal behavior in candid and posed photographs: A study of conversations between university employees. *Sex Roles, 44,* 677–692.

Hall, M. (1994, March 31). Feds, states clash on abortion. *USA Today,* A3.

Hall, N. L. (1984). *The true story of a single mother.* Boston: South End Press.

Hall, R. L., & Greene, B. (1996). Sins of omission and commission: Women, psychotherapy, and the psychological literature. *Women & Therapy, 18,* 5–31.

Halpern, C. T., Udry, J. R., Campbell, B., & Suchindran, C., (1999). Effects of body fat on weight concerns, dating, and sexual activity: A longitudinal analysis of Black and

White adolescent girls. *Developmental Psychology, 33,* 721–736.

Halpern, D. F. (1986). *Sex differences in cognitive abilities.* Hillsdale, NJ: Erlbaum.

Halpern, D. F. (1992). *Sex differences in cognitive abilities* (2nd ed.). Hillsdale, NJ: Erlbaum.

Hamberger, L. K., Saunders, D. G., & Hovey, M. (1992). The prevalence of domestic violence in community practice and rate of physician inquiry. *Family Medicine, 24* (4), 283–287.

Hamer, D. H., Hu, S., Magnuson, V., Hu, N., & Pattatucci, A. M. L. (1993). A linkage between DNA markers in the X chromosome and male sexual orientation. *Science, 261,* 321–327.

Hamilton, M. C. (1988). Masculine generics and misperceptions of AIDS risk. *Journal of Applied Social Psychology, 18,* 1222–1240.

Hamilton, M. C. (1991). Masculine bias in the attribution of personhood: People = male, male = people. *Psychology of Women Quarterly, 15,* 393–402.

Hamilton, M. C., & Henley, N. M. (1982, March). *Detrimental consequences of generic masculine usage: Effects on the reader/hearer's cognitions.* Paper presented at the meeting of the Western Psychological Association, Sacramento, CA.

Hamilton, M. C., & Mayfield, B. (1999). Son-daughter preferences of primiparous married couples, nonpregnant married couples, and college students. Paper presented at the meeting of the Association for Women in Psychology. Providence, RI, March.

Hammer, J. C., Fisher, J. D., Fitzgerald, P., & Fisher, W. A. (1996). When two heads aren't better than one: AIDS risk behavior in college-age couples. *Journal of Applied Social Psychology, 26*(5), 375–397.

Hammer, M. (1970). Preference for a male child: Cultural factor. *Journal of Individual Psychology, 26,* 54–56.

Hammond, J. A., & Mahoney, C. W. (1983). Reward-cost balancing among women coalminers. *Sex Roles, 9,* 17–29.

Hankin, B. L., & Abramson, L. Y. (2001). Development of gender differences in depression: An elaborated cognitive vulnerability-transactional stress theory. *Psychological Bulletin, 127,* 773–796.

Hankin, B. L., Abramson, L. Y., Moffott, T. E., Silva, P. A., McGee, R., & Angell, K. E. (1998). Development of depression from preadolescence to young adulthood: Emerging gender differences in a 10-year longitudinal study. *Journal of Abnormal Psychology, 107,* 128–140.

Hansen, F. J., & Reekie, L. (1990). Sex differences in clinical judgments of male and female therapists. *Sex Roles, 23,* 51–64.

Hanson, K. A., & Gidycz, C. A. (1993). An evaluation of a sexual assault prevention program. *Journal of Consulting and Clinical Psychology, 61,* 1046–1052.

Harding, S. (1986). *The science question in feminism.* Ithaca, NY: Cornell University Press.

Hardy, C. L., Bukowski, W. M., & Sippola, L. K. (2002). Stability and change in peer relationships during the transition to middle-level school. *Journal of Early Adolescence, 22,* 117–142.

Hare-Mustin, R. T. (1983). An appraisal of the relationship between women and psychotherapy: 80 years after the case of Dora. *American Psychologist, 38,* 593–601.

Hare-Mustin, R. T., & Marecek, J. (1988). The meaning of difference: Gender theory, postmodernism, and psychology. *American Psychologist, 43,* 455–464.

Hare-Mustin, R. T., & Marecek, J. (Eds.). (1990). *Making a difference: Psychology and the construction of gender.* New Haven: Yale University Press.

Hare-Mustin, R. T., & Marecek, J. (1997). Abnormal and clinical psychology. In D. Fox & I. Prilleltensky (Eds.), *Critical psychology: An introduction* (pp. 105–120). London: Sage.

Harlan, S. L., & O'Farrell, B. (1982). After the pioneers: Prospects for women in nontraditional blue-collar jobs. *Work and Occupations, 9,* 363–386.

Harlow, H. (1971). *Learning to love.* New York: Albion.

Harlow, S. D., Crawford, S. L., Sommer, B., & Greendale, G. A. (2000). Self-defined menopausal status in a multi-ethnic sample of midlife women. *Maturitas, 36,* 93–112.

Harnack, L., Story, M., Martinson, B., Neumark-Sztainer, D., & Stang, J. (1998). Guess who's cooking? The role of men in meal planning, shopping, and preparation in U.S. families. *Journal of the American Dietetic Association, 98*(9), 995–1000.

Harned, M. S. (2000). Harassed bodies: An examination of the relationships among women's experiences of sexual harassment, body image, and eating disturbances. *Psychology of Women Quarterly, 24,* 336–348.

Harris, B. J. (1984). The power of the past: History and the psychology of women. In

M. Lewin (Ed.), *In the shadow of the past* (pp. 1–5). New York: Columbia University Press.

Harris, M. B. (1992). Beliefs about how to reduce anger. *Psychological Reports, 70,* 203–210.

Harris, M. B., Begay, C., & Page, P. (1989). Activities, family relationships and feelings about aging in a multicultural elderly sample. *International Journal of Aging and Human Development, 29,* 103–117.

Harris, V. R. (1994). Prison of color. In E. Featherston (Ed.), *Skin deep: Women writing on color, culture, and identity* (pp. 8–15). Freedom, CA: The Crossing Press.

Harrison, A. W., Rainer, R. K., Jr., & Hochwarter, W. A. (1997). Gender differences in computing activities. *Journal of Social Behavior and Personality, 12*(4), 849–868.

Harter, S. (1990). Self and identity development. In S. S. Feldman & G. R. Elliott (Eds.), *At the threshold: The developing adolescent* (pp. 352–387). Cambridge, MA: Harvard University Press.

Harter, S. (1999). *The construction of the self: A developmental perspective.* NY: Guilford Press. .

Hartung, C. M., & Widiger, T. A. (1998). Gender differences in the diagnoses of mental disorders: Conclusions and controversies of the DSM-IV. *Psychological Bulletin, 123,* 260–278.

Hartzler, K., & Franco, J. N. (1985). Ethnicity, division of household tasks and equity in marital roles: A comparison of Anglo and Mexican American couples. *Hispanic Journal of Behavioral Sciences, 7,* 333–344.

Harville, M. L., & Rienzi, B. M. (2000). Equal worth and gracious submission: Judeo-Christian atitudes toward employed women. *Psychology of Women Quarterly, 24,* 145–147.

Haslett, B. B., & Lipman, S. (1997). Micro inequities: Up close and personal. In N. V. Benokraitis (Ed.), *Subtle sexism: Current practice and prospects for change* (pp. 34–53). Thousand Oaks, CA: Sage.

Hatch, L. R. (1995). Gray clouds and silver linings: Women's resources in later life. In J. Freeman (Ed.), *Women: A feminist perspective* (5th ed., pp. 182–196). Mountain View, CA: Mayfield Publishing Co.

Hatton, B. J. (1994, March). The experiences of African American lesbians: Family, community, and intimate relationships. Poster presented at the Southeastern Psychological Association Convention. New Orleans, LA.

Hayes, C. L., & Anderson, D. (1993). Psychosocial and economic adjustment of midlife women after divorce. *Journal of Women and Aging, 4,* 83–99.

Hays, S. (1996). *The cultural contradictions of motherhood.* New Haven: Yale University.

Hayward, C., Gotlib, I. H., Schraedly, P. K., & Litt, I. F. (1999). Ethnic differences in the association between pubertal status and symptoms of depression in adolescent girls. *Journal of Adolescent Health, 25,* 143–149.

Healy, S. (1986). Growing to be an old woman: Aging and ageism. In J. Alexander, D. Berrow, L. Domitrovich, M. Donnelly, & C. McLean (Eds.), *Women and aging* (pp. 58–62). Corvallis, OR: Calyx.

Healy, S. (1993). Confronting ageism: A must for mental health. In N. D. Davis, E. Cole, & E. D. Rothblum (Eds.), *Faces of women and aging* (pp. 41–54). Binghamton, NY: Harrington Park Press.

Heaven, P. C. (1999). Attitudes toward women's rights: Relationships to social dominance orientation and political group identities. *Sex Roles, 41,* 605–614.

Hebl, M. R., & Heatherton, T. F. (1998). The stigma of obesity in women: The difference in black and white. *Personality and Social Psychology Bulletin, 24,* 417–426.

Hecht, M. A., & LaFrance, M. (1998). License or obligation to smile: The effect of power and sex on amount and type of smiling. *Personality and Social Psychology Bulletin, 24,* 1332–1342.

Hedges, L. V., & Becker, B. J. (1986). Statistical methods in the meta-analysis of research on gender differences. In J. G. Hyde & M. C. Linn (Eds.), *The psychology of gender: Advances through meta-analysis* (pp. 14–50). Baltimore: Johns Hopkins.

Heenan, C. (2002). Special issue: The reproduction of mothering: A reappraisal. *Feminism and Psychology, 12,* 5–53.

Heilman, M. E., Block, C. J., Martell, R. F., & Simon, M. C. (1989). Has anything changed? Current characterizations of men, women, and managers. *Journal of Applied Psychology, 74,* 935–942.

Heilman, M. E., Simon, M. C., & Repper, D. P. (1987). Intentionally favored, unintentionally harmed? Impact of sex-based preferential selection on self-perceptions and self-evaluations. *Journal of Applied Psychology, 72,* 62–68.

Helgeson, V. S. (1994). Relations of agency and communion to well-being: Evidence and potential explanations. *Psychological Bulletin, 116,* 412–428.

Helmore, E. (2002). U.S. aid cut hits world birth control. *The Observer,* June 30, p. 1.

Helson, R. M. (1978). Creativity in women. In J. Sherman & F. Denmark (Eds.), *Psychology of women: Future directions of research* (pp. 553–604). New York: Psychological Dimensions.

Helson, R. M., & Wink, P. (1992). Personality change in women from the early 40s to the early 50s. *Psychology and Aging, 7,* 46–55.

Helwig, A. A. (1998). Gender-role stereotyping: Testing theory with a longitudinal sample. *Sex Roles, 38,* 403–423.

Hemmer, J. D., & Kleiber, D. A. (1981). Tomboys and sissies: Androgynous children? *Sex Roles, 7,* 1205–1211.

Henderson-Daniel, J. (1994). Exclusion and emphasis reframed as a matter of ethics. *Ethics and Behavior, 4,* 229–235.

Henderson-King, D., Henderson-King, E., & Hoffmann, L. (2001). Media images and women's self-evaluations: Social context and importance of attractiveness as moderators. *Personality and Social Psychology Bulletin, 27,* 1407–1416.

Henley, N. M. (1977). *Body politics: Power, sex, and nonverbal communication.* Englewood Cliffs, NJ: Prentice-Hall.

Henley, N. M. (1989). Molehill or mountain? What we do know and don't know about sex bias in language. In M. Crawford & M. Gentry (Eds.), *Gender and thought* (pp. 59–78). New York: Springer-Verlag.

Henley, N. M., & Freeman, J. (1989). The sexual politics of interpersonal behavior. In J. Freeman (Ed.), *Women: A feminist perspective* (4th ed., pp. 457–469). Mountainview, CA: Mayfield.

Henley, N. M., Meng, K., O'Brien, D., McCarthy, W. J., & Sockloskie, R. (1998). Developing a scale to measure the diversity of feminist attitudes. *Psychology of Women Quarterly, 22,* 317–348.

Henly, J. R. (1997). The complexity of support: The impact of family structure and provisional support on African American and white adolescent mothers' well-being. *American Journal of Community Psychology, 25*(5), 629–655.

Henry, C. (1998, May 10). Community voices—women in the '90s: Names. *The Philadelphia Inquirer,* p. E6.

Hequembourg, A. L., & Farrell, M. P. (1999). Lesbian motherhood: Negotiating marginal-mainstream identities. *Gender and Society, 13,* 540–557.

Herdt, G. (1996). Mistaken sex: Culture, biology, and the third sex in New Guinea. In G. Herdt (Ed.), *Third sex, third gender: Beyond sexual dimorphism in culture and history* (pp. 419–445). New York: Zone Books.

Herdt, G. H., & Davidson, J. (1988). The Sambra "Turnim-man": Sociocultural and clinical aspects of gender formation in male pseudohermaphrodites with 5 alpha-reductase deficiency in Papua New Guinea. *Archives of Sexual Behavior, 17,* 33–56.

Herek, G. M. (2002). Gender gaps in public opinion about lesbians and gay men. *Public Opinion Quarterly, 66,* 40–66.

Herek, G. M. (1993). The context of antigay violence: Notes on cultural and psychological heterosexism. In L. D. Garnets & D. C. Kimmel (Eds.), *Psychological perspectives on lesbian and gay male experiences* (pp. 89–108). New York: Columbia University Press.

Herman, A. (1988). Foreward. In A. Statham, E. M. Miller, & H. O. Mauksch (Eds.), *The worth of a women's work: A qualitative synthesis* (pp. ix–xi). Albany, NY: State University of New York Press.

Hernandez, D. G. (1994). Good and the bad about women's news in newspapers. *Editor and Publisher,* May 21, pp. 17, 41.

Herrett-Skjellum, J., & Allen, M. (1996). Television programming and sex stereotyping: A meta-analysis. In B. Burleson (Ed.), *Communication yearbook 19* (pp. 157–185). Thousand Oaks, CA: Sage.

Hewlett, S. A., & West, C. (1998). *The war against parents: What we can do for America's beleaguered moms and dads.* Boston: Houghton Mifflin.

Heywood, S. (1989). *Fantasy lover.* Ontario, Canada: Harlequin.

Hickman, S. E., & Muehlenhard, C. L. (1997). College women's fears and precautionary behaviors relating to acquaintance rape and stranger rape. *Psychology of Women Quarterly, 21*(4), 527–547.

Highlights of women's earnings in 2001. (Report 960) (2002). Washington, DC: U.S. Department of Labor, Bureau of Labor Statistics.

Hill, D. B. (2000). Categories of sex and gender: Either/or, both/and, and neither/nor. *History and Philosophy of Psychology Bulletin, 12,* 25–32.

Hill, M. (1987). Child-rearing attitudes of black lesbian mothers. In Boston Lesbian Psychologies Collective (Eds.), *Lesbian psychologies* (pp. 215–225). Urbana: University of Illinois Press.

Hill, M., & Ballou, M. (1998). Making therapy feminist: A practice survey. *Women and Therapy, 21,* 1–16.

Hillier, L., & Foddy, M. (1993). The role of observer attitudes in judgments of blame in cases of wife assault. *Sex Roles, 29,* 629–644.

Hite, S. (1976). *The Hite report.* New York: Macmillan.

Hite, S. (1987). *The Hite report: Women and love; a cultural revolution in progress.* New York: Knopf.

HIV/AIDS Among US Women. (2002). Centers for Disease Control and Prevention, National Center for HIV, STD, and TB Prevention, Division of HIV/AIDS Prevention.

Ho, C. K. (1990). An analysis of domestic violence in Asian American communities: A multicultural approach to counseling. In L. Brown & M. P. P. Root (Eds.), *Diversity and complexity in feminist therapy and theory* (pp. 129–150). Harrington Park, NY: Haworth Press.

Hochschild, A. R. (1978). *The unexpected community: Portrait of an old-age subculture.* Berkeley, CA: University of California Press.

Hochschild, A. R. (1989). *The second shift: Working parents and the revolution at home.* New York: Viking.

Hockenberry-Eaton, M., Richman, M. J., DiIorio, C., Rivero, T., & Maibach, E. (1996). Mother and adolescent knowledge of sexual development: The effects of gender, age, and sexual experience. *Adolescence, 31*(121), 35–48.

Hoffman, C., & Hurst, N. (1990). Gender stereotypes: Perceptions or rationalization? *Journal of Personality and Social Psychology, 58,* 197–208.

Hoffman, L. W., & Kloska, D. D. (1995). Parents' gender-based attitudes toward marital roles and child rearing: Development and validation of new measures. *Sex Roles, 32,* 273–295.

Hoffnung, M. (1989). Motherhood: Contemporary conflict for women. In J. Freeman (Ed.), *Women: A feminist perspective* (4th ed., pp. 157–175). Mountain View, CA: Mayfield.

Hollin, C. R. (1987). Sex roles in adolescence. In D. J. Hargreaves & A. M. Colley (Eds.), *The psychology of sex roles* (pp. 176–197). New York: Hemisphere.

Hollingworth, L. S. (1916). Social devices for impelling women to bear and rear children. *American Journal of Sociology, 22,* 19–29.

Holm, K. E., Werner-Wilson, R. J., Cook, A. S., & Berger, P. S. (2001). The association between emotion work balance and relationship satisfaction of couples seeking therapy. *American Journal of Family Therapy, 29,* 193–205.

Homma-True, R. (1990). Psychotherapeutic issues of Asian American women. *Sex Roles, 22,* 477–486.

Hooijberg, R., & DiTomaso, N. (1996). Leadership in and of demographically diverse organizations. *Leadership Quarterly, 7*(1), 1–19.

hooks, b. (1984). *Feminist theory: From margin to center.* Boston: South End Press.

hooks, b. (1989). *Talking back: Thinking feminist, thinking black.* Boston: South End Press.

hooks, b. (2000). *Feminism is for everybody: Passionate politics.* Cambridge, MA: South End Press.

Hornstein, G. A. (2002, January 25). Narratives of madness as told from within. *The Chronicle Review,* B7–B10.

Hort, B., Leinbach, M., & Fagot, B. (1991). Is there a coherence among the cognitive components of gender acquisition? *Sex Roles, 24,* 195–207.

Hort, B. E., & Leinbach, M. D. (1993). *Children's use of metaphorical cues in gender typing of objects.* Paper presented at the meeting of the Society for Research on Child Development, New Orleans, LA.

Hossain, Z., & Roopmarine, J. L. (1993). Division of household labor and child care in dual-earner African-American families with infants. *Sex Roles, 29,* 571–584.

Hostile hallways: Bullying, teasing, and sexual harassment in school. (2001). Washington, D.C.: American Association of University Women Education Foundation.

Houser, B., & Garvey, C. (1985). Factors that affect nontraditional vocational enrollment among women. *Psychology of Women Quarterly, 9,* 105–118.

Houston, S., & Hwang, N. (1996). Correlates of the objective and subjective experiences of sexual harassment in high school. *Sex Roles, 34,* 189–204.

Howard, J. A., & Hollander, J. A. (Eds.). (1997). *Gendered situations, gendered selves: A gender lens on social psychology.* Thousand Oaks, CA: Sage.

Howe, K. G. (1989). Telling our mothers' story: Changing daughters' perceptions of their mothers in a women's studies course. In R. K. Unger (Ed.), *Representations: Social constructions of gender* (pp. 45–60). Amityville, NY: Baywood.

Howe, L. K. (1977). *Pink collar workers.* New York: Putnam.

Howell, M., & Pugliesi, K. (1988). Husbands who harm: Predicting spousal violence by men. *Journal of Family Violence, 3*(1), 15–27.

Hoyt, W. D., & Kogan, L. R. (2001). Satisfaction with body image and peer relationships for men and women in a college environment. *Sex Roles, 45,* 199–215.

Hrdy, S. B. (1988, April). Daughters or sons. *Natural History,* 64–82.

Huang, J. (1993). An investigation of gender differences in cognitive abilities among Chinese high school students. *Personality and Individual Differences, 15,* 717–719.

Huesmann, L. R., & Eron, L. (1992). Childhood aggression and adult criminality. In J. McCord (Ed.), *Facts, frameworks, and forecasts: Advances in criminological theory.* Vol. 3. New Brunswick, NJ: Transaction Publishers.

Hummert, M. L., Gartska, T. A., & Shaner, J. L. (1997). Stereotyping of older adults: The role of target facial cues and perceived characteristics. *Psychology and Aging, 12,* 107–114.

Humphrey, J. A., & White, J. W. (2000). Women's Vulnerability to Sexual Assault from Adolescence to Young Adulthood. *Journal of Adolescent Health, 27,* 419–424.

Hunt, M. (1974). *Sexual behavior in the 1970s.* Chicago: Playboy Press.

Hunter, G. T. (1974). Pediatrician. In R. B. Kundsin (Ed.), *Women and success: The anatomy of achievement* (pp. 58–61). New York: Morrow.

Hunter, J., & Mallon, G. P. (2000). Lesbian, gay, and bisexual adolescent development: Dancing with your feet tied together. In B. Greene & G. L. Croom (Eds.)., *Education, research, and practice in lesbian, gay, bisexual, and transgendered psychology* (pp. 226–243). Thousand Oaks, CA: Sage.

Hunter, M. S. (1990). Psychological and somatic experience of the menopause: A prospective study. *Psychosomatic Medicine, 52,* 357–367.

Huon, G., Gunawardene, A., & Hayne, A. (2000). The gender and SES context of weight-loss dieting among adolescent females. *Eating Disorders: The Journal of Treatment & Prevention, 8,* 147–155.

Hurlbert, D. F., & Whittaker, K. E. (1991). The role of masturbation in marital and sexual satisfaction: A comparative study of female masturbators and nonmasturbators. *Journal of Sex Education and Therapy, 17,* 272–282.

Huselid, B. F., & Cooper, M. L. (1994). Gender roles as mediators of sex differences in expression of pathology. *Journal of Abnormal Psychology, 103,* 595–603.

Huston, A. C., Wright, J. C., Marquis, J., & Green, S. B. (1999). How young children spend their time: Television and other activities. *Developmental Psychology. 35,* 912–925.

Huston, T. L., Caughlin, J. P., Houts, R. M., Smith, S. E., & George, L. J. (2001). The connubial crucible: Newlywed years as predictors of marital delight, distress, and divorce. *Journal of Personality and Social Psychology, 80,* 237–252.

Hyde, J. S. (1981). How large are cognitive gender differences? *American Psychologist, 36,* 892–910.

Hyde, J. S. (1990). *Understanding human sexuality* (4th ed.). New York: McGraw-Hill.

Hyde, J. S., & DeLamater, J. (1997). *Understanding human sexuality* (6th ed.). New York: McGraw-Hill.

Hyde, J. S., & DeLamater, J. D. (2003). *Understanding human sexuality* (8th ed.). New York: McGraw Hill.

Hyde, J. S., Fennema, E., Ryan, M., Frost, L., & Hopp, C. (1990). Gender comparisons of mathematics attitudes and affects: A meta-analysis. *Psychology of Women Quarterly, 14,* 299–324.

Hyde, J. S., & Jaffe, S. R. (2000). Becoming a heterosexual adult: The experiences of young women. *Journal of Social Issues, 56,* 283–296.

Hyde, J. S., & Kling, K. C. (2001). Women, motivation, and achievement. *Psychology of Women Quarterly, 25,* 364–378.

Hyde, J. S., & Linn, M. C. (Eds.). (1986). *The psychology of gender: Advances through meta-analysis.* Baltimore: Johns Hopkins.

Hyde, J. S., & McKinley, N. M. (1997). Gender differences in cognition: Results from meta-analyses. In P. J. Caplan, M. Crawford, J. S. Hyde, & J. T. E. Richardson, *Gender differences in human cognition* (pp. 30–51). New York: Oxford.

Hyde, J. S., Rosenberg, B. G., & Behrman, J. (1977). "Tomboyism." *Psychology of Women Quarterly, 2,* 73–75.

Ihinger-Tallman, M., & Pasley, K. (1987). *Remarriage.* Beverly Hills, CA: Sage.

Imperato-McGinley, J., & Peterson, R. E. (1976). Male pseudohermaphrodism: The complexities of male phenotypic development. *American Journal of Medicine, 61,* 251–272.

Imperato-McGinley, J., Peterson, R. E., Gautier, T., & Sturla, E. (1979). Androgens and the evolution of male-gender identity among male pseudohermaphrodites with 5 alpha-reductase deficiency. *New England Journal of Medicine, 300,* 1233–1237.

Imperato-McGinley, J., Pichardo, M., Gautier, T., Voyer, D., & Bryden, M. P. (1991). Cognitive abilities in androgen-insensitive subjects: Comparison with control males and females from the same kindred. *Clinical Endocrinology, 34,* 341–347.

Inzlicht, M., & Ben Zeev, T. (2000). A threatening intellectual environment: Why females are susceptible to experiencing problem-solving deficits in the presence of males. *Psychological Science, 11,* 365–371.

Island, D., & Letellier, P. (1991). *Men who beat the men who love them: Battered gay men and domestic violence.* Binghamton, NY: Hawthorne Press.

Issues in brief: Abortion in context: United States and worldwide. (1999). New York: The Alan Guttmacher Institute.

Jack, D. C., & Dill, D. (1992). The silencing of the self scale schemas of intimacy associated with depression. *Psychology of Women Quarterly, 16,* 97–106.

Jacklin, C. N. (1981). Methodological issues in the study of sex-related differences. *Developmental Review, 1,* 266–273.

Jackson, A. P. (1997). Effects of concerns about child care among single, employed black mothers with preschool children. *American Journal of Community Psychology, 25*(5), 657–673.

Jackson, J. L., Calhoun, K. S., Amick, A. E., Maddever, H. M., & Habif, V. L. (1990). Young adult women who report childhood intrafamiliar sexual abuse: Subsequent adjustment. *Archives of Sexual Behavior, 19,* 211–221.

Jackson, L. M., Esses, V. M., & Burris, C. T. (2001). Contemporary sexism and discrimination: The importance of respect for men and women. *Personality & Social Psychology Bulletin, 27,* 48–61.

Jackson, M. (1987). "Facts of life" or the eroticization of women's oppression? Sexology and the social construction of heterosexuality. In P. Caplan (Ed.), *The cultural construction of sexuality* (pp. 52–71). London: Tavistock.

Jackson, S. (2001). Happily never after: Young women's stories of abuse in heterosexual love relationships. *Feminism and Psychology, 11,* 305–321.

Jackson-Wilson, A. G., & Borgers, S. B. (1993). Disaffiliation revisited: A comparison of homeless and nonhomeless women's perception of family of origin and social supports. *Sex Roles, 28,* 361–377.

Jacobs, A. (1998, September 13). His debut as a woman. *The New York Times Magazine,* pp. 48–51.

Jaffe, P. G., Suderman, M., Reitzel, D., & Killip, S. M. (1992). An evaluation of a secondary school primary prevention program on violence in intimate relationships. *Violence and Victims, 7,* 129–146.

Jaffee, S., & Hyde, J. S. (2000). Gender differences in moral orientation: A meta-analysis. *Psychological Bulletin, 126,* 703–726.

James, J. (1999). The contribution of women's studies programs. In S. Davis, M. Crawford, & J. Sebrechts (Eds.), *Coming into her own: Encouraging educational success in girls and women* (pp. 23–36). San Francisco: Jossey-Bass.

Jamieson, K. H. (1995). *Beyond the double bind: Women and leadership.* New York: Oxford University Press.

Joffe, H. (1997). Intimacy and love in late modern conditions: Implications for unsafe sexual practices. In J. M. Ussher (Ed.), *Body talk: The material and discursive regulation of sexuality, madness and reproduction* (pp. 159–175). New York: Routledge.

Johansson, C., Mellstrom, D., Lerner, U., & Osterberg, T. (1992). Coffee drinking: A minor risk factor for bone loss and fractures. *Age and Aging, 21,* 20–26.

Johansson, P. (2001). Selling the "modern woman": Consumer culture and Chinese gender politics. In S. Munshi (Ed.), *Images of the modern woman in Asia: Global media, local meanings* (pp. 94–122). Richmond, Surrey, UK: Curzon Press.

John, B. A., & Sussman, L. E. (1984–1985). Initiative-taking as a determinant of role-reciprocal organization. *Imagination, Cognition, and Personality, 4,* 277–291.

John, R., Blanchard, P. H., & Hennessy, C. H. (1997). Hidden lives: Aging and contemporary American Indian women. In J. M. Coyle (Ed.), *Handbook on women and aging* (pp. 290–315). Westport, CT: Greenwood Press.

Johnston-Robledo, I. (2000). From postpartum depression to the empty nest syndrome: The motherhood mystique revisited. In J. C. Chrisler, C. Golden, & P. D. Rozee (Eds.), *Lectures on the psychology of women* (pp. 129–148). Boston, MA: McGraw-Hill.

Joiner, G. W., & Kashubeck, S. (1996). Acculturation, body image, self-esteem, and eating-disorder symptomology in adolescent Mexican-American women. *Psychology of Women Quarterly, 20,* 419–435.

Jones, D. (1996). Physical attractiveness and the theory of sexual selection. Ann Arbor, MI:

Museum of Anthropology, University of Michigan. Cited in K. K. Dion (2002). In G. Rhodes & L. A. Zebrowitz (Eds.), *Facial attractiveness: Evolutionary, cognitive, and social perspectives* (pp. 239–259). Westport, CT: Ablex Publishing.

Jones, L., & Bigler, R. S. (1996, March). Cognitive-developmental mechanisms in the revision of gender-stereotypic beliefs. Poster session presented at the 14th biennial Conference on Human Development, Birmingham, AL.

Jordan, J. V., Kaplan, A. G., Miller, J. B., Stiver, I. P., & Surrey, J. L. (1991). *Women's growth in connection.* New York: Guilford.

Jordan, K. M., & Deluty, R. H. (2000). Social support, coming out, and relationship satisfaction in lesbian couples. *Journal of Lesbian Studies, 4,* 145–164.

Joseph, G. I. (1991). Black mothers and daughters: Traditional and new perspectives. In P. Bell-Scott, B. Guy-Sheftall, J. J. Royster, J. Sims-Wood, M. DiCosta-Willis, & L. P. Fultz (Eds.), *Double stitch: Black women write about mothers and daughters* (pp. 94–106). New York: HarperCollins.

Joseph, G. I., & Lewis, J. (1981). *Common differences: Conflicts in black and white feminist perspectives.* Boston: South End Press.

Joseph, J. (1997). Woman battering: A comparative analysis of black and white women. In G. Kaufman Kantor & J. L. Jasinski (Eds.), *Out of darkness: Contemporary perspectives on family violence* (pp. 161–169). Thousand Oaks, CA: Sage.

Jost, J. T. (1997). An experimental replication of the depressed entitlement effect among women. *Psychology of Women Quarterly, 21,* 387–393.

Jost, J. T., & Banaji, M. R. (1994). The role of stereotyping in system-justification and the production of false consciousness. *British Journal of Social Psychology, 33,* 1–27.

Jost, J. T., & Burgess, D. (2000). Attitudinal ambivalence and the conflict between group and system justification motives in low-status groups. *Personality & Social Psychology Bulletin, 26,* 293–305.

Joyce, P. (1997). Mothers of sexually abused children and the concept of collusion: A literature review. *Journal of Child Sexual Abuse, 6,* 75–92.

Jutras, S., & Veilleux, F. (1991). Gender roles and care giving to the elderly: An empirical study. *Sex Roles, 25,* 1–18.

Kahn, A. S., & Jean, P. J. (1983). Integration and elimination or separation and redefinition: The future of the psychology of women. *Signs, 8,* 659–670.

Kahn, A. S., & Yoder, J. D. (1989). The psychology of women and conservatism: Rediscovering social change. *Psychology of Women Quarterly, 13,* 417–432.

Kahn, J., Smith, K., & Roberts, E. (1984). *Familial communication and adolescent sexual behavior.* Final Report to the Office of Adolescent Pregnancy Programs. Cambridge, MA: American Institutes for Research. Cited in J. Brooks-Gunn & F. F. Furstenberg, Jr. (1989).

Kaiser, C. A., & Miller, C. T. (2001). Reacting to impending discrimination: Compensations for prejudice and attributions to discrimination. *Personality & Social Psychology Bulletin, 27,* 1357–1367.

Kaiser, K. (1990). Cross-cultural perspectives on menopause. In M. Flint, F. Kronenberg, & W. Utian (Eds.), *Multidisciplinary perspectives on menopause. Annals of the New York Academy of Science, 592,* 430–432.

Kakar, S. (1998). The search for middle age in India. In R. A. Shweder (Ed.), *Welcome to middle age: And other cultural fictions* (pp. 75–98). Chicago: University of Chicago Press.

Kanagawa, C., Cross, S. E., & Markus, H. R. (2001). "Who am I?" The cultural psychology of the conceptual self. *Personality and Social Psychology Bulletin, 27,* 90–103.

Kandall, S. R. (1999). *Substance and shadow: Women and addiction in the United States.* Cambridge, MA: Harvard University Press.

Kanekar, S., & Seksaria, V. (1993). Acquaintance versus stranger rape: Testing the ambiguity reduction hypothesis. *European Journal of Social Psychology, 23,* 485–494.

Kanter, R. M. (1977). *Men and women of the corporation.* New York: Basic Books.

Kaplan, A. G., & Surrey, J. L. (1984). The relational self in women: Developmental theory and public policy. In L. E. Walker (Ed.), *Women and mental health policy* (pp. 79–94). Beverly Hills, CA: Sage.

Kaplan, M. M. (1992). *Mothers' images of motherhood.* New York: Routledge.

Karbon, M., Fabes, R. A., Carlo, G., & Martin, C. L. (1992). Preschoolers' beliefs about sex and age differences in emotionality. *Sex Roles, 27,* 377–390.

Karp, S. A., Silber, D. E., Holmstrom, R. W., & Stock, L. J. (1995). Personality of rape survivors and by relation of survivor to perpetrator. *Journal of Clinical Psychology, 51*(5), 587–593.

Karraker, K. H., Vogel, D. A., & Lake, M. A. (1995). Parents' gender stereotyped perceptions of newborns: The eye of the beholder revisited. *Sex Roles, 33,* 687–701.

Katz, B. L. (1991). The psychological impact of stranger versus nonstranger rape on victims' recovery. In A. Parrot & L. Bechhofer, (Eds.), *Acquaintance rape: The hidden crime* (pp. 251–269). New York: Wiley.

Katz, P. A. (1996). Raising feminists. *Psychology of Women Quarterly, 20,* 323–340.

Katz, P. A., & Boswell, S. (1986). Flexibility and traditionality in children's gender roles. *Genetic, Social, & General Psychology Monographs, 112,* 103–147.

Katz, P. A., & Walsh, P. V. (1991). Modification of children's gender stereotyped behavior. *Child Development, 62,* 338–351.

Kaufert, P. L. (1990). Methodological issues in menopause research. In M. Flint, F. Kronenberg, & W. Utian (Eds.), *Multidisciplinary perspectives on menopause. Annals of the New York Academy of Sciences, 592,* 114–122.

Kaufert, P. L., & Gilbert, P. (1986). Women, menopause, and medicalization. *Culture, Medicine & Psychiatry, 10,* 7–21.

Kaw, E. (1994). "Opening" faces: The politics of cosmetic surgery and Asian American women. In N. Sault (Ed.), *Many mirrors: Body image and social relations.* New Brunswick, NJ: Rutgers University Press, pp. 241–265.

Kawakami, C., White, J. B., & Langer, E. J. (2000). Mindful and masculine: Freeing women leaders from the constraints of gender roles. *Journal of Social Issues, 56* (1), 49–63.

Keating, C. T., & Hellman, K. R. (1994). Dominance and deception in children and adults: Are leaders the best misleaders? *Personality and Social Psychology Bulletin, 20,* 312–321.

Keel, P. K., Fulkerson, J. A., & Leon, G. R. (1997). Disordered eating precursors in pre- and early adolescent girls and boys. *Journal of Youth and Adolescence, 26,* 203–216.

Keenan, K., & Shaw, D. (1997). Developmental and social influences on young girls' early problem behavior, *Psychological Bulletin, 121,* 95–113.

Kelle, H. (2000). Gender and territoriality in games played by nine-to-twelve-year-old schoolchildren. *Journal of Contemporary Ethnology, 29,* 164–197.

Keller, H., & Zach, U. (2002). Gender and birth order as a determinant of parental behavior. *International Journal of Behavioral Development, 26,* 177–184.

Kelly, L., & Radford, J. (1996). "Nothing really happened": The invalidation of women's experiences of sexual violence. In M. Hester, L. Kelly, & J. Radford (Eds.), *Women, violence, and male power: Feminist activism, research, and practice.* Buckingham, England: Open University Press.

Keltner, D., Capps, L., Kring, A. M., Young, R. C., & Heerey, E. A. (2001). Just teasing: A conceptual analysis and empirical review. *Psychological Bulletin, 127,* 229–248.

Kemper, V. (2002). Proposal calls fetus a 'child' for health care funding: Bush says rule change would let states offer prenatal services to poor. Abortion rights groups criticize move. *Los Angeles Times,* February 1, p. A30.

Kennedy, C. W., & Camden, C. (1983). Interruptions and nonverbal gender differences. *Journal of Nonverbal Behavior, 8,* 91–108.

Kennell, J., Klaus, M., McGrath, S., Robertson, S., & Hinkley, C. (1991). Continuous emotional support during labor in a US hospital. *Journal of the American Medical Association, 265,* 2197–2201.

Kessler, S. J. (1990). The medical construction of gender: Case management of intersexed infants. *Signs, 16,* 3–26.

Kessler, S. J. (1998). *Lessons from the intersexed.* New Brunswick, NJ: Rutgers University Press.

Kilbey, M. M., & Burgermeister, D. (2001). Substance abuse. In J. Worell (Ed.), *Encyclopedia of Sex and Gender* (pp. 1113–1127). NY: Academic Press.

Kilbourne, J. (2000). *Can't buy my love: How advertising changes the way we think and feel.* New York: Simon & Schuster.

Kiliansky, S. E., & Rudman, L. A. (1998). Wanting it both ways: Do women approve of benevolent sexism? *Sex Roles, 39,* 333–352.

Kimball, M. M. (1995). *Feminist visions of gender similarities and differences.* New York: Harrington Park.

Kimmel, E. (1999). Feminist teaching: An emergent practice. In S. Davis, M. Crawford, & J. Sebrechts (Eds.), *Coming into her own: Encouraging educational success in girls and women* (pp. 57–76). San Francisco: Jossey-Bass.

Kimmel, E. B. (1989). The experience of feminism. *Psychology of Women Quarterly, 13,* 133–146.

Kimmel, M. S. (1996). *Manhood in America: A cultural history.* New York: Free Press.

Kimura, D. (1999). *Sex and cognition,* Cambridge, MA: MIT Press.

King, S. (1974). *Carrie.* New York: Doubleday.

Kinsey, A. C., Pomeroy, W. B., & Martin, C. E. (1948). *Sexual behavior in the human male.* Philadelphia: Saunders.

Kinsey, A. C., Pomeroy, W. B., Martin, C. E., & Gebhard, P. H. (1953). *Sexual behavior in the human female.* Philadelphia: Saunders.

Kinsman, S. B., Romer, D., & Schwarz, D. F. (1998). Early sexual initiation: The role of peer norms. *Pediatrics, 102*(5), 1185–1192.

Kinzer, S. (1993, May 29). German court restricts abortion, angering feminists and the East. *New York Times,* p. A1.

Kirchmeyer, C. (1993). Nonwork-to-work spillover: A more balanced view of the experiences and coping of professional women and men. *Sex Roles, 28,* 531–552.

Kirkpatrick, C. (1936). The construction of a belief pattern scale for measuring attitudes toward feminism. *Journal of Social Psychology, 7,* 421–437.

Kirsh, S. J. (1998). Seeing the world through Mortal Kombat–colored glasses: Violent video games and the development of a short-term hostile attribution bias. *Childhood: A Global Journal of Child Research, 5,* 177–184.

Kishor, S. (1993). "May God give sons to all": Gender and child mortality in India. *American Sociological Review, 58,* 247–265.

Kissling, E. A. (1996). "That's just a basic teenage rule": Girls' linguistic strategies for managing the menstrual communication taboo. *Journal of Applied Communication Research, 24,* 202–309.

Kite, M. E. (1996). Age, gender, and occupational label: A test of social role theory. *Psychology of Women Quarterly, 20,* 361–374.

Kite, M. E. (2001). Changing times, changing gender roles: What do we want women and men to be? In R. K. Unger (Ed.), *Handbook of the psychology of women and gender* (pp. 215–227). New York: McGraw Hill.

Kite, M. E., & Deaux, K. (1987). Gender belief systems: Homosexuality and the implicit inversion theory. *Psychology of Women Quarterly, 11,* 83–96.

Kite, M. E., Deaux, K., & Miele, M. (1991). Stereotypes of young and old: Does age outweigh gender? *Psychology and Aging, 6,* 19–27.

Kite, M. E., & Wagner, L. S. (2002). Attitudes toward older adults. In T. D. Nelson (Ed.), *Ageism: Stereotyping and prejudice against older persons* (pp. 129–161). Cambridge, MA: MIT Press.

Kite, M. E., & Whitley, B. B., Jr. (1996). Sex differences in attitudes toward homosexual persons, behaviors, and civil rights: A meta-analysis. *Personality and Social Psychology Bulletin, 22,* 336–353.

Kityama, S., Markus, H. R., & Kurokawa, M. (2000). Culture, emotion, and well-being: Good feelings in Japan and the United States. *Cognition and Emotion, 14,* 93–124.

Kitzinger, C. (1987). *The social construction of lesbianism.* London: Sage.

Kitzinger, S. (1983). *Women's experience of sex.* London: Dorling Kindersley.

Klein, K. J. K., & Hodges, S. D. (2001). Gender differences, motivation, and empathic accuracy: When it pays to understand. *Personality and Social Psychology Bulletin, 27,* 720–730.

Kline, K. N. (1996). The drama of in utero drug exposure. In R. L. Parrott & C. M. Condit (Eds.), *Evaluating women's health messages* (pp. 61–79). Thousand Oaks: Sage.

Klinger, L. J., Hamilton, J. A., & Cantrell, P. J. (2001). Children's perception of the aggressive and gender-specific content in toy commercials. *Social Behavior & Personality, 29,* 11–20.

Klonoff, E. A., & Landrine, H. (1995). The schedule of sexist events: A measure of lifetime and recent sexist discrimination in women's lives. *Psychology of Women Quarterly, 19,* 439–472.

Klonoff, E. A., Landrine, H., & Campbell, R. (2000). Sexist discrimination may account for well-known gender differences in psychiatric symptoms. *Psychology of Women Quarterly, 24,* 93–99.

Klumb, P. L., & Baltes, M. M. (1999). Time use of old and very old Berliners: Productive and consumptive activities as functions of resources. *Journals of Gerontology: Series B: Psychological Sciences & Social Sciences, 54B,* S271–S278.

Knight, J. L., & Giuliano, T. A. (2001). He's a Laker; She's a "Looker": The consequences of gender-stereotypic portrayals of male and female athletes by the print media. *Sex Roles, 45,* 217–229.

Knudson-Martin, C., & Mahoney, A. R. (1996). Gender dilemmas and myth in the construction of marital bargains: Issues for marital therapy. *Family Process, 35*(2), 137–153.

Kobrynowicz, D., & Branscombe, N. R. (1997). Who considers themselves victims of discrimination? Individual difference predictors of perceived gender discrimination in women and men. *Psychology of Women Quarterly, 21,* 347–363.

Koch, L. (1990). The fairy tale as a model for women's experience of in vitro fertilization. In H. B. Holmes (Ed.), *Issues in reproductive technology I* (pp. 303–320). New York: Garland.

Kohlberg, L. (1981). *The philosophy of moral development: Essays on moral development*, Vols. I & II. San Francisco: Harper & Row.

Koivula, N. (1999). Gender stereotyping in television media news coverage. *Sex Roles, 41*, 589–604.

Kolata, G. (1992, February 12). Track federation urges end to gene test for femaleness. *The New York Times.*

Kong, M-E. (1997). The portrayal of women's images in magazine advertisements: Goffman's gender analysis revisited. *Sex Roles, 37*, 979–996.

Konrad, A. M., Ritchie, J. E., Lieb, P., & Corrigall, E. (2000). Sex differences and similarities in job attribute preferences: A meta-analysis. *Psychological Bulletin, 26*, 593–641.

Kornblut, A. E. (2001, January 23). Bush bans abortion aid overseas stirs an outcry as he restores funding curbs Clinton ended. *The Boston Globe*, p. A1.

Kortenhaus, C. M., & Demarest, J. (1993). Gender role stereotyping in children's literature: An update. *Sex Roles, 28*, 219–232.

Koss, M. P. (1985). The hidden rape victim: Personality, attitudinal, and situational characteristics. *Psychology of Women Quarterly, 9*, 193–212.

Koss, M. P. (1990). The women's mental health research agenda: Violence against women. *American Psychologist, 45*, 374–380.

Koss, M. P. (1992). The underdetection of rape: Methodological choices influence incidence estimates. *Journal of Social Issues, 48*, 61–75.

Koss, M. P., & Burkhart, B. R. (1989). A conceptual analysis of rape victimization. *Psychology of Women Quarterly, 13*, 27–40.

Koss, M. P., & Cleveland, H. H. (1997). Stepping on toes: Social roots of date rape lead to intractability and politicization. In M. Schwartz (Ed.) *Researching sexual violence against women: Methodological and personal perspectives*, 4–21. Sage Publications, Inc., Thousand Oaks, CA.

Koss, M. P., & Gaines, J. A. (1993). The prediction of sexual aggression by alcohol use, athletic participation, and fraternity affiliation. *Journal of Interpersonal Violence, 8*, 94–108.

Koss, M. P., Gidycz, C. A., & Wisniewski, N. (1987). The scope of rape: Incidence and prevalence of sexual aggression and victimization in a national sample of higher education students. *Journal of Consulting and Clinical Psychology, 55*, 162–170.

Koss, M. P., Goodman, L. A., Browne, A., Fitzgerald, L. F., Keita, G. P., & Russo, N. F. (1994). *No safe haven: Male violence against women at home, at work, and in the community.* Washington, DC: American Psychological Association.

Kosson, D. S., Kelly, J. C., & White, J. W. (1997). Psychopathy-related traits predict self-reported sexual aggression among college men. *Journal of Interpersonal Violence, 12*, 241–254.

Kowalski, R. M. (1992). Nonverbal behaviors and perceptions of sexual intentions: Effects of sexual connotativeness, verbal response, and rape outcome. *Basic and Applied Social Psychology, 13*, 427–445.

Kowalski, R. M. (2000). "I was only kidding!" Victims' and perpetrators' perceptions of teasing. *Personality and Social Psychology Bulletin, 26*, 231–241.

Kowalski, R. M., & Chapple, T. (2000). The social stigma of menstruation: Fact or fiction? *Psychology of Women Quarterly, 24*, 74–80.

Kozlowski, J. (1993). Women, film, and the midlife Sophie's choice: Sink or Sousatzka? In J. C. Callahan (Ed.), *Menopause: A midlife passage* (pp. 3–22). Bloomington: Indiana University Press.

Kramarae, C., & Treichler, P. A. (1985). *A feminist dictionary.* Boston: Pandora.

Kravetz, D. (1980). Consciousness-raising and self-help. In A. M. Brodsky & R. Hare-Mustin (Eds.), *Women and psychotherapy* (pp. 267–283). New York: Guilford.

Krieger, S. (1982). Lesbian identity and community: Recent social science literature. *Signs, 8*, 91–108.

Kronenberg, F. (1990). Hot flashes: Epidemiology and physiology. In M. Flint, F. Kronenberg, & W. Utian (Eds.), *Multidisciplinary perspectives on menopause. Annals of New York Academy of Sciences, 592*, 52–86.

Kuebli, J., & Fivush, R. (1992). Gender differences in parent-child conversations about past emotions. *Sex Roles, 27*, 683–698.

Kulick, D. (1997). The gender of Brazilian transgendered prostitutes. *American Anthropologist, 99*, 574–585.

Kunda, A., Sinclair, L., & Griffin, D. (1997). Equal ratings but separate meanings: Stereotypes and the construal of traits. *Journal of Personality and Social Psychology, 72*, 720–734.

Kurdek, L. A. (1988). Perceived social support in gays and lesbians in cohabitating couples.

Journal of Personality and Social Psychology, 54, 504–509.

Kurdek, L. A. (1993). The allocation of household labor in gay, lesbian, and heterosexual married couples. *Journal of Social Issues, 49,* 127–139.

Kurdek, L. A. (1997). Adjustment to relationship dissolution in gay, lesbian, and heterosexual partners. *Personal Relationships, 4,* 145–161.

Kurpius, S. E., Nicpon, M. F., & Maresh, S. E. (2001). Mood, marriage, and menopause. *Journal of Counseling Psychology, 48,* 77–84.

Kuttler, A. F., LaGreca, A. M., & Prinstein, M. J. (1999). Friendship qualities and social-emotional functioning of adolescents with close cross-sex friendships. *Journal of Research in Adolescence, 9,* 339–366.

Kyle, D. J., & Mahler, H. I. M. (1996). The effects of hair color and cosmetic use on perceptions of a female's ability. *Psychology of Women Quarterly, 20,* 447–455.

Laabs, J. (1998). Sexual harassment: New rules, higher stakes. *Workforce,* 34–42.

Lacey, M. (2002, June 15). Fighting light skin as a standard of beauty. *The New York Times,* p. A4.

Lachman, M. E., & James, J. B. (1997). Charting the course of midlife development. In M. E. Lachman & J. B. James (Eds.), *Multiple paths of midlife development* (pp. 1–17). Chicago: University of Chicago Press.

Lackey, P. N. (1989). Adults' attitudes about assignments of household chores to male and female children. *Sex Roles, 20,* 271–281.

Lafontaine, E., & Tredeau, L. (1986). The frequency, sources, and correlates of sexual harassment among women in traditional male occupations. *Sex Roles 15,* 433–442.

LaFrance, M. (1992). Gender and interruptions: Individual infraction or violation of the social order? *Psychology of Women Quarterly, 16,* 497–512.

LaFrance, M. (2001). Gender and social interaction. In R. K. Unger (Ed.), *Handbook of the Psychology of Women and Gender* (pp. 245–255). New York, Wiley & Sons.

LaFromboise, T. D., Berman, J. S., & Sohi, B. K. (1994). American Indian Women. In L. Comas-Diaz & B. Greene (Eds.), *Women of color: Integrating ethnic and gender identities in psychotherapy* (pp. 30–71). New York: Guilford.

LaFromboise, T. D., Choney, S. B., James, A., & Running Wolf, P. (1995). American Indian women and psychology. In H. Landrine (Ed.), *Bringing cultural diversity to feminist psychology* (pp. 191–239). Washington, DC: American Psychological Association.

Lakkis, J., Ricciardelli, L. A., & Williams, R. J. (1999). Role of sexual orientation, and gender-related traits in disordered eating. *Sex Roles, 41,* 1–16.

Lakoff, R. (1975). *Language and woman's place.* New York: Harper & Row.

Lakoff, R. (1990). *Talking power: The politics of language.* New York: Basic Books.

Landa, A. (1990). No accident: The voices of voluntarily childless women–An essay on the social construction of fertility choices. In J. P. Knowles & E. Cole (Eds.), *Motherhood: A feminist perspective* (pp. 139–158). New York: Haworth.

Landrine, H. (1985). Race x class stereotypes of women. *Sex Roles, 13,* 65–75.

Landrine, H. (1987). On the politics of madness: A preliminary analysis of the relationship between social roles and psychopathology. *Psychological Monographs, 113*(3), 341–406.

Landrine, H. (1988). Depression and stereotypes of women: Preliminary empirical analyses of the gender-role hypothesis. *Sex Roles, 19,* 527–541.

Landrine, H. (1989). The politics of personality disorder. *Psychology of Women Quarterly, 13,* 325–339.

Landrine, H. (Ed.). (1995). *Bringing cultural diversity to feminist psychology.* Washington, DC: American Psychological Association.

Landrine, H., & Klonoff, E. A. (1997). *Discrimination against women: Prevalence, consequences, remedies.* Thousand Oaks, CA: Sage.

Landrine, H., & Klonoff, E. A. (2001). Health and health care: How gender makes women sick. In J. Worell (Ed.), *Encyclopedia of sex and gender* (pp. 577–592). NY: Academic Press.

Landrine, H., Klonoff, E. A., & Brown-Collins, A. (1992). Cultural diversity and methodology in feminist psychology: Critique, proposal, empirical example. *Psychology of Women Quarterly, 16,* 145–163.

Landrine, H., Klonoff, E. A., Gibbs, J., Manning, V., & Lund, M. (1995). Physical and psychiatric correlates of gender discrimination: An application of the schedule of sexist events. *Psychology of Women Quarterly, 19,* 473–492.

Laner, M. R. (1983). Courtship abuse and aggression: Contextual aspects. *Sociological Spectrum, 3,* 69–83.

Langhinrichsen-Rohling J., Neidig, P., & Thorn, G. (1995). Violent marriages: Gender differences in levels of current violence and past abuse. *Journal of Family Violence, 10,* 159–176.

Langlois, J. H., Kalakamis, L., Rubenstein, A. J., Larson, A., Hallam, M., & Smoot, M., (2000). Maxims or myths of beauty? A meta-analysis and theoretical review. *Psychological Bulletin, 126,* 390–423.

LaPlante, M. N., McCormick, N., & Brannigan, G. G. (1980). Living the sexual script: College students' views of influence in sexual encounters. *Journal of Sex Research, 16,* 338–355.

Larkin, J., & Popaleni, K. (1994). Heterosexual courtship violence and sexual harassment: The private and public control of young women. *Feminism & Psychology, 4,* 213–227.

LaRossa, R., Jaret, C., Gadgil, M., & Wynn, G. R. (2001). Gender disparities in Mother's Day and Father's Day comic strips: A fifty-four year history. *Sex Roles, 44,* 693–718.

Lauerman, J. (1990, January-February). The time machine. *Harvard Magazine,* pp. 43–46.

Laumann, E. O., Gagnon, J. H., Michael, R. T., & Michaels, S. (1994). *The social organization of sexuality: Sexual practices in the United States.* Chicago: The University of Chicago Press.

Laurance, J. (2001). Doctors must refuse to collude in this abusive practice: 'Genital mutilation is one of many harmful practices affecting women in traditional societies'. *The Independent,* August 22, p. 5.

Laws, J. L., & Schwartz, P. (1977). *Sexual scripts.* Hinsdale, IL: Dryden.

Laws, S. (1983). The sexual politics of premenstrual tension. *Women's Studies International Forum, 6,* 19–31.

Le Maner-Idrissi, G. (2001). Gender role adhesion at 24 months. *Revue Internationale de Psychologie Sociale, 14,* 57–74.

Leaper, C. (1991). Influences and involvement in children's discourse: Age, gender, and partner effects. *Child Development, 62,* 797–811.

Leaper, C. (2000a). Gender, affiliation, assertion, and the interactive context of parent-child play. *Developmental Psychology, 36,* 381–393.

Leaper, C. (2000b). The social construction and socialization of gender during development. In P. H. Miller & E. K. Scholnick (Eds.), *Toward a feminist developmental psychology* (pp. 127–152). NY: Routledge.

Leaper, C., Anderson, K. J., & Sanders, P. (1998). Moderators of gender-effects on parents' talk to their children: A meta-analysis. *Developmental Psychology, 14,* 3–27.

Leaper, C., & Gleason, J. B. (1996). The relationship of play activity and gender to parent and child sex-typed communication. *International Journal of Behavioral Development, 19,* 689–703.

Leaper, C., Tennenbaum, H. R., & Shaffer, T. G. (1999). Communication patterns of African American girls and boys from low-income urban background. *Child Development, 70,* 1489–1503.

Lee, F. (2002). The social costs of seeking help. *Journal of Applied Behavioral Science, 38,* 17–35.

Lee, G. R. (1988). Marital intimacy among older persons: The spouse as confidant. *Journal of Family Issues, 9,* 273–284.

Lee, J. (1995). Beyond bean counting. In B. Findlen (Ed.), *Listen up! Voices from the next feminist generation* (pp. 205–211). Seattle: Seal Press.

Lees, S. (1997). *Ruling passions: Sexual violence, reputation and the law.* Buckingham, UK: Open University Press.

LeGuin, U. K. (1974). *The dispossessed.* New York: Harper & Row.

Leinbach, M. D., Hort, B. E., & Fagot, B. I. (1997). Bears are for boys: Metaphorical associations in young children's gender stereotypes. *Cognitive Development, 12,* 107–130.

Lembright, M. F., & Riemer, J. W. (1982). Women truckers' problems and the impact of sponsorship. *Work and Occupations, 9,* 457–474.

Lemkau, J. P. (1979). Personality and background characteristics of women in male dominated occupations: A review. *Psychology of Women Quarterly, 4,* 221–240.

Lemkau, J. P. (1983). Women in male-dominated professions: Distinguishing personality and background characteristics. *Psychology of Women Quarterly, 8,* 144–165.

Lemkau, J. P. (1988). Emotional sequelae of abortion: Implications for clinical practice. *Psychology of Women Quarterly, 12,* 461–472.

Lemonick, M. D. (2000, October 30). Teens before their time. *Time Magazine,* pp. 66–74.

Leonard, R. (1995). I'm just a girl who can't say "no": A gender difference in children's perception of refusals. *Feminism & Psychology, 5,* 315–328.

Lerman, H. (1986). From Freud to feminist personality theory: Getting there from here. *Psychology of Women Quarterly, 10,* 1–18.

Lerman, H., & Rigby, D. N. (1990). Boundary violations: Misuse of the power of the therapist. In H. Lerman & N. Porter (Eds.), *Feminist ethics in psychotherapy* (pp. 51–59). New York: Springer.

LeVay, S. (1991). A difference in hypothalamic structure between heterosexual and homosexual men. *Science, 253,* 1034–1037.

LeVay, S., & Hamer, D. H. (1994). Evidence for a biological influence in male homosexuality. *Scientific American, 270,* 44–49.

Levenson, R. W., Carstensen, L. L., & Gottman, J. M. (1993). Long-term marriage: Age, gender, and satisfaction. *Psychology and Aging, 8,* 301–313.

Levin, I. (1997). The stepparent role from a gender perspective. *Marriage & Family Review, 26*(1/2), 177–190.

Levine, M. P., & Leonard, R. (1984). Discrimination against lesbians in the work force. *Signs, 4,* 700–710.

Levine, R., Sato, S., Hashimoto, T., & Verma, J. (1995). Love and marriage in eleven cultures. *Journal of Cross-Cultural Psychology, 26*(5), 554–571.

Levy, G. D., Sadovsky, A. L., & Troseth, G. L. (2000). Aspects of young children's perceptions of gender-typed occupations. *Sex Roles, 42,* 993–1006.

Lewin, M., & Tragos, L. M. (1987). Has the feminist movement influenced sex role attitudes? A reassessment after a quarter century. *Sex Roles, 16,* 125–135.

Lewin, T. (2002, July 2). Collegiality as a tenure battleground. *The New York Times,* A12.

Lewis, D. M., & Cachelin, F. M. (2001). Body image, body dissatisfaction, and eating attitudes in midlife and elderly women. *Eating Disorders: The Journal of Treatment and Prevention, 9,* 29–39.

Lewittes, H. J. (1988). Just being friendly means a lot: Women, friendship, and aging. *Women & Health, 14,* 139–159.

L'Hommedieu, T. (1984). *The divorce experiences of working and middle class women.* Ann Arbor: UMI Research Press.

Li, N. P., Bailey, J. M., Kenrick, D. T., & Linsenmeier, J. A. W. (2002). The necessities and luxuries of mate preferences: Testing the tradeoffs. *Journal of Personality and Social Psychology, 82,* 947–955.

Liang, B., Tracey, A., Taylor, C. A., Williams, L. M., Jordan, J. V., & Miller, J. B. (2002). The Relational Health Indices: A study of women in relationships. *Psychology of Women Quarterly, 26,* 25–35.

Liben, L. S., Bigler, R. S., & Krogh, H. R. (2001). Pink and blue collar jobs: Children's judgments of job status and job aspirations in relation to sex of worker. *Journal of Experimental Child Psychology, 79,* 346–363.

Lieberman, M., Gauvin, L., Bukowski, W. M., & White, D. R. (2001). Interpersonal influence and disordered eating behaviors in adolescent girls: The role of peer modeling, social reinforcement, and body-related teasing. *Eating Behaviors, 2,* 215–236.

Lindahl, L. B., & Heimann, M. (1997). Social proximity in early mother-infant interactions: Implications for gender differences. *Early Development & Parenting, 6,* 83–88.

Linnehan, F. (2002). The relation of a work-based mentoring program to the academic performance and behavior of African American students. *Journal of Vocational Behavior, 59,* 310–325.

Linville, P. W. (1985). Self-complexity and affective extremity: Don't put all of your eggs in one cognitive basket. *Social Cognition, 3,* 94–120.

Lipman-Blumen, J., & Leavitt, H. J. (1976). Vicarious and direct achievement patterns in adulthood. *The Counseling Psychologist, 6,* 26–31.

Lippa, R. A. (2002). *Gender, nature, and nurture.* Mahwah, N. J.: Lawrence Erlbaum Associates.

Lippa, R. A., Martin, L. R., & Friedman, H. S. (2000). Gender-related individual differences and mortality in the Terman longitudinal study: Is masculinity hazardous to your health? *Personality & Social Psychology Bulletin, 26,* 1560–1570.

Lippard, L. (1986). Elizabeth Layton. In J. Alexander, D. Berrow, L. Domitrovich, M. Donnelly, & C. McLean (Eds.), *Woman and aging* (pp. 148–151). Corvallis, OR: Calyx.

Lippman, W. (1922). *Public opinion.* New York: Harcourt.

Lips, H. M. (2000). College students' visions of power and possibility as moderated by gender. *Psychology of Women Quarterly, 24,* 39–43.

Liss, M., Hoffner, C., & Crawford, M. (2000). What do feminists believe? *Psychology of Women Quarterly, 24,* 279–284.

Liss, M., O'Connor, C., Morosky, E., & Crawford, M. (2001). What makes a feminist? Predictors and correlates of feminist social identity in college women. *Psychology of Women Quarterly, 25,* 124–133.

Lloyd, S. A. (1991). The dark side of courtship. *Family Relations, 40,* 14–20.

Locher, P., Unger, R. K., Sociedade, P., & Wahl, J. (1993). At first glance: Accessibility of the physical attractiveness stereotype. *Sex Roles, 28,* 729–743.

Lock, M. (1986). Ambiguities of aging: Japanese experience and perceptions of menopause. *Culture, Medicine, and Psychiatry, 10,* 23–46.

Lock, M. (1993). *Encounters with aging: Mythologies of menopause in Japan and North America.* Berkeley & Los Angeles: University of California Press.

Lock, M. (1998). Deconstructing the change: Female maturation in Japan and North America. In R. A. Shweder (Ed.), *Welcome to middle age: And other cultural fictions* (pp. 45–74). Chicago: University of Chicago Press.

Lockheed, M. E. (1985). Sex and social influence: A meta-analysis guided by theory. In J. Berger & M. Zeldich (Eds.), *Status, relations, and rewards.* San Francisco: Jossey-Bass.

Logothetis, M. L. (1993). Disease or development: Women's perceptions of menopause and the need for hormone replacement therapy. In J. C. Callahan (Ed.), *Menopause: A midlife passage* (pp. 123–135). Bloomington: University of Indiana Press.

Loiacano, D. K. (1993). Gay identity issues among Black Americans: Racism, homophobia, and the need for validation. In L. D. Garnets & D. C. Kimmel (Eds.), *Psychological perspectives on lesbian and gay male experiences* (pp. 364–375). New York: Columbia University Press.

Long, J., & Porter, K. L. (1984). Multiple roles of midlife women. In G. Baruch & J. Brooks-Gunn (Eds.), *Women in midlife* (pp. 109–159). New York: Plenum Press.

Lonsway, K. A. (1996). Preventing acquaintance rape through education: What do we know? *Psychology of Women Quarterly, 20,* 229 265.

LoPiccolo, J., & Stock, W. E. (1986). Treatment of sexual dysfunction. *Journal of Consulting and Clinical Psychology, 54,* 158–167.

Lorber, J. (1993a). Believing is seeing: Biology as ideology. *Gender & Society, 7,* 568–581.

Lorber, J. (1993b). *Paradoxes of gender.* New Haven: Yale University Press.

Lorenzi-Cioldi, F. (1993). They all look alike, but so do we . . . sometimes: Perceptions of in-group and out-group homogeneity as a function of sex and context. *British Journal of Social Psychology, 32,* 111–124.

Lott, B. (1978). Behavioral concordance with sex role ideology related to play areas, creativity, and parental sex-typing of children. *Journal of Personality and Social Psychology, 36,* 1087–1100.

Lott, B. (1987). Sexist discrimination as distancing behavior: I. A laboratory demonstration. *Psychology of Women Quarterly, 11,* 47–58.

Lott, B., & Rocchio, L. M. (1997). Individual and collective action: Social approaches and remedies for sexist discrimination. In H. Landrine & E. A. Klonoff (Eds.), *Discrimination against women: Prevalence, consequences, remedies* (pp. 148–171). Thousand Oaks, CA: Sage.

Lowe, R., & Wittig, M. A. (Eds.). (1989). Achieving pay equity through comparable worth. Special issue of the *Journal of Social Issues,* 45.

Lubinski, D., Benbow, C. P., Shea, D. L., Eftekhari Sanjani, H., & Halvorson, B. J. (2001). Men and women at promise for scientific excellence: Similarity not dissimilarity. *Psychological Science, 12,* 309–317.

Lublin, N. (1998). *Pandora's box.* New York: Rowman & Littlefield.

Lueptow, L. B., Garovich, L., & Lueptow, M. B. (1995). The persistence of gender stereotypes in the face of changing sex roles: Evidence contrary to the sociocultural model. *Ethology & Sociobiology, 16,* 509–530.

Lunner, K., Wertheim, E. H., Thompson, J. K., Paxton, S. J., McDonald, F., & Halvaarson, K. S. (2000). A cross-cultural examination of weight-related teasing, body image, and eating disturbance in Swedish and Australian samples. *International Journal of Eating Disorders, 28,* 430–435.

Lutz, W. J., & Hock, E. (1998). Factors that influence depressive symptoms in mothers of infants. *Psychology of Women Quarterly, 22*(3), 499–503.

Lykes, M. B., Brabeck, M. M., Ferns, T., & Radan, A. (1993). Human rights and mental health among Latin American women in situations of state-sponsored violence: Bibliographic resources. *Psychology of Women Quarterly, 17,* 525–544.

Lytton, H., & Romney, D. M. (1991). Parents' differential socialization of boys and girls: A meta-analysis. *Psychological Bulletin, 109,* 267–296.

Maccoby, E. E. (1980). *Social development: Psychological growth and the parent-child relationship.* New York: Harcourt Brace Jovanovich.

Maccoby, E. E. (1988). Gender as a social category. *Developmental Psychology, 24,* 755–765.

Maccoby, E. E. (1998). *The two sexes: Growing up apart, coming together.* Cambridge, MA: Belknap Press of Harvard University Press.

Maccoby, E. E., & Jacklin, C. (1974). *The psychology of sex differences.* Stanford, CA: Stanford University Press.

Macdonald, B., & Rich, C. (1983). *Look me in the eye: Old women, aging and ageism.* San Francisco: Spinsters Ink.

MacFarlane, A. (1977). *The psychology of childbirth.* Cambridge, MA: Harvard University Press.

MacKinnon, C. (1979). *Sexual harassment of working women.* New Haven: Yale University Press.

MacKinnon, C. A. (1994). Sexuality. In A. C. Herrmann & A. J. Stewart (Eds.), *Theorizing feminism: Parallel trends in the humanities and social sciences* (pp. 257–287). Boulder: Westview Press.

MacLeod, C. (2001). Teenage motherhood and the regulation of mothering in the scientific literature: The South African example. *Feminism and Psychology, 11,* 493–510.

MacPherson, K. I. (1993). The false promises of hormone replacement therapy and current dilemmas. In J. C. Callahan (Ed.), *Menopause: A midlife passage* (pp. 145–159). Bloomington: Indiana University Press.

Maddux, H. C. (1975). *Menstruation.* New Canaan, CT: Tobey.

Madson, L. (2000). Inferences regarding the personality traits and sexual orientation of physically androgynous people. *Psychology of Women Quarterly, 24,* 148–160.

Magnusson, D., Strattin, H., & Allen, V. L. (1985). Biological maturation and social development: A longitudinal study of some adjustment processes from mid-adolescence to adulthood. *Journal of Youth and Adolescence, 14,* 267–283.

Mahay, J. W., Laumann, E. O., & Michaels, S. (2001). Race, gender, and class in sexual scripts. In E. O. Laumann & R. T. Michael (Eds.), *Sex, love, and health: Private choices and public policies* (pp. 197–238). Chicago: University of Chicago Press.

Major, B. (1994). From social inequality to personal entitlement: The role of social comparisons, legitimacy appraisals, and group membership. In M. P. Zanna (Ed.), *Advances in experimental social psychology,* Vol. 26 (pp. 293–355). New York: Academic Press.

Major, B., Barr, L., Zubek, J., & Babey, S. H. (1999). Gender and self-esteem: A meta-analysis. In W. B. Swann Jr., J. H. Langlois, & L. A. Gilbert (Eds.), *Sexism and stereotypes in modern society: The gender science of Janet Taylor Spence* (pp. 223–253). Washington, DC: American Psychological Association.

Major, B., Cozzarelli, C., Testa, M., & Mueller, P. (1992). Male partners' appraisals of undesired pregnancy and abortion: Implications for women's adjustment to abortion. *Journal of Applied Social Psychology, 22,* 599–614.

Major, B., Gramzow, R. H., McCoy, S. K., Levin, S., Schmader, T., & Sidanius, J. (2002). Perceiving personal discrimination: The role of group status and legitimizing ideology. *Journal of Personality & Social Psychology, 82,* 269–282.

Makepeace, J. M. (1984). *The severity of courtship violence injuries and individual precautionary measures.* Paper presented at the Second National Family Violence Research Conference, University of New Hampshire, Durham, NH.

Makepeace, J. M. (1986). Gender differences in courtship violence victimization. *Family Relations: Journal of Applied Family and Child Studies, 35,* 383–388.

Malamuth, N. M., Sockloskie, R., Koss, M. P., & Tanaka, J. (1991). The characteristics of aggressors against women: Testing a model using a national sample of college students. *Journal of Consulting and Clinical Psychology, 59,* 670–681.

Malamuth, N. M., & Thornhill, N. W. (1994). Hostile masculinity, sexual aggression, and gender-biased domineeringness in conversations. *Aggressive Behavior, 20,* 185–194.

Malloy, T. E., Fisher, W. A., Albright, L., Misovich, S. J., & Fisher, J. D. (1997). Interpersonal perception of the AIDS risk potential of persons of the opposite sex. *Health Psychology, 16*(5), 480–486.

Malson, H. (1997). Anorexic bodies and the discursive production of feminine excess. In J. M. Ussher (Ed.), *Body talk* (pp. 223–245). London: Routledge.

Mama, A. (2002). Gender, power, and identity in African contexts. *The Wellesley Centers for Women Research and Action Report, 23,* 6–15.

Mangan, K. S. (1999, March 12). Stanford Law School faces tensions over issues of race and gender. *The Chronicle of Higher Education,* p. A12.

Manning, W. D., & Landale, N. S. (1996). Racial and ethnic differences in the role of cohabitation in premarital childbearing. *Journal of Marriage and the Family, 58,* 63–77.

Mansfield, P. K., Koch, P. B., Henderson, J., Vicary, J. R., Kohn, M., & Young, E. W. (1991). The job climate for women in traditionally male blue-collar occupations. *Sex Roles, 25,* 63–79.

Mantecon, V. H. (1993). Where are the archetypes? Searching for symbols of women's midlife passage. In N. D. Davis, E. Cole, & E. D. Rothblum (Eds.), *Faces of women and aging* (pp. 77–88). Binghamton, NY: Harrington Park Press.

Marcus-Newhall, A., Thompson, S., & Thomas, C. (2001). Examining a gender stereotype: Menopausal women. *Journal of Applied Social Psychology, 31,* 698–719.

Marecek, J. (1986, March). *Sexual development and girls' self-esteem.* Paper presented at the Seminar on Girls: Promoting Self-Esteem, sponsored by the Girls' Coalition of Southeastern Pennsylvania, Swarthmore, PA.

Marecek, J. (1989). Introduction to special issue: Theory and method in feminist psychology. *Psychology of Women Quarterly, 13,* 367–378.

Marecek, J. (1993). Silences, gaps, and anxious rhetoric: Gender in abnormal psychology textbooks. *Journal of Theoretical and Philosophical Psychology, 13,* 602–611.

Marecek, J. (2001). Disorderly constructs: Feminist frameworks for clinical psychology. In R. K. Unger (Editor). *Handbook of the psychology of women and gender* (pp. 303–316). NY: Wiley.

Marecek, J., & Kravetz, D. (1998). Putting politics into practice: Feminist therapist as feminist praxis. *Women & Therapy, 21,* 17–36.

Marion, R. (2000, December). The curse of the Garcias. *Discover* (website).

Markens, S. (1996). The problematic of "experience": A political and cultural critique of PMS. *Gender & Society, 10,* 42–58.

Markson, E. W. (1997). Sagacious, sinful, or superfluous? The social construction of older women. In J. M. Coyle (Ed.), *Handbook on women and aging* (pp. 53–71). Westport, CT: Greenwood Press.

Markson, E. W., & Taylor, C. A. (1993). Real versus reel world: Older women and the Academy Awards. In N. D. Davis, E. Cole, & E. D. Rothblum (Eds.), *Faces of women and aging* (pp. 157–172). Binghamton, NY: Harrington Park Press.

Markus, H. R., & Kitayama, S. (1991). Culture and the self: Implications for cognition, emotion, and motivation. *Psychological Review, 98,* 224–253.

Marshall, A. (1997). Who's laughing? Hillary Rodham Clinton in political humor. In N. V. Benokraitis (Ed.), *Subtle sexism: Current practice and prospects for change* (pp. 72–90). Thousand Oaks, CA: Sage.

Martin, C. L. (1989). Children's use of gender-related information in making social judgments. *Developmental Psychology, 25,* 80– 88.

Martin, C. L. (1990). Attitudes and expectations about children with nontraditional and traditional gender roles. *Sex Roles, 22,* 151–165.

Martin, C. L. (1995). Stereotypes about children with traditional and nontraditional gender roles. *Sex Roles, 33,* 727–751.

Martin, C. L. (1999). A developmental perspective on gender effects and gender concepts. In W. B. Swann Jr., J. H. Langlois, & L. A. Gilbert (Eds.). *Sexism and stereotypes in modern society: The gender science of Janet Taylor Spence* (pp. 45–73). Washington, DC: American Psychological Association.

Martin, C. L., & Dinella, L. M. (2001). Gender development: Gender schema theory. In J. Worell (Ed.), *Encyclopedia of Women and Gender* (pp. 507–521). San Diego, CA: Academic Press.

Martin, C. L., Eisenbud, L., & Rose, H. (1995). Children's gender-based reasoning about toys. *Child Development, 66,* 1453–1471.

Martin, C. L., & Fabes, R. A. (1997, April). Building gender stereotypes in the preschool years. Paper presented at the meetings of the Society for Research on Child Development, Washington, DC.

Martin, C. L., & Fabes, R. A. (2001). The stability and consequences of young children's same-sex peer interactions. *Developmental Psychology, 37,* 431–446.

Martin, C. L., Fabes, R. A., Evans, S. M., & Wyman, H. (1999). Social cognition on the playground: Children's beliefs about playing with girls versus boys and their relations to sex segregated play. *Journal of Social & Personal Relationships, 16,* 751–771.

Martin, C. L., & Little, J. K. (1990). The relation of gender understanding to children's sex-typed preferences and gender stereotypes. *Child Development, 61,* 1427–1439.

Martin, J. A., Park, M. M., & Sutton, P. D. (2002). Births: Preliminary data for 2001. *National vital statistics reports, 5,* (10). Hyattsville, MD: Nation Center for Health Statistics.

Martin, K. A. (1996). *Puberty, sexuality, and the self: Girls and boys at adolescence.* London: Routledge.

Martin, S. E. (1988). Think like a man, work like a dog, and act like a lady: Occupational dilemmas of policewomen. In A. Statham, E. M. Miller, & H. O. Mauksch (Eds.), *The worth of women's work: A qualitative synthesis* (pp. 205–224). Albany, NY: State University of New York Press.

Mason, A., & Blankenship, V. (1987). Power and affiliation motivation, stress, and abuse in intimate relationships. *Journal of Personality & Social Psychology, 52,* 203–210.

Mason, D. O., & Lu, Y. (1988). Attitudes toward women's familial roles: Changes in the United States, 1977–1985. *Gender & Society, 2,* 39–57.

Masters, W. H., & Johnson, V. (1966). *Human sexual response.* Boston: Little, Brown.

Masters, W. H., & Johnson, V. (1979). *Homosexuality in perspective.* Boston: Little, Brown.

Mathews, A. M., & Campbell, L. D. (1995). Gender roles, employment, and informal care. In S. Arber & J. Ginn (Eds.), *Connecting gender and aging: A sociological approach* (pp. 129–143). Buckingham, UK: Open University Press.

Mathews, W. S. (1977). Sex-role perception, portrayal, and preference in the fantasy play of young children. *Resources in Education,* August, Document No. ED 136949.

Matschiner, M. & Murnen, S. K. (1999). Hyperfemininity and influence. *Psychology of Women Quarterly, 23,* 631–642.

Matthews, A. P. (1996). How evangelical women cope with prescription and description. In C. C. Kroeger, J. R. Beck, et al. (Eds.), *Women, abuse, and the Bible: How scripture can be used to hurt or to heal* (pp. 86–105). Grand Rapids, MI: Baker Books.

Matthews, W. J. (1984). Violence in college students. *College Student Journal, 18,* 150–158.

Mauthner, N. S. (1998). "It's a woman's cry for help": A relational perspective on postnatal depression. *Feminism & Psychology, 8*(3), 325–355.

Maypole, D. E. (1986). Sexual harassment of social workers at work: Injustice within? *Social Work, 31,* 29–34.

Maypole, D. E., & Skaine, R. (1983). Sexual harassment in the workplace. *Social Work, 28,* 385–390.

Mays, V. M., & Cochran, S. D. (1988). Issues in the perception of AIDS risk and risk reduction activities by black and Hispanic/Latina women. *American Psychologist, 43,* 949–957.

Mays, V. M., Coleman, L. M., & Jackson, J. S. (1996). Perceived race-based discrimination, employment status, and job stress in a national sample of black women: Implications for health outcomes. *Journal of Occupational Health Psychology, 1*(3), 319–329.

McCabe, M. P., Ricciardelli, L. A., & Finemore, J. (2002). The role of puberty, media, and popularity with peers on strategies to increase weight, decrease weight, and increase muscle tone among adolescent boys and girls. *Journal of Psychosomatic Research, 52,* 145–154.

McClelland, D. C., Atkinson, J. W., Clark, R. A., & Lowell, E. L. (1953). *The achievement motive.* Englewood Cliffs, NJ: Prentice Hall.

McCloskey, L. A., & Coleman, L. M. (1992). Difference without dominance: Children's talk in mixed- and same-sex dyads. *Sex Roles, 27,* 241–257.

McCormick, M. J. (2002). The search for the ideal heterosexual role play. In L. Diamant & J. A. Lee (Eds.), *The psychology of sex, gender, and jobs: Issues and resolutions* (pp. 155–170). Westport, CT: Praeger.

McCreary, D. R., & Rhodes, N. D. (2001). On the gender-typed nature of dominant and submissive acts. *Sex Roles, 44,* 339–350.

McDermid, S. A., Zucker, K. J., Bradley, S. J., & Maing, D. M. (1998). Effect of physical appearance on masculine trait ratings of boys and girls with gender identity disorder. *Archives of Sexual Behavior, 27,* 253–267.

McDougall, J., DeWit, D. J., & Ebanks, G. C. (1999). Parental preferences for sex of children in Canada. *Sex Roles, 41,* 615–626.

McFarlane, J. M., & Williams, T. M. (1994). Placing premenstrual syndrome in perspective. *Psychology of Women Quarterly, 18,* 339–373.

McGrath, E., Keita, G. P., Strickland, B. R., & Russo, N. F. (1990). *Women and depression: Risk factors and treatment issues.* Washington, DC: American Psychological Association.

McGrath, J. E. (1986). Continuity and change: Time, method, and the study of social issues. *Journal of Social Issues, 42,* 5–19.

McGuffey, C. S., & Rich, B. L. (1999). Playing in the gender transgression zone: Race, class, and hegemonic masculinity in middle childhood. *Gender & Society, 13,* 608–627.

McGuire, G. M. (2002). Gender, race, and the shadow structure: A study of informal networks and inequality in a work organization. *Gender & Society, 16,* 303–322.

McGuire, J. (1988). Gender stereotypes of parents with two-year-olds and beliefs about gender differences in behavior. *Sex Roles, 19,* 233–240.

McHugh, M. D., Koeske, R. D., & Frieze, I. H. (1986). Issues to consider in conducting nonsexist psychological research: A guide for researchers. *American Psychologist, 41,* 879–890.

McIntosh, P. (1988). *Understanding correspondence between white privilege and male privilege through women's studies work.* (Working paper No. 189). Wellesley, MA: Center for Research on Women, Wellesley College.

McKelvey, M. W., & McKenry, P. C. (2000). The psychosocial well-being of Black and White mothers following marital dissolution. *Psychology of Women Quarterly, 24,* 4–14.

McKinley, N. M. (1998). Gender differences in undergraduate's body esteem: The moderating effect of objectified body consciousness and actual/ideal weight discrepancy. *Sex Roles, 39,* 113–123.

McKinley, N. M., & Hyde, J. S. (1996). The objectified body consciousness scale: Development and validation. *Psychology of Women Quarterly, 20,* 181–215.

McLean, C., Carey, M., & White, C. (Eds.). (1996). *Men's ways of being.* Boulder: Westview.

McMahon, M. (1995). *Engendering motherhood.* New York: Guilford.

Media more likely to show women talking about romance than at a job. (1997, May 1). *The New York Times,* p. B15.

Mellanby, A. R., Phelps, F. A., Crichton, N. J., & Tripp, J. H. (1996). School sex education, a process for evaluation: Methodology and results. *Health Education Research, 11*(2), 205–214.

Mellencamp, P. (2002). From anxiety to equanimity: Crisis and generational continuity on TV, at the movies, in life, in death. In K. Woodward (Ed.), *Figuring age: Women, bodies, generations* (pp. 310–328). Bloomington, IN: University of Indiana Press.

Mennino, S. F., & Brayfield, A. (2002). Job-family trade-offs: The multidimensional effects of gender. *Work and Occupations, 29,* 226–256.

Menon, U. (2001). Midlife adulthood in cultural perspective: The imagined and the experienced in three cultures. In M. Lachman (Ed.), *Handbook of midlife development* (pp. 40–74). NY: Wiley.

Mercer, R. T. (1990). *Parents at risk.* New York: Springer.

Merskin, D. (1999). Adolescence advertising and the ideology of menstruation. *Sex Roles, 40,* 941–957.

Messner, M. A. (1994). Ah, ya throw like a girl! In M. A. Messner & D. F. Sabo (Eds.), *Sex, violence, and power in sports: Rethinking masculinity* (pp. 28–32). Freedom, CA: The Crossing Press.

Messner, M. A., Duncan, M. C., & Jensen, K. (1993). Separating the men from the girls: The gendered language of televised sports. *Gender & Society, 7,* 121–137.

Meston, C. M., Trapnell, P. D., & Gorzalka, B. B. (1996). Ethnic and gender differences in sexuality: Variations in sexual behavior between Asian and non-Asian university students. *Archives of Sexual Behavior, 25*(1), 33–72.

Middlebrook, D. W. (1998). *Suits me: The double life of Billy Tipton.* Boston, MA: Houghton Mifflin.

Miller, B., & Cafasso, L. (1992). Gender differences in care-giving: Fact or artifact. *American Journal of Psychiatry, 32,* 498–507.

Miller, B. C., Benson, B., & Galbraith, K. A. (2001). Family relationships and adolescent pregnancy risk: A research synthesis. *Developmental Review, 21,* 1–38.

Miller, B. D. (2001). Female-selective abortion in Asia: Patterns, policies, and debates. *American Anthropologist, 103,* 1083–1095.

Miller, B. C., Norton, M. C., Curtis, T., Hill, E. J., Schvaneveldt, P., & Young, M. H. (1997). The timing of sexual intercourse among adolescents. *Youth & Society, 29*(1), 54–83.

Miller, D. H. (1996). Medical and psychological consequences of legal abortion in the United States. In R. L. Parrott & C. M. Condit (Eds.), *Evaluating women's health messages* (pp. 17–32). Thousand Oaks: Sage.

Miller, E. K. (1993). Politics and gender: Geraldine Ferraro in the editorial cartoons. In S. T. Hollis, L. Pershing, & M. J. Young (Eds.). *Feminist theory and the study of folklore* (pp. 358–395). Urbana: University of Illinois Press.

Miller, J. B. (1984b). *The development of women's sense of self* (Work in Progress Papers No. 84-01). Wellesley, MA: Wellesley College, The Stone Center.

Miller, J. B. (1986). *Toward a new psychology of women* (2nd ed.). Boston: Beacon Press.

Miller, J. B. (1991). The development of women's sense of self. In J. V. Jordan, A. C. Kaplan, J. B. Miller, I. P. Stiver, & J. L. Surrey (Eds.), *Women's growth in connection: Writings from the Stone Center* (pp. 11–26). New York: Guilford.

Miller, J. B., & Stiver, I. (1997). *The healing connection.* Boston: Beacon Press.

Miller, L. C., Putcha Bhagavatula, A., & Pedersen, W. C. (2002). Men's and women's mating preferences: Distinct evolutionary mechanisms? *Current Directions in Psychological Science, 11,* 88–93.

Mills, C. S., & Granoff, B. J. (1992). Date and acquaintance rape among a sample of college students. *Social Work, 37,* 504–509.

Mintz, L. B., & Kashubeck, S. (1999). Body image and disordered eating among Asian American and Caucasian college students. *Psychology of Women Quarterly, 23,* 782–796.

Mirowsky, J. (1996). Age and the gender gap in depression. *Journal of Health and Social Behavior, 37,* 362–380.

Mirowsky, J., & Ross, K. E. (1987). Belief in innate sex roles: Sex stratification versus interpersonal influence in marriage. *Journal of Marriage and the Family, 49,* 527–540.

Misovich, S. J., Fisher, J. D., & Fisher, W. A. (1997). Close relationships and elevated HIV risk behavior: Evidence and possible underlying psychological processes. *Review of General Psychology, 1*(1), 72–107.

Mitchell, G., Obradovich, S., Herring, F., Tromborg, C., & Burns, A. L. (1992). Reproducing gender in public places: Adults' attention to toddlers in three public locales. *Sex Roles, 26,* 323–330.

Mitchell, V., & Helson, R. (1990). Women's prime in life: Is it the 50's? *Psychology of Women Quarterly, 14,* 451–470.

Miura, I. (1987). The relationship of computer self-efficacy expectations to computer interest and course enrollment in college. *Sex Roles, 16,* 303–312.

Mock, S. E. (2001). Retirement intentions of same-sex couples. *Journal of Gay & Lesbian Social Services, 13,* 81–86.

Modleski, T. (1980). The disappearing act: A study of Harlequin romances. *Signs, 5,* 435–448.

Moen, P., Kim, J. E., & Hofmeister, H. (2001). Couples' work/retirement transitions, gender and marital quality. *Social Psychology Quarterly, 64,* 55–71.

Moen, P., Robison, J., & Fields, V. (1994). Women's work and caregiving: A life course approach. *Journal of Gerontology: Social Sciences, 49,* S176–S186.

Moffat, M. (1989). *Coming of age in New Jersey.* New Brunswick, NJ: Rutgers University Press.

Moller, L. C., Hymel, S., & Rubin, K. H. (1992). Sex typing in play and popularity in middle childhood. *Sex Roles, 26,* 331–353.

Moller, L. C., & Serbin, L. A. (1996). Antecedents of toddler gender segregation: Cognitive consonance, gender-typed toy preferences, and behavioral compatability. *Sex Roles, 35,* 445–460.

Molloy, B. M., & Herzberger, S. D. (1998). Body image and self-esteem: A comparison of African-Americans and Caucasian women. *Sex Roles, 38,* 631–643.

Molm, L. D., & Hedley, M. (1992). Gender, power, and social exchange. In C. L. Ridgeway (Ed.), *Gender, interaction, and inequality* (pp. 1–28). New York: Springer-Verlag.

Mondschein, E. R., Adolph, K. E., & Tamis-LeMonda, C. S. (2000). Gender bias in mothers' expectations about infant crawling. *Journal of Experimental Child Psychology, 77,* 304–316.

Money, J. (1974). Prenatal hormones and postnatal socialization in gender identity differentiation. In J. K. Cole & R. Dienstbier (Eds.), *Nebraska Symposium on Motivation 1973,* Lincoln: University of Nebraska Press.

Money, J., & Ehrhardt, A. (1972). *Man and woman, boy and girl.* Baltimore: Johns Hopkins University Press.

Montgomery, R. J. V., & Kamo, Y. (1989). Parent care by sons and daughters. In J. A. Mancini (Ed.), *Aging parents and adult children* (pp. 213–230). Lexington, MA: Heath.

Mooney, L., & Brabant, S. (1987). Two martinis and a rested woman: "Liberation" in the Sunday comics. *Sex Roles, 17,* 409–420.

Moore, C. L., Dou, H., & Juraska, J. M. (1992). Maternal stimulation affects the number of motor neurons in a sexually dimorphic nucleus of the lumbar spinal cord. *Brain Research, 572,* 42–56.

Moradi, B., Fischer, A. R., Hill, M. S., Jome, L. M., & Blum, A. A. (2000). Does "feminist" plus "therapist" equal "feminist therapist?" *Psychology of Women Quarterly, 24,* 285–296.

Morell, C. (2000). Saying no: Women's experiences with reproductive refusal. *Feminism and Psychology, 10,* 313–322.

Morgan, B. L. (1998). A three generational study of tomboy behavior. *Sex Roles, 39,* 787–800.

Morgan, K. P. (1996). Describing the emperor's new clothes: Three myths of educational (in) equity. In A. Diller, B. Houston, K. P. Morgan, & M. Ayim (Eds.), *The gender questions in education: Theory, pedagogy, and politics* (pp. 105–122). Boulder, CO: Westview Press.

Morgan, K. P. (1998). Women and the knife: Cosmetic surgery and the colonization of women's bodies. In R. Weitz (Ed.), *The politics of women's bodies: Sexuality, appearance, and behavior* (pp. 147–166). New York: Oxford University Press.

Morgan, L. A. (1991). *After marriage ends: Economic consequences for midlife women.* London: Sage.

Mori, D. L., Chaikin, S., & Pliner, P. (1987). "Eating lightly" and the self-presentation of femininity. *Journal of Personality and Social Psychology, 53,* 240–254.

Morris, J. (1974). *Conundrum.* New York: Harcourt Brace Jovanovich.

Morris, J. F., Waldo, C. R., & Rothblum, E. D. (2001). A model of predictors and outcomes of outness among lesbian and bisexual women. *American Journal of Orthopsychiatry, 71,* 61–71.

Morrow, S. L., & Hawxhurst, D. M. (1998). Feminist therapy: Integrating political analysis in counseling and psychotherapy. *Women & Therapy, 21,* 37–50.

Mosher, C. E. (2002). Impact of gender and problem severity upon intervention selection. *Sex Roles, 46,* 113–119.

Moss, J. J. (1997, February 4). *Lesbian baiting in the barracks. The Advocate,* 36–40.

Motenko, A. K., & Greenberg, S. (1995). Reframing dependence in old age: A positive transition for families. *Social Work, 40,* 382–390.

Moya, M., Esposito, F., & Casado, P. (1999). *Women's reactions to hostile and benevolent sexist situations.* Paper presented at the 22nd General Meeting of the European Association of Experimental Social Psychology, Oxford, England. Cited in Glick & Fiske (2001).

Moynihan, D. P. (1965). *The Negro family: The case for national action.* Washington, DC: U.S. Department of Labor.

Muehlenhard, C. L., & Hollabough, L. C. (1988). Do women sometimes say no when they mean yes? The prevalence and correlates of women's token resistance to sex. *Journal of Personality and Social Psychology, 54,* 872–879.

Muehlenhard, C. L., & Rodgers, C. S. (1998). Token resistance to sex: New perspectives on an old stereotype. *Psychology of Women Quarterly, 22*(3), 443–463.

Mueller, K. A., & Yoder, J. D. (1997). Gendered norms for family size, employment, and occupation: Are there personal costs for violating them? *Sex Roles, 36,* 207–220.

Mullen, P. E. (1993). Child sexual abuse and adult mental health: The development of disorder. *Journal of Interpersonal Violence, 8,* 429.

Munshi, S. (2001). Marvellous me: The beauty industry and the construction of the "modern" Indian woman. In S. Munshi (Ed.), *Images of the modern woman in Asia: Global media, local meanings* (pp. 78–93). Richmond, Surrey, UK: Curzon Press.

Murnen, S. K. (2000). Gender and the use of sexually degrading language. *Psychology of Women Quarterly, 24,* 319–327.

Murnen, S. K., & Smolak, L. (1997). Femininity, masculinity, and disordered eating: A meta-analytic review. *International Journal of Eating Disorders, 22,* 231–242.

Murnen, S. K., & Smolak, L. (2000). The experience of sexual harassment among grade-school students: Early socialization of female subordination. *Sex Roles, 43,* 1–17.

Murray, S. B. (1997). It's safer this way: The subtle and not-so-subtle exclusion of men in child care. In N. Benokraitis (Ed.), *Subtle Sexism* (pp. 135–153). Thousand Oaks, CA: Sage.

Murray-Johnson, L., Witte, K., Liu, W. Y., Hubbell, A. P., Sampson, J., & Morrison, K. (2001). Addressing cultural orientation in fear appeals: Promoting AIDS-protective behaviors among Mexican immigrant and African American adolescents and American and Taiwanese college students. *Journal of Health Communication, 6,* 335–358.

Murry-McBride, V. (1996). An ecological analysis of coital timing among middle-class African American adolescent females. *Journal of Adolescent Research, 11*(2), 261–279.

Murstein, B. I. (1986). *Paths to marriage.* Beverly Hills, CA: Sage.

Mustansky, B. S., Bailey, J. M., & Kaspar, S., 2002. Dematoglyphics, handedness, sex, and sexual orientation. *Archives of Sexual Behavior, 31,* 113–122.

Mwangi, M. W. (1996). Gender roles portrayed in Kenyan television commercials. *Sex Roles, 34,* 205–214.

Myaskovsky, L., & Wittig, M. A. (1997). Predictors of feminist social identity among college women. *Sex Roles, 37,* 861–883.

Nacoste, R. W., & Lehman, D. (1987). Procedural stigma. *Representative Research in Social Psychology, 17,* 25–38.

Nadler, A., & Fisher, J. D. (1986). The role of threat to self-esteem and perceived control in recipient reaction to help: Theory development and empirical validation. In L. Berkowitz (Ed.), *Advances in Experimental Social Psychology,* Vol. 19. New York: Academic Press.

Nails, D. (1983). Social-scientific sexism: Gilligan's mismeasure of man. *Social Research, 50,* 643–664.

Nanda, S. (1996). Hijras: An alternative sex and gender role in India. In G. Herdt (Ed.), *Third sex, third gender: Beyond sexual dimorphism in culture and history* (pp. 373–417). New York: Zone Books.

Naples, N. A. (1992). Activist mothering: Cross-generational continuity in the community work of women from low-income urban neighborhoods. Special issue: Race, class, and gender. *Gender & Society, 6,* 441–463.

Nash, H. C., & Chrisler, J. C. (1997). Is a little (psychiatric) knowledge a dangerous thing? The impact of premenstrual dysphoric disorder on perceptions of premenstrual women. *Psychology of Women Quarterly, 21,* 315–322.

Nash, H. C., & Chrisler, J. C. (2001). Personality characteristics and coping styles of women working in and in training for nontraditional blue collar jobs. *Psychological Reports, 87,* 1115–1122.

National Association of Working Women. (2000). Retrieved August 17, 2002, from the World Wide Web: http://www.9to5.org/profile.html.

Needleman, R., & Nelson, A. (1988). Policy implications: The worth of women's work. In A. Statham, E. M. Miller, & H. O. Mauksch (Eds.), *The worth of women's work: A qualitative synthesis* (pp. 293–307). Albany, NY: State University of New York Press.

Neill, C. M., & Kahn, A. S. (1999). The role of personal spirituality and religious social activity on the life satisfaction of older widowed women. *Sex Roles, 40,* 310–329.

Nelson, A. (2000). The pink dragon is female: Halloween costumes and gender markers. *Psychology of Women Quarterly, 24,* 137–144.

Nelson, H. L. (1992). Scrutinizing surrogacy. In H. B. Holmes (Ed.), *Issues in reproductive technology* (pp. 297–302). New York: Garland.

Neppi, T. K., & Murray, A. D. (1997). Social dominance and play patterns among preschoolers: Gender comparisons. *Sex Roles, 36,* 381–393.

Neto, F., & Pinto, I. (1998). Gender stereotypes in Portuguese television advertisements. *Sex Roles, 39,* 153–164.

Nettles, S. M., & Scott-Jones, D. (1987). The role of sexuality and sex equity in the education of minority adolescents. *Peabody Journal of Education, 64,* 183–197.

Neuberg, S. L., Smith, D. M., Hoffman, J. C., & Russell, F. J. (1994). When we observe stigmatized and "normal" individuals interacting: Stigma by association. *Personality and Social Psychology Bulletin, 20,* 196–209.

Nevid, J. S. (1984). Sex differences in factors of romantic attraction. *Sex Roles, 11,* 401–411.

Newton, N. (1970). The effect of psychological environment on childbirth: Combined cross-cultural and experimental approach. *Journal of Cross-Cultural Psychology, 1,* 85–90.

Newtson, R. L., & Keith, P. M. (1997). Single women in later life. In J. M. Coyle (Ed.), *Handbook on women and aging* (pp. 385–399). Westport, CT: Greenwood Press.

Nichter, M., & Vuckovic, N. (1994). Fat talk: Body image among adolescent girls. In N. Sault (Ed.), *Many mirrors: Body image and social relations* (pp. 109–131). New Brunswick, NJ: Rutgers University Press.

Nicolson, P. (1990). A brief report of women's expectations of men's behavior in the transition to parenthood: Contradictions and conflicts for counselling psychology practice. Special Issue: Sexual and marital counselling: Perspectives on theory, research and practice. *Counselling Psychology Quarterly, 3,* 353–361.

Nicolson, P. (1993). Motherhood and women's lives. In D. Richardson & V. Robinson (Eds.), *Thinking feminist: Key concepts in women's studies* (pp. 201–224). New York: Guilford.

Niemann, Y. F. (2001). Stereotypes about Chicanas and Chicanos: Implications for counseling. *Counseling Psychologist, 29,* 55–90.

Niemann, Y. F., O'Connor, E., & McClorie, R. (1998). Intergroup stereotypes of working class Blacks and Whites: Implications for stereotype threat. *Western Journal of Black Studies, 22,* 103–108.

Nieva, V. F., & Gutek, B. A. (1981). *Women and work: A psychological perspective.* New York: Praeger.

Noble, B. P. (1993, April 18). Worthy child-care pay scales. *The New York Times,* 25.

Nolen-Hoeksema, S., & Jackson, B. (2001). Mediators of the gender difference in rumination. *Psychology of Women Quarterly, 25,* 37–47.

Nolen-Hoeksema, S., Larson, J., & Grayson, C. (1999). Explaining the gender difference in depressive symptoms. *Journal of Personality and Social Psychology, 77,* 1061–1072.

Noll, S. M., & Fredrickson, B. I. (1998). A mediational model linking self-objectification, body shame, and disordered eating. *Psychology of Women Quarterly, 22,* 623–636.

Norris, P. (Ed.). (1997). *Women, media, and politics.* New York: Oxford University Press.

Norton, A. J., & Moorman, J. E. (1987). Current trends in marriage and divorce among American women. *Journal of Marriage and the Family, 49,* 3–14.

Norton, K. I., Olds, T. S., Olive, S., & Dank, S. (1996). Ken and Barbie at life size. *Sex Roles, 34,* 287–294.

Novak, L. L., & Novack, D. R. (1996). Being female in the eighties and nineties: Conflicts between new opportunities and traditional expectations among white, middle class, heterosexual college women. *Sex Roles, 35,* 57–77.

O'Brien, M., Peyton, V., Mistry, R., Hruda, L., Jacobs, A., Caldera, Y., Huston, A., & Roy, C. (2000). Gender role cognition in three-year-old boys and girls. *Sex Roles, 42,* 1007–1024.

O'Connell, A. N., & Russo, N. F. (Eds.). (1980). Eminent women in psychology: Models of achievement, Special issue. *Psychology of Women Quarterly, 5.*

O'Connor, A. (1995, April). Tomboys. *Allure,* 68–70.

O'Farrell, B., & Harlan, S. L. (1982). Craftworkers and clerks: The effect of male co-worker hostility on women's satisfaction with nontraditional jobs. *Social Problems, 29,* 252–265.

O'Keeffe, N. K., Brockopp, K., & Chew, E. (1986). Teen dating violence. *Social Work, 31,* 465–468.

O'Laughlin, M. A. (1983). Responsibility and moral maturity in the control of fertility–or, a woman's place is in the wrong. *Social Research, 50,* 556–575.

O'Leary, K. D., Malone, J., & Tyree, A. (1994). Physical aggression in early marriage: Prerelationship and relationship effects. *Journal of Consulting & Clinical Psychology, 62,* 594–602.

O'Sullivan, C. S. (1991). Acquaintance gang rape on campus. In A. Parrot & L. Bechhofer (Eds.), *Acquaintance rape: The hidden crime* (pp. 140–156). New York: Wiley.

O'Sullivan, L. F., Graber, J. A., & Brooks-Gunn, J. (2001). Adolescent gender development. In J. Worell (Ed.) pp. 55–67. *Encyclopedia of women and gender.* San Diego, CA: Academic Press.

Oakley, A. (1974). *The sociology of housework.* New York: Pantheon.

Oakley, A. (1992). Social support in pregnancy: Methodology and findings of a 1-year follow-up study. *Journal of Reproductive and Infant Psychology, 10,* 219–231.

Obermeyer, C. M. (1996). Fertility norms and son preference in Morocco and Tunisia: Does women's status matter? *Journal of Biosocial Science, 28,* 57–72.

Ofosu, H. B., Lafreniere, K. D., & Senn, C. Y. (1998). Body image perception among women of African descent: A normative context? *Feminism & Psychology, 8,* 303–323.

Ogletree, R. J. (1993). Sexual coercion experience and help-seeking behavior of college women. *Journal of American College Health, 41,* 149–153.

Okun, B. S. (1996). Sex preferences, family planning, and fertility: An Israeli subpopulation in transition. *Journal of Marriage & the Family, 58,* 469–475.

Olday, D., & Wesley, B. (1983). Premarital courtship violence: A summary report. Moorehead State University, Moorehead, KY. Unpublished.

Oliver, M. B., & Hyde, J. S. (1993). Gender differences in sexuality: A meta-analysis. *Psychological Bulletin, 114,* 29–51.

Oliver, S. J., & Toner, B. B. (1990). The influence of gender role typing on the expression of depressive symptoms. *Sex Roles, 22,* 775–790.

Olweus, D. (1993). Victimization by peers: Antecedents and longterm outcomes. In K. H. Rubin & J. B. Asendorpf (Eds.), *Social withdrawal, inhibition, and shyness in childhood.* Hillsdale, NJ: Erlbaum.

Oropesa, R. S. (1996). Normative beliefs about marriage and cohabitation: A comparison of non-Latino Whites, Mexican Americans, and Puerto Ricans. *Journal of Marriage and the Family, 58,* 49–62.

Owen, S. A., & Caudill, S. A. (1996). Contraception and clinical science. In R. L. Parrott & C. M. Condit (Eds.), *Evaluating women's health messages* (pp. 81–94). Thousand Oaks: Sage.

Pacheco, S., & Hurtado, A. (2001). Media stereotypes. In J. Worell, Ed. *Encyclopedia of Women and Gender* (pp. 703–708). San Diego, CA: Academic Press.

Padavic, I. (1991). Attractions of male blue-collar jobs for Black and White women: Economic need, exposure, and attitudes. *Social Science Quarterly, 72,* 33–49.

Paetzold, R. L., & O'Leary-Kelly, A. M. (1996). The implications of U.S. Supreme Court and circuit court decisions for hostile environment sexual harassment cases. In M. S. Stockdale (Ed.), *Sexual harassment in the workplace: Perspectives, frontiers, and response strategies* (pp. 85–104). Thousand Oaks, CA: Sage.

Palace, E. M. (1999). Response expectancy and sexual dysfunction in women. In I. Kirsch (Ed.), *How expectancies shape experience* (pp. 173–196). Washington, D.C.: APA Books.

Palmore, E. B. (1997). Sexism and ageism. In J. M. Coyle (Ed.). *Handbook on women and aging* (pp. 3–13). Westport, CT: Greenwood Press.

Paludi, M. (1997). Sexual harassment in schools. In W. O'Donohue (Ed.), *Sexual harassment theory, research, and treatment* (pp. 225–249). Boston: Allyn & Bacon.

Paludi, M. A., & Bauer, W. D. (1983). Goldberg revisited: What's in an author's name? *Sex Roles, 9,* 387–390.

Paludi, M. A., & Fankell-Hauser, J. (1986). An idiographic approach to the study of women's achievement striving. *Psychology of Women Quarterly, 10,* 89–100.

Paludi, M. A., & Strayer, L. A. (1985). What's in an author's name? Differential evaluations of performance as a function of author's name. *Sex Roles, 10,* 353–361.

Papanek, H. (1973). Men, women, and work: Reflections on the two-person career. *American Journal of Sociology, 78,* 852–870.

Parker, S., Nichter, M., Nichter, M., Vuckovic, N., Sims, C., & Ritenbaugh, C. (1995). Body image and weight concerns among African

American and White adolescent females: Differences which make a difference. *Human Organization, 54,* 103–114.

Parlee, M. B. (1975). Review essay: Psychology. *Signs, 1,* 119–138.

Parlee, M. B. (1979). Psychology and women. *Signs, 5,* 121–133.

Parlee, M. B. (1981). Appropriate control groups in feminist research. *Psychology of Women Quarterly, 5,* 637–644.

Parlee, M. B. (1985). Psychology of women in the 80s: Promising problems. *International Journal of Women's Studies, 8,* 193–204.

Parlee, M. B. (1989, March). *The science and politics of PMS research.* Paper presented at the meeting of the Association for Women in Psychology, Newport, RI.

Parlee, M. B. (1990). Integrating biological and social scientific research on menopause. In M. Flint, F. Kronenberg, & W. Utian (Eds.), *Multidisciplinary perspectives on menopause. Annals of the New York Academy of Sciences, 592,* 379–389.

Parsons, E. M., & Betz, N. E. (2001). The relationship of participation in sports and physical activity to body objectification, instrumentality, and locus of control among young women. *Psychology of Women Quarterly, 25,* 209–222.

Parsons, T., & Bales, R. F. (1955). *Family, socialization, and interaction process.* Glencoe, IL: Free Press.

Pastor, J., McCormick, J., & Fine, M. (1996). Makin' homes: An urban girl thing. In B. J. R. Leadbeater & N. Way (Eds.), *Urban girls: Resisting stereotypes, creating identities* (pp. 15–34). New York: New York University Press.

Pasupathi, M., & Lockenhoff, C. E. (2002). Ageist behavior. In T. D. Nelson (Ed.), *Ageism: Stereotyping and prejudice against older persons* (pp. 201–246). Cambridge, MA: MIT Press.

Patterson, M. L., & Werker, J. F. (2002). Infants' ability to march dynamic phonetic and gender information in the face and voice. *Journal of Experimental Child Psychology, 81,* 93–115.

Paxton, S. J., Schutz, H. K., Wertheim, E. H., & Muir, S. L. (1999). Friendship clique and peer influence on body image concerns, dietary restraint, extreme weight-loss behaviors, and binge eating in adolescent girls. *Journal of Abnormal Psychology, 108,* 255–266.

Pearlman, S. F. (1993). Late mid-life astonishment: Disruptions to identity and self-esteem. In N. D. Davis, E. Cole, & E. D. Rothblum (Eds.), *Faces of women and aging* (pp. 1–12). Binghamton, NY: Harrington Park Press.

Pedersen, P., & Thomas, C. D. (1992). Prevalence and correlates of dating violence in a Canadian university sample. *Canadian Journal of Behavioural Science, 24,* 490–501.

Peirce, K. (1990). A feminist theoretical perspective on the socialization of teenage girls through Seventeen Magazine. *Sex Roles, 23,* 491–500.

Peirce, K. (1993). Socialization of teenage girls through teen-magazine fiction: The making of a new woman or an old lady? *Sex Roles, 29,* 59–68.

Peirce, K., & McBride, M. (1999). Aunt Jemima isn't keeping up with the Energizer Bunny: Stereotyping of animated spokescharacters in advertising. *Sex Roles, 40,* 959–968.

Peiss, K. (2001). On beauty . . . and the history of business. In P. Scranton (Ed.), *Beauty and business: Commerce, gender, and culture in modern America* (pp. 7–22). New York: Routledge.

Pence, E., & Shepard, M. (1988). Integrating feminist theory and practice: The challenge of the battered women's movement. In K. Yllo & M. Bograd (Eds.), *Feminist perspectives on wife abuse* (pp. 11–26). Berkeley, CA: Sage.

Peplau, L. A. (1983). Roles and gender. In H. H. Kelley et al. (Eds.), *Close relationships.* New York: W. H. Freeman.

Peplau, L. A., & Cochran, S. D. (1980). Sex differences in values concerning love relationships. Paper presented at American Psychological Association, cited in Peplau, L. A., & Gordon, S. L. (1983). The intimate relationships of lesbians and gay men. In E. R. Allgeier & N. B. McCormick (Eds.), *Changing boundaries: Gender roles and sexual behavior* (pp. 226–244). Palo Alto, CA: Mayfield.

Peplau, L. A., & Cochran, S. D. (1990). A relationship perspective on homosexuality. In D. P. McWhirter, S. A. Sanders, & J. M. Reinisch (Eds.), *Homosexuality/heterosexuality: The Kinsey scales and current research* (pp. 226–244). New York: Oxford University Press.

Peplau, L. A., & Conrad, E. (1989). Beyond nonsexist research: The perils of feminist methods in psychology. *Psychology of Women Quarterly, 13,* 379–400.

Peplau, L. A., & Garnets, L. D. (2000). A new paradigm for understanding women's sexuality and sexual orientation. *Journal of Social Issues, 56,* 329–350.

Peplau, L. A., & Spalding, L. R. (2000). The close relationships of lesbians, gay men, and bisexuals. In C. Hendrick & S. S. Hendrick (Eds.), *Close relationships: A sourcebook* (pp. 111–124). Thousand Oaks, CA: Sage.

Peplau, L. A., & Gordon, S. L. (1985). Women and men in love: Gender differences in close heterosexual relationships. In V. E. O'Leary, R. K. Unger, & B. S. Wallston (Eds.), *Women, gender, and social psychology* (pp. 257–292). Hillsdale, NJ: Erlbaum.

Perkins, K. E. (1992). Psychosocial implications of women and retirement. *Social Work, 37,* 526–532.

Perlmutter, E., & Bart, P. B. (1982). Changing news of "The Change": A critical review and suggestions for an attributional approach. In A. M. Voda, M. Dinnerstein, & S. R. O'Donnell (Eds.), *Changing perspectives on menopause* (pp. 185–199). Austin: University of Texas Press.

Perrone, K. M., Zanardelli, G., Worthington, E. L., & Chartrand, J. M. (2002). Role model influences on the career decidedness of college students. *College Student Journal, 36,* 109–112.

Perry, D. G., Perry, L. C., & Weiss, R. J. (1989). Sex differences in the consequences that children anticipate for aggression. *Developmental Psychology, 25,* 312–319.

Perry, [illegible] ([illegible]). Animated gerontophobia: Ageism, sexism, and the Disney Villainess. In S. M. Deats & L. T. Lender (Eds.), *Aging and identity: A humanities perspective.* Westport, CT: Praeger.

Perun, P. J., & Bielby, D. D. (1981). Towards a model of female occupational behavior: A human development approach. *Psychology of Women Quarterly, 6,* 234–252.

Peters, D. K., & Cantrell, P. J. (1993). Gender roles and role conflict in feminist lesbian and heterosexual women. *Sex Roles, 28,* 379–392.

Petersen, A. C. (1983). Menarche: Meaning of measures and measuring meaning. In S. Golub (Ed.), *Menarche: The transition from girl to woman* (pp. 63–76). Lexington, MA: Lexington Books.

Petersen, A. C. (1987). The nature of biological-psychosocial interactions: The sample case of early adolescence. In R. M. Lerner & T. T. Foch (Eds.), *Biological-psychosocial interactions in early adolescence* (pp. 35–61). Hillsdale, NJ: Erlbaum.

Peterson, C. C. (1999). Grandfathers' and grandmothers' satisfaction with the grandparenting role: Seeking new answers to old questions. *International Journal of Aging & Human Development, 49,* 61–78.

Peterson, E. (1974). Consumer specialist. In R. B. Kundsin (Ed.), *Women and success: The anatomy of achievement* (pp. 78–80). New York: William Morrow.

Peterson, R. F., Basta, S. M., & Dykstra, T. A. (1993). Mothers of molested children: Some comparisons of personality characteristics. *Child Abuse and Neglect, 17,* 409–418.

Peterson, R. E., Imperato-McGinley, J., Gautier, T., & Sturla, E. (1977). Male pseudohermaphrodism due to steroid 5 alpha-reductase deficiency. *American Journal of Medicine, 62,* 170–191.

Petrie, T. A., Austin, L. J., Crowley, B. J., Helmcamp, A., Johnson, C. E., Lester, R., Rogers, R., Turner, J., & Walbrick, K. (1996). Sociocultural expectations of attractiveness in males. *Sex Roles, 35,* 581–602.

Phares, V., & Compas, B. E. (1993). Fathers and developmental psychotherapy. *Current Directions in Psychological Science, 2,* 162.

Phelps, G. C., Andrea, R., Rizzo, F. G., Johnston, L., & Main, C. M. (1993). Prevalence of self-induced vomiting and laxative/medication abuse among female adolescents: A longitudinal study. *International Journal of Eating Disorders, 14,* 375–378.

Phillips, L. (1998). *The girls report: What we know & need to know about growing up female.* New York: National Council for Research on [illegible]

Phillips, R. D., & Gilroy, F. D. (1985). Sex-role stereotypes and clinical judgments of mental health: The Brovermans' findings reexamined. *Sex Roles, 12,* 179–193.

Phillips, S. D., & Imhoff, A. R. (1997). Women and career development: A decade of research. *Annual Review of Psychology, 48,* 31–59.

Phoenix, A., Woollett, A., & Lloyd, E. (Eds.). (1991). *Motherhood: Meanings, practices, and ideologies.* London: Sage.

Phornphutkul, C., Fausto-Sterling, A., & Gruppuso, P. A., 2000. Gender self assignment in an XY adolescent female born with ambiguous genitalia. *Pediatrics, 106,* 135–137.

Pike, K. M. (1995). Bulimic symptomology in high school girls: Toward a model of cumulative risk. *Psychology of Women Quarterly, 19,* 373–396.

Pike, K. M., & Striegel-Moore, R. H. (1997). Disordered eating and eating disorders. In S. J. Gallant, G. P. Keita, & R. Royak-Schaler (Eds.), *Health care for women: Psychological, social, and behavioral influence* (pp. 97–114). Washington, DC: American Psychological Association.

Piliavin, J. A., & Unger, R. K. (1985). The helpful but helpless female: Myth or reality? In

V. E. O'Leary, R. K. Unger, & B. S. Wallston (Eds.), *Women, gender, and social psychology* (pp. 149–190). Hillsdale, NY: Erlbaum.

Pipher, M. (1994). *Reviving Ophelia: Saving the selves of adolescent girls.* NY: G. P. Putnam's Sons.

Pipher, M. (1999). *Another country: Navigating the emotional terrain of our elders.* New York: Riverhead Books.

Piran, N. (2001). Re-inhabiting the body from the inside-out: Girls transform their school environment. In D. Tolman & M. Brydon-Miller (Eds.). *From subjects to subjectivities: A handbook of interpretive and participatory methods* (pp. 218–238). NY: New York University Press.

Piran, N. (2001). Eating disorders and disordered eating. In J. Worell (Ed.), *Encyclopedia of sex and gender* (pp. 369–378). NY: Academic Press.

Pitts, V. L., & Schwartz, M. D. (1997). Self-blame in hidden rape cases. In M. D. Schwartz (Ed.), *Researching sexual violence against women: Methodological and personal perspectives* (pp. 65–70). Thousand Oaks, CA: Sage.

Plant, E. A., Hyde, J. S., Keltner, D., & Devine, P. G. (2000). The gender stereotyping of emotions. *Psychology of Women Quarterly, 24,* 81–92.

Platte, P., Zelten, J. F., & Strunkard, A. J.(2000). Body image in Old Order Amish: A people separate from "the world." *International Journal of Eating Disorders, 28,* 408–414.

Pleck, J. H., Sonenstein, F. L., & Ku, L. C. (1994). Attitudes toward male roles among adolescent males: A discriminant validity analysis. *Sex Roles, 30,* 481–501.

Plous, S., & Neptune, D. (1997). Racial and gender biases in magazine advertising: A content analysis study. *Psychology of Women Quarterly, 21,* 627–644.

Polakow, V. (1993). *Lives on the edge: Single mothers and their children in the other America.* Chicago: University of Chicago Press.

Police say woman, 21, is killed by ex-husband. (1998, July 26). *The New York Times,* p. 1.

Pollitt, K. (1998). "Fetal rights": A new assault on feminism. In R. Weitz (Ed.), *The politics of women's bodies: Sexuality, appearance, and behavior* (pp. 278–287). New York: Oxford University Press.

Pomerantz, E. M., & Ruble, D. N. (1998). The role of maternal control in the development of sex differences in child self-evaluative factors. *Child Development, 69,* 458–478.

Pomerleau, A., Bloduc, D., Malcuit, G., & Cossette, L. (1990). Pink or blue: Environmental gender stereotypes in the first two years of life. *Sex Roles, 22,* 359–367.

Pomerleau, C. S., Zucker, A. N., & Stewart, A. J. (2001). Characterizing concerns about post-cessation weight gain: Results from a national survey of women smokers. *Nicotine and Tobacco Research, 3,* 51–60.

Ponse, B. (1978). *Identities in the lesbian world.* Westport, CT: Greenwood Press.

Pooler, W. S. (1991). Sex of child preferences among college students. *Sex Roles, 25,* 569–576.

Pope, K. (1994). *Sexual involvement with therapists: Patient assessment, subsequent treatment, forensics.* Washington, DC: American Psychological Association.

Pope, K. (2001). Sex between therapist and client. In J. Worell (Ed.), *Encyclopedia of sex and gender* (pp. 955–962). NY: Academic Press.

Popenoe, D. (1987). Beyond the nuclear family: A statistical portrait of the changing family in Sweden. *Journal of Marriage and the Family, 49,* 173–183.

Popenoe, D., & Whitehead, B. D. (1999). *The state of our unions: The social health of marriage in America.* New Brunswick, NJ: National Marriage Project of Rutgers University.

Porter, N., Geis, F. L., Cooper, E., & Newman, E. (1985). Androgyny and leadership in mixed sex groups. *Journal of Personality and Social Psychology, 49,* 808–823.

Poulin-Dubois, D., Serbin, L. A., & Derbyshire, A. (1998). Toddlers' intermodal and verbal knowledge about gender. *Merrill-Palmer Quarterly, 44,* 338–354.

Poulin-Dubois, D., Serbin, L. A., Eichstedt, J. A., Sen, M. G., & Beissel, C. F. (2002). Men don't put on make-up. Toddlers' knowledge of the gender stereotyping of household activities. *Social Development, 11,* 166–181.

Poulin-Dubois, D., Serbin, L. A., Kenyon, R., & Derbyshire, A. (1994). Infants' intermodal knowledge about gender. *Developmental Psychology, 30,* 436–442.

Pour-El, M. B. (1974). Mathematician. In R. B. Kundsin (Ed.), *Women and success: The anatomy of achievement* (pp. 36–37). New York: William Morrow.

Powell, A. D., & Kahn, A. S. (1995). Racial differences in women's desire to be thin. *International Journal of Eating Disorders, 17,* 191–195.

Powell, G. N., Butterfield, D. A., & Parent, J. D. (2002). Gender and managerial stereotypes: Have the times changed? *Journal of Management, 28,* 177–193.

Power, T. (1981). Sex typing in infancy: The role of the father. *Infant Mental Health Journal, 2,* 226–240.

Powlishta, K. K. (1995a). Gender bias in children's perception of personality traits. *Sex Role, 32,* 17–28.

Powlishta, K. K. (1995b). Intergroup processes in childhood: Social categorization and sex role development. *Developmental Psychology, 31,* 781–788.

Powlishta, K. K., Sen, M. G., Serbin, L. A., Poulin-Dubois, D., & Eichstedt, J. A. (2001). From infancy through middle childhood: The role of cognitive and social factors in becoming gendered. In R. K. Unger (Ed.), *Handbook of the Psychology of Women and Gender* (pp. 116–132). NY: Wiley.

Powlishta, K. K., Serbin, L. A., & Moller, L. C. (1993). The stability of individual differences in gender typing: Implications for understanding gender segregation. *Sex Roles, 29,* 723–737.

Press "1" if you're steamed. (2002, July 7). *The New York Times,* p. 8.

Price, S. J., & McKenry, P. C. (1988). *Divorce.* Beverly Hills, CA: Sage.

Prilleltensky, O. (1996). Women with disabilities and feminist therapy. *Women & Therapy, 18,* 87–97.

Pryor, J. B. (1987). Sexual harassment proclivities in men. *Sex Roles, 17,* 269–290.

Pryor, J. B., Giedd, J. L., & Williams, K. B. (1995). A social psychological model for predicting sexual harassment. *Journal of Social Issues, 51,* 69–84.

Pryor, J. B., La Vite, C., & Stoller, L. (1993). A social psychological analysis of sexual harassment: The person/situation interaction. *Journal of Vocational Behavior, 20,* 163–169.

Public Interest Directorate of the American Psychological Association. (1987). Follow-up report to oral presentation of December 2, 1987. Psychological sequelae of abortion.

Pugh, M. D., & Wahrman, R. (1983). Neutralizing sexism in mixed-sex groups: Do women have to be better than men? *American Journal of Sociology, 88,* 746–762.

Purcell, P., & Stewart, L. (1990). Dick and Jane in 1989. *Sex Roles, 22,* 177–185.

Purdy, L. M. (1992). Another look at contract pregnancy. In H. B. Holmes (Ed.), *Issues in reproductive technology* (pp. 303–320). New York: Garland.

Puri, J. (1997). Reading romance novels in postcolonial India. *Gender & Society, 11*(4), 434–452.

Pushkar-Gold, D., Franz, E., Reis, M., & Senneville, C. (1994). The influence of emotional awareness and expressiveness on caregiving burden and health complaints in women and men. *Sex Roles, 31,* 205–224.

Quadagno, J. (1999). *Aging and the life course.* Boston: McGraw Hill.

Quinn, D. M., & Spencer, S. J. (2001). The interference of stereotype threat with women's generation of math problem-solving strategies. *Journal of Social Issues, 57* (1), 55–72.

Quirouette, C. C., & Pushkar, D. (1999). Views of future aging among middle-aged, university-educated women. *Canadian Journal of Aging, 18,* 236–258.

Raag, T. (1999). Influences of social expectations of gender, gender stereotypes, and situational constraints on children's toy choices. *Sex Roles, 41,* 809–831.

Raag, T., & Rackliff, C. L. (1998). Preschoolers' awareness of social expectations of gender relationships to toy choices. *Sex Roles, 38,* 685–700.

Radlove, S. (1983). Sexual response and gender roles. In E. R. Allgeier & N. B. McCormick (Eds.), *Changing boundaries: Gender roles and sexual behavior* (pp. 87–105). Palo Alto, CA: Mayfield.

Radway, J. A. (1984). *Reading the romance: Women, patriarchy, and popular literature.* Chapel Hill, NC: University of North Carolina Press.

Raffaelli, M., & Ontai, L. L. (2001). 'She's 16 years old and there's boys calling over to the house': An exploratory study of sexual socialization in Latino families. *Culture, Health and Sexuality, 3,* 295–310.

Ragsdale, J. D. (1996). Gender, satisfaction level and the use of relational maintenance strategies in marriage. *Communication Monographs, 63*(4), 354–369.

Raja, S. (1998). Culturally sensitive therapy for women of color. *Women and Therapy, 21,* 67–84.

Ralston, P. A. (1997). Midlife and older black women. In J. M. Coyle (Ed.), *Handbook on women and aging* (pp. 273–289). Westport, CT: Greenwood Press.

Ramirez-Valles, J., Zimmerman, M. A., & Juarez, L. (2002). Gender differences of neighborhood and social control processes: A study of the timing of first intercourse among low-achieving, urban, African American youth. *Youth and Society, 33,* 418–441.

Ramos-McKay, J., Comas-Diaz, L., & Rivera, L. (1988). Puerto Ricans. In L. Comas-Diaz &

E. E. H. Griffith (Eds.), *Clinical guidelines in cross-cultural mental health* (pp. 204–232). New York: Wiley.

Randolph, S. M. (1995). African American children in single-mother families. In B. J. Dickerson (Ed.), *African American single mothers* (pp. 117–145). Thousand Oaks: Sage.

Ray, D. C., McKinney, K. A., & Ford, C. V. (1987). Ageism in psychiatrists: Associations with gender, certification, and theoretical orientation. *The Gerontologist, 27,* 82–86.

Raymond, J. G. (1993). *Women as wombs: Reproductive technologies and the battle over women's freedom.* New York: HarperCollins.

Reame, N. K. (2001). Menstruation. In J. Worell (Ed.). *Encyclopedia of women and gender* (pp. 739–742). San Diego, CA: Academic Press.

Reddin, J. (1997). High-achieving women: Career development patterns. In H. S. Farmer (Ed.), *Diversity & women's career development: From adolescence to adulthood* (pp. 95–126). Thousand Oaks, CA: Sage.

Reese, E., Haden, C. A., & Fivush, R. (1993). Mother-child conversations about the past: Relationship of style and memory over time. *Cognitive Development, 8,* 403–430.

Reevy, G. M., & Maslach, C. (2001). Use of social support: Gender and personality differences. *Sex Roles, 44,* 437–459.

Regan, P. C. (1996). Sexual outcasts: The perceived impact of body weight and gender on sexuality. *Journal of Applied Social Psychology, 26*(20), 1803–1815.

Regan, P. C., Levin, L., Sprecher, S., Christopher, F. S., & Cate, R. (2000). Partner preferences: What characteristics do men and women desire in their short-term sexual and long-term romantic partners? *Journal of Psychology and Human Sexuality, 12,* 1–21.

Regan, P. C., Medina, R., & Joshi, A. (2001). Partner preferences among homosexual men and women: What is desirable in a sex partner is not necessarily desirable in a romantic partner. *Social Behavior and Personality, 29,* 625–633.

Reid, P. T. (1993). Poor women in psychological research: Shut up and shut out. *Psychology of Women Quarterly, 17,* 133–150.

Reid, P. T., & Kelly, E. (1994). Research on women of color: From ignorance to awareness. *Psychology of Women Quarterly, 18,* 477–486.

Reid, P. T., Tate, C. C., & Berman, P. W. (1989). Preschool children's self-presentations in situations with infants: Effects of sex and race. *Child Development, 60,* 710–714.

Reid, P. T., & Trotter, K. H. (1993). Children's self-presentations with infants: Gender and ethnic comparisons. *Sex Roles, 29,* 171–181.

Reineke, M. J. (1989). *Out of order: A critical perspective on women in religion.* In J. Freedman (Ed.), Women: A feminist perspective (4th ed., pp. 395–414). Mountain View, CA: Mayfield.

Reiner, W. G., Gearhart, J. P., & Jeffs, R. (1999). Psychosexual dysfunction in males with genital anomalies: Late adolescence, Tanner stages IV to VI. *Journal of the American Academy of Child and Adolescent Psychiatry, 38,* 865–872.

Reinharz, S. (1997). Friends or foes? Gerontological and feminist theory. In M. Pearsall (Ed.). *The other within: Feminist explorations of aging.* Boulder, Co.: Westview Press.

Renzetti, C. M. (1987). New Wave or second stage? Attitudes of college women toward feminism. *Sex Roles, 16,* 265–277.

Renzetti, C. M. (1997). Violence in lesbian and gay relationships. In L. O'Toole, & J. R. Schiffman (Eds.), *Gender violence: Interdisciplinary perspectives* (pp. 285–293). New York: New York University Press.

Reuterman, N. A., & Burcky, W. D. (1989). Dating violence in high school: A profile of the victims. *Psychology: A Journal of Human Behavior, 26,* 1–9.

Rheingold, H. L., & Cook, K. V. (1975). The contents of boys' and girls' rooms as an index of parents' behavior. *Child Development, 46,* 459–463.

Rhoades, J. M. (1989). Social support and the transition to the maternal role. In P. N. Stern (Ed.), *Pregnancy and parenting* (pp. 131–142). New York: Hemisphere.

Rhodes, G., Harwood, K., Yoshikawa, S., Nishitani, M., & McLean, I. (2002). The attractiveness of average faces: Cross-cultural evolution and possible biological basis. In G. Rhodes & L. A. Zebrowitz (Eds.), *Facial attractiveness: Evolutionary, cognitive, and social perspectives* (pp. 35–58). Westport, CT: Ablex Publishing.

Rice, F. P. (1984). *The adolescent: Development, relations, and culture.* Boston: Allyn & Bacon.

Rice, J. (1994). Reconsidering research on divorce, family life cycle, and the meaning of family. *Psychology of Women Quarterly, 18,* 559–584.

Rich, A. (1976). *Of woman born: Motherhood as experience and institution.* New York: Norton.

Rich, A. (1980). Compulsory heterosexuality and lesbian existence. *Signs, 5,* 631–660.

Rich, M. K., & Cash, T. F. (1993). The American image of beauty: Media representations of hair color for four decades. *Sex Roles, 29,* 113–124.

Richeson, J. A. & Ambady, N. (2001). Who's in charge: Effects of situational roles on automatic gender bias. *Sex Roles, 44,* 493–512.

Richman, E. L., & Shaffer, D. R. (2000). "If you let me play sports": How might sports participation influence the self-esteem of adolescent females. *Psychology of Women Quarterly, 24,* 189–199.

Ridgeway, C. L., & Erickson, K. G. (2000). Creating and spreading status beliefs. *American Journal of Sociology, 106,* 579–615.

Rieves, L., & Cash, T. F. (1996). Social developmental factors and women's body-image attitudes. *Journal of Social Behavior and Personality, 11,* 63–78.

Rigby, D. N., & Sophie, J. (1990). Ethical issues and client sexual preference. In H. Lerman & N. Porter (Eds.), *Feminist ethics in psychotherapy* (pp. 165–175). New York: Springer.

Riggs, D. (1993). Relationship problems and dating aggression. *Journal of Interpersonal Violence, 8,* 18–35.

Riggs, D. S., & Caulfield, M. B. (1997). Expected consequences of male violence against their female dating partners. *Journal of Interpersonal Violence, 12,* 229–240.

Riggs, D. S., & O'Leary, K. D. (1989). A theoretical model of courtship aggression. In M. Pirog-Good & J. E. Stets (Eds.), *Violence in dating relationships* (pp. 53–71). New York: Praeger.

Riggs, D. S., & O'Leary, K. D. (1996). Aggression between dating partners: An examination of a causal model of courtship aggression. *Journal of Interpersonal Violence, 11,* 519–540.

Riley, S. (2001). Maintaining power: Male constructions of "feminists" and "feminist values." *Feminism & Psychology, 11,* 55–78.

Rind, B., & Tromovitch, P. (1997). A meta-analytic review of findings from national samples on psychological correlates of child sexual abuse. *Journal of Sex Research, 34,* 237–255.

Rintala, D. H., Howland, C. A., Nosek, M. A., Bennett, J. L., Young, M. E., Foley, C. C., Rossi, C. D., & Chanpong, G. (1997). Dating issues for women with physical disabilities. *Sexuality and Disability, 15*(4), 219–242.

Risman, B. J. (1998). *Gender vertigo.* New Haven: Yale University.

Risman, B. J., & Johnson-Sumerford, D. (1998). Doing it fairly: A study of postgender marriages. *Journal of Marriage and the Family, 60,* 23–40.

Rivers, C. (2000). Mockery of Katherine Harris show double standard. *www.Womensenews.com.* November 29.

Roberts, D. E. (1998). The future of reproductive choice for poor women and women of color. In R. Weitz (Ed.), *The politics of women's bodies: Sexuality, appearance, and behavior* (pp. 270–277). New York: Oxford University Press.

Roberts, T. A., Goldenberg, J. L., Power, C., & Pyszczysnski, T. (2002). "Feminine protection": The effects of menstruation on attitudes toward women. *Psychology of Women Quarterly, 26,* 131–139.

Robin, R. W., Chester, B., Rasmussen, J. K., Jaranson, J. M., Goldman, D. (1997). Prevalence and characteristics of trauma and posttraumatic stress disorder in a southwestern American Indian community. *American Journal of Psychiatry, 154,* 1582–1588.

Robinson, C. C., & Morris, J. T. (1986). The gender-stereotyped nature of Christmas toys received by 36-, 48-, and 60-month-old children: A comparison between nonrequested and requested toys. *Sex Roles, 15,* 21–32.

Robinson, D. T., & Smith-Lovin, L. (2001). Getting a laugh: Gender, status, and humor in task discussions. *Social Forces, 80,* 123–158.

Robinson, J. P., & Milkie, M. A. (1998). Back to the basics: Trends in and role determinants of women's attitudes toward housework. *Journal of Marriage and the Family, 60*(1), 205–218.

Rodeheaver, D. (1990). Labor market progeria. *Generations, 14,* 53–58.

Rodin, J., Silverstein, L. R., Striegel-Moore, R. H. (1984). Women and weight: A normative discontent. In T. B. Sonderegger (Ed.), *Psychology and gender: Nebraska Symposium on Motivation, 1984* (pp. 267–307). Lincoln: University of Nebraska Press.

Rodriguez, C. (1998, November 27). Even in middle school, girls are thinking thin. *The Boston Globe,* pp. B1, B9.

Roff, L. L., & Klemmack, D. L. (1986). Norms for employed daughters' and sons' behavior toward frail older parents. *Sex Roles, 14,* 363–368.

Rohner, R. P., & Veneziano, R. A. (2001). The importance of father love: History and contemporary evidence. *Review of General Psychology, 5,* 382–405.

Romkens, R. (1997). Prevalence of wife abuse in the Netherlands. *Journal of Interpersonal Violence, 12,* 99–126.

Root, M. P. P. (1990). Disordered eating in women of color. *Sex Roles, 22,* 525–536.

Root, M. P. P. (1995). The psychology of Asian women. In H. Landrine (Ed.), *Bringing cultural diversity to feminist psychology: Theory, research, practice* (pp. 265–301). Washington, DC: American Psychological Association.

Rosario, M., Meyer-Bahlburg, H. F. L., Hunter, J., & Exner, T. M. (1996). The psychosexual development of urban lesbian, gay, and bisexual youths. *Journal of Sex Research, 33*(2), 113–126.

Roscoe, B., & Benaske, N. (1985). Courtship violence experienced by abused wives: Similarities in patterns of abuse. *Family Relations, 34,* 419–424.

Roscoe, B., & Kelsey, T. (1986). Dating violence among high school students. *Psychology, 23,* 53–59.

Roscoe, W. (1996). How to become a berdache: Toward a unified analysis of gender diversity. In G. Herdt (Ed.), *Third sex, third gender: Beyond sexual dimorphism in culture and history* (pp. 329–372). New York: Zone Books.

Rose, S., & Frieze, I. H. (1989). Young singles' scripts for a first date. *Gender & Society, 3,* 258–268.

Rose, S., & Zand, D. (2000). Lesbian dating and courtship from young adulthood to midlife. *Journal of Gay and Lesbian Social Services: Issues in Practice, Policy and Research, 11,* 77–104.

Rosell, M. C. & Hartman, S. L. (2001). Self-presentation of beliefs about gender discrimination and feminism. *Sex Roles, 44,* 647–659.

Rosenberg, J., Perlstadt, H., & Phillips, W. R. (1993). Now that we are here: Discrimination, disparagement, and harassment at work and the experience of women lawyers. *Gender & Society, 7,* 415–433.

Rosenberg, R. (1982). *Beyond separate spheres: Intellectual roots of modern feminism.* New Haven: Yale University Press.

Rosenblum, K. E., & Travis, T-M C. (1996). *The meaning of difference: American constructions of race, sex and gender, social class, and sexual orientation.* New York: McGraw-Hill.

Rosenbluth, S. (1997). Is sexual orientation a matter of choice? *Psychology of Women Quarterly, 21*(4), 595–610.

Rosenbluth, S. C., & Steil, J. M. (1995). Predictors of intimacy for women in heterosexual and homosexual couples. *Journal of Social and Personal Relationships, 12*(2), 163–175.

Rosenbluth, S. C., Steil, J. M., & Whitcomb, J. H. (1998). Marital equality: What does it mean? *Journal of Family Issues, 19,* 227–244.

Rosenfeld, M. (1995, December 25). Toys aimed at girls focus on boys. *The Dallas Morning News,* pp. 45A–46A.

Rosenthal, N. B. (1984). Consciousness raising: From revolution to reevaluation. *Psychology of Women Quarterly, 8,* 309–326.

Rosenwasser, S. M., & Patterson, W. (1984–1985). Nontraditional males: Men with primary childcare/household responsibilities. *Psychology and Human Development, 1,* 101–111.

Ross, C. E. (2000). Neighborhood disadvantage and adult depression. *Journal of Health and Social Behavior, 41,* 177–187.

Ross, L., Anderson, D. R., & Wisocki, P. A. (1982). Television viewing and adult sex-role attitudes. *Sex Roles, 8,* 589–592.

Rosser, P. (1992). *The SAT gender gap: ETS responds: A research update.* Washington, DC: Center for Women Policy Studies.

Rosser, P., with the staff of the National Center for Fair and Open Testing (1987). *Sex bias in college admissions tests: Why women lose out* (2nd ed.). Cambridge, MA: National Center for Fair and Open Testing.

Rostosky, S. S., & Travis, C. B. (1996). Menopausal research and the dominance of the biomedical model, 1984–1994. *Psychology of Women Quarterly, 20,* 285–312.

Roter, D. L., & Hall, J. A. (1997). Gender differences in patient-physician communication. In S. J. Gallant, G. P. Keita, & R. Royak-Schaler (Eds.), *Health care for women: Psychological, social, and behavioral influences* (pp. 57–71). Washington, DC: American Psychological Association.

Roth, S., & Lebowitz, L. (1988). The experience of sexual trauma. *Journal of Traumatic Stress, 1,* 79–107.

Roth, S., Wayland, K., & Woolsey, M. (1990). Victimization history and victim-assailant relationship as factors in recovery from sexual assault. *Journal of Traumatic Stress, 3,* 169–180.

Rothblum, E. D. (1983). Sex-role stereotypes and depression in women. In V. Franks & E. D. Rothblum (Eds.), *The stereotyping of women: Its effects on mental health* (pp. 83–111). New York: Springer.

Rothblum, E. D. (2000). Sexual orientation and sex in women's lives: Conceptual and methodological issues. *Journal of Social Issues, 56,* 193–204.

Rothman, B. K. (1988). *The tentative pregnancy: Prenatal diagnosis and the future of motherhood.* London: Unwin Hyman.

Rouselle, R. (2001). "If it is a girl, cast it out:" Infanticide/exposure in ancient Greece. *Journal of Psychohistory, 28,* 303–333.

Rousso, H. (1988). Daughters with disabilities: Defective women or minority women? In M. Fine & A. Asch (Eds.), *Women with disabilities: Essays in psychology, culture, and politics* (pp. 139–171). Philadelphia: Temple University Press.

Rozin, P., Haidt, J., McCaulay, C., Dunlop, L., & Ashmore, A. (1999). Individual differences in disgust sensitivity: Comparisons and evaluations of paper-and-pencil and behavioral measures. *Journal of Research in Personality, 33,* 330–351.

Rubin, G. (1984). Thinking sex: Notes for a radical theory of the politics of sexuality. In C. S. Vance (Ed.), *Pleasure and danger: Exploring female sexuality* (pp. 267–319). Boston: Routledge & Kegan Paul.

Rubin, R. M. (1997). The economic status of older women. In J. M. Coyle (Ed.), *Handbook on women and aging* (pp. 75–92). Westport, CT: Greenwood Press.

Rubin, R. T., Reinisch, J. M., & Haskett, R. F. (1981). Postnatal gonadal steroid effects on human behavior. *Science, 211,* 1318–1324.

Ruble, D. N., Fleming, A. S., Hackel, L. S., & Stangor, C. (1988). Changes in the marital relationship during the transition to first time motherhood: Effects of violated expectations concerning division of household labor. *Journal of Personality and Social Psychology, 85,* 78–87.

Ruddick, S., & Daniels, P. (Eds.). (1977). *Working it out.* New York: Pantheon Books.

Rudman, L. A. (1998). Self-promotion as a risk factor for women: The costs and benefits of counterstereotypical impression management. *Journal of Personality and Social Psychology, 74,* 629–645.

Rudman, L. A., & Borgida, E. (1995). The afterglow of construct accessibility: The behavioral consequences of priming men to view women as sexual objects. *Journal of Experimental Social Psychology, 31,* 493–517.

Rudman, L. A., & Glick, P. (1999). Geminized management and backlash against agentic women: The hidden costs to women of a kinder, gentler image of middle managers. *Journal of Personality and Social Psychology, 77,* 1004–1010.

Rudman, L. A., & Kilianski, S. K. (2000). Implicit and explicit attitudes toward female authority. *Personality & Social Psychology Bulletin, 26,* 1315–1328.

Rudolfsdottir, A. (2000). 'I am not a patient, and I am not a child': The institutionalization and experience of pregnancy. *Feminism and Psychology, 10,* 337–350.

Russell, M., Lipov, E., Phillips, N., & White, B. (1989, Spring). Psychological profiles of violent and nonviolent maritally distressed couples. *Psychotherapy, 26,* 81–87.

Russett, C. E. (1989). *Sexual science: The Victorian construction of womanhood.* Cambridge, MA: Harvard University Press.

Russo, N. F. (1979). Overview: Sex roles, fertility, and the motherhood mandate. *Psychology of Women Quarterly, 4,* 7–15.

Russo, N. F. (1985). *A women's mental health agenda.* Washington, DC: American Psychological Association.

Russo, N. F. (2000). Understanding emotional responses after abortion. In J. C. Chrisler, C. Golden, & P. D. Rozee (Eds.), *Lectures on the psychology of women* (pp. 113–128). Boston, MA: McGraw-Hill.

Russo, N. F., & Denmark, F. L. (1984). Women, psychology, and public policy: Selected issues. *American Psychologist, 39,* 1161–1165.

Russo, N. F., & Dumont, B. A. (1997). A history of Division 35 (Psychology of Women): Origins, issues, activities, future. In D. A. Dewsbury (Ed.), *Unification through division: Histories of the divisions of the American Psychological Association,* Vol. 2. Washington, DC: American Psychological Association.

Rust, P. C. (1993). Neutralizing the political threat of the marginal woman: Lesbians' beliefs about bisexual women. *Journal of Sex Research, 30,* 214–228.

Rust, P. C. (2000). Bisexuality: A contemporary paradox for women. *Journal of Social Issues, 56,* 205–222.

Ruth, S. (1990). *Issues in feminism.* Mountain View, CA: Mayfield.

Ryan, K. M. (1995). Do courtship-violent men have characteristics associated with a "battering personality"? *Journal of Family Violence, 10,* 99–120.

Sadker, M., & Sadker, D. (1994). *Failing at fairness: How America's schools cheat girls.* New York: Scribner.

Sagas, M., Cunningham, G. B., Wiglety, B. J., & Ashley, F. B. (2000). Internet coverage of university softball and baseball websites: The inequity continues. *Society of Sports Journal, 17,* 198–212.

Sakalli, N. (2002). Application of the attribution-value model of prejudice to homosexuality. *Journal of Social Psychology, 142,* 264–271.

Sampselle, C. M., Harris, V., Harlow, S. D., & Sowers, M. (2002). Midlife development and menopause in African American and Caucasian women. *Health Care for Women International, 23,* 351–363.

Sanchez, L., & Thomson, E. (1997). Becoming mothers and fathers: Parenthood, gender, and the division of labor. *Gender & Society, 11*(6), 747–772.

Sanders, G. S., & Schmidt, T. (1980). Behavioral discrimination against women. *Personality and Social Psychology Bulletin, 6,* 484–488.

Sandnabba, N. K., & Ahlberg, C. (1999). Parents' attitudes and expectations about children's cross-gender behavior. *Sex Roles, 40,* 249–263.

Sands, R. G. (1998). Gender and the perception of diversity and intimidation among university students. *Sex Roles, 39,* 801–815.

Sang, B. (1991). Moving toward balance and integration. In B. Sang, J. Warshow, & A. Smith (Eds.), *Lesbians at midlife: The creative transition* (pp. 206–214). San Francisco: Spinsters.

Sapiro, V. (1994). *Women in American society: An introduction to women's studies* (3rd ed.). Mountain View, CA: Mayfield.

Sapp, S. G., Harrod, W. J., & Zhao, L. (1996). Leadership emergence in task groups with egalitarian gender role expectations. *Sex Roles, 34,* 65–80.

Sappington, A. A., Pharr, R., Tunstall, A., & Rickert, E. (1997). Relationships among child abuse, date abuse, and psychological problems. *Journal of Clinical Psychology, 53,* 319–329.

Sarantakos, S. (1991). Cohabitation revisited: Paths of change among cohabiting and noncohabiting couples. *Australian Journal of Marriage and Family, 12,* 144–155.

Sargent, J. D., & Blanchflower, D. G. (1994). Obesity and stature in adolescence and earnings in young adulthood. *Annals of Pediatric Adolescent Medicine, 148,* 681–687.

Satterfield, A. T., & Muehlenhard, C. L. (1997). Shaken confidence: The effects of an authority figure's flirtativeness on women's and men's self-rated creativity. *Psychology of Women Quarterly, 21,* 395–416.

Saunders, D. (2001, November 23). Guns and abayas. *www.Townhall.com.*

Sawyer, R. G., Pinciaro, P. J., Jessell, J. K. (1998). Effects of coercion and verbal consent on university students' perception of date rape. *American Journal of Health Behavior, 22,* 46–53.

Sayers, J. (1997). Adolescent bodies: Boy crazy memories and dreams. In J. M. Ussher (Ed.), *Body talk* (pp. 85–105). London: Routledge.

Scanzoni, L., & Scanzoni, J. (1976). *Men, women, and change: A sociology of marriage and the family.* New York: McGraw-Hill.

Scarborough, E., & Furumoto, L. (1987). *Untold lives: The first generation of American women psychologists.* New York: Columbia University Press.

Scarr, S. (1998). American child care today. *American Psychologist, 53*(2), 95–108.

Scarr, S., Phillips, D., & McCartney, K. (1990). Facts, fantasies and the future of child care in the United States. *Psychological Science, 1,* 26–35.

Schafer, A. T., & Gray, M. W. (1981). Sex and mathematics. *Science, 211,* 231.

Schemo, D. J. (1996, October 18). Among glossy blondes, a showcase for Brazil's black faces. *The New York Times,* p. A13.

Schlesinger, B. (1982). Lasting marriages in the 1980's. *Conciliation Courts Review, 20,* 43–49.

Schlossberg, N. K. (1984). The midlife woman as student. In G. Baruch & J. Brooks-Gunn (Eds.), *Women in midlife* (pp. 315–339). New York: Plenum Press.

Schmader, T. (2002). Gender identification moderates stereotype threat effects on women's math performance. *Journal of Experimental Social Psychology, 38,* 194–201.

Schmitt, M. T., Branscombe, N. R., Kobrynowicz, D., & Owen, S. (2002). Perceiving discrimination against one's gender group has different implication for well-being in women and men. *Personality & Social Psychology Bulletin, 28,* 197–210.

Schneider, K. T., Swan, S., & Fitzgerald, L. F. (1997). Job-related and psychological effects of sexual harassment in the workplace: Empirical evidence from two organizations. *Journal of Applied Psychology, 82,* 401–415.

Schneider, M. S. (1986). The relationships of cohabiting lesbian and heterosexual couples: A comparison. *Psychology of Women Quarterly, 10,* 234–239.

Schnitzer, P. K. (1996). "THEY DON'T COME IN!" Stories told, lessons taught about poor families in therapy. *American Journal of Orthopsychiatry, 66,* 572–582.

Schoen, R., & Wooldredge, J. (1989). Marriage choices in North Carolina and Virginia, 1969–71 and 1979–81. *Journal of Marriage and Family, 51,* 465–481.

Schuler, S. R., Hashemi, S. M., Riley, A. P., & Akhter, S. (1996). Credit programs, patriarchy and men's violence against women in rural Bangladesh. *Social Science Medicine, 43,* 1729–1742.

Schulman, G. I., & Hoskins, M. (1986). Perceiving the male versus the female face. *Psychology of Women Quarterly, 10,* 141–154.

Schultz, M. R. (1975). The semantic derogation of women. In B. Thorne & N. Henley (Eds.), *Language and sex: Difference and dominance* (pp. 64–73). Rowley, MA: Newbury House.

Schwartz, I. (1993). Affective reactions of American and Swedish women to their first premarital coitus: A cross-cultural comparison. *Journal of Sex Research, 30,* 18–26.

Schwartz, M. D. (1989). Asking the right questions: Battered wives are not all passive. *Sociological Viewpoints, 5,* 46–61.

Schwartz, P. (1994). *Peer marriage.* New York: Free Press.

Seagoe, M. V. (1975). *Terman and the gifted.* Los Altos, CA: William Kaufmann.

Searles, P., & Berger, R. J. (1987). The current status of rape reform legislation: An examination of state statutes. *Women's Rights Law Reporter, 10,* 25–43.

Sears, D. O. (1986). College sophomores in the laboratory: Influences of a narrow data base on social psychology's view of human nature. *Journal of Personality and Social Psychology, 51,* 515–530.

Seccombe, K., & Ishu-Kuntz, M. (1991). Perceptions of problems associated with aging: Comparisons among four older age cohorts. *Gerontologist, 31,* 527–533.

Seig, E. (2000). 'So tell me what you want, what you really really want . . .': New women on old footings. *Feminism and Psychology, 10,* 498–503.

Sekaquaptewa, D., & Thompson, M. (2002). The differential effects of solo status on members of high- and low-status groups. *Personality & Social Psychology Bulletin, 28,* 694–707.

Selkow, P. (1984). *Assessing sex bias in testing: A review of the issues and evaluations of 74 psychological and educational tests.* Westport, CT: Greenwood.

Sen, A. (1990, December 20). More than one hundred million women are missing. *New York Review of Books.*

Serbin, L. A., Poulin-Dubois, D., Colburne, K. A., Sen, M. G., & Eichstedt, J. A. (2001). Gender stereotyping in infancy: Visual preferences for and knowledge of gender-stereotyped toys in the second year. *International Journal of Behavioral Development, 25,* 7–15.

Sered, S. (2000). *What makes women sick? Maternity, modesty, and militarism in Israeli society.* Hanover, NH: Brandeis University Press.

Shachar, S. A., & Gilbert, L. A. (1983). Working lesbians: Role conflicts and coping strategies. *Psychology of Women Quarterly, 7,* 244–256.

Shackelford, S., Wood, W., & Worchel, S. (1996). Behavioral styles and the influence of women in mixed-sex groups. *Social Psychology Quarterly, 59,* 284–293.

Shakin, M., Shakin, D., & Sternglanz, S. H. (1985). Infant clothing: Sex labeling for strangers. *Sex Roles, 12,* 955–963.

Shapiro, A. F., Gottman, J. M., & Carrere, S. (2000). The baby and the marriage: Identifying factors that buffer against decline in marital satisfaction after the first baby arrives. *Journal of Family Psychology, 14,* 59–70.

Sherif, C. W. (1979). Bias in psychology. In J. A. Sherman & E. T. Beck (Eds.), *The prisms of sex: Essays in the sociology of knowledge* (pp. 93–133). Madison: University of Wisconsin Press.

Sherif, C. W. (1983). Carolyn Wood Sherif (autobiography). In A. O'Connell & N. F. Russo (Eds.), *Models of achievement* (pp. 279–293). New York: Columbia University Press.

Sheriffs, A. C., & McKee, J. P. (1957). Qualitative aspects of beliefs about men and women. *Journal of Personality, 25,* 451–467.

Sherman, J. A., & Fennema, E. (1978). Distribution of spatial visualization and mathematical problem solving scores: A test of Stafford's X-linked hypothesis. *Psychology of Women Quarterly, 3,* 157–167.

Sherman, P. J., & Spence, J. T. (1997). A comparison of two cohorts of college students in responses to the male-female relations questionnaire. *Psychology of Women Quarterly, 21,* 265–278.

Shields, S. A. (1975). Functionalism, Darwinism, and the psychology of women: A study in social myth. *American Psychologist, 30,* 739–754.

Shields, S. A. (1982). The variability hypothesis: The history of a biological model of sex difference in intelligence. *Signs, 7,* 769–797.

Shields, S. A. (2002). *Speaking from the heart: Gender and the social meaning of emotion.* Cambridge, UK: Cambridge University Press.

Shields, S. A., Steinke, P., & Koster, B. A. (1995). The double bind of caregiving: Representation of gendered emotion in American advice literature. *Sex Roles, 33,* 467–488.

Shih, M., Pittinsky, T. L., & Ambady, N. (1999). Stereotype susceptibility: Identity salience and shifts in quantitative performance. *Psychological Science, 10,* 80–83.

Shipman, G. (1971). The psychodynamics of sex education. In R. E. Muuss (Ed.), *Adolescent behavior and society: A book of readings.* New York: Random House.

Shirley, L. J., & Campbell, A. (2000). Same-sex preference in infancy. *Psychology, Evolution, & Gender,* 2, 3–18.

Showalter, E. (1987). *The female malady: Women, madness, and English culture, 1830–1980.* New York: Pantheon Books.

Shuster, R. (1987). Sexuality as a continuum: The bisexual identity. In Boston Lesbian Psychologies Collective (Eds.), *Lesbian psychologies* (pp. 56–71). Urbana: University of Illinois Press.

Sidanius, J., & Pratto, F. (1999). *Social dominance: An intergroup theory of social herarchy and oppression.* New York: Cambridge University Press.

Siegel, J. (2001, June 28). Modest dress said to cause vitamin deficiency. *Jerusalem Post,* 5.

Siegel, R. J. (1993). Between midlife and old age: Never too old to learn. In N. D. Davis, E. Cole, & E. D. Rothblum (Eds.), *Faces of women and aging* (pp. 173–185). Binghamton, NY: Harrington Park Press.

Siever, M. D. (1994). Sexual orientation and gender as factors in socioculturally acquired vulnerability to body dissatisfaction and eating disorders. *Journal of Consulting and Clinical Psychology, 62,* 252–260.

Signorella, M. L., Bigler, R. S., & Liben, L. S. (1993). Developmental differences in children's gender-schemata about others: A meta-analytic review. *Developmental Review, 13,* 147–183.

Signorielli, N. (1989). Television and conceptions about sex roles: Maintaining conventionality and the status quo. *Sex Roles, 21,* 341–360.

Signorielli, N., & Lears, M. (1992). Children, television, and conceptions about chores: Attitudes and behaviors. *Sex Roles, 27,* 157–170.

Silverstein, L. B. (2002). Fathers and families. In J. P. McHale & W. S. Grolnick (Eds.), *Retrospect and prospect in the psychological study of families* (pp. 35–64). Mahwah, NJ: Lawrence Erlbaum Associates, Inc.

Silverstein, B., Perdue, L., Peterson, B., & Kelly, E. (1986). The role of the mass media in promoting a thin standard of bodily attractiveness for women. *Sex Roles, 14,* 519–532.

Silverstein, B., Peterson, B., & Perdue, L. (1986). Some correlates of the thin standard of bodily attractiveness for women. *International Journal of Eating Disorders, 5,* 895–905.

Silverstein, L. B. (1991). Transforming the debate about child care and maternal employment. *American Psychologist, 46,* 1025–1032.

Silverstein, L. B. (1996). Fathering is a feminist issue. *Psychology of Women Quarterly, 20,* 3–37.

Silverstein, L. B., & Auerbach, C. F. (1999). Deconstructing the essential father. *American Psychologist, 54,* 397–407.

Simes, M. R., & Berg, D. H. (2001). Surreptitious learning: Menarche and menstrual product advertising. *Health Care for Women International, 22,* 455–469.

Simmons, R. G., & Blyth, D. A. (1987). *Moving into adolescence: The impact of pubertal change and school context.* New York: Aldine De Gruyter.

Simmons, R. G., Burgeson, R., & Reef, M. J. (1988). In M. R. Gunnar & W. A. Collins (Eds.), *Development during the transition to adolescence* (pp. 123–150). Hillsdale, NJ: Erlbaum.

Simon, B. L. (1987). *Never-married women.* Philadelphia: Temple University Press.

Simon-Roper, L. (1996). Victim's response cycle: A model for understanding the incestuous victim-offender relationship. *Journal of Child Sexual Abuse, 5,* 59–79.

Simpson, G. (1996). Factors influencing the choice of law as a career by black women. *Journal of Career Development, 22*(3), 197–209.

Sims, M., Hutchins, T., & Taylor, M. (1998). Gender segregation in young children's conflict behavior in a child care setting. *Child Study Journal, 28,* 1–16.

Sinclair, A. H., Berta, P., Palmer, M. S., Hawkins, J. R., Griffiths, B. L., Smith, M. J., Foster, J. W., Frischauf, A. M., Lovell-Badge, R., & Goodfellow, P. N., 1990, A gene from the human sex-determining region encodes a protein with homology to a conserved DNA binding motif. *Nature, 346,* 240–244.

Sinclair, L., & Kunda, Z. (2000). Motivated stereotyping of women: She's fine if she praises me, but incompetent if she criticizes me. *Personality & Social Psychology Bulletin, 26,* 1329–1342.

Skrypnek, B. J., & Snyder, M. (1982). On the self-perpetuating nature of stereotypes about women and men. *Journal of Experimental Social Psychology, 18,* 277–291.

Slaby, R. G., & Guerra, N. G. (1988). Cognitive mediators of aggression in adolescent offenders: I. Assessment. *Developmental Psychology, 24,* 580–588.

Sleek, S. (1994, August). APA amicus brief affects outcome of Va. court case. *American Psychological Association Monitor,* 8.

Smith, B. (1943). *A tree grows in Brooklyn.* New York: Harper & Row.

Smith, E. A. (1989). A biosocial model of adolescent sexual behavior. In G. R. Adams, R. Montemayor, & T. P. Gullotta (Eds.), *Advances in adolescent development* (pp. 143–167). Newbury Park, CA: Sage.

Smith, M. (1997). Psychology's undervaluation of single motherhood. *Feminism & Psychology, 7*(4), 529–532.

Smith, M. D., & Morra, N. N. (1994). Obscene and threatening telephone calls to women: Data from a Canadian national survey. *Gender & Society, 8,* 584–596.

Smith, P. H., Smith, J. B., & Earp, J. A. (1999). Beyond the measurement trap: A reconstructed conceptualization and measurement of woman battering. *Psychology of Women Quarterly, 23,* 177–193.

Smith, P. K. (1987). Exploration, play and social development in boys and girls. In D. J. Hargreaves & A. M. Colley (Eds.), *The psychology of sex roles* (pp. 118–141). New York: Hemisphere.

Smith-Lovin, L., & Brody, C. (1989). Interruptions in group discussions: The effects of gender and group composition. *American Sociological Review, 54,* 425–435.

Smith-Rosenberg, C. (1975). The female world of love and ritual: Relations between women in nineteenth-century America. *Signs, 1,* 1–30.

Smith-Rosenberg, C. (1985). *Disorderly conduct: Visions of gender in Victorian America.* New York: Oxford University Press.

Smolak, L., & Munstertieger, B. F. (2002). The relationship of gender and voice to depression and eating disorders. *Psychology of Women Quarterly, 26,* 234–241.

Smolak, L., Murnen, S. K., & Ruble, A. E. (2000). Female athletes and eating problems: A meta-analysis. *International Journal of Eating Disorders, 27,* 371–389.

Smolak, L., & Striegel-Moore, R. (2001). Body image concerns. In J. Worell (Ed.), *Encyclopedia of sex and gender* (pp. 201–210). NY: Academic Press.

Snizek, W. E., & Neil, C. C. (1992). Job characteristics, gender stereotypes, and perceived gender discrimination in the workplace. *Organization Studies, 13,* 403–427.

Snow, J. T., & Harris, M. B. (1985). Maintenance of weight loss: Demographic, behavioral, and attitudinal correlates. *The Journal of Obesity and Weight Regulation, 4,* 234–255.

Snow, J. T., & Harris, M. B. (1986). An analysis of weight and diet content in five women's interest magazines. *The Journal of Obesity and Weight Regulation, 5,* 194–214.

Snow, J. T., & Harris, M. B. (1989). Disordered eating in Southwestern Pueblo Indians and Hispanics. *Journal of Adolescence, 12,* 329–336.

Snow, M. E., Jacklin, C. N., & Maccoby, E. E. (1983). Sex-of-child differences in father-child interaction at one year of age. *Child Development, 54,* 227–232.

Snyder, M., & Swann, W. B., Jr. (1978a). Behavioral confirmation in social interaction: From social perception to social reality. *Journal of Experimental Social Psychology, 14,* 148–162.

Snyder, M., & Swann, W. B., Jr. (1978b). Hypothesis-testing processes in social interaction. *Journal of Personality and Social Psychology, 36,* 1202–1212.

Snyder, M., Tanke, E. D., & Berscheid, E. (1977). Social perception and interpersonal behavior: On the self-fulfilling nature of social stereotypes. *Journal of Personality and Social Psychology, 35,* 656–666.

Snyder, M., & Uranowitz, S. W. (1978). Reconstructing the past: Some cognitive consequences of person perception. *Journal of Personality and Social Psychology, 36,* 941–950.

Snyder, R., & Hasbrouck, L. (1996). Feminist identity, gender traits, and symptoms of disturbed eating among college women. *Psychology of Women Quarterly, 20,* 593–598.

Snyder, V. N. S., Acevedo, A., Diaz-Perez, M. J., & Saldivar-Garduno, A. (2000). Understanding the sexuality of Mexican-born women and their risk for HIV/AIDS. *Psychology of Women Quarterly, 24,* 100–109.

Sobchack, V. (1999). Scary women: Cinema, surgery, and special effects. In K. Woodward (Ed.)., *Figuring age: Women, bodies, generations* (pp. 200–211). Bloomington, IN: University of Indiana Press.

Sohoni, N. K. (1994). Where are the girls? *Ms., 5* (#1), 96.

Sommer, B. (2001). Menopause. In J. Worell (Ed.), *Encyclopedia of women and gender* (pp. 729–738). San Diego, CA: Academic Press.

Sommer, B., Avis, N., Meyer, P., Ory, M., Madden, T., Kagawa-Singer, M., Mouton, C., Rasor, N. O., & Adler, S. (1999). Attitudes toward menopause and aging across ethnic/racial groups. *Psychosomatic Medicine, 61,* 868–875.

Sommers-Flanagan, R., Sommers-Flanagan, J., & Davis, B. (1993). What's happening on music television? A gender-role content analysis. *Sex Roles, 28,* 745–753.

Sorenson, S. A. (1996, April). Violence against women: Examining ethnic differences and commonalities. *Evaluation Review, 20,* 123–145.

Sorenson, S. B., & Siegel, J. M. (1992). Gender, ethnicity, and sexual assault: Findings from the Los Angeles epidemiological catchment area study. *Journal of Social Issues, 48,* 93–104.

Sorenson, S. B., Upchurch, D. M., & Shen, H. (1996). Violence and injury in marital arguments: Risk patterns and gender differences. *American Journal of Public Health, 86,* 35–40.

Sowers, M., Pope, S., Welch, G., Sternfeld, B., & Albrecht, G. (2001). The association of menopause and physical functioning in women at midlife. *Journal of the American Geriatrics Society, 49,* 1485–1492.

Spence, J. T., & Hahn, D. (1997). The Attitude toward Women Scale and attitude change in college students. *Psychology of Women Quarterly, 21,* 17–34.

Spencer, S. J., Steele, C. M., & Quinn, D. M. (1999). Stereotype threat and women's math performance. *Journal of Experimental Social Psychology, 35,* 4–28.

Spielman, S., & Winfeld, L. (1996). Domestic partner benefits: A bottom line discussion. In A. L. & E. D. B. Riggle (Eds.), *Sexual identity on the job: Issues and services* (pp. 53–78). New York: Harrington Park Press.

Spitzer, B. L., Henderson, K. A., & Zivian, M. T. (1999). Gender differences in population versus media body sizes: A comparison over four decades. *Sex Roles, 40,* 545–565.

Sprecher, S., Barbee, A., & Schwartz, P. (1995). "Was it good for you, too?": Gender differences in first sexual intercourse experiences. *The Journal of Sex Research, 32,* 3–15.

Sprecher, S., & Regan, P. C. (2000). Sexuality in relational context. In C. Hendrick & S. S. Hendrick (Eds.), *Close relationships: A sourcebook* (pp. 217–228). Thousand Oaks, CA: Sage Publications, Inc.

Stack, C. B. (1986). The culture of gender: Women and men of color. *Signs, 11,* 321–324.

Stacy, R. D., Prisbell, M., & Tollefsrud, K. (1992). A comparison of attitudes among college students toward sexual violence committed by strangers and by acquaintances: A research report. *Journal of Sex Education and Therapy, 18,* 257–263.

Stangor, C., Lynch, L., Duan, C., & Glass, B. (1992). Categorization of individuals on the basis of multiple social features. *Journal of Personality and Social Psychology, 62,* 207–218.

Stanley, J. P. (1977). Paradigmatic woman: The prostitute. In D. L. Shores & C. P. Hines (Eds.), *Papers in language variation* (pp. 303–321). University of Alabama: University of Alabama Press.

Stark, E., & Flitcraft, A. (1996). *Women at risk, domestic violence and women's health.* Thousand Oaks, CA: Sage.

Statham, A., Miller, E. M., & Mauksch, H. O. (Eds.). (1988). *The worth of women's work: A qualitative synthesis.* Albany: State University of New York Press.

Stead, B. A., & Zinkhan, G. M. (1986). Service priority in department stores: The effect of customer gender and sex. *Sex Roles, 15,* 601–611.

Steele, B. F. (1986). Notes on the lasting effects of early child abuse throughout the life cycle. *Child Abuse and Neglect, 10,* 283–291.

Steele, C. M. (1997). A threat in the air: How stereotypes shape intellectual identity and performance. *American Psychologist, 52,* 613–629.

Steele, C. M., & Aronson, J. (1995). Stereotype threat and the intellectual performance of African Americans. *Journal of Personality & Social Psychology, 69,* 797–811.

Steele, J., James, J. B., & Barnett, R. C. (2002). Learning in a man's world: Examining the perceptions of undergraduate women in male-dominated academic areas. *Psychology of Women Quarterly, 26,* 46–50.

Steiger, J. (1981). The influence of the feminist subculture in changing sex-role attitudes. *Sex Roles, 7,* 627–634.

Steil, J. M. (1989). Marital relationships and mental health: The psychic costs of inequality. In J. Freeman (Ed.), *Women: A feminist perspective* (4th ed., pp. 138–140). Mountain View, CA: Mayfield.

Steil, J. M. (1994). Supermoms and second shifts: Marital inequality in the 90's. In J. Freeman (Ed.), *Women: A feminist perspective* (5th ed., pp. 149–161). Mountain View, CA: Mayfield.

Steil, J. M. (1997). *Marital equality: Its relationship to the well-being of husbands and wives.* Thousand Oaks, CA: Sage.

Steil, J. M. (2000). Contemporary marriage: Still an unequal partnership. In C. Hendrick & S. S. Hendrick (Eds.), *Close relationships: A sourcebook* (pp. 125–138). Thousand Oaks, CA: Sage.

Steil, J. M. (2001). Family forms and member well-being: A research agenda for the decade of behavior. *Psychology of Women Quarterly, 25,* 344–363.

Steil, J. M., & Turetsky, B. A. (1987a). Marital influence levels and symptomatology among wives. In F. Crosby (Ed.), *Spouse, parent, worker: On gender and multiple roles* (pp. 74–90). New Haven, CT: Yale University Press.

Steil, J. M., & Turetsky, B. A. (1987b). Is equal better? The relationship between marital equality and psychological symptomatology. In S. Oskamp (Ed.), *Family processes and problems: Social psychological aspects* (pp. 73–97). Beverly Hills, CA: Sage.

Steil, J. M., & Weltman, K. (1991). Marital inequality: The importance of resources, personal attributes, and social norms on career valuing and the allocation of domestic responsibilities. *Sex Roles, 24,* 161–179.

Stein, N. (1995). Sexual harassment in schools: The public performance of gendered violence. *Harvard Educational Review, 65*(2), 145–162.

Steinberg, L., & Silverberg, S. B. (1987). Influences on marital satisfaction during the middle stages of the family life cycle. *Journal of Marriage and the Family, 49,* 751–760.

Steinem, G. (1983). *Outrageous acts and everyday rebellions.* New York: New American Library.

Steinmetz, S. (1977–1978). The battered husband syndrome. *Victimology: An International Journal, 2,* 499–509.

Sterk, H. M. (1996). Contemporary birthing practices. In R. L. Parrott & C. M. Condit (Eds.), *Evaluating women's health messages* (pp. 124–134). Thousand Oaks: Sage.

Stermac, L., Du Mont, J., & Dunn, S. (1998). Violence in known-assailant sexual assaults. *Journal of Interpersonal Violence, 13,* 398–412.

Stern, M., & Karraker, K. H. (1989). Sex stereotyping of infants: A review of gender labeling studies. *Sex Roles, 20,* 501–522.

Stevens, D., Kiger, G., & Riley, P. J. (2001). Working hard and hardly working: Domestic labor and marital satisfaction among dual-earner couples. *Journal of Marriage and Family, 63,* 514–526.

Stevens-Long, J., & Commons, M. L. (1992). *Adult life: Developmental processes* (4th ed.). London: Mayfield.

Stewart, A. J., Copeland, A. P., Chester, N. L., Malley, J. E., & Barenbaum, N. B. (1997). *Separating together: How divorce transforms families.* New York: Guilford Press.

Stewart, A. J., & Gold-Steinberg, S. (1990). Midlife women's political consciousness: Case studies of psychosocial development and political commitment. *Psychology of Women Quarterly, 14,* 543–566.

Stewart, A. J., & Vandewater, E. A. (1999). "If I Had It to Do Over Again . . .": Midlife review, midcourse corrections, and women's well-being in later life. *Journal of Personality and Social Psychology, 76,* 270–283.

Stewart, S., Stinnett, H., & Rosenfeld, L. B. (2000). Sex differences in desired characteristics of short-term and long-term relationship partners. *Journal of Social and Personal Relationships, 17,* 843–853.

Stewart, T. L., Vassar, P. M., Sanchez, D. T., & David, S. E. (2000). Attitudes about women's societal roles moderates the effect of gender cues on target individuation. *Journal of Personality & Social Psychology, 79,* 143–157.

Stice, E. (2002). Risk and maintenance factors in eating pathology: A meta-analysis. *Psychological Bulletin, 128,* 825–848.

Stice, E., & Bearman, S. K. (2001). Body-image and eating disturbances prospectively predict increases in depressive symptoms among adolescent girls: A growth curve analysis. *Developmental Psychology, 37,* 597–607.

Stice, E., Haywood, C., Cameron, R. P., Killen, J. D., & Taylor, C. B. (2000). Body-image and eating disturbances predict onset of depression among female adolescents: A longitudinal study. *Journal of Abnormal Psychology, 109,* 438–444.

Stice, E., Presnell, K., & Bearman, S. K. (2001). Relation of early menarche to depression, eating disorders, substance abuse, and comorbid psychopathology among adolescent girls. *Developmental Psychology, 37,* 608–619.

Stice, E., Spangler, D., & Agras, W. S. (2001). Exposure to media-portrayed thin-ideal images adversely affects vulnerable girls: A longitudinal experiment. *Journal of Social & Clinical Psychology, 20,* 270–288.

Stice, E., & Whitenton, K. (2002). Risk factors for body dissatisfaction in adolescent girls: a longitudinal investigation. *Developmental Psychology, 38,* 669–678.

Stoltenberg, J. (1989). *Refusing to be a man: Essays on sex and justice.* New York: Penguin Books.

Stone, L., & McKee, N. P. (2000). Gendered futures: Student visions of career and family on a college campus. *Anthropology and Education Quarterly, 31,* 67–89.

Storms, M. D., Stivers, M. L., Lambers, S. M., & Hill, C. A. (1981). Sexual scripts for women. *Sex Roles, 7,* 699–707.

Straus, M. A., & Gelles, R. J. (1990). *Physical violence in American families: Risk factors and adaptations to violence in 8,145 families.* New Brunswick, NJ: Transaction.

Straus, M. A., Kaufman Kantor, G., & Moore, D. W. (1997). Change in cultural norms approving marital violence from 1968 to 1994. In G. Kaufman Kantor & J. L. Jasinski (Eds.), *Out of darkness: Contemporary perspectives on family violence* (pp. 3–16). Thousand Oaks, CA: Sage.

Streigel-Moore, R. H., McMahon, R. P., Biro, F. M., Schreiber, G., Crawford, P. B., & Voorhees, C. (2001). Exploring the relationship between timing of menarche and eating disorder symptoms among black and white adolescent girls. *International Journal of Eating Disorders, 30,* 421–433.

Stricker, L., Rock, D., & Burton, N. (1992). *Sex differences in SAT predictions of college grades.* New York: The College Board.

Strickland, B. (1988). Sex-related differences in health and illness. *Psychology of Women Quarterly, 12,* 381–399.

Striegel-Moore, R. H., Goldman, S. L., Garvin, V., & Rodin, J. (1996). Within-subjects design: Pregnancy changes both body and mind. In F. E. Donelson (Ed.), *Women's experiences: A psychological perspective* (pp. 430–437). Mountain View, CA: Mayfield.

Striegel-Moore, R. H., & Smolak, L. (1996). The role of race in the development of eating disorders. In L. Smolak, M. Levine, & R. H. Striegel-Moore (Eds.), *The developmental psychopathology of eating disorders: Implications for research, treatment, and prevention* (pp. 259–284). Hillsdale, NJ: Erlbaum.

Strommen, E. F. (1993). "You're a what?": Family member reactions to the disclosure of homosexuality. In L. D. Garnets & D. C. Kimmel (Eds.), *Psychological perspectives on lesbian and gay male experiences* (pp. 248–266). New York: Columbia University Press.

Stueve, A., & O'Donnell, L. (1984). The daughter of aging parents. In G. Baruch & J. Brooks-Gunn (Eds.), *Women in midlife* (pp. 203–225). New York: Plenum Press.

Sugarman, D. B., & Hotaling, G. T. (1989). Dating violence: Prevalence, context, and risk markers. In M. A. Pirog-Good & J. E. Stets (Eds.), *Violence in dating relationships* (pp. 3–32). New York: Praeger.

Suh, M. (1990, September/October). Lesbian battery. *Ms.*

Summit, R. (1983). The child sexual abuse accommodation syndrome. *Child Abuse and Neglect, 7,* 177–193.

A survey finds bias on the front page. (1996, April 17). *The New York Times,* p. A17.

Swaab, D. F., & Hofman, M. A. (1990). An enlarged suprachiasmatic nucleus in homosexual men. *Brain Research, 537,* 141–148.

Swan, S., & Wyer, R. S., Jr. (1997). Gender stereotypes and social identity: How being in the minority affects judgments of self and others. *Personality and Social Psychology Bulletin, 23,* 1265–1276.

Swarz, N., Wagner, D., Bannert, M., & Mathes, L. (1987). Cognitive accessibility of sex role concepts and attitudes toward political participation: The impact of sexist advertisements. *Sex Roles, 17,* 593–601.

Swim, J. K., Aikin, K. J., Hall, W. S., & Hunter, B. A. (1995). Sexism and racism: Old-fashioned and modern prejudices. *Journal of Personality and Social Psychology, 68,* 199–214.

Swim, J. K., & Cohen, L. L. (1997). Overt, covert, and subtle sexism: A comparison between the Attitudes toward Women and Modern Sexism Scales. *Psychology of Women Quarterly, 21,* 103–118.

Swim, J. K., & Hyers, L. L. (1999). Excuse me—What did you say? Women's public and private responses to sexist remarks. *Journal of Experimental Social Psychology, 35,* 68–88.

Swim, J. K., Hyers, L. L., Cohen, L. L., & Ferguson, M. J. (2001). Everyday sexism: Evidence for its incidence, nature and psychological impact from three daily diary studies. *Journal of Social Issues, 57,* (1), 31–54.

Tajfel, H. (1984). Intergroup relations, social myths, and social justice in social psychology. In H. Tajfel (Ed.), *The social dimension.* Cambridge, England: Cambridge University Press.

Takin, H. A., Sanchez, D. T., & Stewart, T. L. (2001). What's in a name? The status implications of students' terms of address for male and female professors. *Psychology of Women Quarterly, 25,* 134–144.

Tang, S., & Zuo, J. (2000). Dating attitudes and behaviors of American and Chinese students. *Social Science Journal, 37,* 67–78.

Tangri, S., Burt, M., & Johnson, L. (1982). Sexual harassment at work: Three explanatory models. *Journal of Social Issues, 38,* 33–54.

Tannen, D. (1994). *Talking from nine to five.* New York: William Morrow.

Tashakkori, A. (1993). Gender, ethnicity, and the structure of self-esteem: An attitude theory approach. *Journal of Social Psychology, 133,* 479–488.

Tasker, F. (1999). Children in lesbian-led families: A review. *Clinical Child Psychology and Psychiatry, 4,* 153–166.

Tasker, F. L., & Golombok, S. (1997). *Growing up in a lesbian family.* New York: Guilford.

Taylor, C. J., Lambert, C., Perry, J., & Tobin, M. (1999, April 16). *The double standard of aging: Perceptions of similarly and dissimilarly aged couples.* Paper presented at the annual meeting of the Eastern Psychological Association, Providence, Rhode Island.

Taylor, M. G. (1996). The development of children's beliefs about social and biological aspects of gender differences. *Child Development, 67,* 1555–1571.

Taylor, R. L. (1997). Who's parenting? Trends and patterns. In T. Arrendell (Ed.), *Contemporary parenting: Challenges and issues. Understanding families* (vol. 9, pp. 68–91). Thousand Oaks, CA: Sage.

Taylor, S. E. (1983). Adjustment to threatening events: A theory of cognitive adaptation. *American Psychologist, 38,* 1161–1173.

Taylor, S. E., Fiske, S. T., Etcoff, N. L., & Ruderman, A. J. (1978). Categorical and contextual bases of person memory and stereotyping. *Journal of Personality and Social Psychology, 36,* 778–793.

Taylor, D. G., & Langer, E. J. (1977). Pregnancy: A social stigma? *Sex Roles, 3,* 27–35.

Tazeau, Y. N., & Gallagher-Thompson, D. (1993). A look at social support, acculturation, and depression in Mexican-American elderly women. *Focus, 7*(2), 12.

Teachman, J. D., & Polenko, K. A. (1990). Cohabitation and marital stability in the United States. *Social Forces, 69,* 207–220.

Teitelbaum, P. (1989). Feminist theory and standardized testing. In A. M. Jaggar & S. Bordo (Eds.), *Gender/body/knowledge* (pp. 324–335). New Brunswick, NJ: Rutgers University Press.

Tenenbaum, H. R., & Leaper, C. (2002). Are parents' gender schema related to their children's gender-related cognitions? A meta-analysis. *Developmental Psychology, 38,* 615–630.

Tennstedt, C., Cafferata, G. L., & Sullivan, L. (1992). Depression among caregivers of impaired elders. *Journal of Aging and Health, 4,* 58–76.

Terman, L. M., & Oden, M. H. (1959). *Genetic studies of genius. V. The gifted group at mid-life: Thirty-five years' follow-up of the superior child.* Stanford, CA: Stanford University Press.

Terwogt, M. M. (2002). Emotional states in self and others as motives for helping in 10-year-old children. *British Journal of Developmental Psychology, 20,* 131–147.

Tevlin, H. E., & Leiblum, S. R. (1983). Sex-role stereotypes and female sexual dysfunction. In V. Franks & E. D. Rothblum (Eds.), *Stereotyping of women: Its effects on mental health* (pp. 129–148). New York: Springer.

Theriault, S. W., & Holmberg, D. (1998). The new old-fashioned girl: Effects of gender and social desirability on reported gender-role ideology. *Sex Roles, 39,* 97–112.

Thibault, J. W., & Kelley, H. H. (1959). *The social psychology of groups.* New York: Wiley.

Thoits, P. A. (1987). Negotiating roles. In F. J. Crosby (Ed.), *Spouse, parent, worker: On gender and multiple roles* (pp. 11–22). New Haven: Yale University Press.

Thomas, J. J., & Daubman, K. A. (2001). The relationship between friendship quality and self-esteem in adolescent girls and boys. *Sex Roles, 45,* 53–65.

Thomas, V. G., & James, M. D. (1988). Body image, dieting tendencies, and sex role traits in urban black women. *Sex Roles, 18,* 523–529.

Thompson, E. H. (1991). The maleness of violence in dating relationships: An appraisal of stereotypes. *Sex Roles, 24,* 261–278.

Thompson, J. K., & Heinberg, L. J. (1999). The media's influence on body image disturbance and eating disorders: We've reviled them, now can we rehabilitate them? *Journal of Social Issues, 55* (2), 339–353.

Thompson, J. K., Heinberg, L. J., Altabe, M., & Tantleff-Dunn, S. (1999). *Exacting beauty: Theory, assessment, and treatment of body image disturbance.* Washington D.C.: American Psychological Association.

Thompson, M., & Sekaquaptewa, D. (2002). When being different is detrimental: Solo status and the performance of women and minorities. *Analysis of Social Issues and Public Policy, 2,* 183–203.

Thompson, M. S., & Keith, V. M. (2001). The blacker the berry: Gender, skin tone, self-esteem, and self-efficacy. *Gender & Society, 15,* 336–357.

Thompson, R. B. (1999). Gender differences in preschoolers' help-eliciting communication. *Journal of Genetic Psychology, 160,* 337–368.

Thompson, S. (1986). Pregnancy on purpose. *Village Voice, 31*(51), 31–37. Cited in Cusick (1987). Sexism and early parenting: Cause and effect? *Peabody Journal of Education, 64,* 113–131.

Thompson, S. (1994). What friends are for: On girls' misogyny and romantic fusion. In

J. Irvine (Ed.), *Sexual cultures and the construction of adolescent identities* (pp. 226–249). Philadelphia: Temple University Press.

Thompson, S. H., Corwin, S. J., & Sargent, R. G. (1997). Ideal body size beliefs and weight concerns of fourth-grade children. *International Journal of Eating Disorders, 21,* 279–384.

Thompson, S. H., Sargent, R. G., & Kemper, K. A. (1996). Black and white adolescent males' perception of ideal body size. *Sex Roles, 34,* 391–406.

Thompson, T. L., & Zerbinos, E. (1995). Gender roles in animated cartoons: Has the picture changed in twenty years? *Sex Roles, 32,* 651–673.

Thompson, T. L., & Zerbinos, E. (1997). Television cartoons: Do children notice it's a boy's world? *Sex Roles, 37,* 415–432.

Thornberry, O. T., Wilson, R. W., & Golden, P. (1986). Health promotion and disease prevention provisional data from the National Health Interview Survey: United States, January-June, 1985. *Vital and Health Statistics of the National Center for Health Statistics, 119,* 1–16.

Thorne, B. (1986). Girls and boys together, but mostly apart. In W. W. Hartup and Z. Rubin (Eds.), *Relationships and development* (pp. 167–184). Hillsdale, NJ: Erlbaum.

Thorne, B. (1993). *Gender play: Girls and boys in school.* New Brunswick, NJ: Rutgers University Press.

Thorne, B., & Luria, Z. (1986). Sexuality and gender in children's daily worlds. *Social Problems, 33,* 176–190.

Tichenor, V. J. (1999). Status and income as gendered resources: The case of marital power. *Journal of Marriage and the Family, 61,* 638–650.

Tiedens, L. Z., Ellsworth, P. C., & Mesquita, B. (2000). Stereotypes about sentiments and status: Expectations about high- and low-status group members. *Personality & Social Psychology Bulletin, 26,* 560–574.

Tiefer, L. (1988). A feminist perspective on sexology and sexuality. In M. Gergen (Ed.), *Feminist thought and the structure of knowledge* (pp. 16–26). New York: New York University Press.

Tiefer, L. (1989, August). Feminist transformations of sexology. In M. Crawford (chair), Feminist psychological science: Frameworks, strengths, visions, and a few examples. Symposium conducted at meeting of the American Psychological Association, New Orleans, LA.

Tiefer, L. (1995). *Sex is not a natural act & other essays.* San Francisco: Westview.

Tighe, C. A. (2001). 'Working at disability': A qualitative study of the meaning of health and disability for women with physical impairments. *Disability and Society, 16,* 511–529.

Tjaden, P., & Rhownnwa, N. (1998). Prevalence, incidence, and consequences of violence against women: Findings from the National Violence Against Women Survey. *Research Brief, November,* U.S. Department of Justice.

Tjaden, P., & Thoennes, N. (1998). *Stalking in American: Findings from the national violence against women survey.* Denver, CO: Center for Policy Research.

Tobach, E., 2001. Development of sex and gender: Biochemistry, physiology, and experience. In J. Worell (Ed.), *Encyclopedia of women and gender: Sex similarities and differences and the impact of society on gender.* (pp. 315–332). San Diego, CA: Academic Press.

Todd, J., Friedman, A., & Kariuki, P. W. (1990). Women growing stronger with age: The effect of status in the United States and Kenya. *Psychology of Women Quarterly, 14,* 567–577.

Tolman, D. L., & Brown, L. M. (2001). Adolescent girls' voices: Resonating resistance in body and soul. In R. K. Unger (Ed.), *Handbook of the psychology of women and gender* (pp. 133–155). NY: Wiley.

Tolman, R. M. (1989). The development of a measure of psychological maltreatment of women by their male partners. *Violence and Victims, 4,* 159–177.

Tong, R. P. (1998). *Feminist thought* (2nd ed.). Boulder: Westview.

Tontodonato, P., & Crew, B. K. (1992). Dating violence, social learning theory, and gender: A multivariate analysis. *Violence and Victims, 7,* 3–14.

Torrez, D. J. (1997). The health of older women: A diverse experience. In J. Coyle (Ed.), *Handbook of women and aging* (pp. 131–145). Westport, CT: Greenwood.

Tougas, F., Brown, R., Beaton, A. M., & Joly, S. (1995). Neosexism: Plus la change, plus c'est pareil. *Personality and Social Psychology Bulletin, 21,* 842–849.

Travis, C. B. (1988a). *Women and health psychology: Biomedical issues.* Hillsdale, NJ: Erlbaum.

Travis, C. B. (2001). Gender development: Evolutionary perspectives. In J. Worell (Ed.), *Encyclopedia of women and gender.* San Diego, CA: Academic Press (pp. 493–506).

Travis, C. B., & Compton, J. D. (2001). Feminism and health in the decade of behavior. *Psychology of Women Quarterly, 25,* 312–323.

Travis, C. B., & Meginnis-Payne, K. L. (2001). Beauty politics and patriarchy: The impact on women's lives. In J. Worell (Ed.), *Encyclopedia of women and gender* (pp. 189–200). San Diego, CA: Academic Press.

Treadway, C. R., Kane, F. J., Jarrahi-Zadeh, A., & Lipton, M. A. (1969). A psycho-endocrine study of pregnancy and puerperium. *American Journal of Psychiatry, 125,* 1380–1386.

Trends in the attendant, place and timing of births in the use of obstetric interventions, United States, 1989–97. (2000). Washington, D.C.: NCHS Public Affairs.

Trent, K., & South, S. J. (1989). Structural determinants of the divorce rate: A cross-societal analysis. *Journal of Marriage and the Family, 51,* 391–404.

Trice, A. D., & Rush, R. K. (1995). Sex-stereotyping in four-year-olds' occupational aspirations. *Perceptual and Motor Skills, 81,* 701–702.

Tronto, J. C. (1987). Beyond gender difference to a theory of care. *Signs, 12,* 644–663.

Trost, J. (1996). Family studies in Sweden. *Marriage & Family Review, 23*(3/4), 723–743.

Trotman, F. K. (2000). Feminist and psychodynamic psychotherapy with African American women: Some differences. In L. C. Jackson & B. Greene (Eds.), *Psychotherapy with African American Women* (pp. 251–274). NY: Guilford Press.

Tsui, L. (1998). The effects of gender, education, and personal skills self-confidence on income in business management. *Sex Roles, 38,* 363–373.

Tulloch, M. I., & Tulloch, J. C. (1992). Attitudes to domestic violence: School students' responses to a television drama. *Australian Journal of Marriage and Family, 13,* 62–69.

Turk, J. L., & Bell, N. W. (1972). Measuring power in families. *Journal of Marriage and the Family, 34,* 215–223.

Turner-Bowker, D. M. (1996). Gender stereotyped assumptions in children's picture books: Does "Curious Jane" exist in the literature? *Sex Roles, 35,* 461–488.

Twenge, J. M. (1997). Attitudes toward women, 1970–1995: A meta-analysis. *Psychology of Women Quarterly, 21*(1), 35–51.

Twenge, J. M. (1999). Mapping gender: The multifactorial approach and the organization of gender-related attributes. *Psychology of Women Quarterly, 23,* 485–502.

Twenge, J. M. (2000). The age of anxiety? Birth cohort changes in anxiety and neuroticism, 1952–1993. *Journal of Personality and Social Psychology, 79,* 1107–1021.

Twenge, J. M. (2001). Changes in women's assertiveness in response to status and roles: A cross-temporal meta-analysis, 1931–1993. *Journal of Personality and Social Psychology, 81,* 133–145.

Twenge, J. M., & Zucker, A. N. (1999). What is a feminist? Evaluations and stereotypes in closed- and open-ended responses. *Psychology of Women Quarterly, 23,* 591–605.

Ulrich, M., & Weatherall, A. (2000). Motherhood and infertility: Viewing motherhood through the lens of infertility. *Feminism and Psychology, 10,* 323–336.

Underwood, M. K., Schockner, A. E., & Hurley, J. C. (2001). Children's response to same- and other-gender peers: An experimental investigation of 8-, 10-, and 12-year-olds. *Developmental Psychology, 37,* 362–372.

Unger, R. K. (1996). Using the master's tools: Epistemology and empiricism. In S. Wilkinson (Ed.), *Feminist social psychologies: International perspectives.* Milton Keynes: Open University Press (pp. 165–181).

Udry, J. R., Talbert, L., Morris, N. M. (1986). Biosocial foundations for adolescent female sexuality. *Demography, 23,* 217–230.

Ullman, S. E., & Knight, R. A. (1995). Women's resistance strategies to different rapist types. *Criminal Justice and Behavior, 22,* 263–283.

Umberson, D., Wortman, C. B., & Kessler, R. C. (1992). Widowhood and depression: Explaining long-term gender differences in vulnerability. *Journal of Health and Social Behavior, 33,* 10–24.

Unger, R. K. (1976). Male is greater than female: The socialization of status inequality. *The Counseling Psychologist, 6,* 2–9.

Unger, R. K. (1978). The politics of gender: A review of relevant literature. In J. Sherman & F. Denmark (Eds.), *Psychology of women: Future directions of research* (pp. 463–517). New York: Psychological Dimensions.

Unger, R. K. (1979a). *Female and male: Psychological perspectives.* New York: Harper & Row.

Unger, R. K. (1979b). Toward a redefinition of sex and gender. *American Psychologist, 34,* 1085–1094.

Unger, R. K. (1981). Sex as a social reality: Field and laboratory research. *Psychology of Women Quarterly, 5,* 645–653.

Unger, R. K. (1983). Through the looking glass: No Wonderland yet! (The reciprocal relationship between methodology and models of reality.) *Psychology of Women Quarterly, 8,* 9–32.

Unger, R. K. (1988). Psychological, feminist, and personal epistemology. In M. M. Gergen (Ed.), *Feminist thought and the structure of knowledge* (pp. 124–141). New York: New York University Press.

Unger, R. K. (1990). Imperfect reflections of reality: Psychology and the construction of gender. In R. Hare-Mustin & J. Marecek (Eds.), *Making a difference: Representations of gender in psychology* (pp. 102–149). New Haven: Yale University Press.

Unger, R. K. (1998a). Positive marginality: Antecedents and consequences. *Journal of Adult Development, 5,* 163–170.

Unger, R. K. (1998b). *Resisting gender: Twenty-five years of feminist psychology.* London: Sage.

Unger, R. K., & Crawford, M. (1989). Methods and values in decisions about gender differences (Review of Alice H. Eagly, *Sex differences in social behavior: A social role interpretation.*) *Contemporary Psychology, 34,* 122–123.

Unger, R. K., & Crawford, M. (1993). Commentary: Sex and gender–The troubled relationship between terms and concepts. *Psychological Science, 4,* 122–124.

Unger, R. K., Hilderbrand, M., & Madar, T. (1982). Physical attractiveness and assumptions about social deviance: Some sex by sex comparisons. *Personality and Social Psychology Bulletin, 8,* 293–301.

Unger, R. K., & Sussman, L. E. (1986). "I and thou": Another barrier to societal change? *Sex Roles, 14,* 629–636.

Urberg, K. A. (1982). The development of the concepts of masculinity and femininity in young children. *Sex Roles, 6,* 659–668.

U.S. Merit Systems Protection Board (USMSPB). (1981). *Sexual harassment in the federal workplace: Is it a problem?* Washington, DC: Office of Merit Systems Review and Studies/Government Printing Office.

U.S. Merit Systems Protection Board (USMSPB). (1987). *Sexual harassment in the federal workplace: An update.* Washington, DC: Office of Merit Systems Review and Studies/Government Printing Office.

Ussher, J. (1989). *The psychology of the female body.* London: Routledge.

Ussher, J. M., & Mooney Somers, J. (2000). Negotiating desire and sexual subjectivity: Narratives of young lesbian avengers. *Sexualities, 3,* 183–200.

Valentine, J. C., Blankenship, V., Cooper, H., & Sullins, E. S. (2001). Interpersonal expectancy effects and the preference for consistency. *Representative Research in Social Psychology, 25,* 26–33.

Valian, V. (1998). *Why so slow? The advancement of women.* Cambridge, MA: MIT Press.

Valkenburg, P. M., Cantor, J., & Peeters, A. L. (2000). Fright reactions to television: A child survey. *Communication Research, 27,* 82–99.

Vance, C. S. (1984). Pleasure and danger: Toward a politics of sexuality. In C. S. Vance (Ed.), *Pleasure and danger: Exploring female sexuality* (pp. 1–27). Boston: Routledge and Kegan Paul.

Vance, E. B., & Wagner, N. N. (1976). Written descriptions of orgasm: A study of sex differences. *Archives of Sexual Behavior, 5,* 87–98.

Vander-Ven, T. M., Cullen, F. T., Carrozza, M. A., & Wright, J. P. (2001). Home alone: The impact of maternal employment on delinquency. *Social Problems, 48,* 236–257.

Vanek, J. (1984). Housewives as workers. In P. Voydanoff (Ed.), *Work and family: Changing roles of men and women* (pp. 89–103). Palo Alto, CA: Mayfield.

Vartaman, T. P., & McNamara, J. M. (2002). Older women in poverty: The impact of midlife factors. *Journal of Marriage and the Family, 64,* 532–547.

Vasquez, M. J. T. (1994). Latinas. In L. Comas-Diaz & B. Greene (Eds.), *Women of color: Integrating ethnic and gender identities in psychotherapy* (pp. 114–138). New York: Guilford.

Vedovato, S., & Vaughter, R. (1980). Psychology of women courses changing sexist and sex-typed attitudes. *Psychology of Women Quarterly, 4,* 587–590.

Veniegas, R. C., & Conley, T. G. (2000). Biological research on women's sexual orientation: Evaluating the scientific evidence. *Journal of Social Issues, 56* (2), 267–282.

Veroff, J., Wilcox, S., & Atkinson, J. W. (1953). The achievement motive in high school and college age women. *Journal of Abnormal and Social Psychology, 43,* 108–119.

Veroff, J., Young, A. M., & Coon, H. M. (1997). The early years of marriage. In S. Duck (Ed.), *Handbook of personal relationships: Theory, research and interventions* (2nd ed., pp. 431–450). Chichester, England: Wiley.

Vicary, J. R., Klingman, L. R., & Harkness, W. L. (1995). Risk factors associated with date rape and sexual assault of adolescent girls. *Journal of Adolescence, 18,* 289–306.

Vida, V. (Ed.). (1978). *Our right to love: A lesbian resource book.* Englewood Cliffs, NJ: Prentice Hall.

Vinick, B. H., & Ekerdt, D. J. (1992). Couples view retirement activities. In M. Szinovacz, D. J. Ekerdt, & B. H. Vinick (Eds.), *Families and retirement* (pp. 129–144). Newbury Park, CA: Sage.

Vobejda, B. (1994, June 16). Abortion rate slowing in U.S., study concludes. *The Washington Post,* p. A13.

Voda, A. M. (1997). *Menopause me and you: The sound of women pausing.* Binghampton, NY: Harrington Park Press.

von Baeyer, C. L., Sherk, D. L., & Zanna, M. P. (1981). Impression management in the job interview: When the female applicant meets the male (chauvinist) interviewer. *Personality and Social Psychology Bulletin, 7,* 45–51.

Vredenburg, K., Krames, L., & Flett, G. L. (1986). Sex differences in the clinical expression of depression. *Sex Roles, 14,* 37–49.

The wage gap by education: 2000. (2001). Washington, DC: National Committee on Pay Equity.

The wage gap over time: In real dollars, women see a continuing gap. (2001). Washington, DC: National Committee on Pay Equity.

Wahrman, R., & Pugh, M. D. (1972). Competence and conformity: Another look at Hollander's study. *Sociometry, 35,* 376–386.

Wahrman, R., & Pugh, M. D. (1974). Sex, nonconformity, and influence. *Sociometry, 37,* 137–147.

Waite, L. J., & Joyner, K. (2001). Emotional satisfaction and physical pleasure in sexual unions: Time horizon, sexual behavior, and sexual exclusivity. *Journal of Marriage and the Family, 63,* 247–264.

Wajcman, J. (1998). *Managing like a man: Women and men in corporate management.* Cambridge: Polity Press.

Waldo, C. R., Berdahl, J. L., & Fitzgerald, L. F. (1998). Are men sexually harassed? If so, by whom? *Law and Human Behavior, 22,* 59–79.

Walker, L. (1979). *The battered woman.* New York: Harper and Row.

Walker, L. (1993). The battered woman syndrome is a psychological consequence of abuse. In R. J. Gelles & D. R. Loseke (Eds.), *Current controversies on family violence* (pp. 133–153). Newbury Park, CA: Sage.

Walker, L. J. (1984). Sex differences in the development of moral reasoning: A critical review. *Child Development, 55,* 667–691.

Walker, L. J. (1986). Experiential and cognitive sources of moral development in adulthood. *Human Development, 29,* 113–124.

Walkerdine, V. (1996). Working class women: Social and psychological aspects of survival. In S. Wilkinson (Ed.), *Feminism and social psychology: International perspectives* (pp. 145–162). Milton Keynes: Open University Press.

Walkerdine, V. (1998). Popular culture and the eroticization of little girls. In H. Jenkins (Ed.), *The children's culture reader* (pp. 254–264). New York: New York University Press.

Wallace, J. E. (2001). The benefits of mentoring for female lawyers. *Journal of Vocational Behavior, 58,* 366–391.

Wallen, K. (1996). Nature needs nurture: The interaction of hormonal and social influences on the development of behavioral sex differences in rhesus monkeys. *Hormones and Behavior, 30,* 364–378.

Wallston, B. S., & Grady, K. E. (1985). Integrating the feminist critique and the crisis in social psychology: Another look at research methods. In V. E. O'Leary, R. K. Unger, & B. S. Wallston (Eds.), *Women, gender and social psychology* (pp. 7–34). Hillsdale, NJ: Erlbaum.

Walter, J. L., & LaFreniere, P. J. (2000). A naturalistic study of affective expression, gender competence, and sociometric status in preschoolers. *Early Education & Development, 1,* 109–122.

Walters, E. E., & Kendler, K. S. (1995). Anorexia nervosa and anorexic like symptoms in a population-based female twin sample. *American Journal of Psychiatry, 152,* 64–71.

Walzer, S. (1998). *Thinking about the baby.* Philadelphia: Temple University.

Ward, I. M., & Caruthers, A. (2001). Media influences. In J. Worell (Ed.), *Encyclopedia of women and gender* (pp. 687–701). San Diego, CA: Academic Press.

Ward, J. V. (1996). Raising resistors: The role of truth telling in the psychological development of African American girls. In B. J. R. Leadbeater & N. Way (Eds.), *Urban girls: Resisting stereotypes, creating identities* (pp. 85–99). New York: New York University Press.

Ward, L. M. (2002). Does television exposure affect emerging adults' attitudes and assumptions about sexual relationships? Correlational and experimental confirmation. *Journal of Youth and Adolescence, 31,* 1–15.

Warren, M. P. (1983). Physical and biological aspects of puberty. In J. Brooks-Gunn & A. C. Petersen (Eds.), *Girls at puberty* (pp. 3–28). New York: Plenum Press.

Waszak, C., Severy, L. J., Kafafi, L., & Badawi, I. (2001). Fertility behavior and psychological stress: The mediating influence of gender norm beliefs among Egyptian women. *Psychology of Women Quarterly, 25,* 197–208.

Watson, G., & Williams, J. (1992). Feminist practices in therapy. In J. M. Ussher & P. Nicolson (Eds.), *Gender issues in clinical psychology* (pp. 212–236). London: Routledge.

Watson, M. S., Trasciatti, M. A., & King, C. P. (1996). Our bodies, our risk. In R. L. Parrott & C. M. Condit (Eds.), *Evaluating women's health messages* (pp. 95–108). Thousand Oaks: Sage.

Watts, Barbara. (1996). Legal issues. In M. A. Paludi (Ed.), *Sexual harassment on college campuses: Abusing the ivory power* (pp. 9–24). Albany: State University of New York.

Watts, C., & Zimmerman, C. (2002). Violence against women: Global scope and magnitude. *Lancet, 359,* 1232–1237.

Weatherall, A., & Walton, M. (1999). The metaphorical construction of sexual experience in a speech community of New Zealand university students. *British Journal of Social Psychology, 38,* 479–498.

Weaver, T. L., Kilpatrick, D. G., Resnick, H. S., Best, C. L., & Saunders, B. E. (1997). An examination of physical assault and childhood victimization histories within a national probability sample of women. In G. Kaufman Kantor & J. L. Jasinski (Eds.), *Out of darkness: Contemporary perspectives on family violence* (pp. 35–48). Thousand Oaks, CA: Sage.

Weber, J. C. (1996). Social class as a correlate of gender identity among lesbian women. *Sex Roles, 35*(5/6), 271–280.

Weber, L. (1998). A conceptual framework for understanding race, class, gender, and sexuality. *Psychology of Women Quarterly, 22,* 13–32.

Weber, L., & Higginbotham, E. (1997). Black and white professional-managerial women's perceptions of racism and sexism in the workplace. In E. Higginbotham & M. Romero (Eds.), *Women and work: Exploring race, ethnicity, and class* (vol. 6, pp. 153–175). Thousand Oaks, CA: Sage.

Weinraub, B. (1994, September 18). Meryl Streep's peculiar career. *New York Times Magazine,* pp. 42–45.

Weiss, M. R., & Barber, H. (1995). Socialization influences of collegiate female athletes: A tale of two decades. *Sex Roles, 33,* 129–140.

Weisstein, N. (1968). *Kinder, Kirche, Kuche as scientific law: Psychology constructs the female.* Boston: New England Free Press.

Weitz, R., & Gordon, L. (1993). Images of black women among Anglo students. *Sex Roles, 28,* 19–34.

Weitzman, L. (1985). *The divorce revolution.* New York: Free Press.

Weitzman, L. J. (1979). *Sex role socialization.* Palo Alto, CA: Mayfield.

Wells, J. D., Hobfoll, S. E., & Lavin, J. (1997). Resource loss, resource gain, and communal coping during pregnancy among women with multiple roles. *Psychology of Women Quarterly, 21,* 645–662.

Werner, P. D., & LaRussa, G. W. (1985). Persistence and change in sex-role stereotypes. *Sex Roles, 12,* 1089–1100.

Wertheim, E. H., Mee, V., & & Paxton, S. J. (1999). Relationships among adolescent girls' eating behaviors and their parents' weight-related attitudes and behaviors. *Sex Roles, 41,* 169–187.

Wertz, D. C. (1992). How parents of affected children view selective abortion. In H. B. Holmes (Ed.), *Issues in reproductive technology* (pp. 161–189). New York: Garland.

Wester, S. R., Crown, C. L., Quatman, G. L., & Heesacker, M. (1997). The influence of sexually violent rap music on attitudes of men with little prior exposure. *Psychology of Women Quarterly, 21,* 497–508.

Whalen, D. M., Bigner, J. J., & Barber, C. E. (2000). The grandmother role as experienced by lesbian women. *Journal of Women & Aging, 12,* 39–57.

Whiffen, V. E. (2001). Depression. In J. Worell (Ed.), *Encyclopedia of Sex and Gender* (pp. 303–314). NY: Academic Press.

Whitam, F., Diamond, M., & Martin, J. (1993). Homosexual orientation in twins: A report on 61 pairs and three triplet sets. *Archives of Sexual Behavior, 22,* 187–206.

Whitam, F. L., Daskalos, C., Sobolewski, C. G., & Padilla, P. (1998). The emergence of lesbian sexuality and identity cross-culturally: Brazil, Peru, the Philippines, and the United States. *Archives of Sexual Behavior, 27*(1), 31–56.

Whitbourne, S. (1986). *The me I know: A study of adult identity.* New York: Springer-Verlag.

White, J. W., & Bondurant, B. (1996). Gendered violence. In J. T. Wood (Ed.), *Gendered Relationships* (pp. 197–210). Mountain View, CA: Mayfield.

White, J. W., Bondurant, B., & Travis, C. B. (2000). Social constructions of sexuality. In C. B. Travis & J. W. White (Eds.), *Sexuality, society and feminism: Psychological perspectives on women* (pp. 11–33). Washington, DC: American Psychological Association.

White, J. W., Holland, L., Mazurek, C., Lyndon, A., Weinstein, A., & Clancey, C. (1998). *Sexual assault experiences among community college students.* Symposium presented at the annual meeting of the North Carolina Coalition Against Sexual Assault, Asheville, NC, October.

White, J. W., & Humphrey, J. A. (1994). *Alcohol/drug use and sexual aggression: Distal and proximal influences.* Paper presented at XI World Meeting: International Society for Research on Aggression. Delray Beach, Florida, July.

White, J. W., & Humphrey, J. A. (1994a, March). *The relationship between perceived justification for forced sexual intercourse and self-reported sexual aggression.* Paper presented at Southeastern Psychological Association, New Orleans.

White, J. W., & Humphrey, J. A. (1995). *Sexual Assault Perpetration and Re-perpetration: From Adolescence to Young Adulthood.* Paper presented at Symposium on Rape and Sexual Assault: Risk Factors and Promising Interventions. National Violence Prevention Conference, Des Moines, Iowa, October 24.

White, J. W., & Humphrey, J. A. (1997). *Vulnerability for sexual assault during adolescence.* Presented at symposium on Factors Related to Sexual Victimization and Revictimization in Women. American Psychological Association, August 19.

White, J. W., & Koss, M. P. (1991). Courtship violence: Incidence in a national sample of higher education students. *Violence and Victims, 6,* 247–256.

White, J. W., & Koss, M. P. (1993). Adolescent sexual aggression within heterosexual relationships: Prevalence, characteristics, and causes. In H. E. Barbarbee, W. L. Marshall, & D. R. Laws (Eds.), *The juvenile sexual offender* (pp. 182–202). New York: Guilford.

White, J. W., Koss, M. P., & Kissling, G. (1991, June). Gender differences in structural models of courtship violence. Poster presented at American Psychological Society, Washington, DC.

White, J. W., & Kowalski, R. M. (1998). Violence against women: An integrative perspective. In R. G. Geen & E. Donnerstein (Eds.), *Perspectives on human aggression.* New York: Academic Press.

Whiting, B. B., & Edwards, C. P. (1973). A cross-cultural analysis of sex differences in the behavior of children aged three through eleven. *Journal of Social Psychology, 91,* 171–188.

Whitley, B. E., Jr. (1985). Sex-role orientation and psychological well-being: Two meta-analyses. *Sex Roles, 12,* 207–225.

Whitley, B. E., Jr., & Lee, S. E. (2000). The relationship of authoritarianism and related constructs to attitudes toward homosexuality. *Journal of Applied Social Psychology, 30,* 144–170.

Wichstrom, L. (1998). Self-concept development in adolescence: Do American truths hold for Norwegians? In E. Skoe & A. von der Lippe (Eds.), *Personality development in adolescence: A cross-national and lifespan perspective* (pp. 98–122). London: Routledge.

Wichstrom, L. (1999). The emergence of gender difference in depressed mood during adolescence: The role of intensified gender socialization. *Developmental Psychology, 35,* 232–245.

Wiest, W. M. (1977). Semantic differential profiles of orgasm and other experiences among men and women. *Sex Roles, 3,* 399–403.

Wilder, D. A. (1986). Social categorization: Implications for creation and reduction of intergroup bias. In L. Berkowitz (Ed.), *Advances in experimental social psychology,* Vol. 19. Orlando, FL: Academic Press.

Wilkinson, S. (1997a). Feminist psychology. In D. Fox & I. Prilleltensky (Eds.), *Critical psychology: An introduction* (pp. 247–264). London: Sage Publications.

Wilkinson, S. (1997b). Still seeking transformation: Feminist challenges to psychology. In L. Stanley (Ed.), *Knowing feminisms: On academic borders, territories and tribes* (pp. 97–108). Thousand Oaks, CA: Sage.

Wilkinson, S., & Kitzinger, C. (Eds.). (1993). *Heterosexuality: A "feminism and psychology" reader.* London: Sage.

Willemsen, T. M. (1998). Widening the gender gap: Teenage magazines for girls and boys. *Sex Roles, 38,* 851–861.

Williams, A., & Giles, H. (1998). Communications of ageism. In M. L. Hecht (Ed.). *Communicating prejudice* (pp. 136–160). Thousand Oaks, CA: Sage.

Williams, C. L. (1992). The glass escalator: Hidden advantages for men in the "female" professions. *Social Problems, 39,* 253–267.

Williams, J. E., & Best, D. L. (1990). *Measuring sex stereotypes: A multination study.* Newbury Park, CA: Sage.

Williams, L. S. (1992). Biology or society? Parenthood motivation in a sample of Canadian women seeking in vitro fertilization. In H. B. Holmes (Ed.), *Issues in reproductive technology* (pp. 261–274). New York: Garland.

Williams, N. (1990). *The Mexican American family: Tradition and change.* New York: General Hall.

Williams, P. J. (1997). My best white friend: Cinderella revisited. In M. Crawford & R. Unger (Eds.), *In our own words: Readings on the psychology of women and gender* (pp. 291–295). New York: McGraw-Hill.

Williams, R., & Wittig, M. A. (1997). "I'm not a feminist but . . .": Factors contributing to the discrepancy between pro-feminist orientation and feminist social identity. *Sex Roles, 37,* 885–904.

Williams, S. S., Kimble, D. L., Covell, N. H., Weiss, L. H., Newton, K. J., Fisher, J. D., & Fisher, W. A. (1992). College students use implicit personality theory instead of safer sex. *Journal of Applied Social Psychology, 22*(12), 921–933.

Williams, W. L. (1986). *The spirit and the flesh: Sexual diversity in American Indian culture.* Boston: Beacon Press.

Williams, W. L. (1987). Women, men, and others: Beyond ethnocentrism in gender theory. *American Behavioral Scientist, 31,* 135–141.

Williamson, A. (2000). Gender issues in older adults' participation in learning: Viewpoints and experiences of learners in the University of the Third Age. *Educational Gerontology, 26,* 49–66.

Wilmott, J. (2000). The experiences of women with Polycystic Ovarian Syndrome. *Feminism & Psychology, 10,* 107–116.

Wilson, A. (1996). How we find ourselves: Identity development and two-spirit people. *Harvard Educational Review, 66*(2), 303–317.

Wilson, B. J., Linz, D., Donnerstein, E., & Stipp, H. (1992). The impact of social issue television programming on attitudes toward rape. *Human Communication Research, 19,* 179–208.

Wilson, M., & Daly, M. (1994). Spousal homicide. *Juristat, 14,* 1–15.

Wilson, R. (1996, February 16). Leading economist stuns field by deciding to become a woman. *The Chronicle of Higher Education,* pp. A17, A19.

Winkel, W., & DeKleuver, E. (1997). Communication aimed at changing cognitions about sexual intimidation: Comparing the impact of a perpetrator-focused versus a victim-focused persuasive strategy. *Journal of Interpersonal Violence, 12,* 513–529.

Witkin, H. A., Mednick, S. A., Schulsinger, F., Bakkestrom, E., Christiansen, K. O., Goodenough, D. R., Hirschhorn, K., Lundsteen, C., Owen, D. R., Philip, J., Rubin, D. B., & Stocking, M. (1976). Criminality in XXY and XYY men. *Science, 193,* 547–555.

Wolf, S. (1985). A multi-factor model of deviant sexuality. *Victimology: An International Journal, 10,* 359–374.

Wolfe, N. (2001). *Misconceptions: Truth, lies, and the unexpected on the journey to motherhood.* New York: Doubleday.

Women's Action Collective. (1992). 75 Reasons why angry Cornell women (your worst nightmare) are exercising their freedom of speech. Women's Action Collective: Author.

Wood, A. D., & McHugh, M. C. (1994). Woman battering: The response of the clergy. *Pastoral Psychology, 42,* 185–196.

Wood, K. C., Becker, J. A., & Thompson, J. K. (1996). Body image dissatisfaction in preadolescent children. *Journal of Applied Developmental Psychology, 17,* 85–100.

Wood, W., & Karten, S. J. (1986). Sex differences in interactive style as a product of perceived sex differences in competence. *Journal of Personality and Social Psychology, 50,* 341–347.

Wood, W., & Rhodes, N. (1992). Sex differences in interaction style in task groups. In C. L. Ridgeway (Ed.), *Gender, interaction, and inequality* (pp. 97–121). New York: Springer-Verlag.

Wooley, H. T. (1910). Psychological literature: A review of the recent literature on the psychology of sex. *Psychological Bulletin, 7,* 335–342.

Wooley, S. C., & Wooley, O. W. (1980). Eating disorders: Anorexia and obesity. In A. M. Brodsky & R. Hare-Mustin (Eds.), *Women and psychotherapy* (pp. 135–158). New York: Guilford.

Woollett, A., White, D., & Lyon, L. (1982). Fathers' involvement with their infants: The role of holding. In N. Beail & J. McGuire (Eds.), *Fathers: Psychological perspectives.* London: Junction.

Worell, J. (1988). Women's satisfaction in close relationships. *Clinical Psychology Review, 8,* 477–498.

Worell, J. (1996). Opening doors to feminist research. *Psychology of Women Quarterly, 20,* 469–485.

Worell, J., & Johnson, D. (2001). Therapy with women: Feminist frameworks. In R. K. Unger (Ed.), *Handbook of the psychology of women and gender* (pp. 317–329). NY: Wiley.

Workman, J. E., & Johnson, K. K. P. (1991). The role of cosmetics in attributions about sexual harassment. *Sex Roles, 24,* 759–769.

World Wire. (1993, December 21). China proposed eugenics law. *The Wall Street Journal,* p. A6.

Worth, D. M., Matthews, P. A., & Coleman, W. R. (1990). Sex role, group affiliation, family background, and courtship violence in college students. *Journal of College Student Development, 31,* 250–254.

Wright, J. C., Huston, A. C., Vanderwater, E. A., et al. (2001). American children's use of electronic media in 1997: A national survey. *Journal of Applied Developmental Psychology, 22,* 31–47.

Wyatt, G. (1991). Sociocultural context of African American and White American women's rape. *Journal of Social Issues, 48,* 77–92.

Wyatt, G. E. (1985). The sexual abuse of Afro-American and White-American women in childhood. *Child Abuse and Neglect, 9,* 507–519.

Wyatt, G. E., Guthrie, G., & Notgrass, C. M. (1992). Differential effects of women's child sexual abuse and subsequent sexual revictimization. *Journal of Consulting and Clinical Psychology, 60,* 167–173.

Wyatt, G. E., & Riederle, M. H. (1994). Reconceptualizing issues that affect women's sexual decision-making and sexual functioning. *Psychology of Women Quarterly, 18,* 611–626.

Wyche, K. F. (1996). Conceptualization of social class in African American women: Congruence of client-therapist definitions. *Women & Therapy, 18,* 35–43.

Wyche, K. F. (2001). Sociocultural issues in counseling women of color. In R. K. Unger (Ed.), *Handbook of the psychology of women and gender* (pp. 330–340). NY: Wiley.

Wyche, K. F., & Crosby, F. (Eds.). (1996). *Women's ethnicities: Journeys through psychology.* Boulder, CO: Westview.

Wyche, K. F., & Rice, J. K. (1997). Feminist therapy: From dialogue to tenets. In J. Worell & N. G. Johnson (Eds.), *Shaping the future of feminist psychology: Education, research, and practice* (pp. 57–71). Washington DC: American Psychological Association.

Wynn, R. L., & Fletcher, C. (1987). Sex role development and early educational experiences. In D. B. Carter (Ed.), *Current conceptions of sex roles and sex typing: Theory and research* (pp. 79–88). New York: Praeger.

Xu, X., & Lai, S. C. (2002). Resources, gender ideologies, and marital power: The case of Taiwan. *Journal of Family Issues, 23,* 209–245.

Yama, M. F., Tovey, S. L., & Fogas, B. S. (1993). Childhood family environment and sexual abuse as predicting of anxiety and depression in adult women. *American Journal of Orthopsychiatry, 63,* 136–141.

Yanovski, S. Z. (1993). Binge eating disorder: Current knowledge and future directions. *Obesity Research, 1,* 305–324.

Yee, B. W. K. (1990). Gender and family issues in minority groups. *Generations, 14,* 39–42.

Yee, D. (1997). Issues and trends affecting Asian Americans, women, and aging. In J. M. Coyle (Ed.), *Handbook on women and aging* (pp. 316–334). Westport, CT: Greenwood Press.

Yllo, K. (1993). Through a feminist lens: Gender, power, and violence. In R. J. Gelles & D. R. Loseke (Eds.), *Current controversies on family violence* (pp. 47–62). Newbury Park, CA: Sage.

Yoder, J. D. (1985). An academic woman as a token: A case study. *Journal of Social Issues, 41,* 61–72.

Yoder, J. D. (2002). Context matters: Understanding tokenism processes and their impact on women's work. *Psychology of Women Quarterly, 26,* 1–8.

Yoder, J. D., Adams, J., Grove, S., & Priest, R. F. (1985). To teach is to learn: Overcoming tokenism with mentors. *Psychology of Women Quarterly, 9,* 119–132.

Yoder, J. D., & Aniakudo, P. (1996). When pranks become harassment: The case of African American women firefighters. *Sex Roles, 35,* 253–269.

Yoder, J. D., & Kahn, A. S. (1992). Toward a feminist understanding of women and power. *Psychology of Women Quarterly, 16,* 381–388.

Yoder, J. D., Schleicher, T. L., & McDonald, T. W. (1998). Empowering token women leaders: The importance of organizationally legitimated credibility. *Psychology of Women Quarterly, 22,* 209–222.

Yoder, J. D., & Sinnett, L. M. (1985). Is it all in the numbers? A case study of tokenism. *Psychology of Women Quarterly, 9,* 413–418.

Young, I. M. (1998). Breasted experience: The look and the feeling. In R. Weitz (Ed.), *The politics of women's bodies: Sexuality, appearance, and behavior* (pp. 125–136). New York: Oxford University Press.

Youngblut, J. M., Singer, L. T., Madigan, E. A., Swegart, L. A., & Rodgers, W. L. (1997). Mother, child, and family factors related to employment of single mothers with LBW preschoolers. *Psychology of Women Quarterly, 21*(2), 247–263.

Zak, A., & McDonald, C. (1997). Satisfaction and trust in intimate relationships: Do lesbians and heterosexual women differ? *Psychological Reports, 80,* 904–906.

Zanna, M. P., & Pack, S. J. (1975). On the self-fulfilling nature of apparent sex differences in behavior. *Journal of Experimental Social Psychology, 11,* 583–591.

Zebrowtiz L. A., & Montepare, J. M. (2000). Too young, too old: Stigmatizing adolescents and elders. In T. F. Heatherton, R. E. Kleck, M. L. Hebl, & J. G. Hull (Eds.), *The social psychology of stigma* (pp. 334–373). New York: Guilford Press.

Zelnik, M., Kantner, J. F., & Ford, K. (1981). *Sex and pregnancy in adolescence.* Beverly Hills, CA: Sage.

Zernike, K. (1999, March 21). MIT women win a fight against bias. *The Boston Globe,* pp. F1, F4.

Zimmerman, L., Mitchell, B., Wister, A., & Gutman, G. (2000). Unanticipated consequences: A comparison of expected and actual retirement timing among older women. *Journal of Women & Aging, 12,* 109–128.

Zimmerman, M. K. (1987). The women's health movement: A critique of medical enterprise and the position of women. In B. B. Hess & M. M. Ferree (Eds.), *Analyzing gender* (pp. 442–472). Newbury Park, CA: Sage.

Zinkhan, G. M., & Stoiadin, L. F. (1984). Impact of sex role stereotypes on service priority in department stores. *Journal of Applied Psychology, 69,* 691–693.

Zita, J. N. (1993). Heresy in the female body: The rhetoric of menopause. In J. C. Callahan (Ed.), *Menopause: A midlife passage* (pp. 59–78). Bloomington: University of Indiana Press.

Zlotnick, C., Kohn, R., Peterson, J., & Pearlstein, T. (1998). Partner physical victimization in a national sample of American families. Relationship to psychological functioning, psychosocial factors, and gender. *Journal of Interpersonal Violence, 13,* 156–166.

Zucker, A. N., Harrell, Z. A., Miner-Rubino, K., Stewart, A. J., Pomerleau, C. S., & Boyd, C. J. (2001). Smoking in college women: The role of thinness pressures, media exposure, and critical consciousness. *Psychology of Women Quarterly, 25,* 233–241.

Zucker, A. N., Ostrove, J. M., & Stewart, A. J. (2002). College-educated women's personality development in adulthood: Perceptions and age differences. *Psychology and Aging, 17,* 236–244.

Zucker, K. (2001). Biological influences on psychosexual differentiation. In R. K. Unger (Ed.), *Handbook of the psychology of women and gender* (pp. 101–115), NY: Wiley & Sons.

Zucker, K. J., Wild, J., Bradley, S. J., & Lowry, C. B. (1993). Physical attractiveness of boys with gender identity disorder. *Archives of Sexual Behavior, 22,* 23–36.

Zucker, K. J., Wilson-Smith, D. N., Kurita, J. A., & Stern, A. (1995). Children's appraisals of sex-typed behaviors in their peers. *Sex Roles, 33,* 703–725.

Zweig, J. M., Barber, B. L., & Eccles, J. S. (1997). *Journal of Interpersonal Violence, 12,* 291–308.

Credits

Photos

Figure 1.2: © The New-York Historical Society; **Page 25 box:** (left) Courtesy of Dr. Karyn Boatwright/Kalamazoo College, (right) Courtesy of Wellesley College Archives. Photograph by Partridge.; **Figure 2.1:** Dancers of the Third Age. Photographer: Dennis DeLoria. All rights reserved 1981 Liz Lerman Dance Exchange, Inc.; **Figure 2.3:** (left) © Jeff Mitchell/Reuters NewMedia Inc./CORBIS, (right) © Thomas Coex/AFP/CORBIS; **Figure 2.5:** © Joel Gordon; **Figure 2.6:** © 1999 MAK; **Figure 2.7:** © 1993 Time Inc./Getty Images; **Page 45 box:** © Trapper Frank/Corbis Sygma; **Figure 2.8:** © Paolo Cocco/Reuters Newsmedia Inc./ CORBIS; **Figure 2.9:** © Noel Quidu/Gamma Liaison; **Figure 3.3:** © Fred Mertz; **Page 93 box:** (top) The Oswego Historical Society, (bottom) The Oswego Historical Society; **Figure 3.6:** © Professor Caroline Keating/Colgate University/2003; **Page 107 box:** © Greta Pratt, 1998; **Figure 4.6:** Women's College Coalition; **Figure 4.7:** © Digital Vision; **Figure 5.4:** The Intersex Society of North America; **Page 153 box:** © Mike Geissinger; **Figure 5.7:** © W. Van Capellon/Saba/CORBIS; **Figure 5.9:** © 2003 Banco de Mexico Diego Rivera & Frida Kahlo Museums Trust. Av. Cinco de Mayo No.2, Col. Centro, Del. Cuauhtemoc 06059, Mexico, D.F. Courtesy, Instituto Nacional de Bellas Artes Y Literatura, Mexico. Digital file courtesy of Munson Graphics.; **Figure 5.10:** © The Philadelphia Inquirer/Barbara Demick; **Figure 6.1:** United Nations (1991). "Women: Challenges to the Year 2000." N.Y. UN Publications; **Figure 6.4:** (left) Kenya James courtesy CED Talent Agency, Inc. Jack Carroll courtesy Ford Management. Photograph © Robert Trachtenberg, (right) Dexter Summers courtesy Nell Scovell. Annie LaZebnik courtesy Claire LaZebnik. Photograph © Robert Trachtenberg.; **Figure 6.5:** (left) © Powerstock/SuperStock, (top right) © Dennis Galante/Taxi/Getty Images, (bottom right) © Susie Fitzhugh; **Figure 6.8:** © FOX-TV/The Kobal Collection; **Figure 6.9:** © Simons/Corbis Sygma; **Figure 6.10:** © Stuart Isett/Polaris Images; **Page 210 box:** Courtesy, Global Health Council; **Figure 7.2:** © Anita Kunz; **Figure 7.5:** © Wartenberg/Picture Press/CORBIS; **Page 239 box:** © AP/Wide World Photos; **Figure 7.7:** © Bonnie Burton; **Page 271 box:** © AP/Wide World Photos; **Page 298 box:** © AP/Wide World Photos; **Page 322 Box 10.1:** Hollingworth, 1916; **Figure 10.4:** © Suzanne Arms/The Image Works; **Figure 10.6:** © Judy Chicago/Through the Flower; **Page 354 box:** © AP/Wide World Photos; **Figure 10.8:** © Steve Jacobs/Albany Times Union; **Page 365 Box 11.1:** © Richard Freeda/AP/Wide World Photos; **Page 369 box:** © AP/Wide World Photos; **Page 371 Box 11.2:** Photo by Sigrid Estrada. Courtesy of Henry Holt & Company.; **Figure 12.1:** © 1998 Time Inc./Getty Images; **Figure 12.9:** © Newsweek, Inc. All rights reserved. Reprinted by permission.; **Page 433 box:** © AP/Wide World Photos; **Figure 12.10:** (top left) © Michael C. York, (top right) © Fred R. Conrad/The New York Times, (center right) © Fred R. Conrad/The New York Times, (bottom left) © Carol Halebian, (bottom right) © Fred R. Conrad/The New York Times; **Figure 12.11:** © Elizabeth Layton; **Page 442 box:** © 1991 Time Inc./Getty Images; **Figure 13.2:** © Michael Siluk/The Image Works; **Figure 13.3:** Courtesy of White Ribbon Campaign; **Figure 13.5:** © Donna Ferrato, 1991; **Page 479 box:** © Bettmann/CORBIS; **Figure 14.4:** © AP/Wide World Photos; **Page 522 box:** © AP/Wide World Photos.

Text

Table 2.1: Adapted from S. Coltrane & M. Messineo (2000), "The perpetuation of subtle prejudice: Race and gender imagery in 1990s television advertising," *Sex Roles,* 42. Reprinted by permission of Kluwer Academic/Plenum Publishers. **Table 2.2:** From K. Deaux, W. Winston, M. Crowley, & L. L. Lewis "Level of categorization and content of gender stereotypes," *Social Cognition,* 3. Copyright © 1985. Reprinted by permission of The Guilford Press. **Figure 3.1:** From Quinn, D. M. & Spencer, S. J. (2001). The interference of stereotype threat with women's generation of math problem-solving strategies. *Journal of Social Issues,* 57 (1), 55–71. Reprinted by permission of the publisher, Blackwell Science. **Figure 3.7:** From "Beyond Prejudice as Simple Antipathy: Hostile and Benevolent Sexism Across Cultures," by Peter Glick et al., 2000, *Journal of Personality and Social Psychology,* 79, p. 770. Copyright © 2000 by the American Psychological Association. Reprinted with permission. **Figure 4.1:** From *The Gender Question in Education: Theory, Pedagogy and Politics* by Ann Diller. Copyright © 1996 by Westview Press, a member of Perseus Books, L.L.C. Reprinted by permission of Westview Press, a member of Perseus Books,

L.L.C. **Figure 4.5:** From Eccles and Jacobs's, "Social Forces Shape Math Attitudes and Performance," *Signs*, 11, pp. 367–389, 1986. University of Chicago Press. Reprinted by permission of the authors. **Table 5.1:** From Blackless, M., Charuvastra, A., Derryck, A., Fausto-Sterling, A., Lauzanne, K., & Lee, E., 2000. "How sexually dimorphic are we? Review and synthesis." *American Journal of Human Biology*, 12. Copyright © 2000 John Wiley & Sons. Reprinted by permission of Wiley-Liss, Inc., a subsidiary of John Wiley & Sons, Inc. **Table 5.2:** From Diamond, "Biological aspects of sexual orientation and identity," in *The Psychology of Sexual Orientation, Behavior, and Identity*, L. Diamant & R. McAnulty (eds). Copyright © 1995 by Louis Diamant and Richard D. McAnulty. Reproduced by permission of Greenwood Publishing Group, Inc., Westport, CT. **Page 160:** From John Colapinto, "The True Story of John/Joan." Reprinted by permission of International Creative Management, Inc. Copyright © 1997 by John Colapinto. First appeared in *Rolling Stone.* **Table 6.1:** From "Gender essentialism in cognitive development" by S. A. Gelman & M. G. Taylor, in *Toward a Feminist Developmental Psychology* by P. H. Miller & E. J. Scholnick, eds. Copyright © 2000. Reproduced by permission of Routledge/Taylor & Francis Books, Inc. **Table 6.2:** From P.A. Katz, "Raising Feminists," *Psychology of Women Quarterly*, 20, 1996, pp. 323–340. Copyright © 1996. Reprinted by permission of the publisher, Blackwell Science. **Pages 216–217:** From *Reviving Ophelia* by Mary Pipher, Ph.D. Copyright © 1994 by Mary Pipher, Ph.D. Used by permission of G. P. Putnam's Sons, a division of Penguin Group (USA) Inc. and the author. **Pages 222–225:** From *Puberty, Sexuality, and the Self: Girls and Boys at Adolescence* by Karin A. Martin. Copyright © 1996. Reproduced by permission of Routledge/Taylor & Francis Books, Inc. **Pages 225–226:** From *A Tree Grows in Brooklyn* by Betty Smith, p. 212. Copyright © 1943, 1947 by Betty Smith. Copyright renewed 1971 by Betty Smith (Finch). Reprinted by permission of HarperCollins Publishers Inc. and in the United Kingdom by permission of the William Morris Agency on behalf of the author. **Page 227:** From *Puberty, Sexuality, and the Self: Girls and Boys at Adolescence* by Karin A. Martin. Copyright © 1996. Reproduced by permission of Routledge/Taylor & Francis Books, Inc. **Table 7.1:** From Rieves & Cash, "Social developmental factors and women's body-image attitudes," *Journal of Social Behavior and Personality*, 11, 1996. © *Journal of Social Behavior & Personality.* Reprinted by permission of Select Press. **Table 8.1:** Adapted from Mahay, J. W., Laumann, E. O., & Michaels, S., "Race, gender, and class in sexual scripts," in E. O. Laumann & R. T. Michael (eds), *Sex, Love, and Health: Private choices and public policies* (2001). University of Chicago Press. Reprinted by permission of University of Chicago Press. **Page 255:** From *Song of Love* by Rachel Elliott. © 1988 Rachel Elliot. Used by permission of the publisher, Harlequin S.A. **Page 255:** From "Student Sexual Autobiography." Moffatt, Michael, *Coming of Age in New Jersey.* © 1989 by Rutgers the State University. Reprinted by permission of Rutgers University Press. **Pages 261–262:** Reprinted by permission of Sage Publishing Ltd. from *The Social Construction of Lesbianism* by Celia Kitzinger, 1987, pp. 43, 99, 110. © 1987 Celia Kitzinger. **Pages 282–283:** From *Fantasy Lover.* Copyright © 1988 Sally Heywood. Used by permission of the publisher, Harlequin S.A. **Page 284:** From *American Couples* by Philip B. Blumstein and Pepper S. Schwartz, pp. 53, 57–58, 150, 318 and adaptation of figs. on pp. 308, 315. Copyright © 1983 by Philip B. Blumstein and Pepper S. Schwartz. Reprinted by permission of HarperCollins Publishers, Inc. (William Morrow) and by International Creative Management. **Page 292:** From *American Couples* by Philip B. Blumstein and Pepper S. Schwartz, pp. 53, 57–58, 150, 318 and adaptation of figs. on pp. 308, 315. Copyright © 1983 by Philip B. Blumstein and Pepper S. Schwartz. Reprinted by permission of HarperCollins Publishers, Inc. (William Morrow) and by International Creative Management. **Figure 9.5:** From *American Couples* by Philip B. Blumstein and Pepper S. Schwartz, pp. 53, 57–58, 150, 318 and adaptation of figs. on pp. 308, 315. Copyright © 1983 by Philip B. Blumstein and Pepper S. Schwartz. Reprinted by permission of HarperCollins Publishers, Inc. (William Morrow) and by International Creative Management. **Figure 10.7:** The Alan Guttmacher Institute, "Teenagers' sexual and reproductive health," *Facts in Brief*, New York: The Alan Guttmacher Institute, 2001. **Pages 352–354:** From Gillian Darley's essay in *Balancing Acts: On Being a Mother* by Katherine Gieve, pp. 127–128, 124. Reprinted by permission of PFD on behalf of Gillian Darley. © 1989, Gillian Darley; From Elizabeth Peretz's essay in *Balancing Acts: On Being a Mother* by Katherine Gieve, pp. 114; From Jennifer Uglow's essay in *Balancing Acts: On Being a Mother* by Katherine Gieve, pp. 159; From *Balancing Acts: On Being a Mother* by Katherine Gieve, pp. 41, 51, 45. Reprinted by permission of Katherine Gieve; From Jean Radford's essay in *Balancing Acts: On Being a Mother* by Katherine Gieve, pp. 138–139, 140, 143–144. Reprinted with permission of the author; From Hilary Land's essay in *Balancing Acts: On Being a Mother* by Katherine Gieve, pp. 77; From Victoria Hardie's essay in *Balancing Acts: On Being a Mother* by Katherine Gieve, pp. 53–54. **Table 11.1:** Reprinted from *The Career Psychology of Women* by Betz & Fitzgerald, p. 143. Copyright © 1987, with permission from Elsevier and the author. **Table 12.1:** From "Historical Terminology Used to Represent Older People," Rosalie A. Kane, *Gerontologist*, 28, 1988, 291–297. Copyright © 1988 by Gerontological Society of America. Reproduced with permission of Gerontological Society of America in the format Textbook via Copyright Clearance Center. **Figure 12.5:** *Newsweek*, July 22, 2002. © 2002 Newsweek Inc. All rights reserved. Reprinted by permission. **Table 12.2:** From P. B. Bart & M. Grossman (1978), "Menopause," in M. T. Notman & C. C. Nadelson (eds), *The Woman Patient: Medical and Psychological Interfaces.* Copyright © 1978 Plenum Publishing Corporation. Reprinted by permission of Kluwer Acedemic/Plenum Publishers. **Figure 12.7:** Reprinted by permission of New York Times Graphics. **Figure 13.2:** www.whiteribbon.com/educational_materials/wrcposter.gif. Reprinted with permission. **Figure 13.4:** From R. J. Gelles & D. R. Loseke (eds), *Current Controversies on Family Violence*, pp. 47–62. Used by permission of the Minnesota Program Development, Inc. **Table 14.1:** From S. L. Morrow & D. M. Hawxhurst (1998), "Feminist therapy: Integrating political analysts in counseling and psychotherapy. *Women & Therapy*, 21, p. 43. Used by permission of The Haworth Press, Inc., Binghamton, N.Y.

Name Index

Subject Index